HER MAJESTY QUEEN VICTORIA.

QUEEN VICTORIA

Her Life and Reign

A STUDY OF

MONARCHICAL INSTITUTIONS IN BRITISH COUNTRIES AND HER MAJESTY'S IMPERIAL INFLUENCE.

BY

J CASTELL HOPKINS

*Author of the "Life of Sir John Thompson," "Life and Work of Mr. Gladstone,"
"The Sword of Islam," etc., etc.*

WITH A PREFACE BY

THE MARQUESS OF DUFFERIN AND AVA, K.P., G.C.B., ETC.
Late Governor-General of Canada and Viceroy of India.

THE QUEEN PUBLISHERS,
TORONTO AND BRANTFORD
1901.

PREFACE

TWO statements may be made in regard to the Victorian era, both of which will meet with universal acceptation. The first is that Her Majesty's reign has been not only longer, but also more prosperous than that of any of her predecessors; and, the second, that the Sovereign herself has led a more blameless life in her public capacity as Queen, and in her domestic relations as a woman, than any monarch of whom history has taken note. As a consequence, the autumn of her life has mellowed beneath the sun of a universal popularity—a popularity not confined to her own dominions, but which prevails wherever the English language is spoken—while she is regarded by all the European rulers and statesmen of the day with the profoundest veneration. Nor need we be surprised that this should be the case. Endowed by nature with a quick intelligence and a strong understanding, she was initiated in the duties of her regal office by advisers of the greatest capacity and the highest integrity, and, within the sanctuary of her home, she was blessed with the sympathy of a husband as instructed and as wise as he was devoted.

Indeed, all her life Queen Victoria has been in close and intimate official relations with the most sagacious and experienced ministers that have ever served the English Crown. Her early steps in the art of government were guided with generous and paternal solicitude by Lord Melbourne. To him succeeded a long line of illustrious and loyal counsellors—the Duke of Wellington, Sir Robert Peel, Sir James Graham, Lord John Russell, Lord Aberdeen, Sidney Herbert, Lord Derby, Lord Beaconsfield, and many others—to mention only those that have passed away. Each of these gave her of his best, without reticence or reserve; and the profound affection she inspired in the breasts of every one of them is in itself a proof of the honest and keen appreciation with which she assimilated their advice. But, besides these, there have been many others, men eminent in every branch of human knowledge—fathers both of the Anglican and of the Scottish Church, experts in science and philosophy, men of the world, as well as an equal number of good, high-minded, and noble women, who, being admitted to her intimacy, repaid her gracious benignity by placing their garnered gifts at her disposal.

As a result, at this moment Queen Victoria has come to be considered the best equipped and the most experienced ruler of her age. But, apart from these endowments, she has created for herself a better title to the love and admiration of mankind in the transparent simplicity of her unresting and unfaltering devotion to duty, which has been the mainspring of all her actions and her unerring guide through the thorny and complicated mazes of her public and official as well as of her private life. Nowhere has the appreciation of these qualities been more intense than in Canada; for by Canadians Her Majesty is not only regarded as their Sovereign, but as the founder and nursing mother of their great Dominion. It has been under her auspices that the discordant and fragmentary elements have been united into a mighty state, its constitutional liberties confirmed and enlarged, its status as an independent member of the British Empire assured, and its territories extended from the Atlantic to the Pacific.

And what is true of Canada may be said of all the other British colonies and possessions in every part of the globe; for, to one and all of them, Queen Victoria's Imperial throne, or rather the august presence that adorns it, is the outward and visible bond of sympathy between all their English-speaking inhabitants, the reflex of what they most venerate in the past, and the focus of their aspirations for the future. Although at present scarcely amounting to more than an inarticulate murmur, an imperceptible afflatus,—the British Empire is undoubtedly pervaded by a certain instinctive desire for a closer and more pronounced unity between its members than it has yet been able to develop. And in producing this result we have in a great measure to thank Her Majesty's noble interpretation of what are the duties and what should be the bearing of a constitutional Sovereign. At last it has come to be understood that the political system which prevails in England, and which has been imitated by her colonies, is in its true aspects more frankly democratic than that of any Republic. In other words, the will of the people and the popular verdict of the constituencies, as represented by their Parliaments, is much more rapidly carried into effect and transmuted into legislative enactments in all those regions which owe allegiance to the British Crown, than even in the United States of America. Under these circumstances, it need not be a matter of surprise that Queen Victoria, as the impersonation of this well-ordered system of government, should be beloved by the millions who have planted the laws, liberties and freedom of England in all the four quarters of the globe. When she began to reign her title was that of Queen, but during the span of sixty years that she has borne the burthen of power, the confines of her oversea dominions have been so widely extended, and their inhabitants have so increased in numbers, in wealth, and in power, that she has been saluted by universal consent, not only as Queen of England, but as the wide-ruling Empress of a Greater Britain.

The foregoing few words, I feel, is all that is required to comply with the request with which the author has honoured an ex-Governor-General, to add a few introductory sentences to his valuable volume, and it only remains for me to say that in doing so, although I can, of course, in no way hold myself responsible for any statement or opinion which the book may contain, I have such confidence in his ability and good faith as to be able to heartily recommend the work to the better judgment of the general English-speaking reader, whether in the States, the Colonies, or at home.

Dufferin and Ava

AUTHOR'S INTRODUCTION.

In presenting to a public which has proved unusually appreciative and kind, a new edition of this work, the author may be permitted a few words of congratulation to its publishers and of explanation to an increasing circle of readers. This is really an Imperial edition. It seems to be required by the general demand for a volume which will treat, in this year of an Empire's celebration, of the Sovereign's influence outside of the British Isles as well as of her personal character and career. It will, I think, be the first Canadian work which has found a place for itself amid the pulsing life and vigour of Australasia and the bounding development of South Africa. It is therefore an apparent embodiment of the closer sympathy and the Imperial sentiment which is now permeating the minds of British peoples everywhere; and in so far as it may prove even the faintest influence in extending inter-colonial knowledge and broadening this Imperial appreciation of the link which binds together our widely scattered realms, will I have strong reasons for feeling proud and grateful.

I have pointed out in a few prefatory words to the previous edition that a large number of biographies of the Queen have been published, and have proved in their different ways both useful and interesting. But in none of them, so far as careful research and examination will reveal, has there been any real effort made to treat at the same time of the domestic detail of Her Majesty's life, the historic environment of her career, and the Imperial influence of her personality and work. The latter, especially, is a branch of the subject which appears to have been almost entirely overlooked. It seems strange that such should have been the case. As the head of a vast and ever broadening Empire, as the centre of the greatest constitutional and governmental system in the world or the world's history, as the theme of an almost universal literature, and the basis of an Imperial loyalty which girdles the earth with British liberty and power, one would think the topic of such importance as to have demanded almost continuous consideration.

The fact seems to be, however, that this negligence is a survival of the old school of indifference to Imperial expansion and power. The British people have awakened, it is true, to the advantage of having a great Empire and the necessity of preserving its unity and promoting its inter-dependence. They have been satisfactorily aroused from the slumber of secure isolation to which the magnetic eloquence of Bright, the cosmo-politan effect of Cobdenism, and the narrow theories of the Manchester school, once sub-jected their minds and national policy. The statesmen of to-day appreciate to the fullest extent the Queen's influence in developing this changed condition just as they comprehend and admire her statesmanlike ability in a thousand other historic directions, and are proud to receive and benefit by her experience and advice in the diplomatic and world-wide complications incident to such an Empire as that of Britain.

But the press, the platform, and the people have not yet risen to quite the level of the occasion. In this year of Her Majesty's Diamond Jubilee she shows her comprehension of the greatest event of her reign, and a clear insight into the causes which will make its greatness a permanent element in the future, by giving the leaders and troops of British Colonial States a foremost official place in the celebrations of the 22nd of June. Yet to-day, as ten years since, we find that the press of her realms continues to treat of the Queen' personal virtues and her noble domestic example and influence, in terms which though just and timely in themselves, yet fail in a full measure of appreciation for the great ability which has in so many crises controlled foreign affairs; for the tact which has guided political parties and leaders out of so many home difficulties and complications; for the personal and royal influence which has more than once averted war abroad and held war-like cabinets in check at home; for the Imperial personality which has made the British monarchy a world-strong institution, and killed republicanism at home while harmonising it in the colonies with a general system of broad and free constitutional government.

There is, of course, much excuse for this condition of affairs. Her Majesty's immense correspondence over a long term of years with prime ministers and ministers, with viceroys of India and Ireland, and with governors of all the large dependencies of the Crown have been published in only a very few cases, and then under the most rigid scrutiny and with the certainty that nothing connected with myriad possibilities in home and foreign politics was thrown into the crucible of publicity. Still, the Memoirs of Lord Palmerston, Lord John Russell, Sir George Gray, Earl Grey, the Duke of Wellington, Lord Aberdeen, Lord Ellenborough, and Lord Malmesbury, to say nothing of the Prince Consort's Life by Sir Theodore Martin, indicate sufficiently this phase of Her Majesty's career to make one wonder at the comparatively little attention which has been paid to it.

So far as may be possible in a limited space—after prolonged study and much valuable help given during a recent visit to England by many officials and public men—I have with all diffidence endeavored to draw attention to this particular topic and to indicate the immense influence of the Queen in moulding the opinion and policy of her ministers; to prove the personal and practical share of Her Majesty in the government of the Empire; to show her actual work in constructive legislation and diplomatic arrangements; to embody, especially, the strong and pronounced Imperialism of the Queen's character and labours.

Of what the British Empire really owes to the Queen it is difficult to speak fully. We know that in a certain sense its institutions and unity depend upon the Crown as a centre and that colonial loyalty to the Sovereign will strengthen a connection which the establishment of a republican system in Great Britain would break like pack-thread. We are aware that no colonial state would consent to owe an hour's allegiance to an official elected by the votes of a part of the British people in the Isles at home. And the Queen's interpretation of monarchical institutions has made a British Republic as visionary and useless a thing as would be the establishment of cable communication with the moon. We know that Her Majesty's influence has been ever on the side of peace—which Lord Salisbury and Lord Rosebery unite in declaring to be the great present requirement of our Empire and people. And history, so far as it has yet revealed its secrets to us, indicates at least three wars which have been averted by her personal intervention and authority.

Canada owes directly to Her Majesty the visit of the Prince of Wales in 1860 and a keen personal appreciation of its Imperial policy in railway development and provincial

THE EARL OF ABERDEEN, G.C.M.G.

J. CASTELL HOPKINS, F.S.S.

unity. South Africa owes to the Queen the several visits of the Duke of Edinburgh, and her sympathy with Imperialistic governors such as Sir George Grey and statesmen such as Mr. Cecil Rhodes. The public appreciation accorded to the latter by the Prince of Wales, and the practical co-operation given him in his great policy of expansion by the Duke of Fife, could never have been exhibited without Her Majesty's approval. Australasia owes to her the compliment of many royal visits, the kindly personal treatment of its leaders, and an earnest desire for its unity in one great and growing British nationality—British in allegiance and connection and power; Australian in local authority, patriotism and development. India is indebted to its Queen-Empress for continued sympathy and advice to its Governors-General; for the modification of the Royal proclamation after the Mutiny into phraseology which rendered the new conditions of allegiance comprehensible and satisfactory; for the important visit of the Prince of Wales in 1877; and for the support of Lord Beaconsfield's general Imperial policy which made the purchase of the Suez Canal shares possible and the ultimate acquisition of Egypt a necessity. The Colonies, as a whole, owe to their Queen a condition of government which has made peaceful constitutional development possible, and evolution rather than revolution the guiding principle of this century. To her warm sympathy with personal exertions upon behalf of Imperial unity, they are indebted for the compliment involved in the calling to her own Privy Council at the heart of the Empire of such men as Sir John A. Macdonald, Cecil J. Rhodes, and W. Bede Dalley.

But there is more than this. During the period between 1840 and 1870, when the Manchester school of disunion and ignorance was in full popular swing, there is now little doubt that the Queen's great personal influence with political leaders was thrown into the scale on behalf of the Colonies and Imperial unity. She was indeed a pioneer in the cause which the late Lady Tennyson once told me was the dominant passion of her great husband's life and work: which Lord Beaconsfield so devotedly encouraged and developed; and which Lord Rosebery has publicly declared to be worth living for, and, if need be, dying for. During all these years of anti-colonial sentiment and a dead level of Imperial ignorance, which is still voiced by a few men like Henry Labouchere, Her Majesty was quietly working upon the minds of those around her—and for sixty years be it remembered every week has seen a different member of the current administration in close attendance upon the Sovereign—while by correspondence, the sending of her sons to the outskirts of the Empire, and a judicious distribution of personal compliments and honours, she has helped to keep alive the embers of Colonial loyalty during that most trying of periods.

And now, when the spirit of unity controls the policy of all these great and scattered states; when the free yet dignified principle of a limited constitutional monarchy has become engraved upon the hearts of British peoples everywhere; when the life-work of the Queen is beginning to be appreciated in the fullest and broadest sense—as that of a great statesman as well as a model woman—the people of the British Empire will do well to look into this Imperial phase of Her Majesty's reign more closely and carefully than has yet been done.

I will venture one word more in conclusion. Thanks to the many who have helped me in this work would be invidious and impossible, though I may perhaps acknowledge the kind assistance of His Excellency the Earl of Aberdeen, Governor-General of Canada; His Excellency the Earl of Glasgow, Governor of New Zealand;

Lord Balfour of Burleigh, Secretary of State for Scotland; the Earl of Jersey, late Governor of New South Wales; Lord Tennyson; Colonel Sir C. E. Howard Vincent, M.P.; the Earl of Hopetoun, lately Governor of Victoria; the Earl of Northbrook, formerly Viceroy of India; Lord Harris, lately Governor of Bombay, and Sir Charles Tupper, lately Prime Minister of Canada. And, although my task has not been an easy one and the authorities consulted have run far into the hundreds of volumes, it has been an extremely interesting and pleasant one. The reward will certainly be ample if readers in any of the great States of our Empire find in its pages the slightest impetus to their loyalty, or any fresh light upon the great services of Her Majesty to this nation and realm.

J. CASTELL HOPKINS.

Toronto, Canada.

PREFACE TO THE MEMORIAL EDITION.

The Queen is dead ! No words regarding any possible event in the history of present humanity could mean so much to so many people as did this simple sentence on January 22nd, 1901. To men and women and children in all parts of the world the passing of their venerated Sovereign involved the breaking of a tie in which family and national sentiment had been commingled as far back as their memories could go and even beyond that to where personal affection had become a family tradition and inheritance.

To more than four hundred millions of people it meant the breaking of a link with the greatest era in the world's annals—a period of popular progress, of constitutional development, of Imperial growth, of material prosperity, of national unity and power. The Queen's reign has indeed meant much to her subjects. It has stamped the power and perpetuation of monarchical principles upon the Empire and, in doing so, has provided a permanent centre for the loyalty of distant nations and the unity of vast and diverse countries. It has incorporated democracy with monarchy, liberty with loyalty, and has made the Crown a pledge of national stability, settled government and high ideals of honour in public life. To the Queen's wise statesmanship much of the good government and contented loyalty of British countries has been due—as the pages of this volume must amply prove. To her Imperial aspirations and earnest belief in the growth of a greater and better Empire-system is due much of the marvellous feeling which now binds the Motherland and Colonies in bonds of unbreakable strength. To her personal example and noble character is due a respect for the Monarchy and a loyalty to the Monarch which exceeds even the loftiest traditional and historical sentiments of other ages.

The Diamond Jubilee of a few years since revealed the passionate pride of the people in the greatness of the Empire, gave a noble picture to the world of military splendour and naval supremacy, and illustrated the loyalty of the masses to the Crown. The death of the Queen has now given a final and still more marked proof of the personal affection of the people for their Sovereign and has shown that she lives in their hearts from London to Toronto, from Vancouver to Melbourne, from Calcutta to Cape Town. She leaves to them the legacy of a great name, a noble life, an united Empire, and a successor trained in the best principles of British rule and world-wide statecraft. With deep sorrow the people of British realms have heard that their Queen is dead, but with loyal confidence they can still say in words which echo round the world : " God Save the King."

J. CASTELL HOPKINS.

LIST OF ILLUSTRATIONS

TABLE OF CONTENTS

CHAPTER IV.

THE YOUNG QUEEN.

National conditions. The Government. Popularity of the youthful Sovereign. Ways and means. Relations with Lord Melbourne. His character, life, and capacity as a confidential adviser. The Queen and the Court. Stories of the period. Political events. The leaders of Parliament and the people. Names which seem like ancient history. Royal duties and daily work. A bright and joyous Court. Balls, concerts, and functions. The Queen fond of gaiety and riding at this time. Her Majesty at home. Lessons to her statesmen. Stories of youthful exuberance. A constitutional crisis. Melbourne and Peel. The Queen's sorrow at any prospect of losing Melbourne. Natural under the circumstances. Admirable conduct of Peel.

CHAPTER V.

BETROTHAL AND MARRIAGE.

A Royal love story. Education and surroundings of Prince Albert. His character and appearance. Aspirants for the Queen's hand. Policy of the Duchess of Kent. Baron Stockmar's remarkable qualities and career. The Queen hesitates about marriage. Visit of the Prince and sudden termination of the Royal hesitancy. Courtship and engagement. Letter from Her Majesty to King Leopold. Joy of the Prince. Romantic memories, and the evidence of beautiful personal qualities. Declaration to Parliament. A strange popular misconception. Unfortunate political incidents. The coming of the Prince. Great reception by the people. An ideal romance merges into a happy marriage.

CHAPTER VI.

HOME LIFE AND PUBLIC WORK.

A picture of domestic happiness. Difficulties of the Prince's public position. His letter to the Duke of Wellington. The Royal example to the people. The Prince at home and in the hunting field. Birth of the Princess Royal. Visit to Lord Melbourne. Fall of the Ministry. The new Government. Increasing popularity of Prince Albert. Birth of the Prince of Wales. Royal anxieties and national troubles. The Plantagenet Ball. Attempts to murder the Queen. Birth of Princess Alice. Chartist riots. Visit to Scotland. The Corn Laws and Sir Robert Peel. In the grounds at Buckingham Palace. Birth of Prince Alfred. Visit to France and Belgium.

CHAPTER VII.

ROYAL FUNCTIONS AND DUTIES.

Visit to Cambridge. Absence of the Prince for a brief period. The Emperor of Russia arrives. His character and intentions. The Queen's estimate. The King of Saxony. Visit of the Prince of Prussia and the King of the French. Opening of the Royal Exchange, London. The Queen and Prince are entertained at Burleigh, and Stowe, and Strathfieldsaye. Speech by Sir R. Peel. Political events. Royal visit to Cobourg. Up the Rhine. Pleasures of the trip. The Corn Law crisis. The Queen and Sir Robert Peel. A new Government. Birth of Princess Helena. Visit to Hatfield House and Arundel Castle. Christmas at Osborne.

CHAPTER VIII.

An Eventful Period.

Troubles with France in 1846. Various minor events. Social and personal. Political upheaval in Europe. Storm and stress everywhere. Overthrow of Louis Philippe. Birth of Princess Louise. At Balmoral Castle. Visit to Ireland. Birth of Prince Arthur. The Queen and Lord Palmerston. Death of Queen Adelaide. The Exhibition of 1851. Fancy dress ball. Louis Napoleon and France. Death of the Iron Duke and sorrow of the Queen. Changes in the Administration. Approach of the Crimean War. Character of Lord Aberdeen, and the Queen's high opinion of him. Birth of Prince Leopold. Unremitting labours of the Queen and Prince.

CHAPTER IX.

The Queen and the Crimean War.

The Aberdeen Ministry. Royal review of troops. Questions at issue with Russia. Prince Albert on the situation. The Queen's letter to Lord Aberdeen. Memorandum by the Prince. Letter from the Queen to Emperor Nicholas. Declaration of war against Russia. Letter from the King of Prussia, and reply by the Queen. Her Majesty's opinion of the war. Advice to Lord Aberdeen. The Queen on the Battle of Alma. Royal anxiety about the troops. The Battle of Inkerman. The Queen and Austria. Help to the soldiers. Influence of the Prince Consort. Resignation of Lord Aberdeen. The Queen and the crisis. A new Government. Letter to Lord Panmure regarding hospitals. Emperor Napoleon visits the Queen. Continuation of the war. Russian losses. The Queen visits France. Fall of Sebastopol. Letter from Napoleon III., and the Queen's reply. The Prince and Napoleon. Another Royal letter. Peace at last.

CHAPTER X.

Education and Training of the Royal Family.

Their responsibilities greatly felt by the Queen and Prince. Systematic plans carefully carried out. Baron Stockmar's advice. The Queen to Lord Melbourne. Her Majesty's memorandum. Lady Lyttelton chosen as governess. Training and instruction of the Prince of Wales—religious, scientific, and otherwise. His tutors, and early friends. Stories of a Royal childhood. Happy children in a happy home. The Royal family in its earlier years. Their characters and qualities. Mutual affection. Respect and obedience and kindliness constantly inculcated. Simplicity of life in the Royal household. Difficulties in training Royal children. Surrounded by temptation. Her Majesty's firmness and discipline. A Queen of the home as well as the nation.

CHAPTER XI.

Last Days of Wedded Life.

Betrothal of the Princess Royal. Visit of the King of Sardinia. The Queen opens Parliament. Reviews the Crimean regiments. Birth of Princess Beatrice. The title of " Prince Consort." Visit of the French Emperor and Empress to Osborne. The Indian Mutiny. Marriage of the Princess Royal. Lord Derby becomes Prime Minister. Royal visit to Cherbourg. The Queen's letter to the Emperor of Austria. Mr. Disraeli to the

on their return.   Opening of the Law Courts.   Death of the Duke of Albany.   Sincere
national regret.   Loss to the Queen.   Marriage of Princess Beatrice.   Opens the Parliament of 1886.   The Colonial and Indian Exhibition.   Royal visit to Liverpool.   The
Holloway College.   The Jubilee celebrations at home and abroad.   A world-wide event.
The Imperial Institute.   Memories of the past.   The Queen visits Birmingham.   Addresses
the London Corporation.   Opens the People's Palace.   The Jubilee service in Westminster
Abbey.   Grand State celebration.   Marvellous demonstrations of popularity.   Jubilee
reviews.   Addresses and replies.   Mr. Gladstone on the Queen's reign.   Letter to the
nation.   Visit to Lord Salisbury.   The Shah of Persia in England.

CHAPTER XVI.
The Queen and the Constitution.

National conditions at the Accession.   Popular conceptions of Sovereignty.   The
Queen's view of her position and duties.   At first she learns from others—the Duchess of
Kent, King Leopold, and Lord Melbourne.   Then she improves upon the previous system.
Becomes the permanent head of her Ministry.   Relations with Ministers.   Peel and
Wellington.   Palmerston and Russell.   Lord Aberdeen.   Gladstone and Beaconsfield.
Often the adviser of her own Cabinet.   Continuous growth of personal influence within the
limits of strict constitutionalism.   Effect of this upon politics and events.   The Queen's
place in the Constitution.   Her rights in choosing a Prime Minister.   Instances to the
point.   Rise of Parliamentary power.   Increase of Royal influence as opposed to the open
exercise of Royal power.   Her Majesty a great statesman in the fullest meaning of the
word.

CHAPTER XVII.
The Prince of Wales.

His early life and character.   Careful training in Royal duties.   Difficult position of
an heir apparent.   His youthful travels and pursuits.   With Dean Stanley in the
Holy Land.   The loss of his noble father.   Journeys in Europe.   Visit to Canada and
the United States.   Marriage to the Princess Alexandra.   Her character and life work.   At
Sandringham.   Its beauty and charm.   The rising family.   Their training and home life.
Marlborough House as a centre of public work and duty.   The Prince in society.   His
place in charitable and philanthropic work.   His fondness for sport.   Hard, unremitting
labours of his position.   Unfair criticism and false statements.   The death of Prince
Albert Victor, and marriage of the Duke of York.   Environments of Royalty.   Responsibility and restriction.   The Prince in Germany, India, and Russia.   Popularity at home,
and influence abroad.   The Royal Derby, and the marriage of Princess Maud.

CHAPTER XVIII.
The Court and the Sovereign.

The Court in the early part of the century.   George IV. and William IV.   The
Queen makes a great change.   Its lasting importance.   Prince Albert helps in purifying
and elevating the environment of the throne.   It becomes an example to the nation.
The Queen in society.   Before and after the Prince Consort's death.   State
ceremonials and Court functions.   Her Majesty upholds the dignity of the Crown and adds

prestige to the position of her country. Questions of morality and etiquette. Conversation and amusements. Art, science, and literature. The bestowal of honours. Wordsworth, Tennyson, and Austin. Difference between the Court of Victoria and that of the Empress Eugenie, or those of European sovereigns of to-day. Effect of Her Majesty's example and views upon public morals and living. Divorce laws as an instance. A higher ideal of private and domestic life.

CHAPTER XIX.

IRELAND AND THE MONARCHY.

Susceptible character of the Irish people. Possibilities of loyalty. The troubles of 1848. Visit of the Queen and Prince Albert. Enthusiastic reception. Queenstown and Cork and Dublin. A memorable sight in Kingstown Harbour. A continued Jubilee in the Irish capital. The Levee, and review of troops. Speech by the Prince Consort. Visit to Ulster. Great reception at Belfast. Opinion of Lord Clarendon. Letter from Prince Albert. In Ireland again (1853). Influence of the Queen's visits. What might have been. A Royal visit in 1861. The Lakes of Killarney. The loyal peasantry. Troubles of the people. Agitators and agitations. Home Rule and its leaders. Visits of the Prince of Wales. Popular receptions. Advantage of Monarchical institutions to the Irish people. Union with England. The duties of Royalty. An Irish residence. The Queen's sympathies. Her influence upon the masses.

CHAPTER XX.

CANADA UNDER THE QUEEN.

British America in 1837. Influence of the Monarchical principle. The Rebellion. and Lord Durham. Resolution in Legislature of Lower Canada. The Prince of Wales in Canada. Loyal receptions. Letters from the Duke of Newcastle to the Queen. Lord Elgin. Confederation and the Queen. Canada and the Royal titles. Her Majesty's representatives. Value of their work and influence. The Princess Louise at Ottawa. Visits of Prince Arthur and Prince Leopold. The Queen and Sir John Macdonald. Growth of popular loyalty. Effect upon national unity and our relations with the States. Lord Dufferin's view of the Queen's influence. A crowned Democracy. The Colonial Conference of 1887. The Queen's Jubilee. Resolutions—Parliamentary and general. Celebrations in Canada. The development of a half century. Visit of Prince George. Imperial Conference of 1894. Sir John Thompson at Windsor. Memories of Royal sympathy. The Crown and the Canadian people.

CHAPTER XXI.

AUSTRALASIA UNDER THE QUEEN.

The Australian character. Difficulties of development. Value of the stable Monarchical principle amidst the wildly fluctuating progress of the Colonies. Victoria named after the Queen. Her Majesty also names Queensland. Growth of constitutional rule. The Governors of the Colonies and their excellent work. The Peerage scheme. Visits of the Duke of Edinburgh, Prince Albert Victor, and Prince George. Recent invitation to the Duke of York. Federation Conference. Australian statesmen and the Queen. The Jubilee celebrations. Loyal addresses. The Australian Centenary. Telegram from the Queen. The Soudan contingent. Marvellous evidences of loyalty and enthusiastic British sentiment. The Colonial Conference and Naval Defence Fund. Some recent Governors. Lord Jersey, Lord Carrington, Lord Hopetown. In New Zealand. Development and history of the New England of the southern seas. The Queen and the Maoris. Lord Onslow and the Queen's Jubilee. The general position of Australasia and the influence of Her Majesty's name, and life, and popularity in moulding its past and future.

CHAPTER XXII.

South Africa Under the Queen.

A glimpse of South African history. Influences of Monarchy amongst savage races. The countries and peoples of South Africa. Sir George Grey's scheme of federation. Visit of the Duke of Edinburgh. Letter from Sir George Grey. The Prince and the Natives. Kaffir letter. The Prince Consort and Cape Colony. Statues of the Queen. Growth of British territory. Sir Bartle Frere. Lord Carnarvon tries his hand at federation. Zululand and the Transvaal. The Boers and the Natives. Appeals from the latter to the Queen. The Jubilee of the Queen's reign. South Africa at the conferences in London and Ottawa. Mr. Hofmeyr. Trouble with the Boers. Their history and characteristics. Rise of Cecil Rhodes. His ambitious schemes and patriotic motives. Successes and failures. The Jameson raid. The Queen's place in South African history. The Monarchy and its share in giving free Government to the Cape and Natal.

CHAPTER XXIII.

India Under the Queen.

Prestige of Royalty amongst the millions of Hindostan. From the Company to the Queen. Memories of the past. Lord Ellenborough's letters to the Queen. The Indian Mutiny. Royal anxieties. Correspondence between Lord Canning and the Queen. Prince Albert on the situation. Constant advice from Her Majesty. Parliamentary debates. Transfer from the East Indian Company to the Crown. The Queen's proclamation to the people. Change in its wording. Immediate and beneficial effect. Her interest in Indian problems. Lord Dalhousie and the Queen. Letters to Lord Lawrence. The Prince of Wales visits India. Enthusiastic reception everywhere. Good done by the tour. Lord Beaconsfield's far-sighted policy. The Queen made Empress of India. The Royal proclamation. Lord Lytton and the native Princes. Evidences of loyalty. The people of India and Russian invasion. Romantic ideas of the Queen's personality. Letter to the author from Lord Northbrook. Her Majesty's Viceroys. Lord Dufferin and Burmah. Value of Imperial rule in India, and potentiality for good of the Queen's name.

CHAPTER XXIV.

The Queen's Influence Upon Foreign Affairs.

Monarchical institutions and diplomacy. Importance to a world-wide empire of a stable centre from which to deal with foreign powers. The personal influence of the Queen a growing quantity during fifty years. Lord Palmerston first feels the weight of her displeasure. Added experience brings more and more power. Family connections steadily increase this influence. Her Majesty's correspondence with King Leopold. Her letters to

Louis Philippe. Her advice to the Emperor of Austria. Letters to the Czar of Russia during the Crimean War. Correspondence with Napoleon III. Opinions upon foreign questions. Italian Independence and the French alliance. Ambition of Napoleon III. Relations with United States. The Schleswig-Holstein question. The Queen and her Minister of Foreign Affairs. Liking for Palmerston's later policy, and for Lord Beaconsfield's ideas of expansion. A thorough Imperialist. Her Majesty's wide knowledge of European diplomacy. Her present influence with the Emperors of Germany and Russia. Her wide foreign correspondence. Important services to the nation and the cause of peace·

CHAPTER XXV.

THE QUEEN AND THE UNITED STATES.

Past relations between Great Britain and the Republic. What they should be in future. Differences in Government, life, character, and modes of thought. The Queen ever a friend to peace and desirous of cultivating the closest and kindliest ties with the Republic. Her special courtesy to Americans. Opinions of Emerson, Motley, Hawthorne, and Holmes. Letter from the Queen to President Buchanan. Visit of the Prince of Wales to the United States. Cordial reception. The Queen's letter to Mrs. Lincoln. George Peabody and his London charities. Kindness of Her Majesty. The Queen and Mrs. Garfield. Many instances of sympathy. Her sentiments regarding slavery and the Civil War. Lowell, Phelps, and Bayard at the Court of St. James. The other side of the shield. Abuse of Royalty. False stories of the Prince of Wales and the Royal family. The American press and the British Monarchy. Ignorance and prejudice. Attitude towards Canada and the Empire. Questions of arbitration and friendship. Mutual toleration required. England anxious to be friends with the Republic. A great ideal, but one which requires a clearer American perception of British institutions. The Queen and the future of the race.

CHAPTER XXVI.

THE QUEEN AT HOME.

Domestic life in Royal palaces. External glitter and pomp, internal simplicity and peace. The Queen's favourite residences. Windsor as the abode of Royal state and ceremony. Its grandeur and historic fame. Buckingham Palace, the London residence and occasional home of the Court. Changes since Prince Albert's time. Kensington Palace—the great and homely abode of the youthful Princess. Now occupied chiefly by Lord Lorne and the Princess Louise. Osborne and Balmoral the favourite abodes of Her Majesty. Beauty of the Highland scenery at Balmoral. Osborne the result of the united plans and work of the Prince Consort and the Queen. Rare art works in the Royal palaces. Hampton Court and the great painters. Rare china, great curiosities, national trophies. The home life of the Queen and daily pursuits. In youth and in old age. A gulf of sorrows and splendours between. Visit of M. Guizot to Windsor. Lady Canning's letters. Other reminiscences. A great life amid great surroundings.

CHAPTER XXVII.

THE ROYAL FAMILY.

Their varied lives and characters. Incidents of travel and work. Constant toil an essential of Royal existence. The Queen's influence over her surviving children. Her many griefs and losses.   Happy marriages and scattered homes.   The Princess Royal and Germany.   The late Princess Alice at Hesse-Darmstadt.   The Duke of Edinburgh at Clarence House and in Cobourg.   The Princess Louise at Kensington and in Ottawa. The Duke of Connaught at Bagshot Park.   The brief and noble life of the Duke of Albany.   The good work of the Princess Helena (Princess Christian).   Princess Beatrice and her loving service to the Queen.   Her Majesty's many grandchildren and great-grand-children.   Princess Alix upon the throne of Russia.   William II. and the Empire of Germany.   The Duke and Duchess of York.   Their popularity and wide public duties. The late Duke of Clarence.   Physcial weakness and high character.   The Queen's regard for him.   Mr. Gladstone's tribute.   A widely scattered family, influenced in their varied spheres of work and rule by the life and teachings of England's Queen.

CHAPTER XXVIII.

HER MAJESTY'S FRIENDS AND CONTEMPORARIES.

The memorable period during which the Queen has reigned.   Her intimacy with the leaders in literature and art, politics and international statecraft, during several generations. Natural ability combined with lofty position gave her this distinction.   Dean and Lady Augusta Stanley.   Lord Tennyson.   The Duke of Wellington.   Sir Robert Peel and Lord Aberdeen.   Mr. Gladstone and Lord Beaconsfield.   Lord Lytton.   Thomas Carlyle and his rugged genius.   Mr. W. H. Smith.   Charles Dickens.   Mr. W. E. Forster.   Sir Bartle Frere.   Lord Cross.   Reminiscences of Sir Archibald Allison.   The Queen's Prime Ministers.   Lord Malmesbury's diary.   Lord Palmerston.   As the years pass Her Majesty's friends have disappeared.   New friendships have been formed and again shattered by the hand of death.   The late Sir Henry Ponsonby the last of Her Majesty's trusted servants from the days of Prince Albert.   Three generations of British leaders have come and gone.   The sovereigns of Europe all changed since the Queen's accession.   Five Russian rulers since 1837.   Wide experience, however, and much pleasure gained from so prolonged an acquaintance with the genius and greatness of the world.

CHAPTER XXIX.

MODERN DEMOCRACY AND THE QUEEN.

The Throne and the people.   A stable centre around which democracy can develop. A rampart against revolution, and a permanent strength to the State in its external rela-tions.   The pivot of Imperial supremacy.   Burke on Monarchical institutions.   Their limitations, as now understood in England, make them the happy medium between unbridled republicanism and immoderate despotism.   Views of the Prince Consort.   Mr. Gladstone on the Monarchy.   Lord Beaconsfield's opinion.   The sentiment of loyalty. The place of the Peers in British public life.   Value of their work and functions.   Parlia-ment and the Queen.   Records of futile Republican agitation.   Dilke and Labouchere. The Queen as the source of honour.   The Church and the Crown.   The spirit of democ-racy.   Not necessarily opposed to Monarchy.   True patriotism combines national freedom with national dignity.   The latter not visible in Republican institutions.   The British limited Monarchy under the Queen's interpretation combines liberty, dignity, stability, and diplomatic power.

CHAPTER XXX.

The Queen and the Empire.

Empires of the past.   Inherent seeds of disintegration.   The adaptability of the British Constitution.   Its easy adjustment to new conditions and distant countries.   Elastic nature of the relationship between the colonies and the Mother Country.   Monarchical institutions and the unity of the empire.   The Queen's wide influence.   Resolutions of conferences and public bodies.   The Jubilee celebrations an evidence of the strength of this element of union.   The representatives of the Queen.   Old-time character of the men sent out.   The new type of governors.   Value of their presence in the colonies and importance of their work.   A training school for statesmen.   The Colonial Secretaries of the past and present.   Change in the position and its duties.   Imperial influence of Lord Beaconsfield. Rise of the Rosebery-Chamberlain type of leader.   British foreign policy now controlled by colonial interests.   The Queen, the Monarchy, and the New Empire.

CHAPTER XXXI

A Glorious Sunset.

Last years of a great reign.   Lord Salisbury, Lord Rosebery, Mr. Balfour, and Mr. Chamberlain rise to the surface of affairs.   The Queen visits Wales.   The German Emperor arrives in England.   The Duke of Clarence—betrothal and death.   The Queen opens the Imperial Institute.   State functions and Royal marriages.   Princess Louise, of Wales, Princess Marie, of Edinburgh, the Duke of York, Princess Victoria, of Edinburgh, and other members of the Royal Family, married amid popular rejoicings.   The Queen's health.   Her occasional appearance in public.   Loyalty of the people at home and abroad. Affection felt for her personally in all the homes of her vast empire.   Continued influence for peace in the world and good in the nation.   Labouring still for the welfare of her people.   Loss of Prince Henry of Battenberg.   Death from time to time of her favourite grandchildren and children.   Lonely splendour of the Throne.   A solace in the affection of millions, and the veneration of the world.

CHAPTER XXXII.

The Diamond Jubilee.

The greatest day in British history.   Far-reaching importance of the event.   Enthusiasm throughout the Empire.   Elaborate preparations for the celebration.   Popular generosity to charitable projects.   The Queen leaves Windsor.   Amongst her people for a brief moment.   State receptions at Buckingham Palace.   The Colonial Premiers honoured. The great procession starts on the 22nd of June.   The Queen's message to an Imperial people.   The Colonial Contingents' magnificent greeting from the British masses.   Sir Wilfrid Laurier and Lord Roberts the popular favourites amongst the notabilities present. Marvellous demonstration of love and loyalty to the Queen.   Ceremonies at St. Paul's Cathedral.   Magnificence of the scene.   Description of the great procession and the wild enthusiasm.   Fêtes, State Banquets and Royal Receptions.   Return to Windsor.   The Naval Review and its splendid proof of British power.   The universal welcome to the Colonial Premiers.   A week's Jubilee festivities.   Continued compliments to the Colonial visitors.   Around the Empire.   The Jubilee in Africa, India, Canada, Australia and the Isles of the Seas.   The greatest Sovereign in the world fittingly acclaimed by the world's greatest Empire.

CHAPTER XXXIII.

The Close of a Noble Life.

Last years of work and thought. The Duke and Duchess of York in Ireland. Death of the Princess Mary of Teck. The Queen and Mr. Gladstone. Her Majesty's 80th Birthday. The Queen's relation to South African Policy. Royal Visit to Ireland. Death of Prince Christian Victor in South Africa. Reception of returning troops. The Queen and the Empire's Soldiers. Announcement of the Duke and Duchess of York's visit to Australia. The Queen and the new Commonwealth. The Irish soldiers and the Royal Shamrock order. Death of the Duke of Edinburgh and Saxe-Coburg-Gotha. The Queen and her troops. The loyalty of Canada and the Battle of Paardeberg. The Royal Canadian Regiment reviewed by Her Majesty. Rumours of illness. The deathbed of a great ruler. Scenes of mourning throughout a vast Empire. The funeral of the Queen. Tributes of her army, navy, people and far-flung realm. Resting in peace.

H.R.H. FIELD MARSHAL THE DUKE OF KENT.
THE FATHER OF QUEEN VICTORIA.

AN EARLY PORTRAIT OF PRINCESS VICTORIA.

H.R.H. THE DUCHESS OF KENT, THE MOTHER OF QUEEN VICTORIA.

CHAPTER I.

THE MONARCHY:

HE life of Queen Victoria has impressed itself upon the character, the social customs, the moral environment, and the home institutions of British peoples throughout the world. Her long reign and personal influence has modified the nature of Monarchical government; has transfused its constitutional forms throughout the national life of great and widely scattered communities; has developed its best and noblest elements in harmony with the instincts of a progressive civilization; has combined liberty with stability, and transmuted the loyalty due to a lofty principle of traditional rule into devoted allegiance to the personality and power of a great modern ruler. And, during this most memorable period the British realm has seen a march of commerce, an expansion of territory, a development of thought, a growth of Imperial power, unequalled in its own or any other history.

Through all these various phases of progress may be seen the influence of the Monarchical principle, the living power of personal loyalty to a great Sovereign or a splendid ideal. Whether it be the sentiment felt by the soldier standing with his comrades upon the burning sands of Africa; the feeling of allegiance which prevented the Canadian settler in earlier days from joining in rash revolutionary movements for the redress of admitted local grievances; or the prestige gathering around the name of the Queen-Empress as the proclamation of her Imperial rule closed the melancholy incidents of the Indian Mutiny, this influence of the Monarchy upon the events of many succeeding years has been as great as its moulding effect upon the character, manners, and customs of the masses has been elevating and beneficial. The British Sovereign has, in fact, and in the truest sense of the term, led her people forward during the last sixty years, and has distinctly embodied in her policy and rule the highest aspirations of the best minds in the nation.

To a greater extent than is, indeed, generally understood in these democratic days the Monarchy in Great Britain has, during a thousand years, permeated the national development and expansion. Through nearly all British history the Sovereign has either represented the popular instincts of the time or else led in the direction of extended territory and power under the forceful influence of royal valour or statecraft.   The history of England is not, of course, confined to the biography of its Kings and Queens, but it would be as absurd to trace those annals without extended study of the rulers and their characters as it would be to write its records without reference to the people.   And the Monarchy has done much for the British Isles.   Its influence has affected their whole national life in war and in peace, in religion and in morals, in literature and in art.   The individual achievements and actions of some of these rulers are to be found as the very foundation stones in the structure of modern British power.   Others again have helped to build the walls of the edifice, while the Sovereign at the close of the Nineteenth century has become the pivot upon which turns the constitutional unity of the Empire and which forms the only possible centre for a common allegiance amongst its peoples.

At first this Monarchical principle was embodied in the form of military power, was based upon feudal loyalty, and was hedged in with the noble ideals, but somewhat reckless practices, of mediæval chivalry.   The victories of Egbert and Alfred the Great transformed the Heptarchy into a substantial English Kingdom.   The military skill of William the Conqueror gave an opportunity to blend the graces of Norman chivalry and a somewhat higher form of civilization with the rougher virtues of the Saxon character.   Henry II. personally illustrated this combination, with his ruddy English face and strong physical powers, and impressed himself upon British history by the conquest of Ireland.   Richard Coeur de Lion gave his country many famous pages of Crusading in the East, and embodied in his life and character the adventurous and daring spirit of the age.   Edward I. dominated events by his energy and ability, subdued Wales, and for a time conquered the Kingdom of Scotland.   Edward III., in his long reign of fifty years, carried the British flag high over the fields of France, and won immortality at the battles of Crecy and Poictiers.   Henry V. gained the victory of Agincourt, and won and wore the title of King of France.   Then came the Wars of the Roses and the turbulent termination to a period of six centuries during which the English monarchs had represented the military spirit of their time, and had led in the rough process of struggle and conquest out of which was growing the United Kingdom of to-day.

With the reign of Henry VIII. commenced the period of religious change, the struggles of religious liberty against ecclesiastical dominance.   Limited as were the achievements of Henry and Elizabeth, in this respect, by prevailing bigotry and narrowness of view, they none the less did great service to the country and the people.   The rule of Cromwell—who, in the exercise of Royal power, and the possession of regal personal ability, may properly be included in such a connection—gave that liberty of worship to the masses with which previous Sovereigns had more especially endowed the classes.   During the reigns of the Stuarts religious discussions, and ecclesiastical controversies, and intermittent persecutions, illustrated the predominant passion of the period, and forced the weak or indifferent monarch of the moment to be an unconscious factor in the progress towards that general toleration which the Revolution of 1688 and the crowning of William III. finally accomplished. But whether it was Henry persecuting the monks, or Elizabeth the Roman Catholics, or Mary the Protestants, or Cromwell the Episcopalians, or Charles II. the Dissenters, each ruler was being led, to a great degree, by the undercurrents of surrounding bigotry, and was in the main representing some strong, popular sentiment of the time. Henry voiced the national uprising against Rome, just as the second Charles embodied popular reaction against the Puritans, and William of Orange was enabled to lead a successful opposition to the gloomy and personal bigotry of the last of the royal Stuarts.

The third period of British Monarchical history was that marked by the growth toward Constitutional government under the sway of the House of Hanover. Coupled with this was the equally important foundation of a great Colonial empire, and the loss of a large portion of it in the reign of George III. But the development of Constitutional rule under the Georges must not be confounded with the growth of that popular system which exists to-day. The latter is a progressive evolution out of the aristocratic and oligarchical government of the Hanoverian period, just as it had been a step from the kingly power of the Tudors and the Stuarts, which, in turn, had arisen upon the ruins of feudalism and military monarchical power. It is this gradual growth—this " gently broadening down from precedent to precedent "—which makes the British constitution of to-day the more or less perfected fabric of centuries of experience and struggle. But that result has only been made possible by the peculiar series of national adjustments in which the power of the monarchs has been modified from time to time to suit the will of the people, while the ability of individual sovereigns has been given full scope in which to exercise wise kingcraft or pronounced military skill. It has, in fact, been a most elastic system, and to that elasticity has been due its prolonged stability of form under a succession of dynastic changes.

It would be a mistake to minimize the importance and value of the aristocratic rule by which the government of England was graded down from the high exercise of royal power under the Tudors and Stuarts to that beneficial exercise of royal influence which marks the close of the present period. To the aristocracy of these two centuries is mainly due the fact that the growth from paternal government and personal rule to direct popular administration was a gradual development, through occasional scenes of storm and stress, instead of being a constant succession of revolutions alternating with civil war. Somers and Godolphin, Walpole and Chatham, Pitt and Shelburne, Eldon and Canning, Grey and Liverpool, Wellington and Durham, Melbourne and

Palmerston were all of this class, though of varying degrees in rank and title. They filled the chief places in the Government of the country during a period when the people were being slowly, and perhaps painfully, trained in the perception and practice of constitutional and religious liberty. At the best such processes are difficult, and often prove bitter tests of national endurance; but it was well for Great Britain that these two centuries produced a class of able and cultured men who—though naturally Tory at heart—were upon the whole honestly bent upon furthering the best interests of the masses. And this despite the mistakes of a Danby or a North.

Yet, even towards the close of this period of preparation, popular government as now practised was neither understood by the immediate predecessors of Queen Victoria, nor by the nobles who presided over the changing administrations of the day. It was not clearly comprehended by men like Russell and Grey, it was feared by Wellington and the Tories as being republican and revolutionary, it was dreaded by many who could hardly be called Tories, and who, in the condition of things then prevalent, could scarcely even be termed loyalists. Writing in 1812, Charles Knight, the afterwards veteran author, describes the fierce national struggle of the previous twenty years with Napoleon, and expresses a longing wish for the prop of a sincere and spontaneous loyalty to the throne in the critical times that must follow. But such a sentiment of loyalty was not then expressed, and could hardly have been publicly evoked by a ruler of the type of George IV., whether governing as prince regent or as king.

There is, however, no doubt of its having existed, and there seems to have been through all these troubled years an inborn spirit of loyalty to the Crown as being the symbol of the State and public order. Its wearer might make mistakes, and be personally unpopular, but he represented the nation as a whole, and must consequently be respected. This powerful feeling has often in English history made the bravest and strongest submit to slights from their sovereign, and has won the most disinterested devotion and energetic action from men who have never even seen the monarch in whose personal character there was sometimes little to evoke or deserve such faith and sacrifice. For ages this loyalty had been the preservative of society in England, and it is still indispensable to the tranquillity and permanence of a state, whether given to the sovereign of Great Britain, or to the elective and partisan head of a modern republic.

At that time, as well as in the middle ages and at the present moment, loyalty was, and is, a sincere and honest patriotism, refining the instincts and elevating the actions of those who were willing to waive self-interest on any given occasion in order to guard what they believed to be the true basis of national stability and order. Certainly a monarchy which could survive the

HIS MAJESTY GEORGE THE FOURTH,
KING OF GREAT BRITAIN AND IRELAND.

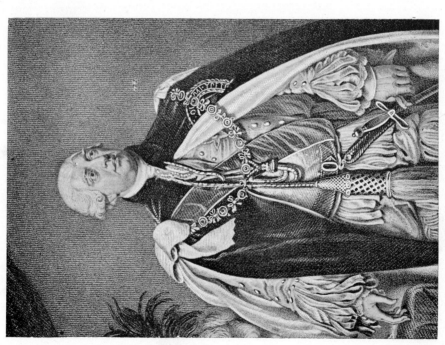

HIS MAJESTY GEORGE THE THIRD,
KING OF GREAT BRITAIN AND IRELAND.

HIS MAJESTY WILLIAM THE FOURTH.
KING OF GREAT BRITAIN AND IRELAND.

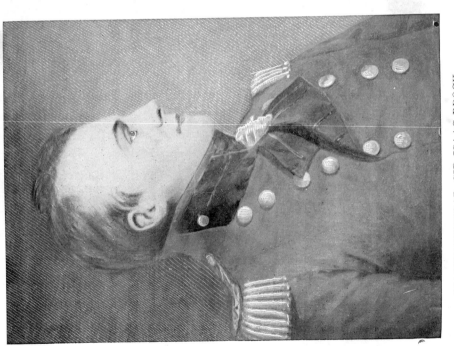

MAJOR GENERAL, SIR ISAAC BROCK.

wars and European revolutions, the internal discontents and personal deficiencies, of the period which commenced with the reign of George I. and closed with that of William IV. must have possessed some inherent strength greater than may be gathered from many of the superficial works which pass for history. But whatever that influence was it does not appear to have been personal. With the close of the reign of Queen Anne the brilliant prestige of personal authority and power wielded by the sovereign passed quietly away, and up to the death of William IV. had not yet been replaced by the vast influence of a constitutional ruler.

The earlier sovereigns of the House of Hanover, George I. and George II., were unfortunate rather than blameworthy. They came to the throne without having been imbued by education or training with the national spirit and traditions which might have made them distinguished without being great. They were—with certain important exceptions—usually content to be guided and governed by the aristocracy of the realm, and perhaps, in the transition state of affairs which then existed, this was best for the nation and best for the monarchy. But it steadily undermined the personal element, which had hitherto been so strong a pillar of the monarchical principle. George III. was doubly unfortunate in having a strong will of his own, in exercising it honestly but mistakenly, and in going down to posterity with an undeserved reputation for despotism, and a responsibility for acts and conditions often due to his advisers, or to the dominance of the Prince Regent in the King's sorrowful closing years. His education had been lacking in almost every element which should properly have been present, with the exception of religious sentiment and observance. His father, Frederick, Prince of Wales, died before coming to the throne; but, during his career, had made his royal residence the headquarters of the Opposition of the day, much as the future George IV., in long-after years, was to make Carlton House the centre of a similar antagonism.

George III. was brought up in utter ignorance of constitutional rule, or the history of European governments, and even of the conditions under which his family had come to the throne, and by which he should have been guided. With all these early deficiencies, however, he proved himself a thorough Englishman, and all the more so for possessing the faults as well as the virtues of such a character. He voiced the prejudices as well as the determination of the people. He was temperate, frugal, devout, courageous, affectionate, and hard-working. And in the war policy against the American colonies he represented the feelings of the nation as a whole—feelings which not even the thundering echoes of Chatham's magic voice could sway in the opposite direction. It is forgotten now, or partially concealed in the mass of hostile literature created by the split in the race, that the King of England acted from as patriotic motives, in that memorable struggle with the thirteen colonies, as ever actuated a ruler in history. He indeed believed the prosperity of the Empire to be as thoroughly involved in the maintenance of his American dominion as ever Abraham Lincoln felt the prosperity of the great Republic to depend upon the preservation of its union.

For years, by the pure force of his own will, he persevered in these unfortunate hostilities, but in doing so he was emphatically the leader of the masses in England as against the classes. " Before I will hear of any man's readiness to come into office," he once wrote Lord North, " I will expect to see it signed under his hand that he is resolved to keep the empire entire." Writing on June 12th, 1781, he declared that " we have the greatest objects to make us zealous in our pursuit, for we are contending for our whole consequence, whether we are to rank amongst the great powers of Europe, or be reduced to one of the least considerable." Again, on November 3rd, he wrote to Lord North, " I feel the justice of our cause ; I put the greatest confidence in the valour of our Army and Navy, and, above all, in the assistance of Divine Providence." And, whether his policy was unwise or not in its ultimate result, the motives of George III. seem to have been worthy of a king, while his character has deserved far greater praise than it usually receives.

In following years he stood firmly and strongly behind Pitt, and supported that brilliant leader through all his stupendous struggles with Napoleon, and in his hardly less difficult conflicts at home with the eloquence of Fox or the truculence of Burke. In a constitutional sense he still appears with distinctness as having sometimes supported the people against the Peers, during a period in which the latter seemed almost supreme ; and as having preserved a homely, simple style of living, amid surroundings of corruption and debauchery. In the latter years of his long reign insanity gave the Crown into the practical keeping of the son who, in 1820, became George IV. Little can be said in favour of this dissipated, frivolous, but marvellously polite personage. His appearance was good, and his manners so charming that they won him the title of "the first gentleman in Europe." His reign is chiefly marked and marred by the disgraceful controversy with his wife, the unpleasant domestic details of his life, and the unfortunate qualities and career of her who should have been the recognized Queen of England—Caroline of Brunswick. He had, however, strong ideas regarding monarchical power, and more than once vented a personal prejudice in excluding Canning from Ministries which his eloquence would have adorned and his liberalized Toryism have greatly benefited.

He was also opposed to the recognition of the South American colonies in their struggle against Spain, and in this had the sympathy of the Duke of Wellington. But Lord Liverpool, the Premier, held different views, and, with Canning, believed that England should act with, and not against, the embryo republics, in order to keep them from " consolidating their system and policy with the United States of America." Writing to the Duke, on December 8th, 1824, Lord Liverpool observed: "I am quite aware that the King has strong prejudices on this subject ; I am very sorry for it, but I am satisfied that they originate partly in mistake as to the origin of the separation of the colonies from the mother country (Spain). I think he should be set right upon this point, as well as made to feel that the opinions which he sometimes avows on the subject of legitimacy would carry him to the full length of the principles of the Emperor of Russia and Prince Metternich." •

This is strong language from a Tory Premier, and shows what might have been expected had George IV. lived till the days of the Reform Bill. And the Duke of Wellington had a similar experience in connection with the influence of the Duke of Cumberland over his royal brother. "Between the King and his brothers," wrote Wellington in 1828, "it is next to impossible to govern this country." So with Peel and Canning in their prolonged efforts to carry Catholic emancipation in face of the King's hostility. Fortunately for the welfare of the Monarchy and the country his successor did not prove so bent on exercising the Royal prerogative, although at times he showed himself quite able and willing to do so. Hence perhaps the fact that this nineteenth century in England has been one of peaceful evolution and progress. This development has, in the main, been guided by wisdom and modified by experience, and, if the negative virtues of William IV. enabled the process to commence, the positive qualities of Queen Victoria have accelerated its growth and aided its beneficial application. The Duke of Clarence, indeed, made quite a popular King during the greater part of his reign. The contrast with his predecessor had possibly something to do with this feeling, and his coronation was certainly not attended with such remarks as that of Stratford Canning, the Lord Stratford de Redcliffe of a later time, who recorded the accession of George IV. in his diary with the remark: "God grant that this may not prove a disastrous day for the British Monarchy."

King William's bluff and hearty manners were a relief after the graceful hypocrisy of his brother, and his undoubted benevolence of disposition and supposed tendency to Liberalism, in the non-partisan sense of that word, helped the popularity which he soon obtained. Many stories are told of him, and one of these shows how strongly he felt and spoke upon occasion, and how well he voiced the manners of a period which too often practised roughness of language and a certain disregard of the forms of courtesy. The late Archbishop Tait of Canterbury records in his diary the ceremony which took place in 1856, upon his appointment as Bishop of London. He describes the Act of Homage to the Queen, and then adds: "Longley, the new Bishop of Durham, who had accompanied me, then went through the same ceremony. He had not escaped so quietly when he had been consecrated Bishop of Ripon. His oath was then taken to William IV., and no sooner had he risen from his knees than the King suddenly addressed him in a loud voice :—'Bishop of Ripon, I charge you, as you shall answer before Almighty God, that you never, by word or deed, give encouragement to those d——d Whigs, who would upset the Church of England.'"

William IV. was fortunate in commencing his reign with such a dignified courteous, and tactful Minister as Earl Grey, but he was unfortunate, during the Reform crisis, in having his heart with the Opposition, while the growing environment of constitutional government compelled him to give his hand to the Ministry of the moment. In this difficult position he has never been accused of treachery, although he held out against the Reform Bill until almost the last external ramparts of royal power were pulled down, and amid the flames of Bristol and the ruins of Nottingham a revolution seemed to be imminent. "I went home," says a Whig diarist in May, 1832, "turning in my mind what place of refuge I should seek with my family on the Continent." Eventually, however, the King gave way, Earl Grey was given the privilege of naming the necessary number of Peers, and the Reform Bill passed the House of Lords through the abstention of its opponents, and without the carrying out of such a drastic and desperate expedient.

Two years later the King used his prerogative in a way which precedent then justified, but which practice has now rendered dormant, and excusable or possible only under circumstances of great national moment. Writing to Lord Melbourne on Nov. 14th, 1834, he referred to the apparent unpopularity of his Ministry in the country and its narrow majority in the House, and added: " His Majesty, therefore, under this view, and the apprehension of contingencies which the King has expressed to Lord Melbourne personally, does not think it would be acting fairly or honourably by his Lordship to call upon the Viscount for the continuance of his services in a position of which the tenure appears to the King so precarious." The result in the end proved an increase of strength to Melbourne and the Whigs, and the return of the former to power after a general election. But despite this very considerable exercise of power the King retained much of his popularity, and his character has in recent years been relieved of some of the unjust charges which the Greville memoirs have rendered current. He was, in fact, a typical Englishman of the day, and, with all his faults, gloried in his country and served it, so far as his faculties would permit, faithfully, honestly and loyally. Such then, were the general precedents and methods of governing when Queen Victoria came to the Throne in 1837, and attained

"The slippery tops of human state,
The gilded pinnacles of fate."

But this event, so fortunate for the nation and the Monarchy, seems, in looking back, to have been almost the sport of chance, if indeed, it were not the deliberate design of Providence. Up to 1817, the heiress to the Throne had been Princess Charlotte, the only child of George IV., and the victim from her birth of all manner of misfortunes, of contaminating surroundings, of undignified and altogether wretched family quarrels. That in spite of these influences, and the environment of an evil Court, she should have become a sweet and promising young woman, with distinct abilities and an excellent disposition, opens up one of the most pathetic pages in all the royal history of Shakespeare's sceptred Isle. The character of her father all the world knows. The misfortunes of her mother and her character of weakness verging upon something worse, and combining a superficial cleverness with an absolute want of tact and refinement, is also pretty well known. Born at Carlton House in 1796, the Princess grew up amid every possible element of family discord, alternating with periods of rigid control such as those with which the somewhat narrow-minded Queen Charlotte delighted to surround the child of her wayward son. With a strong sense of duty, and a loving, truthful, and generous disposition, the young Princess derived from her mother a somewhat quick and vehement temper, but she was always anxious to do right, had a very full and vivid sense of her responsibility as a possible Queen of England, and loved her country so fervently, that despite the remonstrances of her family and every pressure which could be brought to bear, she broke off an engagement with the Prince of Orange in 1814, rather than risk the chance of having to live for any length of time out of England.

Her political education was as peculiar and erratic as was the moral example set her by the nearest members of her own family. Instead of being trained to an impartial perception of the national conditions and the position of a modern limited monarchy, she was at first taught the extremest Whig partisanship. Speaking in 1812, the Prince Regent, who then affected Whiggism, as he probably would have supported anything in opposition to his father, said, "I have made it my care to instil into the mind and heart of my daughter the knowledge and love of the true principles of the British constitution; and I have pointed out to her young understanding, as a model for study, the political conduct of my most revered and lamented friend, Mr. Fox, who has asserted and maintained with such transcendent force the just principles under which the Government ought to be administered."

Not long after this the Prince Regent changed his views, but found it difficult to effect any modification in those of his daughter. Writing to the Earl of Albemarle on Jan. 17th, 1812, she spoke of Fox's "great name and great deeds"; of his "uncorrupted integrity," of his denunciations of the slave trade and wise advocacy of religious liberty, and of "his laudable exertions for universal toleration and comfort to our unfortunate and grossly abused sister kingdoms." For a girl of sixteen these were pretty strong expressions, and, coupled with a strength of character which enabled her upon occasion to defy her whole family and to assert that, "I am not one of those Princesses who mean to leave the choice of their husbands to others," seem to indicate that there might have been some stormy scenes had she ever ascended the Throne. Upon the other hand, however, it is not unlikely that age would have mellowed the mind, while her happy marriage with Prince Leopold of Saxe-Coburg would have placed her more and more, as time passed by, under the influence of the ripe intellect which in succeeding years was to make him a royal statesman of the first rank.

But, after one brief year of wedded happiness, she passed away on Nov. 6th, 1817, amidst a sentiment of national grief so sincere and universal as to well prove the depth and strength of British loyalty when it has a really bright and hopeful personality to look up to and respect. Popular sentiment had indeed gradually wound itself around the fair young heiress to the Throne, as the one pleasing spot in a dark background, and had commenced to look upon the Princess Charlotte as a future Queen Elizabeth. Hence the plaintive lines of Southey in memory of " The Flower of Brunswick":

> " Late with youth and splendour crown'd,
> Late in beauty's vernal bloom,
> Late with love and joyance blest ;
> Never more lamented guest,
> Was in Windsor laid to rest."

Leaving aside this young Princess, the heirs to the throne after King George IV. were his six brothers, in the following order :

Field Marshal, the Duke of York ; Admiral, the Duke of Clarence ; Field Marshal, the Duke of Kent ; the Duke of Cumberland ; Field Marshal, the Duke of Cambridge ; and the Duke of Sussex. Yet, in 1817, not one of these royal personages had been legally married—the Marriage Act forbidding their union with a subject of the Crown—and the direct line of succession was threatened with extinction. In the succeeding year, therefore, the Dukes of Clarence, Kent, Cumberland, and Cambridge were married to various German Princesses. But the children born to the Duke and Duchess of Clarence died in infancy, and the Duke of York followed in 1827, leaving behind a reputation for intense Toryism, and keen memories of his bigoted opposition to Catholic emancipation, together with an excellent military record—one which made the *Examiner*, a Radical paper of the day, declare that, " take him all in all he was the best Commander-in-Chief the army has ever had. He did much for the private soldier in securing to him the regular receipt of his pay, a clear view of his regimental accounts, and in providing for his comforts."

Ten years later the Duke of Clarence died as King William IV. Of the Duke of Kent it is difficult to speak too highly. He was not a favourite with his father, he was strongly disliked by his brother, George IV., and was too sincere and straightforward to get on with either the Ministers of the day or with the intriguing politicians, who sought to make Royalty the tools of the partisan rather than the leaders of the people. He served with distinction in Germany and in the West Indies, and as Commander-in-Chief of the forces in Nova Scotia, British America, and at Gibraltar. He had thus served abroad for thirteen years, when, in 1798, an accidental fall from his horse in Halifax caused his return to England, and the passage in the Nova Scotian Legislature of a resolution offering His Royal Highness an expression of its "high respect," and "the grateful sense it entertains of the very essential services rendered (by him) to the Province." A grant of 500 guineas was also made. At Gibraltar he had afterwards to encounter a condition of the most scandalous insubordination and drunkenness amongst the soldiers, and even amongst many of the officers. These evils were soon partially remedied, but the unwelcome change resulted in a rising which, though quickly suppressed, gave his enemies at home a chance to obtain his recall from a not unwilling King.

He was charged with undue severity, yet two years before, when he had left British America for the last time, the Lieutenant-Governor and Council at Halifax presented him with an address which stated that " To your benevolence the indigent have owed their support, the tradesmen and mechanics employment, and the industrious of every description the means of reaping the recompense of their skill and diligence." Writing many years afterwards, Sir Brenton Haliburton, who knew the Duke well, declared that "a tale of woe always interested him deeply, and nothing but gross misconduct could ever induce him to abandon any whom he had once been induced to befriend." The Duke, however, seems to have always laboured under financial difficulties. He does not appear to have been placed upon any kind of equality in money matters with the other members of the Royal family, and therefore, during his whole career, suffered greatly from the limitations which are naturally entailed by a position of exalted poverty. In 1815 the situation became so acute that he resolved to leave England and live on the Continent, where he might dispense with the most of his servants and greatly limit his expenditure.

The Duke therefore assigned the chief part of his income to a committee of friends to apply on outstanding debts, and went to reside in Brussels. Before going, however, the City Council of London resolved that " In consideration of the distinguished manner in which their Royal Highnesses, the Dukes of Kent and Sussex, have exerted themselves to promote every object of benevolence throughout the United Kingdom, and especially within the City, thereby adding to the lustre of their high birth and meriting in an eminent degree the sincere respect and gratitude of the City of London, the freedom of the City be presented in a suitable manner to each of their Royal Highnesses." Eventually the death of Princess Charlotte brought the Duke within measurable distance of the throne ; and his marriage, in 1818, to Her Serene Highness, Mary Louisa Victoria, sister of Prince Leopold of Saxe-Coburg, and widow of the late Prince of Leiningen, made it absolutely necessary for Parliament to grant him some adequate provision.

Lord Liverpool, in proposing a vote of 6,000 pounds a year in the House of Lords, stated that the Duke of Kent " had suffered considerable embarrassments; but they arose from no improvidence on his part, but solely from his having been left for several years without any provision." This statement was echoed in the Commons by Lord Castlereagh, who added that His Royal Highness had met his difficulties in " the most manly and honorable way." All the speakers referred to his personal worth ; and Brougham, for once in his life, became actually eulogistic. " He would venture to say that no man had set a brighter example of public virtue. no man had more beneficially exerted himself in his high station to benefit every institution with which the best interests of the country and the protection and education of the poor were connected, than H.R.H. the Duke of Kent." Such was the father of the future Queen and Empress, and the royal exponent of views upon public questions which are well embodied in the following extract from one of his speeches : " I am the friend of civil and religious liberty all the world over. I am an enemy to all religious tests. I am a supporter of a general system of education. All men are my brethren ; and I hold that power is delegated only for the benefit of the people. These are the principles of myself and of my beloved brother, the Duke of Sussex. They are not popular principles just now—that is, they do not conduct to place or office. All the members of the Royal family do not hold the same principles. For this I do not blame them ; but we claim for ourselves the right of thinking and acting as we think best."

Very different in character and career was the Duke of Cumberland, who, in 1837, succeeded William IV. as King of Hanover, by virtue of the Salic law which forbade a female sovereign in that country. The records of the time indicate that he was not only intensely unpopular, but that in many quarters he was absolutely hated. He was not only a Tory of the Tories, in a time when that was beginning to mean opposition to the distinct will of the masses, but had announced his intention of " cutting the wings of the democracy " in Hanover, and by implication in England—if he ever obtained the chance. He was Grand Master of the Orangemen at a period when that body was growing by leaps and bounds; but not even such a position of influence seems to have had any effect upon the reputation of " the most unpopular man in England." It was widely alleged and believed, in 1835, that he was connected with a plot to set aside Princess Victoria in favour of himself, as the next heir to the throne. Though this charge appears to have been untrue, it is evident that had anything occurred to the youthful Princess within the next few years the result of the Duke's accession would have been more than disastrous. And his private virtues appear to have been as limited as was his public popularity.

Another son of George III. was the Duke of Sussex. Unlike His Grace of Cumberland, whom Lord Brougham had once characterized as "the illustrious by courtesy," he did honour to his position and to the opportunities for doing good which it presented. Unlike the most of his royal brothers he was honestly and heartily Liberal in his opinions, and was not afraid to put his views into practical form. He supported the Reform Bill, and in 1831 declared emphatically: "I always was a Reformer, I am a Reformer, and I shall always be a Reformer." It was the fashion and recognized privilege of royalty in those days to take part in politics, and it is not necessary to say that such an attitude as his, in such a critical period, made him highly popular with a large section of the people. But, aside from this, and his unaffected interest in everything which might improve and better the welfare of the masses, he was, like the Duke of Kent, distinctly moral in life and character, plain, honest, and charitable in disposition. Hence the genuine public sorrow at his death in 1843.

Of a somewhat similar character was King George's youngest son, the Duke of Cambridge, father of the popular Princess Mary of Teck, and of the veteran Commander-in-Chief of after years. Like the Dukes of York and Kent he had seen active service upon more than one foreign field, and eventually attained the rank of Field Marshal in the army. Like the Dukes of Kent and Sussex he devoted himself, in the later years of his life, to the higher duties of royalty—the promotion of the welfare of the people—and became extremely popular with all classes of the community. His Royal Highness died in 1850, and his career was thus characterized by *The Times*: "The Duke was a zealous and indefatigable supporter of all our great public charities, and was a warm advocate of their claims. His firm and yet suave manner always exercised a composing effect upon any differences that arose in connection with the management of the many institutions under his patronage. He was thoroughly English in habits, disposition, and bearing, and seemed at all times at home with the English people."

It will thus be seen that the principles, the functions, the constitutional position, and work of British royalty in the early part of the century was entirely different from the conception which prevails, and the situation which exists, in its closing years. And it also appears evident that a loyalty which could endure in practical form through some of the events and environments of that day and the previous century must have been stronger than is usually supposed, and must have been based upon principles rather than persons; upon belief in a system of government rather than affection for a mere hereditary succession—important though that sentiment was, and is.

Yet upon the whole the records of Monarchy in England have been such as to warrant British pride in the past, and to promote the perpetuity of the principle in the future. It unquestionably gave glory to a great military period, and has brought together the countries which now form the United Kingdom, and constitute the pulsing heart of a vast Empire. It promoted religious independence under Henry VIII. and Elizabeth, and popular worship under Cromwell and William III. It protected arts, and sciences, and literature from the earliest times, and has thus glorified the Court of Queen Anne as it cast a halo of beauty over those of the first Stuarts through the brushes of Lely and Kneller. It has in recent centuries given a stable centre of government around which and with which a popular system could be woven in peace and reasonable harmony. It has given the English people the inestimable blessings of evolution without revolution; a union of the British Isles for all time to come; a history replete with gallant and royal deeds side by side with the brave achievements of knight and noble and common soldier; a power of diplomatic action and well directed war against foreign foes; independence of all foreign ecclesiastical domination; and much aid in the foundation of the external British empire through personal encouragement to adventurous spirits from the days of Drake to those of Rhodes. There are some shameful pages in our royal annals, but if Magna Charta had to be forced from King John it was preserved to the people by more than one of his successors, and, if Charles II. allowed the Dutch to flaunt themselves at the mouth of the Thames, William III. sent the British flag flying over the Continent and the channel, while under George II. it swept over the plains of India and climbed the Heights of Quebec.

And to-day, when we find the British Monarchy graven deep in the affections as well as the reason of its subjects, it is possible to look back through this mist of centuries and echo with increased force and meaning the statement of Macaulay, that " no other society has yet succeeded in uniting revolution with prescription, progress with stability, the energy of youth with the majesty of immemorial antiquity."

PRINCESS VICTORIA IN 1834.

H.R.H. PRINCE ALBERT, THE QUEEN'S CONSORT.

CHAPTER II.

PRINCESS VICTORIA.

THE Duke of Kent was very fortunate in his choice of a wife. The Princess of Leiningen had been brought up in one of the few German Courts which did not in those days imitate the looseness of the French Court and adapt itself to the social coarseness of the time. She possessed in a signal degree the sound sense, prudence, and strength of character which had already enabled her brother, Prince Leopold, to win the sincere respect of Englishmen during his brief residence at Claremont as the husband of the Princess Charlotte. Though a widow with two children she was, in 1818, still young, and, as she always remained, a handsome and stately woman.

For a while after their marriage the royal couple lived quietly at the Castle of Amorbach, in Bavaria, but early in 1819 returned to England, and at Kensington Palace, on May the 24th, the future Queen was born. The desire of the Duke that his child should be British-born was thus realized; his other hope that she might inherit the Crown of the realm was also destined to be fulfilled, though many years after his own premature death. In the quaint-looking, comfortable abode at Kensington, far from the strife of politics and the whirl of courts, the royal infant passed her early years. Here she was baptized in great pomp. The gold font, which had long been unused, was brought from the Tower of London; the Archbishop of Canterbury officiated, and the Prince of Wales stood as sponsor; while the Duke of York represented the Emperor of Russia, after whom it was proposed to partly name the child. Her godmothers were the Duchess-Dowager of Coburg—who was not only her own maternal grandmother, but also grandmother to Prince Albert—and the Queen of Wurtemberg.

It was by the purest chance that the infant received the name which has since been given to the age in which she lived. The Duke of Kent, with a watchful eye to the future, wished to call her Elizabeth, thinking, rightly enough, that such a name would help to endear her to a people whom he firmly believed she would some day rule over. Of an athletic physique, which he had never deranged by dissipation, he even thought himself to have a good chance of coming to the throne. " My brothers," he once remarked, " are not as strong as I am, and have not lived so regular a life. I expect to outlive them all. The crown will come to me and my children." But in the matter of the name he was over-ruled, and it was decided to call her Alexandrina, after the Russian Emperor, and Georgiana, in compliment to the Prince Regent. Fortunately, at the last moment, the latter objected to his name being given second place, and suggested in its stead the name of the Duchess of Kent—Victoria. And so the child of many hopes was christened, with the words of its grandmother in Coburg yet ringing in the mother's ears: "May God's blessing rest on the little stranger! Again a Charlotte, destined, perhaps, to play a great part one day, if a little brother is not born to take it out of her hands. The English like a Queen, and the niece of the ever-lamented, beloved Charlotte will be most dear to them. I need not tell you how delighted everybody is here."

The first event of importance in the infancy of the Princess was her journey to Sidmouth, in Devon, during December of the same year. To this place she was taken by her parents in order to escape the rigours of the London winter, and here, during what proved to be his last days, the Duke of Kent watched and guarded his precious infant with most unusual fondness. He was always thinking of the child, its health, its training, its future. To one of his friends, just before they left Kensington Palace for this fatal visit to Devon, he said with simple earnestness: "Don't pray simply that hers may be a brilliant career, and exempt from those trials and struggles which have pursued her father, but pray that God's blessing may rest on her, that it may overshadow her, and that in all her coming years she may be guided and guarded by God."

Unfortunately the season about Sidmouth proved very inclement, and one day on his return from a walk through mingled rain and snow the Duke went straight to the nursery to see his child and remained some little time playing with the babe without giving a thought to his own wet boots and the need of changing his clothes. As with so many apparently robust persons the chill thus received affected him quickly and fatally. The situation was not improved by the copious bleeding to which he was subjected, after the fashion of the day, and on January 23rd, 1820, the Duke of Kent died, leaving his widow practically a stranger in a strange land, and his child depending upon remote contingencies, and the apparent favour of a fickle ruler and dissipated Court. But good qualities and education had made the Duchess a woman worthy of her mission and work in life. Though not greatly beautiful she was attractive in appearance, charming in manner, sincere, sensitive, and warmly affectionate, and thenceforward every good quality she possessed and every aim in life were centred upon the bringing up of the youthful Princess.

Without waiting in useless sorrow for sympathy or help in the financial difficulties with which she was surrounded, the Duchess promptly returned to Kensington, and almost as promptly received from Prince Leopold an allowance of £3,000 a year. Her brother's wise generosity—he was in receipt of £25,000 a year from Great Britain as the consort of the late Princess Charlotte—enabled her, with the personal jointure of £6,000 from Parliament, to live quietly until, in 1825, that body granted another £6,000 for the training and nurture of the Princess Victoria. At Kensington the Duchess received the formal condolences of the nation, and intimated the intention of devoting herself to the care and education of her child. Here she resolved to live and give the little Princess a thoroughly British environment. And here she at once received—and retained for some ten years—the constant and wise advice of Prince Leopold. It is, indeed, not often that a child, in either humble or royal life, has such an uncle to take the place of so good a father. He had become a naturalized Englishman, and, like another Prince Consort of twenty years later, had given great thought and study to the constitutional history of England, and the duties and responsibilities of a constitutional monarch.

And what in these early years he taught his niece he afterwards practised as King of the Belgians, until he had won a reputation, as a constitutional and wise ruler, only second to that of the Queen herself. Her Majesty in later life has told us that she " adored her uncle," and in naming her youngest son Leopold announced it to be "the name which is dearest to me after Albert." During these years the atmosphere of the Court was stormy and unpleasant, but the little Princess was kept resolutely from it, though some consolation came in the kindness and consideration of the Duke of York—whose death in 1827 was the child's first great sorrow—and in the loving tenderness of Queen Adelaide, the consort of William IV. The loss of her own children seems to have had none of the effect upon her character which might have come to meaner natures, and her simple words to the Duchess of Kent, " My children are dead, but yours lives, and she is mine, too," afford the keynote to her affectionate treatment of the child who was to take the great place she had hoped her own little girl would one day fill.

Many are the simple stories told of the baby and child life of "the little Drina," as she was called in the home circle. Her large blue eyes, blooming face, and fair complexion are said to have made her a model of infantine beauty, and there are many memories of her appearance and actions still extant. Upon one occasion a private soldier, named Maloney, caught the child up in his arms as she was thrown from a tiny pony carriage, and probably saved the life of one whom he was long afterwards astonished to know as the Queen of the realm. At another time an accidental charge of shot from the gun of some hunter in the neighbourhood passed through a window of the Palace, and just over the head of the playing child. William Wilberforce, writing on July 21st, 1820, says : " In consequence of a very civil message from the Duchess of Kent I waited on her this morning. She received me with her fine, animated child on the floor by her side with its playthings, of which I soon became one."

The life at Kensington during succeeding years was very quiet, very well ordered, and very simple. Breakfast was served at eight o'clock, the Princess having her bread and milk and fruit placed on a small table by her mother's side. An hours' walk or drive with her governess followed, and then a couple of hour's personal instruction from the Duchess. Then the child was allowed to play till her plain dinner at two o'clock, after which came a couple of hours of lessons. Then a visit, or a drive, or ride, or walk. On fine evenings the whole party would sit under the trees on the lawn, and at dinner the Princess would be given a light supper at her mother's side, retiring at nine o'clock to a bed placed during all the years of her youth beside that of her mother. The Earl of Albemarle tells us in his Recollections of these years that (December, 1826) :—

"One of my occupations on a morning while waiting for the Duke (of Sussex) was to watch from the window the movements of a bright, pretty little girl, seven years of age. She was in the habit of watering the plants immediately under the window. It was amusing to see how impartially she divided the contents of the watering-pot between the flowers and her own little feet. Her simple but becoming dress contrasted favourably with the gorgeous apparel now worn by the little damsels of the rising generation—a large straw hat, and a suit of white cotton ; a coloured *fichu* round the neck was the only ornament she wore."

Upon one or two occasions she was taken to Court, though not as often as King George IV. would have liked. He was inclined to be somewhat jealous of his little niece ; yet he was still more jealous of the seclusion in which she was kept, and the influence which Prince Leopold had over her education. An instance of the child's ready wit is recorded in connection with one of these rare visits. The King had entered the drawing-room, leading the Princess by the hand. The band was stationed, as usual, in the adjoining conservatory. "Now, Victoria," said His Majesty, "the band is in the next room, and shall play any tune you please; what shall it be ?" "Oh, uncle," was the reply, "I should like ' God save the King ' better than anything else."

But she was not confined to Kensington Palace all the time. The Duchess took her every year either to some quiet spot at the seaside or to Prince Leopold at Claremont. This place Her Majesty afterwards described as possessing "a peculiar charm" for her, and as bringing back recollections of "the happiest days" of her childhood, besides reviving many memories of her uncle's wise kindliness of disposition. Everyone seems to have been won by the beauty and charm of the child. Leigh Hunt, who had dealt with the Prince Regent in terms of cruel sarcasm, and who had no particular affection for royalty, states somewhere how well he remembered "the peculiar kind of personal pleasure which it gave us to see the future queen the first time we ever did see her." Charles Knight, in his "Passages of a Working Life," gives a pleasant glimpse of the Princess as he saw her in 1827. "I delighted to walk in Kensington Gardens," he observes. "As I passed along the broad central walk I saw a group on the lawn before the palace which to my mind was a vision of exquisite loveliness. The Duchess of Kent and her daughter, whose years then numbered nine, are breakfasting in the open air—a single page attending upon them at a respectful distance; the matron looking on with eyes of love, whilst 'the fair, soft, English face' is bright with smiles. What a beautiful characteristic it seemed to me of the training of this royal girl that she should not have been taught to shrink from the public eye; that she should not have been burdened with a premature conception of her probable high destiny; that she should enjoy the freedom and simplicity of a child's nature; that she should not be restrained when she starts up from the breakfast table and runs to gather a flower in the adjoining parterre; that her merry laugh should be as fearless as the notes of the thrush in the groves around her. I passed on and blessed her; and I thank God that I have lived to see the golden fruits of such a training."

The young Princess was taught to be kind, and charitable, and thoughtful of those around her. Many are the stories of her affectionate disposition and kindliness. When the Duke of York was dying in 1827, she carried his favourite flowers to him every day, and charmed the last hours of a life whose faults were largely the product of his surroundings, and whose good qualities were all his own. But her sympathies were very catholic, and almost from the bedside of the heir to the throne, she would go to those of the son and daughter of an old soldier, named Hillman, who had faithfully served under her father at Gibraltar, and would nurse and cheer them in their prolonged and hopeless illness. Two days after her accession to the Throne, she sent to the daughter who still survived, a book of Psalms, with a marker she had herself worked, and the message by one of the ladies of the Court, that though now Queen of England and obliged to leave Kensington, " she had not forgotten " the sufferers.

She had been fortunate during these years in having with her the Princess Feodore, her own half-sister. Though a good deal older than the English Princess, the former was young enough to be a companion and, later on, a friend. This pleasant bond was partially broken, however, in 1828, by the marriage of the Princess Feodore to the Prince Hohenlohe-Langenbourg. It was about this time that the little Princess paid one of her rare visits to Court and was dazzled by the reception given to the child-Queen of Portugal, who wore a dress blazing with crown jewels, and was led into the ball-room by the King himself. George IV. was greatly annoyed at the same time by someone asking him to see " the two little Queens dancing together."

Another glimpse of her appearance is given us by Miss Jane Porter, the talented author of " The Scottish Chiefs," in a private letter written at the time of the Queen's accession. " In describing the infancy of the Princess," wrote Miss Porter, " I would say she was a beautiful child, with a cherubic form of features, clustered round by glossy, fair ringlets Her complexion was remarkably transparent, with a soft, but often heightening tinge of the sweet blush-rose upon her cheeks, that imparted a peculiar brilliancy to her clear blue eyes. Whenever she met any strangers in her usual paths she always seemed, by the quickness of her glance, to inquire who and what they were! The intelligence of her countenance was extraordinary at her very early age, but might easily be accounted for on perceiving the extraordinary intelligence of her mind."

And any precocity which existed in the child was taken full advantage of by her mother. The Duchess of Kent seems to have realized that true education does not consist in the acquisition of stilted accomplishments and dry facts, but in the formation of character, the discipline of the nature, and the application of wise principles wisely inculcated in the childish mind. The Princess possessed a transparently truthful disposition, and her mother trained her so carefully in this direction, that Mr. Bright, with all his Quaker-like belief in the exact truth, and the whole truth, has stated the vivid impression which this characteristic in the Queeen left upon his own mind. She was never allowed to buy anything on credit or exceed her own limited allowance, and was taught that to live beyond one's means, or to incur debts which it was impossible to pay, was distinctly dishonest and dishonourable. There are many cases on record of the little Princess having to relinquish the purchase of a trifling article because she had not money enough to pay for it. Upon one occasion, at Tunbridge Wells, she so far went beyond her rules and self-control as to ask the shopkeeper to reserve some greatly desired toy until she had received a fresh installment of her allowance. And as soon as she had obtained the money, the child appeared in the shop at seven o'clock in the morning to claim possession of the object of her wishes.

Both the Duchess of Kent and the Princess were fortunate in having the Baroness Lehzen as governess for the latter. She was the daughter of a Hanoverian clergyman, and had first come to England in 1818 in charge of the Princess Feodore. In 1824, by command of the King and the wish of the Duchess she entered upon her duties with the Princess Victoria, then five years of age. Three years afterwards she was raised to the rank of Baroness in the auxiliary Kingdom of Hanover, and remained in her position of royal instructress until 1837. For some years after the accession she continued at Court as a faithful and respected friend of Her Majesty. Another tutor was found in the Rev. George Davys, afterwards Bishop of Peterborough. He had charge of what may be termed the more solid and weighty portion of the instruction which it was deemed necessary to give the Princess, and which expanded as she came nearer and nearer the Throne, until it included everything, from " a box of letters to the delivery of a Queen's speech." The Baroness presided over the lighter subjects, such as music, singing, dancing, etc., and though specialists had to be more or less employed under her supervision, the young Princess was hardly ever out of sight of the Duchess or the governess. Sir Walter Scott, in fact, wrote in his diary after a visit to Kensington that, "the little lady is educated with such care, and watched so closely, that no busy maid has a moment to say, 'You are the heir of England.'"

Under the careful instruction of Mr. John Bernard Sale, assisted by the famous vocalist, Luigi Lablache, the Princess became an accomplished musician, with a carefully cultivated mezzo-soprano voice of considerable flexibility and richness. Her riding-master was a proficient in his art; and a most pleasing picture in the early days of Her Majesty's reign was that of the young Queen galloping in the Row, amidst the general admiration of those who witnessed the ease and grace of her carriage. For many years Mr. Richard Westall, R.A., was her drawing-master, and under his instruction she became quite an expert in painting and sketching. Indeed, Mr. Westall—who would never accept any remuneration for his services—was fond of saying that the Princess showed such natural talent as to indicate that if she had not been born to wear the crown she would have become the first woman-artist of the day.

Even in those early years the Queen could write a good letter, and the subjects who have so often read Her Majesty's sympathetic letters to her people in after life can appreciate the remarks of William IV., when receiving upon his accession a letter written entirely by herself, and so well done that the King expressed publicly his pleasure "at the eloquence and spirit of its diction, and its penmanship." By the time she had reached her eleventh year the Princess had studied mathematics to a considerable extent ; was able to speak French, Italian, and German, as well as English ; had made some progress in Latin— reading Virgil and Horace with ease ; and had made a fair commencement with Greek. It was at this date that she entered upon the study of the English Constitution, under the direction of a gentleman deeply versed in the subject, and with the indirect but, perhaps, more valuable counsels of her uncle—Prince Leopold.

The little Princess had in these years a very clearly defined will of her own, and to properly modify and direct it was perhaps the most difficult part of the Baroness Lehzen's duties. With the help of a wise mother and her own tact she succeeded. But the incidents told of childish wit and quickness in the royal pupil show how gentle and considerate the means adopted were. For instance, the first lessons upon the piano were found to be monotonous, and she quickly grew impatient. The instructress told her that it was absolutely necessary that she should become "mistress of the piano."

"Oh, I am to be mistress of my piano, am I ?" was the response.

"Yes, indeed, Princess."

"Then what would you think of me if I became mistress at once ?"

"That would be impossible. There is no royal road to music. Experience and great practice are essential."

"Oh, there is no royal road to music, eh ? No royal road ? And I am not mistress of my pianoforte ? But I will be, I assure you ; and the royal road is this"—and she closed the piano, locked it, and put the key in her pocket. "There ! That is being mistress of the piano ! and the royal road to learning is never to take a lesson till you are in the humour to do it." Needless to say this little ebullition of the Brunswick spirit did not last long, and the Princess soon volunteered to go on with her lesson. Upon another occasion she asked a gentleman to tell her a story, but was told that he had none to relate—she had heard them all. " Well, can't you make one up ?" said the Princess. " But then it would not be true," was the reply. " Oh, that doesn't matter—very few are," returned the Princess ; "that is why they are called stories." Miss Porter, who has been already quoted, says that her brother, Sir Robert, when in England, often had the honour of dining at Claremont, and of listening to the young Princess singing in company with her mother and Prince Leopold. And the same chronicler tells us of another branch of the royal studies:

" She read general history under the guidance of one of England's best scholars in that essential branch of education—and, more especially, she fixed the eyes of her mind on the ancient annals of her own future dominions. Not being satisfied with our celebrated historians, Hume, Rapin, and others of modern date, she sought after the original authorities ; and these venerable pen-men, in *black-letter*, were constrained to give up their lore to the youthful heiress of their almost worshipped themes—our Saxon Alfred, our Norman Henries and Edwards. Succeeding chroniclers also yielded to her the same genuine tribute, till they told of the happily united royal streams in the bosoms of the Stuart and the Brunswick race—herself a nobly conscious daughter of both."

It was not till 1831, the year after William the Fourth's accession, and when she was just twelve years old, that the Princess was informed of her nearness to the Throne. Of her position as a member of the Royal family she was quite aware, and could not well avoid being so, from the degree of respect shown her wherever she went. But at Court the belief was industriously kept up for a long time after this that the King and Queen might yet have children, and thus change the succession away from her. It was fortunate that this idea did prevail, as it enabled the Duchess to keep her child at home, and in comparative retirement. At last, however, the time had come, and Baroness Lehzen, in a letter to the Queen—written many years afterwards, and published by authority of Her Majesty—tells us the charming story of how the news was broken to the little heiress of England. After consultation with the Duchess, the governors placed the genealogical table in the historical book.

" When Mr. Davys was gone the Princess opened the book again, as usual, and seeing the additional paper said, 'I never saw that before.' 'It was not thought necessary you should, Princess,' I answered. 'I see I am nearer the Throne than I thought.' 'So it is, madam,' I said. After some moments the Princess answered, ' Now, many a child would boast, but they don't know the difficulty. There is much splendour, but there is more responsibility.' The Princess, having lifted up the forefinger of her right hand while she spoke, gave me that little hand, saying, 'I will be good. I understand now why you urged me so much to learn even Latin. My aunts Augusta and Mary never did, but you told me Latin is the foundation of English grammar, and of all the elegant expressions, and I learned it as you wished it; but I understand all better now.' And the Princess gave me her hand again, repeating 'I will be good.'

"I then said, 'But your aunt Adelaide is still young and may have children, and, of course, they would ascend the Throne after their father, William IV., and not you, Princess.' The Princess answered, 'And if it was so I should never feel disappointed, for I know by the love Aunt Adelaide bears me how fond she is of children.' "

From this time her studies were broadened, her appearances in public became more numerous, and the Dowager Duchess of Northumberland was placed in charge of the royal pupil in all matters relating to state ceremonies. In view of the contingency of Princess Victoria coming to the Throne before she was of age, Parliament also passed a bill by which the Duchess of Kent was to be guardian of the Princess and regent of the kingdom, with the assistance of a council of regency drawn from the Royal Family and the Ministers of State. Shortly afterwards a sum of £10,000 a year was voted, in addition to the original grant of £6,000, for the support of the dignity of the heiress presumptive, and her further education.

On the 24th of February, 1831, the Princess made her first appearance at Court during the new reign. It was at a drawing-room held by Queen Adelaide in celebration of her own birthday, and during the reception Princess Victoria stood on the Queen's left hand, clad in a simple white frock, with a pearl necklace and a rich diamond ornament in her fair hair. She thoroughly enjoyed the splendour of the occasion, as she did the more simple pleasure of a juvenile ball which the Queen gave in her honour about the same time. But she was not present at the coronation, which gave rise to an unusual amount of gossip and criticism. Amidst a multitude of reasons given came the final statement from the Duchess that, on account of her daughter's delicate health, she had obtained the King's sanction to her absence.

During the years immediately following this the Princess was taken by her mother on a number of little tours and visits throughout England and Wales. They visited in this way Lord Liverpool at Buxted Park, the Duke of Wellington at Walmer Castle, the Marquess of Westminster at Eaton Hall the Earl of Shrewsbury at Alton Towers, the Duke of Devonshire at Chatsworth, Earl Somers at Eastnor Castle, Earl Beauchamp at Madresfield Court, and the seats of the Earls of Harewood and Fitzwilliam, and the Duke of Rutland. But these excursions were not limited to the magnificent homes of the nobility. In the summer months of 1832 they travelled through many Welsh counties, visiting Coventry, Shrewsbury, Powis Castle, Wynnstay and Beaumaris, where all kinds of historical, statistical, and industrial information was picked up. Later they visited the Isle of Anglesey, and during an autumn tour of the Midland counties the Princess officiated at more than one of those functions which afterwards became so familiar and frequent to the Queen. She manifested great interest in the most diverse matters. At Lichfield Cathedral it was Chantrey's sculptured group of the " Sleeping Children "; at Bromsgrove it was the ironworks and the making of nails; at Oxford University it was, naturally, the memories of an historic past. Here she was presented with a magnificent Bible, together with a history of the royal visit printed on white satin.

In 1833 the mother and daughter spent some months at a beautiful place in the Isle of Wight—Norris Castle—and delighted in long walks and excursions, unincumbered by ceremonial or social trammels. Visits were also paid to Southampton, Carisbrooke, Winchester, Plymouth, and Torquay. At this latter place the Duchess of Kent, in reply to an address, said : "It has ever been my pride to lead the Princess to regard with warm feelings all the recollections that belong to the naval service of the country." It was on the return from this trip that the *Emerald* yacht ran into some other vessel, and the pilot had just time to spring forward, seize the Princess, and leap to a place of safety, when a great block of wood fell upon the spot where she had been standing.

Then followed various public occurrences, including a visit with the King and Queen to Westminster Abbey, and a State attendance at the Ascot races, where the sixteen-year-old Princess received a wonderfully enthusiastic welcome. Her costume upon this occasion was a rose-coloured satin dress, a pelerine cape trimmed with black lace, and a large pink bonnet. Her appearance was so altogether charming that N. P. Willis, a visiting American author, declared her to be " much better looking than any picture in the shops, and for the heir to such a Crown as that of England unnecessarily pretty and interesting." On the 30th of August, 1835, the Princess was confirmed in the Chapel Royal, St. James, by the Archbishop of Canterbury and the Bishop of London, in the presence of her mother, the King and Queen, and some other members of the Royal Family. The scene is said to have been very touching, and the pathetic exhortations of the Archbishop upon the great responsibilities of her future position so moved the sensitive heart of the girl that she laid her head upon her mother's shoulder and sobbed aloud.

A very different scene was that described by Greville, in his famous

Memoirs, as taking place at Windsor on August 21st, 1836. The Sailor King was subject to violent outbreaks of temper and the exercise of a singularly undignified and inappropriate facility of speech. For some years he had been growing more and more jealous of his youthful successor, and annoyed at the policy pursued by her mother. The simple, retired life led by the Princess seemed to him a deliberate effort by the Duchess of Kent to keep the child away from Court, from his personal influence, and from those whom he thought entitled to share in her training. And in this supposition His Majesty was probably not very far astray. Added to this, however, was a ridiculous dislike to the public and private visits made by the Duchess and her daughter in the wise process of education which the former had set before herself. But these "royal progresses," as they were termed around his Court, made the King exceedingly angry.

Finally came the climax in the scene described by Greville, when at a dinner in honour of the King's birthday, and in the presence of some hundred guests, with the Duchesss of Kent on one side [of him and the Princess Victoria opposite, he delivered the extraordinary speech which follows:

"I trust in God that my life may be spared for nine months, after which period, in the event of my death, no regency would take place. I should then have the satisfaction of leaving the royal authority to the personal exercise of that young lady (pointing to the Princess), the heiress presumptive of the Crown, and not in the hands of a person now near me, who is surrounded by evil advisers, and who is herself incompetent to act with propriety in the station in which she would be placed. I have no hesitation in saying that I have been insulted—grossly and continually insulted—by that person; but I am determined to endure no longer a course of behaviour so disrespectful to me. Amongst other things, I have particularly to complain of the manner in which that young lady has been kept away from my Court; she has been repeatedly kept from my drawing-rooms, at which she ought always to have been present; but I am fully resolved that this shall not happen again. I would have her know that I am King, and I am determined to make my authority respected; and for the future I shall insist and command that the Princess do upon all occasions appear at my Court, as it is her duty to do."

Such a tirade from an English king had never been heard before in modern days, and, it is safe to say, will never be heard again. But the hasty temper of William IV. had been probably stirred up to bursting point by the rumours and gossip of a Court circle which naturally disliked the Duchess, which feared her influence, and was prevented from obtaining any degree of intimacy or acquaintance with the future Queen. Perhaps nothing could have more absolutely vindicated the wisdom of her mother in keeping Princess Victoria away from Court than this unfortunate scene. Shortly before this the Duke of Cobourg, accompanied by his two sons, Prince Ernest and Prince Albert, had visited England, and stayed at Kensington Palace for nearly four weeks with the Duchess of Kent. There is no doubt now that both the Duchess and

Prince Leopold hoped for some such result of this meeting of the young people as did ultimately transpire ; but the world at large and the Princess herself had no thought of anything of the kind. The royal party during this month of activity and pleasure visited the chief sources of attraction and interest in the city, were present at the anniversary of the London Charity Schools at St. Paul's, and attended a luncheon afterwards given by the Lord Mayor at the Mansion House. Contemporary accounts indicate that everyone was charmed with the fresh, youthful beauty of the Princess, and the frank, kindly manners of her cousins from Cobourg.

On the 24th of May, 1837, the young girl, who now, all unconsciously, stood upon the very steps of the Throne, attained her legal majority, and received from the King a magnificent birthday present in the form of a pianoforte, valued at 200 guineas. It is also said that, with his old feelings of hostility to the Duchess still in mind, he offered his niece a personal allowance of £10,000 if she would let him name the officers of her household. Of course, the offer was refused. Meanwhile, London, for the first time, was celebrating the now familiar 24th of May: a grand State ball was given at the Palace of St. James ; while Parliament adjourned in honour of the occasion. At this ball the Princess, for the first time, took precedence of her mother, and occupied the central Chair of State in the enforced absence of the King and Queen, through the illness of the former. There were also demonstrations throughout the country, and addresses of congratulation from the City Council of London and many other organizations. In reply to the former, the Duchess of Kent observed :

"I have, in times of great difficulty, avoided all connection with any other party in the State ; but if I have done so, I have never ceased to impress on my daughter her duties, so as to gain by her conduct the respect and affection of the people. This I have taught her should be her first earthly duty as a constitutional Sovereign. The Princess has arrived at that age which now justifies my expressing my confident expectation that she will be found competent to execute the sacred trust which may be reposed in her ; for communicating, as she does, with all classes of society, she cannot but perceive that the greater the diffusion of religion, knowledge, and the love of freedom in a country, the more orderly, industrious, and wealthy is its population ; and that, with the desire to preserve the constitutional prerogatives of the Crown, ought to be co-ordinated the protection of the people."

Within a month the maiden of eighteen who had blushingly and timidly replied to these addresses with the simple statement that : "My mother has expressed all my feelings," was sitting upon one of the great thrones of the world, receiving the acclamations of a nation, and entering upon a career so lofty as almost to transcend imagination, and so great in its environment, and power for good or evil, as to appal even the vigorous intellect of a Carlyle, and win the republican sympathies of a Harriet Martineau.

THE QUEEN ON THE MORNING OF HER ACCESSION, JUNE 20, 1837.

HER MAJESTY'S FIRST COUNCIL AT KENSINGTON PALACE JUNE 20, 1837.

CHAPTER III.

ACCESSION AND CORONATION.

IT was in the early morning light of a June day that the Princess Victoria heard of the death of her uncle, the King, and of her own transformation into the Queen of a great realm, the head of the Church of England, the cynosure of the eyes of the world. William IV. died at half-past two on June 20th, 1837, and within a couple of hours the Archbishop of Canterbury and Lord Conyngham were on their way from Windsor to Kensington Palace. There are two accounts of what then transpired, which, though different in detail, corroborate each other in the main particulars. Greville tells us that the important messengers of State immediately desired to see "the Queen." They were ushered into an apartment, and in a few minutes the door opened and she entered, wrapped in a dressing-gown, and with slippers on her naked feet. Lord Conyngham, in a few words, told their errand, and as soon as he uttered the words "Your Majesty" she put out her hand to him, intimating that he was to kiss hands before he proceeded.

He dropped on one knee, kissed her hand, and then went on to tell her of the late King's death. She presented her hand to the Archbishop, who likewise kissed it. Miss Wynn, in her well-known diary, adds that after the Primate had formally announced to the Princess her accession to the throne she was deeply agitated, and that her first words were, "I ask your prayers on my behalf." The Prime Minister, Lord Melbourne, was then sent for, and a meeting of the Privy Council summoned for eleven o'clock. Meanwhile the Queen wrote to her aunt, Queen Adelaide, a tender letter of condolence, and it is not difficult to imagine the mingled dignity and humility of this epistle. In directing it she wrote, "To Her Majesty the Queen," instead of "To Her Majesty the Queen-Dowager." When someone ventured to draw attention to the fact the young Sovereign merely said that she was quite aware of the matter, but "would not be the first to remind Queen Adelaide" of her changed position.

The memorable Council which followed has made an impression on the literature and correspondence of that day almost as great as the Coronation, though necessarily confined to a more limited circle of observers. Greville, who was Clerk of the Privy Council, says that there "never was anything like the first impression she produced, or the chorus of praise and admiration which is raised about her manner and behaviour, and certainly not without justice. Her youth and inexperience, and the ignorance of the world concerning her, naturally excited intense curiosity to see how she would act on this trying occasion, and there was a considerable assemblage at the Palace, notwithstanding the short notice that was given." After certain formalities had been gone through with, the doors were thrown open and the Queen entered the room, in which were gathered nearly a hundred of the leaders of England. Amongst those present were the Duke of Wellington, the Royal Dukes of Cumberland and Sussex, the Duke of Argyle, the Marquess of Lansdowne, and the Marquess of Salisbury, Earl Grey, and Lord Lyndhurst, the Earl of Aberdeen, Lord Melbourne, and Sir Robert Peel. Many of the names in the complete list sound like those of another age ; many of them represented the fathers or grandfathers of the men of to-day.

Upon entering, Greville tells us, the Queen was met by the Duke of Cumberland—who had now become King of Hanover—and her other uncle, the Duke of Sussex. "She bowed to the Lords, took her seat, and then read her Speech in a clear, distinct, and audible voice, and without any appearance of fear or embarrassment. She was quite plainly dressed, and in mourning." The document thus presented to her Council and the nation is of historic interest and importance, and reads as follows :

" The severe and afflicting loss which the nation has sustained by the death of His Majesty, my beloved uncle, has devolved upon me the duty of administering the government of this empire. This awful responsibility is imposed upon me so suddenly, and at so early a period of my life, that I should feel myself utterly oppressed by the burden were I not sustained by the hope that Divine Providence, which has called me to this work, will give me strength for the performance of it, and that I shall find in the purity of my intentions and in my zeal for the public welfare that support and those resources which usually belong to a more mature age and to longer experience.

" I place my firm reliance upon the wisdom of Parliament, and upon the loyalty and affection of my people. I esteem it also a peculiar advantage that I succeed to a Sovereign whose constant regard for the rights and liberties of his subjects, and whose desire to promote the amelioration of the laws and institutions of the country, have rendered his name the object of general attachment and veneration.

" Educated in England, under the tender and enlightened care of a most affectionate mother, I have learned from my infancy to respect and love the Constitution of my native country.

" It will be my unceasing study to maintain the Reformed religion as by law established, securing at the same time to all the full enjoyment of religious liberty ; and I shall steadily protect the rights and promote to the utmost of my powers the happiness and welfare of all classes of my subjects."

After this speech had been delivered, and the oath for the security of the Church of Scotland had been taken, the Privy Councillors were sworn—the two royal dukes first. Greville says that as these two old men, her uncles, knelt before her, swearing allegiance and kissing her hand, he saw her blush up to the eyes, as if she felt the contrast between their civil and their natural relations.

But this appears to have been the only sign of emotion she evinced. Her manner to them was " very graceful and engaging "; she kissed them both, rising from her chair to move towards the Duke of Sussex, who was somewhat infirm. The same chronicler tells us that she seemed rather bewildered by the multitude of men who were sworn, but did not make any difference in her manner to any individual, of whatever rank, station, or party. " She went through the whole ceremony with perfect calmness and self-possession, but at the same time with a graceful modesty and propriety particularly interesting and ingratiating."

Harriet Martineau, though she could not have been present, voiced the appreciation of the moment when she wrote, not long after this event : " If the millions who longed to know how the young Sovereign looked and felt could have heard her first address it would have gone far to satisfy them. Her manner was composed, modest, and dignified ; her voice firm and sweet ; her reading, as usual, beautiful." Mr. Disraeli has told us how he accompanied Lord Lyndhurst as far as the Palace, and how deeply impressed that statesman was by the striking scene and the homage of so many illustrious subjects given to a simple maiden, who yet, by her position, voiced all the concentrated power of the British realm. Lord Stratford de Redcliffe—then Sir Stratford Canning— wrote to his brother that "nothing could be more satisfactory than the demeanour of our young Queen at the Council this morning. She has really gained every- one's good-will by her modest self-possession and the excellent manner in which she delivered her declaration. I was present and can honestly bear witness to the truth."

Earl Grey, the veteran premier of preceding reigns, wrote to the Princess Lieven that "when called upon for the first time to appear before the Privy Council, and to take upon herself the awful duties with which at so early an age she has been so suddenly charged, there was in her appearance and demeanour a composure, a propriety, an *aplomb*, which were quite extraordinary. She never was in the least degree confused, embarrassed, or hurried ; read the Declaration beautifully ; went through the forms of business as if she had been accustomed to them all her life." After dining at the Palace in the following spring, Lord Grey's impressions were fully confirmed ; and he adds, " I was charmed, as every one is, with our little Queen's appearance and manner."

Lord Palmerston, writing to the Earl Granville of that day, observed that " The Queen went through her task with great dignity and self-possession ; one saw she felt much inward emotion, but it was fully controlled. Her articulation was peculiarly good, her voice remarkably pleasing." He then refers to her reception of the Foreign ministers, who were introduced one by one, and " the easy, dignified, and gracious manner " with which she went through this impor- tant function. Sir Robert Peel expressed to a friend his amazement at her mingled modesty, firmness, and sense of responsibility. The Duke of Wellington declared himself as proud of her as if she had been his own daughter. Lord Campbell proclaimed himself quite in raptures over the deportment of the young Queen : "Nothing could be more exquisitely proper ; she looked modest, sorrowful, dejected, diffident, but at the same time she was quite cool and collected, and composed, and firm."

But there was another and more touching side to the picture. Careful training, strong sense of responsibility, and strength of character enabled Her Majesty to go through many of these early and great functions with the dignity and composure admired by so many contemporaries. But it seems probable that much was due to the education which a wise mother had given her, and about which those who then surrounded her knew so little as to be fairly amazed at the result. And though a great Queen she was still but a young girl ; and there are, at least, two recorded incidents which show that nature had its limits of repression. The first occurred on the day following the Council, when, standing at an open window of St. James' Palace, surrounded by members of the Royal family, the Officers of the Household, and Ministers of State, and faced by a multitude of people, she was proclaimed as "our only lawful and rightful liege Lady, Victoria I., Queen of Great Britain and Ireland, Defender of the Faith."

It was a pathetic picture. Dressed in deep mourning, with a white tippet, white cuffs, and a border of white lace under a tiny black bonnet, she seemed so small and delicate in stature, and so graceful and pleasing in appearance, as to win instant sympathy and admiration. The burden of so great a place in life seemed as if it must be too heavy to be borne by her ; and when, at the conclusion of the Proclamation, the band struck up the National Anthem, the guns in the Park and at the Tower thundered their reply, and the air was rent with the cheers of tens of thousands of her subjects, it proved too much for their youthful Sovereign. Turning to her mother, she buried her face in her bosom and wept unrestrainedly. It was one of those spectacles which make all natures kin, and unite the sympathies and sentiment of all sections of struggling humanity. Mrs. Browning has beautifully commemorated the incident :

> "God save thee, weeping Queen !
> Thou shalt be well-beloved ;
> The tyrant sceptre cannot move
> As those pure tears have moved !
> The nature in thy eyes we see
> Which tyrants cannot own,
> The love that guardeth liberties.
> Strange blessing on the nation lies,
> Whose Sovereign wept,
> Yea, wept to wear a crown."

Towards the end of that eventful and pregnant day, when the young Queen found herself for a brief time free from the duties of solemn ceremonial, she sought her mother's apartments in the Palace, and, we are told, expressed herself as even yet unable to realize the full responsibilities of her position. "But in time," she said to the Duchess, "I shall become accustomed to my change of character; meanwhile, since it is really so, and you see in your little daughter the Sovereign of this great country, will you grant her the first request she has had occasion in her regal capacity to put to you? I wish, my dear mamma, to be left for two hours alone." And in that brief period, no doubt, the youthful monarch, who in early days had said "I will be good," communed with herself upon the future, and, perhaps, mourned over the free and joyous past, which must now have seemed so far away.

But she was much too natural in herself, and had been too carefully trained for the position to let it change her character or disposition. With all her added dignity, the Queen was still full of the high spirits of youth, and was, fortunately for herself, able to bear the burdens of the moment with a keen appreciation of the pleasures which came with them. Henry Crabb Robinson, the poet, gives us in his diary an amusing illustration of this lightsomeness. "The Bishop of London told Amyot," he says, "that when the bishops were first presented to the Queen, she received them with all possible dignity, and then retired. She passed through a glass door, and, forgetting its transparency, was seen to run off like a girl, as she is." And he adds, "This is just as it should be. If she had not now the high spirits of a girl of eighteen, we should have less reason to hope she would turn out a sensible woman at 30." Miss Martineau also notes that, in this early part of the reign, it so happened that she never saw the Queen when she was not laughing or talking and moving about.

It must be mentioned here that, by a happy personal decision, Her Majesty had made her first official signature "Victoria," instead of "Alexandrina Victoria," which it had been supposed would be her name and style. Although this necessitated a number of changes in the forms of oath, and some considerable trouble at the moment to those in charge of the functions connected with the accession, it was something upon which succeeding generations of the Victorian era have reason to congratulate themselves and the tactful young Sovereign. There is much in a name; and no more inspiring and gracious word could have been selected for a British monarch than that which the Queen was so fortunate as to possess and so wise as to use. But Her Majesty showed in many ways, and from the first moment of assuming power, that her position and its responsibilities were perfectly familiar to her mind and heart.

She very soon had the Court thoroughly in hand, and controlled in a way which somewhat astonished, and probably greatly angered, many of the courtiers of the previous reigns. She snubbed *intriguantes*, resented carelessness or lack of punctuality, treated her mother with all imaginable consideration, but did not seek her advice upon affairs of State; introduced new codes of Sabbath observance, bestowed the Grand Cross of the Bath upon that most brilliant Radical and unfortunate statesman, the Earl of Durham; showed great regard 'or Lord Melbourne, and great care in the consideration of all the questions which came before her; provided for her father's debts, appointed Miss Davys a Maid of Honour, and promoted Dr. Davys to the Bishopric of Peterborough, provided liberally for her royal relatives, and, withal, managed to enjoy herself thoroughly. Upon this point, Greville says that everything was new and delightful to her: " She is surrounded with the most exciting and interesting enjoyments; her occupations, her pleasures, her business, her Court—all present an increasing round of gratifications. With all her prudence and discretion, she has great animal spirits, and enters into the magnificent novelties of her position with the zest and curiosity of a child."

On the 17th of June, Her Majesty went from Buckingham Palace, where she had taken up her residence, to dissolve Parliament. The day was exquisite, and the first of many which has made " Queen's weather " a household phrase. All along the route were dense crowds of people shouting and cheering, as the great procession and its central figure passed through their serried ranks. The Queen was attired in a splendid white robe, with the ribbon of the Garter crossing her shoulder, a necklace and stomacher of large brilliants, and a splendid tiara of diamonds on her head. About three o'clock, amidst a flourish of trumpets, and preceded by the heralds and great officers of State, she entered the House of Lords, and ascended the Throne. Over her shoulders, as she took her seat, was thrown a royal mantle of crimson velvet. It is said that the silent, intense observation of the brilliant gathering present so disconcerted her for the moment that she forgot they were all standing, until reminded by Lord Melbourne, who stood at her side. Then came the gracious inclination of the head, and the low tones of the command, " My lords, be seated."

Her Majesty read the Speech in that clear voice which seems to have been a characteristic from her earliest days. Charles Sumner, the distinguished American statesman, who was present, wrote to a friend that he was " astonished and delighted. Her voice is sweet, and finely modulated, and she pronounced every word distinctly and with a just regard to its meaning. I think I never heard anything better read in my life than her Speech." Upon the general ceremony of dissolution, another American, Miss Greenwood, with true feminine disregard of the great principles concealed under Constitutional forms, has commented very amusingly. She states how strange it seemed to her to think of " that slight girl of eighteen coming in upon that great assembly of legislators, many of them grey, and bald, and pompous, and portly, and gravely telling them that they might go home ! " In addressing Parliament upon this occasion the Queen used words perhaps advised by her Ministry, but which must have also represented with great accuracy her own feelings:

" I ascend the Throne with a deep sense of the responsibility which is imposed upon me ; but I am supported by the consciousness of my own right intentions, and by my dependence upon the protection of Almighty God.   It will be my care to strengthen our institutions, civil and ecclesiastical, by discreet improvement, wherever improvement is required ; and to do all in my power to compose and allay animosity and discord.   Acting upon these principles, I shall, upon all occasions, look with confidence to the wisdom of Parliament and the affections of my people, which form the true support of the dignity of the Crown, and ensure the stability of the Constitution."

It is said that even the Duchess of Kent herself was surprised at the composure of the Queen during this ceremony, and the musical tones of the familiar voice.   Fanny Kemble, who was one of those present at this historic event, describes Her Majesty as being not exactly handsome, but very pretty, while the singularity of her great position seemed to give a sentimental and poetic charm to her youthful face and figure.   " The serene, serious sweetness of her candid brow and clear, soft eyes, gave dignity to the girlish countenance ; while the want of height only added to the effect of extreme youth of the round but slender person, and gracefully moulded hands and arms."   She also describes the voice as exquisite, with perfect enunciation and melodious intonation.   " I think," she concludes, " it is impossible to hear a more excellent utterance than that of the Queen's English by the English Queen."

In August, Her Majesty removed with the Court to Windsor Castle, taking possession of that historic home of British royalty for the first time.   There she received, shortly afterwards, her much loved Uncle Leopold, now King of the Belgians, together with his consort, Queen Louise.   During the autumn she visited Brighton, and then returned to London for Lord Mayor's Day, and participation in another great function.   It was the Queen's first State visit to the City; and for that reason, as well as the magnificence of the ceremonial and celebration, proved a really memorable 9th of November.   From Buckingham Palace to the Guildhall there was a long line of cheering people, their voices mingling merrily in the sunny air with the peals of Church bells, and fitting harmoniously with the flags and heraldic banners which everywhere waved in honour of the occasion.   The Queen, who was magnificently dressed in " pink satin shot with silver," seemed in high spirits, and acknowledged constantly the enthusiastic greetings of her subjects.

A very amusing feature of the demonstration was the spectacle of the Lord Mayor and Aldermen mounting and riding their chargers.   The unaccustomed exercise proved too much for at least one of them, who was sent sprawling while attempting to recognize some fair acquaintance.   Sundry functions followed, such as receiving the keys of the City from the Lord Mayor, and their return by Her Majesty, and the reception of an address delivered by one of the scholars on behalf of the boys of Christ's Hospital.   A pretty description of the scene during the procession has been left us by Mrs. Newton Crosland, who declared that she would never forget the appearance of the maiden Sovereign. " Youthful as she was, she looked every inch a Queen. Seated with their backs to the horses were a lady and gentleman in full Court dress (the beautiful Duchess of Sutherland, Mistress of the Robes, and the Earl of Albemarle, Master of the Horse), and in the centre of the opposite seat, a little raised, was the Queen. All I saw of her dress was a mass of pink satin and swan's-down. The swan's-down encircled her throat, from which rose the fair young face—the blue eyes beaming with goodness and intelligence—the rose-bloom of girlhood on her cheeks, and her soft light brown hair, on which gleamed a circlet of diamonds, braided as it is seen in the early portraits."

After reaching the Guildhall, and the receipt of further loyal addresses dinner was served in the great dining-room. Hangings and gildings, mirrors and lustres, gold and silver plate (valued at £400,000), which had been in part lent by noblemen and gentlemen for the occasion, transformed the place into a perfect bower of beauty. From the roof hung immense chandeliers of stained glass and prisms, which, with innumerable other lights, and the combination of gorgeous Court dresses, and the finest old diamonds of the realm, made the scene one of infinite and fairy-like splendour. And when the Queen appeared, a sweet chorus of hidden voices sang lines such as these :

> " O happy fair !
> Your eyes are lodestars, and your tongue's sweet air
> More tunable than lark to shepherd's ear,
> When wheat is green, when hawthorn buds appear."

Seated upon a throne-like chair of exquisite proportions, which had been placed on an elevated platform, and immediately surrounded by the Dukes of Sussex and Gloucester; the Duchesses of Kent, Gloucester, Cambridge, and Sutherland ; Prince George and Princess Augusta of Cambridge, and the Countess of Mulgrave, Her Majesty received the renewed homage of those privileged to be present, accepted the loyal toasts, drank to the City of London in sherry said to have been a hundred and twenty years old, and knighted the Sheriffs of London—one of whom was Sir Moses Montefiore. And then, amid the fresh acclamations of the assembled crowd out of doors, the Queen drove away from a scene which has seldom been excelled in England for magnificence, and which must have seemed to the young Sovereign like a glimpse of the Eastern world, or a page from some new Arabian Nights.

Time now passed rapidly amidst a constantly changing round of pleasures and duties, of important functions, and unseen, but perhaps still more important details, to the great event of the coronation. The personal popularity of the Queen, the well defined statements of her independence in character and action, the difference between past coronations and the circumstances surrounding the coming one, and the romance attached to this particular occasion, aroused the expectations of the people to fever heat, and, as the 28th of June, 1838, approached, made the public appear almost " coronation mad." Indeed that phrase has been freely and truthfully applied to the popular condition at the time. There were many interesting preliminaries to arrange. An ancient custom which involved the appearance of a feudal-looking champion on horse-back, whose duty it was to present a public challenge in the name of England and the Sovereign, by casting upon the ground a gauntlet which he dared any one to pick up, was dispensed with by royal proclamation. So was the time-honoured custom through which the Peers of the realm did homage by kissing the left cheek, as well as touching the Crown of the Sovereign. The young Queen might have endured such a ceremony if limited to her two royal uncles; but it was a different matter with six hundred Peers—spiritual and secular. The crown worn by George IV. and William IV. at their respective coronations was, like some of these ancient customs, found to be rather inappropriate. Its weight of seven pounds, to say nothing of its large size, made the use of it in the existing form quite impossible. It was therefore made over, and the £112,760 worth of jewels rearranged.

The eventful day broke fair and beautiful, and London seemed to contain and centre within itself a whole world of people. It was a surging, orderly, enthusiastic mass of men, women and children. From Hyde Park corner to the Abbey every house had a scaffold, while every window and conceivable place for looking on was a living mass of humanity. Waving flags, loyal and costly decorations, beautiful banners, flowers without end, strains of music everywhere, a sea of waving handkerchiefs and hats, bursts of artillery, lines of soldiers, a veritable ocean of seething spectators constituted the outside environment of the occasion.

The procession started from Buckingham Palace at 10 o'clock, after a royal salute of twenty-one guns, the hoisting of the Imperial standard, and the simultaneous entry of Her Majesty into the gorgeous State coach. Drawn by eight cream-colored horses, it was preceded by trumpeters and a detachment of Life Guards; by the members of the Royal family and the Royal household; by the State officers, and the foreign ministers and ambassadors. The Royal personages received their share of applause; the gorgeously-attired representatives of foreign nations were cheered; Marshal Soult received an unexpected and splendid welcome; and the Duke of Wellington was accorded the applause which he always obtained from any gathering of Englishmen. But the enthusiasm of the masses when their young Queen came in sight was absolutely overpowering, and evidently most delightful to herself. As the procession

" With slow, but stately pace kept on its course,
　　While all tongues cried, ' God save thee,'
　　You would have thought the very windows spake,
　　So many greedy looks of young and old
　　Through casements darted their desiring eyes,
　　　　And that all the walls

With painted imagery had said at once,
　　　　'Jesu preserve thee.'"

But the scene of beauty along the route, where, it has been said, every window was a bouquet and every balcony a parterre of living loveliness, was nothing to the enchantment of the grand old Abbey and its embodiment of national greatness, living and dead.

The specially erected galleries, covered with crimson and gold cloth, were crowded with spectators—admitted, of course, by ticket—brilliantly clad, and including the members of the House of Commons, ambassadors, and other persons of distinction. The stone floor of the Abbey was spread with matting and purple and crimson cloth. The platform upon which stood the golden "Chair of Homage" was also carpeted with cloth of gold, while within the chancel and near the altar stood the quaint old chair in which the Sovereigns of England since Edward the Confessor have been crowned, and the famous "Stone of Scone," which had served the same purpose for the ancient Kings of Scotland. Harriet Martineau, who has recorded her observations during the weary hours which preceded the entrance of the Queen, says that, "About nine o'clock the first gleams of the sun started into the Abbey, and presently travelled down to the peeresses. I had never before seen the full effect of diamonds. As the light travelled, each lady shone out as a rainbow. The brightness, vastness and dreamy magnificence of the scene produced a strange effect of exhaustion and sleepiness. . . . The guns told when the Queen set forth, and there was universal animation. The Gold Sticks flitted about; there was tuning in the orchestra; and the foreign ambassadors and their suites arrived in quick succession. Prince Esterhazy, crossing a bar of sunshine, was the most prodigious rainbow of all. He was covered with diamonds and pearls; and as he dangled his hat it cast a dazzling radiance all around. At half-past eleven the guns told that the Queen had arrived."

Amongst the superb procession which then entered was all that Great Britain could boast in royal birth, in hereditary greatness, in State position, in military prowess, in ancient ceremonial, in historic prestige, in the formal honour of foreign powers. The swords of investiture, the sceptre, and other national regalia, were born by the Duke of Roxburgh, the Duke of Cleveland, Lord Byron, the Duke of Devonshire, the Marquess of Westminster, and the Duke of Sutherland. The Princes of the blood royal, the great officials of the three kingdoms, Bishops of the Established Church, Lord Melbourne, and the Duke of Wellington, were there—all in brilliant robes of State or office. Then came Her Majesty the Queen, supported on one side by the Bishop of Bath and Wells, and on the other by the Bishop of Durham; attired in a royal robe of crimson velvet, furred with ermine and bordered with gold lace and wearing the collars of her Orders and a circlet of gold upon her head. Her train was borne by eight young ladies selected from the noblest families in the kingdom, and she looked as thoroughly royal as her surroundings were magnificent.

Amid the musical notes of the National Anthem, and a mighty storm of cheers from within and without the gray old walls of the Abbey, the Queen had entered, and as she advanced slowly towards the choir, the anthem "I was glad" rang out upon the trembling air, and was followed by "Vivat Victoria Regina." Amidst the booming of guns and the renewed acclamations of the brilliant multitude, Her Majesty reached the recognition chair, and then knelt for a few moments on the faldstool and engaged in silent prayer. The Archbishop of Canterbury, accompanied by some high officials of State, then approached the Sovereign and formally recognized her by saying to the people:

"Sirs, I here present unto you Queen Victoria, the undoubted Queen of this realm; wherefore, all you who are come this day to do your homage, are you willing to do the same?"

A similar "recognition" was made to the other three sides of the Abbey, and received the same enthusiastic response of "God save Queen Victoria." Then followed all manner of ceremonies, including the placing on the altar before the kneeling Sovereign of the Bible and chalice borne in the procession, the delivery of the regalia to the Primate, the reading of the Litany and the Communion service. At the conclusion of the latter, the Archbishop addressed the Queen, and, being assured of her readiness to take the oath, said: "Will you solemnly promise and swear to govern the people of the United Kingdom of Great Britain and Ireland, and the dominions thereto belonging, according to the statutes in Parliament agreed on, and the respective laws and customs of the same?"

The Queen replied that she would promise so to do, and gave the same answer to the charge that she should, to the extent of her power, cause law and justice to be properly executed. Then the Archbishop proceeded:

"Will you, to the utmost of your power, maintain the laws of God, the true profession of the Gospel, and the Protestant reformed religion established by law? And will you maintain and preserve, inviolably, the settlement of the united Church of England and Ireland, and the doctrine, worship, discipline, and government thereof, as by law established, within England and Ireland and the territories thereunto belonging? And will you preserve unto the Bishops and clergy of England and Ireland, and to the churches there committed to their charge, all such rights and privileges as by law do or shall appertain to them or any of them?"

To this Her Majesty clearly and firmly assented. Preceded by the Sword of State and the higher officials, she then passed to the altar again and took the Coronation oath. And now came an interesting ceremony. Sitting in what is known as King Edward's chair, a rich cloth of gold was held over the Queen's head by four Knights of the Garter—the Dukes of Buccleuch and Rutland and the Marquesses of Anglesey and Exeter—while the Archbishop, with a gold anointing spoon, anointed her head and hands with oil, marking them in the form of a cross, and saying:

" Be thou anointed with holy oil, as kings, priests, and prophets were anointed. And as Solomon was anointed King by Zadoc the priest and Nathan the prophet, so be you anointed, blessed, and consecrated Queen over this people, whom the Lord your God has given you to rule and govern. In the name of the Father, and of the Son, and of the Holy Ghost. Amen."

Then followed some curious incidents and ceremonial. Gold spurs were presented to the Queen, and duly returned, as was the Sword of State borne by Lord Melbourne, with the injunction from the Primate to " do justice, stop the growth of iniquity, protect the holy Church of God, help and defend widows and orphans, restore the things that are gone to decay, maintain the things that are restored, punish and reform what is amiss, and confirm what is in good order." The investiture of Her Majesty with the orb, another royal robe, and the ring and sceptre, followed, and then came the placing of the Crown upon her head by the Archbishop of Canterbury and Primate of all England. Simultaneously with the crowning of the Sovereign, the peers in the chapel and the peeresses in the gallery donned their flashing, gleaming coronets, the multitude shouted " God save the Queen," the orchestra pealed forth deafening strains of musical splendour, the guns of the tower, and city, and national fortresses roared their recognition, and the scene in the Abbey became one of indescribable excitement, grandeur, and enthusiasm. The Queen was visibly moved during the long-continued acclamations; and while she struggled strongly and successfully to suppress her emotions, the Duchess of Kent gave way and sobbed audibly. Even ordinary spectators say that the strain of the sustained splendour of the scene was more than their nerves could bear.

Then came the ceremony of homage to the Queen, who had again taken her seat, or been " enthroned "—after a brief Episcopal exhortation, an anthem, and a benediction. One by one the Archbishops and Bishops, or Lords Spiritual, knelt and kissed the Queen's hand. The Dukes of Sussex and Cambridge then knelt, removed their coronets, touched them to the Crown, pledged their allegiance, and kissed their royal niece on the left cheek. One by one the Peers Temporal came forward, touched Coronet to Crown, kissed the little white hand, and repeated the quaint old Saxon oath:

" I do become your liegeman of life and limb, and of earthly worship; and faith and truth I will bear unto you, to live and die, against all manner of folks. So help me God ! "

Several pretty and characteristic incidents took place during this elaborate function. When the good old Duke of Sussex, feebly and with difficulty, ascended the steps of the Throne, the Queen gave way for the moment to natural emotion, threw her arms round his neck, and kissed him on the cheek. An oft-described scene was that connected with old Lord Rolle's effort to do homage. He had to be partially carried up to the Throne, and, by some mischance, slipped and fell. Again he tried, but found it impossible to touch the Crown. Upon seeing this, Her Majesty rose, leaned forward, and gave him her hand, dispensing with the rest of the ceremony. In connection with this, and the fact that the Duke of Norfolk had not long before presented the Queen with a glove, as being the custom under which he held the Manor of Worksop, a foreigner, who was present, gravely informed his countrymen that rolling down the steps of the Throne at a Coronation was the means by which, and from which, the Lords Rolle held their title !

At the close of the homage further brief ceremonies followed, and then, attired once more in the royal robe, as distinguished from the mantle of State worn during the Coronation, Her Majesty walked to the west door of the Abbey, wearing upon her head the Crown with its silver and velvet, its ball of flashing diamonds, its Maltese cross of brilliants, its sapphires, and rubies, and emeralds, and exquisite pearls, and carrying in one hand her sceptre, and in the other the orb. About four o'clock, and thus attired, she entered her carriage and drove home through many more thousands of her waiting subjects. So ended the prolonged tension of a stately and splendid ceremonial—one which makes us wonder how the central and frail figure of the great occasion was able to endure it all. Anna Jamieson has described, in a letter written at the time, the orderly enthusiasm of the populace ; and concludes with what seems significant truth :

"As to the Queen, poor child, she went through her part beautifully ; and when she returned, looking pale and tremulous, crowned, and holding her sceptre in a manner and attitude which said ' I have it, and none shall wrest it from me ! ' even Carlyle, who was standing near me, uttered with emotion a blessing upon her head."

But it was all over at last, and the young Queen had now fully and formally entered upon what was destined to be so glorious a reign and so great an era.

CHAPTER IV.

THE YOUNG QUEEN.

THE general position of affairs in 1837 was not one which can be looked back upon with any degree of pleasure. The people were dissatisfied, though they hardly knew why or wherefore. The monarchy itself had been for many years weak in appearance, though probably strong in reality. The net result, however, of a system which commended itself to public reason, while excluding itself from popular sympathy, was a development of republicanism, and consequent strong expressions of disloyalty at more than one public meeting. The country was also on the verge of the prolonged Corn Law crisis; the Canadian rebellion, in all its greatly exaggerated and misunderstood details, was in full swing; and the disastrous Afghan war was on the horizon. The Government, controlled by Lord Melbourne, was Whig in politics, and existed chiefly on the reputation and memory of the Reform Bill. Its majority had been over a hundred, but in the general elections resulting from Her Majesty's accession the figures fell to thirty-eight. In composition this first government of a great reign was fairly strong, as the names will indicate:

Premier and First Lord of the Treasury -	Lord Melbourne.
Lord Chancellor - - - -	Lord Cottenham.
Lord Privy Seal - - - -	Lord Duncannon.
Chancellor of the Exchequer - -	Mr. Spring-Rice.
Home Secretary - - - -	Lord John Russell.
Foreign Secretary - - -	Lord Palmerston.
Secretary for War and the Colonies - -	Lord Glenelg.
Lord Lieutenant of Ireland - -	Marquess of Normanby.
Chief Secretary for Ireland - - -	Lord Morpeth.

Upon the thrones of Europe there were a few really notable personages, but none of them now survive in the places of power. In Sweden, Charles Bernadotte remained as the last relic of the Napoleonic empire. In Russia, Nicholas I. was Czar, whilst Austria, with the Emperor Ferdinand I. at its head, still held the primacy amongst German countries. Prussia, under Frederick William III., had not yet felt the touch of Bismarck's genius, and for some time to come would have to continue upon the verge of first-class national strength. Belgium was ruled, fortunately for itself, by Leopold I.; and France was under the peaceful and somewhat feeble guidance of Louis Philippe.

The accession of the young Queen worked a revolution in the popular

HENRY, LORD BROUGHAM.

LORD LYNDHURST.

British ideas of royalty, as well as in the duties of statesmen and the procedure of the Court. Month by month public interest grew in connection with her appearance, her actions, her words, and everything that she did, until it culminated during the wildly enthusiastic days of the Coronation. Old people wondered at her vast responsibilities and opportunities for good; the young dreamed of her reputed beauty, and goodness, and fairy-like surroundings of greatness. She stirred the hearts of statesmen and poets, and the most practical of men into a feeling of almost romantic loyalty. Veteran soldiers, like Wellington, and *blasé* men of the world, like Lord Melbourne, were alike moved to sympathy and unselfish action. O'Connell declared that if the Duke of Cumberland should cause trouble, as was rumoured, " I can get 500,000 brave Irishmen to defend the life, the honour, and the person of the beloved young lady by whom England's throne is now filled." Charles Dickens thought so much of the fanciful and romantic nature of her position and destiny as to become almost monomaniac, and everywhere, in politics and at Court, a sentiment of courtesy and chivalry developed to an extent hitherto unknown.

A writer in *Blackwood* described the Queen during this period as " winning all sorts of golden opinions from all sorts of people by her affability, the grace of her manners, and her prettiness." Her appearance seems, indeed, to have been very much what the coins of that time and of to-day indicate. Another description refers to Her Majesty as "really a very lovely girl, with a fine, delicate, rose-bloom complexion, large blue eyes, a fair, broad brow, and an expression of peculiar candour and innocence." And the charming stories told of her enhanced the popular interest and liking. One represented her as having a magnificent throne set up in the Throne-room of Buckingham Palace, covered with crimson velvet and silk, and with gold embroideries, and laces and tassels and fringes galore. When ready she is said to have tried it, and declared that she " never sat upon a more comfortable throne in all her life."

Another, and a true one, is the story of the first court-martial death sentence presented her for confirmation. With tears in her eyes, she asked the Duke of Wellington if nothing could be said in favour of the man.

" Nothing; he has deserted three times," was the reply.

"Oh, your Grace, think again! "

" Well, your Majesty, he certainly is a bad soldier, but there was somebody who spoke as to his good character in private life."

" Oh, thank you ! " exclaimed the Queen, and dashed the word " Pardoned " and her signature across the terrible document.

Finally Parliament relieved her of the duty of deciding in such cases, by enabling a Royal Commission to sign the ordinances of death. It also became known that she had paid her father's debts out of her own private resources, and had substituted a system of careful financial management throughout her whole business affairs.   Parliament in the meantime fixed her Civil List at £385,000 per annum, as compared with the £1,030,000 given George III. and George IV., and the £510,000 paid William IV.   The private Royal estates were, by arrangement, made over for this reign into the care of Parliament, and the returns from them, ere many years passed, almost sufficed to cover the expenses of the Civil List itself.

But the central feature of this first year in the reign, and of several following, was Her Majesty's relations with Lord Melbourne, and the effect of his political teachings and guidance upon the formation of her character, and the development of those principles of public duty which the labours of the Duchess of Kent had so well initiated.   The Premier was a man of remarkable ability, and possessed of qualities which made him capable of rendering the young Queen almost incalculable service.   A thorough man of the world, and possessed of mingled geniality and culture, he was able to instruct while he appeared to entertain.   A man of broad mind, and without the modern tendency to bitter or narrow partisanship, he was fitted to assume a sincere position of impartial counsel upon the motives and principles of all parties in the State.   And his sound judgment and varied store of political and historical knowledge was freely put to the best of all uses—the instruction of a Sovereign who was destined for sixty years to lead the statesmen of the realm.   The opportunity did Lord Melbourne himself untold service.   It has enabled history to dissipate the false impressions of contemporaries, and to destroy the one-time wide belief that he was a man of reckless indolence and selfish indifference to everything in the State except his own personal comfort and welfare.

The supposed presence of these qualities is now well known to have been the result of his indifferent, blasé manners.   The seventh Duke of Somerset, a Tory of the Tories, declared in this connection—November 29th, 1848—that " One great characteristic of Melbourne's mind was the absence of prejudice and the great readiness with which he listened to very opposite views and appreciated the merits of his opponents.   This made him so useful to the Queen ; and there was hardly another public man who could have spoken so fairly upon difficult and disputed questions as he did."   Archbishop Whately, in 1846, spoke of him as a man of " perfect good temper, of varied and extensive knowledge, and generally of sound judgment."   He thought that Melbourne's " odd but clever way of putting things " must have made the Queen like him.

Greville adds in his diary that " No man is more formed to ingratiate himself with her than Melbourne.   He treats her with unbounded consideration and respect, he consults her tastes and her wishes, and he puts her at her ease by his frank and natural manners, while he amuses her by the quaint, queer, epigrammatic turn of his mind and his varied knowledge upon all subjects." More than this, he was exceedingly handsome and charming, even on the verge of sixty. The reverse side of the picture is found in the fact that Lord Melbourne had led emphatically a life of pleasure, and that his moral character had been warped by the possession of a wife who in earlier years had brought him bitter sorrow and much trouble. But of these shadows the young Queen knew nothing, and certainly appears to have had no reason at any time to suspect them. And her influence upon him was as beneficial and elevating as his experience was useful to her.

Her Majesty most emphatically possessed and exhibited at this time a strong will of her own, though it was in the main an intelligent, prudent, and educated will. It won the immediate and sincere respect of her Premier and the Court. Greville prophesied that " she will some day play a conspicuous part, and has a great deal of character "; and declared that Melbourne " thinks highly of her sense, discretion, and good feeling." Those who had been upon specially good terms with the Duchess of Kent had expected to obtain high favour under the new *regime*. Sir John Conroy, her private secretary and adviser, anticipated much, even to a peerage and the private secretaryship to Her Majesty. But he was calmly dismissed with a pension and a baronetcy. Lord Durham, his unfortunate and brilliant friend, was given an order of knighthood when he hoped for much more, and shortly afterwards disappeared in the gulf of the Canadian Governership. The Duchess of Kent was made affectionately aware that she could no longer be her daughter's adviser upon affairs of State, and the almost insuperable difficulty of appointing a private secretary to a youthful and inexperienced Sovereign was obviated for the time being by Lord Melbourne's performance of the more important public part of the duties, Baroness Lehzen's aid in the social matters, and the unostentatious, but useful and effective advice of that wise and valued friend of the Queen and Prince Albert in after years—Baron Stockmar.

It was not long before the whole Court felt the effect of her rule. One of its proudest official ladies, for instance, received a very direct intimation that punctuality was expected in all her relations with the Queen. Upon this occasion—not the first on which tardiness had occurred—she found the Queen regarding her watch in a rather significant manner, and said in tones of apology that she feared she had kept Her Majesty waiting.

" Yes ; full ten minutes," was the reply : " and I beg that in future you will be more punctual."

Needless to say the offence was not repeated. This and similar incidents created an impression at Court very well voiced by Greville, who observes that " In the midst of all her propriety of manner and conduct, the young Queen begins to exhibit signs of a peremptory disposition, and it is impossible not to suspect that, as she gains confidence, and as her character begins to develop, she will evince a strong will of her own." So in other matters, the Queen displayed a mixture of caution and self-will. The Princess Lieven, a clever character, somewhat like the Madam Novikoff of later years, sought to obtain information in a private interview which might prove useful in her varied political intrigues. But, to her great chagrin, Her Majesty "talked of nothing but commonplaces," and so dismissed the rather dangerous visitor. Upon another occasion, some months later, Lord Melbourne wanted the Queen to review some troops. She consented, but added the wish to do so on horseback. The Premier intimated his belief that it would be better for her to review them from a carriage. "Very well, my lord," was the prompt reply, "but remember: no horse, no review." She seems to have also enjoyed a joke as well as anyone in her *entourage*, and we are told that one Sunday a very strong sermon was preached by Dean Hook, in the course of which he told the Queen that the Church would endure, no matter what happened to the Throne. On returning from the Chapel Royal to Buckingham Palace, Lord Normanby, who had been in attendance, said, "Did not your Majesty find it very hot?" to which he received the quick reply, "Yes, and the sermon was very hot, too." Such were the Queen and her chief Minister when they commenced to act together in the government of the Empire.

The first event in the political history of the reign was the general election of 1837, and here the Whigs committed a serious blunder, and one which seems curious in view of Lord Melbourne's personal impartiality and wise attitude towards the Queen. They made public use of his official position and of the fact that Her Majesty had voluntarily retained King William's ministry. They pointed to the friendly relations existing between the young Sovereign and her Minister, and to the well-known Whig tendencies of the Duke and Duchess of Kent, as reasons for claiming the support of the electorate. To thus represent directly or indirectly that the Queen had Whig opinions and wanted Whig ministers was neither wise nor constitutional, and laid the foundation for some undeserved unpopularity in succeeding years. It certainly estranged the Tories, and this to such an extent that the Court gradually became permeated with adherents of the other faction, while Her Majesty for the first and last time in her life was hissed, in 1839, when visiting Ascot, and certain Tory gatherings drank to the toast of "Queen Adelaide" with fervency and in marked contrast to their reception of Queen Victoria's name. All this was, of course, very silly, and the feeling soon passed away, but for a time it seemed a real grievance. During the elections it found incipient expression in a rather clever epigram:

> "'The Queen is with us' Whigs insulting say;
> 'For when *she found us in* she let us stay';
> It may be so; but give me leave to doubt
> How long she'll keep you when *she finds you out.*"

On the 20th of November the young Queen opened her first parliament, with accompaniments of brilliant weather, immense crowds along the route from Buckingham Palace, and a House of Lords in which the galleries were packed with peeresses and leaders in every branch of the national life. The Speech was read by Her Majesty with the musical elocution which appears to have been so noteworthy, and amid an intense silence which made the self-possession of that slender, graceful personage, with her magnificent robes and surroundings, seem so remarkable. The membership of this parliament is of more than usual interest. Under the auspices of the Queen and with the aid of the men who appeared upon this scene of passing splendour, the Empire of to-day has been built up, and its foundations laid in varying stages of agitation and legislation; amid occasional error and not infrequent neglect.

Nearly all have done their work and run their course, and the statesmen in 1896 are, in many cases, the sons and grandsons of the leaders of 1837. Many even have been forgotten by all but the chronicler of the past and the lover of history. In the House of Lords the great figures of Wellington and Lyndhurst stood out in their grim diversities of character upon the canvass of Conservative leadership. With them were the Duke of Rutland, the Earl of Aberdeen, the Marquess of Bute, the Earls of Stanhope and Devon, Lords Strangford, Alvanley and Redesdale. Upon the other side of the House were the *debonair* and handsome Melbourne, the aristocratic, somewhat silent, and thoughtful figure of Earl Grey, the sensitive, sarcastic, erratic, and utterly unmanageable Brougham, the brilliant Earl of Durham, the aged and popular royal Duke of Sussex, the fluent, elegant, and experienced Marquess of Lansdowne, the now familiar name of Lord Rosebery, the Earls of Gosford, Minto, Shrewsbury and Lichfield, the Marquess of Sligo, the Marquess of Northampton, and Lords Lyndoch and Portman. Archbishop Howley, a man of mediocre ability, sat as the Primate of all England, while Bishop Philpotts, of Exeter, was the eloquent and sophistical champion of the Church.

In the House of Commons were the real leaders of the people. The most of them were of that aristocratic lineage and character which has stamped the government of the Empire all through the reign, and which lost force in 1868 only to regain it in 1874, and obtain increased influence in 1895. Of this stamp were the leaders on both sides. Sir Robert Peel was the idol of the Tories. Good-looking and with a finely proportioned physique, full round face, and red hair, he made a strong and respected leader. With him were Henry Goulburn, the exponent of extreme Toryism; Sir Henry Hardinge, the Waterloo veteran; Sir Robert Inglis, the defender of the Church; Colonel Sibthorpe, the honest and eccentric and notorious, the Marquess of Chandos, whom Disraeli has pilloried for all posterity as the Marquess of Carabas; Mr. Spring Rice, a courteous Irishman, with an affection for dandyism and rings; and—unnoticed amid the throng—Mr. Disraeli himself. Lord Stanley—another future Conservative Premier, as Earl of Derby—was known to fame, but it was as a rising Whig Minister. The Lord Salisbury of to-day was in the nursery, while his opponent, Lord Rosebery, as well as Mr. Balfour and Mr. Chamberlain, were not yet born.

Upon the Liberal, or Whig, side of the House were some equally striking figures. First and foremost was Lord John Russell, small, slender, and weakly, but with ability and determination and family influence sufficient to keep him in the front. Lord Palmerston, like Disraeli and many others of the time, was a dandy, vain of admitted accomplishments and of his tall, handsome figure, pleasing face, and fine black hair. Though Foreign Secretary, he had not yet won any particular reputation. Sir John Campbell was a rising lawyer, with a Scotch accent and plenty of Scotch ambition—even to expectations of the wool-sack. Daniel O'Connell, with an ability rising into genius, was now alternately supporting the Whigs and praising the Queen, while Richard Lalor Shiel, offering, with his small figure and piercing eyes, a remarkable contrast to his colleague's athletic frame and ruddy face, gave the benefit of his impulsive eloquence to the "Cause of Ireland." Macaulay, young and full of learning, and possessed of the very genius of literary expression, came home from India about this time, and soon electrified the House by his eloquence. Lord Morpeth —afterwards Earl of Carlisle—embodied the spirit of aristocratic politics and culture, while Lord Howick, destined in years to come, as Earl Grey, to be a prominent Colonial Secretary, was reckoned a man of distinct ability and promise. Mr. Poulett Thompson was still busy with commercial questions, and utterly unaware of his future mission in distant Canada, as Lord Sydenham and Governor-General.

Scattered through the House were many men of the future and of the past— Roebuck, the cynical Radical; Codrington, the hero of Navarino; Feargus O'Connor, the Chartist; Edward Lytton Bulwer, the author of "Pelham," but without political repute as yet, or the addition of the surname which has become more famous than that he had so far borne; Henry Lytton Bulwer, handsome and, like his brother, inclined to foppishness, and not himself aware perhaps of the diplomatic talents afterwards recognized in Lord Dalling and Bulwer; Joseph Hume, the economist; Grote, the historian of Greece; Charles Buller, the promise of great things which never came; Sir Francis Burdett, and Sir William Follett. Mr. Gladstone was there, but it was as a rising hope of the sternest Tories, and as a young man of religious views, and prejudices so strong as to make many fear that his ability might be wasted and the promises of greatness fail to be realized.

During the months immediately following the opening of Parliament—in which the Whigs had a small majority—the Queen was worried by a number of more or less crazed individuals who would have liked to share her greatness.

This mania to marry the young Sovereign took various forms. One man used to drive his phæton in front of, or behind, the royal carriage whenever an opportunity offered, and make a nuisance of himself by waving or kissing his hand to Her Majesty. Another lunatic went through a sort of dumb show of the same kind in the Chapel Royal, while a commercial traveller, named Willets, galloped alongside the Queen's carriage, and almost over her attendants, in his mad desire to reveal the state of what he might have termed his heart. These men were dealt with in ways best suited for the disposal of harmless monomaniacs; but there were others who proved less amusing. In 1837, a German imbecile, named Stuber, declared his intention of shooting the Queen and her mother, and was sent to a lunatic asylum. A little later in the year, Captain John Goode sprang one day at the Queen's open carriage, and shook his fist at her, exclaiming, " I'll have you off the Throne, and your mother too." He was adjudged insane, as was a fellow, in the spring of 1839, who hurled a stout paper packet into the Queen's face as she was driving past Apsley House.

Meanwhile the Queen was living an orderly, busy, and pleasant life. The arrangement of time at Windsor was methodical and careful. Her Majesty rose about eight o'clock, breakfasted in her own room, and employed the whole morning in transacting business, which included the reading of despatches and the consideration of matters of interest and importance in every department of the Government. At eleven or twelve the Premier would come and spend an hour with her, or more if the business in hand required it. After luncheon she would ride for two hours at a full gallop, and with a numerous suite in attendance. Lord Melbourne would generally be at her left hand, and an equerry-in-waiting on her right. Upon returning from this excursion she would spend the rest of the afternoon with music and singing, and perhaps playing with children, of whom she was very fond—generally contriving to have some at the Castle.

Dinner usually commenced at eight o'clock, the Lord-in-waiting having previously instructed the gentlemen as to whom they were to take in. When the guests had all assembled Her Majesty would enter, preceded by the gentlemen of the household and followed by the Duchess of Kent and all her ladies. To each lady she spoke briefly, bowed to the men and led the way to the dining-room, generally taking the arm of the man of highest rank present. After dinner, which lasted the usual time, the men would very soon be called to the drawing-room, instead of being allowed to dawdle over their wine. Music and whist filled in the evening till about half-past eleven, when the Queen retired. This regularity was, of course, frequently broken in upon by functions of varying degrees of importance. In May, 1838, for instance, a State ball was given by the Queen at Buckingham Palace, followed by a State concert and a drawing-room.

The ball was on a scale of regal magnificence, and was opened by the Queen in person, who took Prince George of Cambridge—the Field Marshal and Duke of later years—for a partner.   Her Majesty wore white satin, trimmed with silver and lace and blush roses, and scattered over with diamonds.   The head-dress was of roses, the centre formed of brilliants.   During the evening the Queen danced with Prince Esterhazy—who still sparkled with jewels, as he had done on Coronation day, the Marquess of Douro, the Earl of Uxbridge and other noblemen.   And right royally she kept the dancing and merriment up, until, at four o'clock she took part in the last piece on the programme with unabated and girlish animation.   At her first birthday celebration London was ablaze with illuminations.   In Regent street one enterprising firm displayed a transparency of Her Majesty, robed and seated on the Throne, with the British lion at her feet, repelling the hydra-headed demon of anarchy.   The motto " Hail, Star of Brunswick," surmounted the device in fiery letters.   Elsewhere, variegated oil lamps, blazing stars, crowns, rosettes, festoons, and the initials " V. R." appeared in multitudinous forms.

The State concert was held at the palace, and amongst the great names on the programme were those of Grisi, Persiani, Rubini, Lablache, and Costa.   Other balls followed, in one of which Prince Esterhazy fairly out-did and out-shone himself—and no more can be said.   His sword-belt was studded with diamonds, the hilt of the sword and the scabbard were crusted with brilliants.   His Hussar cap was almost concealed in glimmering pearls, and numerous stars and orders around his neck, or upon his breast, blazed with precious stones.   A more quiet and homely scene about this time was that of the Queen sitting to Sir David Wilkie for a portrait.   His description is alike loyal and courtly. He speaks of Her Majesty as having " all the buoyancy and singleness of heart of youth, with a wisdom and decision far beyond her years."   Elsewhere he writes :

" Having been accustomed to see the Queen as a child, my reception had a little of the air of an early acquaintance.   She is eminently beautiful, her features nicely formed, her skin smooth, her hair worn close to her face in a most simple way ; glossy and clean looking.   Her manner, though trained to act the Sovereign, is yet simple and natural. She has all the decision, thought, and self-possession of a Queen of older years ; has all the buoyancy of youth, and from the smile to the unrestrained laugh is a perfect child."

Illustrations of the truth of Wilkie's description are many.   One day while another painter was engaged upon a portrait of Her Majesty and was using his daughter as a temporary model, the Queen suddenly entered the room where Miss Sully was sitting on the Throne with the royal robes wrapped around her. In great confusion the girl was about to descend, when the gay young Queen stopped her, saying : " Pray stay as you are ; I like to see how I look."   But the leaven of firmness and determination were there, mingling pleasantly with the natural lightsomeness of a youthful disposition.   Upon one occasion Lord Melbourne placed a certain paper before her for signature, explaining what he thought was the *expediency* of the measure. The comment was prompt and somewhat crushing: " I have been taught, my Lord, to judge between what is right and what is wrong, but expediency is a word I neither wish to hear nor to understand." On another occasion, the Prime Minister used all his eloquence in vain to obtain the royal sanction to a certain document, and when he found it was useless to press the matter, declared it not to be one of paramount importance. " It is with me," said the Queen, " a matter of the most paramount importance whether or not I attach my signature to a document with which I am not thoroughly acquainted."

The whole world has heard the story of Her Majesty's refusal to transact certain business on Sunday, her instructions to the clergyman who preached that day to the royal household to deal with the duties of the Sabbath, and her intimation afterwards that at any hour next morning—seven o'clock, if the Premier liked—she was prepared to go into the papers with him. But the statesman found they were not so pressing as to require attention before nine o'clock. Two or three unfortunate events occurred at this time, which it is not necessary to go into. The Lady Flora Hastings' case was an incident of misfortune which now seems to have been as unavoidable as the measures taken by Lord Melbourne on behalf of the Queen were necessary. The curious storm raised in certain quarters over the presentation of that eccentric individual, Robert Owen, to Her Majesty was one which partakes more of small partisanship than of historic interest.

But petty scandals, and other matters of graver political import, had steadily weakened Lord Melbourne's administration, and on the 6th of May, 1839, Lord John Russell only obtained a majority of five for the Bill suspending the Constitution of Jamaica. The Government promptly resigned office and brought the Queen face to face with her first political crisis. The prospect of losing Lord Melbourne's advice and aid was undoubtedly a great grief to her, but she knew the Constitution and was determined within all recognized limits to abide by it. Writing to Lord J. Russell, who had been the medinm of communicating the Cabinet's resignation to Her Majesty, she said :

" The Queen received this morning Lord John Russell's letter, and she can assure him she never felt more pain than in learning from him yesterday that the Government had determined to resign.

" Lord John is well aware, without the Queen's expressing it, how much she was satisfied with the manner in which he performed his duties, which were performed in a manner which has greatly tended to the welfare and prosperity of this country."

The Queen at once sent for the Duke of Wellington, who advised her that, while his services in any capacity were always at her disposal, he thought it would be wiser to call in Sir Robert Peel, as being the party leader in the Commons, where the chief troubles of the Administration would be. Peel was then sent for, and undertook the task with every apparent prospect of success. But a hitch came when he proposed that the Ladies of the Bedchamber and the Household should be changed. The trouble which followed, and which has been labelled by history "The Bedchamber Plot," was due partly to the young Queen's inexperience, and partly to that unfortunate quality which the Iron Duke hit off when, in referring to their relations with a female Sovereign, he said: "I have no small talk, and Peel has no manners." Like most epigrams, this is only half true; but there is little doubt that had Peel possessed half the tact of Melbourne, the difficulty would never have occurred. To the Queen it was hard enough to part with her old advisers, without asking her to dismiss all her companions and the friends whose sympathy she had felt, and with whose characters and faces she was now so familiar. To have strange advisers was a Constitutional necessity; but why should she have her Court and Household filled also with strangers?

To Peel it was equally clear that government would be impossible, with ladies in close and constant attendance upon Her Majesty who were allied in relationship and opinion with his strongest political opponents. Both in a sense were right; and the misfortune of the situation seems to have been that the Queen thought all her ladies were to be removed, while Peel would have been, in reality, satisfied with the dismissal of the chief ones. The intervention of Lord Ashley—afterwards Earl of Shaftesbury—was sought by Sir Robert; but neither his persuasions nor the arguments of Wellington could induce Her Majesty to recede from her position; and the result was a formal letter to Peel, stating her inability to consent to a course which she considered contrary to usage, unnecessary, and repugnant to her feelings.

At the same time she wrote Melbourne in terms which Elizabeth or Anne might have used. "Do not fear," she said, "that I was not calm and composed. They wanted to deprive me of my ladies; and I suppose they would deprive me next of my dresses and my housemaids; they wished to treat me like a girl; but I will show them that I am Queen of England." This indicates a personal feeling which could only be the outcome of distinct misunderstanding, as had, in fact, been shown in her previous statement to Peel, that "You must not expect me to give up the society of Lord Melbourne." The fact of the matter is that the young Queen had come to regard her Premier almost as a father, and that everything done by his opponents assumed to her a suspicious and unpleasant appearance. In after days, when Wellington became her greatest friend and Peel one of those whom she could regard with personal confidence as well as respect, this passing difficulty no doubt seemed absurdly small.

But at the moment it was exceedingly important. Peel could not, of course, form a Government under the circumstances; and with every expression of regret, and the hope "that whatever arrangements your Majesty may be enabled to make may be most conducive to your Majesty's personal comfort and happiness, and to the promotion of the public welfare," he resigned his commission. The Queen promptly sent for Melbourne, who had been meanwhile consulting with his colleagues. They had decided to stand by their youthful Sovereign in the difficult circumstances in which she was placed. Of this determination Earl Spencer, a Liberal leader, who, as Lord Althorp, held the respect of the whole country, expressed to Lord J. Russell the belief that "as gentlemen they could not do otherwise." Lord Palmerston, writing to Earl Granville on the same day (10th May), throws further light upon the situation :

"The Queen, alone and unadvised, stood firm against all assaults, showed a presence of mind, a firmness, a discrimination far beyond her years, and had much the best of it in her discussion with Peel and the Duke. She sent Peel this morning her final refusal to comply with this condition, and Peel thereupon resigned his commission. We shall, of course, stand by the Queen, and support her against this offensive condition which the Tories wanted to impose upon her, and which her youth and her isolated position ought to have protected her from. It remains to be seen whether this House of Commons will support us in supporting her ; and if it will not, whether this House does or does not faithfully represent the opinion of the country."

Looking back through the constitutional march of nearly fifty years, it is easy now to agree with Peel and Wellington in their refusal to act as the advisers of a Sovereign who would soon have been surrounded by an inner circle of opposing intrigue. At the same time, it is equally impossible to look back at that frail figure of nineteen in her position of lofty loneliness without feeling a thrill of strong, personal sympathy with her objection to a Court environment of altogether strange and unfamiliar people. And there was much of human nature and instinctive kindliness in Lord Melbourne's acceptance of his old position and responsibilities under circumstances which he knew would greatly discredit him, and which, in fact, have been enshrined in literature under the misleading designation of a "plot." Subsequent events indicate that he did not inspire the Queen's action, and his character, as now known, proves anything so contemptible to have been utterly foreign to his nature. His announced reasons for the resumption of office are therefore worthy of all credence :

"I resume office unequivocally and solely for this reason, that I will not desert my Sovereign in a situation of difficulty and distress, especially when a demand is made upon Her Majesty with which, I think, she ought not to comply ; a demand inconsistent with her personal honour, and which, if acquiesced in, would render her reign liable to all the changes and variations of political parties, and make her domestic life one constant scene of unhappiness and discomfort."

For the next two years his Ministry struggled along in ever increasing weakness and unpopularity. A tacit understanding was, however, come to, that whenever a change of government should take place a few of Her Majesty's chief Ladies would be expected to retire. Where Peel's bluntness could never have succeeded, Melbourne's tact and urbanity, aided by Stockmar's diplomacy, made the settlement easy. This was the last of the "Bedchamber question." But the discussions and difficulties of her solitary position were so brought home to the Queen by the whole incident that it is little wonder if her thoughts were turned, against her own will, to the necessity of a suitable marriage. Fortunately the question once raised in her mind was destined to an easy, a natural, and a most beneficial solution.

THE QUEEN AND THE WOUNDED SOLDIERS FROM THE CRIMEA.

THE DUKE OF WELLINGTON, K.G.

CHAPTER V.

BETROTHAL AND MARRIAGE.

THE love-story of England's Queen forms one of the most charming romances of the ages. The marriage itself voiced the truest and highest conception of that relationship, and stands out upon the pages of history as a signal instance of royal happiness and beauty of life. When Prince Albert, and his brother Ernest, visited the old Palace at Kensington in 1836, they were mere boys, and seem to have enjoyed themselves and the society of their charming little cousin, as such. There is no doubt that Princess Victoria liked the Prince, and, perhaps, in a misty sort of way, considered it possible that in the distant future she might marry him—if she had to marry some one. But, though they were brought together purposely by King Leopold and the Duchess of Kent, nothing more than friendship seems to have been the immediate result.

In the opinion of those most directly interested in the future happiness of the young Princess, it was clear that no better match could be suggested. For the Queen—as she became in the succeeding year—to marry a Crowned head would have been provocative of many and serious complications—to say nothing of the lack of eligible rulers. And the minor Courts of Germany did not at this time furnish very hopeful or beneficial surroundings for developing the qualities and character suitable for such a position. One of the exceptions was the Court of Coburg. It had already given Leopold to the lamented Charlotte of England, and later to the Throne of Belgium. It had preserved an atmosphere of home life and honest statesmanship which did honour to the good old Dowager-Duchess, of whom Prince Albert and the Queen were in after years so fond. From this environment had come the Duchess of Kent, and many of the beneficent influences with which she and her brother Leopold had surrounded the Princess Victoria in her childhood and youth.

It was, therefore, very natural that these careful guardians should have looked upon a possible union of the scion of this princely house with the Queen, as a security for much that was good and against much that was dangerous. But there were many other suitors. Not often in history does such an opportunity occur for obtaining what might be termed matrimonial greatness, as here presented itself. It is needless to say there were many who desired to win the prize without much care as to the accompanying responsibilities. A catalogue of the royal personages who at one time or another deemed themselves eligible filled sixteen pages of a work published in 1840. It included the names of Prince George of Cumberland and Prince George of Cambridge, the Duc d'Orleans, the eldest son of the Prince of Orange, the Duke of Brunswick, the Duc de Nemours, and King Otho of Greece. Amongst others, Prince Adalbert of Prussia, with the sanction of the Court of Berlin, and through the intermediation of the British Ambassador there, asked permission from the Duchess of Kent to present his addresses to the young Princess. The answer was characteristic, and shows clearly that Her Royal Highness' policy was to discourage every one—except the fortunate scion of the House of Coburg. "I will candidly tell your Lordship," was the reply, written within a month of the accession, "that I am of opinion that the Princess should not marry till she is much older. I will also add that in the choice of the person to share her great destiny I have but one wish—that her happiness and the interest of the country be realized in it."

Meanwhile, amid the whirl of international and political intrigue, the happy plans of the Duchess and her royal brother were being quietly carried out. Unaware of it himself, Prince Albert was being trained for his future position with care similar to that bestowed upon the education of the Princess. From his earliest years his disposition seems to have been susceptible of good impressions, and from boyhood he was distinguished for perfect moral purity, an eager desire to do good to others, and sincere gratitude for any act of kindness shown to himself. His education, as well as that of Prince Ernest—who afterwards, as the elder brother, became Duke of Saxe-Coburg-Gotha, and was destined to be succeeded in long after years by his nephew, the Duke of Edinburgh—was of the broad character suited to their position, and included history, geography, mathematics, religion, Latin, philosophy, the modern European languages, and natural history, music, and drawing—for which latter studies Prince Albert showed a marked inclination.

During these years Baron Stockmar took great interest in the young Prince and his future. This remarkable man was one of those makers of history who appear but little on the surface of affairs. His life was devoted to the extension of constitutional government everywhere. His personal services, and sincerest, strongest, affections, were given to the House of Coburg in its various spheres of influence. His work, through intimate relationship with the statesmen and princes of Europe, and clearness of intellect and disinterested honesty, made him one of the chief unseen political forces of the Continent. His passionate desire was to see German unity achieved under the headship of Prussia; to aid in creating a close alliance between Germany and England; to help in harmonizing the principles of monarchy and democracy in Great Britain, Germany, and Belgium. To him King Leopold owed much in the building up of Belgic constitutionalism; to him Prince Albert owed much of his fundamental conception of free government; to him the Queen was greatly indebted for early secretarial assistance and constant advice.

He made mistakes like every other man, and his position was one which at times seemed to lack dignity, and which was always incapable of definition—besides being often the source of natural suspicion to Englishmen as a whole. But he had a sort of rugged indifference to feelings of this sort, and went on performing services which could never be adequately appreciated by the public or rewarded by those who received and benefited by them. The Queen has declared that at the beginning of her reign " Lord Melbourne had the greatest regard and affection for, and the most unbounded confidence in him." And Lord Aberdeen in after years told Her Majesty that " I have known men as clever, as discreet, as good, and with as much judgment; but I never knew any one who united all these qualities as he did. He is a most remarkable man." Lord Palmerston did not, on the other hand, like him, although he respected his ability, and it is, perhaps, not altogether surprising. Indeed, his position of unofficial adviser to Prince Albert, and, indirectly, to the Crown, while of great and undoubted value, seems difficult to harmonize with the perfect constitutional government which he himself aimed at. But perfect methods cannot always be employed in the attainment of desirable ends.

Baron Stockmar's services, as a whole, were, however, such as to effectually cancel any errors of heart or judgment in this particular direction, and it is not difficult to find excuses for a man who could write the Prince—January 25th, 1854—that " In my eyes the English Constitution is the corner and copestone of the entire political civilization of the human race, present and to come." Perhaps no clearer indication of his mental powers can be found than his analysis of Prince Albert's character as contained in a letter written to King Leopold in 1836, the year of the visit to Kensington. He describes him as a fine young fellow, with agreeable and valuable qualities, and the possibility of developing into a strong, handsome man, of kindly, simple, yet dignified demeanour. " Externally, he therefore possesses all that pleases the sex, and at all times and in all countries must please." And then he goes on to express some doubt concerning his capacity and character. They are still, he thinks, immature.

" He is said to be circumspect, discreet, and even now cautious. But this is not enough. He ought to have not merely great ability, but a *right* ambition and great force of will as well. To pursue for a lifetime a political career so arduous demands more than energy and inclination—it demands also that earnest frame of mind which is ready of its own accord to sacrifice mere pleasure to real usefulness. If he is not satisfied hereafter with the consciousness of having achieved one of the most influential positions in Europe, how often will he feel tempted to repent what he has undertaken ? If he does not from the very outset accept it as a vocation of grave responsibility, on the fulfilment of which his honour and happiness depend, there is small likelihood of his succeeding."

The Prince must at this time have been given some glimmering view of his destined future, and his visit to England left an impression of the fair Princess upon his mind which, no doubt, was sufficiently defined to give pleasure to all these busy and kind conspirators. But no one knew better than they the slips which might yet occur, and there could be no security where there was still absolute uncertainty as to the feelings of the Princess. Meanwhile, she ascended the Throne, and amongst the myriad congratulations of the moment was a significant one from the Prince to his "dearest cousin," in which he says : "You are now Queen of the mightiest land of Europe ; in your hand lies the happiness of millions. May Heaven assist you and strengthen you in that high but difficult task. . . . May I pray you to think likewise sometimes of your cousins in Bonn, and to continue to them that kindness you favoured them with till now. Be assured that our minds are always with you."

Following this discreet epistle came a prolonged tour through Italy and Switzerland, and the visit to the Rhine, interspersed with studies of Roman law, political economy, anthropology, and other serious subjects. A letter of Stockmar's, written upon the Prince's return from Italy, describes him as intelligent and amiable ; with good intentions but lacking in determined effort ; with a not very strong constitution ; an utter indifference to politics, and a disposition rather sensitive and retiring. All these deficiencies, however, were such as would naturally disappear, and did disappear, under the influence of great responsibilities and a devoted love. But in the meantime the Prince's position was a difficult one, and, for a man, decidedly unpleasant. He was the possible husband of a great sovereign, and to that end he knew his own training and education were being directed. Yet the whole affair seemed in a decidedly nebulous condition.

The young Queen was at first too full of the excitements and pleasures and duties of her position to even think of marriage, and she wrote her uncle Leopold very frankly that "the change had put all ideas of marriage out of her mind." When, in 1838, he pressed for "some decisive arrangement" Her Majesty demurred upon nominal grounds which reflect great credit upon her sound practical judgment, and which were, of course, accepted by the King. She stated that they were both too young ; that the Prince had still a very imperfect knowledge of the English language ; and should also have time to obtain a wider experience, more practical habits of observation, and more self-reliance than he could have yet attained. Of course this very practical method of dealing with the matter proves clearly enough that the royal maiden was still "fancy free," and, like the most humble of her subjects, desired to be won by personal impressions and intercourse, and not married as a mere affair of State importance or wise counsel. Indeed, the whole proposal threatened to fall through at one moment, and the Prince wrote to a friend that "the Queen declared to my uncle of Belgium that she wished the affair to be considered as broken off, and that for four years she would think of no marriage ; and," adds the Prince, in naturally aroused pride, "I must, therefore, with quiet but firm resolution declare on my part that I also withdraw entirely."

Such was the situation when, in October, 1839, King Leopold decided to take a determined step, in view of the state of politics in England, and bring the young couple together. He, therefore, wrote to the Queen a note, in which he described the Princes—who were themselves to carry the letter—as " good and honest, sensible and trustworthy" ; commending them, at the same time, to her kindness. As the Queen received her visitors, on October 10th, at the top of the grand staircase of Windsor, and amid suitable surroundings of State, the thoughts of the two chief personages in that commencement of the old, old story must have been curious as well as interesting. Both knew the reason for that meeting, and each was very doubtful of the result. But since they had met a great and hitherto unknown change had come over them. Three years makes wonderful alterations in a youth of seventeen and a maiden of the same age, whether it be in a royal palace or a humble cottage. In this case the shy, retiring, and slightly awkward Prince had grown tall and manly-looking, with a face in which gentleness of expression was united with a peculiar sweetness of smile. His clear blue eyes and expansive forehead embodied deep thought and high intelligence, while his manner was charming and his conversation cultured and interesting.

The Queen, on the other hand, had developed greatly in feature and expression and general appearance from the little Princess of a few years before. Apart from the statements of contemporaries, it is not difficult to realize how great responsibilities had brought dignity to the youthful face and form, while knowledge and experience, far greater than the mere passage of years, had stamped more firmly upon her life and appearance those qualities of sincerity, kindliness, and strength of affection which were only maturing in the merry months at Kensington. And during the days that now followed the two saw much of each other. The gay and happy Queen made a gay and happy Court, and a something in the air which whispered of the future made all devote themselves to creating entertainment and pleasure. In the morning Her Majesty would breakfast in her private apartments, and then the Princes would afterwards pay her a visit. At two o'clock they had luncheon with her and the Duchess of Kent, and then they all went riding, accompanied by Lord Melbourne and a large cavalcade of ladies and gentlemen. Every evening there was a great dinner, followed very frequently by a dance.

The result hoped for by so many soon became apparent, and the young couple, almost unconsciously, drifted into an attachment which time has sanctified and a nation honoured, one which the poet might well have anticipated when he said :

> " Love rules the Court, the camp, the grove,
> And men below and saints above ;
> For love is heaven and heaven is love."

To the mind of the youthful Queen the change of thought and intention must have come very quickly. The day after his arrival she wrote King Leopold that " Albert's beauty is most striking, and he is most amiable and unaffected—in short, very fascinating," and then, by a sort of afterthought of charming modesty, she adds that "the young men are very amiable, delightful companions, and I am very happy to have *them* here." In a few days from this the crisis came. Both had made up their minds, the clouds of doubt and ignorance of each other had blown away, and the four years by which the Queen had been inclined to put the whole suggestion aside had vanished into dreamland.

But it was a difficult position for the maiden Queen. The exigencies of Royal State made it necessary for her to ask the question which custom and modesty and precedent make incumbent upon the opposite sex in private life. General Grey, in his " Early Years of the Prince Consort," written, as it was, under the direct authority of the Queen, merely tells us that on the 15th of October "the Prince had been out hunting early with his brother, but returned at twelve, and half an hour afterward obeyed the Queen's summons to her room, where he found her alone. After a few minutes' conversation on other subjects, the Queen told him why she had sent for him." This is all, and we might well be content to draw the veil over what was said and felt, were it not for the interest which all must take in this most royal romance. We, indeed, get many glimpses into the heart of things, though they are necessarily little more than side-lights. One pretty little story tells us that during one of the dances given at Windsor about this time the Queen presented the exquisite bouquet she was carrying to her royal cousin. He might well have felt awkward at the unexpected compliment, for his uniform jacket was fastened up to the chin after the Prussian fashion, and there seemed no possible place to put the precious gift. But inspiration came to him, as it sometimes does to less exalted mortals, and he seized a penknife, slit an aperture in his dress over his heart, and placed the gift in its most appropriate place.

Other stories relate how the Queen led up to the declaration by asking him "if he would like to live in England," and by saying, " It depends on you to make it your home." But the fact must be as Her Majesty states in her own journal and elsewhere, and as she told her aunt, the Duchess of Gloucester, the day before making the " declaration " to the Privy Council. The Duchess asked her if the prospect did not make her nervous. To this the Queen said, " Yes ; but I did a much more nervous thing a little while ago." " What was that ? " " I proposed to Prince Albert." The breaking of the news was characteristic. The Queen had told her faithful friend, Lord Melbourne, of her intention the previous day, and he had—according to Her Majesty's journal—expressed great and almost paternal satisfaction : " I think it will be very well received ; for I hear there is great anxiety now that it should be, and I am very glad of it. You will be much more comfortable ; for a woman cannot stand alone for any time, in whatever position she may be." To King Leopold she wrote the very day of her betrothal :

"Windsor Castle, Oct. 15, 1839.

" MY DEAREST UNCLE.—This letter will, I am sure, give you pleasure, for you have always shown and taken so warm an interest in all that concerns me. My mind is quite made up, and I told Albert this morning of it. The warm affection he showed me gave me much pleasure. He seems perfection, and I think I have the prospect of very great happiness before me. I love him *more* than I can say, and shall do everything in my power to render this sacrifice (for such in my opinion it is) as small as I can. He seems to have great tact, a very necessary thing in his position. These last few days have passed like a dream to me, and I am so much bewildered by it all that I know hardly how to write ; but I do feel very happy. . . . " Lord Melbourne has acted in this business, as he has always done toward me, with the greatest kindness and affection. We also think it better, and Albert quite approves of it, that we should be married very soon after Parliament meets, about the beginning of February.

" Pray, dearest uncle, forward these two letters to uncle Ernest (of Saxe-Coburg-Gotha), to whom I beg you will enjoin strict secrecy, and explain these details which I have not time to do, and to faithful Stockmar. I think you might tell Louise of it, but none of her family.

" I wish to keep the dear young gentlemen here till the end of next month. Ernest's sincere pleasure gives me great delight. He does so adore dearest Albert.

" Ever, dearest uncle, your devoted niece,

V. R."

To Baron Stockmar, upon whom she had so recently and strongly impressed the fact that marriage, for a long time, was out of the question, she wrote at the same time with very naive embarrassment. " I *do* feel so guilty, I know not how to begin my letter," she declared, " but I think the news it will contain will be sufficient to ensure your forgiveness. Albert has completely won my heart, and all was settled between us this morning. . . . I feel certain he will make me very happy. I wish I could say I felt as certain of my making him happy, but I shall do my best." The next day Prince Albert wrote to Stockmar that " Victoria is so good and kind to me that I am often puzzled to believe that I should be the object of so much affection. I know the interest that you take in my happiness, and therefore pour out my heart to you. . . . More, or more seriously, I cannot write ; I am at this moment too much bewildered to do so.

Heaven opens on the ravished eye,
The heart is all entranced in bliss."

It is difficult to know which is most striking and admirable in this and other correspondence of the moment—the affection or the humility which the Queen and the Prince each display. In Her Majesty's Journal is the straightforward and simple entry, " How I will strive to make him feel as little as possible the great sacrifice he has made! I told him it *was* a great sacrifice on his part, but he would not allow it." Such language indicates the depth of true affection evoked in one who could thus forget self and sink her great position in sincere personal devotion. To the world at large the match meant the union of a great Sovereign with a young and almost penniless Prince—his income was £2400 a year. To the Queen it meant his assumption of all the innumerable worries and responsibilities of a great position : the exchange of a life of care and tranquility for one full of burdens, and the ceaseless anxiety of living within the light which beats upon the thrones of the world.

To the Prince there was both advantage and sacrifice in the marriage. He had the privilege of possessing that " love and affection " of which he wrote to his grandmother when he described the betrothal and spoke of the Queen as having declared that " I had gained her whole heart and would make her intensely happy if I would make her the sacrifice of sharing her life." He had untold possibilities of doing good and achieving honour and fame. But coupled with this prospect of domestic love and human greatness was the pain which a sensitive man feels at living in a constant blaze of publicity ; which a good man feels at being subject to persistent and serious misrepresentations ; which a man of home tastes and simple life feels at the prospect of leaving the quiet country of his fathers for a land of ceaseless activity, and struggle, and almost complete strangeness. But in the end the result was what the wise uncle of both had expected, and which he so well embodied in his reply to the Queen's letter announcing her betrothal.

" You say most amiably that you consider it a sacrifice on the part of Albert. This is true in many points, because his position will be a difficult one ; but much, I may say *all*, will depend on your affection for him. If you *love* him and are *kind* to him he will easily bear the bothers of his position, and there is a steadiness, and, at the same time, a cheerfulness in his character which will facilitate this."

During the month which followed time passed in a whirl of gayety and nominal secrecy as to the royal engagement. But one can easily imagine the degree of privacy which would surround such an event in the most important court circle of Europe. The two were constantly together, and we are told of a beautiful emerald ring which the Prince presented to his betrothed. They played and sang, and rode and danced together until the time of departure came and the young bride—to be—was left desolate in her splendid halls and amid all her brilliant company. But many and constant were the letters exchanged " That I am the object of so much love and devotion," writes the Prince one day, " often comes over me as something I can hardly realize. My prevailing feeling is, What am I that such happiness should be mine? For excess of happiness it is for me to know that I am so dear to you." And again he tells her, "How often my thoughts are with you! The hours I was privileged to pass with you in your dear little room are the radiant points of my life."

With the Queen herself, stern duties had to break in upon the pleasant intercourse of the pen and the romantic dreams of lovers. On November 23rd, Her Majesty made the formal declaration of the proposed marriage to her Council, which had been called together at Buckingham Palace. More than eighty members—leaders in the public thought of the nation—were present. Amongst them were Wellington, Clarendon, Palmerston, Melbourne, Russell, Lyndhurst, Brougham, Cowley, Abinger, and Macaulay. Yet of all that stately throng not one survives to-day—save only the central figure of the scene! Grenville says of what followed: "The folding doors were thrown open, and the Queen came in attired in a plain morning gown, but wearing a bracelet containing Prince Albert's picture. She read the declaration in a clear, sonorous, sweet-toned voice, but her hands trembled so excessively that I wonder she was able to read the paper which she held." Her Majesty refers to the occasion in her Journal in a very similar way, and tells us that, "I went in; the room was full, but I hardly knew who was there. Lord Melbourne I saw looking kindly at me with tears in his eyes, but he was not near me. I then read my short declaration. I felt my hands shake, but I did not make one mistake. I felt happy and thankful when it was over."

She adds that Lord Lansdowne then rose and asked permission in the name of the Privy Council to print "this most gracious and most welcome communication." The declaration itself simply announced her intention to marry the Prince Albert of Saxe-Coburg and Gotha, and proceeded to say that "Deeply impressed with the solemnity of the engagement which I am about to contract, I have not come to this decision without mature consideration, nor without feeling a strong assurance that, with the blessing of Almighty God, it will at once secure my domestic felicity and serve the interests of my country." This announcement was repeated when the Queen opened Parliament in person on the 16th of January, 1840. The news was variously received. By the nation as a whole the proposed marriage was welcomed, but there was a very strong undercurrent of misconception, prejudice, and bitterness, which soon found expression in Parliament.

The public mind was susceptible at the moment to all kinds of rumours, and the mistake had been made of not declaring the Prince to be a Protestant. The Queen and Lord Melbourne thought that the strong sympathies of the House of Coburg were sufficiently well known, and they supposed the people would understand that by the constitution of the realm the Queen's consort must be a Protestant. But common sense had very little to do with the situation, and a violent debate in Parliament was the result. Then the Tories were so embittered by the Queen's supposed partiality for the Whigs and by memories of the Bed-chamber Plot, that they seemed ready for any antagonistic action which might present itself. On the other hand, the government was tottering to its fall, and its partisans were so much in the habit of using Her Majesty's name and of appealing to Irish support that, as Lady Holland wittily remarked, they would soon have " nothing to rely upon but the Queen and Paddy." There was also a section of society, and a by no means small class in the country, which resented the rules of the new Court, and its habits of quietness and of antagonism to the old roystering system of the last two reigns. To further complicate matters, the Whigs themselves did not seem to care much for the personality of the young Prince, while a financial crisis and general commercial stagnation intensified the irritation of the one party and the indifference of the other. Enthusiasm was left to what these politicians would have called the common people.

Meanwhile Parliament acted as might have been expected under such cir-cumstances. In the Commons Lord John Russell proposed on behalf of the Gov-ernment an allowance to Prince Albert of £50,000 a year. This sum was the same as that voted Prince Leopold upon his marriage with Princess Charlotte. Prince George of Denmark, the husband of Queen Anne, and several Queens consort had received a similar amount. But during the debate which followed many sharp and unpleasant things were said, and it was soon evident that a combination of motives and reasons, from partisan bitterness to the real stress of hard times, would force a reduction in the amount. The Government, however, would not meet this feeling, and, after defeating the Radical motion to reduce the grant to £21,000, an Opposition resolution to place it at £30,000 was carried by 262 to 158. Sir Robert Peel supported this strongly, and the vote showed that he had with him many Whigs as well as the Radicals.

There was too much reason for this reduction in the severe national depression, chronic deficits, and falling revenue to make it necessary for either the Queen or Prince to look back of the situation into the more partisan issues of the moment. Certainly Prince Albert never showed the slightest soreness to Peel or the Tories in his subsequent treatment of them, although there is no doubt that many expected, and some hoped, to see a still further estrangement between that party and the Crown. But in the end the reverse was the case. A more important matter in the opinion of the Queen was the question of the Prince's official precedence. The proper thing to do, and what the ministry at first desired, was to give the Prince, by law, his natural position immediately following the Queen; and the Bill for the Prince's naturalization contained a clause to this effect. The King of Hanover, however, raised furious objections against the proposal, and was supported by some of his Royal brothers. The Duke of Wellington opposed it in the Lords on the ground that Her Majesty could herself settle the question by placing the Prince where she liked. As he said upon another occasion, when the Earl of Albemarle, who was very sensitive about his precedence as Master of the Horse, complained of some supposed slight: "The Queen can make Lord Albemarle sit at the top of the coach, under the coach, behind the coach, or wherever else Her Majesty pleases."

The ministry was too weak to carry the proposal against the Duke's opposition; so it was, perforce, abandoned. The immediate result was an order in council settling the Prince's place as immediately following that of the Queen. The ultimate consequence was that through the greater part of his life complications were constantly arising from the fact of the Prince having *legally* no rank higher than that of a scion of the House of Coburg. In a memorandum by the Queen, given to Sir Theodore Martin in this connection, is the statement that much difficulty resulted during the Royal visits to Prussia and France from the refusal of various royal personages to take a position lower than that of one whom international etiquette recognized as of very inferior rank. Meanwhile Prince Albert was on his way to England, and at Aix heard of the unexpected situation of affairs. He at once wrote the Queen expressing his sympathy and regret, and adding the expressive sentence: "All I have time to say is that while I possess your love they cannot make me unhappy."

The Prince arrived at Dover on February 6th, and soon found that the politicians, in this instance at least, did not represent the populace. From the moment he landed upon English soil, an English welcome awaited him. Cheering crowds were everywhere, in hamlet, village, or town—from the sea-port to Buckingham Palace—and everywhere the pleasant-spoken, good-looking Prince seemed to win popular approval. Upon the various members of the Royal family whom he visited on the 9th of the month his frank and manly bearing made a most favourable impression. The next day was the wedding morn, and, somewhat like the married life which followed, it opened with clouds and closed in glorious sunshine. The first action of the Prince was to write his much-loved grandmother of Saxe-Coburg: "In less than three hours I shall stand at the altar with my dear bride. In these solemn moments I must once more ask your blessing . . . God be my stay." Meanwhile, it is said, the Queen was having an interview with the Primate, who came to ask if he should omit the word "obey" from her part of the ceremony. The reply was characteristic of Her Majesty's whole life and views in this connection: "It is my wish to be married, not as a Queen, but as a woman."

It was really a most interesting event. For the first time in more than a century the reigning Queen of England was to be married amid every accompaniment of State ceremonial and popular demonstration. The youth and grace of Her Majesty, and the youth and good looks of the Prince, were also sufficient to add greatly to the loyal interest and enthusiasm of the dense crowds which greeted the Royal procession, as it left Buckingham Palace at about twelve o'clock, surrounded it along the entire route, and swelled into greater volume as the Queen reached St. James' Palace. Her Majesty was accompanied by the Duchess of Kent and attended by the Duchess of Sutherland. Dressed in white satin trimmed with the most exquisite and costly lace, and wearing a wreath of orange blossoms, a veil of Honiton lace, and a diamond necklace and earrings, the Royal bride is described as looking pale and agitated when she started, but as brightening up with blushes and smiles as the ringing cheers and waving handkerchiefs continued through all the crowded streets.

The Prince, who was accompanied by his father, the Duke of Saxe-Coburg-Gotha, his brother Ernest, and their suites, preceded the Queen to St. James' and in his entrance to the Chapel Royal. His Royal Highness wore a Field Marshal's uniform and the star and ribbon of the Garter, which had been a short time before conferred upon him, and carried in his hand a Bible bound in velvet. He received an enthusiastic welcome from the audience; and an onlooker describes him as looking like the Queen, save that he was of lighter complexion, and "as though neither care nor sorrow had ever ruffled or cast a cloud over his placid and reflective brow. There is an unmistakable air of refinement and rectitude about him, and every year will add intellectual and manly beauty to his very interesting face and form." In his seat, to the left of the altar, the Prince awaited the arrival of the bride. And very shortly, amid floods of sunshine streaming through the windows over all the gorgeous scene, the procession came up the aisles of the chapel. It included the Royal Household, the members of the Royal family, the twelve beautiful young bridesmaids, the Ladies of the Bed-chamber, the Maids of Honour:

> "I pass their form, and every charming grace—
> Less than an angel would their worth debase;
> But their attire, like liveries of a kind,
> Simple but rich, is fresh within my mind;
> In satin white as snow the troop was gown'd,
> The seams with sparkling emeralds set around."

The Royal bride was given away by her aged uncle, the Duke of Sussex, and the words of the simple and solemn service of the Church were used by the Archbishop of Canterbury, without change or modification. To the ordinary questions Prince Albert replied in firm and clear tones, and then came the corresponding inquiries to Her Majesty: "Victoria, wilt thou have Albert to thy wedded husband, to live together after God's ordinance in the holy estate of matrimony? Wilt thou obey him and serve him, love, honour, and keep him in sickness and in health, and, forsaking all other, keep thee only unto him so long as ye both shall live?" With a look at the groom which spoke more than words, the Queen's musical voice rang softly but clearly through all the crowded chapel as she said " I will." While the Prince, a little later, placed the ring upon his wife's finger, the artillery of the tower and the park fired a royal salute, and the bells of all the churches rang out in still more cheerful peals of gratulation.

At the conclusion of the ceremony the procession re-formed, this time with the Queen and Prince hand in hand; and so they passed out and on to the Throne-room. Here the marriage register was signed by the unfamiliar style of Alexandrina Victoria Guelph, and Francis Albert Augustus Charles Emanuel Busici. An interesting incident of the Royal departure from the chapel was the spontaneous outburst of enthusiasm when the Duke of Wellington, who had not appeared in the procession, came within view of the company. Everyone rose, as if moved by one single impulse, and cheered the now feeble footsteps of the aged hero. The Duke was amongst those who signed the marriage register, as he had also attested his Sovereign's birth.

Back through the city and its thronging multitudes the Royal couple proceeded, and two days later went to Windsor, where addresses had to be received from Parliament and many other public bodies. Thus ended the three years of Royal loneliness and solitary splendour; a period of which the Queen said, in an after time, that "a worse school for a young girl—one more detrimental to all natural feelings and affections—cannot well be imagined than the position of a Queen at eighteen, without experience and without a husband to guide and protect her." Thus began a prolonged period of unique happiness, during which the two streams of life, and thought, and sentiment, merged and harmonized in one long and beautiful Royal romance. To this beginning, and to the end which came in the death of the noble husband, may be applied the eloquent words of a Canadian poet—William Wilfrid Campbell:

" Love came at dawn when all the world was fair,
    When crimson glories, bloom and song were rife ;
Love came at dawn when hope's wings fanned the air,
    And murmured, ' I am life.'

Love came at even, when the day was done,
    When heart and brain were tired and slumber pressed ;
Love came at eve, shut out the sinking sun,
    And whispered ' I am rest.' "

CHAPTER VI.

HOME LIFE AND PUBLIC WORK.

AMID all that makes existence happy the young Queen and her royal consort commenced their career of harmonized life and work. Bounding health, and hope, and present joy were theirs, together with an almost ideal affection and mutual trust. And not the least important influence during the years which followed was the constant, ever-present labour and responsibility of their great position, and the consequent necessity of being always ready to meet the exacting demands of its vast and varied duties. To the Queen, however, the change from her previous loneliness gave an impetus which reflected upon public affairs as well as upon her own disposition and character. The light-hearted girl became gradually transformed into the dignified but still beautiful matron, with a heart and life wholly centred in her home, her husband, and her duties.

Writing the day after the wedding to Baron Stockmar she declared that " there cannot exist a purer, dearer, nobler being in the world than the Prince." And this feeling lasted with intensified strength throughout all her future life. Like a true-hearted woman, and wife of the highest type, Her Majesty has always represented Prince Albert as the adviser, promoter, and director in the changes brought about by their joint efforts ; in the improvements effected throughout public affairs and in Court life by their combined labours ; in the increase of popular loyalty caused by their personal virtues, executive ability, and constitutional conduct. But, in fact, it was the Queen's own character that made all this possible, and enabled her to wield the authority of the State between jealous and rival parties at home as she did its influence among rival nations abroad. She made the Prince one with herself, yet so fully did her own character act and react upon him that, except in one or two important cases, the naturally anti-foreign instincts of the English people found no cause for complaint in his relations with a wife who was also their Sovereign.

Difficulties they had to contend with, and but for the perfect love and confidence existing between them these early troubles might have proved great, and almost insuperable. For a time, and owing to the peculiar composition of the royal household, the Prince, as he said in a private letter, was " the husband but not the master in his own house." A carefully planned re-organization of the Court and its officers eventually remedied this difficulty, and through the Prince's executive tact made it by far the best ordered royal establishment in

HAWARDEN CASTLE,

SEAT OF THE LATE RIGHT HON. W. E. GLADSTONE.

HUGHENDEN MANOR,
SEAT OF THE LATE EARL OF BEACONSFIELD.

Europe. And, if the Queen in these years was everything that a loving, self-sacrificing wife could be, the Prince, on his side, was a model of domestic virtue and self-abnegation. His course of action in public and private life was outlined in a letter to the Duke of Wellington—April 8th, 1850—which not only shows the character and policy of the Prince, but affords some idea of the difficulties he had to contend with.

"This position," he observed, "is a most peculiar and delicate one. Whilst a female sovereign has a great many disadvantages in comparison with a king, yet if she is married, and her husband understands and does his duty, her position, on the other hand, has many compensating advantages, and in the long run will be found even to be stronger than that of a male sovereign. But this requires that the husband should entirely sink his *own individual* existence in that of his wife; that he should aim at no power by himself or for himself; should shun all ostentation; assume no separate responsibility before the public; fill up every gap which, as a woman, she would naturally leave in the exercise of her regal functions; continually and anxiously watch every part of the public business in order to be able to advise and assist her at any moment in any of the multifarious or difficult questions or duties brought before her, sometimes international, sometimes political, or social, or personal. As the natural head of her family, superintendent of her household, manager of her private affairs, sole, *confidential* adviser in politics, and only assistant in her communications with the officers of the government, he is, besides, the husband of the Queen, the tutor of the royal children, the private secretary of the sovereign, and her permanent minister."

To this incisive and able summary of his position the Prince lived up nobly and well. As it worked out, no objection could be taken to any word contained in the letter, with perhaps the exception of an admittedly technical one, which Mr. Gladstone raised long afterwards, regarding the phrase "permanent minister." Meanwhile Lord Melbourne advised Her Majesty to communicate all foreign dispatches to the Prince, if she so desired, and he commenced at once to take great interest in that branch of the Government, putting his views on paper in such a way that they could be acted upon without committing himself or the ministry. And he tells us that they often were accepted. His household was appointed soon after the marriage, and Mr. Anson, the Premier's secretary, was made private secretary to the Prince. At first the latter demurred to the selection—fearing a political appointment above all things—but, in the end, it proved a wise and serviceable choice. The Queen wanted him also to have the title of King Consort, but the matter was deferred, and eventually (1857) she created him Prince Consort, a more popular though not more suitable designation. Her Majesty had already given him the Garter, and she also proceeded to make him a Field Marshal, a Knight Grand Cross of the Bath, and a Privy Councillor. No doubt, too, she would have quite liked to create some extra and special orders with which to further decorate the handsome and beloved Prince, upon whom she declared, woman-like, that everything looked so becoming and altogether charming.

The years upon which England now entered constituted a period in which the Throne was to be either a power for good or a power for evil. Had it been filled by one who thought little of its responsibilities and much of its pleasures, it would have had a hard struggle to survive the storms of 1840-48. As it was, the affection and clear practical judgment of the Queen, aided by the steadily maturing mind and devoted labours of the Prince, combined to give an example of home life and royal love of duty which soon entered into the very hearts of the people, and gave the British Monarchy strength sufficient to withstand the shock of any severe revolutionary storm. The Chartists were at this time in the first flush of a design to overturn the Constitution by—if need be—fire and sword, and in South Wales, and a little later at Birmingham, showed the miserable strength of their powers of violence. Ireland was being inflamed by the menacing language of O'Connell, while France was trying to establish Egypt under Mehemet Ali as a sort of subsidiary maritime power in the Mediterranean. Lord Palmerston, however, who was now getting well established as a skilful Foreign Secretary, soon checkmated the French attack upon the British route to India, by arranging for a Turkish protectorate of Egypt under the terms of a treaty between Russia, Prussia, Austria, and Great Britain. But so bitterly did France resent this diplomatic reversal that for some time war seemed imminent, and the dangers of the situation, as well as its anxieties, become clear from the playful words of the Queen on October 16th, 1840, in a letter to King Leopold: "I think our child ought to have, besides its other names, those of Turko-Egypto, as we think of nothing else." Meanwhile the Prince was making his first essay in public speaking—the subject being the abolition of the slave trade. Like all his subsequent efforts it was carefully committed to memory, and in this case, the Queen tells us in her Journal, was repeated to her beforehand. He had also, on July 13th, been named Regent in the possible event of the Queen's death, leaving issue. Both Houses concurred unanimously in the arrangement—with the exception of the aged Duke of Sussex, who considered himself overlooked; and this caused both the Queen and the Prince very great pleasure.

About the same time Her Majesty, while out driving, was fired at twice by a youth named Oxford. He was adjudged insane and committed to the Asylum for life. The effect of this mistaken clemency was seen in the attempts made by Francis and Bean in 1842. None of them seem, however, to have been really dangerous outrages. Desire for notoriety in at least one case was acknowledged, and in the other two the cowardly object of frightening the Queen, rather than of killing her, was probably the cause. In August Her Majesty prorogued Parliament with all possible state, and by her side in a splendid chair, placed a little lower than the Throne, sat her handsome husband. On November 21st came the first birth in the household—the arrival of the Princess Royal. During his wife's illness the Prince was indefatigable in his devotion and kindness, and, as Her Majesty tells us in her Journal, was content to sit with her in a darkened room, to read to her, or to write for her. " No one but himself ever lifted me from my bed to my sofa, and he always helped to wheel me in my bed or sofa into the next room." And as years went on and he became overwhelmed with work, it was always the same in any illness which came to her. " In short," the Queen adds, " his care of me was like that of a mother, nor could there be a kinder, wiser, or more judicious nurse."

And here let it be said that for all the sweetness of his nature there was no lack of manliness in the Prince. He was at this period passionately fond of riding, although time was all too scarce for its constant enjoyment, and when a little later they commenced their visits to the homes of the nobility, Prince Albert distinguished himself, even amongst English cross-country riders, by his prowess in fox-hunting. The little Princess was christened at Buckingham Palace on February 10th, 1841, a few days after the opening of Parliament, which the Queen had attended in person. The names chosen were those of Victoria Adelaide Mary Louisa, and the little one's sponsors were the Duke of Wellington, the King of the Belgians, the Queen Dowager Adelaide, the Duchess of Kent—who now lived at Ingestre House, but was still constantly to be seen with her daughter—the Duchess of Gloucester, and the Duke of Sussex.

Meantime, the Melbourne Ministry was visibly nearing its end, and the Premier made every effort, backed by Prince Albert and the alert Stockmar, to prepare the Queen for the inevitable change. And now that she had the Prince to confide in, and talk to, the matter was made comparatively easy, and the loss of Melbourne—for some years the only person in her kingdom to whom she could talk confidentially—was minimized. It was, indeed, in acting as a confidant, even more than as an adviser, that the Prince became so valuable to the Queen in critical affairs of State. No Minister could fill this necessity. As Her Majesty said at this juncture, in a letter to King Leopold : "Albert is, indeed, a great comfort to me. He takes the greatest possible interest in what goes on, feeling with me and for me, and yet abstaining, as he ought, from biassing me either way, though we talk much on the subject, and his judgment is, as you say, good and calm."

But before the crisis came the Queen and Prince were able to make a tour through part of the country, and to confer one last personal honour upon Lord Melbourne. They visited Lord and Lady Cowper at Panshanger, the Duke of Bedford at Woburn Abbey, and the Duke of Devonshire at Chiswick, passing thence to the home of the Premier at Brocket Hall. Everywhere the Royal couple were received with the warmest demonstrations of loyalty and pleasure. So enthusiastic were the popular greetings at the various towns and villages as to make it clear, whatever might be said to the contrary by Chartists and agitators, that the hearts of the masses were hardly touched by the canker of disloyalty which had lately been somewhat industriously cultivated. At Brocket Hall decorations, arches, and every form of welcome was found awaiting them. With the Queen were the Duchess of Sutherland, Lady Palmerston, and Lady Lyttelton, while the Prince, who was riding, had Lords de Grey, Palmerston, Cowper, and Charles Russell in attendance. Here, amid the sylvan beauties of his park, under the great oaks and beeches near the house, and within its ancient and interesting walls, Lord Melbourne received his Sovereign and celebrated the sunset of his political life.

After a brief stay at Brocket the Royal party visited Hatfield House, the superb seat of the Cecils, and thence returned to Windsor. Writing on August 3rd, 1841, to King Leopold, the Queen says of this little trip that "nothing could be more enthusiastic or affectionate than our reception *everywhere*, and I am happy to hear that our presence has left a favourable impression. The loyalty in this country is certainly very striking." At the same time, in a letter to his father, the Prince notes that "there is beyond all question a great depth of devotion towards the Throne, the Constitution, and the Church in the English rural population, which it is most touching to witness." Meanwhile, the general elections had decided the fate of the Melbourne Ministry, and on August 19th Parliament was opened by the Queen. Shortly afterwards Lord Melbourne accepted his defeat with characteristic stoicism, and repaired to Windsor to present his resignation. It was a trying moment for the young Sovereign, but was brightened by Melbourne's tactful praises of the Prince Consort, whom he described as understanding everything, as having "a clever, able head," and as promising to be a very great support to Her Majesty. For himself he had little to say, excepting that it was the breaking of a tie of close friendship which he should greatly feel, and by which he had been greatly honoured. In reality the separation from official life which this parliamentary majority of eighty against him had involved meant more than the veteran statesman would acknowledge, even to himself.

Gradually he drifted out of politics and into retirement. More active natures and House of Commons leaders crowded him naturally to the wall, and the genial, cultured, able, but indolent Melbourne reached, in a year or two, that dreaded period in the life of a man of affairs when the echo of his name no longer resounds through Parliament and the press, or is heard in potent whispers at Court or Council.

> "Then all was blank, and bleak, and grey,
>   It was not night, it was not day,
>   But vacancy absorbing space,
>   And fixedness without a place,
>   A sea of stagnant idleness
>   Blind, boundless, mute and motionless."

For a time he kept up appearances, but the iron had entered his soul, and he finally retired to his lonely home and his books, passing quietly away in the autumn of 1848. But though men may come and men may go, the Queen's Government must be carried on, and Sir Robert Peel had meanwhile formed a strong Ministry, and one which lasted unchanged till the beginning of 1846. It was constituted as follows:

First Lord of the Treasury	Sir Robert Peel.
Lord Chancellor	Lord Lyndhurst.
Chancellor of the Exchequer	Mr. Henry Goulburn.
Secretary for Home Affairs	Sir James Graham.
Secretary for Foreign Affairs	Earl of Aberdeen.
Secretary for War and the Colonies	Lord Stanley.
President of the Board of Trade	Earl of Ripon.
Secretary at War	General Sir H. Hardinge.
Vice-President of the Board of Trade	Mr. Gladstone.
Lord Privy Seal	Duke of Buckingham.
President of the Council	Lord Wharncliffe.
Lord Lieutenant of Ireland	Earl de Grey.
Chief Secretary for Ireland	Lord Elliot.
President of the Board of Control	Lord Fitzgerald.

The Duke of Wellington was, of course, leader in the Lords, with a seat in the Cabinet without portfolio. Sir J. Graham and Lords Ripon aud Stanley were converts from Whiggism.

The Ministry kissed hands upon their appointment on the 3rd of September, and from that time there seems to have developed the feeling in the mind of Her Majesty that all the leaders of the State were, or should be, her personal friends, or, at the least, be placed upon terms of personal confidence during their terms of office. At first, Greville tells us, she found Sir Robert Peel somewhat shy, and he adds that this made her shy, and so increased the temporary embarrassment of their intercourse. If this was so it soon wore away, and Peel seems to have taken an immediate liking to Prince Albert, which greatly facilitated matters. To a friend, indeed—Mr. Pemberton, afterwards Lord Kingsdown—he described His Royal Highness about this time as " one of the most extraordinary young men I have ever met with." And one of his earliest executive acts was to mark the public appreciation of Prince Albert's interest in music and painting by making him chairman of a Fine Arts Commission, upon which the leading men of the day had been placed.

On November 9th, following all these political changes, the hopes of the Queen and Prince were crowned by the birth of an heir to the Throne. There was great and genuine happiness over the event, and two weeks later the Queen records in her Journal that " Albert brought in dearest little Pussy (Princess Victoria) in such a smart white merino dress, which Mamma had given, and a pretty cap, and placed her in my bed, seating himself next to her, and she was very dear and good, and as my precious, invaluable Albert sat there, and our little love between us, I felt quite moved with happiness and gratitude to God." Writing to King Leopold, on the 4th of December, Her Majesty said, like many another mother : " I wonder very much whom our little boy will be like. You will understand how fervent are my prayers, and I am sure everybody's must be, to see him resemble his father in *every, every* respect, both in mind and body."

The little Prince was shortly afterwards created by Royal patent Prince of Wales and Earl of Chester. In the words of the curious old-time phraseology, the Queen declared her intent " to ennoble and invest him with the said principality and earldom, by girding him with a sword, by putting a coronet on his head, and a gold ring on his finger, and also by delivering a gold rod into his hand, that he may preside there, and may direct and defend those parts." He also became Duke of Saxony, Duke of Cornwall and Rothesay, Earl of Carrick, Baron of Renfrew, Lord of the Isles, and Great Steward of Scotland. And, having been thus christened by the State, he was baptized into the Church on January 25th, 1842, in St. George's Chapel, Windsor Castle, by the simple names of Albert Edward. The one was, of course, after his father, the other after his maternal grandfather, the Duke of Kent.

Amongst the sponsors was the King of Prussia, who, as the leading Protestant monarch of the Continent, had been specially selected and invited to Windsor. After the christening His Majesty was made a Knight of the Garter, and then entertained at a grand banquet, where the display of gold plate is said to have been amazing—one gold vessel capable of containing thirty dozens of wine being filled with mulled claret. The total expenses in connection with this splendid ceremony, and the State reception to the Prussian King, are said to have exceeded £200,000. The Queen seems to have liked Frederick William, and says in her Journal that he was very witty and amusing, while Baroness Bunsen tells us that she saw Her Majesty conversing eagerly with him, in " perfect grace and dignity," and as " laughing heartily (no *company* laugh) at things he said to entertain her." And, despite some passing troubles, this seems to have been a particularly happy and joyous time with the Queen. Writing to Leopold of Belgium she observes significantly that :

" We must all have trials and vexations ; but if one's home is happy, then the rest is comparatively nothing. . . . I had this autumn one of the severest trials I could have, in parting with my Government, and particularly from our kind and valued friend, and I feel even now this last very much ; but my happiness at home, the love of my husband, his kindness, his advice, his support, and his company, make up for all and make me forget it."

Parliament was opened on February 3rd by Her Majesty in person, and with the usual accompaniments of state and splendour. Baroness Bunsen, whose husband was for many years Prussian Minister in London, and who saw much of everything during that time, has recorded her impressions of the Queen's entry, "looking worthy and fit to be the converging point of so many rays of grandeur." And, continues this observer, "the composure with which she filled the Throne while awaiting the Commons was a test of character—no fidget and no apathy. Then her voice and enunciation could not be more perfect. In short, it could not be said that *she did well*, but she *was* the Queen; she was, and felt herself to be, the acknowledged chief among grand national realities." It was one of the many serious moments of this critical period. Personal loyalty throughout the kingdom was growing; but so was the terrific pressure of hard times and the growl of Chartist disaffection. The people might be loyal to the Throne in a sentimental sense, and they really were so; but pressure of low wages, high-priced food, and scarcity of work; paralysis in trade, in manufactures, and in national revenue; together with the great strikes in the coal districts, made the very air black with gloom. And, at the same time, military forces were required in Ireland, in China, in Afghanistan, and at the Cape.

The anxieties of the Queen and Prince may therefore be understood; and in every possible way they helped Sir Robert Peel in his important financial policy of establishing an income-tax and of steadily lowering the duties upon various articles of manufacture, commerce, and food. There is no doubt that they were both inclined to the free-trade policy which Peel, aided by Gladstone, now began to evolve. Her Majesty intimated her intention of not claiming any exemption from the income-tax, and this announcement had considerable effect in reconciling public opinion to what is always unpopular—a new imposition of taxes. And the tide of depression and discontent began to turn after a few anxious months, partly because of the splendid harvests of 1842; partly from the impetus given to manufactures by new and steadily improving machinery. Meantime, the Court had done everything possible to give a stimulus to trade in London. Dinners, balls, concerts, and festivities of all kinds followed each other in rapid succession; and many were the rejoicing tradesmen as a consequence.

The historic centre of these events was that known as "the Queen's Plantagenet Ball." It was, perhaps, the most brilliant fancy dress ball ever given in London, and in the spacious halls of Buckingham Palace a past age was revived with more than picturesque splendour. Her Majesty appeared as Queen Philippa, and Prince Albert as her kingly husband, Edward III. Enormous sums were spent upon dresses, diamonds, and jewels of every conceivable value and kind. The Queen's dress was made of materials manufactured at Spitalfields, and in her crown she wore but one diamond—valued at £10,000. All the leading characters of that dimly distant Court and age were represented, and by the leading men and women of the passing era. It was a few weeks after this event that the miscreant Francis shot at the Queen, and, whether really intending murder or not, failed to do harm through his pistol flashing in the pan. The leniency shown him and to Oxford some time before probably caused the hunchback Bean, on July 3rd following, to make a similar attempt. In this case also the pistol did not go off.

Though there is a ludicrous side to these various and pitiable occurrences, there is the serious consideration of the effects which such attempts might have had upon any character less strong than that of Her Majesty. She was still a very young woman—only twenty-three—in the full flush of domestic happiness, and the consciousness of maternal as well as national responsibilities. It is therefore a marvellous evidence of her fortitude and courage that, although more than once in a poor state of health when these outrages occurred, she was able to face them calmly, and continue to cheerfully perform her public duties with the full consciousness that at any moment some crank or miserable lunatic might again attempt her life. And, so long as the punishment for high treason was the only one which could be meted out to wretches who were not declared insane, there seemed a natural objection to convicting them, as there was on the part of the Queen to having them summarily dealt with. In July, however, the Premier introduced, and Parliament accepted, a measure providing for transportation, imprisonment, or whipping, for such attempts at crime. This proved salutary, although it did not yet entirely check the trouble. To the Queen there was also something more important in these affairs than any purely personal consideration, and Lord Fitzgerald refers to it in a private letter written at this time: " It was," he observes, " in every respect a childish affair, but it has naturally excited uneasiness and alarm in the palace. I do not mean in the breast of the Queen ; hers is a spirit unconscious of fear for herself, but she is haunted with a notion of danger for her husband and children."

Fortunately, however, hers was not a character which permitted much nervousness, and life also was too brimful of occupation to allow of brooding over possibilities, had she even desired to do so. For the autumn a visit to Scotland had been arranged, but after the prorogation of Parliament early in August by the Queen, Chartist and other riots—inspired by the combination of dear bread and cheap machinery—became so serious as to make the prospect of getting away seem doubtful. " The evil spirit," wrote Sir Robert Peel to Her Majesty, " has spread into the West Riding of Yorkshire ; Huddersfield has been attacked by the mob, and other towns are threatened." But vigorous measures, and the signs of harvest abundance, checked the threatened uprising, and on August 29th the Queen and Prince Albert, accompanied by the Duchess of Norfolk and the Earl of Morton, embarked at Woolwich on the Royal George yacht. Off Tilbury Fort, so associated with the name of Elizabeth, the Queen was received with a royal salute. At Gravesend and elsewhere she was welcomed with enthusiasm and plenty of powder, while every tower and beacon along the coast blazed forth its loyalty in honour of the passing Sovereign and her squadron.

On September 1st Her Majesty landed at Granton pier and proceeded direct to Dalkeith Palace, the magnificent home of the Dukes of Buccleuch. Edinburgh that night was brilliantly illuminated, and from even the remotest districts of the north people journeyed to swell the vast concourse which soon assembled to see the Queen. The State procession through the streets to Edinburgh Castle was an immense success from every point of view, and Her Majesty was accompanied during that event and much succeeding ceremonial by Sir R. Peel, the Earl of Aberdeen, the Earl of Liverpool, the Duke and Duchess of Buccleuch, the Duchess of Norfolk, and the Duke and Duchess of Argyll. And close beside her, and always with her, was the Prince. On leaving Edinburgh the Royal party paid a brief visit to the Earl of Rosebery—predecessor of the future Premier—at Dalmeny Park, and from thence returned to Dalkeith, where, on September 5th, a reception was held and attended by an extraordinarily large number of the nobility and gentry of Scotland.

Addresses followed from the different universities and the authorities of Edinburgh. A visit was then paid to Perth; to Scone Palace, the ancient seat of the Earl of Mansfield; and to Taymouth Castle, where the Queen was magnificently entertained by the Marquess of Breadalbane. Subsequently, Lord Willoughby d'Eresby was visited at Drummond Castle, as were the towns of Sterling and Falkirk. On their return to Dalkeith, Prince Albert was given the freedom of the city of Edinburgh and the honorary degree of LL.D. by the University. Her Majesty left for home on the 15th, after causing the Earl of Aberdeen to write the following letter:

"The Queen cannot leave Scotland without a feeling of regret that her visit on the present occasion could not be further prolonged. Her Majesty fully expected to witness the loyalty and attachment of her Scottish subjects; but the devotion and enthusiasm evinced in every quarter, and by all ranks, have produced an impression on the mind of Her Majesty which can never be effaced."

The bracing northern air had done both the Queen and Prince good, and not very long after their return, while resting at Walmer Castle, came the welcome news of the conclusion of the disastrous Afghan war, the settlement of difficulties with the United States, and of peace with China. The combined effect of the successful Scotch visit, the suppression of Chartist troubles, and the lifting of the foreign cloud, revived the health and spirits of Her Majesty, and made even that incorrigible Radical and agitator—George Jacob Holyoke— declare in his diary, with reference to some public ceremonial of the moment, that he was "agreeably surprised at her. The breezes of Blair Athol have left her quite blooming, and her pretty Saxon-looking face, beaming with both maternal affection and thought, quite prepossessed me in her favour." Parliament met on February 2nd, 1843, to receive some good news and to fight over the corn laws, but for the first time the Queen was unable to open the Session. Meanwhile, Peel had proved himself as great an adept at pleasing his Sovereign as he had already proved in passing important legislation in the face of his own previous opposition. No doubt his manners had greatly improved in the new atmosphere of the Court, and since the days of the Iron Duke's epigram; but it must have required more than mere surface politeness or attention to so greatly influence a keen participator in the politics of the world, such as the young but now experienced Queen, and induce her to write King Leopold at this time that her Premier seemed to be "undoubtedly a great statesman, a man who thinks but little of party, and never of himself." Upon the whole, this verdict, given by a Sovereign who had not at first liked him, will be accepted by history as substantially accurate.

Another addition came to the Royal family on April 25th, and the little Princess was christened by the good old English names of Alice, Maud, Mary. About this time also the Queen and the Prince determined to encourage fresco painting by having some of it done in connection with a summer pavilion in the grounds of Buckingham Palace. His Royal Highness had already, with success, urged the adoption of patriotic designs for similar application to the Houses of Parliament; and for the work on the pavilion, Landseer, Maclise, Unwins, Eastlake, Ross, and other eminent artists received commissions. Their progress was closely watched by Her Majesty and the Prince. Mr. Unwins, in a private letter dated 15th August, 1843, has left us the following charming sketch of the Royal couple :

"The opportunity lately afforded me of becoming acquainted with the habits, tastes, and, in some degree, with the intellectual acquirements of the Queen and Prince has greatly increased my respect for them.

History, literature, science, and art seem to have lent their stores to form the mind of the Prince. He is really an accomplished man, and, withal, possesses so much good sense and consideration, that, taken apart from his playfulness and good humour, he might pass for an aged and experienced person, instead of a youth of two or three and twenty.

The Queen, too, is full of intelligence, her observations very acute, and her judgment apparently matured beyond her age.

It has happened to me in life to see something of many Royal personages, and I must say, with the single exception of the Duke of Kent, I have never met with any, either in England or on the Continent of Europe, who have impressed me so favourably as our reigning Sovereign and her young and interesting husband.

Coming to us twice a day, unannounced and without attendants, entirely stript of all state and ceremony, courting conversation and desiring reason rather than obedience, they have gained our admiration and love. In many things they are an example to the age. They have breakfasted, heard morning prayers with the household in the private chapel, and are out some distance from the Palace talking to us in the summer-house before half-past nine o'clock—sometimes earlier. After the public duties of the day, and before their dinner, they come out again, evidently delighted to get away from the bustle of the world to enjoy each other's society in the solitude of the garden."

Such a picture could hardly be improved upon, and gives a very clear idea of the young Queen and her husband. Meanwhile, during the earlier part of 1843, the veteran and really noble Duke of Sussex had passed away, and the Princess Augusta of Cambridge had been married to the Grand Duke of Mecklenburg-Strelitz at the new Chapel Royal of Buckingham Palace, and in the presence of the Queen, Prince Albert, the Duchess of Kent, and the King and Queen of the Belgians. Later on in the year Her Majesty and the Prince went on a yachting expedition round the Isle of Wight, and subsequently visited Dartmouth, Plymouth, and Falmouth. At this latter place the crowd in the harbour was so tremendous, and the desire to see the Queen so great, that there was serious danger to many people amidst the general crush of boats and barges. It was here that the Mayor, who was a Quaker, received permission from the Queen to present an address with his hat on.

Leaving Falmouth, the Royal party sailed for Cherbourg, where they were to pay a long-desired visit to the French King and Queen. Louis Philippe, when Duc d'Orleans, in days gone by, had been an intimate friend of the late Duke of Kent, as well as of the youthful Princess Charlotte and her husband, Prince Leopold. The latter, in 1832, had married, for a second time, the Princess Louise of Orleans, so that the relationship of the King and Her Majesty of England was fairly close. Apart from this, however, the Queen had long entertained a sincere respect—perhaps not altogether deserved—for one whom she now described in her Journal as " the good, kind King." Louis Philippe and Queen Amalie, accompanied by the Prince de Joinville, the Duc d'Aumale, the Duc de Montpensier, Lord Cowley the British Ambassador, and various Ministers of State, met the Royal party at Cherbourg, and there, for the first time since the Field of the Cloth of Gold, an English and a French monarch met upon French soil, while the Royal Standards of the two countries floated amicably side by side.

The landing was made amid cheering people and troops crying, " Vive la Reine " and " Vive le Roi," until, as the Journal tells, Her Majesty was well-nigh overcome. For five days the visit lasted, and many pleasant but quiet hours were spent by the Queen and Prince with their kindly hosts. To the former it was a period of undoubted enjoyment. She liked what her Journal terms, "this admirable and truly amiable family," and appreciated the friendly home-like feeling which it was possible to have with them. An interesting minor incident was the visit to a little Catholic chapel full of painted windows and pictured saints—the first Her Majesty had ever seen. To their Royal hosts the intercourse must have given a still keener pleasure. They felt, and had some reason to feel, that for the thirteen years of their reign the exclusive Courts of Europe had more or less boycotted them, or failed to recognize their regal position in other than the most formal manner. Therefore, as Prince Albert noted in a private letter at this time, "they rate very highly the visit of the most powerful Sovereign in Europe. The King said this to me over and over again."

But the visit was useful as well as mutually agreeable. It not only strength-ened Royal friendships, but allayed some of the friction prevalent between the two countries, and, had Louis Philippe been wise in adhering to the pledge made at this time in a conversation with the Queen, the Prince, and Lord Aberdeen, it might have averted the disasters which afterwards came through his attempt to place a son upon the throne of Spain. From Cherbourg the English Royal couple went on a brief tour of Belgium, where they were received with the greatest enthusiasm by the people, and with more than pleasure by their uncle, King Leopold. Bruges, Ghent, Brussels, and Antwerp were visited, and it is not difficult to imagine how delightful to the Queen was this view of a country so rich in art and historical associations, made, as it was, under the guidance of one who had been a father to her, and with the companionship of her princely consort. On the 21st of September the whole party were back at Windsor, and while the newspapers were variously speculating upon the international reasons for the trip, and its possible consequences, Lady Canning was recording in a letter to a friend that " Our Belgian travels were very enjoyable and amusing, but I wondered how we had strength to stand such constant fatigue. The Queen bore it better than anyone. We had a very rough crossing to Ostend, and all were sick but the Queen and me."

THE QUEEN AT CHURCH IN 1846.

THE QUEEN AND PRINCE ALBERT IN IRELAND IN 1849.

CHAPTER VII.

ROYAL FUNCTIONS AND DUTIES.

UPON their return from France the Queen and Prince Albert visited Cambridge, where they were most warmly welcomed—the latter being given the degree of LL.D. amid the wildest acclamations. "I seldom remember more enthusiasm," wrote the Queen a few days afterwards. From the loyal shouts of the undergraduates they proceeded to the quiet hospitality of Drayton Manor, on a brief visit to Sir Robert Peel. Thence the Royal party went to join a brilliant assemblage of leading Whigs at Chatsworth, where they were received by the Duke of Devonshire. At Belvoir, the ducal seat of the Rutlands, were gathered a little later all the fashionable sporting men of Melton and Leicester. Incidentally, Prince Albert paid a much-appreciated visit to the manufactories of Birmingham. Early in 1844 the Duke of Saxe-Coburg-Gotha died after a few hours' illness. His son's sorrow was very great, and the sympathy of the Queen induced her to consent to his absence for a short time, in order to attend the funeral. Every day they wrote each other, and Lady Lyttleton tells us that the Queen literally counted the hours until her husband's return. In these last cynical and *blasé* years of the century, when emotion is deemed reprehensible, and the exhibition of pleasure or sorrow a social crime, it is interesting to read such letters as passed between these royal lovers. Writing from his vessel in Dover harbour on the day of departure the Prince says:

"I have been here about an hour, and regret the lost time which I might have spent with you. Poor child! You will while I write be getting ready for luncheon, and you will find a place vacant where I sat yesterday. In your heart, however, I hope my place will not be vacant. I, at least, have you on board with me in spirit.

"I reiterate my entreaty, 'Bear up!' and do not give way to low spirits, but try to occupy yourself as much as possible. You are even now half a day nearer to seeing me again; by the time you get this letter you will be a whole one—thirteen more and I am within your arms."

The Prince had not been very long back from this melancholy duty when, on May the 30th, came the intelligence that the Emperor of Russia was on his way to visit the British Sovereign, and might be expected at any moment. The King of Saxony was also expected for the 1st of June. For the next few weeks, therefore, all was excitement and gayety and gorgeous ceremonial. The Czar of all the Russias was an exceedingly handsome, cold, hard, and ambitious man. He was in all respects an Eastern autocrat, accustomed to absolute power, but clothing his strong passions in a garb of cynical civility. At times he could be courteous and charming in manner to a degree seldom equalled—and this was one of the occasions. He never did anything without an object, and his admitted reason for this visit was to detach England from her steadily increasing friendship with France, and direct her into a sort of alliance with himself for the immediate preservation, and eventual partition, of Turkey. To Sir Robert Peel he declared that "By personal intercourse I trust to annihilate prejudices. For I esteem England highly ; but as to what the French say of me I care not. I spit upon it."

He was received by the Queen at Buckingham Palace, entertained at Windsor—which he thought the noblest of all royal residences—given a review of troops in the Park, and taken to the Opera by the Queen and Prince Albert. On the 9th of June he departed, leaving behind him very varied impressions, and carrying away very distinct ones. The people liked him as a whole—his stately presence and courteous manner being quite captivating to the masses. But the Queen, in spite of his judicious and, no doubt, sincere praise of Prince Albert, and despite a personal liking for him, which was natural under the circumstances, showed all her usual judgment in a letter to King Leopold, from which the following is an extract :

"A great event, and a great compliment, his visit certainly is, and the people here are extremely flattered at it. He is certainly a very striking man, still very handsome ; his profile is beautiful, and his manners most dignified and graceful ; extremely civil, quite *alarmingly* so, as he is so full of attentions and *politenesses*. But the expression of the eyes is severe, and unlike anything I ever saw before. He gives Albert and myself the impression of a man who is not happy, and on whom the burden of his immense power and position weighs heavily and painfully. He seldom smiles, and when he does the expression is not a happy one."

Could Her Majesty, in penning this very accurate picture, have looked into the future she would have seen how truly that alarming civility was the cover for deep designs, and that remarkable expression in the eyes a sad premonition of coming and hereditary madness. Nicholas I., on his part, went away delighted with his reception, and misconstruing it into a tacit acceptance and endorsation of his policy in the East. Prince Albert he greatly admired, and told Lord Aberdeen he should like to have him for his own son. And the Court, as a whole, he thought, was conducted on the noblest scale of any in Europe. The unassuming and greatly pleased King of Saxony remained a week or so longer, and left just as the Queen and her Government found themselves face to face with a crisis in foreign affairs. It arose through the French annexation of Tahiti, and assumed serious form in an outrage perpetrated there upon the British Consul. Eventually, after violent passions had been aroused on both sides, the matter was settled without war, and largely through the mediation of the Queen and Leopold of Belgium, with their mutual and personal friend, the King of the French

The latter expressed himself very clearly to Her Majesty during his subsequent visit to England, when he wished the whole affair "was at the bottom of the sea."

On August 31st another Royal visitor arrived upon English shores. It was the Prince of Prussia—the future unifier and Emperor of Germany. Few, indeed, could have looked ahead and anticipated the results of his wise government in Prussia, but the Queen once more showed her discernment by the comments made in her Journal. "I like him very much," she writes on the day of his arrival at Windsor. " He is extremely amiable, agreeable, and sensible." A later entry describes him as " very amusing, sensible, and frank. On all public questions he spoke most freely, mildly, and judiciously, and, I think, would make a steadier and safer king than the present." Before leaving England he attended the christening of Her Majesty's second son, Alfred Ernest Albert, who had been born on the 6th of the month.

After a brief period of rest in the Highlands, where the scenery and air, the fishing and shooting, the free and untrammelled life, proved as intensely pleasant as they were clearly healthful, the Queen and Prince Albert returned to the Castle in order to receive the King of the French on October 8th. Accompanied from Portsmouth by the Prince and the Duke of Wellington, Louis Philippe was welcomed by Her Majesty at Windsor. Lady Lyttleton's description of this scene is both characteristic and picturesque. "I found the Court in the corridor," she tells us, "and we waited an hour, and then the Queen of England came out of her room to go and receive the King of France; the first time in history. From the Armoury, amidst all the old trophies, and knights' armour, and Nelson's bust, and Marlborough's flag, and Wellington's, we saw the first of the escort enter the quadrangle, and down flew the Queen, and we after her, to the outside of the door on the pavement of the quadrangle, just in time to see the escort clattering up, and the carriage close behind. The old man was much moved, I think, and his hand rather shook as he alighted, his hat quite off, and gray hair seen. His countenance is striking, much better than the portraits, and his embrace of the Queen was very parental and nice. Montpensier is a handsome youth, and the courtiers and ministers very well-looking, grave, gentlemenlike people. It was a striking piece of *real* history—made one feel and think much."

The King's reception was very cordial, and his visit lasted for a week. He did not go to London, as the Queen had not yet visited Paris; but the Corporation of the capital paid him the unique compliment of coming in full civic state to Windsor, for the purpose of presenting him with an address of congratulation. In his reply he declared that France had nothing to ask of England and England had nothing to ask of France but cordial union. His Majesty took great interest in the historic associations of Windsor, and was especially pleased when the Queen invested him with the Order of the Garter. This royal order—perhaps the most valued and loftiest in the world—had been instituted by Edward III. after the victory of Crecy, and its earliest Knights were the Black Prince and his companions. But time had brought its revenge, and now a French King received the honour from the hands of the Sovereign of Great Britain as a token of personal amity and international peace.

Following this event came the opening of the new Royal Exchange by the Queen in State. It was a public holiday, and the proceedings, as Her Majesty said in a letter to King Leopold, were "splendid and royal in the extreme." She goes on to say that it was "a fine and gratifying sight to see the myriads of people assembled, more than at the Coronation even, and all in such good humour and so loyal. I seldom remember being so pleased with any public show, and my beloved Albert was enthusiastically received by the people." Baroness Bunsen, in a letter written at the time, declared that she had never seen such a mass of human beings, and that they crowded to the very roofs of the houses. The Queen was greeted by the crash of the church bells, by the singing of a great assemblage of children in the Strand, by the music of the city bands, by civic addresses and continual popular plaudits. At the Exchange she accepted a luncheon of which 1,200 persons partook.

A couple of weeks later, Her Majesty passed through Northampton, the home and centre of Radicalism, on her way to visit the Marquess of Exeter at Burleigh. An unexpectedly strong demonstration of loyalty was given here. And along the roads which had once been so bad that Queen Elizabeth in a Royal progress to this mansion—when held by another and a greater Cecil—had been obliged to ride a pillion behind the Lord Steward, Queen Victoria now drove in her splendid carriage, between long lines of cheering people. Early in the new year a similar visit was paid to the Duke of Buckingham at Stowe. The splendour of the reception upon this occasion has become historic, its brilliance and beauty the theme of many pens, its cost the object of much speculation and comment. Ranking with Chatsworth and Hatfield, and a few other magnificent places, Stowe gave every facility for display, and the Duke certainly excelled in his expenditure and the lavishness of his welcome. A two days' visit to the Duke of Wellington at Strathfieldsaye followed and was as characteristic of the Iron Duke as the reception at Stowe had been of its owner. He wanted no publicity and would permit none. One newspaper representative, in asking for the privileges usually given the press on such occasions, received this gentle intimation : "Field Marshal the Duke of Wellington presents his compliments to Mr.——, and begs to say that he does not see what his house at Strathfieldsaye has to do with the public press."

Parliament was again opened by Her Majesty on the 4th of February, 1845. The Royal speech referred to the recent visits of the Emperor of Russia and the

King of the French, to the proposed extension of the income tax, and to academical education in Ireland. In connection with the first mentioned matter, Sir Robert Peel took occasion to pay a deserved tribute to the Queen's financial management.

"Here," said the Premier, "I may be permitted to say that any Executive Government that would have a due regard to the exercise of a wise and judicious economy could not do better than follow the example which has been set them by the control exercised over her own expenditure by the Sovereign. A settlement was made of the Civil List on her accession to the Throne. On the occasion of her marriage no addition was made to the Civil List. It has pleased God to bless that marriage by the birth of four children, which has made a considerable additional demand upon the Civil List. In the course of last year three Sovereigns visited this country, two of them the most powerful Sovereigns in the habitable globe—the Emperor of Russia and the King of the French. Those visits, of necessity, created a considerable increase of expenditure; but through that wise system of economy, which is the only source of true magnificence, Her Majesty was enabled to meet every charge, and to give a reception to those Sovereigns which struck every one by its magnificence, without adding one tittle to the burdens of the country.

"I think that to state this is only due to the personal credit of Her Majesty, who insists upon it that there shall be every magnificence required by her station, but without incurring a single debt."

During these years Peel's general policy had been working wonders. From the Income Tax, and despite the enormous reductions of the tariff in 1842, had come a surplus in 1845 of nearly six millions sterling, and a growing degree of prosperity in the country and of confidence amongst all classes of the community. Part of his surplus he now proposed to devote to the increase of the navy, and the rest to a still further reduction in fiscal duties. But in spite of his successful policy the Maynooth question had brought upon him much sectarian abuse—and the incidental retirement of Mr. Gladstone—while the more pronounced Protectionists now showered invective and reproach upon him for his desertion of old-time principles.

So pronounced did this grow that the Queen felt, and tried to express, great sympathy with the much-burdened Premier. "Peel works so hard," wrote Her Majesty on March 25th, "and has so much to do that sometimes he says he does not know how he is to get through it all." And then she adds: "In these days a Minister *does* require some encouragement, for the abuse and difficulties he has to contend with are terrible." In accordance with this feeling she sent Sir Robert a letter received from King Leopold, speaking very highly of his statecraft; intimated her intention of acting as sponsor to his grandchild—the son of Lord and Lady Villiers; and a little later offered him through Lord Aberdeen the unique honour of the Garter. To no other Commoner in modern times has that Order been proffered. But Peel, actuated by mingled modesty and indifference to titles or distinctions, declared that all he wished was to be remembered as a faithful servant of the Crown and people. "He looks to no other reward, apart from your Majesty's favourable opinion, than that posterity shall hereafter confirm the judgment of King Leopold, that Sir R. Peel was a true and faithful servant of your Majesty, and used the power committed to him for the maintenance of the honour and just prerogatives of the Crown and the advancement of the public welfare."

Meanwhile he struggled on, and carried sundry important measures through Parliament, but it was by means of the most fluctuating and varied support. To quote Prince Albert, in a letter written on July 28th, "His party is quite broken up, and the Opposition has as many different opinions and principles as heads." A political crisis was therefore on the horizon, but this was not allowed to interfere with a magnificent costume ball given by Her Majesty at Buckingham Palace on June 6th. The period represented was the ten years from 1740 to 1750, in the reign of George II. There were 1,200 guests present, amongst others the Duke and Duchess de Nemours and the Prince of Leiningen, and great was the display of powder and hoops and stomachers, glowing jewelry and rich and exquisite lace, brocades and velvets and gorgeous embroideries. The men all wore powdered wigs and coats of velvet—crimson, black, or blue—adorned with gold and silver. The Queen was dressed magnificently, and much as the Queen Charlotte of a hundred years before would have appeared on some state occasion.

On August 9th Her Majesty prorogued Parliament in person, and then at once set sail for Antwerp on her first German tour—with every confidence in Sir Robert Peel's statement that the country was both prosperous and happy and that nothing serious was likely to occur in her absence. Accompanied by the Prince and Lord Aberdeen, Lord Liverpool, Lady Gainsborough, Lady Canning, Mr. Anson, and Sir James Clark, the Queen reached the shores of Belgium next day, and was met at Malines by the King and Queen, who travelled some little distance further with them. At the Prussian frontier the Royal party was met by Lord Westmoreland, the Ambassador at Berlin, and an escort of gentlemen from the Prussian Court.

"To hear the people speak German," wrote the Queen in her Journal, " and to see the German soldiers, etc., seemed to me so singular. I overheard people saying that I looked very English." The King and Prince of Prussia met Her Majesty at Aix-la-Chapelle, and with a numerous suite accompanied her to Cologne, Ehrenbreitstein, and other places. At the former city the reception was enthusiastic, the flags and streamers innumerable, while the whole roadway was sprinkled with Eau de Cologne. In the evening the place was brilliantly illuminated, the houses in many cases looking like walls of fire, while the majestic Cathedral literally glowed with flaming decorations. The visit to the Cathedral was a great source of enjoyment to the Queen, as was a delightful concert in her honour conducted by Meyerbeer in person, and shared in by Jenny Lind, Viardot, and Francois Liszt. The Palace of Brühl was the next point reached, and here the Prussian King—well known as a graceful speaker—excelled himself during the grand banquet which he tendered his Royal guests. In proposing their healths he declared that "There is a word of inexpressible sweetness to British as well as to German hearts. Thirty years ago it echoed on the heights of Waterloo from British and German tongues, after days of hot and desperate fighting, to mark the glorious triumph of our brotherhood in arms. Now it resounds on the banks of our fair Rhine, amidst the blessings of that peace which was the hallowed fruit of the great conflict. That word is *Victoria*. Gentlemen, drink to the health of Her Majesty the Queen of Great Britain and Ireland, and to that of her august Consort."

The Queen was greatly affected by the kindness of the toast and the courteous terms in which the compliment was tendered. Then came a Royal progress up the Rhine, and it is safe to say that not even the waters of that historic stream had ever before carried a more distinguished gathering. In the party were the King and Queen of Prussia, the King and Queen of the Belgians, Queen Victoria and Prince Albert, the future Emperor and Empress of Germany, the Archduke Frederick of Austria, Baron Von Humboldt, and many others. Past the varied and exquisite Rhine landscapes the Prussian royal yacht steamed; past Ehrenbreitstein, where 20,000 troops made the air lurid with the noise and smoke of apparent battle; past many scenes and places of historic interest, till Stolzenfels was reached, and Her Britannic Majesty was left with the Prince Consort to proceed alone with their escort towards the Coburg which both were dreaming of, and longing to see.

At Mayence they were met by Prince William of Prussia, Prince Charles of Hesse, and the Austrian Commander, and witnessed a march-past of troops, besides receiving a most brilliant serenade in the evening from combined Austrian and Prussian bands. Here, also, they saw Prince Louis of Hesse—a future son-in-law—whom the Queen describes in her Journal as "a very nice boy of eight—nice, and full of intelligence." Thence in travelling carriages they passed through a number of German and Bavarian towns; through crowds of picturesque and most interesting and diverse people; through most varied scenery, some charming, some wild, some commonplace, until, as the Queen writes, " I began to feel greatly moved—agitated, indeed, in coming near the Coburg frontier. At length we saw flags, and people drawn up in lines, and in a few minutes more we were welcomed by Ernest (the Duke of Coburg) in full uniform." And at the Palace they found King Leopold and Queen Louise of Belgium, the Duchess of Kent, the Duchess and Dowager-Duchess of Coburg, and a whole host of more or less distant relatives.

During the brief visit which followed both the Queen and the Prince seem to have experienced intense pleasure—the one from seeing for the first time the home of her mother and her uncle Leopold, and the birthplace of her beloved husband; the other from reviving the cherished memories of the past, and visiting the haunts and scenes of childhood in company with his Royal wife. One shadow there was for both in the recent death of the father of the Prince and uncle of the Queen, who had so eagerly hoped to some time welcome them to the ancestral home. But beautiful Rosenau, where they stayed, could not fail to soon drive away any haunting shadow of sorrow. Here the Queen occupied the very room in which Prince Albert had been born, and here for some days they wandered through the exquisite woodlands and surrounding scenery, until, as Her Majesty's Journal tells us, it became "like a beautiful dream."

Of course there were also the inevitable functions, and concerts, and receptions, and Prince Albert wrote Stockmar that "Victoria seems to have pleased everybody, and is herself satisfied and extremely interested in all she sees or has seen. The mass of Royal personages, who stream in from all sides, is somewhat oppressing, although their *impressement* cannot be otherwise than flattering." But, so far as Coburg was concerned, the end soon came, and the last evening was spent in "dear, dear, peaceful Rosenau." A brief visit to the Duke of Meiningen was followed by a stay at Gotha, which, next to Coburg, was the point of special personal interest. Here they spent much time with the Dowager-Duchess, a charming old lady of seventy-four, the grandmother of Prince Albert and his brother, the Duke of Saxe-Coburg-Gotha, and mother of King Leopold. She had long been known to the Queen through intimate correspondence, and because of her deep affection for the Prince Consort. Here also the Queen met again for the first time in some years her faithful governess of days gone by, Baroness Lehzen. Then ensued delightful excursions in the Thuringian Forest, a splendid ball at Gotha, a brief visit to the Grand Duke of Wiemar, and to the great fortress of Wartburg. At Frankfort they dined with the eccentric King of Bavaria and met Prince Mettenich, the apostle of modern absolutism, who was also a guest.

Upon reaching Deutz, after the return trip down the Rhine, despatches were received from Sir Robert Peel, giving the Queen assurances that things were going well in England and Ireland. A flying visit was then made to the Chateau d' Eau, where Louis Philippe was very anxious to have Her Majesty stay for even the briefest period—as a sort of popular set-off to the German visit. Into the one day spent upon French soil, however, the King crowded much entertainment, and took occasion, also, to emphatically declare that he would never consent to Montpensier's marriage with the Infanta of Spain—a question which was coming to the front as an incipient storm-cloud. The next morning they set sail for England on the royal yacht, "the sea like a lake, and of deepest blue," and soon afterwards disembarked at Osborne, where—the Queen's Journal tells us— "stood the four children looking like roses, so well, and so fat."

The Queen arrived home only to find herself confronted with the political crisis which for some months had been impending. The country occupied an attitude towards the Corn Laws which can only be described as one of animated expectancy. Public opinion, after long and stormy agitation, was now in the main favourable to their abolition, but politicians and leaders had become so pledged to maintain them that it seemed a matter of serious difficulty for either party to take the first step. Everything and every one was, therefore, waiting—like Micawber—for something to happen, when suddenly and unexpectedly, to most people, the storm broke. Prince Albert's Journal early in October has the significant entry: "Very bad news from Ireland—fears of a famine." And silently but swiftly the shadow of that terrible disaster swept over the land, and, to quote Mr. Disraeli in his biography of Lord George Bentinck, "agitated England, perplexed the sagacious Tuilleries, and disturbed even the serene intelligence of the profound Metternich." Peel had no doubt of the course to take. He had already done much to widen the bounds of free trade, and had incurred severe contumely for his efforts. But the principle of protection to the farmer still remained untouched, and his Government had been placed in office as a result of distinct pledges to uphold that principle. Hence his special difficulty at a crisis when cheap and plentiful food was an instant and absolute necessity. He did not hesitate, however, and the following letter to the Duke of Wellington indicates the proposed course, as well as his immediate difficulties:

"My Dear Duke:

In the enclosed memorandum are contained the reasons which induce me to advise the suspension of the existing Corn Laws for a limited period. . . . I thought it right to mention confidentially to the Queen that I feared there were serious differences in the Cabinet as to the measures which the present emergency requires. Believe me, etc.,

ROBERT PEEL."

For the moment, however, he could not get his Ministry to agree upon this course, and retirement seemed inevitable. With a few exceptions its members did not appreciate the serious nature of the crisis. Wellington had replied in characteristic terms: "A good government for the country is more important than the Corn Laws or any other consideration; and as long as Sir Robert Peel possesses the confidence of the Queen and the public, and he has strength to perform the duties, his administration of the Government must be supported." Lord Ripon felt in much the same way. "I cannot look," he declared, "without the greatest apprehension upon the evils which may fall upon the Queen and country if you are withdrawn from the guidance of public affairs." To Lord Wharncliffe there was another consideration. Writing to Peel on December 1st, he asked if there were not reasons in respect to the Queen which should prevent the Government being hastily broken up. "We have enjoyed up to this moment her entire confidence, and she has a right to ask from us the utmost caution and deliberation before we take the extreme step of resigning our offices." But Sir Robert found it impossible to carry his Cabinet, as a whole, with him, and was therefore obliged to repair to Osborne and tender his resignation. The following extract from his Memoirs describes what occurred there:

" In the course of the interviews with Her Majesty which took place after my arrival at Osborne, on the 5th of December, I trust I satisfied the Queen that I was influenced by considerations of public interest, and not by the fear of responsibility or of reproach, in humbly tendering my resignation of office. Her Majesty was pleased to accept it with marks of confidence and appreciation, which, however gratifying, made it a very painful act to replace in Her Majesty's hands the trust she had confided in me. I will not say more than that the generous support which I had uniformly received from Her Majesty and the Prince, and all that passed on the occasion of my retirement, made an impression on my heart which can never be effaced."

The Queen at once sent for Lord John Russell, who was completely taken by surprise. In spite of recent declarations in favour of the abolition of the Corn Laws, he found himself somewhat disturbed and in grave difficulties as to future and useful colleagues. After some delay he secured Lord Lansdowne, the influential and experienced Whig leader in the Lords, who had already served as a Cabinet Minister in four reigns; but his efforts broke down upon the disagreement of Lord Grey and Lord Palmerston regarding the Foreign Office. Finally, on the 29th of December, he had to admit failure and return his commission to the Queen. The Prince Consort's diary records what followed : " Sir Robert Peel comes down in the afternoon ; is very much excited, but declares that he will not desert the Queen, and will undertake the Government." His Ministry was at once reorganized, and all the old members excepting Lord Stanley—who was replaced at the Colonial Office by Mr. Gladstone—now agreed to stand by him, not only in the suspension but the abolition of the Corn Laws. Writing two days after the resumption of office, Her Majesty describes her Premier as " a man of unbounded loyalty, courage, patriotism, and high-mindedness. And then she adds significantly : " I have never seen him so excited and so determined, and such a good cause must succeed."

These latter words indicate what there is little reason to doubt, that the Queen for some years had been a free-trader from conviction. Lord Campbell said in his diary during 1849 that " the Queen and Prince Albert are both genuine free-traders." Mr. Cobden, speaking at Manchester on July 2nd, 1846, supported the suspension of the Anti-Corn Law League in view of its work being now accomplished, and declared that "they were indebted to the Queen, who had favoured their cause as one of humanity and justice." Three hearty cheers were thereupon given Her Majesty. But before this occurred Peel had to face a campaign, Parliamentary and otherwise, such as few men have ever come through with either reputation or success. His financial policy, and scheme for the entire abolition of the Corn Laws within three years, passed through both Houses, and became law despite all the brilliant bitterness of Disraeli, the consequent disruption of the Tory party, and the wholesale charges of falseness and fraud against the Prime Minister. There is no doubt that Bulwer Lytton hit off Peel's character, as then understood by the masses, and in connection with Catholic emancipation as well as the Corn Laws, in those well-known lines :

> " At each new thought he paused, and feared, and trembled,
> And while he doubted, with himself dissembled ;
> But when conviction was from doubt evolved,
> It filled, it ruled him, and he stood resolved."

That the Queen believed otherwise—and has left that belief on record—is an additional and very strong proof that the verdict of history is often different from the immediate judgment of the masses. And her opinion has in itself contributed much to the change of view. As with Wellington, Peel seems to have looked for his immediate duty, and carried it out regardless of the past or future. In such a position consistency had at times to be disregarded, though when national necessity takes its place abundant excuses are available. In his general policy at this moment Peel made some serious mistakes. The Corn Laws, as they stood, had unquestionably to go, but it was not necessary to leave the agricultural interest almost entirely without protection, nor was it advisable to abolish absolutely that discrimination in favour of colonial food products which—slight as it might have been in some new form—would in these later days have been such an untold blessing to England and her colonies, and such an immense factor in cementing the unity of the Empire. But excuses are not difficult to find, even in these connections, and time may bring its own revenges.

As might have been expected, the moment his great measure had passed, the Protectionist Tories joined the Whigs and defeated the Government upon some proposal regarding Ireland. There was nothing for it but resignation, and the triumphant yet defeated Minister was succeeded by Lord John Russell, who, by playing the Conservative protectionists against the free-trade wing of the party, managed to hold office until 1852. His Ministry was formed on June 28th, 1846, as follows :

First Lord of the Treasury	Lord John Russell.
Lord Chancellor	Earl of Cottenham.
Chancellor of the Exchequer	Sir Charles Wood.
Secretary for Home Affairs	Sir George Grey.
Secretary for Foreign Affairs	Lord Palmerston.
President of the Council	Lord Lansdowne.
Lord Privy Seal	Earl of Minto.
Colonial and War Secretary	Earl Grey.
Secretary at War	Mr. Fox Maule.
President Board of Control	Sir J. C. Hobhouse.
First Lord of the Admiralty	Lord Auckland.

President of the Board of Trade - -	Earl of Clarendon.
Vice-President of the Board of Trade -	- Mr. Milner Gibson.
Commissioner Woods and Forests - -	- Lord Morpeth.
Paymaster-General - - -	Mr. T. B. Macaulay.

Shortly afterwards Her Majesty, in writing to King Leopold, declared that " Yesterday was a hard day for me. I had to part with Sir Robert Peel and Lord Aberdeen, who are irreparable losses to us and the country. They were both so overcome that it quite upset me. We have in them two devoted friends. We felt so safe with them. Never during the five years that they were with me did they ever recommend a person or a thing that was not for my or the country's best, and never for the party's advantage only. . . . I cannot tell you how sad I am to lose Aberdeen." But these partings had to come, and as the years went on and they became more frequent by death as well as by political removal, Her Majesty found herself so supremely fortunate as to realize that, with few exceptions, the men who replaced them were worthy of all friendship and personal trust, whatever might be their views upon national or party questions.

Meanwhile, on May 25th, another Princess had been born, and christened a little later as Helena Augusta Victoria. Early in August the Court retired to Osborne with the King and Queen of the Belgians, and within the next few weeks the Queen and Prince Albert took little yachting excursions to various points along the coast. In September they stayed with the Queen Dowager at Cashiobury for a few days, and then proceeded for a brief visit to Hatfield House, where they were met by the Marquess of Salisbury, the Duke of Wellington, Lord John Russell, and last, but not least, Lord Melbourne. The ex-Premier had so completely dropped out of the Queen's life, and out of national politics, that the meeting must have caused a mutual revival of many old and pleasant memories —on the one side of devoted service, on the other of friendly and confidential intercourse. To Melbourne it was almost the last flicker in the flame of his public and social career. After a longer stay at Hatfield than was usual upon these occasions, the Queen went on December 1st to Arundel Castle, where elaborate preparations had been made by the Duke of Norfolk to receive and entertain his royal guests. Christmas was spent at Osborne amid the domestic comforts and pleasures of the new palace—which owed so much to the Prince's artistic taste—and the home-like surroundings which Her Majesty knew so well how to create and control.

VISCOUNT MELBOURNE, K.G.,
THE QUEEN'S FIRST PRIME MINISTER.

RIGHT HON. SIR ROBERT PEEL, BART., M.P.

CHAPTER VIII.

An Eventful Period.

THE opening of the New Year of 1847 was darkened by the pestilence and famine in Ireland, by the distress and high price of food in England, and by the shadow of diplomatic trouble with France. To the Queen it was a matter of intense disappointment that Louis Philippe—whom she had hitherto esteemed as a Sovereign of the highest personal character—should have deliberately broken his pledge to her regarding his son's marriage with the sister of the young Queen of Spain. By this union the Duc de Monpensier became the husband of the heiress to the Spanish Crown, while, as if to outrage all international opinion and all domestic sentiment, Queen Isabella was married to a cousin—the Duc de Cadiz—who possessed neither moral, physical, nor mental qualifications for the position, and was notoriously an object of dislike to the young Queen.

It was a small, shabby policy on the part of the Ministers of Spain and France, and one which antagonized the public opinion of Europe, and alienated the friendship of England, at a time when the King of the French was in need of all the support he could receive. No doubt he had thought the alliance would strengthen his throne and family; but how such honourable men as he and M. Guizot had hitherto proved themselves to be could have carried out such a scheme is hard to understand. "Tell M. Guizot from me," said Prince Metternich, when he heard of the marriage, "that one does not with impunity play little tricks with great countries. He knows I do not think much of public opinion; it is not one of my instruments; but it has its effect. The English Government have done their best to establish Louis Philippe in public opinion. They can withdraw what they gave." Queen Victoria did at once express what she felt, and her letter to Queen Marie Amelie, read between the lines of the friendship which had hitherto existed, and compared with former letters, indicates the contempt felt by Her Britannic Majesty, and thoroughly voices the opinion of her own subjects. It was, perhaps, characteristic of the French King that he placed the writing of the communication making this unpleasant announcement upon his wife's shoulders. The reply, however, is sufficiently explicit for both, and is dated from Osborne, Sept. 10th, 1846:

" I have just received Your Majesty's letter of the 8th inst., and I hasten to thank you for it. You will perhaps remember what passed at Eu between the King and myself; you are aware of the importance which I have always attached to the maintenance of our cordial understanding, and the zeal with which I have laboured to this end. You have, no doubt, been informed that we refused to arrange the marriage between the Queen of Spain and our cousin Leopold (which the two Queens had eagerly desired), solely with the object of not departing from a course which would be more agreeable to the King, although we could not regard the course as the best. You will therefore easily understand that the sudden announcement of this double marriage could not fail to cause us sorrow and very keen regret.

"I crave your pardon, Madam, for speaking of politics at a time like this, but I am glad that I can say for myself that I have always been *sincere* with you."

The sting in that last little word must have been severe to two sovereigns whose whole policy had been one of cultivating the English alliance, and whose whole lives, with the exception of this regrettable incident, had been marked by kindliness and decorum. But to Queen Victoria the occurrence had been a painful shock in a personal as well as national sense, and the rebuke was certainly deserved. Meanwhile, in this tenth year of her reign, the young Queen and her husband were becoming more and more fitted for the performance of their great work. Baron Stockmar, in one of his analytical criticisms of the Prince Consort's character at this time, declared that he had "made great strides of late," had gained in self-reliance and activity, and had shown a keen and sure eye in politics. "The Queen also," he adds, "improves greatly. She makes daily advances in discernment and experience ; the candour, the love of truth, the fairness, the considerateness with which she judges men and things, are truly delightful, and the ingenious self-knowledge with which she speaks about herself are simply charming." Early in February the Prince received a much appreciated honour in his election as Chancellor of the University of Cambridge by a majority of 116 over the Earl of Powis. He had, of course, taken no personal part in the contest. To the Queen the result was very pleasant as indicating his increasing popularity, and she wrote to King Leopold saying that "We have been gratified at the great kindness and respect shown towards Albert by such numbers of distinguished people."

The public ceremony of installation on July 5th was marked by a great popular reception to the Queen and the Prince at Cambridge. The events of the visit included a concert in the Senate Hall, the conferring of honorary degrees, a banquet at Trinity Hall, and a Levee held by Prince Albert. It was made memorable also by a beautiful Installation Ode from Wordsworth, the veteran poet-laureate—then in his seventy-seventh year. One verse referring to Her Majesty was most eloquent in word and thought :

"Infancy by wisdom mild,
Trained to health and artless beauty ;
Youth by pleasure unbeguiled
From the love of lofty duty ;
Womanhood in pure renown

Seated on her lineal throne ;
Leaves of myrtle in her crown
Fresh with lustre all their own.
Love the treasure worth possessing
Less than all the world beside ;
This shall be her dearest blessing,
Oft to Royal hearts denied."

A little later the Queen prorogued Parliament in person—an event followed by the elections and a further strengthening of the Liberals and Lord John Russell's Government. Then came a holiday yachting tour on the Victoria and Albert around the coast of Scotland, including visits to the Isle of Man, and Iona, and Fingall's cave. After a short period at Osborne, the Court came up to Windsor for Christmas, and with the early weeks of 1848 came the first shock of revolution upon the continent—the overthrow and flight of the King of the French, the arrival of the Duc de Nemours at Dover, and the imprisonment of Guizot, together with the death of Her Majesty's much-loved grandmother, the Duchess of Gotha. To quote a private letter of Prince Albert's on February 29th: "France is in flames ; Belgium is menaced. We have a Ministerial, money, and tax crisis; and Victoria is on the point of being confined. My heart is heavy." Amid all this storm and stress the Princess Louise was born a few weeks later—March 18th, 1848. Meantime Lombardy, and Venice, and Tuscany had broken out in rebellion against Austria ; the Dukes of Modena and Parma were driven from their dominions ; Metternich the all-powerful was compelled to flee from Vienna ; Hungary rose in a national struggle for independence ; the principalities of Germany were the seat of innumerable small revolutions ; and all Europe, with the exception of England and Belgium, seemed to be on fire. A few disturbances incited by the Chartists occurred in Great Britain, but the masses as a whole proved themselves opposed to revolution and loyal to the Throne. Writing privately on May 18th, Prince Albert summed up the exact situation, and explained in a phrase the country's comparative immunity from trouble when he said : " We are quite well, and monarchy never stood higher in England than it does at this moment."

Then followed the troubles in Ireland, the suppression of the attempted rebellion led by Smith O'Brien, and the prorogation of Parliament by the Queen on September 5th. Upon this occasion the new House of Lords was used for the first time, and amid surroundings of beauty within, brightness of weather without, and immense throngs of cheering people all along the route, Her Majesty was able to lead the ceremony of the day and declare, amid the crash of European thrones, that " The strength of our institutions has been tried and has not been found wanting. I have studied to preserve the people committed to my charge in the enjoyment of that temperate freedom which they so justly value." Immediately afterwards the Queen and Prince Albert visited the north of Scotland and there rented the estate of Balmoral, with which they had become delighted, as a future residence.   Needless to say, it was purchased ere long and soon became a favourite spot for occasional rest and recreation.

Towards the end of the year matters settled down somewhat upon the continent, though Italy, Austria, and Germany still remained in more or less of a ferment, and the Queen was incidentally able to renew in their time of sorrow and desolation her old friendship with Louis Philippe and his wife and scattered family.   On the 24th of November Lord Melbourne died after a companionless old age, cheered only by books and memories of the past and an occasional letter from the Queen.   " Truly and sincerely," writes Her Majesty in her Journal, "do I deplore the loss of one who was a most kind and disinterested friend of mine and most sincerely attached to me.   He was, indeed, during the first two years and a half of my reign, almost the only friend I had, except Stockmar and Lehzen, and I used to see him constantly, daily."

Early in 1849 occurred the first Royal visit to Ireland, under circumstances of sorrow and suffering in that country which made the prospect a singularly unpleasant one to the Queen, but all the more a duty which she would be the last to overlook.   In its results it was beneficial in the extreme, and produced an ebullition of loyalty as strong as it was unexpected.   Following this came, in October, the first appearance of the little Prince of Wales and the Princess Royal at a public function—the opening of the New Coal Exchange—while in accordance with that strange mixture in Royal lives, " 'Tis here a bridal and there a burial," came the sickness and death of the Dowager Queen Adelaide.   " I love her so dearly " wrote the Queen from the bedside at Stanmore Priory, and a little later she paid a deserved tribute to the good consort of King William IV. in a characteristic letter to Leopold of Belgium :

" I know how truly you will grieve with us for the loss of our dearly beloved Queen Adelaide ; though for her we must not repine.   Though we daily expected this sad event, yet it came as suddenly, when it did come, as if she had never been ill, and I can hardly realize the truth now.   You know how *very* kind she was at all times to me, and how admirably she behaved from the time the King died.   She was truly motherly in her kindness to us and to our children, and it always made her happy to be with us and to see us ! She is a *great* loss to us both, and an irreparable one to hundreds and hundreds.   She is universally regretted, and the feeling shown is very gratifying.   Her last moments were, thank God, very peaceful."

On the first of May, 1850, which happened to be the eighty-first birthday of the Duke of Wellington, came the seventh child to the Royal household.   He was baptized Arthur William Patrick Albert—the first name in honour of the great general who, with the future Emperor, William I. of Germany, acted as his sponsor—and at least one of the others in memory of the Irish visit and in compliment to Irish loyalty.   About this time there commenced an acute stage in the interference which Lord Palmerston had considered it his duty to make in Greece in connection with certain claims for damages presented by Don Pacifico, a British subject, against the Government of that country. Without going into details, it may be said that the Foreign Secretary took a characteristically high hand and an undoubtedly patriotic position, but that while his brilliant speech carried the Commons and his policy carried the country, its peculiarly irritating enunciation almost brought about war with France, while its diplomacy was conducted with a disregard of the Queen and his colleagues which almost brought matters to a crisis at home. It was the first marked stage in a prolonged difficulty between Her Majesty and this able but imperious Minister. Writing on the 14th of May, in reply to the Premier's announcement that the French Ambassador had been recalled, Prince Albert wrote to Lord John Russell that "Both the Queen and myself are *exceedingly sorry* at the news your letter contained. We are not surprised, however, that Lord Palmerston's mode of doing business should not be borne by the susceptible French Government with the same good humour and forbearance as by his colleagues."

In the end the affair turned out well, and Lord Palmerston's motto of "*Civis Romanus Sum*," as applied to Britons and the protection of British life and property, has become historic, and an invaluable basis for all true Imperialism. Following these occurrences Sir Robert Peel met with the unfortunate accident which cut short a life of crowded work and performance, and took from the Queen one whom she both trusted and esteemed. A letter of Prince Albert's at this time undoubtedly indicates Her Majesty's opinion as well as his own: "We have lost our truest friend and trustiest counsellor; the throne, its most valiant defender; the country, its most open-minded and greatest statesman." There were other troubles besides this. The Prince was in the throes of his effort to organize the first great Exhibition, and was meeting with much popular hostility and criticism. The Queen was attacked, as she left Cambridge House from a mission of inquiry concerning her uncle, by a strange character named Pate, who struck her with a walking-stick across the face, and received seven years' transportation to Australia for his cowardly outrage. There he died in 1845, a wealthy and, it is said, a respected man. Shortly afterwards the Duke of Cambridge died, leaving alive only two others of the fifteen children of George III.—the King of Hanover and the Duchess of Gloucester.

Meanwhile Her Majesty's differences with Lord Palmerston had reached a crisis at last. The Foreign Secretary had not for some years been carrying out the Queen's wishes; had written hasty despatches upon important subjects without referring them to her; had altered others after they were approved, or had omitted to make alterations as directed in the draft; had refused even to accept the Premier's intervention and direct statement that he—Lord J. Russell —concurred in Her Majesty's views. Finally, on August 12th, 1850, the Queen sent to the Premier the following important memorandum, which summed up what she considered should be the relationship between herself and the Foreign Secretary:

"With reference to the conversation about Lord Palmerston, which the Queen had with Lord John Russell the other day, and Lord Palmerston's disavowal that he ever intended any disrespect to her by the various neglects of which she has had so long and so often to complain, she thinks it right, in order to prevent any mistake for the future, to explain what it is she expects from the Foreign Secretary.

She requires:

I. That he will distinctly state what he proposes in a given case, in order that the Queen may know as distinctly to what she has given her Royal sanction.

II. Having once given her sanction to a measure, that it be not arbitrarily altered or modified by the Minister. Such an act she must consider as failure in sincerity towards the Crown, and justly to be visited by the exercise of her Constitutional right of dismissing that Minister. She expects to be kept informed of what passes between him and the Foreign Ministers before important decisions are taken based upon that intercourse, to receive the foreign despatches in good time, and to have the drafts for her approval sent to her in sufficient time to make herself acquainted with their contents before they must be sent off. The Queen thinks it best that Lord John Russell should show this to Lord Palmerston."

There is no doubt that Lord Palmerston's immediate predecessors—notably Lord Aberdeen—had been more than willing to consult Her Majesty and give her every possible facility in sharing the conduct of foreign affairs. He himself in his former tenure of office—1837-41—had not been disinclined to the same course. But power and popularity had combined to render him independent and careless, and the result was an historic vindication and exercise of the Queen's authority. For the moment he gave way and apologized. But it was not long before a fresh illustration of his characteristic carelessness took place. A despatch was being sent to the Austrian Government expressing the formal regret of the British Government for the public assault upon General Haynau in the streets of London. Lord Palmerston sent to the Premier and the Queen the draft of a proposed communication. It contained, however, a paragraph which the Queen and Lord John Russell both agreed " to be derogatory to the honour of the nation." This opinion was advised to Lord Palmerston, when it turned out that the note had actually been sent *before* the draft had been submitted to Her Majesty for approval. This was too much, and the Foreign Secretary was informed that he must recall the note and substitute an amended one. He threatened to resign, but finally submitted.

During the ensuing year matters went on in a not very satisfactory way, but the climax came when in December, 1851, at the time of the *coup d'etat* in

Paris, and the sudden, not to say alarming, ebullition of Napoleonic policy upon the French stage, Her Majesty wrote to the Premier that "The Queen has learned with surprise and concern the events which have taken place at Paris. She thinks it of great importance that Lord Normanby (the British Ambassador) should be instructed to remain *entirely passive*, and should take no part whatever in what is passing." This was, undoubtedly, the wise and correct policy; yet almost at the moment the above words were written Lord Palmerston had assured M. Walewski, the French Ambassador in London, that he entirely approved the action of the President. A week later, and without submission to the Queen, he wrote a despatch expressing satisfaction at the success of the *coup d'etat*. Only one result was possible, and Lord Palmerston's resignation was at once asked for and received.

Meanwhile, Louis Philippe and the Queen of the Belgians, both personal friends of the Queen, had followed the Duke of Cambridge, Sir Robert Peel, and Queen Adelaide to the land from which there is no return. In February, 1851, a Ministerial crisis of unusual severity had occurred, mainly from the mixed up state of parties and the complications arising out of the Ecclesiastical Titles Bill. It was a time of great anxiety to the Queen. Writing to Lord John Russell on the 27th of the month, Her Majesty says: "All possible combinations have failed in their turn. First, you declared your inability to carry on the Government on account of hostility displayed towards it in Parliament. Second, Lord Stanley declined forming a Government of his party until every other possibility should have been exhausted. Third, you have failed to reconstruct the Government by a combination with Sir Robert Peel's friends. Fourth, Lord Aberdeen did not think it possible to form a Government with his friends alone. Fifth, Lord Stanley has failed in the attempt to construct a Government by a junction with some of Sir Robert Peel's friends, or of his party alone. . . . The Queen would therefore wish to pause before she entrusted the commission of forming an administration to anybody till she has been able to see the result of to-morrow evening's debate." Ultimately, on March 3rd, and over a week after their resignation, Lord J. Russell and his colleagues were invited to resume office, and did so, thus settling for the time a most perplexing situation.

During all this period Prince Albert was labouring at the great Exhibition, and amid discouragements of every kind was pushing it on to success. "Just at present," he wrote on April 15th, "I am more dead than alive from overwork," and the fact is not difficult to apprehend. "The opponents of the Exhibition," he added, "work with might and main to throw all the old women into panic, and to drive myself crazy." On May 1st this pioneer International Exhibition was opened by the Queen in person, amid the cheers of 25,000 people in the great building erected by Sir Joseph Paxton, and of 700,000 persons on the road from Buckingham Palace; amid the waving palms, the myriad flowers, the exquisite statues, and the surrounding wonders of art and industry. "The great event has taken place," says the Queen's diary, " a complete and beautiful triumph— a glorious and touching sight, one which I shall ever be proud of for my beloved Albert and my country. . . . Yes! it is a day which makes my heart swell with pride and glory and thanksgiving." Congratulations poured in upon every side, and Prince Albert realized at last the splendid fulfilment of his two years' work and foresight. Amongst the letters received by the Queen was one from Lady Lyttelton, and others from Lord Russell and Lord Palmerston and the King of the Belgians. To the first she replied, in characteristic terms, that it was "the proudest and happiest day of my happy life. . . . To see this great concep- tion of my beloved husband's mind, which is always labouring for the good of others—to see his great thought and work crowned with success, in spite of difficulties and opposition of every imaginable kind, and of every effort which jealousy and calumny could resort to to cause its failure—has been an immense happiness to us both. But to me the glory of his dear name, united with the glory of my dear country . . . is a source of pride, happiness, and thank- fulness which none but a wife's heart can comprehend."

The Exhibition of 1851 was a complete success—in a popular, industrial, financial, and every other sense. It did not create universal peace, but it pro- moted universal imitation and better international relations. A few ensuing weeks in August and September spent at Balmoral were followed by State visits to Liverpool and Manchester, and one to Croxteth Park, the seat of the Earl of Sefton, and to Lord Ellesmere at Worsley Hall. Thence they went to Windsor, after what the Prince has described as " a most brilliant and enthusiastic recep- tion in Lancashire." Early in the succeeding year the Russell Ministry finally collapsed, and the Earl of Derby (Lord Stanley), though in a Parliamentary minority, consented to form a Government—with Mr. Disraeli as leader in the Commons—which lasted until December, when Lord Aberdeen formed his famous Coalition Administration of Peelites, or Conservative free-traders, such as himself, and Gladstone, and Newcastle, and Sidney Herbert, and Cardwell, together with Liberals like Palmerston, Russell, Wood, Granville, Arygll, and Lowe.

The year 1852 was marked by a revival in trade, the influx of gold from Australia, and a social season of unusual gaiety and animation. A Militia Act was passed to take advantage of the wave of volunteer enthusiasm, and the elections were held resulting in the above-mentioned accession of Lord Aberdeen to power. After a sojourn at Osborne, the Queen and Prince, in August, ran over to Belgium and spent a brief season with King Leopold at Laeken. Then came a stay at Balmoral, and the curious leaving of his whole personal estate to the Queen—at least £250,000—by Mr. John Camden Nield. But the chief event of the year was the death of the Duke of Wellington, a stately figure of historic greatness, who had served not only as a link connecting two centuries and a living memorial of great deeds, but as a friend, counsellor, and almost father to the Sovereign of the realm.

"I am sure," wrote the Queen on Sept. 17th to Leopold of Belgium, "you will mourn with us over the loss we and the whole nation have experienced in the death of the dear and great Duke of Wellington. . . . He was the pride and good genius, as it were, of this country ; the most loyal and devoted subject, and the staunchest supporter, the Crown ever had. He was to us a true friend and most valuable adviser . . . We shall soon stand sadly alone. Aberdeen is almost the only personal friend of that kind left to us—Melbourne, Peel, Liverpool, now the Duke—all gone. Albert is much grieved. The Duke showed him great confidence and kindness."

And with her Ministers and her people the Queen joined in giving every possible honour in death to one who had received every available honour and title in life, from England, and his Sovereign, and the rulers of Europe. The funeral was a memorable one, and Her Majesty sorrowfully watched the procession, as it passed Buckingham Palace on its way to place the remains of perhaps the greatest Englishman of modern times in his tomb beneath the dome of the stately Cathedral of St. Paul's, and not far from that of the other British national hero—Nelson. Prince Albert's personal view of the Duke is interesting in this connection. "He is a fresh illustration," wrote the Prince to Stockmar, "of the truth that to achieve great results, and to do great deeds, a certain one-sidedness is essential. That feature of his character, to set the fulfilment of duty before all other considerations, and in fulfilling it to fear neither death nor the devil, we ought all of us to be certainly able to imitate, if only we set our minds to the task."

On the 7th of April, at Buckingham Palace, a fourth son was born to the Queen, and duly christened as Leopold George Duncan Albert, and a few months later reviews of troops by Prince Albert, and a great Naval review of 40 warships by the Queen, indicated the revival of England's martial ardour and demonstrated the success of the efforts against the " peace at any price " party, referred to in a letter from the Queen to King Leopold on August 10th: "When I think that this camp and all our large fleet are without doubt the result of Albert's assiduous and unceasing representations to the late and present Government, without which I fully believe very little would have been done, one may be proud and thankful." Meanwhile, the Crimean War was upon the horizon, public sentiment was becoming embittered against Russia, the Government was getting more and more divided in opinion, and the Queen—while having every confidence in Lord Aberdeen—was being kept upon a rack of anxiety by the myriad phases of the preliminary diplomatic period.

No Minister and no Cabinet ever faced a great war with better prospects of organized success than did Lord Aberdeen and his Government in the early fifties. The Premier possessed the entire confidence of the Queen and a prolonged personal experience of foreign affairs and foreign travel.   He was not popular with the masses, but he had the leading favourites of the people in his Ministry.   Mr. Gladstone was in the first flush of his great financial triumphs, and Lord Palmerston was the idol of all who liked spirit and patriotism in the conduct of foreign policy—although he was not himself in charge of that depart-ment during this period.   The public feeling of England was heartily with the cause of Turkey as against Russia, and the more pronounced the aggressions of the latter power, the stronger grew the flame of British hostility.   Lord Aberdeen also had the advantage—one not always appreciated by him, however, and very often minimized and restricted—of having at Constantinople, in Lord Stratford de Redcliffe, the greatest Minister whom England has ever sent to the East, with the possible exception of Lord Dufferin.   But, it may be said in passing, no com-parison between these two men is possible.   One was all daring and energy and aggressive force of character—dominating opposition by pure power of will. The other has always been the embodiment of courteous and skilful diplomacy —the iron hand if you like, but one concealed within a glove of velvet, and act-ing under the soft sheen of silken words.

As time passed in the varied complications of 1852 and 1853, the difficulties which Lord Aberdeen had to encounter grew apace, and become to the historical eye as evident as were his advantages.   Louis Napoleon was at best a doubtful ally.   In the first stages of the struggle he went into it largely from the personal motives of resentment against the Czar for a haughty indifference to his new Imperial style and position; of a desire to establish his dynasty in French opinion by playing with the edge-tools of a great war; and perhaps because he had an admitted liking—which he proved in 1860 by accepting the Cobden com-mercial treaty—for an English alliance.   But when war really broke out he aimed chiefly at winning personal prestige from it and cared little for the vital causes at the root of the conflict.   Hence his anxiety in the end to get away from it without standing by England in obtaining the results for which she, at least, had fought.

Lord Stratford, too, was a character hard for any Government to get on with, unless its mind was thoroughly made up—in the direction which Lord Stratford wished to move.   This was notoriously not the case with the Aberdeen Ministry. The Premier did not like the Turks, did not like war in either the abstract or in practice, did not even think Russia entirely in the wrong.   To a certain extent Lord J. Russell and Mr. Gladstone agreed with him, while Lord Palmerston kept to his desk at the Home Office and said little.   In such circumstances a hesitating policy, and eventually a sudden plunge, were inevitable.   Writing to Lord Clarendon, the Foreign Secretary, on July 9th, Lord Stratford indicates the situation with characteristic vigour.   "Surely it is time," said the great Eltchi, " to come to a decision which may give consistency, *ensemble*, and energy to our proceedings. I am as much for peace as any man; but if the object at stake is to be maintained, as I think it ought, there should be a limit to attempts which can only prove nugatory in the end and turn to the benefit of uncompromising Russia."

Eventually the Russian armies invaded Moldavia and Wallachia, and Lord Stratford was given what the Prime Minister described as "a fearful power"—the right to call the British fleet from Malta and bring it through the Dardanelles in case of emergency. From this time war became inevitable, and a letter written by Prince Albert on September 21st illustrates the anxieties of the period. "Louis Napoleon," observed the Prince, "wishes for peace, enjoyment, and cheap corn. The King of Prussia is a reed shaken by the wind. We are paralyzed through not knowing what our agent in Constantinople is doing or is not doing. The Divan (Turkish Government) has become fanatically warlike and headstrong, and reminds one of Prussia in 1806. The public here is furiously Turkish and anti-Russian. All this makes Aberdeen's bed not one of roses." Then came the battle of Sinope in December, the destruction of the Turkish fleet, a wild outburst of indignation in England, the sending of the French and English fleets into the Black Sea, the practical abandonment of negotiations, and, finally, on February 27th, 1854, an ultimatum from Lord Clarendon to Count Nesselrode, Russian Minister of Foreign Affairs, declaring that :

" The British Government, having exhausted all the efforts of negotiation, is compelled to declare to the Cabinet of St. Petersburg that if Russia should refuse to restrict within purely diplomatic limits the discussion in which she has for some time past been engaged with the Sublime Porte, and does not by return of the messenger who is the bearer of my present letter announce her intention of causing the Russian troops under the orders of Prince Gortchakoff to commence their march with a view to recross the Pruth, so that the Provinces of Moldavia and Wallachia shall be completely evacuated on the 30th of April next, the British Government must consider the refusal or the silence of the Cabinet of St. Petersburg as equivalent to a declaration of war, and will take its measures accordingly."

Of course, no one really expected Russia and its haughty ruler to do anything else but accept the ultimatum and fight to the end. There is now no doubt that this war resulted from a general game of deceit and misapprehension. The Czar at first mistakenly believed, through some tentative words let fall by Ministers when he was in England, that he would be supported there in a general division of Turkey. The Emperor Napoleon deceived the British Government during the final negotiations towards the close of the struggle, as he is said to have deceived that of Russia by attempted negotiations for an alliance *against* England at the beginning. Prussia seems to have played fast and loose with every one, and to have engaged to support Austria should that power be attacked by Russia, while pledging support to the latter power should it be attacked by Austria. The Austrian Government acted uncertainly all through the negotiations, but undeniably gave Lord Westmoreland, the British Ambassador, assurance of its support to the British summons for the evacuation of the provinces. And it was only after the ultimatum was actually despatched that the Cabinet learnt that the "support" would be only diplomatic.

Great Britain, however, entered upon the conflict with distinct points for settlement. These famous "Four Points" had been the centre and theme of negotiation from the time of Russia's first overt action against the Turks, and they included demands for the Russian abandonment of all control over the Provinces of Moldavia, Wallachia, and Servia; the relinquishment of all claim to control the mouths of the Danube; the abrogation of all treaties giving Russia a preponderance in the Black Sea, together with its consequent neutralization; the renunciation of the now historic Russian claim to an exclusive right in the protection of Christians under Turkish rule. Failing to obtain these demands, and feeling that the integrity of the Turkish Empire—the possession by Russia of Constantinople and the Dardanelles, with the approaches to the Mediterranean—was threatened, no British Government could have refused under existing conditions of popular approval, French alliance, and, apparently, general European support, to send the ultimatum, already quoted, and to declare war when no attention was paid to its message. Hence the Queen's announcement to the House of Lords on March 27th that:

"In this conjunction Her Majesty feels called upon, by regard for an ally, the integrity and independence of whose Empire have been recognized as essential to the peace of Europe, by the sympathies of her people with right against wrong, by a desire to avert from her dominions most injurious consequences, and to save Europe from the preponderance of a power which has violated the faith of treaties and defies the opinion of the civilized world, to take up arms in conjunction with the Emperor of the French for the defence of the Sultan. Her Majesty is persuaded that in so acting she will have the support of her people; and that the pretext of zeal for the Christian religion will be used in vain to cover an aggression undertaken in disregard of its holy precepts, and of its pure and beneficent spirit."

Meanwhile the Queen's share in the worries and correspondence and negotiations of this trying period had been very considerable, and will require more extended consideration than can be given at the close of a chapter. But concurrently with these vital matters of national concern had gone on the ordinary routine of daily work and ceremonial, the reading and signing of multitudinous despatches, the study of the political changes in each passing day, the many inevitable anxieties of family life, the sharing in all the joys and sorrows of Prince Albert's strenuous career. Sir Theodore Martin gives us in one of his crowded pages a glimpse of the kind of work done by the Prince Consort during these years. On the 15th of October (1852) he distributed the prizes of the Windsor Royal Association. The next day he met Lord Derby, Lord Hardinge, Lord J. Manners, the Duke of Norfolk, and various officials, to settle the complicated arrangements for the funeral of the Duke of Wellington. On the 19th he was busy with negotiations for the purchase by the Exhibition Commissioners of land at Kensington. Next day found him preparing a singularly able report as to the disposal of the Exhibition surplus—a question of some complication and importance. A little later in the same day he had to show his mastery of the Cambridge University Commission's Report, and to communicate the results to its authorities as Chancellor of the University. On the 22nd came further arrangements for the great funeral. Two days afterwards, in a personal interview with the Premier, he went into the details of various Government measures dealing with taxation, and free trade, and manufactures, and agriculture—no doubt for the purpose of furnishing the Queen with much boiled-down and necessary information. On the 29th he presided at a meeting of the Exhibition Commissioners, and persuaded them to adopt his plans concerning the surplus and the purchase of land. The work for the fortnight was closed by an inspection of experiments being made with shrapnel shells at Woolwich, upon his recommendation; the furnishing of an elaborate paper to the military authorities upon the subject; a discussion with the Chancellor of the Exchequer upon financial details of the question of national defence; and, finally, a settlement of the music to be played at the Duke's funeral.

These are only indications of the work done by him day in and day out, but they sufficiently prove his devotion to duty and the service of the country— a devotion which was put to still further tests of patience and endurance in the ensuing Crimean war, and was destined to triumph over both critics and circumstances.

CHAPTER IX.

The Queen and the Crimean War.

THROUGH the wreck of national reputations caused by the conduct of the war in the Crimea, the Queen's name stands out clearly and brightly. Where she interfered, good results seem to have followed, and soldiers and people and politicians all have cause to appreciate the varied influence which Her Majesty exerted during that trying period. Out of the struggle, Lord Aberdeen, and Lord John Russell, Mr. Gladstone, and the Duke of Newcastle came with the lustre of their reputations dimmed, the public opinion of their ability greatly lessened, and the public faith in their characters, for the time being, materially affected. Through it Lord Palmerston alone, of all the members of that brilliant Government, emerged with increased popularity and power.

At its very commencement Prince Albert had to encounter and overcome one of those outbursts of public slander and temporary dissatisfaction, to which he was subject during the first dozen years of his residence in England. It originally arose out of the enforced retirement of Lord Palmerston in 1851, and the popular misapprehension of its meaning and cause, together with the current rumour—which in certain quarters was industriously cultivated into a belief— that His Royal Highness was a sort of power behind the Throne and above the Ministers. It expanded into a volume of noisy declamation, when, in December, 1853, the same statesman again resigned. The absurd charge was made that the Prince Consort was in league with the enemies of the country against the Ministers of the Queen, and especially against the popular and powerful Minister who had just retired from his post. When, shortly afterwards, Lord Palmerston returned to office, some newspapers withdrew their statements; but, meantime, as the *Spectator* put it, "a whisper, which was first insinuated for party purposes, has grown into a roar, and a constructive hint has swelled into a positive and monstrous fiction." A story was circulated, and actually believed for the moment, that Prince Albert had been impeached for high treason and committed to the Tower.

The basis for this curious wave of popular sentiment was, of course, the known ability of the Prince; the closeness of the tie which bound him to the Sovereign, and the consequent influence which he was supposed to have over her; the false impression of his personal hostility to Lord Palmerston; and vague rumours of the copious Memoranda upon passing events which we now

ALEXANDER II., EMPEROR OF RUSSIA.

ALEXANDER III., EMPEROR OF RUSSIA.

know him to have frequently submitted to the Government—sometimes by request and sometimes not, but always receiving and meriting the closest consideration, and not infrequent acceptance, by the Cabinet. Of course the details could not then be known to the public, and only the wildest suppositions and silliest stories were available for discussion. And in some peculiar way the popular though vague impression grew broadcast over the country that the work, and influence, and correspondence, and study which we now understand so clearly to have been devoted to advancing the welfare of England had all been used against the realm of his own wife and the home of his children. It was an almost inexplicable situation, and is hard to understand, even after forty years have passed away.

Writing to Stockmar early in January, 1854, the Prince tells him that Louis Napoleon and Palmerston are the idols of the public—"the favourites for the Derby," and that "the unceasing attacks upon me in the press have really reached an incredible height." He adds that when Parliament met on the 31st Lord Aberdeen and Lord John Russell were to undertake his defence. To the Queen all this was exceedingly painful, more so, perhaps, than to the Prince. He had always a certain amount of German stoicism in his disposition, but she was so intensely proud of her husband, so anxious for his reputation and popularity, so sensitive to any wound inflicted upon him in feeling or character, that she must have felt this period of undeserved censure and suspicion very keenly.

To Lord Aberdeen, on January 4th, Her Majesty declared plainly that, "In attacking the Prince, who is one and the same with the Queen herself, the Throne is assailed ; and she must say she little expected that any portion of her subjects would thus requite the unceasing labours of the Prince." In his reply the Premier referred to the undeniably anomalous position of Prince Albert in connection with the constitution and constitutional functions, and declared his personal pleasure at the Queen having possessed "so able, so zealous, and so disinterested an adviser." And then he continued : " The Prince has now been so long before the eyes of the whole country, his conduct is so invariably devoted to the public good, and his life so perfectly unattackable, that Lord Aberdeen has not the slightest apprehension of any serious consequences arising from these contemptible exhibitions of malevolence and faction." A little later Her Majesty writes that "coming as it does at a moment of such *intense* political anxiety, when this country is on the verge of a war, and anything but prepared for it, it is overwhelming and depresses us sadly."

When Parliament assembled the leaders of the Government took the first opportunity to prick the bubble of calumny. Wherever charges had assumed a definite form they were disposed of by a statement of fact. Where they were confined to insinuation they could only be dealt with by the declaration of absolute faith in the loyalty and honour of the Prince. The Premier and Lord John

Russell were supported by Lord Derby, and Lord Campbell, and Mr. Spencer Walpole, in their explanations, and although Mr. Disraeli said nothing he had written to a friend some days before that "the opportunity which office has afforded me of becoming acquainted with the Prince filled me with a sentiment towards him which I may describe without exaggeration as one of affection." The result of the Parliamentary discussion was very satisfactory, and at once cleared the air. The Queen was delighted, and on February 10th—the anniversary of the royal marriage—she wrote to Baron Stockmar, then suffering from a prolonged and painful illness : "This blessed day is full of joyful and tender emotions. Fourteen happy and blessed years have passed, and I confidently trust many more will, and find us in old age, as we are now, happily and devotedly united ! Trials we must have ; but what are they, if we are together ?"

What the Premier had designated as "a signal example of popular delusion," and an instance of "stupid credulity," now passed away very quickly, and was soon forgotten for a time in the greater excitement of the conflict in the Crimea. The first event following the declaration of war was the assemblage of a stately fleet at Spithead, carrying 2,000 guns and 21,000 men, and intended, under Sir Charles Napier, to do great deeds in the Baltic—an intention which for various reasons can hardly be said to have been carried out. On March 11th the Queen visited the squadron in the royal yacht *Fairy*, and went through the magnificent ceremony of thunderous salutes and slowly defiling warships. In an ensuing private letter the Queen speaks of her enthusiasm for "my dear army and navy," and characteristically adds, "I know I shall suffer much when I hear of losses among them." Meanwhile diplomacy was still active. Certain proposals made by the Czar had been rejected by the Court of Vienna, as one of the united powers, and in accordance with a decision of a Conference of Ambassadors then being held. This induced the King of Prussia, always friendly to his Russian neighbour and brother-in-law, to attempt a personal mediation, and he, therefore, wrote two letters to Queen Victoria—one official, the other personal. The first was short, and was briefly and formally answered. The second, which was, of course, also submitted to the Cabinet, required more careful consideration.

In it, with an eloquence which usually marked both his speech and pen, the King embodied an equally characteristic weakness of will in connection with that concerted action of Europe to which he was considered bound. His words were fair. "When the vocation of diplomacy ceases," he rather cleverly remarked, "the special province of the sovereign begins." Then he points out the terrible nature of the coming war, and denounces it as being only for an idea. "The preponderance of Russia is to be broken down ! Well ! I, her neighbour, have never felt this preponderance and have never yielded to it. . . . But, above all, suffer me to ask, does God's law justify a war for an idea ?" Then he speaks of the Russian proposals, and urges Her Majesty to "order them to be probed to the bottom, and see that this is done in a desire for peace. Cause what may be accepted to be winnowed from what appears to be objectionable, and set negotiations on foot upon this basis." As for himself, the King declared that he and his people both desired and intended to preserve complete neutrality. To this the Queen replied in German, and with the most admirable tact and patriotism. The letter may be given almost in full, as an interesting illustration of Her Majesty's style and ability in such correspondence :

"Osborne, 17th March, 1854.

" DEAR BROTHER,—General Graf von Groben has handed to me the official as well as private letter of your Majesty, and I send your friendly messenger back to you with answers to both. He will be able to tell you by word of mouth what I can only do imperfectly in writing, how deep is my regret that after we have gone hand in hand loyally until now you should separate from us at this critical moment. My regret is all the greater by reason of my inability even to comprehend the reasons which induce your Majesty to take this step.

" The recent Russian proposals came as an answer to the very last attempt at a compromise which the Powers considered they could make with honour, and they have been rejected by the Vienna Conference, not because they were merely at variance with the language of the programme, but because they were directly contrary to its meaning. Your Majesty's envoy has taken part in this Conference and its decision, and when your Majesty says, ' Where the vocation of diplomacy ends there that of the sovereign may with propriety begin,' I cannot concur in any such line of demarcation, for what my ambassador does he does in my name, and consequently I feel myself not only bound in honour, but also constrained by an imperative obligation to accept the consequences, whatever they may be, of the line which he has been directed to adopt.

" The consequences of a war, frightful and incalculable as they are, are as distressing to me to contemplate as they are to your Majesty. I am also aware that the Emperor of Russia does not wish for war. But he makes demands upon the Porte which the united European Powers, yourself included, have solemnly declared to be incompatible with the independence of the Porte, and the equilibrium of Europe. In view of this declaration, and of the presence of the Russian army of invasion in the Principalities, the Powers must be prepared to support their words by acts. . . . Your Majesty calls upon me to probe the question to the bottom in the spirit of love and peace, and to build a bridge for the Imperial honour. All the devices and ingenuity of diplomacy, and also of good will, have been squandered during the last nine months in vain attempts to build up such a bridge! *Projets de notes.* Conventions, protocols, etc., etc., by the dozen have emanated from the Chanceries of the different Powers, and the ink that has gone to the penning of them might well be called a second Black Sea. But every one of them has been wrecked upon the self-will of your Imperial brother-in-law.

" When your Majesty tells me that you are now determined to assume an attitude of complete neutrality, and that in this mind you appeal to your people, who exclaim with sound, practical sense, ' It is to the Turk that violence has been done ; the Turk has plenty of good friends, and the Emperor has done us no harm,' I do not understand you. Had such language fallen from the King of Hanover or of Saxony I could have understood it. But up to the present hour I have regarded Prussia as one of the five great

Powers, which since the Peace of 1815 have been the guarantors of treaties, the guardians of civilization, the champions of right, and ultimate arbitrators of the nations ; and I have, for my part, felt the holy duty to which they were thus divinely called, being at the same time perfectly alive to the obligations, serious as these are, and fraught with danger, which it imposes.   Renounce these obligations, my dear brother, and in doing so you renounce or Prussia the *status* she has hitherto held.

"Let not your Majesty think that my object in what I have said is to persuade you to change your determination ; it is a genuine outpouring from the heart of a sister who is devoted to you, who could not forgive herself if, at such an eventful moment, she did not lay bare her inmost soul to you.   So little have I it in my purpose to seek to persuade you that nothing has grieved me more than the suspicion expressed through General Von Groben, in your name, that it was the wish of England to lead you into temptation by the holding out of certain advantages.   The groundlessness of such an assumption is apparent from the very terms of the treaty which was offered to you, the most important clause of which was that by which the contracting parties pledged themselves *under no circumstances to seek to obtain from the war any advantage to themselves*.   .   .   .

"But now to conclude.   You think that war might even be declared ; yet you express the hope that, for all that, it might still not break out.   I cannot, unfortunately, give countenance to the hope that the declaration will not be followed by immediate action.   Shakespeare's words—

> ' Beware
> Of entrance to a quarrel ; but, being in,
> Bear it, that the opposer may beware of thee '—

have sunk deeply into every Englishman's heart.   Sad that they should find their application here, when, in other circumstances, personal friendship and liking would alone prevail ! What must be your Majesty's state of mind at seeing them directed against a beloved brother-in-law, whom yet, much as you love him, your conscience cannot acquit of the crime of having, by his arbitrary and passionate bearing, brought such vast misery upon the world !

"May the Almighty have you in His keeping !   With Albert's warmest remembrances, and our united greetings to the dear Queen, I remain, my dear brother, your Majesty's faithful sister and friend,

Victoria R."

A draft of this communication was sent to Lord Clarendon, as Foreign Secretary, and he transmitted a copy to Lord Aberdeen.   Judging it upon the basis of dignified argument and keen criticism combined, it is little wonder that Lord Clarendon should have written the Prince Consort that he " read it with sincere pleasure and admiration.   It is probably the first time that a faithful picture of his conduct and position has been presented to the King."   There can be no doubt that, as the Queen had intimated in this letter, the position of Prussia was one of unenviable weakness.   In his famous conversations with Sir Hamilton Seymour, the Russian Emperor had not even thought of that country as an international factor, and had Austria thrown herself into the war, as at first seemed probable, such action would have made the success of the allies much greater, while re-establishing Austrian influence in Germany at the expense of Prussia.　With such a result the modern history of Europe might have been changed.

But Russia was aggressive, Austria nervous, and Prussia weak, so the war commenced with England and France as allies, and was carried on with only the subsequent assistance of little Sardinia—anxious to assert itself and take a place amongst the nations of Europe.　Meanwhile the English people had received the declaration of definite hostilities with determination, and there has probably never been a contest in British history when such entire unanimity existed amongst every class of the population.　For the time even Mr. Bright and Mr. Cobden became objects of public coldness and dislike, while the "peace at any price" party was absolutely overwhelmed.　In the House of Lords, during the debate following the Queen's formal announcement of the beginning of war, the Premier had stated that it was proposed to have a "day of humiliation and prayer" for the success of our arms by land and sea.　To this particular phrase the Queen at once objected in a letter to Lord Aberdeen on April 1st, and still more strongly criticized the forms of prayer usually adopted by the Church upon such occasions.

The language employed by Her Majesty in this connection illustrates her strong opinion regarding the conflict and its causes: "To say (as we probably should) that the *great sinfulness of the nation* has brought about this war, when it is the selfishness, and ambition, and want of honesty of *one man* and his servants which has done it, while our conduct throughout has been actuated by unselfishness and honesty, would be too manifestly repulsive to the feelings of everyone, and would be a mere bit of hypocrisy."　In a further letter the Queen made certain suggestions as to the choice of prayers, etc., for the consideration of the Archbishop, and they were ultimately carried out, to the general improvement of the occasion.　Following this period of religious and military preparation in England, and the despatch of Sir C. Napier to the Baltic, came distinct evidence of the King of Prussia being a mere tool in the Russian Emperor's hands.　The Queen's letter had been without apparent effect, and before long he showed his policy in both an effective and hostile manner.　Baron Bunsen, the popular Prussian Minister in London, was recalled for having previously opposed the policy of Russia; other Ministers at home in Berlin were dismissed from office for the same reason; and the Crown Prince (afterwards William I. of Germany) became so disgusted that he left the Capital.　The whole policy of Frederick IV. in this connection proves the truth of Prince Albert's exclamation in a private note on April 28th, that "if there were a *Germany* and a *German* Sovereign in Berlin" the war could never have occurred!

In a letter written on May 24th following, and as a reply to one from the Prussian King, Her Majesty speaks very plainly regarding these changes.　"If such men as these," she says, speaking chiefly of the Crown Prince, "have felt themselves constrained to part from you at a momentous crisis, this is a *serious symptom*, which may well give your Majesty occasion to take counsel with your-self, and to test with anxious care whether the hidden source of evils, past and present, may not perhaps be found in your Majesty's own views." Meanwhile the war dragged on its course. The Austrians, though not taking part openly in the contest, aided the allies by a threatening movement of troops which com-pelled the Czar to recross the Pruth. A joint effort of English and French forces was rendered necessary in Greece by that country's determination to attack Turkey. Odessa and Bomarsund were taken by storm, and the campaign in the Crimea commenced. By invitation of the French Emperor, and, after consultation with the Cabinet, Prince Albert in September paid a visit to Boulogne, reviewed the troops there, and had some very important inter-views with Napoleon.

Then followed the great series of battles around Sebastopol. News of Bal-aclava, and Inkerman, and the Alma, were received with pride and pleasure in England, mixed, however, with sorrow at the whisperings of privation and suffer-ing amongst the troops. In a letter to King Leopold on October 13th, the Queen voices the general feeling. "We are," she declares, "entirely engrossed with one idea, one anxious thought, the Crimea." Speaking of "the splendid and decisive victory of the Alma," Her Majesty goes on to say that " My noble troops behaved with a courage and determination truly admirable. . . . Lord Raglan's behaviour was worthy of the old Duke's—such coolness in the midst of the hottest fire. I feel so proud of my dear noble troops, who, they say, bear their privations and the sad disease which still haunts them with the greatest courage and good humour." Another month passed and still Sebastopol was untaken, and the Queen again writes : "Such a time of suspense, anxiety, and excitement I never expected to see, much less to *feel.*"

Of these troubles not the least was the state of the army. So keenly was the necessity of strengthening it felt that on November 11th the Prince, by Her Majesty's request, wrote Lord Aberdeen urging immediate inspection and organ-ization of the militia, the giving of power to send militia regiments to the Crimea, and the obtaining of the right to enlist foreigners. The Cabinet did not altogether like the suggestions, but within a few weeks they were forced by events to accept and carry them out. Meanwhile, the reinforcements in men and pro-visions were despatched, but, through unforeseen contingencies, were delayed on the way, and the battle of Inkerman marked the interval. Writing on Novem-ber 28th, the Queen says to her uncle of Belgium : "Since I wrote we have received all the details of the bloody but glorious action of Inkerman ; 60,000 Russians defeated by 8,000 English and 6,000 French is almost a miracle. The Russians lost 15,000. They behaved with the greatest barbarity ; many of our poor officers who were only slightly wounded were brutally butchered on the ground. Several lived long enough to say this."

During this whole period, it may be said here, the Queen and Prince Albert were not only a unit in their views of foreign policy, but the able memoranda and State papers prepared by the latter were the frequent basis for Cabinet decision and action. For instance, on November 19th, His Royal Highness submitted an elaborate document upon the principles which should underlie any negotiations for peace, and defining the relations and position of Austria to the questions at issue. During two days it was considered in Council, and then Lord Aberdeen writes the Queen that :

" The Cabinet yesterday and to-day was occupied in the consideration of the answer to be given to the despatch of Count Buol to Count Colleredo, requesting explanations from the allied Powers, previous to signature of the proposed treaty between them and Austria. The answer contained in a despatch to Lord Westmoreland has been mainly founded upon an excellent Memorandum by the Prince to Lord Clarendon, which appears to embrace the whole subject, and to take a perfectly just view of the position of the two parties."

While, therefore, the Queen, as a matter of course, followed the foreign policy of the moment, and guided it in many important matters herself, she was strongly assisted at this critical time by the sound sense and deep study of the Prince Consort. Had they been able to control some of the Departments of the Government as they influenced its foreign affairs, the Crimean War would not embrace such a record of mingled glory and shame. What they could do to alleviate the collapse of the Commissariat and the mortality amongst the troops they did. A Royal Commission was formed, with the Prince at its head, to collect what soon became known as " The Patriotic Fund " for the relief of the orphans and widows of those who had fallen, or might fall, during the war. Upwards of £1,250,000 were obtained. Every support was given Miss Nightingale in her noble mission, and various suggestions were made the Duke of Newcastle regarding methods of further alleviation. Writing to Lord Raglan, the Commander of the Crimean forces, early in January, 1855, Her Majesty declared that " the sad privations of the army, the bad weather, and the constant sickness are causes of the deepest concern and anxiety to the Queen and Prince. The braver her noble troops are, the more patiently and heroically they bear all their trials and sufferings, the more miserable we feel at their long continuance. The Queen trusts that Lord Raglan will be *very* strict in seeing that no *unnecessary* privations are incurred by any negligence of those whose duty it is to watch over their wants."

On January the 30th, Lord Aberdeen tendered his resignation to the Queen. The causes were many, but the immediate ones were Mr. Roebuck's threatened motion to inquire into the conduct of the war; Lord J. Russell's untimely and unwise retirement ; and other dissensions within the Cabinet itself. The popular dissatisfaction was universal and deep, at not only the privations of the troops, but at the slowness of the siege of Sebastopol. For it all Lord Aberdeen, the Duke of Newcastle, and Mr. Sidney Herbert were blamed—unjustly, but naturally. The fact is that they had inherited from the days of Wellington an army system utterly unsuited to the wants of the present, and one which broke down when put to the test of a great war. The troops were all right, but the organization was fatally defective. When the test came the Ministers named toiled day and night to modify evident weaknesses and meet the new demands which were springing up in every quarter. There is no doubt that amid all the racking anxieties of that period they did their fullest duty. But it none the less remains clear that someone was to blame for the condition of affairs and that it was natural for the public to throw it upon those who were at least nominally responsible.

The truth appears to be that the war was not prepared for in time, and that to this extent the Aberdeen Ministry must bear the historic responsibility. The Premier did not want war—which was perhaps well—but he did not like to think of its possibility—which was certainly and inevitably disastrous. To quote Prince Albert on March 23rd, 1854, he looked upon it even then "like a civil war, a war between England and Scotland." Months later the Queen herself had to impress upon the Premier the unwisdom of defending Russia publicly in connection with some particular phase of the contest. Naturally, therefore, in a Government whose leading members notoriously disliked all wars, the proper preparations were not made for an event which they hoped would never take place. And, equally as a matter of course, when disaster came, and our starving, freezing troops were winning battles in the teeth of privations which made men at home shiver to even think of, the public blame fell heaviest upon the leaders identified with that sentiment and the neglect of the past— though during the time of actual war they may have done everything that men could do.

To the Queen the situation was a very trying one. The Coalition Government was broken up, and neither the Peelites (Free Trade Conservatives), the Liberals, nor the Conservatives had a distinct majority in the House. Lord Derby was first called on to form an administration, but Lord Palmerston refused to join it, even though Mr. Disraeli offered to give up to him the leadership in the Commons. And it was Palmerston the country wanted. But he was not the leader of any party, and could hardly form a Government without Lord J. Russell, who had been instrumental in carrying the Roebuck motion and was known to want the opportunity himself. After a consultation, therefore, with the veteran statesman, Lord Lansdowne, Her Majesty wrote Lord John, giving him the commission, and stating that "it would give her particular satisfaction if Lord Palmerston would join in this formation."

The latter was naturally much pleased at such an intimation, in view of what had occurred in other years, and hastened to show his satisfaction by promising to take office if desired by Lord John. But the latter found it impossible to overcome his own personal unpopularity, and the effect of his hasty action in wrecking the late Ministry. When, therefore, men like Lansdowne, Grey, and Clarendon refused to join him he abandoned the task, and on the 6th of February —after a week had practically passed without a Government—Lord Palmerston was called upon and succeeded in forming one. It was much the same in composition as Lord Aberdeen's, and the late Prime Minister, with the Duke of Newcastle, showed singular nobility at a critical period, in urging their friends— Gladstone, Herbert, and the Duke of Argyll—to join the Cabinet which was being formed as the result of a Parliamentary vote really directed against themselves. Following this political crisis came a time of wild discussion and the more or less envenomed criticism of public men. Once more Prince Albert became subject to a series of stupid attacks—somewhat similar to that of an intelligent, educated man, like Mr. John Arthur Roebuck, who, in an interview with the Duke of Newcastle, actually expressed his belief that the Prince had determined the Crimean expedition should not succeed, and had worked to that end! Then came the unexpected death of the Russian Czar and some futile efforts at peace. A little later a number of wounded and disabled troops from the Crimea reached home and were reviewed at Chatham by the Queen and Prince Consort. Two days afterwards—March 5th—Her Majesty wrote to Lord Panmure, Secretary-at-War, the following letter:

"The Queen is very anxious to bring before Lord Panmure the subject which she mentioned to him the other night, viz., hospitals for our sick and wounded soldiers. These are absolutely necessary, and *now* is the moment to have them built; for, no doubt, there would be no difficulty in obtaining the money requisite for the purpose, so strong is the feeling now existing in the public mind for improvement of all kinds connected with the army, and the well-being and comfort of the soldier.

"Nothing can exceed the attention paid to these poor men in the barracks at Chatham, and they are in that respect very comfortable—but the buildings are bad—the wards more like prisons than hospitals, with the windows so high that no one can look out of them— and the most of the wards are small, with hardly space to walk between the beds. There is no dining-room or hall, so that the poor men must have their dinners in the same room in which they sleep, and in which some may be dying, or at any rate suffering, while others are at their meals."

The result of this very practical intervention was an immediate consideration of the matter and the ultimate establishment of the great Military Hospital at Netley. On April 16th the Emperor Napoleon arrived at Windsor on a visit to the Queen, and in response to an invitation extended during the Prince Consort's stay at Boulogne. He was given the same suite of rooms which had previously been occupied by a common enemy—the late Czar of Russia—and by his own predecessor, King Louis Philippe. In London he received a tremendous popular ovation, and at Windsor seems to have made a very favourable personal impression upon the Queen. In her Journal she describes the first meeting in state as being very agitating; speaks of the Empress as " gentle, graceful, and evidently very nervous "; while " Vicky " (the Princess Royal), in being presented, is pictured as making low courtesies " with very alarmed eyes." The Emperor at dinner spoke of his former residence in England, and asked the Queen if she knew that he had been sworn in as a special constable during the troubles of 1848 ! Her Majesty's Journal describes him as " very quiet and amiable and easy to get on with." His voice was " soft and low," and she repeats elsewhere that nothing could be " more civil or amiable or more well-bred than the Emperor's manner—so full of tact."

This is rather high praise from one who was accustomed to judging men, and it should go far to relieve Napoleon III. from a popular impression that he was a sort of *parvenu* monarch—a man lifted by events above his natural position. There can be no doubt that this is an error, and that although he may have made many great mistakes and proved a fickle and troublesome ally he was, upon the whole, a ruler of ability and personal dignity. During this visit he was entertained and cheered to the uttermost. State entertainments in the city; an address from the Corporation of London; a grand ball at Windsor; investment with the Order of the Garter by the Queen; a State luncheon at the Guildhall; a visit to the opera through what Her Majesty describes as "a sea of human beings, cheering and pressing near the carriage "; a visit to the Crystal Palace amid renewed demonstrations of popularity. Finally, on April 20th, a Council was held to consider plans for future operations in the Crimea, and there were present the Queen, the Prince Consort, the Emperor of the French, Marshal Vaillant, Lords Palmerston, Panmure, and Clarendon. It must have been an interesting as well as important occasion.

Next day the Emperor left for home; first writing in the Queen's album : "I tender to your Majesty the feelings which one entertains for a Queen and a sister, respectful devotion, tender friendship.—Napoleon." It had been a most successful visit in a public sense, and to the Queen a most interesting and delightful experience. "It is a dream, a brilliant, successful, pleasant dream," says the royal Journal. "I am glad to have known this extraordinary man, whom it is certainly impossible not to like when you live with him, and even to a considerable extent to admire." The impression produced on the Emperor seems to have been even stronger. He speaks in a letter, written shortly after his return, of Her Majesty's reception, as "so full of grace and affectionate kindness," and declares that it is in truth "impossible to live for a few days as an inmate of your home without yielding to the charm inseparable from the spectacle of the grandeur and the happiness of the most united of families."

Meanwhile Austria—fearing that she might now be dragged into the war under the terms of the treaty made with the Powers on 2nd December, 1854— proposed a new arrangement with Russia, which, though favoured by the special

English and French Plenipotentiaries in Vienna, was seen to be entirely unsuited to the contingency. Without going into details it may be said that immediately on receipt of the proposals Her Majesty wrote to her Foreign Secretary : " The Queen has received Lord Clarendon's letter with extreme concern. How Lord John Russell and M. Drouyn de Lhuys can recommend such proposals to our acceptance is beyond her comprehension. The Prince has summed up the present position of the question in a few sentences, which the Queen encloses, and which she thinks might be communicated to the Cabinet, and perhaps to the Emperor." This was done, and the decision was in harmony with the Queen's impressions and the Prince's advice. Napoleon also agreed in the rejection of the proposals, and Count Walewski was appointed to succeed M. Drouyn de Lhuys as French Minister of Foreign Affairs. Unfortunately for himself Lord John Russell did not look at the failure of his mission in the same light, and continued to retain his place in the British Ministry.

Early in May Lord Lansdowne stated in the Upper House that the losses of the Russians had so far been threefold that of the Allies, and estimated the total figures at 240,000 men. But Russia could not yet be brought to accept the principle of neutralization in the Black Sea, and so the war went on. Prince Albert wrote on May 30th, after a brief stay at Osborne, that "to-morrow, alas ! our holiday is at an end, and then new fatigues and exertions of every kind, in temper, mind, and body, await us in London. Of our negotiations for peace nothing has come." Following the opening of Parliament came a prolonged debate on the inadmissible terms suggested by Russia and seconded by Austria. Greatly to the regret of the Queen and Prince Consort, Mr. Gladstone, and Mr. Sidney Herbert, and Sir J. Graham, joined Cobden and Bright in urging their acceptance—fortunately without success. On the 29th of June news arrived of the death of the brave old soldier who had endured so patiently all the anxieties of the siege of Sebastopol. To Lady Raglan the Queen at once wrote : " Words cannot convey all I feel," said Her Majesty, " at the irreparable loss you have sustained, and I and the country also, in your noble, gallant, and excellent husband, whose loyalty and devotion to his sovereign and country were unbounded." Of Lord Raglan the Prince added in a letter to Stockmar, and with much truth : "Spite of all that has been said and written against him, an *irreparable loss* for us."

Then came the promised Royal visit to Paris. Napoleon had wished it to be a protracted one, but on July 7th Lord Clarendon wrote Lord Cowley, the British Ambassador, explaining the necessity for restricting its length : "The Emperor is, I believe, aware that the Queen's life is one of incessant occupation and fatiguing business, but he may, perhaps, not know that it is absolutely indispensable for her health to pass some weeks in Scotland, and to be invigorated by the mountain air." The visit was therefore arranged for the 18th and 27th of August inclusive, and events in connection with the war —the destruction of Sweaborg, the success at Riga, the defeat of the Russians at Tschernaja—made the occasion an especially auspicious one. The Queen was accompanied by Prince Albert, the little Prince of Wales, and the Princess Royal, and it goes without saying that Paris was *en fête* when reached by the Royal visitors. Banners, flags, arches, illuminations, flowers, the roar of cannon, bands and drums, and cheering people, rendered the occasion indescribable as well as memorable.

The Queen's Journal records some charming instances of passing compliments in which truth and flattery were delightfully mixed : " Maréchal Magnan told me that such enthusiasm as we had witnessed had not been known in Paris, not even in the time of the Emperor Napoleon's triumphs ; and General Lowstein said that all France would have come if there had been time." A perhaps more accurate and interesting statement is that of General Canrobert, who had just returned from the Crimea, and after a long conversation with the Queen told Lord Aberdeen " that he had talked to many people, military and civil, but to none so thoroughly well-informed about the Crimea, the siege, and the armies, as Her Majesty." State visits were paid to the chief sights of Paris, to Versailles, to the Grand Opera, and to the beautiful Tuileries—now, like St. Cloud, where the Queen stayed, a mass of ruins. A brilliant Ball was given at the Hotel de Ville, and another at Versailles. The Queen on both occasions danced with the Emperor, and amongst those presented to her was Count Bismarck, then Prussian Minister at Frankfort, but just returned from a mission to St. Petersburg, and whom the Royal diary describes as "very Russian," and as saying to her that Paris was " even more beautiful that St. Petersburg."

Upon one occasion while the Emperor was driving Her Majesty through the Park of St. Cloud in his own phaeton, a conversation took place upon the Orleanist Princes : the Queen's friendship for them—which she explained was personal and not political ; and the recent confiscation of their property. The Queen thought that they were not guilty of conspiracy, but states in her Journal, with characteristic courage, that " I, however, added that naturally all exiles were inclined to conspire, which he did not deny, and which indeed he had practised himself ! " When the time to depart came, after a final round of festivities, the Emperor accompanied his visitors to the coast, and upon the very spot where Napoleon I. had assembled his troops for the invasion of England the Queen now reviewed 36,000 infantry, besides cavalry, lancers, and dragoons. " We drove down the lines," says the Journal, " which were immensely deep, quite a forest of bayonets. The effect they produced, with the background of the calm blue sea and the setting sun, which threw a glorious crimson light over all, was most magnificent."

From the French coast the Queen and her family travelled straight to

Balmoral, and there came the welcome news of the fall of Sebastopol. And in the two months which immediately followed, the Emperor Napoleon pressed the importance of taking advantage of this success to obtain peace. His Minister of Foreign Affairs favoured some fresh Austrian proposals, and would not accept the modifications suggested by England. Finally, Lord Palmerston had to write declaring that rather than consent to an inadequate settlement England would carry on the war alone. The result was a long personal letter from Napoleon to the Queen, explaining his view of the situation and his reasons for thinking that the war should now be terminated. On receiving it Her Majesty sent for Lord Palmerston and Lord Clarendon and laid it before them together, with an outline of her proposed reply. In the latter the matters under discussion were summed up as follows:

"Passing over all these considerations, I am sincerely anxious to be at one with your Majesty. All that is required to enable my Government to do so is: First, that we should not be bound to the letter of the proposal, of which we have had no opportunity of discussing the meaning or the import. Second, that Austria should agree to abide, under all circumstances, by her Ultimatum, and not to bring us back counter-proposals from St. Petersburg, which we, yourself and I, should have to accept or to refuse, whereby we should be replaced again in the same bad position we found ourselves in last year. Third, that the Neutralization Treaty should be made a reality, and not something merely illusory, which it would inevitably be if, as proposed, it were left as a separate treaty existing merely between Russia and Turkey."

The letter, as a whole, was satisfactory to the Emperor, and he promptly let it be known that whatever might be rumoured to the contrary he would not be a party to any peace of which England did not approve. On January 31st, 1856, and amid indications that the war was at last over, through Russian willingness to accept the Four Points, the Queen opened Parliament in person. About the same time Lord Clarendon departed for Paris bearing a personal letter from Her Majesty to Napoleon III., in the course of which she spoke strongly of the necessity of united action in the coming peace negotiations, and declared that "The operations of our combined armies and fleets under a divided command have been subjected to enormous difficulties, but these difficulties have been happily overcome. In diplomacy, as in war, the Russians will have a great advantage over us in their unity of plan and action, and I believe that they are stronger here than in the field of battle; but, beyond all doubt, we shall continue to be as victorious here as elsewhere, if we can prevent the enemy from dividing our forces, and fighting us in detail." The Conference which followed justified the wise and timely words of the Queen, and the Treaty of Paris was the result of the earnest labours of Lord Clarendon and the Plenipotentiaries there assembled. Upon the whole, the points fought for had been gained, and the British Minister of Foreign Affairs was fully justified in the terms of the following letter, written on March 30th, and announcing the signing of the Treaty and the closing of a blood-stained but noble chapter in British history :

"Lord Clarendon presents his humble duty to your Majesty, and humbly begs to congratulate your Majesty upon the signature of Peace this afternoon. It is not to be doubted that another campaign must have brought glory to your Majesty's arms, and would have enabled England to impose different terms upon Russia ; but setting aside the cost and the horror of war, in themselves evils of the greatest magnitude, we cannot feel sure that victory might not have been purchased too dearly.

"Lord Clarendon would not make such an assertion, but he feels convinced that your Majesty may feel satisfied with the position now occupied by England. Six weeks ago it was a painful position here ; everybody was against us, our motives were suspected, and our policy was denounced ; but the universal feeling now is that we are the only country able, ready, and willing, if necessary, to continue the war ; that we might have prevented peace, but that having announced our readiness to make peace on honourable terms we have honestly and unselfishly acted up to our word. . . .

"Lord Clarendon, therefore, ventures to hope that the language in England with respect to the peace will not be apologetic or dissatisfied. It would be unwise and undignified, and would invite criticism, if such language were held before the conditions are publicly known."

This letter brought a congratulatory reply from the Queen, and a personal one to the Emperor Napoleon ; and with the French ruler's appreciative answer, and an incidental reference to his indebtedness to Prince Albert for wise views and advice, the curtain may be said to have fallen upon the Crimean war, with all its mingled glories and disasters. Through them all, however, can be traced the distinct and beneficial influence of Her Majesty—always for good, always for the honour of her country, always for the welfare of her soldiers, always for the dignity of the Crown and nation.

HER MAJESTY AND THE PRINCE CONSORT ETCHING.

HER MAJESTY'S SITTING ROOM, OSBORNE HOUSE, ISLE OF WIGHT.

CHAPTER X.

EDUCATION AND TRAINING OF THE ROYAL FAMILY.

THE Queen and the Prince Consort were from the first permeated with a deep sense of their responsibilities in the bringing up of an heir to the throne, and in the education of those who might help to surround him with other bright family examples, and the potent force of high aims and actions. To the humblest of Her Majesty's subjects, and in the lowliest as well as in the highest of spheres, such matters as the training of children are of grave import. How much more so to a Christian and keenly conscientious mother who was also a great Queen! Her first-born son would, in all human probability, become the Sovereign of a constantly growing Empire, and the wielder of vast and increasing responsibilities. Her other children, as they took their places upon the high stage of life to which they were born, would become instruments for much of good to the people and the world, or else possible elements of evil in a sphere from which they could not well be removed, and in which they could scarcely be concealed from the public eye or that blazing light which surrounds all who stand in proximity to the throne.

Hence the thoughtful and careful manner in which the royal couple early entered upon the study of the problems connected with the education of children. They probably felt with Locke that "to neglect beginnings is the fundamental error into which most parents fall." They must have keenly appreciated the inattention which George III.—with all the well-merited popular belief in his domestic virtues—bestowed upon some members of his family in this connection. They knew that of his sons only three were brought up in England, and that the Dukes of Kent, Cumberland, Sussex, and Cambridge were in the main trained upon the Continent, and amid surroundings certainly not conducive to the cultivation of the home and family virtues. They knew something of the moral faults of George IV., and William IV., and the Duke of York, and were determined that, so far as in them lay, the Royal family of the present and future should have very different surroundings and a very different system of instruction.

Baron Stockmar was consulted, and in a memorandum—rather ponderous in its terms—dealt with the whole question at some length. His conclusions may be summed up in the general statement that there should be " placed about children only those who are good and pure, who will teach not only by precept, but by living example; for children are close observers, and prone to imitate whatever they see or hear, whether for good or evil." The early regulation of the child's natural instincts in a pure and right direction was the keynote of what followed; and certainly the Royal family of to-day owe much to the devotion of their mother and the earnest sympathy of their father during these years. The first and pressing question was that connected with the infant Princess Royal and the Prince of Wales. Writing from Windsor on March 24th, 1842, the Queen confided her troubles to Lord Melbourne in the following interesting letter:

"We are much occupied in considering the future management of our nursery establishment, and naturally find considerable difficulties in it. As one of the Queen's kindest and most impartial friends, the Queen wishes to have Lord Melbourne's opinion upon it. The present system will not do, and must be changed. . . . Stockmar says, and very justly, that our occupations prevent us from managing these affairs as much our own selves as other parents can, and therefore that we must have some one in whom to place *implicit confidence*. He says a lady of rank and title with a sub-governess would be the best. But where to find a person so situated, fit for the place, and, if fit, one who will consent to shut herself up in the nursery and entirely from society, as she must if she is *really* to superintend the whole, and not accept the office, as in my case, Princess Charlotte's, and my aunt's, merely for title, which would be only a source of annoyance and dispute.

"My fear is that, even if such a woman were found, she would consider herself not only as responsible to the Prince and Queen, but more to the country, and nation, and public; and I feel she ought to be responsible only to *us*, and *we* to the country and nation. A person of less high rank, the Queen thinks, would be less likely to do that, but would wish to be responsible only to the parents. Naturally, too, we are anxious to have the education as simple and domestic as possible. Then, again, a person of lower rank is less likely to be looked up to and obeyed than one of some name and rank. What does Lord Melbourne think?"

The Prime Minister fully recognized the importance of the matter and the nature of the difficulties so spontaneously suggested by the Queen. Upon the whole, his reply approved Baron Stockmar's idea of a person in good rank and position. In the end a most excellent choice was made. Lady Lyttelton, a daughter of the second Earl Spencer, and wife of the third Lord Lyttelton—who had for eleven years been a lady-in-waiting—accepted the post, and from April, 1842, until December, 1850, filled it with wisdom and discriminating zeal. When she retired, at an age which needed rest, her young charges parted from her with sadness, and the Queen expressed her highest appreciation of the services rendered. But though an onerous position, it could not have been an unpleasant one. The Governess to the royal children had constant proofs of the anxious affection of the Queen mother, and the advantage of her wise advice and frequent assistance. And Lady Lyttelton has also spoken of the ready helpfulness and constant kindness of Prince Albert—his candour, truth, prudence, and manliness. Occasionally, too, Her Majesty, amid all the stress of myriad duties and responsibilities, would issue a memorandum concerning the children.

In one of these, dated March 4th, 1844, she declares the "greatest maxim of all" to be a simple and domestic training, frequent presence with their parents—so far as it did not interfere with lessons—and the inculcation of perfect confidence in their father and mother. The teaching of religion was a matter of constant and earnest thought. The Queen's own conviction was that daily instruction at a mother's knee was the best and truest method; and she has placed on record her keen regret that other occupations made it impossible for her, as a rule, to hear the little Princess Royal's evening prayers. In this connection, too, there was always the desirability of preventing the minds of the children, as the years rolled on, from being unduly affected by waves of sectarian thought in the Established Church. To teach Christianity and the broad faith of the Church of England, without reference to current subjects of controversial theology and ceremonial observance, was the policy of the Queen and the Prince Consort; and it was not altogether an easy one to pursue. In a memorandum concerning the child who was to one day be Empress of Germany, the Queen says at this time—November, 1844:

"I am *quite* clear that she should be taught to have great reverence for God and for religion, but that she should have the feeling of devotion and love which our Heavenly Father encourages His earthly children to have for Him, and not one of fear and trembling; and that the thoughts of death and an after life should not be represented in an alarming and forbidden view; and that she should be made to know, as yet, no difference of creeds, and not think that she can only pray on her knees, or that those who do not kneel are less fervent and devout in their prayers."

Such was the wise and simple religious instruction given to the royal children. They were, of course, trained in the principles of the Church of England, but they seem to have been from the first taught to view that and the other creeds of the nation from the broadest and most liberal standpoint. The national position of the Church was one thing, the general basis upon which all Christianity rests was another. The former should be preserved in the interests of the people, the latter was wide enough to include all sects and all degrees of genuine religious thought. As early as 1846 these considerations were brought out in a document, prepared by Stockmar, concerning the future education of the Prince of Wales—then five years old. This was supplemented by able and elaborate papers prepared at the Queen's request by Bishop Wilberforce, of Oxford, and Sir James Clark.

Two years later the time had come for the young Prince to be placed in the hands of a tutor; and, after much anxious thought, the Queen and Prince Albert decided to appoint Mr. Henry Birch, an under-master at Eton, who had taken high honours at Cambridge, and whose personality had impressed the Prince Consort very favourably. Announcing the selection to the Dowager Duchess of Gotha, the latter speaks of him as "a young, good-looking, amiable man, whose pupils (at Eton) have won especial distinction"; and added, with his usual keen sense of responsibility: "It is an important step, and God's blessing be upon it; for upon the good education of princes, and especially of those who are destined to govern, the welfare of the world in these days very greatly depends." Under Mr. Birch the Prince's studies were conducted until 1851, when Mr. Gibbs, his classical tutor, was appointed and continued in charge until 1858. Of course each department of study was in the hands of a specialist, and drawing, French, and other branches of instruction were carefully looked after. But, both in his early years and when under advanced tutors, the young Prince and his brothers and sisters were constantly in the society of their parents. Here, indeed, as may well be imagined, the most valuable part of their education took place.

A man of such wide and varied learning and accomplishments as Prince Albert could not fail to exercise the best of influences upon his children, while the Queen's love of home and high example and Christian character gave an added beauty to the domestic surroundings of their family. It was through his father's love of the arts and sciences that the Prince of Wales was taken to places where culture of a sort not then very general amongst young Englishmen was fostered—before, indeed, such subjects had come fully within the scope of academic training and honours, through the Prince Consort's influence as Chancellor of the University of Cambridge. Incidentally, too, the royal children were in these early years given many quiet glimpses of the people and the country. During the autumn of 1846 the two eldest ones were taken on the tour which included Portland, Weymouth, Guernsey, Plymouth, and various places in Cornwall. The Queen's Journal tells us how anxious the people were to see the Duke of Cornwall—the little Prince's second title. At Penrhyn, for instance, the corporation came on board the royal yacht with an address, and asked for him; "so I stepped out of the pavilion with Bertie, and Lord Palmerston told them that was the Duke of Cornwall; and the old mayor of Penrhyn said that he hoped he would grow up to be a blessing to his parents and to his country."

Again, they were taken on a trip to the Channel Islands, and in 1847 along the coast of Wales, and thence to Scotland. Meanwhile Lady Lyttelton had been succeeded as governess to the younger children by Lady Caroline Barrington—a sister of the late Earl Grey. In writing to Mr. Greville during 1852, the former declared that "the Queen is very fond of her children, but severe in her manner, and a strict disciplinarian." She described the Prince of Wales as "extremely shy and timid, with very good principles, and particularly an exact observer of truth; the Princess Royal is remarkably intelligent." About the same time Lady Canning gives us another pretty little glimpse of the Prince. "Mr. Birch left yesterday," she records in her diary. "It has been a terrible sorrow to the Prince of Wales, who has done no end of touching things since he heard that he was to lose him three weeks ago.   He is such an affectionate, dear little boy; his little notes and presents which Mr. Birch used to find on his pillow were really too moving."   Two years later, in another letter to a friend, Lady Canning affords a picture of domesticity at Windsor which is charming :

"We assembled in the corridor at seven this evening for the Christmas tree and to receive presents.   Everybody had very pretty things, and the children quantities of toys and books.   There were pictures and things, from Balmoral for the Queen and Prince, and no end of *surprises of work* from the children to them.   A great drawing of Mary, Queen of Scots, and a poem illustrated by the Princess Royal were full as good as Lou could have done at her age, perhaps in some ways better, and done quite by herself, at fourteen."

Writing to his wife on March 19th, 1854, the Duke of Somerset, then Lord Seymour, spoke of dining at Windsor the night before, there being present the Duchess of Kent, Lord Aberdeen, Lord and Lady Claude Hamilton and others, and then adds: "The little Princesses, Helena and Louise, went in to dinner and stood by the side of their parents, 'because it was Louise's birthday.'   They are very like the Queen, but I suppose will be taller eventually. . . After dinner in the gallery the little Prince of Wales came to me to enquire after Edward ; the Queen also said the Princes were very desirous to have him again to play with them."

But simple, and healthy, and wholesome as their life was, the very environment of Windsor and other royal palaces was productive of a certain amount of ceremony and formality.   It was, therefore, the great delight of the children as well as of the Queen and Prince Consort to get away for their annual sojourn in the Highlands.   There they seem to have lived in absolute simplicity, and to have entirely dispensed with the formalities of Court life.   The Queen and her daughters would visit the poor in their cottages, and make garments for the children or do some knitting for the older persons.   To the Princess Louise especially, these wild and romantic surroundings and picturesque scenery gave great enjoyment.   Amongst the hills, and rocks, and glens she loved to wander, and there she developed the artistic instincts which were afterwards exhibited to such a considerable extent and in such excellent work.   Her Majesty's Journal records an early appreciation of this talent and many references to the sketching done by the little Princess.   No doubt, too, she had the strong sympathy and tasteful instruction of a father who loved art in the warmest sense of the word.

During these years the children were, undoubtedly, a very great source of comfort to their Royal parents.   Lady Canning, who was then in constant attendance at Court, speaks on January 1st, 1855, of a few days' stay at Osborne—in the quietness of home and country life—as being good for the Queen and Prince, "for all their troubles (Crimean war, etc.) keep them awake at night."   And the spirit shown in the Queen's private reference to Prince Albert, "Trials we must have; but what are they if we are together !" speaks eloquently of the closeness of the family tie at this time and afterwards. One of the most pleasant features of this home training was the custom amongst the children of celebrating family anniversaries by some pretty theatrical performance—sometimes going to much patient toil and study for the purpose of preparing a surprise for their father and mother. Of one of these the Baroness Bunsen, a frequent and favourite guest of the Queen, furnishes a bright and pleasant picture. The occasion was Her Majesty's wedding day, and the incident exhibits both graceful and sympathetic characteristics in the children :

"We followed the Queen and Prince Albert a long way, through one large room after another, till we came to one where hung a red curtain, which was presently drawn aside, for a representation of the Four Seasons, studied and contrived by the Royal children as a surprise to the Queen, in celebration of the day. First appeared Princess Alice as the Spring, scattering flowers and reciting verses, which were taken from Thomson's ' Seasons '; she moved gracefully, and spoke in a distinct and pleasing manner, with excellent modulation, and a tone of voice sweet and penetrating, like that of the Queen. Then the curtain was drawn and the scene changed, and the Princess Royal represented Summer, with Prince Arthur stretched upon the sheaves, as if tired with the heat and harvest work; another change, and Prince Alfred, with a crown of vine leaves and the skin of a panther, represented Autumn—looking very well. Then followed a change to a winter landscape, and the Prince of Wales represented Winter, with a cloak covered with icicles (or what seemed such), and the Princess Louise, a charming little muffled-up figure, busy keeping up a fire ; the Prince reciting (as all had done) passages more or less modified from Thomson. Then followed the last change, when all the Seasons were grouped together, and far behind, on a height, appeared Princess Helena, with a long white veil hanging on both sides down to her feet, holding a long cross, and pronouncing a blessing upon the Queen and Prince. These verses were composed for the occasion."

Taken altogether, the home of the Royal family was not only a happy one, but an almost ideal one. The Princess Helena (Princess Christian of Schleswig-Holstein), in her Memoir of Princess Alice, speaks of the daily intercourse with their parents ; the many walks and drives and journeys, taken with them and the other brothers and sisters ; the occupations and amusements, "all watched over and shared in by the Queen and the Prince Consort "; as making up the sum of " a most perfectly happy childhood and youth." Prince Albert, indeed, seems to have inspired his family, as he did the nation, with the deepest affection and respect. Of Princess Alice, who in a subsequent mournful period proved her sympathetic love so strongly, Princess Helena says that " Her adoration for her father became the one leading star through all her life ; it influenced her every thought and action ; and to the end of her short stay on earth she strove to act up to what he would have thought right. He was her highest ideal of all that was perfect, beautiful, and good, and even on her deathbed his loved name was the last she ever uttered."

The Queen's Journal contains many references to these years, and the literature of the period is full of quaint stories about the Royal family. As with other children, in humbler homes, there were pet names employed in place of the formal baptismal designations. The Prince of Wales was " Bertie," the Princess Royal in early days was called " Pussy," and in after years " Vicky." And so with some of the others. Speaking of the two eldest, Miss Tytler tells us that they delighted to stand still and quiet in the music-room at Windsor in order to hear " the Prince-father discourse sweet sounds on the organ and the Queen-mother sing with one of her ladies." She adds that they furnished a never-ending series of merry anecdotes. " Now it was the little Princess, a quaint, tiny figure, in dark-blue velvet, white shoes, and yellow gloves, keeping the nurseries alive with her sports, showing off the new frock she had got as a Christmas box from her grandmother, the Duchess of Kent, and bidding Mrs. Liddell *put one on*. Now it was the Queen offending the dignity of her little daughter by calling her ' Missy,' and being told in indignant tones, ' I'm not Missy, I'm the Princess Royal ! ' "

This future Empress had indeed quite a will of her own in these days. It is stated that when Dr. Brown entered the Royal service the little Princesses, hearing their father address him as " Brown," adopted the same form, or lack of form, in speaking to him. The Queen corrected them, and all obeyed, by addressing him as Mr. Brown, except the Princess Royal, who maintained her right to use the name as her father did. One day the Queen heard her and declared that if she again addressed the physician in that manner she should go to bed. Next morning, however, on his presenting himself, the young Princess said, " Good morning, Brown ! " then, meeting her mother's look, added, " And good night, Brown, for I am going to bed." And to bed she accordingly went.

Meanwhile, the children passed through the ordinary phases of child life. As they grew older amusements were given them in the broadest sense, and they were allowed all the more innocent enjoyments and experiences of a lofty position. On Prince Arthur's fifth birthday—May 1st, 1854—a ball was given in his honour to two hundred children at Buckingham Palace, and Her Majesty took occasion to write Lord Aberdeen a brief note of graceful invitation, in the hope of relieving him for the moment from his burdens of work and responsibility : " Though the Queen cannot send Lord Aberdeen *a card for a child's ball*, perhaps he may not disdain coming for a short time to see a number of happy little people, including some of his grandchildren, enjoying themselves." It is most probable that the present Earl, and Governor-General of Canada—then seven years old—was one of the children referred to. In July, 1855, the four younger members of the family caught scarlet fever and gave their parents the usual period of care and anxiety. The Prince of Wales and Princess Royal were shortly afterwards taken on the Queen's visit to Paris, and allowed to see all the splendours of State receptions and national fêtes. During the previous year the Heir Apparent had taken his place for the first time beside the Queen and Prince Albert upon the Throne at the opening of Parliament.

In 1856, the Queen and Prince Albert became occupied with plans concerning Prince Alfred—then twelve years of age. He had expressed a rather decided liking for the Navy, besides showing a marked taste for music. It was therefore decided to give him a separate establishment, where, under a suitable Governor, and away from the crowded functions and attractions of the Court and Palace, he could study in quiet and without interruption. Much depended, of course, upon the selection made to preside over this work, and, finally, the appointment of Lieutenant Cowell—afterwards Major-General Sir John Cowell, K.C.B., Master of the Queen's household—was made. The Prince Consort announces the arrangement in the following portion of a private letter :

" The latest news I have to give about ourselves is that I have succeeded in getting a distinguished and most amiable young officer of Engineers as Affie's (Prince Alfred's) tutor, one Lieutenant Cowell, who was Adjutant of Sir Harry Jones at Bomarsund, and before Sebastopol, and is well spoken of by everybody. He is only twenty-three, and has had the highest scientific training. By this a great load has been taken off my heart. Cowell comes to us at once to learn the working of our system, and will afterwards take up his quarters with Affie in the Royal Lodge in Windsor Park."

During the succeeding year arrangements were made with Captain Elphinstone (afterwards General Sir Howard Elphinstone, V.C., K.C.B.) to take charge of the future studies of Prince Arthur. This he did in 1859, when the young Prince was nine years old, and continued to superintend them until his pupil grew to manhood. Meanwhile Prince Alfred succeeded excellently in his naval studies, and the Queen's Diary says—August 31st, 1858—that when they landed at Portsmouth, on returning from a visit to Berlin, " Sir George Seymour gave us the delightful news that Affie had passed an excellent examination, and received his appointment. He had just gone to report himself on board the *Euryalus*, and would meet us at Osborne." There they found him on the private pier, " in his Middie's jacket, cap, and dirk, half blushing and looking very happy. He is a little pulled from these three days' hard examination, which only terminated to-day. . . . We felt very proud, as it is a particularly hard examination." The total percentage of clear and distinct answers given by the young Prince was eighty, while fifty would have been thought good ; and Lord Derby, after looking over the papers, rather humorously wrote the Prince Consort that it would be very difficult, indeed, to form an Administration if its members had to pass through such an ordeal.

During the years immediately following, and in view of the distractions and recklessness of life on board ship and in the rough work of naval training, the Prince Consort was very desirous that his son's religious principles should be deeply seated and clearly defined. He was anxious—to quote his own words— that the young man should feel convinced that " sin is not positive, but something transitory, the struggle between the animal nature and the moral law, which begins with the moral law and ends with the victory over mere impulse, which Christ has won for us by His teaching, life, and death, if we only follow Him." And, writing to his daughter in Berlin—July, 1860—he declares his belief that "Alfred fully recognizes his personal responsibility for his own conduct and his own happiness. It is to this that we must look for safety for him in the future struggles of life."

As time passed on the education of the Prince of Wales had also become a matter of increasingly anxious thought to his father. In 1858 Mr. Gibbs retired from his position of tutor, and was succeeded as director of studies and chaplain by the Rev. Canon Tarver, who accompanied the Prince to Rome, Spain, and Portugal, and remained with him afterwards at Edinburgh until the autumn of 1859, when his university education began. Before this, however, and at the age of seventeen, the young Prince was confirmed with all state and solemnity. His preliminary examination by the Archbishop of Canterbury, the Queen, and the Prince Consort, lasted a full hour; and the latter declares that " Bertie acquitted himself *extremely well*." The day after the Confirmation the first Communion was administered, and the religious character of this Royal household is beautifully illustrated by a Memorandum from the Queen, in Sir Theodore Martin's work, to the effect that the Prince Consort "had a very strong feeling about the solemnity of this act, and did not like to appear in company either the evening before or on the day on which he took the sacrament; and he and the Queen almost always dined alone on these occasions."

Following this event, in 1858, it was arranged that, after a brief run into Ireland, the young Prince should take up his residence at the White Lodge in Richmond Park, so as to be away from the world and devote himself entirely to study, and the immediate preparation for a military examination. As companions —to quote a letter of the Prince Consort's—"we appointed three very distinguished young men, of from 23 to 26 years of age, who are to occupy in monthly rotation a kind of equerry's place about him, and from whose more intimate intercourse I anticipate no small benefit to Bertie." One of these was Lord Valletort, eldest son of Lord Mount-Edgecumbe, who succeeded his father in 1861, after two years in the Commons, and has since been Lord Chamberlain and Lord Steward of the Household. Another was Major Teesdale, R.A., of Kars celebrity—now a Major-General, a K.C.M.G., and a V.C. The third was Major Lloyd-Lindsay, V.C.—afterwards a K.C.B., and for many years member of Parliament. In 1885 his services to the militia and volunteers were rewarded with a peerage and the title of Lord Wantage. The Prince Consort was therefore fully justified in his praise of these young men's ability and qualifications.

A little later, all concerned were benefited by the appointment of Colonel Bruce—a brother of Lord Elgin, and his secretary while in Canada—as Governor to the young Prince.   He is described as having all the amiability of his sister, Lady Augusta—who both before and after her marriage with Dean Stanley was such an intimate friend of the Queen's—and as possessing much of the ability of his brother.   At this time the Prince seems to have had a pretty stiff course of study. Dr. Lyon (now Lord) Playfair gave him lectures on chemistry in relation to manufactures, and he was taken at the same time to see the practical working of the problems dealt with.   Dr. Schmitz, the Rector of the High School at Edinburgh, gave him lectures on Roman history.   Italian, German, and French were also being studied, while Mr. Fisher, his future tutor at Oxford, instructed him in law and history generally.   At the same time he was being trained in military evolutions and exercises with the 16th Hussars.

In December, 1859, he went to Oxford, and about the same time Prince Albert writes of another member of the Royal family: " Vicky has developed greatly of late, and yet remains quite a child—of such is the Kingdom of Heaven."   Another note says that " Baby (Princess Beatrice) is the liveliest, cleverest, child I have ever seen," and adds that " the Prince of Wales is working hard at Oxford.   Alfred is in Corfu, and has made the tour of Greece."   In her Diary on the 1st of January following, the Queen observes that " I never remember spending a pleasanter New Year's Day, surrounded by our children and dear Mama.   It is really extraordinary how much our good children did for the day, in reading, reciting, and music."   A little later, on April 25th, she pens a few more characteristic lines—in this case about a member of the Royal family who seems to have been as particularly regarded within the household as she was without.

" To-day is our dear and sweet Alice's sixteenth birthday !   I can hardly believe it possible.   She is a great treasure, and a child who only is a comfort and pleasure to us. May God leave her long with us, and may she ever be blessed, preserved, and protected ! We wished one another warmly joy.   Put on a new dress.   When dressed, we went to fetch our dear, dear Alice, gave her a nosegay, and took her with all the children to the breakfast room."

The two younger children—Prince Leopold, who had been born in 1853, and Princess Beatrice, born in 1857—must have seemed almost like a new family springing up beside the other rapidly growing ones.   It was fortunate for the first-named that he had a father in his early years who was content to watch and wait, and not attempt to force the intellect too soon at the expense of a naturally weak and feeble physique.   This bright and gentle Prince, who was known in after years and until his early death as Duke of Albany, was educated cautiously and with much fear and trembling on his parents' part.   Fond as he was of books they were often kept from him in order to prevent his over-doing a limited store of physical power.   The Prince Consort did not worry him about a future profession or definite work in life, but up to the time of his own death, when the little Prince was nine years old, simply encouraged his progress in a quiet way—

leading him in the direction which makes a man good and leaves greatness of achievement to come after, if it will. How nobly Prince Leopold in his few short years of public life carried out this ideal all the world knows.

The Princess Beatrice knew little of her father. When he died she was only four years old, but with her brother Leopold she naturally became after that sad event a most constant companion of the Queen. And, bitterly as the little Prince at first mourned his father, he was, after all, but a child, and before long had regained a cheerfulness which was natural to his gentle disposition, and which, no doubt, proved a balm to the deeply wounded Queen. Fond of music, and of poultry, and of watching dogs and birds—and games in which sickness so often prevented him from joining—he was at the same time always kind and affectionate, and when in really good health was as exuberant and full of pranks as any other schoolboy. In these years the Royal family saw but little of the bright gaiety and social pleasures which had marked the childhood of its older members, and Prince Leopold was consequently given full opportunity to study, as he grew older, that history and higher constitutional lore which he loved.

But he also devoted himself as strenuously as health would permit to the study of languages, music, and mathematics. And, if there were fewer Court functions and entertainments in these sad years at Windsor and elsewhere, there was much more communication and intercourse on the part of the Queen with private friends and men of note. From these Prince Leopold was quick to benefit, and both Professor Tyndall and Dean Stanley have testified to his ability and studious enthusiasm. From the Dean, his mind is said to have taken such a deep religious impress that at one time he thought seriously of becoming a clergyman. There is certainly no doubt of his love for sacred things, and his frequent conversations upon religious subjects. One great hardship which he had to endure was the impossibility of satisfying a constant longing to see foreign lands and soft southern seas and skies, which the stern necessities of ill-health prevented. With his appearance at Oxford in 1872 ends the home training of this young Prince—the one most like his father in character and pursuits. One reminiscence, however, of those earlier days may be given from the pen of Professor Tyndall :

" It is now more than twenty years since I was invited, with three or four very distinguished men, to go down to Osborne and talk to the children of the Queen upon matters connected with science. Taken from my studies, I did not expect more than familiar conversations; but I found that I had to lecture before Her Majesty herself, and, being entirely undisciplined in the manners of a Court, I fear my behaviour in the presence of the Queen was not what it ought to have been, and my uncertainty in this respect was a source of intense discomfort to me. But on the following morning the discomfort melted away like a cloud in the presence of the cordial, merry laughter and pleasant conversation of the Prince (Leopold), then a little boy. The Prince took me over his little garden, showed me his implements of husbandry, wheelbarrows, spades, rakes, and hoes allotted to him, his brothers, and his sisters, by their most noble and wise father. He showed me their museum and told me to whom each of the objects belonged, and it was a profound comfort to me, for I felt that I was standiug, not in the presence of any hollow artificiality, but in the presence of Royal persons who had changed hollowness and artificiality for the cultivation of those virtues which lie in the power of any upright, wise man, in any grade of society."

It is impossible, of course, to do justice in a limited space to the system of training thus pursued by the Queen and Prince Consort, or to properly describe the home life which environed the Royal family during its period of growth and development. Much that has taken place in this domestic circle has never become known, and never will be; but the Queen herself, in published Journals, and through the Memoranda given to the world in connection with her princely Consort, has furnished sufficient hints for us to understand something at least of the beneficent example and bright home surroundings with which her sons and daughters have been blessed—and through them the Courts and peoples of many another land in Europe. The Royal household under Queen Victoria has not, in fact, resembled that of any other in history or in contemporary records. It has been an example, and many have since followed it, but at the time it was without precedent. The dignity of the Court was one thing, the sacredness of the home another. The Royal children were taught as children, and trained in the ordinary duties and principles of humanity and Christianity before being burdened with Royal functions, and ideas of dignity and splendour suited to their future, but not their present.

They were not, as in some European Courts, appointed to the command of regiments whilst lying in the cradle, or made to drill soldiers before they could walk properly without support. And despite the fact that both the Queen and Prince took their education so seriously—the latter almost looking upon it as the chief business of his life—the young princes were not forced overmuch in their studies, as is the modern custom in ordinary life. They were given plenty to do, and more and more as they grew older and their capacities became known. But it was not a system of burdensome work and severe mental training; it was rather one of developing the mind and body together, and with a view to the just division of work and play, of study and the learning which only comes from experience, and travel, and intercourse with older people. Needless to say also that the princes were trained in a just perception of their constitutional place and duties as soon as they were old enough to understand and appreciate their position. And, as they grew older, it is hard to estimate the value of such practical teachings as both the Queen and their father could give them.

Needless to say also that the Queen looked after the proper domestic training of her daughters. They were taught to do plain sewing as well as fancy work, to play hymns as well as lighter music, to cook every variety of plain food, and to understand the ordinary principles and practice of nursing. They were never taught the principle of marriage for the convenience of the State. To the

Queen a union without love and mutual respect was, and is, abhorrent. Her own marriage had been so perfectly, ideally, happy that she would have been the last in all her dominions to dream of marrying a child for money, or rank, or power. In this she set an example which might well be followed amongst many humbler circles than those of royalty. And in this sentiment, there is no doubt, Prince Albert strongly shared. Lord Carendon, in 1855, told Mr. Greville that the Prince had assured him that there was not a word of truth in the prevailing report of the engagement of the Princess Royal to the young Prince of Prussia. " Nothing," he added, " has ever passed between the parents on the subject, and the union never will take place unless the children should become attached to each other. *There will be no more political marriages.*"

Certainly, if the world can judge—and it has every opportunity of doing so in the brilliant light flashing around a throne—there have not been any such unions in the present Royal family of England. No doubt, reasons of State might have prevented such happy marriages as those of Princess Alice, or the Princess Louise, or the Princess Beatrice. Much higher positions might have been won for her daughters by a little gentle coercion on the part of the Queen, or by a judicious training in the old-time principles of national expediency. But to Her Majesty the home was first, and domestic happiness could not be obtained without mutual affection. Hence one great illustration of the benefits coming from a really royal sentiment working into royal practice, and pervading the lives of innumerable descendants in the minor, as well as the greater, Courts of Europe.

Industry, economy, method, and observance of all Christian duties were scrupulously taught. The Queen's private secretary in the early years of her married life—Mr. George Anson—is authority, in 1847, for the statement that " the Queen's affairs are in such good order and so well managed that she will be able to provide for the whole expense of Osborne out of her income without difficulty." And this involved a cost of at least £200,000. The example thus set must have been brought home to the Prince of Wales through the further fact that £100,000 had already been saved for him at that date from the revenues of the Duchy of Cornwall. But so it was in everything. The Queen and her Royal husband laid the plans and carried out the system of education with earnest care, giving personal attention as well as general supervision, and, above all, offering the potent force of living example as well as wise precept. Hence it is that the name of Her Majesty has become one around which the most cherished sentiments of the home circles of her vast empire can centre as the embodiment of domestic virtue, and the medium through which its blessings have radiated down into every strata of modern society and life.

CHAPTER XI.

Last Days of Wedded Life.

DURING the latter days of the Crimean war a pretty little romance had been going on at Balmoral—not unknown nor unwatched by the royal parents, who had themselves gone through a similar experience some eighteen years before. Prince Frederick William of Prussia was a young man of the highest accomplishments, and possessed of an ability and patriotism which all the world came to afterwards recognize, both in the Franco-German war, and in his brief reign as Frederick I. of Germany. The Princess Royal, in 1855, was little more than a child, but her fifteen years of life had crowned her with a dignity beyond her age, and she was noted for varied accomplishments and a frank kindliness of nature, united with singular self-possession.

It was one of those cases where true love *does* run smooth, and there had been every desire on the part of the Prince of Prussia—afterwards Emperor William I., and a frequent visitor in England—that the match should one day take place. But although the Queen and Prince Albert were not unwilling, they had determined long since to promote no union in which mutual affection was not the central motive and reason. No difficulties were, however, placed in the way of the young people meeting, and on September 20th the Prince Consort wrote to Stockmar that the Prussian Prince was staying at Windsor, that he was greatly attracted by Princess Victoria, and had come, with the consent of his parents and the King of Prussia, to ask for her hand. "I have been much pleased with him," adds Prince Albert, "his chiefly prominent qualities are great straightforwardness, frankness, and honesty. He appears to be free from prejudices and pre-eminently well-intentioned." He then states that "we accepted it (the offer) for ourselves, but requested him to hold it in suspense as regards the other party till after her Confirmation. Till then all the simple unconstraint of girlhood is to continue undisturbed. . . . The seventeenth birthday is to come off before the actual marriage is thought of."

The Prince Consort soon found, however, as so many other parents have done before and since, that such little arrangements—prudent as they might be—would not quite work out in practice, and on the 25th he writes again that "Victoria is greatly excited—still all goes smoothly and prudently. The Prince is really in love, and the little lady does her best to please him. . . . The day after to-morrow the young gentleman takes his departure." But on

THE EARL OF ABERDEEN, K G.

THE EARL OF DERBY, K.G.

the 29th of September he was still there, and the result is recorded in Her Majesty's Journal:

"Our dear Victoria was this day engaged to Prince Frederick William of Prussia, who has been on a visit to us since the 14th. He had already spoken to us on the 20th of his wishes; but we were uncertain, on account of her extreme youth, whether he should speak to her himself, or wait till he came back again. However, we felt that it was better he should do so, and, during our ride up *Craig-na-Ban* this afternoon, he picked a piece of white heather (the emblem of good luck), which he gave to her; this enabled him to make an allusion to his hopes and wishes as they rode down *Glen Gerrioch*, which led to this happy conclusion."

To the Prince Consort and the Queen the match was pleasing upon personal grounds, the former writing on the 2nd of October that "the young people are ardently in love with one another, and the purity, innocence, and unselfishness of the young man have been on his part equally touching." But it was also a matter of gratification on national grounds. Lifted above the natural anti-Prussian feelings of the day in England, and knowing from the relative strength and resources of Prussia and Austria that under a strong ruler the former would eventually come to the top in Germany, they could not but see that the alliance might be good for England in the future, and would certainly result very differently from the unwise anticipations of the *Times*— which took advantage of some rumours about the royal engagement to make a most bitter attack upon Prussia, and upon the young Prince in particular, as a probable "exile and fugitive" in days to come. When the marriage took place, however, three years later, this was all forgotten, or consigned to the oblivion of unrealized and prejudiced prophecies.

Soon after this domestic incident, and the ensuing confirmation of the young Princess, came a visit from the King of Sardinia, whose troops had distinguished themselves in the Crimea, and whose personal ability was to make him famed in history as Victor Emmanuel I.—the King of a free and united Italy. He stayed only a short time, but was shown much during the interval. On December 1st the Queen and Prince Albert took him to Woolwich, the next day to Portsmouth, and thence to London. There the Corporation presented an address; the Queen gave a reception at Buckingham Palace, and conferred the Order of the Garter upon him, besides giving a final great banquet in his honour. The King was accompanied by Count Cavour, and left England on the 5th of the month, after a pleasant and generally beneficial visit—one which included many talks over the situation in the Crimea, and doubtless gave the Queen a further insight into the conditions in Italy, which, during another decade, were to throw Europe into a flame of war and diplomatic discord.

In January the Queen opened Parliament, and during the next two months was deeply concerned in the peace negotiations going on at Paris, and in the result which put an end to the long and disastrous, yet triumphant, Crimean war.   During March an heir to the throne was born in France, and the congratulations of Her Britannic Majesty were so warmly couched that Napoleon replied in terms which sufficiently indicate the personal relations existing between them—even at a time when the diplomatic ties had been very considerably strained.   " I have been greatly touched," wrote the Emperor, " to learn that all your family have shared my joy; and all my hope is that my son may resemble dear little Prince Arthur, and that he may have the rare qualities of your children.   The sympathy shown on this last occasion by the English people is another bond between the two countries, and I hope my son will inherit my feelings of sincere friendship for the Royal family of England, and of affectionate esteem for the great English nation."   In the fine young Prince Imperial's death, while fighting on the sands of Africa under the British flag, this wish was long afterwards mournfully and truly realized.

Meanwhile politics at home had entered upon that period of rest and reaction which followed naturally upon the complications of the Crimean contest, and which, with his diplomatic skill and inimitable personality, helped to keep Lord Palmerston in power—with one brief exception in 1858-9—until his death in 1865.   He had developed in many ways since his controversies with the Queen had shown the faults in his character; and during this long period of power he seems to have steadily risen in her estimation and confidence, until his death came to her as a shock and personal loss only second to the feeling with which she had met the deaths of Sir Robert Peel or the Duke of Wellington.   On April 11th of this year (1856) Her Majesty did a graceful act in writing the Premier and offering him the most coveted of all British honours —the blue ribbon of the Garter—in recognition of the close of the war and his services in that connection.   His reply is an evidently spontaneous expression of mingled pleasure and surprise, and declares in part that:

" The gracious communication which he has this morning received from your Majesty will be preserved by him as in his eyes still more valuable even than the high honour which it announces as your Majesty's intention to confer upon him.   That high and distinguished honour Viscount Palmerston will receive with the greatest pride as a public mark of your Majesty's gracious approbation ; but he begs to be allowed to say that the task which he and his colleagues have had to perform has been rendered comparatively easy by the enlightened views which your Majesty has taken of all the great affairs in which your Majesty's Empire has been engaged, and by the firm and steady support which, in all these important transactions, your Majesty's servants have received from the Crown."

During April the Queen and Prince Albert visited Chatham to inspect the hospital arrangements there ; and Her Majesty's intervention resulted in several practical benefits, to say nothing of the impalpable but powerful influence of kindly smiles and gracious words to the suffering, and worn, and wounded heroes of the war.   From there they went to Aldershot, now becoming a military camp of first-class importance.   On reaching it—April 18th—the

Queen left her carriage and mounted a richly-caparisoned chestnut charger, upon which she reviewed some 14,000 troops—presenting a front of a mile and a half in length. As Her Majesty rode down the long line, with the bayonets flashing in the sun, flags waving, and the bands of twenty regiments giving a musical welcome, the scene must have been very inspiring. Next day the Queen—clad in a Field-Marshal's uniform, the star and ribbon of the Garter, and a dark blue riding skirt—watched the march-past and a series of succeeding manœuvres. A few days later the royal party reviewed the great fleet which had been collected at Spithead to the number of 240 ships-of-war; and as the Queen in her yacht passed down the long line of ships, the flying flags, the roar of the guns, and the cheering of the sailors produced an almost bewildering effect.

Immediately preceding these events, the Queen had anticipated and endeavoured to avert that wholesale reduction of the national armament which the peace and economic school of politicians was now calling for—headed, unfortunately, by Mr. Gladstone, then in the prime and flush of a great financial reputation—and which, a year or two later, became so serious a matter during the Indian mutiny. Writing Lord Palmerston on April 12th, she expressed the hope and expectation that any proposed retrenchments would be made "with great moderation and very gradually; and that the difficulties we had had and the sufferings which we had endured might not be forgotten. To the miserable reductions of the last thirty years," continued the Queen, "are entirely owing our state of helplessness when the war began; and it would be unpardonable if we were to be found in a similar condition when another— and who can tell how soon there may be one?—breaks out. . . . We ought and must be prepared for every eventuality; and we have splendid material in that magnificent little army in the Crimea." The result of this was an attempt at reorganization by the military officials, checked, however, in its fruition by financial considerations—so called. A month later the close of the war was celebrated by a great ball which the Queen gave in the newly completed ball-room of Buckingham Palace.

In July the Queen reviewed the returned Crimean troops at Aldershot, Woolwich, and London. The first occasion was the most noteworthy. Accompanied by the Prince Consort, the Prince of Wales, the King of the Belgians, the Duke of Cambridge, and Lord Panmure, Her Majesty arrived on the grounds during a short break in what had not been "Queen's weather." After the evolutions had been watched for a while, the Crimean regiments were advanced so as to form three sides of a square around the royal carriage; and the officers who had been under fire, together with four men of each troop and company, stepped forward. The Queen then rose in her carriage and addressed the following words to them in that clear, silvery sweetness of voice for which she has always been so distinguished :

"Officers, non-commissioned officers, and soldiers! I wish personally to convey through you to the regiments assembled here this day my hearty welcome on their return to England in health and full efficiency. Say to them that I have watched anxiously over the difficulties and hardships which they have so nobly borne, that I have mourned with deep sorrow over the brave men who have fallen in their country's cause, and that I have felt proud of their valour, which, with their gallant allies, they have displayed on every field.

"I thank God that your dangers are over, while the glory of your deeds remains ; but I know that should your services be again required you will be animated with the same devotion which in the Crimea has rendered you invincible."

The scene which followed was of that emotional, spirit-stirring kind that only a great principle or great cause can properly arouse. The cry of "God save the Queen" echoed from every heart and lip, while helmets and bearskins, shakos and sabres, were waved enthusiastically in the air and kept pace with the long-continued acclamations. Next day—July 9th—London and the Queen and Prince Consort joined in welcoming the Guards. The weather was brilliant and the people enthusiastic, and these two facts speak volumes upon such an occasion. On the previous day a sad incident occurred while Lord Hardinge, the Commander-in-Chief of the army, was having an audience of the Queen. He was standing at a table and speaking, when a stroke of paralysis came without a moment's warning. It was the practical ending of a most useful life, and as Her Majesty very justly said in accepting his resignation shortly afterwards, "The loss of Lord Hardinge's services will be immense to the Queen, the country, and the army." And then she added the kindly hope that "she might still reckon on his advice and assistance on matters of importance, though he will no longer command her noble army." But it was not to be, and two months later he had passed away.

During August a visit was paid England by the Prince and Princess of Prussia, and the public announcement made of the Princess Royal's engagement to their son. A very different visitor at Balmoral in the succeeding month was Miss Florence Nightingale, from whom the Queen heard with intense interest an account of her experience and work in the Crimea, and of whom the Prince Consort writes in his Diary : "She put before us all the defects of our present military hospital system and the reforms that are needed. We are much pleased with her ; she is extremely modest." Early in 1857 following, Lord Palmerston appealed to the country upon his China war policy, and was strongly supported —prominent peace advocates like Bright and Cobden and Milner-Gibson being defeated by large majorities. The Queen and Prince Consort were in complete sympathy now with the Palmerstonian policy, and the latter wrote significantly to the Dowager-Duchess of Coburg on April 9th, that "the apostles of peace have been turned out by the people neck and crop. Not because the people do not love peace and are not greedy of money, but because they love their own importance and their own honour, and will not submit to be tyrannized over by the peace-at-any-price people."

On April 14th another daughter was born to the Queen, and baptized as Beatrice Mary Victoria Feodore. The first name, wrote the Queen to her uncle Leopold on May 5th, was "a fine old name, borne by three of the Plantagenet Princesses." Mary was after Her Majesty's aunt, the Duchess of Gloucester, Victoria came from the Duchess of Kent, and Feodore was in remembrance of the Queen's half-sister. The same day that this letter was written, Prince Albert unveiled a statue of the Queen at Salford, and made a brief and thoughtful speech, about which the *Spectator* declared: "There are few men who could put the pith of our Constitution into a sentence so tersely and clearly as the first gentleman in our commonwealth." The phrase so much praised by this critical organ expressed the hope that the future inhabitants of Salford would find, in contemplation of the statue, "an assurance that when loyalty and attachment to the Sovereign, *as the representative of the institutions of the country*, are linked to an ardent love of progress, founded upon self-reliance and self-improvement, a country cannot fail to prosper under favour of the Almighty."

The coming marriage of the Princess Royal now rendered it necessary that some provision should be made by Parliament; and Prince Albert, with that foresight which is such an important part of true statesmanship, desired to obviate the necessity of future appeals for grants, by a settlement providing for all the Royal children as they attained their majority or were married. Such an arrangement would have been both dignified and beneficial, and would have represented the wish of a great mass of the people—then and since. But, from some feeling of timidity or misgiving, the Cabinet could not agree upon the subject, and Parliament was therefore simply asked for the individual dowry of £40,000, and an annuity of £4,000. It was granted by a vote of 321 to 14 in the House of Commons, and with a good-will which showed that Prince Albert was right in thinking that this was the time to have settled the whole question. A letter, written by him immediately afterwards, says that "this only shows how little politicians, in their over-anxiety, often know what the feeling of the country is. Seeing how marked was the desire to keep questions relating to the Royal family aloof from the pressure of party conflict, and to have them *settled*, it would, I believe, have been an easy matter to have carried through the future endowments of them all, according to the Chancellor of the Exchequer's (Sir Cornewall Lewis) and Palmerston's original plan, which was subsequently dropped by the Cabinet; and I more than regret that this was not done."

During June, the Court at Windsor and in London was very gay and busy. The Crystal Palace festival, and a Royal visit to Manchester, the christening of Princess Beatrice, and various balls, concerts, and *levées*, the visits of Prince

Frederick (or, as he was called in the home circle, "Fritz") of Prussia, King Leopold of Belgium, Dom Pedro of Portugal, and the Archduke of Austria, al followed and crowded upon each other. The coming of the Archduke Maximilian bears a most mournful memory. He was only twenty-five years old at this time, and had just been betrothed to Princess Charlotte of Belgium. The Queen had congratulated the latter personally, and, during this brief visit of the Archduke to London, seems to have been very favourably impressed with his bearing and character. Writing to King Leopold, shortly afterwards, she declares it impossible to say how much they like him, "he is charming, so clever, natural, kind, and amiable, so English in his feelings and likings, and so anxious for the best understanding between England and Austria." Even so critical an observer as the Prince Consort was completely won over by his manner and personality. "You have conquered my sincerest friendship," he wrote him, later on, "which, resting, as it does, on a similarity of taste and thinking, promises to be firmly knit for life by the ties of kinship." The Princess Charlotte also came to England for a few days, and the Royal letters of the moment describe a bright and happy girl of seventeen, devoted to her lover, and with every prospect of a long and prosperous career. Yet in six years from this time the unfortunate Emperor of Mexico had been murdered by a portion of his own subjects, while carrying out his ambitious but noble aim of making a strong and united country out of inconceivably warring elements—and the poor Empress Charlotte had become insane for life.

On the 26th of June, amidst a vast concourse of 100,000 people concentrated in Hyde Park; surrounded by 4,900 troops, and accompanied by a brilliant suite ; Her Majesty decorated sixty-two Crimean veterans with the Victoria Cross. Seated on horseback, she pinned this mark and token of exceptional bravery and devotion to their country, with her own hand, upon the breast of the hero who had won it. It was the first investiture of this much-prized decoration, and the wisdom of creating it by royal warrant in the previous year has been fully justified by the pride felt in receiving and holding what has come to be a greater honour to the soldier or the sailor than the Garter is to a nobleman. The latter is only conferred when no additional title can enhance the reputation or the position of the recipient, and is valued as indicating that fact. The former stamps a great deed with national approval, and lifts a perhaps otherwise humble hero into the full blaze of fame. The day before this event the Queen had conferred upon Prince Albert by her own volition the title of Prince Consort—which had long been his popular designation. "I think," she says, in a letter to Leopold of Belgium, "it is wrong that my husband should not have an English title. I should have preferred its being done by Act of Parliament."

In August the French Emperor and Empress came over on a private visit to the Queen at Osborne. As a result of various complications with Austria and Prussia and Russia, Napoleon wished to secure himself against misunderstandings, and also to strengthen the English alliance by a personal talk with Her Majesty. On the 20th of May previously, Lord Clarendon had written Prince Albert that:

"M. de Persigny describes the Emperor as being intent upon this project, and as attaching the utmost importance to it in order to *clear* his own ideas, to guide his policy, and to prevent by personal communication with the Queen, your Royal Highness and Her Majesty's Government, the disagreements and misunderstandings which the Emperor thinks will arise from the want of such communication. . . In the Emperor's present frame of mind and his evident alarm lest it should be thought that the alliance has been in any way shaken, I cannot entertain a doubt that much good might be done, or, at all events, that much mischief might be averted, by the Emperor being allowed to pay his respects to Her Majesty in the way he proposes."

The visit was a most successful one, and in long and confidential conversations with the Queen and Prince Albert the existing difficulties were modified or removed from the Emperor's mind, and his letter to the Queen after his departure indicates the cordial nature of his sentiments. "I believe," he says, "that after passing a few days in your Majesty's society one becomes better." And Lord Clarendon, writing to the Queen on August 20th, declares that "one cannot over-estimate the importance of the recent visit, for *the Emperor is France*, and France, moreover, in her best form, because he is thus capable of generous emotions and of appreciating the truth, and her alliance with England has consequently been re-toned and invigorated at Osborne." Meanwhile, the mutiny had broken out in India, and the Queen's correspondence of the period shows how deep were her anxieties, and how excellent was the advice given to her ministers—to say nothing of the personal encouragement afforded Lord Canning during that fiery ordeal. More active work and increased reinforcements was the Queen's motto during the early stages of the rebellion, and at a time when even the Cabinet thought it would be easy to crush the rebels.

Toward the end of August the Queen and Prince Albert paid a brief yachting visit to Alderney and Cherbourg, and were enthusiastically received by the peasantry and hospitably entertained by the local officials. The colossal nature of the works and fortifications in connection with Cherbourg caused Her Majesty some anxiety in the event of any possible and sudden descent being made from there upon English shores. Immediately upon her return detailed reports were called for as to the progress of the defence works at Portsmouth, the number of ships in commission, and other particulars of the kind. The mere enquiry did good, and the pressure of increasingly bad news from India did more. Of the latter trouble, Her Majesty wrote the King of the Belgians on September 2nd, that "we are in sad anxiety about India, which engrosses all our attention. . . The horrors committed on the poor ladies, women and children, are unknown in these ages, and make one's blood run cold. Altogether the whole is so much more distressing than the Crimea, where there was glory and honourable warfare, and where the poor women and children were safe."

With the new year of 1858 came the preparations for the first of those Royal weddings which have since been so familiarized and brought home to the nation. The earliest public function in connection with it was a Royal visit to Her Majesty's Theatre, where Mr. and Mrs. Keeley, Miss Helen Faucit, and Mr. Phelps performed, and at which a brilliant and overflowing audience was present. The Queen says in her Diary, and with truth, that when the National Anthem was sung, "all the house rising and the vast stage crowded with those who could not find room in the body of the house, the scene was one not readily to be forgotten, as it certainly could not have found its parallel in Europe." A great ball followed at Buckingham Palace, with 1,000 guests in attendance, and this was succeeded by an equally imposing State dinner during the next evening. Various entertainments ensued and several more visits to the opera, until at last the wedding day arrived, and the Queen's Journal of January 25th says:

"The second most eventful day in my life as regards feelings. I felt as if I were being married over again myself, only much more nervous, for I had not that blessed feeling which I had then, which raises and supports one, of giving myself up for life to him whom I loved and worshipped—then and ever. . . . Got up, and, while dressing, dearest Vicky came to see me, looking well and composed, and in a fine quiet frame of mind. She had slept more quietly and better than before. Gave her a pretty book called 'The Bridal Offering.' "

The wedding took place in the Chapel Royal at St. James' Palace, and the procession passed in state through throngs of cheering people, and under the pleasant influences of a bright, clear day. The Queen wore a train of lilac velvet, with a petticoat of lilac and silver moire antique, a flounce of Honiton lace, and a corsage ornamented with diamonds. The Koh-i-noor was worn as a brooch, and a diadem of diamonds and pearls as a head-dress. The Prince Consort and King Leopold wore Field Marshal's uniforms, and to the latter Her Majesty refers, in her description of the event, as "himself the widower of Princess Charlotte of this country, and Mama's brother, and one of the wisest kings in Europe." The Princesses Alice, Helena, and Louise walked hand in hand behind their mother in the procession up the church, and wore white lace over pink satin, with daisies in their hair. The bridegroom looked very stately, and a thorough soldier, in his uniform of a Prussian general. The bride wore a white dress of moire and Honiton lace, with wreaths of orange and myrtle blossoms, and a train borne by eight bridesmaids, whom the Queen's Journal describes as "looking charming in white tulle, with wreaths and bouquets of pink roses and white heather."

The marriage was performed by the Archbishop of Canterbury, who was assisted by the Bishops of London, Oxford, and Chester, and the Dean of

LORD STRATFORD DE REDCLIFFE, K.G., G.C.B.

RIGHT HON. SIR PHILIP CURRIE, G.C.B.

Windsor. A scene of genuine emotion followed the close of the ceremony, and was succeeded by a tremendous popular reception from the multitude assembled in front of Buckingham Palace when the Royal party returned from the chapel. So continuous was the cheering that Her Majesty and the children, and the newly-married couple, at last appeared on the balcony and bowed to the enthusiastic people. Meantime the day had been celebrated as a general holiday throughout the United Kingdom, and in the evening London was brilliantly illuminated. The brief honeymoon was spent at Windsor, and on the 31st of January the young couple left for Berlin, after the Prince had been made a Knight of the Garter. For a time the Queen felt her daughter's loss keenly, but it was gradually made up to her by the growing and sympathetic influence of Princess Alice. In a public sense the Royal wedding was eminently popular. Most of the old prejudices of Crimean days were gone, and the Prince Consort was able to tell Stockmar, on February 3rd, that "Of the touching enthusiasm and sympathy of all ranks of the people you can form no conception. Down to the humblest cottage the marriage has been regarded as a family affair."

Meanwhile Lord Palmerston had been dealing with the preliminaries of a political crisis. His influence, though still great in the country, was waning in Parliament, partly from causes inseparable from restless Liberal organizations ; partly from his too dictatorial and assured personal manner. When, therefore, the Orsini bomb explosion took place in Paris, its ultimate effect was a political explosion and upheaval in London. Napoleon III. very naturally asked for some law by which assassins, or attempted assassins, like Orsini, should be prevented from making England their place of refuge and plotting headquarters. Very naturally, Lord Palmerston, who had always liked the Emperor, responded with a bill in the House of Commons—though without answering the despatch. Very naturally, also, people woke up suddenly and strongly to an idea that the French Emperor was dictating English legislation. That settled the matter, and on February 19th the Conspiracy Bill was defeated by a majority of nineteen. Nothing was left but resignation, although Lord Derby, who was immediately sent for by the Queen, told Her Majesty in a subsequent communication that Lord Clarendon had just " made an admirable speech in explanation of the course which the late Government had pursued, and which, had it been delivered in the House of Commons on the subject of the amendment, would probably have deprived Lord Derby of the honour of addressing your Majesty on the present occasion."

For the moment, however, Palmerston was under a dark cloud, and the new administration had anything but an easy road to run—with a normal Liberal majority in the Commons of two to one. Nor was the Cabinet very strong individually. With an interval of one year the Conservatives had not been in office since 1846, and their supply of first-class or experienced men was small. Mr.

Disraeli, of course, as Chancellor of the Exchequer, was a host in himself, but the Peelites—Gladstone, Sidney Herbert, the Duke of Newcastle, and Earl Grey —definitely refused to join, and became finally merged in the Liberal ranks. Lord Malmesbury was Foreign Secretary, Mr. Walpole Home Secretary, Sir John Pakington First Lord of the Admiralty, General Peel Secretary for War. Lord Ellenborough was at the Board of Control, Sir Frederick Thesiger became Chancellor with the title of Lord Chelmsford, while Mr. (afterwards Earl) Cairns took the first step in a great political and judicial career by becoming Solicitor-General.

Following this event came the readjustment of affairs in India, and the transferring of the Government from the East India Company to the Crown. Without going into the details of the successive bills which were introduced before the final settlement was effected, it may be said that Her Majesty took no small part in the work of reorganization. In the first measure presented to Parliament, Lord Ellenborough, whose department then controlled Indian affairs, had included a provision for certain *elected* members of the Indian Council. As soon as the draft reached the Queen she urged that this proposal be reconsidered by the Cabinet, but, upon being assured that the clause was absolutely necessary to the passage of the bill, refrained from doing more than to write Lord Ellenborough that she:

"Felt the greatest apprehension as to the political soundness and wisdom of giving to the ten pound householders of Manchester, Liverpool, Belfast, Glasgow, and the city of London, the election of five members of the Council, the constituency not being either directly interested in India, or at all peculiarly fit to judge of Indian matters, and the arbitrary selection of five towns out of the three kingdoms not appearing to the Queen a just distribution of an important political right. She is afraid that these elections will be turbulent and democratic, and that the effect of an inadequate popular representation will be a future desire to give the nine seats to be filled by the nomination of the Crown to other great towns, which the Crown will have difficulty in resisting, as the principle of an English Parliamentary constitution is admitted into the bill."

The proposal was, of course, soon found to be impracticable, and even the Radicals would have nothing to do with it—Mr. Bright calling that particular clause "claptrap." Eventually a satisfactory measure was passed by the agreement of both parties, and the curtain rung down upon the great history of the East India Company, and the stormy scenes of slaughter and suffering which had shrouded the preceding year in gloom. On June 14th, the Queen and Prince Albert escaped from the heat and fatigues of the London season for a brief visit to Lord Leigh at Stoneleigh Abbey, and to Lord Warwick at Warwick Castle. In passing through Birmingham a tremendous reception was given the Queen, and some of the mottoes and scrolls are worth remembering. "Victoria, the People's Friend," was one. "The Queen, Our Nation's Pride," and "Victoria, the Queen of Peace," were others. At least one effort was made at poetry in honour of the recent Royal wedding. It was sufficiently striking—

> " God bless Prince Frederick of Prussia's bright star !
> Health to the blooming Rosebud afar."

At Stoneleigh Her Majesty found genuine pleasure in what her Journal calls the cool and refreshing air, and the reception prepared at this " stately home of England," and spontaneously seconded by cheering thousands on the roads and in the park, was all that even such a Sovereign could desire—although some of its latter manifestations became perhaps a little irksome. Following this came a State visit to Cherbourg, where a great French naval display was about to take place in honour of the completion of the works. Although originally built as a menace to England, they could hardly be considered such so long as Napoleon was friendly; and, as Lord Malmesbury wrote the Queen on June 24th, "Nothing has so favourable an influence on the Emperor's mind as these personal interviews with your Majesty." Hence the visit which took place on August 4th— the Queen, Prince Albert, and the Prince of Wales sailing from Osborne in the Royal yacht, and being received at Cherbourg by the Emperor and Empress of the French. It was a great reception.

The *Times* declared that it surpassed expectation as it defied description. The thunderous salutes of the great guns were absolutely unique in the volume of sound produced ; and the same paper says that " the ring of fire seemed not only to embrace the town, but to extend far into the country, up among little ravines where no one ever dreamed that guns lay lurking ; at the top of picturesque eminences, where one fancied only villages and rural cottages could exist ; around thick clumps of trees and flanking yellow cornfields came the same dreadful uproar ; till it seemed as if all France, even from her hills and mountain-tops, were doing honour to the advent of the Queen of England." One of the incidents of the visit was a State dinner on board the French Admiral's ship, at which both the Emperor and the Prince Consort had to make speeches. As the eyes of Europe were turned upon Cherbourg at the moment, it was a somewhat trying occasion, and the Queen's Journal records her intense nervousness during the meal and while the Prince was speaking. Her Majesty adds that when it was all over they discussed the emotion they had undergone, the Emperor having " changed colour," and the Empress having also been very nervous. " I shook so I could not drink my cup of coffee." The departure came on the 6th, after a brilliant display of fireworks and an illumination which turned night into day.

A few days later a brief visit was paid the Prince and Princess of Prussia at Babelsberg—their country house near Potsdam—and the Queen and Prince Consort had the pleasure of also seeing their daughter, surrounded by every evidence of popularity and happiness and good work. Berlin was then visited, and many memorials of Frederick the Great inspected with warm interest. The

King did not welcome them in person—indeed, the mental aberration which had long been threatening made the appointment of a Régent necessary two months later. Greatly to the pleasure of the Queen, the position was filled by the heir to the throne and father-in-law of the Princess Royal. Following this period of pleasure came one of prolonged anxiety over the situation in Europe. The French were restless and wanted war of some sort. The Emperor was anxious to keep his position secure and popular. Italy was in a turmoil under the domination of Austria. Hence the danger of a French war with Austria on behalf of Italy, and the efforts now made by the Queen to promote peace.

Her Majesty first wrote to Napoleon on February 4th, 1859, and then a little later sent Lord Cowley on a confidential mission to Vienna, bearing an autograph letter to the Austrian Emperor, in which the Queen offered to personally mediate between the two Powers. For the time negotiations were renewed, but by May it was seen that they were useless, and the war inevitable. Austria and France had 220,000 troops in Sardinian territory by this time, and before long the conflict took its course. About this period a great debate took place in the Commons, which Mr. Disraeli, as the leader of the House, described in one of those daily reports to the Queen which now occupy such an historically valuable place in the archives of Windsor—including as they do the summarized and crystallized opinion of passing events formed by British leaders from the beginning of the reign. It was the 22nd of March, and he wrote as follows:

"A night of immense power and excitement. Two of the greatest speeches ever delivered in Parliament—by Sir Edward Lytton and the Solicitor-General. . . . Deaf, fantastic, modulating his voice with difficulty, sometimes painful—at first almost an object of ridicule to the superficial—Lytton occasionally reached even the sublime, and perfectly enchained his audience. His description of the English constitution, his analysis of democracy—as rich and more powerful than Burke's. Sir Hugh Cairns devoted an hour to a reply to Lord John Russell's resolution, and to a vindication of the Government (Reform) Bill, which charmed everyone by its lucidity, and controlled everyone by its logic. When he had in the most masterly manner, and with a concinnity which none can equal, closed the business part of his address, he directed himself to the political portion of the theme, and having literally demolished the mover of the amendment sat down amid universal cheers."

But this was the beginning of a crisis, and all Mr. Disraeli's characteristic brilliancy could not, and probably did not, attempt to disguise the situation from the Queen. It may be said in this connection that it was the incisive and clever style of these daily letters which first attracted Her Majesty to the character and views of the great leader who was now forcing his way to the front. His bitter attacks upon Sir Robert Peel in a previous decade had been more than unpleasant to her, and it is probable that up to this time he had been very far indeed from being a favourite in any sense of the word. During April the House was dissolved as a result of the defeat of the Ministry on their Reform

Bill, and a Liberal majority once more returned. The Queen opened Parliament on the 7th of June, and a non-confidence motion was at once carried in the Commons. The resignation of Lord Derby, which followed, placed Her Majesty in an awkward position between the rival and equal claims of Lord Palmerston and Lord John Russell.

It therefore appeared to the Queen that a middle course would be best, and she sent for Lord Granville, writing autograph and personal letters to the other two statesmen asking their co-operation. Lord Palmerston consented to serve, but Lord John refused to take a place under Lord Granville. Palmerston was accordingly called upon, and formed a Ministry which lasted till his death in 1865. Unfortunately, Lord John Russell insisted upon having the Foreign Office, and this necessitated the leaving out of Lord Clarendon, a most able Minister, who naturally would not take another post. But it was a strong Government, including, as it did, all sections of the Liberal party. The old Whigs were represented by Lord Granville, Lord Campbell, Sir G. C. Lewis, Sir George Grey, and Sir Charles Wood—afterwards Lord Halifax. The Dukes of Newcastle and Argyll, Lord Elgin, Mr. Gladstone, Mr. S. Herbert, and Mr. Cardwell represented the Peelites. The Duke of Somerset and Mr. Milner-Gibson conciliated the extreme Radicals. Mr. Cobden refused a place in the Ministry.

During September and October, the Queen and the Prince Consort stayed at Balmoral for a time, and the latter did much deer-stalking in the Highlands. They also opened the Glasgow Waterworks at Loch Katrine, paid a brief visit to Edinburgh and one to Chester—near which they stopped at Penrhyn Castle, the seat of Mr. Douglas Pennant—afterwards Lord Penrhyn. Later on the Prince and Princess Frederick of Prussia stayed for nearly a month at Windsor. With the new year came many perplexing problems in Italy, Austria, and France, and much correspondence and study in the same connection. The Queen opened Parliament on the 24th of January, 1860, and about two weeks later wrote Lord John Russell a pretty sharp letter relating to the French Emperor's designs upon Savoy. It began by stating that " Lord Cowley's report, and the telegram following it, are most unsatisfactory. We have been made regular dupes (which the Queen apprehended and warned against all along). The return to an English alliance, universal peace, respect for treaties, commercial fraternity, etc., etc., were the blinds to cover before Europe a policy of spoliation." Other communications followed, upon this vexed question, and on June 23rd, as an outcome of the situation, Her Majesty reviewed a body of 20,000 volunteers in Hyde Park, and a few days later opened the first meeting of the National Rifle Association at Wimbledon.

These functions gave a great impetus to the already enthusiastic and growing volunteer movement, and in a speech at the Trinity House dinner following the review Prince Albert referred to the latter as "a scene which will never fade from the memory of those who had the good fortune to be present—the representatives of the independence, education, and industry of this conntry in arms, to testify their devotion to their country and their readiness to lay down their lives in its defence." Following this, in August, came a great review of Scotch volunteers at Edinburgh, an immense popular reception to the Queen, and a brief stay at Holyrood Palace. There were 22,000 volunteers and 200,000 spectators at this review and, says the Prince Consort in a private letter, " the French are as much out of humour at this demonstration as Messrs. Cobden and Bright." After a sojourn at Balmoral in September, the Queen and Prince, accompanied by Princess Alice and a large suite, left for a visit to Coburg. Though very enjoyable, it was marred by an accident in which Prince Albert was nearly killed. He was alone in an open carriage drawn by four horses, with the driver on the box-seat, when the animals took fright and became uncontrollable. Seeing a railway-crossing before them—closed with a bar and with a wagon standing in front of it—the Prince very wisely jumped out before the maddened horses could reach the obstacle. He was only bruised, while some of the horses were killed, the coachman seriously wounded, and the carriage smashed to pieces.

About this time the Princess Alice became engaged to Prince Louis of Hesse—a young man of good family, character, and ability. The Queen's Journal of November 30th, some little time after their return from Germany, records the event. " After dinner, while talking to the gentlemen, I perceived Alice and Louis talking before the fireplace more earnestly than usual, and when I passed to go to the other room both came up to me, and Alice, in much agitation, said he had proposed to her, and he begged for my blessing. I could only squeeze his hand and say ' certainly,' and that we would see him in our room later." To Baron Stockmar the Prince Consort announced this family occurrence three days later :

" Close on the heels of my last letter comes this to announce to you the betrothal of Alice to Prince Louis of Hesse. You, like ourselves, will have expected this event, but you will not the less share our joy at it when you are told that the young people are sincerely attached to each other, and justify the hope that they will one day find their mutual happiness in marriage. We like Louis better every day because of his unaffectedly genial and cordial temper, his great modesty, and a very childlike nature, united with strict morality, and genuine goodness and dignity."

The Parliamentary grant asked for by the Ministry early in 1861 was £30,000, and £6,000 as the annuity. The Prince once more tried to get the question of other dowries settled for good, but, as a private letter says : " Gladstone, however, sees the greatest difficulties, which are probably imaginary." On the 16th of March following, in this year so stamped with sorrow for the Queen, she lost her much-loved mother—the Duchess of Kent. It had not been a prolonged illness, though a somewhat painful one, and up to the last day no fatal termination was expected. Her Majesty felt it terribly. "I went into the room again after a few minutes," says the Royal diary, "and gave one look. My darling mother was sitting as she had done before, but was already white! O God! How awful! How mysterious! But what a blessed end! Her gentle spirit at rest, her sufferings over. But I . . . who had lost the mother I so tenderly loved, from whom for these forty-one years I had never been parted, except for a few weeks, what was my case? My childhood—everything seemed to crowd upon me at once. I seemed to have lived through a life, to have become old. What I had dreaded and fought off, the idea of years, had come and must be borne. The blessed future meeting and *her* peace and rest must henceforth be my comfort."

The death of the Duchess excited deep and sincere sympathy in the country. Her life had been so noble in deed and so prolific of good in the principles taught her child that universal respect and esteem had justly been her lot. Both Houses of Parliament at once voted addresses of condolence, and through the speeches of Lord Granville and Lord Derby, and particularly Mr. Disraeli, further proferred their sympathies. The latter's speech beautifully voiced the popular sentiment. "The ties," said he, "which united Her Majesty to her lamented parent were not only of an intimate, but a peculiar character. In the history of our reigning house none were ever placed as the widowed Princess and her Royal child. Never before devolved on a delicate sex a more august responsibility. How these great duties were encountered—how fulfilled—may be read in the conscience of a grateful and loyal people." And then he added, in words which had a touching application to the even greater loss which was to follow, "It is generally supposed that the anguish of affection is scarcely compatible with the pomp of power, but that is not so in the present instance. She who reigns over us has elected, amid all the splendour of empire, to establish her life on the principle of domestic love."

The brief period which followed between the death of the Queen's mother and the fatal illness of the Prince Consort was passed by the latter in almost continuous labour. He had by this time assumed so many public and private duties, and carried on his immense work so systematically and steadily, that it is a question if even the Queen knew what a strain it was upon his mental, nervous, and physical system. The Duchess of Kent had now left him sole executor of the property which she had willed the Queen, and the consequent examination of many documents, and financial arrangements in connection with the estate, added one more burden to his strenuous and crowded life. But no single duty can be blamed for the result; it was the accumulation of responsibilities and work which hastened the inevitable break-down of a system never very strong.

CHAPTER XII.

DEATH OF THE PRINCE CONSORT.

FOR many years Prince Albert had been piling one duty upon another; one burden on top of the other. Constant in every possible mark of affection to his royal wife; unceasing in his devotion to the family which had grown up around them; anxious to an extreme degree about the condition and progress of the people; active in every kind of good work and charitable deed; busy in a never-ending and ever-increasing round of public functions and speech-making; studious in the widest literary and intellectual sense; watchful of all foreign politics and home affairs; it is little wonder that a never very powerful physique should have at last given way, and collapsed with a suddenness which crushed the heart of the Queen and left a nation mourning the loss, which in all its measure of greatness was soon brought home to them.

The disposition of the Prince Consort seems to have been such that he was continually spurred on to fresh work and wider fields of activity by a keen sense of the responsibilities of his high position as well as by circumstances which—arising naturally from time to time—afforded such splendid scope for his useful ambitions. But it was also inevitable that nature would sooner or later assert itself, and either check the continued accretion of fresh labours which was going on by a prolonged illness, or, as unfortunately happened, touch with fatal accuracy the springs of life itself. For years past the Prince had been adding to his stores of knowledge in every direction. To quote the tribute of Sir Theodore Martin:

"Ministers of State found him as familiar as themselves with the facts immediately connected with the working of their own departments. Ambassadors returning from their legations were struck to find how completely he had at command every significant detail of what had happened within the sphere of their special observations. Diplomatists proceeding for the first time to some foreign court learned, in an interview with the Prince, not merely the exact state of affairs which they would find awaiting them, but very frequently the character of the Sovereign and statesmen with whom they would have to deal."

Such a mastery of details could only result from a steady and systematized labour in itself enough for a man's whole time. But when there were combined with this the claims of politics and constitutional development at home; the questions of science and art, and social improvement; the management of an immense correspondence; the duties of an affectionate husband and father,

JOHN EARL RUSSELL, K.G., G.C.M.G.

THE BLUE DRAWING-ROOM AT BUCKINGHAM PALACE.

and those of a practically confidential secretary to the Queen; it became too much for even the most robust health to endure year in and year out. Up to within a few weeks of his death he was busy arranging the future household for the Princess Alice, and the details of Prince Leopold's journey to Cannes, where he was to spend the winter. Then he had made several visits to London to inspect alterations in progress at Buckingham Palace, and preparations which were being made to fit Marlborough House as a residence for the Prince of Wales, who was now entering his twenty-first year. About the same time, also, he presided over the annual meeting of the Agricultural Society, and took an active part in arrangements for the great International Exhibition of 1862, which had been fortunate enough to procure his patronage as honorary president.

Though feeling very unwell—"weak and tired," as the Queen's Diary of November 23rd, 1861, says—and being greatly troubled with sleeplessness, he was even then taking an active part in public matters. The last service he rendered the State was indeed a characteristic one. The Trent affair had just occurred, and the rash action of the American man-of-war in taking the Confederate envoys, Mason and Slidell, out of a British ship had thrown the relations of the two countries into a seething cauldron of warlike controversy. Public opinion in England was greatly excited; preparations for war were being pushed on apace, and it was currently believed that the seizure was a deliberate insult offered by direct orders from the Washington Government. Even Lord Palmerston believed this to be the case, and Lord Lyons, the British Minister to the United States, wrote on the 19th of November that there was little probability of the attack upon "the Trent" being disavowed. "I don't think it likely they will give in," he observed, "but I do not think it impossible they may do so, particularly if the next news from England brings note of warlike preparation and determination on the part of the Government and the people."

It was under these circumstances that the Cabinet met on the 29th of November, and, as Lord Palmerston wrote to the Queen, concluded that Her Majesty "should be advised to demand reparation and redress." They were to meet again the next day, he added, to consider a despatch embodying their conclusions for submission to the Queen. It reached her in due course, and so anxious was the Prince regarding the affair that he got out of his bed, "looking very wretched," and, in a handwriting which shows visible weakness in the original draft, penned his last political Memorandum. It was written in the Queen's name, and, as now seen, includes sundry changes made by Her Majesty afterwards in the text. The suggestions breathed a restraint and wisdom which were lacking in the proposed despatches to Lord Lyons, and, in fact, left a loophole by which a proud and sensitive people might escape from the mess they had got into without disgrace. The Cabinet were quick to see and accept the alterations advised, and the course thus proposed by the Prince and accepted by the Queen and her Ministry resulted in the release of Mason and Slidell, and averted an almost imminent war. A little more than a month later, and after the Prince Consort's lamented death, Lord Palmerston wrote in this connection to the Queen, as follows:

"There can be no doubt that, as your Majesty observes, the alterations made in the despatch to Lord Lyons contributed essentially to the satisfactory settlement of the dispute. But these alterations were only one of innumerable instances of the tact and judgment, and the power of nice discrimination, which excited Lord Palmerston's constant and unbounded admiration."

But this was the last effort of a keen intelligence, the final bit of work wrung from a weakened frame. From that day until December 14th, when the end came, the Prince grew worse—fitfully at first, steadily towards the last. On Sunday, the 1st of December, he was able to go to the Windsor chapel with the Queen, looking, however, as Her Majesty's Diary says, "very wretched and ill." Shivering fits, sleeplessness, restlessness, and depression followed. Feverish symptoms were not immediately observed by Dr. Jenner and Sir James Clark, who were in attendance, and he told them, in connection with news of the death of the King of Portugal—a great friend of himself and the Queen's—that it was just as well *his* trouble was not typhoid, as it would, he felt sure, prove fatal.

It is a curious fact that not very long before this illness he had said to the Queen: "I do not cling to life. You do, but I set no store by it. If I knew that those I loved were well cared for, I should be quite ready to die to-morrow." And he added prophetically, "I am sure if I had a severe illness I should give up at once." The truth is that although up to a few weeks of the attack he had been as active as he ever was in his life—hunting, shooting, and walking in moments of enforced freedom from work—his vitality was really gone, and when the fatal fever finally developed out of an enfeebled condition there was no available fund of strength to fight it with. Day by day he seemed to grow worse, though with alternations of transient improvement and hopefulness. From the 7th of December the result became more than doubtful, and the agonizing anxiety of the Queen was only soothed by the watchful, constant care of the Princess Alice, whose unselfish love for her mother made her put aside the keen sense of her own bitter pain in the effort to alleviate the sufferings of another.

Though only eighteen, the characteristics which afterwards showed themselves in times of war in her husband's country, and in days of sorrow within her own household, now won the admiration and sympathy of everybody. As the *Times* well said: "It is impossible to speak too highly of the strength of mind and self-sacrifice shown by Princess Alice during these dreadful days. Her Royal Highness has certainly understood that it was her duty to be the help and support of her mother in her great sorrow, and it was in a great measure due to her that the Queen has been able to bear with such wonderful resignation the irreparable loss that so suddenly and terribly befell her." During his last Sunday on earth the Prince was moved into a more comfortable room —as it happened, the one in which George IV. and William IV. had died. Princess Alice was with him, the Queen being for the moment almost prostrated with grief—living, as her Diary puts it, "in a dreadful dream." The Princess played his favourite hymns, while he gazed out of the window at the sky and fleeting clouds. It was during these last days that his deep religious feeling came to him as an unutterable blessing. "Were you asleep, dear papa?" asked the Princess on this particular afternoon, as he lay with his eyes closed and hands folded. "Oh, no," was the reply, "but I had such sweet thoughts."

And often during the brief period that followed, in varying but always characteristic ways, this inward peace subdued the restlessness and feverish irritability caused by disease. The end came on the 14th of December. During the morning of the day the Queen had retired for a little into the adjoining room, but hearing the Prince's breathing become worse she hurried back and found him bathed in perspiration, which the doctors, with a pitiable attempt at consolation, said might be an effort of nature to throw off the fever. Bending over the dying man, she whispered: "'Tis your own little wife!" and he bowed his head and kissed her. As night drew near, and the darkness of death came down upon that chamber in England's royal home, the Queen, and the Prince of Wales, the Princess Alice, and the Princess Helena, knelt by the bedside in speechless sorrow, while physicians and attendants stood near by. Let Sir Theodore Martin's beautiful words draw the veil over that last sad scene:

"In the solemn hush of the mournful chamber there was such grief as has rarely hallowed any deathbed. A great light which had blessed the world, and which the mourners had but yesterday hoped might long bless it, was waning fast away. A husband, a father, a friend, a master, endeared by every quality by which man in such relations can win the love of his fellow-men, was passing into the Silent Land, and his loving glance, his wise counsels, and his firm, manly thought should be known among them no more. The Castle clock chimed the third quarter after ten. Calm and peaceful grew the beloved form; the features settled into the beauty of a perfectly serene repose; two or three long, but gentle, breaths were drawn; and that great soul had fled to seek a nobler scope for its aspirations in the world within the veil, for which it had often yearned, where there is rest for the weary, and where 'the spirits of the just are made perfect.'"

It is impossible to describe the feeling which swept over the nation at the news of the Prince's death, and which has since crystallized into universal reverence, and become a form of distinct hero-worship. Slow as the people had been to grasp the real greatness and goodness of the Prince Consort, it had now for ten years been growing steadily into their inner consciousness, and impressing itself upon their hearts, and in their very lives. He had, like the Queen, become a part of England, and his example, his life, his character, and his utterances had become woven into the warp and woof of English society in its every phase and form. The expression of public sorrow was absolutely unique. It was distinct from that felt at the death of a national hero, such as Wellington, in being a personal sorrow, a home grief, an almost domestic sentiment. The great Duke had been an historical character, a man far beyond the allotted span of life, and one whose death might be expected at any moment. Moreover, he was far above the masses in policy and feeling, and was removed for many years from active public life.

But the Prince Consort and the Queen embodied the home thought and sentiment of the nation. He had been handsome and pre-eminently lovable in character and disposition. He had been also mixed up in all kinds of popular interests and movements, and was daily before the people, and with the people, in pulpit and in prayer, in the press and upon the platform. Sir Frederick Pollock's Diary, on December 22nd, states that he is writing " at the close of the saddest day I ever saw in London. The signs of general grief have been everywhere seen and heard ; all the public offices have been closed ; nearly all shops shut ; all faces wear an expression of sorrow and concern. Posthumous praise has never been so well deserved as in the case of all the encomiums which have been written on the Prince Consort." Lord Houghton, in his Diary of the previous day, declares that " Prince Albert's death is a national tragedy. The peasants in the cottages talk as if the Queen was one of themselves. It is the realest public sorrow I have ever seen—quite different from anything else."

From an Australian visitor, in England at this time, comes an equally strong picture of the national grief. " It is beautiful," says Sir Henry Parkes in his Autobiography, "to see how the poor lose sight of their own privations and sufferings in the gloom of a mighty sorrow such as then fell upon the heart and home of Queen Victoria. It seemed as if death had entered every household in the land. Rich and poor, high and low, all joined in the national mourning." To a friend in New South Wales, the same political leader asserted that "never in English history has any death been so visibly felt by all ranks of the English people. It is not by closed shutters and doors, by habiliments of mourning, by the tolling of church bells, and by drooping flags wreathed with crape, that the national sorrow is most touchingly expressed. You see it everywhere in the grief-burdened faces of the people." Dean Alford, writing on December 29th, declares it "a terrible blow, and the loss will be spread over years to come. The Queen bears up very tolerably, I hear ; and the family are admirable. You never saw anything like the sorrow here in England. I remember nothing like it since the Princess Charlotte's death in 1817, which I do remember well."

To many the shock and the sorrow were personal, and not merely sympathetic in their nature. Lord Shaftesbury writes in his Diary, on December 16th, that he "heard this morning the Prince was dead. Short of my own nearest and dearest, the shock could not have been greater!" And, like everyone else, he thought of the Queen, and goes on to speak of the desolation in her heart and life—the deathblow to her happiness on earth. "The disruption of domestic existence unprecedented in Royal history, the painful withdrawal of a prop, the removal of a counsellor, a friend in all public, in all private affairs ; the sorrows she has, the troubles that await her—all rend my heart as though the suffering were my own."

Lord Malmesbury, in the same way, records his feeling that "she has lost everything that could make life valuable to her, as all her happiness was centred in her husband." As Mr. Disraeli so truly said, at the time of the Duchess of Kent's death, Her Majesty had chosen to establish her life upon the principle of domestic love ; and now the sorrow from this shattering blow was terrible in proportion to its depth. Assisted, however, by the force of character, and tact, and judgment shown by Princess Alice, the Queen went through the first few days and months of her loneliness and grief in apparent calmness. Undoubtedly the popular sympathy did much to comfort her, and those exquisite lines by Tennyson voiced a religious sentiment, which also proved a strong staff and consolation :

> " Break not, O woman's heart, but still endure ;
> Break not, for thou art Royal, but endure,
> Remembering all the beauty of that star
> Which shone so close beside thee that ye made
> One light together, but has passed and leaves
> The Crown a lonely splendour.
>
>   May all love,
> His love, unseen but felt, o'ershadow thee,
> The love of all thy sons encompass thee,
> The love of all thy daughters cherish thee,
> The love of all thy people comfort thee,
> Till God's love set thee at his side again ! "

The funeral took place on December 3rd with all possible state and ceremony, but in private, and a year later the magnificent mausoleum at Frogmore marked the grave of the Prince and embalmed in monumental form the love of the Queen. Meanwhile the nation proferred every tribute of reverence to his memory and of loyalty to their bereaved Sovereign. Addresses of deepest regret and sympathy were passed in both Houses of Parliament when they met in February. As Mr. Disraeli well said in the House of Commons : "The counties, the cities, the corporations of the realm—those illustrious associations of learning, and science, and art, and skill, of which he was the brightest ornament and the inspiring spirit, have bowed before the Throne. It does not become the Parliament of the country to be silent.   To-night the two Houses sanction the expression of public sorrow, and ratify, as it were, the record of a nation's woe."   But the great, the most memorable, speech of the occasion was that of Lord Dufferin.

"Never before, my Lords," said he, "has the heart of England been so greatly stirred, and never yet has such signal homage been more spontaneously rendered to unpretending intrinsic worth.   Monarchs, heroes, patriots, have perished from among us, and have been attended to their grave by the respect and veneration of a grateful people.   But here was one who was neither king, nor warrior, nor legislator—occupying a position in its very nature incompatible with all personal pre-eminence ; alike debarred the achievement of military renown and political distinction ; secluded within the precincts of what might easily have become a negative existence ; neither able to confer those favours which purchase popularity, nor possessing in any particular degree the trick of manner which seduces it— who, nevertheless, succeeded in winning for himself an amount of consideration and confidence such as the most distinguished or the most successful of mankind have seldom attained.   By what combination of qualities, a stranger and an alien, exercising no definite political function ; ever verging on the peril of a false position ; his daily life exposed to ceaseless observation ; shut out from the encouragement afforded by the sympathy of intimate friendship, the support of partisans, the good-fellowship of society ; how such an one acquired so remarkable a hold on the affections of a jealous, insular people might well excite the astonishment of anyone acquainted with the temper and the peculiarities of the British nation."

And then the speaker dealt with the qualities which had brought about this result—those principles which had enabled the Prince to tread day by day, and hour by hour, patiently, humbly, and faithfully, the uninviting path of duty, amid all the bewildering temptations and distractions, luxury and splendour, of his Royal position.   Above all, he dwelt upon the way in which Prince Albert had sustained the great trust confided to him twenty-two years before—the domestic happiness of their youthful Queen.   "So bright has shone the flame of that wedded love, so hallowing has been its influence, that even its reflected light has gladdened and purified many a humble household, and at this moment there is not a woman in Great Britain who will not mournfully acknowledge that as in life he made our Queen the proudest and the happiest, so in death he has left her the most afflicted lady in her kingdom."   What Lord Dufferin so beautifully said then, a whole vast empire and the world at large has since come to fully realize.

But for the Queen there was no real rest or retirement.   From mere public functions she might and did withdraw, but they only constituted a small portion of her Royal duties.   Lord Houghton had asked in his Diary, a week after the Prince's death, what it would be like "when the lonely and responsible daily life" of the present and the future opened out before her ?   The answer comes to us, through many years of time, in Lord Malmesbury's Journal of December 20th— six days after the sad event : "We continue to receive good accounts of the Queen. . . . She has signed some papers and seen Lord Granville."   And on December 28th he adds : "I hear that Ministers have signed a memorial to the Queen refusing to transact business with her through Sir Charles Phipps (the Private Secretary). This, though right, is certainly cruel under the circumstances." Her Majesty's position made it, in fact, out of the question for work to be done by or through others; and much of that confidential labour which the Prince had been able to do now came upon her with redoubled weight. Despatches and international complications and all the anxieties of so great a place in the world had to be considered and borne. Perhaps, upon the whole, it was good for the Queen, and in the end for her people, that circumstances forced these matters into immediate prominence and confined her grief to the few hours of privacy and rest.

But everywhere she missed the watchful eye and helpful hand of the loving husband. To Dean Stanley, in 1863, Her Majesty mournfully observed that: " Lord Melbourne was very useful to me, but I can never be sufficiently thankful that I passed safely through those two years to my marriage. Then I was in a safe haven, and there I remained for twenty years. Now that is over and I am again at sea, always wishing to consult one who is not here, groping by myself, with a constant sense of desolation." These words to one who was worthy and capable of being a Sovereign's confidant in time of trouble—there are but few such men—indicate the first feelings of loneliness and sorrow, but hardly reveal that sense of duty and love of country which actuated the Queen through all the ensuing years.

They do, however, afford some insight into the value of the Prince Consort's advice and opinions during the period which had passed away, and they are amply borne out by Sir Theodore Martin's volumes of Royal correspondence and memoranda—the greatest and most enduring of all the many memorials erected to the Prince by a grateful and appreciative nation. From these some quotations have already been made, but they have only given the faintest idea of his skilled statecraft and almost scientific study of diplomacy and government. His Memoranda submitted from time to time for the consideration of the British Cabinet contain a complete code of constitutional liberty and an elaborate history of the rise and fall of modern European States. They were written in English, and deal with these lofty topics in a way one would think only possible from a man who had been permeated, through birth and ancestry and environment, with the very spirit of English institutions and development. The fact is that King Leopold's early teachings had done much in this direction; Baron Stockmar's friendship and instruction in youthful days had done more; and the adaptive intelligence of the Prince, acted upon by the British feelings and knowledge of the Queen, had responded until he became a thorough Englishman in the best and highest sense of the name. As an illustration of this fact, a paragraph may be cited from a letter to Lord John Russell upon Italian affairs—September 5th, 1847:

" England has, by her own energies and the fortunate circumstances in which she has been placed, acquired a start in civilization, liberty, and prosperity over all other countries. Her popular institutions are most developed and perfected, and she has run through a development which the other countries will yet in succession have to pass through. England's mission, duty, and interest is to put herself at the head of the diffusion of civilization, and the attainment of liberty. Let her mode of acting, however, be that of fostering and protecting every effort made by a State to advance in that direction, but not of pressing upon any State an advance which is not the result of its own impulse. Civilization and liberal institutions must be of organic growth, and of national development, if they are to prosper and lead to the happiness of a people. Institutions not answering the state of society for which they are intended *must work ill*, even if these institutions should be better than the State that society is in. Let England, therefore, be careful (in her zeal for progress) not to push any nation beyond its own march, and not to *impose* upon any nation what that nation does not itself *produce.*"

These were wise words, and especially applicable to the situation of Italy and England at the time. Especially admirable are they when we remember that the Prince was then only twenty-eight years of age. But this was not an isolated instance. A week later he wrote a long memorandum regarding affairs in Germany, which is of standard value to-day, as constituting a clear analysis of the elements then working towards popular government and the united Germany of twenty odd years afterwards. Following this came his interesting correspondence with Baron Stockmar, which, spread over a series of years, covers the whole ground of European politics and history, and shows the pupil rapidly becoming the master in a department of study and experience which effectually marks out the statesman from the mere politician. His letters and suggestions regarding the improvement of the educational system at Cambridge at this time also indicate wide knowledge of the true requirements of higher education and university training.

Then, in 1850, his correspondence with the Duke of Wellington throws a flood of light upon the difficulties of his position, the purity of his motives, and the clearness of his views. The Duke was very anxious to retire from the position of Commander-in-Chief in favour of the Prince, and in accordance with his belief that the Sovereign should be the real commander of the army and navy. For this purpose the Duke proposed that a Chief of the Staff should be created, combining under him the offices of Adjutant and Quartermaster-General, thus preparing the way for the ultimate assumption of his own office by the Prince Consort. Several conversations—memoranda of which have been preserved—took place, and finally Prince Albert wrote a now historic letter declining to take the position on constitutional grounds, and because of the complications which would inevitably follow from his being a servant of the State and the husband of his Sovereign at the same time. Other notable memoranda and letters by the Prince dealt with various phases of the Crimean war ;

BUCKINGHAM PALACE.

GENERAL, THE RIGHT HON. SIR HENRY PONSONBY, G.C.B.

the relations of Austria, Prussia, Russia, and France to each other, and to England; the Eastern Question in all its various and complicated forms; the character of Napoleon III.; and the condition of the British army and navy.

He very seldom complained in his own private correspondence of the difficulties of his position, and the extravagant misconceptions which he had to live down; but on one occasion, in a letter to Stockmar, he does summarize the situation—24th January, 1854: "A very considerable section of the nation," wrote the Prince, "had never given itself the trouble to consider what really is the position of the husband of a Queen Regnant. When I first came over here, I was met by this want of knowledge and unwillingness to give a thought to the position of this luckless personage. Peel cut down my income, Wellington refused me my rank, the Royal family cried out against the Foreign interloper, the Whigs in office were only inclined to concede to me just as much space as I could stand upon. The Constitution is silent as to the Consort of the Queen; even Blackstone ignores him, and yet there he was, and not to be done without." Years of patience, and work, and study, and the influence of natural ability and innate modesty, eventually conquered all these difficulties, and transferred doubt into absolute faith, suspicion into sincere affection. But it was a struggle, none the less felt because of a silent and self-contained character.

His letters to King Leopold of Belgium were replete with valuable suggestions upon the constantly changing situation in Europe, and there is little doubt that the personal influence and correspondence of the Prince with Napoleon of France, and the Crown Prince of Prussia, did much to oil the wheels of European diplomacy, and prevent them from being rusted by suspicion and clogged with mutual prejudices. Nicholas I. of Russia held a very high opinion of his abilities, while Napoleon III. constantly availed himself of his advice and friendship. In the latter connection there is an interesting letter, dated April 28th, 1857, and written during a time of alleged intrigue and closer relations between Russia and France, in which Prince Albert warns the Emperor that the English public can understand the basis of an alliance between England and France, but that if they look for the basis for such a relationship between England and France and Russia "they find there is a complete dissimilitude of views, of feelings, of ideas; that in the eyes of Russia western civilization, far from having any title to be encouraged, is the enemy that, above all others, ought to be resisted, and that there exists between the two such an absence of mutual interests that, in truth, if the one ceased to exist the other would scarcely be affected." It was letters such as this, and conversations of still greater frankness, which helped during many years to keep Napoleon attached to the English alliance; made him write to Her Majesty upon one occasion of "the various knowledge and the exalted judgment" of the Prince; and enabled Lord Cowley to write Lord Clarendon on August 18th, 1857, after one of Napoleon's visits to England: "You are already aware of the high opinion which the Emperor entertained of the Prince Consort's judgment and abilities, and this opinion appears, if possible, to have been augmented."

But the Prince's work abroad was only a branch of his many activities. He was never weary of labour for the poor and suffering, the ignorant and unfortunate. His sympathies were as wide as the influence he wielded soon became effective and useful. In June, 1863, a memorial, which amply illustrated this fact, was presented to the Queen from the ballast-heavers of the Port of London. They declared that to the Prince was due "eight years contented life in our hard labour, after a long time of misery from which he relieved us." Before that they could only get work through a body of middlemen who were mostly river-side publicans, and who forced the men to spend half their wages on drink.

"Your Majesty," continued the Memorial, "we tried hard to get rid of this cursed system ; we appealed to men of all classes, and opened an office ourselves ; but we got no help till we sent an appeal to your late Royal Consort on his election to the Mastership of the Trinity House. He at once listened to us. Your Majesty, he loved the wife of his own bosom, and he loved the children of his love ; he could put himself down from the throne he shared to the wretched home of us poor men, and could feel what we and our wives and children were suffering from the terrible truck-drinking system that had dragged us in the mire. . . . With his counsel a clause was put into the Merchant Shipping Act, 1853, which placed us under the control of the Corporation of the Trinity House. At once our wrongs were redressed, and the system that had ruined us swept away."

This was one of myriad instances which might be quoted of work well done or influence well used. Sir John Simon, the great authority on Sanitary science, tells us in the " Life of Lord Sherbrooke" that certain important changes in a Parliamentary measure under consideration in 1858 were " due to a conversation which, in the interval, my political chief (Lord Derby) had had with the late Prince Consort, whose highly informed statesman's mind, always bent upon objects of public good, had long been interested in the cause of Sanitary science, and whose opinion expressed on such a point as this in question was likely to be conclusive." In these and many other cases—such, for example, as the co-operative movement—the Prince was quick to see either material good, or opportunity for creating better social and humanitarian relations between the various classes of the community. For this latter purpose were his words addressed in May, 1848, to a meeting called by the Society for improving the condition of the working classes, of which the Prince was President. To dispel ignorance and to show how man can help man he declared to be the special duty of those who enjoyed station, wealth, and education. They should at the same time avoid dictatorial interference with labour and employment, which only frightened away capital, and destroyed freedom of thought and independence of action. Only by united exertions and combined action, however, could the natural imperfections of humanity be improved and its wants fully satisfied, and for this end self-reliance and confidence in each other were essential.

It must have been sentiments such as these, coupled with years of added experience, and culture, and mental growth, which made De Tocqueville write on June 29th, 1857, after an interview with Prince Albert in Manchester, that he could not describe how much he was struck and charmed by his sound sense. " I have rarely met a man so distinguished," he added, " and I have never met a Prince who seemed to me, take him for all in all, so remarkable ; and I was able to say without flattery, as I parted from him, that of all the things worthy of remembrance which I had come across in England that which impressed me the most was the conversation we had just had. You are happy in having such a man so near the Throne." Such praise from such a man was indeed notable and eminently expressive.

During his latter days the Prince experienced intense pleasure in corresponding with his daughter, the Princess Royal, wife of Prince Frederick of Prussia, who became, in 1860, Crown Prince and heir apparent. He took great interest in her settlement amongst a strange people, and in a foreign country, and his letters breathe much anxiety for her popularity and influence for good. Writing to her on February 11th, 1858, he speaks of the cordial welcome given to her everywhere in Prussia, and hopes that it has kindled and confirmed within her the determination to be worthy of such feelings of trust and friendliness. But he does not urge her to this in any work outside of a woman's proper place, or inside what the so-called advanced females of to-day consider a " woman's sphere."

" You have received from heaven," he writes, " the happy task of effecting this object by making your husband truly happy, and of doing him at the same time the best service, by aiding him to maintain and to increase the love of his countrymen. That you have everywhere made so favourable an impression has given intense happiness to me as a father. Let me express my fullest admiration of the way in which you have kept down and overcome your own little personal troubles. . . . This is the way to success, and the *only* way. If you have succeeded in winning people's hearts by friendliness, simplicity, and courtesy, the secret lay in this, that you were not thinking of yourself. Hold fast this mystic power, it is a spark from heaven."

So in much other correspondence of a similar nature he seems to search the heart of his daughter and cultivate the highest aspirations of her nature. Writing to her in July, 1859, he speaks of the reward due to faithful servants—a matter often neglected by Princes as well as more humble personages—and then proceeds, in words which have become almost classical, to declare that " without the love of others man cannot be happy, and one must himself be capable of loving, and must love, in order to be loved." It is interesting to note, in passing from domestic details to public matters, that the Prince was at this time a free trader. Writing to his daughter on March 7th, 1860, he states that " protected industries do not thrive because, but in spite of, protection. This is a theorem that has been proved to a demonstration." Of course, England was at this time in the first flush of its industrial supremacy, and had almost complete command of the markets of the world. But it is, perhaps, a little to be wondered at that so far-seeing a man should not have perceived that the United States, and Germany, and France were bound to some day seek industrial power and to obtain it by means of protection. He does not, however, seem to have gone very deeply into the question; hence the acceptance of a narrow proposition then almost universally believed in England.

In his public speeches the Prince was always clear, pleasing, and patriotic. They stand out distinctly as voicing common-sense views of the position at the moment, and as being delivered with that slow, careful, and effective enunciation which Englishmen like so much. Yet, though he appeared to speak easily, it was in reality an exceedingly difficult and painful ordeal. His private letters refer to the " torture " of making speeches which every hearer enjoyed at the time, and which the press afterwards greatly praised. The reception given his remarks seems to have always surprised him, while his pleasure when through with the ordeal was as great as his preparations had been careful. One illustration may be given here of his style in speaking. It was at a banquet tendered on October 25th, 1850, by the Lord Mayor of York, and the mayors of other chief cities and towns in the United Kingdom, to the Lord Mayor of London. In the course of his reference to the recent death of Sir Robert Peel, the Prince made the following clear analysis of the English character and national position :

" Warmly attached to his institutions, and revering the bequests left to him by the industry, wisdom, and piety of his forefathers, the Englishman attaches little value to any theoretical scheme. It will attract his attention only after having been for some time placed before him; it must have been thoroughly investigated and discussed before he will entertain it. Should it be an empty theory it will fall to the ground during this period of probation ; should it survive this trial it will be on account of the practical qualities contained in it ; but its adoption in the end will entirely depend upon its harmonizing with the national feeling, the historic development of the country, and the peculiar nature of its institutions.

" It is owing to these national qualities that England, while constantly progressing, has still preserved the integrity of her constitution from the earliest times, and has been protected from wild schemes whose chief charm lies in their novelty, while around us we have, unfortunately, seen whole nations distracted, and the very fabric of society endangered, from the levity with which the result of the experience of generations, the growth of ages, has been thrown away to give place to temporarily favourite ideas."

In line with all his thoughts and aspirations were the International Exhibitions of 1851 and 1862. He was the father of this great idea, and in all its extended ramifications in after years the trade of the world and the spread of knowledge owes much to the Prince Consort.   But little more can be said here, and only the briefest sketch of his life-work has in any case been possible.   His characteristics were such as all men could comprehend—if they wished to.   With a noble presence, and a figure which denoted more strength and stamina than in his last years he really possessed, was coupled a face which appeared emphatically clear, open, pure-minded, and honest.   He possessed extreme quickness of mind, great ability in serious conversation, much patience in bearing criticism and contradiction, and keen delight in graceful wit or humour.   His sense of duty and love of liberty are now writ largely upon the pages of history.   Closely united with them was a hatred of prejudice or intolerance, and a love of England which yet never made him forget his birthplace—that beautiful Coburg which he and the Queen so delighted to visit.   He was shy and sensitive by nature, reserved yet joyous in temperament, and possessed a horror of flattery or of meanness in any form.   Altogether the Prince Consort had a very simple, lovable character, one which makes it easy to understand the happy home life of the Royal family; the abiding love of the Queen for his memory and qualities; the deep reverence of the people amongst whom he lived, and moved, and worked for twenty years of an unselfish, generous, and noble life.

CHAPTER XIII.

Mingled Joys and Sorrows.

THE curtain of death and destiny had now fallen upon twenty years of happiness, but it was only to rise again upon a far longer period of royal duty and resignation. It must have been very hard at first to endure the fresh load of lonely responsibility; to begin to reign again without the aid of a Lord Melbourne or a Prince Consort; to pick up in solitary state the thread of what had so long been united thought and aim and sentiment. For a time, King Leopold came from Brussels and gave Her Majesty the support of his silent strength and wise words, and that loving friendship and kindness of which the Queen has always thought so much. And the Princess Alice was everywhere, soothing, arranging, and managing in the first months of grief and desolation. The Ministers might not and could not, as Lord Malmesbury hints, even in these first days of sorrow, communicate to any great extent with the Queen through her Private Secretary, but they were able and willing to do so through Princess Alice.

With the opening of 1862 came a calamity which plunged many a cottage home into the same trial through which the royal widow and family had just passed. The Hartley Colliery accident, by which 250 miners were buried alive —dying to a man before rescue could come—sent a thrill of horror throughout the land, and brought a message from the Queen declaring that her " tenderest sympathy is with the poor widows and mothers, and her own misery only makes her feel the more for them." A subscription headed by Her Majesty soon ran up to £81,000, and gave some sorrowful satisfaction to those who had been left without the means of subsistence. About the same time the cotton famine in Lancashire commenced, and called for every sympathy and aid which it was possible to give. A committee headed by Lord Derby collected £407,000, and the one organized by the Lord Mayor of London obtained £236,000, for the aid of the gallant operatives. Unable to obtain cotton to work upon in the mills, on account of the American Civil War, they yet stood to their guns as bravely and truly as ever the men of the Northern States did, and refused to propose or support a British war policy which, while freeing the trade in cotton with the South, would have probably put back the American slave in bondage and kept him there. Yet they have received little thanks or appreciation from the nation whose unity they helped to preserve and for whom they suffered so greatly. It must be remembered, in passing, that the influence of Lancashire thrown into

RIGHT HON. JOHN BRIGHT, M.P.

RICHARD COBDEN, M.P.

the scale for war would in that critical period have probably forced it on, and have saved the South through the joint intervention of England and France.

Meanwhile the last product of Prince Albert's thought and work—the International Exhibition of 1862—was opened on May 1st with an Inaugural Ode by the Poet Laureate, in which he referred to the "silent father of our Kings to be," and recalled his many triumphs on behalf of peace, and civilization, and national culture. It was about this time also, and during the widowed Queen's first visit to that home at Balmoral so endeared to her by memories of the Prince, that Dr. Norman Macleod accompanied her as chaplain in attendance, and by his direct and fearless preaching won Her Majesty's favour and lasting regard. "I am never tempted," he wrote, "to conceal my conviction from the Queen, for I feel sure she sympathizes with what is true and likes the speaker to utter the truth exactly as he believes it." His further description of an interview is interesting. "I was summoned unexpectedly to the Queen's room," he says. "She was alone. She met me, and with an unutterably sad expression, which filled my eyes with tears, at once began to speak about the Prince. . . . She spoke of his excellences, his love, his cheerfulness, how he was everything to her. She said she never shut her eyes to trials, but liked to look them in the face; how she would never shrink from duty, but that all was at present done mechanically; that her highest ideas of purity and love were obtained from him, and that God could not be displeased with her love. But there was nothing morbid in her grief."

At Balmoral the Queen devoted herself to much charity and sympathetic work amongst the poor and suffering, and it seemed in some degree a relief to her own sorrow. Many are the stories told in this and following years of the darkly clad royal lady reading the Bible to the sick and dying, or bearing material comforts to the humble cottager or peasant. And everywhere the sweet, sad face taught the lesson of equality in grief and patience in trouble. At Netley Hospital, which was visited a little later, Her Majesty is described as bearing in her face "the marks of a heartfelt and abiding sorrow. Her smile was, however, as gracious as ever, and her voice, though low and very gentle, had all its old sweetness and clearness." But the duties of a Sovereign were carried on despite private sorrows and personal charities. The Prince of Wales was sent on his tour to Egypt and the East, and arrangements were made for the marriage of the Princess Alice. The ceremonious work of holding drawing-rooms and presiding at popular festivities was, of course, abandoned; but, to quote the Duke of Argyll, the serious responsibilities of a Sovereign were fully and nobly borne.

"I think it a circumstance worthy of observation," he states, "and one which ought to be known to all the people of this country, that during all the years of the Queen's affliction, during which she lived necessarily in comparative retirement, she has omitted no part of that public duty which concerns her as Sovereign of this country; that on no occasion during her grief has she struck work, so to speak, in those public duties which belong to her exalted position; and I am sure that when the Queen reappears again on more public occasions, the people of this country will regard her only with increased affection, from the recollection they will have that during all the time of her care and sorrow she has devoted herself, without one day's intermission, to those cares of government which belong to her position as Sovereign of this country."

And the Duke of Argyll knew what he was discussing. He was at this time, and during many years to come, a greatly respected member of the Cabinet, and a student and writer and speaker of weight, upon all constitutional topics. Later in the year the Prince of Wales returned from his important and interesting visit to Egypt, Constantinople, Greece, Palestine, and the Crimea, and Sir Henry Holland, the eminent physician, stated in a private letter that the Prince was proving " a great comfort to the Queen " since he got back, and that she was " still deeply sorrowing over what is hardly less a grief to the country than to herself." But, he goes on to say, " she does her public work admirably, as usual." The wedding of the Princess Alice had been a very quiet affair, but it was an additional and serious loss to the Queen at this juncture. As the daughter who had been such a comfort and help to her was leaving for the Continent, Her Majesty must have felt again as she did some months before—in that burst of sentiment which proved the woman in the Sovereign—" I have no one to call me Victoria now." That phrase, touching and simple as it is, carries a world of meaning to those who live, or have ever lived, in the atmosphere of a Court. The marriage took place at Osborne on July 1st, and was of the most private character. The Princesses Helena, Louise, and Beatrice, and Princess Anna of Hesse were the bridesmaids, and the Prince of Wales and his brothers attended with the Queen, who was dressed in deepest mourning. Prince Louis of Hesse had the rank of Royal Highness conferred on him before he departed with his bride, amid the best wishes of the people, and an affection for the gentle Princess which *Punch* beautifully voiced in the lines:

> " Dear to us all by those calm earnest eyes,
> And early thought upon that fair young brow;
> Dearer for that where grief was heaviest thou
> Wert sunshine, till He passed where suns shall rise
> And set no more; thou, in affection wise
> And strong, wert strength to Her who even but now
> In the soft accents of thy bridal vow
> Heard music of her own heart's memories."

Early in September the Queen left for a visit to Germany accompanied by several members of the family, and during a brief stay with King Leopold at Laeken met for the first time the Princess Alexandra of Russia, who was soon to become Princess of Wales, the source of much pleasant companionship, and the object of an affection which finds abundant expression throughout Her Majesty's journals in such phrases as " Dear, sweet, gentle Alix." From there she went to Reinhardtsbrunn in Thuringia, where the Crown Prince and Princess of Prussia and their children, with Prince Louis and Princess Alice, soon joined the family party. A little later—on December 18th—the Prince Consort's remains were moved from St. George's Chapel to the magnificent mausoleum which the Queen had erected at Frogmore at a personal expense of £200,000. The Royal family were present, and Princess Alice came home for the mournful event and a brief visit to her mother. But before this a constant correspondence had taken place between them, and the following letter must be quoted as embodying characteristics of great beauty. It was written by the Princess on July 24th, hardly a month after her marriage, and is published in the Princess Helena's Memoirs of her sister:

" You tell me," she writes, " to speak to you of *my* happiness—our happiness. You will understand the feeling which made me silent towards you, my own dear bereaved Mother, on this point; but you are unselfish and loving and can enter into my happiness, though I could never have been the first to tell you how intense it is, when it must draw the painful contrast between your past and present existence. If I say I love my dear husband, that is scarcely enough—it is a love and esteem which increases daily, hourly; which he also shows to me by such consideration, such loving, tender ways. What was life before to what it has become now? There is such blessed peace being at his side, being his wife; there is such a feeling of security; and we two have a world of our own when we are together, which *nothing* can touch or intrude upon."

This outpouring of a warm heart marked the beginning of what was a durable happiness—one which lasted through much of trouble and trial till her own death in 1873. And, taken in connection with the happy marriage of the Princess Royal, such a letter and such sentiments offered an excellent omen for the coming wedding of the heir to the throne. The preliminaries of this event had been arranged in September, as the result of a meeting between the Prince of Wales and the Princess Alexandra at Heidelberg, in Germany, during the autumn of 1861. A mutual attachment seems to have then been formed and the engagement arranged, although the Prince Consort's death had postponed its public announcement. On the 4th of November, 1862, however, the *Gazette* stated that Her Majesty had consented to the marriage, and five days afterwards the young Prince completed his twenty-first year amid popular rejoicings in London and elsewhere. Then the Princess Alexandra came to Osborne on a brief visit, and in February following a special Message from the Queen announced the intended marriage to Parliament. Lord Palmerston at once proposed that, in addition to the revenues from the Duchy of Cornwall, the Prince of Wales should receive £40,000, and the Princess £10,000 a year from the Consolidated Fund. A Bill to this effect passed both Houses unanimously and received the Royal assent.

Such are the bare details of an event round which romance has wreathed many a story, and over which all England rejoiced for a period. The young Danish Princess was at this time only eighteen; beautiful, it was said, to a degree beyond comparison; simple in her tastes and training, though amply cultured so far as education was concerned; popular in her own country, though destined to exceed that popularity in the land of her adoption. Born as the daughter of a Prince who appeared for years to stand further away from the throne of Denmark than ever did the Duke of Kent from that of England; brought up in simplicity and almost poverty; trained in every household duty, as well as given a thorough education by a father who thought he would have little else to give; she was now engaged to the heir of the greatest throne in the world, and the subject of most elaborate preparations by a whole nation.

It was an undeniably popular marriage. The English people liked the Danes, and they knew how to appreciate the simple upbringing of the Princess. Her beauty was evident, and her photographs alone were sufficient to charm a nation as they would have won the admiration of an individual. More than all, the Prince was believed—and there was every reason for the belief—to have chosen his own bride in his own way. There are stories which, of course, cannot be proven, of his having quite by accident seen a photograph of the Princess, and become so impressed with it that he determined to meet and win the original. However that may be, the reception prepared for her voiced a perfect wave of enthusiasm which swept over England. Everyone was interested in the event. The natural love of romance, and beauty, and happiness stirred the hard-working factory girl, or the poor woman with her large family, as much as it did the peeress or the society leader—possibly a good deal more. It was to multitudes like a lovely fairy tale, and the knowledge of the beautiful home life of the Queen made the people hope that this was the prelude to another prolonged love story.

It is said that the Princess Alexandra had not the least idea of the grandeur of the preparations going on in England, or that she was to make a Royal progress from Gravesend equal to any by Queen Elizabeth; and amid such cheering thousands on the shores, the country roads, and the thoroughfares, as to make it seem as if the whole nation had turned out to prove the Poet Laureate's welcome:

> " The Sea-King's daughter, as happy as fair,
>   Blissful bride of a blissful heir ;
>   Bride of the heir of the Kings of the sea—
>   Oh, joy to the people and joy to the throne,
>   Come to us, love us, and make us your own ;
>   For Saxon, or Dane, or Norman, we,
>   Teuton, or Celt, or whatever we be,
>   We are each all Dane in our welcome of thee,
>   Alexandra ! "

With the Princess from Copenhagen came her father—who within a few months became King of Denmark—her mother and her brother. They stayed at Brussels a couple of days with King Leopold, and then at Antwerp found the Queen's yacht, accompanied by several men-of-war, awaiting them. On the 6th of March they reached the Nore, and were met by illuminations everywhere along the beach during the night which followed. Next morning the shore and the countryside were simply a mass of people, and one description of what followed is probably as nearly accurate as such accounts ever are. At any rate it is interesting, and correct in the main: "Those upon the shore saw a pretty sight—a timid girlish figure dressed entirely in white who appeared on the deck at her mother's side, then, returning to the cabin, was seen first at one window, then at another, the bewitching face framed in a little white bonnet. . . . The Prince's yacht approached that of his bride, the gangway was thrown down, and immediately he was seen by all these thousands to rush across it, and, waiting for no formal word of greeting, caught the Princess in his arms and kissed her, 'just,' as an honest Yorkshire man said to me in describing the scene, 'as though she were any other lass.'"

Thence the Royal party drove through Gravesend, amid great crowds of people, and with roses strewn along the way of the carriages, to the railway station, and from there went by train to the Bricklayer's Arms station in London, where they were met by the Duke of Cambridge, the Prince of Prussia, the Duke of Saxe-Coburg, the Lord Mayor and Sheriffs, and other personages. Addresses were presented and the drive then began through the chief streets of the metropolis to Paddington. To the simple Danish Princess it must have been a great sight, accustomed though she was to the affectionate welcome and cheering of the population in her own land. Street after street was decorated with flags and garlanded in flowers; triumphal arches and festooned bands of music were everywhere; flashing sabres, and uniforms, and all the paraphernalia of civic splendour was combined with the real enthusiasm of the people, and with such evidences of solid power as the 17,000 volunteers drawn up in Hyde Park.

On the way to Windsor the crowds continued, and, at Eton, 800 boys cheered enthusiastically, while the illuminations at the Castle in the evening could be seen for twenty miles around. The Queen's reception was motherly in the extreme, and the Princess must have felt herself at home once more after the tremendous excitement of a most eventful day. Next morning the officials of London came to Windsor and presented her with a diamond necklace and earrings valued at £10,000, and on the 10th the marriage took place in the Chapel Royal—the first occurrence there of such a ceremony in seven hundred years—with the Archbishop of Canterbury, the Bishops of London and Chester, and the Dean of Windsor officiating. The Queen took no part in the brilliant ceremonial, though she was present in a secluded enclosure. The Prince of Wales wore a general's uniform, with several orders and the mantle of the Garter. The bride wore a dress of white satin and Honiton lace, with a silver moire train, and a number of costly necklaces, bracelets, and other jewelled presents.

A wedding breakfast followed, and then the Royal couple departed for their honeymoon at Osborne. Meanwhile London and other large towns were illuminated, and the rejoicings continued for some days afterwards. During August and September following, the Queen and some of the Royal family visited King Leopold once more, and then went on to Coburg. While there Her Majesty stayed at Rosenau—the birthplace of the Prince Consort—and received visits from the King of Prussia and the Emperor of Austria. In October she went to Aberdeen to unveil in person the statue of the Prince Consort. The occasion was to her a very melancholy one, the day was wet and gloomy, and she trembled and felt very nervous in carrying out the ceremony—the first public function since her husband's death. But it was not by any means the first Memorial to the Prince. Statues dotted the land, and in all the chief towns his memory had been, or was yet to be, honoured in some such lasting form. Perhaps the best of them all, in a certain sense, was the Queen's own creation, the Albert medal. This decoration was intended to be awarded to persons who risked their lives in endeavouring to save others from shipwreck or the various perils of the sea, and it has since been an honour and source of pleasure to many an otherwise obscure hero.

The Prince of Wales now began to assume many of the functions of Royalty, and in this way greatly aided the Queen, while the birth of Prince Albert Victor on the 8th of January, 1864, gave her much pleasure. Writing not long before in his Diary, Sir Charles Lyell, the eminent geologist, states that in an interview with Her Majesty " she asked me a good deal about the Darwinian theory, as well as the ' Antiquity of Man.' She has a clear understanding and thinks quite fearlessly for herself, and yet very modestly. . . . I do not think she has given way more than is perfectly natural ; all necessary duties she has performed." And she had certainly retained her interest in everything affecting the welfare of the people. During July of the previous year a woman walking on a tight-rope, blindfolded, in Birmingham, was dashed to the ground and instantly killed. The Queen at once wrote the Mayor, through her secretary, a very characteristic letter, and one which did much good :

" Her Majesty cannot refrain from making known to you her personal feelings of horror that one of her subjects, a female, should have been sacrificed to the demoralizing taste unfortunately prevalent for exhibitions attended with the greatest danger to the performers. Were any proof wanting that such exhibitions are demoralizing, I am commanded to remark that it would be at once found in the decision arrived at to continue the festivities, the hilarities, and the sports of the occasion after an event so melancholy. The Queen trusts that you, in common with the rest of the townspeople of Birmingham, will use your influence to prevent in future the degradation of such exhibitions in the Park

EDWARD JENNER, M.D.

RUDYARD KIPLING.

SIR WALTER SCOTT

WILLIAM WORDSWORTH.

—which was gladly opened by Her Majesty and the beloved Prince Consort, in the hope that it would be made serviceable for the healthy exercise and rational recreation of the people."

There is much in this communication which might be borne in mind by the British people of thirty years after, and in very different countries and conditions.   On January 1st, 1865, the Queen again intervened publicly in connection with the railway accidents which were becoming all too frequent.   Through Sir Charles Phipps she wrote a letter to the directors of the leading railway companies, which was received with respect and attention by both the railways and the press. "It is not for her own safety," wrote the Private Secretary, " that the Queen has wished to provide in thus calling the attention of the company to the late disasters ; Her Majesty is aware that when she travels extraordinary precautions are taken ; but it is on account of her family, and those travelling upon her service, and of the people generally, that she expresses the hope that the same security may be insured for all as is so carefully provided for herself.   The Queen hopes that it is unnecessary for her to recall to the recollection of the railway directors the heavy responsibility which they have assumed since they have succeeded in securing the monopoly of the means of travelling of almost the entire population of this country."

The warning was effectual, and means were taken to place the railways in the splendid position they are in to-day, when, by virtue of overhead bridges and solid construction, the security of the passengers and the public is guarded to an extent unknown upon the American continent.   Following this occurrence came a Royal visit to the Consumption Hospital at Brompton on March 14th, with pleasant words and kindly smiles for many a suffering patient.   In August the Queen went to Coburg again, when a splendid statue of the Prince Consort was unveiled, and, after a brief stay with King Leopold, spent the autumn in the Highlands.   With the widowed Duchess of Athole Her Majesty there stayed some time.   During this visit, says the Royal Journal, " there were long drives, rides, and rows on the lake, sometimes in mist and rain, among beautiful scenery, like that which had been a solace in the days of deepest sorrow ; tea amongst the bracken or the heather, or in some wayside house ; friendly chats, peaceful readings."

During this year two men passed away—one having a great name, the other filling a great position.   Mr. Cobden died on April 2nd, and Lord Palmerston on October 18th.   The Premier's death was not only a great loss to the country ; it was the falling away of the last dyke of resistance to Mr. Gladstone's progressive Liberalism and practical leadership of his party.   It cannot truly be said that the Queen mourned or missed Cobden, but she certainly did Palmerston. The former had never been a member of any Government, and, though Her Majesty was a free-trader on principle, she had always strongly opposed the peace-at-any-price policy of which Cobden and Bright were the able exponents. But with Lord Palmerston it was different. During the last few years she had seen much of him, and his matured judgment had prevented the rash diplomacy of old, while his undoubted Imperialism had commended him, personally and politically, to the Queen. In spite of a tentative wish expressed by him to the contrary, Her Majesty, therefore, desired his burial in Westminster Abbey, and there his remains were finally placed amidst the sincere sorrow of the nation, the representatives of many countries, the presence of the chief men in England, and of the Prince of Wales and the Duke of Cambridge as mourners.

Another death at this time was that of the wise and kindly King of the Belgians. To Her Majesty he had been more than an uncle; for many years he had really been a father to her and a friend of the sincerest, noblest type. Princess Alice, in writing to her mother on December 11th, very truly declared that "the regret for dear uncle Leopold is universal—he stood so high in the eyes of all parties; his life was a history in itself—and now that book is closed. Oh, it is so sad, and he is such a loss. . . . I do feel for you so much, for dear uncle was indeed a father to you." With the death of Lord Palmerston came the accession of Lord John (soon to be Earl) Russell to the Premiership, and the selection of Mr. Gladstone as leader of the House of Commons and the real leader of the Liberal party in the country. The newly-organized Ministry included such older leaders as Lord Granville, the Duke of Argyll, Mr. Gladstone, Sir George Grey, Lord Clarendon—who now became Foreign Secretary—Cardwell, Milner-Gibson and Villiers; and new men, mostly in subordinate offices, such as Mr. Goschen, Lord Hartington, Lord Dufferin, Mr. W. E. Forster, and Mr. Chichester Fortescue—afterwards Lord Carlingford. Lord Cranworth was Lord Chancellor, and Earl de Grey and Ripon—now Marquess of Ripon—was Secretary-at-War.

But the real power in the party and country was Mr. Gladstone, just as Mr. Disraeli now stood as the vital force of Conservatism. The two men were thus, at last, fairly and squarely opposed to each other. For a long time they had veiled their mutual antagonism under the guise of belonging to the free-trade and protectionist wings of the same party. But the Aberdeen coalition had given a blow to this fiction, and the refusal of Gladstone and his friends to join Lord Derby in 1859 had finally severed the former from the slightest tie of union with the Conservative party. The fact is that there was not, and could not be, room in the same political organization for Gladstone and Disraeli. General causes might have combined to bring about this condition. The friendship of the one for Sir Robert Peel, and the bitter attacks by the other upon that statesman and his life and policy; the championship of free trade by the one, and of protection by the other; the conscientious, religious, and sometimes sombre disposition of Mr. Gladstone, and the brilliant, witty, man-of-the-world style of Mr. Disraeli;

the commercial training and financial nature of the one, the romantic characteristics and broad sympathies of the other; all tended to help the divergence from
the time when they stood shoulder to shoulder behind the battlements of Toryism. Without all this, however, the natural and intense ambition of the two men
would have driven them ultimately into antagonism. Of course, it might have
been veiled, as was the feeling during many years between Gladstone and Palmerston, and no doubt would have been had they not started together, or almost
together, upon the ladder of political life. As it was, one would have had to
climb over the other had they remained in the same party. But many things
prevented such a result, and they now stood with clashing swords ready for a
struggle of sixteen years' duration.

On the 6th of February, 1866, and for the first time since the Prince
Consort's death, Her Majesty opened Parliament in person, amid enthusiastic
crowds along the route and a scene of splendour in the House of Lords. The
first Royal arrivals were the Prince and Princess of Wales, and for them the
whole glittering and jewelled audience stood, as they did again a minute later
when the Queen —clad in a deep purple velvet robe trimmed with white miniver,
a white lace cap *à la* Marie Stuart, a collar of brilliants, and the blue riband of
the Garter—entered, preceded by the great officers of State. The Speech was
read by the Lord Chancellor, and included a statement that " Her Majesty had
recently declared her consent to a marriage between the Princess Helena and
Prince Christian of Schleswig-Holstein-Sonderburg-Augustenburg, and trusted
the union would be prosperous and happy. The death of her beloved uncle, the
King of the Belgians, had filled her with profound grief; but she felt confident
that the wisdom he had evinced during his reign would animate his successor."
A reference was made to the Fenian agitation as being adverse to authority and
religion ; and to the cattle disease, then widely prevalent.

It was during this year that some west-end tradesmen in London, and some
political malcontents elsewhere, began to murmur that the Queen was not quite
doing her duty in not making more public appearances and taking a more public
part in national affairs. They were ignorant then, as many are still, that the
chief part of the Sovereign's work was being performed in silence and retirement,
and under circumstances of continued toil, day in and day out. The feeling,
however, at last found vent in a speech by Mr. Ayrton, M.P., to a great meeting
of the trades-unions during December, at St. James' Hall, London. The speech
had been made and the accusations duly formulated, when no less a personage
than John Bright—the tribune of the people and uncompromising advocate of
democracy—rose to his feet and uttered words of loyal defence which will never
be forgotten.

" I am not," said the great orator, "accustomed to stand up in defence of
those who are possessors of crowns. But I could not sit and hear that observa-

tion without a sensation of pain and of wonder. I think there has been, by many persons, a great injustice done to the Queen, in reference to her desolate and widowed position. And I venture to say this, that a woman—be she the Queen of a great realm or the wife of one of your labouring men—who can keep alive in her heart a great sorrow for the lost object of her life and affection is not at all likely to be wanting in a great and generous sympathy." The result of these simple words was instantaneous. Rising to their feet, the immense audience made the building ring with their cheers, and from cheering they passed on to " God save the Queen "—utterly refusing to even hear Mr. Ayrton in self-defence. Two years later, it may be stated here and in this connection, Her Majesty gave to the *Times* a statement which was of the most intense interest and importance. It indicated what people did not then know, that the Queen was not, and is not, a mere *roi faineant*, but a working, ruling Sovereign in the most practical sense of the word. It is sufficiently noteworthy to be given in full :

" An erroneous impression seems generally to prevail, and has lately found frequent expression in the newspapers, that the Queen is about to resume the place in society which she occupied before her great affliction; that is, that she is about to hold *levées* and drawing-rooms in person, and to appear, as before, at Court balls, concerts, etc. This idea cannot be too explicitly contradicted.

" The Queen appreciates the desire of her subjects to see her, and whatever she can do to gratify them in this loyal, affectionate wish she will do. Whenever any real object is to be obtained by her appearing on public occasions, any national interest to be promoted, or anything to be encouraged which is for the good of the people, Her Majesty will not shrink, as she has not shrank, from any personal sacrifice or exertion, however painful.

" But there are other and higher duties than those of mere representation, which are now thrown upon the Queen, alone and unassisted—duties which she cannot neglect without injury to the public service—which weigh unceasingly upon her, overwhelming her with work and anxiety. The Queen has laboured conscientiously to discharge these duties till her health and strength, already shaken by the utter and abiding desolation which has taken the place of her former happiness, have been impaired.

" To call upon her to undergo, in addition, the fatigue of those mere State ceremonies which can be equally well performed by other English members of her family is to ask her to run the risk of entirely disabling herself for the discharge of those other duties which cannot be neglected without serious injury to the public interests. The Queen will, however, do what she can—in the manner least trying to her health, strength, and spirits—to meet the loyal wishes of her subjects ; to afford that support and countenance to society, and to give that encouragement to trade, which is desired of her.

" More the Queen cannot do ; and more the kindness and good feeling of her people will surely not exact of her."

The publication of this remarkable State paper or Royal manifesto did much good, but it remained for the publication of Sir Theodore Martin's " Life of the Prince Consort " to clearly indicate the wide and varied nature of the Queen's duties and work. Meantime—to return to the session of 1866—the prolonged and brilliant debates on the Reform Bill had taken place, and resulted in the defeat of the Gladstone policy and the Russell Ministry. Lord Derby at once assumed office on the call of the Queen, and formed a Government composed of Lord Chelmsford, Mr. Disraeli, Lord Malmesbury, the Duke of Buckingham, Mr. Walpole, General Peel, Lord Carnarvon, Sir Hugh Cairns, and others. The chief new men were Mr. Gathorne Hardy (Lord Cranbrook), Sir Stafford Northcote (Lord Iddesleigh), Lord Naas—afterwards Earl of Mayo, and Viceroy of India—Mr. Ward Hunt, Lord Stanley, and the Duke of Marlborough. Another Reform Bill was introduced, and this "leap in the dark," as Lord Derby had called it, was ultimately passed by the Lords in August, 1867, and after nearly six months' discussion and consideration.

Meanwhile, the Queen had in the spring of the year twice visited Aldershot and reviewed the troops in garrison, besides presenting the 89th Regiment with a new pair of colours, in place of the shattered and battered fragments which it had carried for thirty-three years in all parts of the world. In June the Princess Mary of Cambridge, a cousin of the Queen, was married to H.S.H. the Prince of Teck—now the Duke of Teck—in the presence of Her Majesty; and on July 5th the Princess Helena was united to Prince Christian in St. George's Chapel, Windsor Castle, the Queen giving the bride away. During this period the war between Prussia and Austria had dragged in most of the petty German States on one side or the other, and the Princess Royal and Princess Alice had the misfortune to see their husbands fighting on opposite sides. The Austrians had much the worst of it from the beginning, and Hesse-Cassel became not only a centre of struggle and the scene of invasion, but was ultimately annexed to Prussia. Prince Louis fought bravely but uselessly, and, amid the clash of swords and roar of cannon, a child—the Princess Irene— was at this time born to his wife.

The anxiety for her husband, the work for the wounded, and the worry over the future of their little State made it indeed a bitter time for the gentle English Princess. But one of her letters to the Queen is none the less beautifully characteristic. "Baby is well," she writes on July 19th, "and very pretty. The time she came prevented a thought of disappointment at her being a girl. Only gratitude to the Almighty filled our hearts, that I and the child were well, and that dear Louis and I were together at the time. The times are hard; it wants all a Christian's courage and patience to carry one through them; but there is one Friend who in time of need does not forsake one, and He is my comfort and support. God bless you, my own Mama, and pray for your child."

In October following the Queen opened the fine new waterworks at Aberdeen, and, speaking for the first time in public since her husband's death, declared that she felt it was right for her to make some exertion during the present anxious discussions regarding the public health, in order to testify to her sense of the importance of such sanitary works. During the ensuing February she had opened Parliament again in person, and on May 20th laid the foundation of the great building at Kensington now known as the Royal Albert Hall of Arts and Sciences. Her Majesty was enthusiastically received by a vast audience, and was attended by most of the members of the Royal family's home circle. In June the Queen of Prussia arrived at Windsor on a visit, and during the following month the Sultan of Turkey received a hearty, but hardly deserved, welcome from the Queen and the nation.

Abdul-Aziz was at that time entirely misunderstood in England. It was generally supposed that his visit to Europe meant an adoption of European customs and a modified development of freer government. He was consequently fêted at Windsor and in London, and left England apparently greatly impressed. The result was a policy of mixed civilization and barbarism. Lawlessness and extortion and murder continued in his dominions side by side with the building of railways and the borrowing of money. In this latter European art he learned to excel. During the years 1854-74 the national debt was run up from $15,000,000 to $900,000,000—most of the increase being under Abdul-Aziz. He held an Exhibition at Constantinople, and then, as if to equalize things, permitted or directed the Bulgarian massacres. But most of this was still in the womb of the future, and at the time, as we know from a reliable source, he returned from Europe profoundly impressed—with the beauty of the Empress Eugènie! And this, with the Turkish loans of the future, seems to have been the net result of his tour.

During August of this year the Queen visited the Duke and Duchess of Roxburgh at Floors Castle—the procession from Kelso being led by fifty girls dressed in white, wearing chaplets of ivy and strewing the road with exquisite bouquets of flowers. During the first night beacon fires were lit on the hilltops of the countryside over a wide area, and blazed a welcome from the Eildons to the Cheviot Hills. Abbotsford, Melrose Abbey, and Jedburgh were also visited, and at the famous seat of Sir Walter Scott Her Majesty consented to write her name in the great novelist's Journal. After a brief stay at Glenfiddich, the shooting-lodge of the Duke of Richmond, the Queen went to Balmoral, and on October 15th—the anniversary of her engagement—unveiled another statue of the Prince Consort. In February of the following year (1868) an address of loyalty and affection, signed by 22,603 Irish residents of London, was presented as a protest against the Fenian conspiracies and outrages of the moment.

With the opening of Parliament came the retirement of Lord Derby on account of ill-health, and the calling of Mr. Disraeli to the leadership of the Government. It was the triumph following long years of labour and endurance, of struggle and success, of discouragement upon every side, and friendship from but a few. It was the beginning of a career of genuine greatness, and wide aspirations, and the inauguration of an Imperial policy. But it was only the beginning. In his first speech as Premier Mr. Disraeli referred to the situation in Ireland, and before the session was over Mr. Gladstone had introduced his Church Disestablishment proposals and unhorsed his rival. Circumstances, however, connected with the franchise or Reform Bill, and the advisability of not appealing to the people until it could be done under the terms of that act and to the new electorate, carried the Government from this defeat in April until the elections in November. Incidentally, it caused an important debate in the House upon the relations of the Government and the Queen. When Mr. Gladstone's disestablishment proposals were carried against the Ministry in April, the Premier had, of course, proferred his resignation to the Crown, and its acceptance would have been the only constitutional course were it not that no appeal to the new constituencies was possible for some months to come, and that the Premier had, under the circumstances, the right to demand an immediate dissolution, which would necessarily have shut out the new voters from the franchise for years to come. Hence the compromise by which the Queen asked a defeated Premier to retain his office. Mr. Disraeli's reference to the matter is interesting.

"I told Her Majesty," said the Premier, "that under the circumstances the advice which her Ministers would, in the full spirit of the constitution, offer her would be that Her Majesty should dissolve this Parliament and take the opinion of the country upon the conduct of her Ministers, and upon the question at issue. But at the same time, with the full concurrence of my colleagues, I represented to Her Majesty that there were important occasions on which it was wise that the Sovereign should not be embarrassed by personal claims, however constitutionally valid and meritorious ; and that if Her Majesty was of opinion that the question at issue could be more satisfactorily settled, or that the interests of the country would be promoted by the immediate retirement of the present Government from office, we are prepared to quit Her Majesty's service immediately, with no other feeling but that which every Minister who has served the Queen must entertain, viz., a feeling of gratitude to Her Majesty for the warm constitutional support which she always gives to her Ministers, and I may add—for it is a truth that cannot be concealed—for the *aid and assistance which any Minister must experience from a Sovereign who has such a vast experience with the public affairs.*"

This curious and little-remembered constitutional incident ended in the refusal of the resignation, and shows how elastic the powers of the Sovereign really are, while the last words quoted indicate the Queen's personal influence— an influence great in 1867, and necessarily infinitely greater in 1896. What Mr. Disraeli could then say Lord Rosebery or Lord Salisbury can corroborate with redoubled force in these later days.

CHAPTER XIV.

GLADSTONE AND BEACONSFIELD.

WITH the closing days of 1868 came the end of what may be termed Mr. Disraeli's preliminary Ministry, and the inauguration of Mr. Gladstone's "Golden era of Liberalism." The elections had given the latter leader an enormous majority—393 to 265— and it seemed as if the people really wished him to do as he liked with the Irish Church and with various other threatened institutions. It was indeed the beginning of an era of reform and change and so-called progress, just as the triumph of the Tory leader in 1874 commenced an equally distinct era of Imperialism and the growth of external power and prestige. Thus the two schools of thought and action had their innings, and each voiced the sentiments of the nation for the time being, and prevented the country from settling into a permanent groove of domestic narrowness or branching out into a policy of continued aggression.

The Gladstone Government was a strong one. During its five years of power there were many changes in its construction, but the chief members, aside from the Premier, were Lord Hatherley, the Lord Chancellor, who was afterwards succeeded by Lord Selborne—well known in those days as Sir Roundell Palmer; the Foreign Secretary, Lord Clarendon, who died in 1870, and was succeeded by Lord Granville; the Earl of Kimberley, as Colonial Secretary; Mr. Lowe, as Chancellor of the Exchequer; Mr. H. A. Bruce, as Home Secretary—a new man, afterwards created Lord Aberdare; Lord Cardwell, as Secretary for War; and the Duke of Argyll, as Indian Secretary. Mr. Bright was in the Ministry for a couple of years; Lord Dufferin was at the Duchy of Lancaster until he left for Canada; Lord Hartington was Irish Secretary, in succession to Chichester Fortescue (Lord Carlingford); Mr. Goschen and Mr. Childers, Mr. Forster and Mr. Grant-Duff, all held different posts at different times. Lord Halifax was Lord Privy Seal, and Lord Lansdowne and Lord Northbrook commenced their public careers in subordinate posts. Mr. W. E. Baxter, Mr. Adam, Mr. Stansfeld, Mr. Ayrton, Mr. Monsell, Mr. Knatchbull-Hugesson, Mr. Shaw-Lefèvre, and Dr. Lyon (now Lord) Playfair, were also included in the list.

Meanwhile the Queen's movements had not been very varied. In May, 1868, she had laid the foundation stone of St. Thomas' Hospital, and in June had reviewed 27,000 volunteers in Windsor Park. During August, in company

THE EARL OF BEACONSFIELD, K.G.

RIGHT HON. WILLIAM EWART GLADSTONE.

with Princesses Louise and Beatrice, and Prince Leopold, she paid her first visit to Switzerland, travelling *incognita* as Duchess of Kent, and going by way of Paris, where she had a private visit from Empress Eugènie at the English Embassy. The autumn was spent at Balmoral as usual, and in December Her Majesty made her first appearance as an authoress in her "Leaves from the Journal of Our Life in the Highlands." It was a simple and unpretentious, but valuable and altogether charming, Diary of daily life in the retirement of Balmoral during many years of her union with Prince Albert. This was not, however, the first time that the Queen had taken the nation into her confidence. The "Early Years of the Prince Consort," published in 1867, was compiled by General Grey under the Queen's personal direction, and is full of her private notes and Memoranda, besides being instinct with her own love and admiration for the deceased Prince.

Of the literary style of the "Leaves from the Journal" and other subsequent publications of a similar nature, it would be absurd to speak critically. To be of any value, a Diary has to breathe the thoughts of a hasty moment, jotted down without study of style or suspicion of public intrusion or examination. This necessity the Queen's Journals most assuredly meet, and although Her Majesty is known to have a thorough belief in her own lack of literary talents most people feel inclined to enjoy these obviously sincere and simple records without trying to tear them into tatters by the art of the critic. The *Athenæum*, which is certainly able to judge upon this point, says of the Queen's literary modesty that "Our own opinion is that the belief rests on no better foundation than that pleasing, natural diffidence which is felt by every true artist when he ventures on a new path. . . . In all the Queen's writing there is a freshness which compensates a reader for the absence of severer and more conscious art." Although looking forward some six years, reference may be made here to another work of great value—historically, constitutionally, and personally—which the Queen overlooked in person, and for which she provided and selected the material. Sir Theodore Martin's "Life of the Prince Consort" was really the completion of the Queen's literary work. In this book he officially edited and arranged a vast mass of correspondence and memoranda, which may be said for a time to have revolutionized the public conception of royalty and its functions. It is now, however, relegated too often to the forgotten book-shelf, and is not as well known in America—Canada and the United States—as it should be. A striking letter from the Queen to Princess Alice on January 1st, 1875, explains her reasons for the publication of this work :

"Now as regards the book. If you will reflect a few minutes, you will see how I owed it to beloved papa to let his noble character be known and understood, as it now is, and that to wait longer, when those who knew him best—his own wife, and a few (very few there are) remaining friends—were all gone, or too old, or too far removed from that time to be able to present a really true picture of his most ideal and remarkable character, would have been really wrong. He must be known for his own sake, for the good of England, and of his family, and of the world at large. Countless people write to say what good it does and will do. And it is already thirteen years since he left us !

" Then you must also remember that endless false and untrue things have been written and said about us, public and private, and that in these days people will write and will know ; and therefore the only way to counteract this is to let the real full truth be known, and as much be told as can be told with prudence and discretion, and then no harm, but good, will be done. Nothing will help me more than that my people should see what I have lost."

And there is no doubt the Queen was right. In still another way the publications did good. The simpler ones illustrated the beautiful domestic character of the Sovereign ; the more elaborate work, in spite of every effort at personal effacement, brought out the strong statesmanlike qualities and abilities of the Queen herself. Thus in knowing the Prince Consort people came to know his Royal widow. But to return to the events of the day. The Queen had intended to open Mr. Gladstone's first Parliament in person, but was prevented by the illness of Prince Leopold, as just a year before she had been worried by the attempted assassination of the Duke of Edinburgh at Sydney, in Australia. The latter occurrence was an outcome of the Fenian troubles, but fortunately the shot, though intended to be fatal, did not touch a vital spot, and the Prince's recovery was rapid. O'Farrel, the would-be murderer, was found guilty and executed. Around this Parliament of 1869 cluster many memories of the Irish Church and its summary disestablishment by Mr. Gladstone. And not the least important are those connected with the Queen and her personal intervention between the contending parties.

There is no question now about Her Majesty's opinions in the matter. She did not like the disestablishment proposals, and did not like Mr. Gladstone's Irish policy. But as a constitutional ruler she bowed from the first to the recognized will of the people as expressed in the elections, and was consequently opposed to the uncompromising attitude which the Church of England, and the Peers, and many Conservatives, intended to assume. She believed that moderate counsels should prevail and the decision of the people be recognized, and that in this way much modification in terms might be obtained. She saw, also, that a conflict between the two Houses, upon this particular question, meant a critical contest between the Peers and the people, and that it would be a distinctly unnecessary and useless one. Hence the important part which she took in the ensuing controversy through the Archbishop of Canterbury. The latter was, of course, a strong sympathizer with the doomed Establishment, and had been appointed to his high position as one of Mr. Disraeli's last recommendations. But, to all intents and purposes, he became the leader of the moderates in the House of Lords during all the heated discussions which followed.

The position taken by the Queen was one midway between the policy of absolute obstruction and opposition—proposed by Church leaders such as the eloquent Bishop of Peterborough—and the headlong use of an obedient majority in the Commons, intended by Mr. Gladstone. Through the Archbishop she arranged meetings between him and the Premier, and indirectly influenced the policy of Mr. Disraeli—as is shown by correspondence since published. In a letter from Osborne, on February 15th—the day before Parliament was opened—Her Majesty wrote to the Primate as follows;

" The Queen must write a few lines to the Archbishop of Canterbury on the subject of the Irish Church, which makes her very anxious. . . . The Queen has seen Mr. Gladstone, who shows the most conciliatory disposition. He seems to be really moderate in his views, and anxious, so far as he can properly and consistently do so, to meet the objections of those who would maintain the Irish Church. He at once assured the Queen of his readiness—indeed, his anxiety—to meet the Archbishop, and to communicate freely with him on the subject of this important question ; and the Queen must express her earnest hope that the Archbishop will meet him in the same spirit. The Government can do nothing that would tend to raise a suspicion of their sincerity in proposing to disestablish the Irish Church, and to withdraw all State endowments from all religious communions in Ireland ; but were these conditions accepted all other matters connected with the question might, the Queen thinks, become the subject of discussion and negotiation. The Archbishop had best now communicate with Mr. Gladstone direct as to when he can see him."

Much correspondence followed between Mr. Gladstone and the Archbishop, and Mr. Disraeli and the Queen, through the Archbishop. Meanwhile the Bill was introduced by the Premier in a great speech, and accepted by the majority of the Commons in detail and principle. Very few modifications were made, and early in June it passed up to the Lords. Here came the danger of a collision. Either the Lords would throw it out altogether upon the second reading, or else propose amendments impossible of acceptance by the Commons. The first point was to prevent its absolute rejection—the Queen's idea being that a compromise could be effected upon the subsequent amendments in committee. And this was Archbishop Tait's feeling also. Writing to His Grace on June 4th, by order of the Queen, General Grey declared that " Mr. Gladstone is not ignorant (indeed the Queen has never concealed her feelings on the subject) how deeply Her Majesty deplores the necessity under which he conceived himself to lie, of raising the question as he has done; or of the apprehensions, of which she cannot divest herself, as to the possible consequences of the measure which he has introduced."

And then the writer gives expression to Her Majesty's constitutional views of the issue. " Considering the circumstances under which the measure has come to the House of Lords, the Queen cannot regard, without the greatest alarm, the probable effect of its absolute rejection in that House. Carried as it has been by an overwhelming and steady majority, through a House of Commons chosen expressly to speak the feelings of the country on the question, there seems no reason to believe that any fresh appeal to the people could lead to a different result." This important letter went on to point out that a collision between the two Houses would prevent a modification of the measure, and urged that a committee of the Lords might make the Bill "less objectionable." The stormy debates which followed in the Upper House showed the necessity of milder counsels, and proved, by a majority for the Government of 179 to 146, how greatly the Queen's influence must have told upon the members as a whole. Though nominally a private correspondence, there is no doubt that the Archbishop used Her Majesty's wishes and arguments to influence the result. Bishop Wilberforce and several Conservative Peers withdrew without voting on this second reading, while staunch Tories such as Lord Salisbury, Lord Bath, Lord Devon, Lord Carnarvon, and Lord Nelson actually *supported* the Government. Then came the long battle over amendments. For more than a month the struggle was maintained, until on July 11th Her Majesty addressed another letter —this time a personal one—to the Primate :

"The Queen thanks the Archbishop very much for his letter. She is very sensible of the prudence and at the same time the anxiety for the welfare of the Irish Establishment which the Archbishop has manifested in his conduct throughout the debates, and she will be very glad if the amendments which have been adopted at his suggestion lead to the settlement of the question ; but, to effect this, concessions, the Queen thinks, will still have to be made on *both* sides. The Queen must say that she cannot view without alarm the possible consequences of another year of agitation on the Irish Church, and she would ask the Archbishop seriously to consider, in case the concessions to which the Government may agree should not go so far as he may himself wish, whether the postponement of the settlement for another year would not be likely to result in worse rather than in better terms for the Church. The Queen trusts, therefore, that the Archbishop will himself consider, and, as far as he can, endeavour to induce others to consider, any concessions that may be offered by the House of Commons in the most conciliatory spirit."

Mr. Gladstone's language in the House, however, indicated no intention to compromise, and the debate upon the amendments of the Lords waxed hot and furious. Finally the measure went back to the Peers, with some of their changes accepted and others rejected. Upon the whole, the Premier had given way more than his words had indicated, and the struggle now entered on its last phase. For some days it looked like war to the knife. The Peers insisted upon all their amendments, and the Archbishop was striving with might and main to mediate between the two parties as represented by Lord Cairns and Mr. Gladstone. He was in almost hourly communication with the Queen, and his Diary of July 19th declares it to be " a great blessing that the Queen takes such a vivid interest in the welfare of her people, and is so earnest to ward off a collision between the two Houses of Parliament." Finally, both Mr. Gladstone and the Peers gave way, and on July 22nd the compromise was effected, and the measure passed through the Upper House. To the Queen this triumph of moderation was really due, and the whole incident furnishes a striking illustration of the Sovereign's influence within the limits of constitutional government, and through the medium of personal argument and advice.

In November of this year Her Majesty opened Blackfriar's Bridge and the Holborn Viaduct amid the most beautiful weather and multitudes of cheering people. During 1870 the Gladstone Government carried through their great measures dealing with the Irish Land Laws and the educational system generally. The former has been disappointing in its results; the latter, with some exception in details, has been an undoubted benefit to the people. But the great event of the year, and a very painful one to the Queen, was the war between France and Prussia, including, as it did, the revolution in Paris and the exile of the Emperor and Empress. The correspondence of that period has not been published, and the public have as yet no way of knowing the exact part taken and felt by Her Majesty. It is certain that she greatly liked the Empress Eugènie, and in many ways admired Napoleon III. While they were on the Throne she had an undoubted influence over them, and through that influence a means of maintaining the alliance and friendship between the two nations. On the other hand, the war was an aggressive and foolish one on the part of France, and King William of Prussia—Emperor William of Germany—was not only the father of her daughter's husband, but a personal friend and greatly respected ruler.

Whatever the circumstances, however, the Emperor and Empress were most hospitably received in England—though not officially—and after they had taken up their residence at Chiselhurst, where Napoleon was so soon to die, the ex-Empress and the Queen became close friends, and have remained so ever since. The loss of the *Captain* and its five hundred men, in the autumn of 1870, was a disaster which evoked the strongest expressions of sympathy from Her Majesty. During the succeeding May the Queen opened the new buildings of the University of London, and in June had the misfortune to lose Sir James Clark, her veteran physician and true friend. Meanwhile the question of purchase in the army had aroused a prolonged Parliamentary and political discussion, and was finally terminated by Mr. Gladstone advising the use of the Queen's prerogative. This remarkable advice, for a Liberal leader to give, was accepted by Her Majesty, who in all probability sympathized with the very many deserving and distinguished officers who were debarred from promotion because of being too poor to purchase it. The result was the abolition by Royal warrant, and without Parliamentary sanction, of the system of buying commissions, followed by severe criticism of the Premier upon the constitutional point and his alleged inconsistency. In the autumn, announcement was made of the engagement of Princess Louise to the Marquess of Lorne—eldest son of the Duke of Argyll. To the public it was pleasant news, and there is little doubt that alliances between the Royal family and the nobility of the realm would be continu-ously popular if they could be arranged with the same propriety and discretion. To the Queen it meant the loss of another daughter, and one who had proved a close and valued companion for some years. A note in the " Leaves from My Journal " declares that " though I was not unprepared for this result, I felt pain-fully the thought of losing her."

The wedding took place on March 21st, 1871, at St. George's Chapel, Windsor, and was celebrated with all possible pomp. The Queen and all the family were present—even the two little grandchildren, Prince Albert Victor and Prince George of Wales, clad in Highland costume, and looking very cheerful and happy. Her Majesty had known the bridegroom from childhood ; but it is interesting to note the anxious enquiries she made about him at the time of the engagement. She could not have gone to a better source than Dr. Macleod. " I asked him," says the Royal Diary, " about Lord Lorne, and he said he had a very high opinion of him." A little later the Queen adds that " He again told me what a very high opinion he had of Lord Lorne ; how good, excellent, and superior he thought him in every way ; and the whole family so good." Shortly before this event the Queen had personally opened Parliament; and shortly after it she attended the inauguration of the Royal Albert Hall. On June 21st Her Majesty opened St. Thomas' Hospital, three years after laying its foundation stone. In the autumn she suffered from a serious illness, and had not long recovered from it when news came, on November 23rd, that the Prince of Wales was suffering from an attack of typhoid fever.

The Princess Alice was at this time, with her children, staying in England ; and, on November 9th, had written her mother from Sandringham that " Bertie and Alix are so kind, and give us so warm a welcome, showing how much they like having us, that it feels quite like home. . . . They are both charming hosts, and all the party suit well together." Two weeks later she had to hurriedly carry her children back to Windsor ; and from the 29th of November to the 19th of December the Queen was at Sandringham, helping to nurse her son, with agonizing apprehension and the keenest memories of that other dreadful case of fever ten years before. At first it was not supposed that there was any danger ; and the Marquess of Lorne, speaking at a Scotch gathering on the 30th of the month, announced that the Prince had passed a quiet and favourable day. But a week later a relapse occurred, and the bulletins stated that the patient's life was in imminent danger. All the members of the Royal family were soon gathered at Sandringham, the papers were full of the Prince's illness, and the nation seemed to think and talk of nothing else.

While the anxiety of both family and nation was at its height the cause of the illness became known. The Prince had been visiting Lord Londesborough at Scarborough, and it was soon found that a guest at the same time—Lord

Chesterfield—and the Prince's groom, Blegg, were suffering from the same trouble. The Peer and the peasant died. But the Prince still lived, although on Saturday, the 9th of December, it was announced that while the fever had exhausted itself the patient's strength was also exhausted. The next day all England prayed in all the churches of the land for the recovery of the Prince of Wales. On Monday the best that the *Times* could say was that "the Prince still lives, and we may therefore still hope." Restless nights and days of exhaustion followed, and as the anniversary of his Royal father's death came on many millions wondered if the fatal omen would be realized. But the day so dreaded by the Queen and the people in this connection passed, and gradually a slow improvement became perceptible, until on Christmas day danger seemed to be passed, and the Princess of Wales and Princess Alice, smiling, but pale with watching and weariness, attended the distribution of presents to the labourers on the estate and gave them a message from the Prince.

The news created intense enthusiasm everywhere, and the London theatres went wild—as only a London theatre can do—when the announcement was made on the evening of Boxing day, amid the strains of " God bless the Prince of Wales." On the 26th Her Majesty published a letter to her people, written in simple and moving terms :

" The Queen," it stated, " is very anxious to express her deep sense of the touching sympathy of the whole nation on the occasion of the alarming illness of her dear son, the Prince of Wales. The universal feeling shown by her people during those painful, terrible days, and the sympathy evinced by them with herself and her beloved daughter, the Princess of Wales, as well as the general joy in the improvement of the Prince of Wales' state, have made a deep and lasting impression on her heart, which can never be effaced. The Queen wishes to express at the same time, on the part of the Princess of Wales, her feelings of heartfelt gratitude, for she has been as deeply touched as the Queen by the great and universal manifestations of loyalty and sympathy.

" The Queen cannot conclude without expressing her hope that her faithful subjects will continue their prayers to God for the complete recovery of her dear son to health and strength."

On February 27th, 1872, a national thanksgiving was held at St. Paul's, and, it would not be too much to say, throughout all the country. The Queen had at first intended to have little more than a private service, attended by herself, and the family, and Court. But as the day approached the magnitude of the celebration grew until it burst all bounds and assumed the form of a popular and national festival. The streets of London were covered with decorations and crowded with cheering thousands. The great Cathedral, though capable of seating 13,000 people, was, of course, full to the doors. A special prayer was offered by the Primate, and a hymn sung which had been composed for the occasion. The enthusiasm of the people was marvellous, while the leading men of the country in every rank and every department of human effort came also to take part in this demonstration of loyalty and affection—a combined evidence of feeling which made Her Majesty once more address a letter of thanks and gratitude to the nation. "Words are too weak," she declared, "for the Queen to say how very touched and gratified she has been by the immense enthusiasm and affection exhibited towards her dear son and herself, from the highest down to the lowest, on the long procession through the capital; and she would earnestly wish to convey her warmest and most heartfelt thanks to the whole nation for this great demonstration of loyalty." A couple of days later an unpleasant incident occurred, when a young man named O'Connor rushed to the side of the Queen's carriage, pointing a pistol with one hand and holding out a parchment in the other. John Brown seized him, while Her Majesty looked on without flinching or showing a sign of fear—even when face to face with the pistol. The lad turned out to be a Fenian, and the paper a petition for the Clerkenwall prisoners. As the pistol proved to be unloaded he was only given a good birching and a year's imprisonment at hard labour.

Early in the succeeding year Napoleon III. died from the painful malady which for years had caused him considerable suffering, and by acute torture during that eventful day at Sedan may have affected the result of the war. He was buried with every mark of respect and regard in the presence of the Prince of Wales, the Duke of Edinburgh, and some 40,000 people, including two thousand Frenchmen. On April 2nd the Queen visited Victoria Park, a favourite resort of the people in the east end of London, and received a popular ovation. During the autumn the Court went to Balmoral, and Her Majesty paid a visit to the Pass of Glencoe and climbed the ground at the head of Loch Shiel, where Prince Charlie saw the gathering of the clans in August, 1745. "I thought," says the Royal Diary, "that I never saw a lovelier or more romantic spot, or one which told its history so well. What a scene it must have been in 1745! and here was I, the descendant of the Stuarts and of the very king whom Prince Charles sought to overthrow, sitting and walking about quite privately and peaceably."

But the events of these years can only be skimmed over. The death of little Prince "Frittie" of Hesse, in May, caused the Princess Alice keen sorrow. The unfortunate boy fell out of an upper window while trying to save a toy, and died shortly afterwards. In June the Shah of Persia visited England by invitation of the Queen, and was received in state at Windsor Castle. This remarkable potentate, "the King of Kings and Lord of Lords," really believed himself to hold some such position, and during his tour of Europe did and said the most extraordinary things. Upon one occasion, after having been brilliantly entertained in Russia, Nasr-ed-Deen is stated to have taken leave of the Czar by saying: "I have noticed the way in which you govern this great country. I am well satisfied with it; you may continue to govern it, for you do so very well, and

I am entirely pleased with you." After a warm welcome in Berlin, Vienna, and Brussels, the Shah-in-Shah received an invitation from Her Britannic Majesty, through Sir Henry Rawlinson, and declared that the chief object of his journey was to pay a visit to England and pay his respects to its Sovereign.

On his way across the channel the Eastern monarch and his bejewelled suite were welcomed, and nearly frightened to death, by a fleet of British iron-clads—the first they had ever seen. The Shah stood the sight of these monsters bearing down upon them with dignity, though he turned as pale as death, but for his followers the salute of the great guns was too much, and under its effects they finally collapsed. He was given Buckingham Palace to stay in, after being formally received by the Queen, and the wreckage which ensued is historical. So also should be his remark, after having been sumptuously entertained by the Duke of Sutherland at Trentham, that his host ought to be put out of the way, as being too wealthy and influential for the safety of the State! Following this curious visitation came the marriage of the Duke of Edinburgh and the Grand Duchess Marie, only daughter of the Emperor Alexander II. of Russia. It was solemnized with great pomp on January 23rd, 1874, at the winter Gardens in St. Petersburg, and was the first wedding in her family which the Queen had been unable to attend. She was personally represented by Lord Sydney and Lady Augusta Stanley, and the service was performed according to the rites of both the Anglican and Greek Churches—the former ceremony being conducted by Dean Stanley under special commands from the Queen. The Prince and Princess of Wales, Prince Arthur, and the Imperial Crown Prince and Princess of Germany were present, as well as the Russian Royal family.

In England, despite various causes for national ill-feeling, the bride was given not only a cordial but a splendid welcome. The State entry into London on March 7th was a most imposing event, although snow covered the ground, and made the country look, as one spectator said, like " one vast bride cake." None the less, people thronged the streets and every available balcony and housetop, and received the Queen and Princess Beatrice and the Royal couple with continued acclamations. Some weeks after this Her Majesty reviewed the troops which, under Sir Garnet Wolseley, had just returned from Ashantee, and with her own hand fastened the Victoria Cross upon the breast of young Lord Gifford, who had greatly distinguished himself by his bravery. About this time, also, the Queen wrote to the President of the Society for the Prevention of Cruelty to Animals—taking advantage of a congress of home and foreign dele-gates, and the jubilee of the association—and desired him to give public expression to Her Majesty's warm interest in their efforts, and to accept a donation of £100 towards its funds. The letter continued : " The Queen reads and hears with horror of the sufferings which the brute creation often undergo from the thoughtlessness of the ignorant, and she fears, also, sometimes from experiments in the pursuit of science. For the removal of the former the Queen trusts much to the progress of education, and in regard to the pursuit of science she hopes that the entire advantage of these anæsthetic discoveries, from which man has derived so much benefit himself in the alleviation of suffering, may be fully extended to the lower animals."

On May 13th the Czar of Russia arrived on a visit to his daughter and the Queen. Everything was done in ceremonial and reception and entertainment to make his stay pleasant. In his last speech, addressed to the Lord Mayor and citizens of London at a banquet in the Guildhall, he concluded by thanking England for its good feeling " towards my beloved daughter," and by expressing the hope that " the affectionate home she finds in your country will strengthen the friendly relations now established between Russia and Great Britain." To-day the Empress of Russia is a granddaughter of the Queen, and the Emperor a personal friend of the Prince of Wales.

Meantime there had been a political crisis in 1873, when Mr. Gladstone resigned office on account of an accidental defeat, but had to resume it on the refusal of Mr. Disraeli to take any responsibility against a normal Liberal majority in the House. It was during the debate on this question—the Irish university endowment scheme—that Mr. Disraeli launched some fierce attacks upon the Administration. " You have had four years of it," he declared in one speech. " You have despoiled churches. You have threatened every corporation and endowment in the country. You have examined into everybody's affairs. You have criticized every profession and vexed every trade. No one is certain of his property, and nobody knows what duties he may have to perform to-morrow." The constitutional point involved in the Conservative leader's refusal to assume office turned upon the condition of public business, which he thought made it impossible to advise an immediate dissolution of Parliament, and equally impossible for him to carry on the Government without a majority. Several interviews of consequence took place with the Queen, and the result was as stated. A year later Mr. Gladstone appealed to the country, and was as badly beaten as he had five years ago beaten his great opponent.

Mr. Disraeli then became Prime Minister with a Government composed of Lord Cairns, as Lord Chancellor; the Duke of Richmond and Lord Malmesbury; Lord Derby, as Foreign Secretary—succeeded in 1878 by Lord Salisbury, who had meantime been Secretary for India; Lord Carnarvon, and afterwards Sir M. E. Hicks-Beach, as Colonial Secretary; Gathorne Hardy (Lord Cranbrook), as Secretary for War; Mr. (now Lord) Cross, as Home Secretary; Sir Stafford Northcote, as Chancellor of the Exchequer; and Lord John Manners, as Post-master-General. Other members of the Administration were Mr. Ward Hunt Lord Sandon (now Earl of Harrowby), Sir Charles Adderley (Lord Norton) and Mr. Sclater Booth. Some of the new or rising men were Lord George

Hamilton, Mr. W. H. Smith, Colonel Frederick Stanley—afterwards Lord Stanley of Preston and Earl of Derby—Mr. James Lowther, and Mr. Edward Stanhope. It was a Government of Imperial instincts and constitutional protection. To quote Mr. Disraeli, the aristocratic principle was to be preserved, the Commons prevented from becoming an indiscriminate multitude of ignorant partisans, the national Church was to be maintained, the functions of corporations, the tenure of landed property, and the sacredness of endowments was in each case to be strengthened and consolidated. To quote the policy which followed, the Queen was to become Empress of India and thus assert a new monarchical authority and influence ; the Prince of Wales was to travel in the great Eastern dominions as Her Majesty's special representative ; the Suez Canal was to be controlled, and the egg of a northern African empire laid ; the Princess Louise and the Marquess of Lorne were to go to Canada as an impressive evidence of the interest taken by the Royal family in the Colonies ; the power of England was to be reasserted in Europe ; and its Imperial influence felt on the shores of the Black Sea and throughout the countries of the world, by the appearance of the British fleet in the Golden Horn during the Russo-Turkish conflict, by the landing of Indian troops in Malta, and by Lord Beaconsfield's brilliant policy at the Congress of Berlin.

But these events took years to accomplish. In February, 1875, and following the accession of Mr. Disraeli to power, the Queen had intended to open Parliament, but the serious illness of Prince Leopold—this time from typhoid fever—once more prevented her. During September Her Majesty visited the Duke and Duchess of Argyll at Inverary Castle. In February of the succeeding year she again opened Parliament, attended a grand concert in the Albert Hall, and in March opened the new wards of the London Hospital, besides unveiling the statue of the Prince Consort which forms part of the magnificent memorial in Hyde Park. A visit to Germany followed, and while in Paris on the way home Her Majesty received Marshal MacMahon, the President of the Republic, on a private visit. During May she attended a review at Aldershot, and on August 17th was present at the unveiling of the statue to Prince Albert in Edinburgh. In the succeeding month she gave new colours to " The Royal Scots "—her father's regiment—and reminded them in a few clear and musical words that the Duke of Kent " Was proud of his profession, and I was always told to consider myself a soldier's child."

During the next few years public and private events crowded upon one another, but the political interest of the period in connection with the Queen remains a sealed page until her State documents and letters are made public. One thing we do know. Lord Beaconsfield, as the Premier became in 1876, was in complete accord with Her Majesty, and was a man whose patriotism and Imperialism she delighted to honour. Even in his Turkish policy he seems to have had her sympathy and the Duke of Somerset, who was in a position to know, wrote his wife on December 11th, 1878, saying that "When I went to the House of Lords on Monday the Prince of Wales came to me in the ante-room, and said he was very much pleased with what I had said on Thursday. It is obvious that the Prince as well as the Queen are entirely with Beaconsfield." It could not well be otherwise. Both Sovereign and Minister were strongly Imperialistic in their views, and extremely anxious to advance the external influence and power of England.

Hence the personal regret which Her Majesty must have felt in 1880 at his defeat—a feeling, however, which has never been allowed to transcend the bounds of constitutional decorum. Hence also the Royal visit to Hughenden Manor in December, 1877, and the Garter bestowed upon the hero of "Peace with Honour" in 1878. Hence the Queen's wreaths upon the bier of the dead statesman in 1881, composed in one case of primroses, and bearing the inscription, "His favourite flowers from Osborne, a tribute of affection from Queen Victoria," and, in the other case, of bay leaves and everlasting flowers, with the words, "A mark of true affection, friendship, and respect from the Queen." Hence the presence of the Prince of Wales, the Duke of Connaught, and Prince Leopold—the latter directly representing the Sovereign—at his funeral in Hughenden Church. Hence the unaccepted offer of a place in Westminster Abbey, and the private, mournful visit of the Queen and Princess Beatrice to the tomb in that little country church some days later, in order to place upon the coffin a last wreath and cross of flowers. Hence the monument afterwards erected to the memory of Lord Beaconsfield, "by his grateful and affectionate Sovereign and friend, Victoria R.I.," with the additional inscription: "Kings love him that speaketh right." Hence also the beautiful letter to Dean Stanley which follows, and which more than speaks for itself:

"OSBORNE, April 21st, 1881.

"DEAR DEAN,—Thank you very much for your sympathy in the loss of my dear, great friend, whose death on Tuesday last completely overwhelmed me.

"His devotion and kindness to me, his wise counsels, his great gentleness combined with firmness, his one thought of the honour and glory of the country, and his unswerving loyalty to the Throne, make the death of my dear Lord Beaconsfield a national calamity. My grief is great and lasting.

"I know he would wish to rest with the wife he loved so well, and not in Westminster Abbey, where, however, I am anxious that a monument should be erected to his memory.

"Ever yours affectionately,   V. R. and I."

Meantime many things had occurred in the Royal family. Prince Louis of Hesse became Grand Duke in 1877, through his father's death, and a year afterwards he lost his loving wife, the Queen a wonderfully sympathetic daughter and companion, the British people a Princess whom everyone admired and many loved. The peculiarly sad and pathetic death of Princess Alice was indeed a lasting sorrow to the Queen, and to the country a source of sincere and evident regret. Practically she had laid down her life in nursing her children through that dread disease, diphtheria—and the end came on the very anniversary of the Prince Consort's death. In 1879 Her Majesty joined in the sorrow of the Empress Eugènie for the death of her only son—the heir to all the hopes of the Imperialists of France—upon the plains of Southern Africa. During this year, also, on March 13th, the Duke of Connaught was married at St. George's Chapel, Windsor, to Princess Louise Margaret of Prussia. The usual State ceremonies were observed, and the Queen and Royal family were nearly all present. During February, 1881, the son of the Princess Royal and grandson of the Queen—now Emperor William II.—was married in great pomp at Berlin, Her Majesty being represented by the Prince of Wales. A little later Dean Stanley followed his wife to the tomb, and the Queen lost two devoted and faithful friends. At the end of April Prince Leopold—who had just been created Duke of Albany—was married to Princess Helen of Waldeck-Pyrmont, and on May 6th the Queen went in State to Epping Forest, and, in the presence of a multitude of her subjects, dedicated it to the perpetual use and enjoyment of the people. In August she replaced the colours lost by the brave Berkshire, or 66th, Regiment at Maiwand.

With these functions ended an historic period full of memorable national incidents and important domestic events. It had seen the oratorical leadership of Gladstone, and the brilliant statecraft of Disraeli; the inauguration of a new era in Ireland, and the most active page in the history of British Liberalism; the Imperial policy of the Conservatives, and the gradual decadence of the Manchester school; the beginning of a new system in India, and the lifting of England into its old-time position as a great European power. To the Queen it was a period of more or less domestic sorrow. Death had visited her family in various directions, sickness had been the source of many keen anxieties, and even the joyful weddings of the time became to her a natural cause of severance in home ties—troubles which had, however, to be endured in order to advance the welfare and happiness of her large but scattered family circle.

CHAPTER XV.

LATER EVENTS AND THE ROYAL JUBILEE.

MEANWHILE the Gladstone Government of 1880-1885 had been formed upon the temporary wreck of Lord Beaconsfield's policy and aspirations. It was essentially a retrogressive Ministry in its control of Foreign Affairs. The British protectorate over Asia Minor, which had been arranged by the Anglo-Turkish Convention of 1878, and by which the Armenian atrocities of a later date might have been averted, was abandoned. The war in Afghanistan was hurried to a close, and Candahar, which had been considered essential to the security of India from Russian invasion by a certain important route, was given up to the Afghans. The troubles with the Boers came and went, and the Transvaal was handed back to the Dutch farmers, whose courage had asserted itself so conclusively at Majuba Hill, but whose ideas of liberty were, and are, confined to the privilege of oppressing the natives and foreign residents to the full extent of their own selfish interests. Egypt, it is true, was conquered under stress of peculiar circumstances, and the Soudan invaded several times, but General Gordon was also sent to his destiny of abandonment and death at Khartoum, and the whole unsystematized campaign carried on without any apparent comprehension of what England really wanted or how far she was prepared to go.

But though it was not a progressive Government in any Imperialistic sense of the word, it was certainly one in composition and domestic policy. Mr. Gladstone was for two years Chancellor of the Exchequer as well as Prime Minister, and in 1882 was succeeded by Mr. H. C. E. Childers. Lord Selborne made a great Lord Chancellor; Lord Spencer was President of the Council until, in 1882, he became Lord Lieutenant of Ireland and the centre of most virulent Irish Home Rule abuse; Lord Northbrook was head of the Admiralty; Lord Granville, Foreign Secretary; Lord Hartington was at first Secretary for India, and then for War; Mr. Bright was at the Duchy of Lancaster until conscientious scruples connected with the war in Egypt compelled his resignation in 1882; Sir William Harcourt was Home Secretary; Lord Kimberley, Colonial Secretary, and afterwards Secretary for India; and the Duke of Argyll was Lord Privy Seal for a time, as was Lord Carlingford later on. The distinctly progressive and Radical element in the Government was Mr. Chamberlain, the President of the Board of Trade; Sir Charles Dilke, the Under Foreign Secretary until December, 1882, when he became President of the Local Government

RIGHT HON. JOSEPH CHAMBERLAIN, M.P.

THE EARL OF ROSEBERY, K.G., K.T.

Board; Mr. Mundella, the Vice-President of the Council; and Mr. Fawcett, the Postmaster-General.   They represented the new Radicalism; the semi-socialistic sentiment of the party; the domestic home policy and municipal legislative ideas of contemporary Liberalism.   That Mr. Chamberlain has since developed out of this chrysalis stage of politics and become a broad-minded statesman of the true Imperial type illustrates the expansive possibilities of British public life, while proving the intellectual acuteness of the one-time Radical leader.

Sir Charles Dilke had perhaps equal ability and opportunities at this period, and it was for some years an open question in the minds of many as to which would ultimately forge ahead of the other.   But the latter had limitations which were bound to hamper his rise.   Aside from the lamentable moral episodes of an after-time, he had in 1873 shown a singular lack of wisdom, and a distinct absence of political tact and knowledge of public feeling, by entering upon an anti-monarchical campaign, and in giving—or attempting to give—a series of addresses which included much abuse and personal misrepresentation of the Queen. Closed as the incident was by the lapse of years and the practically complete abandonment of his republican ideas, it none the less leaves an unpleasant impression, and one which statesmen, in the proper sense of the word, never desire to leave.   Certainly, Mr. Chamberlain did not make any such mistake, and, even though his earlier career shows no strong sympathy with the unity and extension of the Empire, it was one of intense preoccupation in more local matters, and he never placed himself on record as against what is now the predominant public principle in England and in his own life.

Another leader who was destined to come to the surface of affairs with almost unexampled rapidity was the Earl of Rosebery, who, early in 1885, became Lord Privy Seal and Chief Commissioner of Works, after having some years before filled a minor office for a short period.   Young, able, popular, and a most eloquent speaker, he was an especial favourite of Mr. Gladstone, frequently his host at Dalmeny, and the practical leader of the Scotch Liberals.   Other members of this Government were Mr. (now Sir) H. Campbell-Bannerman, Lord Wolverton, Mr. (now Sir) G. Osborne Morgan, Mr. Grant-Duff, Lord F. Cavendish—who was so brutally murdered in Dublin—Mr. Shaw-Lefèvre, Mr. L. H. Courtney, Mr. Adam, Mr. (now Sir) G. O. Trevelyan, and Mr. Dodson.   This first Parliament of Mr. Gladstone's second Ministry had been opened by the Queen on February 5th, 1880.   The two years that followed have been already partially referred to, and included the marriage of the Duke of Albany and the loss of many of Her Majesty's friends— especially the Earl of Beaconsfield.

The beginning of 1882—March 2nd—was marked by another attempt upon Her Majesty's life.   With the Princess Beatrice she was driving from the train to Windsor Castle, when a young man named Roderick Maclean pointed a revolver and fired. The man was at once secured, and declared that he only wished to frighten the Queen and not to injure her. Ultimately he was adjudged insane, and confined to prison as a dangerous lunatic. At the Castle little fuss was made over the matter, but in Parliament, and amongst the people, and in all parts of the Empire, much was said and written upon this seventh personal attack to which the Queen had been subjected. Addresses of sympathy and gratulation poured in, and Parliament acted in the same spirit. Earl Granville, in the House of Lords, spoke of the Queen's admitted bravery :

" I remember as if it were yesterday," he said, " that in 1850 Lord John Russell, a man of singularly calm and collected character, told me, immediately after an outrage on the Queen, that he was perfectly astonished at the courage Her Majesty exhibited at that moment. Thirty-two years have elapsed since that time, and it is possible that Her Majesty has suffered some diminution of physical strength, but the same brave spirit that characterized Her Majesty at that time has remained to this day. The first enquiry of the Queen was whether anyone was hurt. She next expressed her appreciation of the courage of the Princess Beatrice. It is with the highest satisfaction that I state—and I state it on the highest authority, that of the illustrious Prince who has only just left the Queen—that after this attempt, which was enough to shock the nerves of the bravest man, he left Her Majesty in the enjoyment of the same health as she had possessed before the attempt."

Mr. Gladstone and Sir Stafford Northcote made similar remarks in the Commons, while from all the chief rulers of the world and public bodies of every kind came sympathetic words or resolutions. Everywhere in England and the Empire the National Anthem was sung with enthusiasm, and prayers offered in church on the succeeding Sunday amid sincere and spontaneous emotion. A visit to Mentoné followed, the Queen travelling as Countess of Balmoral, and thus waiving State ceremonial—although it was impossible to really conceal her identity. Meanwhile Ireland was the storm-centre of politics, as Egypt was of international complications. Conciliation borne to the unhappy people of the former, as an olive branch in the hands of Lord Frederick Cavendish—a most estimable politician, and brother to the present Duke of Devonshire—was answered by his cruel assassination, and was followed by a renewed recourse to coercion. In the land of the Nile the war with Arabi had run its course, and Sir Garnet Wolseley, in storming the heights of Tel-el-Kebir, had given the rebels a final blow.

By the Queen the campaign was followed with much interest—enhanced by the fact that the Duke of Connaught had accompanied the expedition, in command of the first battalion of the Scots Guards, and was taking an active and distinguished part in its operations. It is understood that the Prince of Wales was anxious to go also, but this was naturally not deemed expedient by the Queen, and the heir to the Throne could only accompany his brother to the point of embarkation. Her Majesty also visited the ships as they lay off Cowes, and inspected the troops before their departure. When the forces were really engaged with the enemy the Queen suffered intense anxiety, and more than once the memory of the poor Prince Imperial, whose mother was then visiting the spot where he had been killed, came to this other Royal mother, and to the wife and sister who were with her.   On the 11th of September a cipher telegram arrived from Sir John McNeill, saying that it was intended to attack the enemy two days later.   Her Majesty's Diary speaks of the hours which followed.   " How anxious we felt I need not say ; but we tried not to give way.   Only the ladies dined with us.   I prayed earnestly for my darling child, and longed for the morrow to arrive.   Read Korner's beautiful ' Prayer before the Battle.'   My beloved husband used to sing it often.   My thoughts were entirely fixed on Egypt and the coming battle.   My nerves were strained to such a pitch by the intensity of my anxiety and suspense that they seemed to feel as if they were all alive."

The next morning—this was at Balmoral—the Queen was up early for her usual morning walk, and found a telegram saying the troops had marched out on the previous night.   But there was not then much time for reflection.   After breakfast the inevitable morning's work of reading despatches, writing letters and memoranda, and signing papers, required attention.   Then came a telegram saying that the battle was going on, and finally the despatch from Sir John McNeill : " A great victory ; Duke safe and well."   From Sir Garnet Wolseley there shortly arrived a longer one, written on the field at Tel-el-Kebir, describing the conflict, and concluding with those joyful words to the waiting hearts : " Duke of Connaught is well, and behaved admirably, leading his brigade to the attack."   Two months later Her Majesty, accompanied by the Empress of Germany, who was paying a visit to Windsor, and the Duke and Duchess of Connaught, witnessed at Victoria Station the return of the Grenadier and Scots Guards.   Shortly afterwards 8,000 of the troops who had served in Egypt were reviewed in St. James' Park, while medals and the Distinguished Service Order were personally bestowed by the Queen upon various officers and men.

On December 4th the new Courts of Justice, which had been built upon the site of Temple Bar, were opened by Her Majesty in great state and splendour.   Though the weather was bad the streets were crowded, and the people as enthusiastic as ever, while the decorations were striking, and the scene in the great hall during the ceremony was gorgeous with vivid colours and costumes, contrasting, as they did, with the black gowns of the barristers and the sombre effect of the building itself.   Early in 1883 a daughter was born to the Duke and Duchess of Albany, and baptized with those names of Alice Mary, around which so many cherished memories clung.   Not long afterwards the Queen slipped while ascending the stairs at Windsor, and sprained her knee so severely that for several months walking or standing was very painful.   A good deal of popular anxiety was felt regarding the result, as checking exercise and thus affecting the general health, but nothing more serious than inconvenience and some suffering came from it.

Just in the midst of this personal trouble, however, came the death of John Brown—the faithful servitor who had devoted himself, as only such a servant can do, to the comfort and well-being of his Royal mistress. "His loss to me," she wrote in "More Leaves from My Life in the Highlands" some eight months later, "ill and helpless as I was at the time, is irreparable, for he deservedly possessed my entire confidence, and to say that he is daily, nay, hourly, missed by me, whose lifelong gratitude he won by his constant care, attention, and devotion, is but a feeble expression of the truth." Unlike so many Sovereigns— and people of lesser rank—the Queen has never forgotten faithful service, and has certainly always received it from those who are too often overlooked and disregarded, but who, humble though they may be, are yet able to add much to the comfort of even a Royal life and home. The dedication of the volume just quoted from is made to her "Loyal Highlanders, and especially to her devoted personal attendant and faithful friend, John Brown." In these democratic days, this tribute of regard to a domestic servant is a characteristic of Her Majesty which should be remembered. Her dignity is safe, her position above attack, and she fears neither to be royal to the great nor appreciative to the humble. How true the following words were—as finally used by the Queen, in connection with Brown—no one probably knows as fully as she does:

> "A truer, nobler, trustier heart,
> More loyal, and more loving, never beat
> Within a human breast."

With the spring of 1884 came a loss of greater and more serious import to the already grief-burdened Queen. The Prince Consort was gone; the Princess Alice had been a martyr to personal affection and heroism; Prince Leopold, the delicate and carefully guarded favourite of his mother, was now to join the others, after a brief career of wedded happiness and the clear promise of distinction in all good words and work. From infancy, the Duke of Albany had been the victim of ill-health, and his natural sweetness of disposition and intellectual sensibility only increased the constant anxiety of those around him. Early in the new year he had reluctantly been compelled to leave his wife, whose health was not then very good, and spend the rigorous season at Cannes. For a time all went well, and he entered into the various simple amusements of the place with zest. The day before his death he watched the Battle of Flowers from his balcony with great pleasure, and expressed an intention of taking part in it. While descending the stairs, however, he slipped and hurt his knee severely, but was able to send off some telegrams and write a long letter to the Princess. Then he went to bed, and after a few hours' sound sleep passed suddenly away. The funeral at Windsor was a solemn and stately event and the sorrow of the people expressive and sincere, while their appreciation of the young Prince's life and character was well indicated by the *Times*:

"Almost on the threshold of a life rich for its brief duration in performance, and richer still in promise, death has suddenly removed a gifted, high-minded Prince, to whose future all subjects of the Queen looked forward with unfeigned pleasure and hope. . . . The career which was plainly marked out for him, and which he had already made his own, was not unworthy for any English Prince, however ambitious, to aspire to. His tastes were, for the most part, those of the scholar. In all his speeches was heard a rare note of culture, refinement, and reflection. He delighted in the pursuits which his father had followed; and, English by birth, he was able to throw himself completely into our literary and social movements. . . . His services, we all know, were cheerfully given whenever they could advance the literary, scientific, and philanthropic objects which he had so much at heart; and on these subjects he uniformly spoke with a clearness and force which promised that when with full experience his faculties had mellowed he would be a potent power and influence for good."

Addresses of condolence with Her Majesty and the widowed Duchess were at once passed by both Houses of Parliament, and in a thousand minor, but none the less pronounced, ways the sympathy of the public was shown. Following this event came a natural period of retirement, and it was not until the opening of Parliament on January 21st, 1886, that the Queen made any really important public appearances, although she had in the previous spring paid a brief visit to the Continent, and later on had distributed medals to the Egyptian troops and spoken gentle words to the invalid soldiers at Netley Hospital. On July 23rd, 1885, she had also been present at Whippingham Church, in the Isle of Wight, where her last unmarried daughter and most faithful companion was wedded to Prince Henry of Battenberg—a handsome Prince, and brother to the gallant Alexander of Bulgaria, who did so much to develop national life and unity out of the crushed races of a country long cursed by Turkish tyranny and crime. The brief Parliament which Her Majesty now opened in great state and amid a most brilliant environment of dignitaries, great men and beautiful women, bright costumes and flashing jewels, was a very short-lived one. It had succeeded the five-year House which Mr. Gladstone had held in his hand until in its latter days a combination of causes—Irish discontent, general dissatisfaction at the death of Gordon, and the conduct of the Soudan campaign as a whole—resulted in his defeat upon a clause of the Budget, the taking of office by Lord Salisbury, and an appeal to the country.

The elections had resulted in a victory for the Liberals with a decreased majority. Though a short-lived Parliament it was destined to be a stormy one. The new Gladstone Government, which had, of course, been formed, included some new names, and gave high posts to some of the rising men. Lord Rosebery became Foreign Secretary, and distinguished himself by proclaiming the necessity of continuity and non-partisanship in foreign affairs. Sir William Harcourt was Chancellor of the Exchequer; Mr. Campbell-Bannerman, Secretary for War; Mr. Trevelyan, Secretary for Scotland. But even in the composition of the Ministry there were ominous hints of what was to follow. Home Rule was in the air, and old Liberals were afraid of the rumours current as to Mr. Gladstone's intentions, while Conservatives unhesitatingly declared that his majority depended upon the Irish contingent and the Irish vote in the House. However that may be, leaders like John Bright and the Duke of Argyll were not in the Government ; Lord Selborne refused to accept the Lord Chancellorship, and it was given to Lord Herschell ; the Marquess of Hartington—soon to be Duke of Devonshire by his father's death—declined office; and Mr. Chamberlain accepted it under conditions which left him free to act when the time came.

There were some prominent men in the Government for the first time. Mr. H. H. Fowler and Mr. J. T. Hibbert; Mr. Bryce and Mr. Jesse Collings ; Sir Charles Russell, now Lord Russell of Killowen and Lord Chief Justice ; Lord Dalhousie, whose premature death soon after closed a most promising career ; held various positions, while Lord Aberdeen became Lord Lieutenant of Ireland. In two months from the formation of this Ministry on February 1st, the Home Rule Bill had been introduced and the Liberal party disrupted. Bright and Hartington, Chamberlain and Collings, Argyll and Selborne, Northbrook and Goschen, and many more of the brightest men in the Liberal ranks, went into permanent opposition and organized the Liberal-Unionist party. The Bill was eventually defeated and an appeal made to the country. A majority was given to the Unionists of over one hundred, and Mr. Gladstone promptly resigned. Lord Salisbury—after offering to serve under Lord Hartington as Premier—formed a Government, which, for six years, directed the affairs of the nation.

It was the first real opportunity which this heir of the Cecils, and of Burleigh's name and Burleigh's fame, had been given of showing his faculty for government. He had proved himself against Disraeli, as against Gladstone, a master of sarcastic oratory and forceful speaking. He had with Beaconsfield proved himself at Berlin, and in control of the Foreign Office generally, a master of skilled diplomacy. He had impressed himself upon contemporary opinion as a sort of constitutional sheet-anchor, a product in some sense of the past, and a preservative of its best influences and traditions. His Government was, upon the whole, a strong one. For a few months Lord Iddesleigh—the Sir Stafford Northcote of old—was Foreign Secretary, and on his retirement the post was assumed by the Premier. Lord Randolph Churchill, who had come to the front with a bound, became Chancellor of the Exchequer, but only held the position for a short time, when he was succeeded by Mr. Goschen—the first Liberal-Unionist to join a Conservative cabinet. Lord Cranbrook and Mr. W. H. Smith; Lord Cross, Lord George Hamilton, and Lord Ashbourne, Sir M. E. Hicks-Beach, and Lord John Manners, were other familiar names. Sir Henry Holland, afterwards Lord Knutsford, was Colonial

Secretary for the greater part of this period, while Mr. Matthews—now Lord Llandaff—Mr. C. T. Ritchie, Mr. Cecil Raikes, Sir James Fergusson, Sir John Gorst, and Sir Richard Webster, the Attorney-General, were some of the newer men.

But the great reputation made in this Government and Parliament was won by Mr. Balfour. Beginning as Secretary for Scotland and with a popular belief in his unfitness for any real duties of statesmanship, he soon took the hardest post in the Cabinet—the Secretaryship for Ireland—and, after a time of brilliant administration there, closed the Parliamentary period as First Lord of the Treasury and leader of the House of Commons. The policy of the Government was essentially an Imperial one. It did not palter much with domestic legislation. As usual, after a long experience of Liberal rule, the people received and probably desired a rest in that respect. But abroad the foreign policy of the country was made a strong and efficient one, and received, in 1892, the public praise of Lord Rosebery himself. Africa was staked out amongst the Powers in what were called "spheres of influence," and millions of square miles were practically brought within the beneficent scope of British civilization and commerce. In India, Lord Dufferin's hands were strengthened, and Burmah annexed to the Crown. In America, the United States was warned out of the Canadian seal fisheries, and the Behring Sea arbitration resulted in a victory for the British and Canadian contention. In Egypt British influence and good government were developed, while at home the Colonial and Indian Exhibition and the Colonial Conference did much to promote the unity of the Empire.

It must have been a pleasant period for the Queen, with her strong Imperial sympathies. The Prince of Wales had begun to take a deeper and deeper interest in all national and Imperial movements, and—following in his father's footsteps—had shown intense interest in various great exhibitions. The Fisheries Exhibition of 1883, the Health Exhibition of 1884, the Inventions Exhibition of 1885, were succeeded by the greatest and best—the Colonial and Indian Exhibition of 1886. They all owed much to the Prince, but the latter was his special creation, as was the Imperial Institute, which grew out of it, and which was intended to make its benefits and Imperial influences permanent. The Exhibition was opened by Her Majesty on May 4th, amid every possible accessory of pomp and splendour. She came from Windsor attended by the Crown Princess of Germany and the Princess Beatrice, and the route of the royal procession from Paddington was alive with people, the air filled with fluttering flags, the houses, especially in South Kensington, gaily decorated with crimson cloth and varied hangings. The Queen was received by the Prince of Wales as Executive President, and after walking through the Exhibition and taking her place on the dais of the Royal Albert Hall found herself surrounded by representative men from every part of her vast Empire, and by most substantial personal evidences of its ethnographical variety and complex unity.   The National Anthem, first in English and then in Sanskrit, greeted Her Majesty as she took her seat, and was followed by a prolonged burst of cheers from the great audience. Then came that exquisite Ode written by Lord Tennyson at the request of the Prince, set to music by Sir Arthur Sullivan, and sung by Madame Albani amidst the enthusiastic appreciation of the audience and the very evident pleasure of the Queen herself.   It embodied in beautiful words that unity of the Empire which the Sovereign represented and which the Poet Laureate had so long and so earnestly struggled to promote, and was most eloquently appropriate to the occasion.   The first verse ran as follows:

> " Welcome, welcome with one voice!
>   In your welfare we rejoice,
>   Sons and brothers that have sent,
>   From isle and cape and continent,
>   Produce of your field and flood,
>   Mount and mine and primal wood,
>   Works of subtle brain and hand,
>   And splendours of the Morning Land,
>   Gifts from every British zone!
>   Britons, hold your own."

Then came a lengthy address, presented by the Prince of Wales to his Royal mother, and concluding with the hope that the Exhibition would illustrate and record the Imperial development of the immediate past ; would stimulate commercial interest, knowledge, and intercourse within the Empire ; would augment the warm and sympathetic feeling between all parts of her dominions ; and would " still further deepen that steadfast loyalty which we who dwell in the Mother Country share with our kindred who have elsewhere so nobly done honour to her name."   In replying, the Queen expressed her warm pleasure at seeing the success of the enterprise, as well as the part which her son had taken in leading the movement, and concluded by declaring that: " I cordially concur with you in the prayer that this undertaking may be the means of imparting a stimulus to the commercial interests and intercourse of all parts of my dominions, by encouraging the arts of peace and industry, and by strengthening the bonds of union which now exist in every portion of my Empire."   With " Home, Sweet Home," from Madame Albani, after the Exhibition had been declared open, and a bow from Her Majesty to the enthusiastically cheering audience, the Royal party left the building amid the farewell strains of "Rule, Britannia."

On the 14th of May following a Royal visit was paid to Liverpool, the first since 1851.   The Queen was accompanied by the Duke of Connaught and the Prince and Princess Henry of Battenberg, and on arriving early in the morning was received enthusiastically by a vast gathering of people.   Later in the day a State procession was made from Newsham House to the Exhibition of Naviga-

NICHOLAS II., EMPEROR OF RUSSIA.

LORD STANLEY OF PRESTON, 16th EARL OF DERBY, G.C.B.

tion, Commerce, and Industry, which, with all due formality, was opened by the Queen amid the strains of an orchestra composed of the philharmonic societies of the city, the chorus from Mendelssohn's " Hymn of Praise," and the National Anthem. A brilliant illumination of the city took place in the evening, and during all the next day Liverpool remained *en fête*. After this event a brief period was spent at Balmoral, followed on June 30th by the opening of Holloway's Royal College for the Education of Young Women at Egham, and by a review of troops at Aldershot on July 2nd. Three days later a number of Colonial and Indian visitors were entertained at Windsor by Her Majesty.

It had been a very busy season for all the members of the Royal family, and in every direction they were deep in the work of attending conferences, and opening bridges, buildings, institutions, and public improvements of every possible nature. During August the Queen visited Edinburgh, stayed at Holyrood Palace, and attended the International Exhibition of Industry, Science, and Art. The streets of the city were beautifully decorated, and the loyalty of the people perfectly exuberant—unusually so for a race so little given to enthusiastic manifestations. Received by the Marquess of Lothian, Her Majesty was escorted to the great hall, where a dais and throne had been erected, and where, amid a distinguished gathering, she received an address, made a brief reply, and accepted a gold casket and badge. After visiting various parts of the Exhibition, the Royal party returned to Holyrood through great masses of cheering people, and in the evening witnessed illuminations of the most brilliant nature and effect, the hills overlooking the Palace appearing to be literally ablaze with lights and coloured fires.

With the beginning of 1887 came preparations for the greatest national celebration in all the history of the British Isles. Upon the 20th of June the Queen would complete the fiftieth year of her reign—a half century of such Imperial expansion, such constitutional progress and reform, such territorial and commercial growth, such literary and scientific and artistic achievements, as the world had never seen. Upon that date she would illustrate the completion of a period which her qualities had adorned, her statesmanship illumined, and her domestic example improved. With her the people of a great Empire could join in congratulations which were at the same time personal and national. In the one sense they could appreciate a development and progress which had helped them as individuals, brightened their homes, and lightened their lives. In the other they could feel as patriotic citizens a pride as potent as ever inspired the Roman or the Greek in the national power of their Sovereign's sceptre and the might and majesty embodied in the throne of their realm. In the former sense they could feel with Lewis Morris' " Song of Empire," which formed one of the many poetic tributes to the occasion :

" Thy life is England's. All these fifty years

Thou from thy lonely Queenly place
Hast watched the clouds and sunshine on her face,
Hast marked her changing hopes and fears ;
Her joys and sorrows have been always thine.
Always thy quick and royal sympathy
Has gone swiftly to the humblest home,
Wherever grief or pain or suffering come."

And in the sense of Imperial pride and progress they could say with truth :

" We hold a vaster Empire than has been !
Nigh half the race of man is subject to our Queen !
Nigh half the wide, wide world is ours in fee !
And where her rule comes all are free.
And therefore 'tis, O Queen ! that we,
Knit fast in bonds of temperate liberty,
Rejoice to-day and make our solemn Jubilee."

No other monarch in English history, with three exceptions, had reigned so long, and certainly none had reigned so beneficially. Henry III. had completed fifty-six years, but he came to the throne at nine years of age. Edward III. had just reigned the half century, while George III., who completed his sixty years, was insane for more than a decade of that period. It was therefore very natural that the proposal to celebrate such an occasion should call forth a national demonstration as great as British power and as wide as the world in its sympathetic strength. And it was equally fitting that while British citizens everywhere were discussing ways and means of embodying this national senti-ment, the Prince of Wales should suggest at least one method which would have the special advantage of being personally agreeable to Her Majesty. Hence the inception of the Imperial Institute at a meeting held on January 12th at St. James' Palace, presided over by His Royal Highness and attended by many eminent men. In the Chairman's opening address he described his idea of developing the Colonial and Indian Exhibition into a permanent exhibit—housed in suitable form and dignity—of the whole vast resources of the Empire, and contributed to by all its parts so as to prove at once the vitality and loyalty of the British realms.

" In order," said the Prince, " to afford the Queen the fullest satisfaction, the pro posed memorial should not merely be personal in its character, but should tend to serve the interests of the entire Empire, and to promote a feeling of unity among the whole of Her Majesty's subjects. The desire to find a fitting means of drawing our Colonies and India into closer bonds with the mother country, a desire which of late had been clearly expressed, met with the Queen's warmest sympathy. . . . From the close relation in which he stood to the Queen, there could be no impropriety in his stating that if her subjects desired, on the occasion of the celebration of her fiftieth year as Sovereign of this great Empire, to offer her a memorial of their love and loyalty, she would specially value one which would pro-mote the industrial and commercial resources of her dominions in various parts of the world, and which would be expressive of that unity and co-operation which Her Majesty desired should prevail among all classes and races of her extended Empire."

The success which followed this initiatory movement need not be referred to at this stage, but it was certainly not the least striking evidence of the world-wide British desire to honour the Queen as she would have liked to be honoured. During February and March various State functions took place at Windsor, and on the 23rd of the latter month Her Majesty visited Birmingham, where five miles of streets had been superbly decorated with flags and festoons and banks of flowers, triumphal arches, and trophies emblematic of the industries and inventions of the great Midland metropolis. In spite of a severe personal cold and a storm of wind, the Queen set out from Windsor at the hour appointed. Fortunately, by the time the Royal party reached Birmingham the sun had shone through the clouds and brightened the day and the scene for a multitude of at least half a million people who thronged its streets. A very striking feature of the reception was a semicircle of 15,000 school children, a mile long, with the teachers standing behind each school, and the groups keeping up all along the line a continuous strain of " God save the Queen." At the town hall an address was presented by the Corporation, and a reply read by Her Majesty, which concluded with these words : " During the long and eventful period, now extending over fifty years, through which my reign has continued, the loyalty and affection of my faithful people have been a constant source of support in difficulty and sorrow, and consolation in affliction."

After luncheon the Queen proceeded with her suite to the pavilion covering the site of the future Law Courts, and, amid the usual ceremonial, laid the foundation stone. A brief visit to the Continent followed, and in April a Colonial Conference was held in London, which was destined to be famous as the second of the links in the chain of closer Imperial unity. On the 4th of May the delegates were received at Windsor, and presented an address to the Queen, dilating upon the expansion, progress, and constitutional stability of the Empire during her prolonged reign. The celebrations now commenced in earnest. A Jubilee Exhibition illustrative of progress in arts and manufactures during the Victorian era was held at Manchester, and opened by the Prince and Princess of Wales. On May 9th a large deputation representing the Corporation of London waited on Her Majesty at Buckingham Palace and presented a loyal address of congratulation. In her reply reference was made to " the sympathy which has united the Throne and the people," and to her hope that this cordial feeling would always continue unbroken.

On the following day a most brilliant drawing-room was held, and a private visit paid to Westminster Abbey in connection with the forthcoming Jubilee service. Meantime, and through many succeeding weeks of ceremonial and State duties, the daily routine of correspondence and reading despatches, signing papers, and the making of memoranda of opinions and instructions upon all manner of important State matters, had to be attended to, as well as the pressure of public engagements in connection with the Jubilee. On May 14th Her Majesty opened the People's Palace in Whitechapel, the Royal procession passing through streets of garlands and banners, drapery and decorations of every conceivable kind, together with at least 15,000 troops arranged along the route in most effective and imposing style. Many were the evidences of loyalty and affection shown, and especially in the great East-end thoroughfare. The usual loyal address, enthusiastic cheers from the audience, and sympathetic reply from the Queen followed, and after the Prince of Wales, in Her Majesty's name, had declared the building open, an adjournment was made to the Mansion House, where great preparations had been going on to formally receive the Sovereign.

Some seven hundred invited guests were present, including the Aldermen in their scarlet robes and chains, and the Lord Mayor in his state robes of crimson velvet and ermine. The latter official received Her Majesty, who was accompanied by the Prince and Princess of Wales and other members of the Royal family. Refreshments were then served, and after a brief stay the party left amid enthusiastic cheers from the crowds outside. Six days later the Queen received deputations at Windsor from the London and Edinburgh Universities, the English Presbyterians, the Society of Friends, and various Nonconformist bodies. The address from the Friends was peculiarly interesting both from its contents and from being read by Mr. John Bright, a political veteran whose views upon some topics were narrow and harmful, but whose character and oratory have been undoubted ornaments to the nation. On Sunday, May 12th, occurred the central event of the series of celebrations now commencing. The House of Commons on that day attended Church in a body at St. Margaret's, Westminster, for the first time since May 4th, 1856, on the conclusion of the Crimean struggle. But for the House to meet in state and go to Church in order to offer solemn thanksgivings on the jubilee of the Sovereign's reign was absolutely unique. The Speaker, Mr. Peel, led the way, and the members followed four abreast—the first four being Mr. Gladstone, Mr. W. H. Smith, Mr. Courtney, and Lord Hartington. The Queen's Westminster volunteers, headed by Colonel (now Sir) C. E. Howard Vincent, formed a guard of honour, and the sermon was preached by the eloquent Bishop of Ripon.

Many other commemorations followed in the form of banquets, assemblies, balls, and public festivities of every kind and character, from the feeding of 6,000 poor people in Glasgow to a Jubilee yacht race around the United Kingdom. Meantime presents of every sort and value had been pouring in from individuals and collective bodies, princes and potentates in the east and the west, and men, women, and children in all parts of the Empire. A typical one was the "Woman's

Jubilee Offering," which was to be contributed to by British women and girls, and the nature of which was to be decided by the Queen herself.   But the pivotal event of a celebration extending from India to Canada, and from Africa to Europe, was the Thanksgiving Jubilee service of June 21st, attended by the Queen and Royal family, the King and Queen of the Belgiums, the King of Denmark, the King of Saxony, the King of Greece, the Crown Princes of Austria and Sweden, the Crown Prince of Portugal, the Crown Prince and Princess of Germany, the members of Royal families in nearly every state of Europe, the afterwards unfortunate Queen of Hawaii, the brother of the King of Spain, the uncle of the Mikado of Japan, the Maharajahs of Kuch Behar and Indore, the Rao of Kutch, and many other Indian princes, as well as the men of light and leading in the British realm, and representatives from all its great Colonial States.

The thoroughfares through which the series of brilliant processions passed from Buckingham Palace to the Abbey were decorated in a way impossible to describe.   Any previous demonstration of the kind was eclipsed and obliterated. It was one long array of brilliant colouring, shifting and gleaming brightness, waving flags and banners, and an almost Oriental display of magnificence.   The day broke fair and beautiful, and Westminster Abbey had been prepared at a cost of £17,000 for the reception of 9,000 or 10,000 persons.   The Queen left the Palace at half-past eleven in a carriage drawn by six cream-coloured horses, attended by walking footmen, guarded by the Duke of Cambridge and an escort, and immediately followed by a bodyguard of Princes—the heir to the throne being mounted on a golden chestnut horse and the recipient of many and frequent cheers.   But throughout that marvellous journey, amid millions of her subjects standing in serried masses of loyal enthusiasm, our Sovereign Lady was the central figure, and the one to whom all eyes and hearts were first turned.   It was the greatest popular demonstration in all history, and little wonder that Her Majesty was visibly affected by the evidences of a great people's sympathetic joy.

At the Abbey the scene was one which even that accustomed centre of historic splendour had never seen equalled.   Waiting the arrival of Her Majesty were various Episcopal dignitaries clad in the rich vestments of their office, the heralds in blazoned tabards, the Court officials in full uniform, the visiting rulers in brilliant costumes, the members of every British order of Knighthood in all the chivalric insignia of their rank, the peers and prelates in their robes of State, and the women in the audience dressed with a magnificence which only such an occasion could call forth.   As the Queen walked up the Abbey to her place, followed and surrounded by all this gorgeous array, it was seen that her face literally beamed with pleasure—a reflection, no doubt, of the happiness occasioned by such a reception as had just been given her—and that her dignity of bearing was unaffected by age and responsibilities and sorrows. Clad in black attire, relieved, however, by the brilliant insignia of many orders, and a head-dress of white lace sparkling with diamonds, she looked thoroughly worthy of her great Imperial position, and the lustre of a half century's glorious reign.

The solemn service proceeded, and was echoed in every church and religious meeting-house throughout the British Empire, while during the ensuing evening the British Isles were illumined with festal fires, and on every cliff, and hill, and lofty heath or mountain peak there blazed great bonfires. From sea to sea, from Hampstead and the Cathedral at Ely to the Orkneys or the Malvern Hills, flared these evidences of popular pleasure. On the day following Her Majesty formally received and inspected a vast number of gifts. Later in the day she drove in State down a long and happy line of 27,000 school children, who had been given a Jubilee banquet and various amusements, together with some 40,000 toys, through a representative Committee organized by Mr. (now Sir) Edward Lawson, presided over by the Prince of Wales, and including the Duchess of Abercorn, the Duchess of Manchester, Lady Rosebery, Mrs. Lawson, the Duchess of Westminster, Lady Spencer, Lady Rothschild, and others. After the Queen had driven through the children's ranks to the flagstaff, the Royal ensign was hoisted, the National Anthem sung, and a specially manufactured Jubilee mug presented by Her Majesty with some kind words to a little girl who had attended school for seven years—she was then twelve—without missing a single attendance. Miss Lawson then presented a bouquet of orchids bearing the inscription: " Not Queen alone ; but Mother, Queen, and Friend in one." Amid the strains of " Rule, Britannia," followed by the singing of "God Bless the Prince of Wales," the Royal party left to pay a visit to Eton, where the reception by nine hundred boys—the flower of British youth—was more than enthusiastic. In a myriad of other forms the Jubilee continued to be celebrated, long after the Queen had issued a personal letter of thanks to her loyal subjects, which, in most expressive words, read as follows :

" Windsor Castle, June 24th, 1887.

" I am anxious to express to my people my warm thanks for the kind, and more than kind, reception I met with on going to and returning from Westminster Abbey, with all my children and grandchildren. The enthusiastic reception I met with then, as well as on all these eventful days, in London as well as at Windsor, on the occasion of my Jubilee, has touched me most deeply. It has shown that the labour and anxiety of fifty long years, twenty-two of which I spent in unclouded happiness, shared and cheered by my beloved husband, while an equal number were full of sorrows and trials, borne without his sheltering arm and wise help, have been appreciated by my people.

" This feeling, and the sense of duty towards my dear country and subjects, who are so inseparably bound up with my life, will encourage me in my task—often a very difficult and arduous one—during the remainder of my life. The wonderful order preserved on this occasion, and the good behaviour of the enormous multitudes assembled, merits my highest admiration.

"That God may protect and abundantly bless my country is my fervent prayer.

"VICTORIA R. and I."

Following this came a great garden party at Buckingham Palace; a Royal reception at Windsor to Indian chiefs and princes and municipal corporations bearing addresses; a review of 28,000 volunteers in the metropolis; the laying of the foundation stone of the Imperial Institute; a review of 56,000 volunteers at Aldershot; the laying of the foundation stone at Windsor of a statue to the Prince Consort, which was to be erected out of a portion of the £80,000 presented as the Women's Jubilee Offering; a grand review of 135 warships at Spithead, amid innumerable smaller vessels, 30,000 spectators, and royal salutes which made a roar like many thousand thunders. On July 15th, Her Majesty paid a second visit to Hatfield House, but her first to the present Marquess of Salisbury. Accompanied by several members of the Royal family, she was enthusiastically received by masses of people in the little town, and in the Park which had been thrown open to them. The Premier, of course, made his magnificent mansion and its historic accessories do every possible honour to the occasion. During the succeeding year a second visit was received in England by the Queen from the Shah of Persia.

Meanwhile the ring of joyous celebration had extended like a girdle round the earth, and the Queenly woman and womanly Queen who was the centre of such universal gratulation was going on with her quiet and almost imperceptible labours in the direction and control of her vast Empire. Perhaps of all the tributes paid to her personal qualities and regnant work none was at this time more important and interesting than that of the statesman who had entered Parliament at her accession and had impressed all British politics since with his vitality and force. In a speech on the Queen's reign, delivered at Hawarden, Mr. Gladstone depicted her career and influence as a monarch, and added: "I beseech you, if you owe the debt of gratitude to the Queen for that which I have described, for her hearty concurrence in the work of public progress and improvement, for the admirable public example which her life has uniformly set, for her thorough comprehension of the true conditious of the great covenant between the throne and the people—if you owe her a debt of gratitude for these, may I say to you, try to acknowledge that debt by remembering her in your prayers." This request illustrates a peculiar phase in Mr. Gladstone's own character, as it certainly marks one of the greatest forces in that of the Queen—the combination of religious sincerity with personal ability and great individual influence.

CHAPTER XVI.

THE QUEEN AND THE CONSTITUTION.

THE influence of a British Sovereign upon and within the constitution of the realm is not at all in accordance with some modern popular impressions. That constitution is clearly defined within certain limits, but outside of this field of operation there stretches a vast area of possible action and of room for the exercise of Royal power. Much depends upon the personality of the ruler, and when that ruler possesses such varied experience, such wide knowledge of politics and modern history, such intimate acquaintance with the secret springs and mechanism of all modern government, such prolonged intercourse with the great men of the nation during the longest reign in British annals, as Queen Victoria admittedly possesses, it is almost impossible to over-estimate her influence and power. But, aside from this personal view, the monarch has great reserve powers, which have been seldom, and in some cases never, used, but which are available in any important crisis, should the occasion demand their exercise. The position in this respect has been clearly defined by Mr. Gladstone—September, 1878—in words of weight and authority:

" The Sovereign in England is the symbol of the nation's unity, and the apex of the social structure; the maker (with advice) of the laws; the supreme governor of the Church; the fountain of justice; the sole source of honour; the person to whom all military, all naval, all civil service is rendered. The Sovereign owns very large properties; receives and holds, in law, the entire revenue of the State; appoints and dismisses ministers; makes treaties; pardons crime, or abates its punishments; wages war or concludes peace; summons or dissolves the Parliament; exercises these vast powers for the most part without any specified restraint of law; and yet enjoys, in regard to these and every other function, an absolute immunity from consequences. There is no provision in the law of the United Kingdom for calling the Sovereign to account; and only in one solitary and improbable, but perfectly defined case—that of his submitting to the jurisdiction of the Pope—is he deprived by statute of the Throne."

This is the theory upon which the Queen reigns, and these are the powers which she can or does wield. No one disputes this primary constitutional condition, but where the skill and statesmanship of the Sovereign, the honour and patriotism of her Ministers, and the discretion and wisdom of the people have been shown is in the practical working of the system so as to completely combine the interests of the Crown and the nation. Under our modern development the Sovereign is still hedged in with the attributes and dignity, though not exactly with the old-time application of the principle of divine right; and the idea that

NICHOLAS I., EMPEROR OF RUSSIA, 1825-55.

LOUIS PHILIPPE, KING OF THE FRENCH, 1830-18.

NAPOLEON III., EMPEROR OF THE FRENCH, 1852-70.

EUGENIE, EMPRESS OF THE FRENCH.

"the King can do no wrong" is imbedded in the system of ministerial responsibility, and in the necessity of obtaining advisers who are willing to assume the actions of the Sovereign as theirs and accept such responsibility before Parliament and the people. That Her Majesty has never taken a course in which she was unable to obtain such advisers is the real triumph of her constitutional career and personal statecraft. When she has differed with her Ministers she has either influenced them into the acceptance of her views or found others who would carry those views into effect.

The Queen has never been a constitutional figurehead in any sense of the word. This fact cannot be too strongly stated and reiterated, because it is one which many people who can hardly be termed ignorant along general lines—and yet who are emphatically so in this connection—believe in many parts of Her Majesty's dominions. The Sovereign accepts the will of the popular majority when voiced in important legislation representing their wishes. But long before that legislation is carried into effect it has been discussed in detail with the Queen, and probably as much advice given as is received. In such matters she has a great advantage. The position of the monarch is a permanent one, that of the Ministers is transitory; she speaks from a station immeasurably higher, and representative not of a party, but of the nation and the Empire; she takes, and has always taken, a calm survey of the whole situation, unworried by partisan difficulties and hasty deductions. The Queen had great tact before she obtained great experience, and her political interventions have therefore been generally successful and far-seeing. She possessed weight of character and untiring industry, together with habitual presence at the seat of government and in the very heart of public affairs, so that her *influence* almost from the first corresponded with her lofty position and made it, as a rule, unnecessary to exercise her *powers*. Ministers might come and go, Premiers, and governors, and parties, and politicians might rise and fall, but their Sovereign and Queen was always working and watching at the helm of the State.

The educating influences of King Leopold and the Duchess of Kent early operated upon the mind of the Queen. She was trained in a clear perception of constitutional rule and of the English character from the first, and the combination of these two lines of thought and precept have greatly helped her throughout the reign. It is one thing to comprehend the dignity of a throne, the dormant powers of a constitution, and the inherent strength of a royal position. It is another to comprehend the power of the people, the character and idiosyncrasies of a nation, the nature of the compromises under which an unwritten constitution must be worked. The Queen learned both elements in the governing problem, and to that is due much of her marvellous success. Lord Melbourne proved an ideal successor to the Duchess and her uncle of Belgium. From him the youthful Sovereign undoubtedly obtained much information and experience;

and if to-day Lord Salisbury or Lord Rosebery are glad to receive the practised advice and opinions of their Queen in many more matters than the world ever dreams of, it is because of the development from out of this initiatory stage of study and instruction. Incidentally, Lord Melbourne was connected with the first public constitutional difficulty of the reign. The Bedchamber Question has been referred to elsewhere, but the following letter illustrates the nature of the incident and the reasonable objections of the Queen. It was written by Lord Palmerston to Lord Granville, on May 10th, 1839—after the resignation of the Melbourne Ministry on account of the Jamaica question:

" The Tories have failed to make a government, not from any difference between themselves, but from a difference with the Queen. They insisted on the removal of the Ladies of the Bedchamber. The Queen declared she would not submit to it; that it would be too painful and affronting to her; that those ladies have no seats in Parliament; that the object in view in dismissing them was to separate her from everybody in whom she could trust. . . . They came three times to the charge. First, Peel made the demand singly, then he brought to his aid the Duke of Wellington, and again he came back with the unanimous opinion of his Cabinet that was to be. The Queen, alone and unadvised, stood firm against all these assaults, showed a presence of mind, a firmness, a discrimination far beyond her years, and had much the best of it in her discussion with Peel and the Duke. She sent Peel this morning her final refusal to comply with their condition, and Peel thereupon resigned his commission to form a government. We shall, of course, stand by the Queen and support her against this offensive condition which the Tories wanted to impose upon her. . . . It remains to be seen whether this House of Commons will support us in supporting her, and, if it will not, whether this House does or does not faithfully represent the opinion of the country."

This is evidently a partisan letter, and written under the feelings of the moment; but in the end the Queen maintained her right to appoint the chief officials about her person; her refusal to allow them to be turned into political appointments; and the chief points of the position stated by Lord Palmerston. There were, of course, two sides to the question, and Sir Robert Peel had good reasons for not liking to see the youthful Sovereign surrounded by Whig appointees—in some cases the wives or daughters of former Ministers. But as the Queen assumed and asserted her own judgment and place in the constitution, and showed distinctly that she was not a Queen Anne, to be influenced by female favourites, or a Queen Elizabeth, to be swayed by male friends, the situation naturally adjusted itself, and no one in later days would dream of thinking that any action or policy of Queen Victoria could be moulded by the views of a Lady of the Bedchamber, or by anything apart from herself and the constitution, as she understands and interprets it. In the Ministerial crises and changes which more immediately followed, the Queen proved her absolute political impartiality, and showed that, while firm as a rock where she believed her rights to be invaded, she was flexible to a degree in subordinating personal sympathies to national necessities.

Lord Melbourne had to ultimately go, and be succeeded by Sir Robert Peel, but though it was a keenly-felt separation the new Premier received the same measure of confidence and support as the old, and in time became as close a personal friend. And so with the ensuing change to Lord John Russell. During this period, however, and for over twenty years, the Queen had the advantage of Prince Albert's wise help and counsel. With characteristic self-effacement, she has always exaggerated the effect and value of the Prince Consort's share in this portion of her life-work. It was undeniably a great and important part, and not the less so for leaving ample room for the play of Her Majesty's own faculties and royal functions. Sir Archibald Allison, the eminent historian, says in his Memoirs—speaking of a visit to Balmoral in 1849— that : " I sat opposite the Queen at dinner on both days, and as the party was small the conversation was general. . . . The Queen took her full share in the conversation, and I could easily see from her quickness of apprehension and the questions which she put to those around her that she possessed uncommon talents, a great desire for information, and in particular great rapidity of thought ; a faculty often conspicuous in persons of her rank, and arising not merely from natural abilities, but from the habit of conversing with the first men of the age."

And, while Prince Albert was of immense help in the consideration of foreign affairs during nearly the whole of their wedded life, it must be remembered that in the first years of that period he was—despite the early and valuable counsels of Stockmar and King Leopold—really only a student of British political life, and it is quite probable that the Queen moulded his views of constitutional practice, as distinct from constitutional precept, to at least as great a degree as he ever influenced her opinions upon foreign policy. This is clearly enough indicated in the " Early Years of the Prince Consort," where it is stated that " for the first year or two the Prince was not, except on rare occasions, and by special invitation, present at the interviews of the Queen with her Ministers. Though taking, the Queen says, great pains to inform himself about everything, and though Lord Melbourne expressed much anxiety that the Queen should tell him and show him everything connected with public affairs, he did not at this time take much part in the transaction of business." This work being supervised by Her Majesty personally, the statement shows conclusively that the Prince learned, in the long run, as much from the Queen as she ever derived from him. And it is also apparent from what we have been allowed to learn of Her Majesty's intervention in statecraft long after his death, and following the period covered by this volume and the publication of Sir Theodore Martin, that her views of government, and what may be termed ability in administration and international diplomacy, were not dependent upon his presence and guiding influence, important as they admittedly were.

An illustration of the Queen's political power is seen in the crisis of 1852, when the coalition which had so brilliant a beginning and so disastrous an ending was practically arranged by the Sovereign. For some years the Government had been carried on by one or other of the two parties without any definite majority, or, as it would now be called, mandate from the people. The free-trade element in the old Tory party had not yet found its final resting-place in the bosom of the Liberals, and all was fluctuation and confusion. Writing under the direct authority of the Queen, Sir Theodore Martin tells us that she felt, upon the resignation of Lord Derby in the year mentioned, that "the time had come for the formation of a strong administration, and for closing the unsatisfactory epoch of government upon sufferance." With this view she called to her counsels the two veteran leaders in the Conservative and Liberal parties—Lord Aberdeen and Lord Lansdowne. The latter was too ill to come, but the former did so. On December 19th Lord John Russell received a letter from the Queen, dated at Osborne, and declaring her opinion that the moment had arrived when "a popular, efficient, and durable government could be formed by the sincere and united efforts of all parties professing Conservative and Liberal opinions. The Queen, knowing that this can only be effected by the patriotic sacrifice of personal interests and feelings to the public, trusts that Lord John Russell will, as far as he is able, give his valuable and powerful assistance to the realization of this object." The ultimate result was the "Cabinet of all the Talents," and a note from the Queen to Leopold of Belgium on December 28th, saying that "The success of our excellent Aberdeen's arduous task, and the formation of so brilliant and strong a Cabinet, would, I am sure, please you. It is the realization of the country's and our own most ardent wishes. . . . It has been an anxious week, and just on our happy Christmas eve we were still uneasy." The part which Her Majesty took in the ensuing Crimean war was continuous, earnest, and effective. Much of it properly comes into the consideration of Foreign Affairs during her reign, but as an illustration of her careful and close watchfulness over public matters the following letter—June 26th, 1854—is of vital interest:

"The Queen is very glad to hear that Lord Aberdeen will take an opportunity to-day of dispelling misapprehensions which have arisen in the public mind in consequence of his last speech in the House of Lords, and the effect of which has given the Queen very great uneasiness. She knows Lord Aberdeen so well that she can fully enter into his feelings and understand what he means; but the public, particularly under the strong excitement of patriotic feeling, is impatient, and annoyed to hear at this moment the first Minister of the Crown enter upon an impartial examination of the Emperor of Russia's character and conduct.

"The qualities in Lord Aberdeen's character which the Queen values most highly, his candour and his courage in expressing opinions, even if opposed to general feelings at the moment, are in this instance dangerous to him, and the Queen hopes that in the vindication of his own conduct to-day, which ought to be triumphant, as it wants, in fact, no vindication, he will not undertake the ungrateful and injurious task of vindicating the Emperor of Russia from any of the exaggerated charges brought against him and his policy, at a time when there is enough in that policy to make us fight with all our might against it."

This was a distinct and very direct letter of advice from the Sovereign to her chief Minister, and to the fact that it was closely followed was due a successful speech and a cessation of many calumnious attacks. In the formation of the Government which succeeded the Coalition, in 1855, Her Majesty had a most anxious and responsible part. It was in the middle of a great war, and while all kinds of complications were growing upon the foreign horizon, that the party leaders fell to quarrelling among themselves, so that after nearly two weeks of a Ministerial crisis Lord Cowley wrote from Paris to Lord Clarendon : " I wish to heaven that a Government of some sort was formed. I cannot exaggerate the mischief that the state of things is causing to our reputation as a nation, or the disrepute into which it is bringing constitutional government." Meanwhile the Queen had tried Lord Derby, Lord Lansdowne, and Lord John Russell. Each had failed to form a Ministry or effect an arrangement, and the crisis was only settled by the final calling in of Lord Palmerston. Of a similar nature to these anxieties was the Queen's continuous interest in her troops. Her correspondence with the Ministers of War and Foreign Affairs, the Viceroys of India and Governors of the Colonies, teem with references to the services of her soldiers and with schemes for their welfare or reward.

Writing to Lord Palmerston on January 14th, 1858, she declared that "the question of rewarding the gallant men who have done such wonders in the East is one of great importance. It will not be possible to take the whole of the claims into account as yet, but . . . the Queen hopes that Lord Palmerston will, with Lord Panmure, Mr. Vernon Smith, and the Duke of Cambridge, go into the question and make her an early report." The succeeding paragraph is interesting as anticipating her future action—and perhaps as indicating her own opinion upon the system of purchase in the army. " The Queen would likewise recommend that the opportunity should not be lost for obtaining by ' promotion for distinguished services ' some younger and abler general officers, whom our system affords no other means of bringing forward." It was this sympathetic feeling that induced her to found the Victoria Cross and the Distinguished Service Order; and which in a wider sense, and applicable to far-distant subjects of the Crown, led her to institute the Order of the Indian Empire and the Imperial Order of the Crown of India. In this connection it may be said that Her Majesty's share in the government of the great Eastern dominions of England has been as important as her part in home administration. The correspondence of Indian Governors-General teem with suggestions from the Queen, and especially during the mutiny was Lord Canning indebted for much cordial co-operation in the crucial days of the conflict—when the Government in London did not appear to be sufficiently alive to the issue. But of this more anon.

In all questions of foreign policy the Queen's interest has been keen and her participation constant. The dismissal of Lord Palmerston from office in 1851 for not furnishing immediate drafts of important despatches for the Queen's consideration, before they were sent abroad, is an historic illustration of the fact. One of many other evidences may be quoted here. The following letter was written at a time when Napoleon III. was proving too ambitious for the peace of Europe and was threatening to follow the example of his great Imperial exemplar —or at least to make the attempt. Dated at Buckingham Palace on 27th March, 1860, it shows that Her Majesty was not only a constitutional ruler, but a Sovereign who could think and speak for herself.

" The Queen has read with much pleasure Lord John Russell's speech of last night, and from the way in which it was received in the House of Commons she is certain that the country feels the danger which a supposed intimate and exclusive alliance with France has for the interests of Europe and of England.

" It is a belief in this alliance which makes the rest of Europe powerless and helpless, nay, drives it to enter into separate secret bargains with France, from a knowledge that an united resistance is impossible, and from a fear of England's full acquiescence in the various schemes of the Emperor. As the English press and general public were favourable to the Italian revolution and the loss of the Italian provinces by Austria, and are supposed to be so with regard to the separation of Hungary from Austria, and of Poland from Russia, the Emperor Napoleon has the more chance of keeping up the distrust of the Continental Powers in England. Fear being the worst counsellor, we cannot be astonished that the Powers should follow an unwise policy. But once reassured as to the views of England, they would, the Queen feels certain, readily rally round her and follow her lead."

A further illustration of the necessity and ability of the Queen to act for herself is shown in the crisis of 1859. Lord Derby's Government had resigned, and the question of the Premiership lay between Lord John Russell, who had been a Liberal leader for twenty years, and Lord Palmerston, who had held the post for four years. Neither would give way to the other, so far as the leadership of the Commons was concerned, so that the position of the Queen was a very delicate one. She at first tried a middle course by sending for Lord Granville, the Liberal chief in the House of Lords. He found it, however, impossible to harmonize the claims of the two rivals, and had to give up the attempt, thus throwing the distinct responsibility of a choice upon the Queen. As Lord John Russell put it in a private letter : " I am afraid Her Majesty must encounter the difficulty of making a choice. But I do not think either Lord Palmerston or I should be inclined to do otherwise than to submit with respect and loyal duty to Her Majesty's decision." The Queen awarded the apple of supremacy to Palmerston, and from that time until his death, in 1865, he reigned without dispute in his party and in Parliament. Then came the turn of Lord John— who meanwhile had become Earl Russell. Writing to him on December 19th from Balmoral, the Queen referred to " the melancholy news of Lord Palmerston's death," spoke of it as the breaking of another link with the past, declares that she felt deeply, "in her desolate and isolated condition," how one by one her tried servants and advisers were being taken from her, and added that she "could turn to no other than Lord John Russell, an old and tried friend of hers, to undertake the arduous duties of Prime Minister and to carry on the government."

In 1866 another crisis occurred—this time over the Reform Bill proposed by Lord Russell and Mr. Gladstone. During the whole of the stormy debates which took place in the Commons upon this question, the Queen wrote constantly to her Ministers in the course of business, and always urged compromise and conciliation. Prussia and Austria were just then preparing for a struggle of which no one could see the end, and Her Majesty naturally desired to have a stable Government in power, and to avert a political crisis. Lord Russell's letters to the Queen, however, indicate a rather uncompromising spirit, and for a time evidenced his belief that they would pull through all right. Finally, the vote upon Lord Dunkellin's amendment and the consequent defeat of the Ministry resulted in a letter of resignation on June 19th, which was answered in the following expressive terms :

"The Queen has received Lord Russell's letter with the greatest concern. The adverse vote in the House of Commons, and the step which the Ministers have thought it right to take in consequence, have taken her completely by surprise, having understood from Lord Russell, and others of the Government, whom she saw before going to Scotland, that there was no fear of a crisis. In the present state of Europe, and the apathy which Lord Russell himself admits to exist in the country on the subject of Reform, the Queen cannot think it consistent with the duty which the Ministers owe to herself and the country that they should abandon their posts in consequence of their defeat on a matter of detail (not of principle) in a question which can never be settled unless all sides are prepared to make concessions; and she must therefore ask them to reconsider their decision."

The Cabinet responded to this command by an endeavour to hold their own, but as day after day passed it was seen to be impossible for them to continue under existing conditions, and the Queen ultimately accepted the resignation, and called in Lord Derby and Mr. Disraeli. By the exercise of Her Majesty's policy of conciliation and compromise, the new Ministers finally carried a Reform Bill which, in another shape, the Russell-Gladstone Government had failed to do. With the accession of Mr. Gladstone to power three years later, there came a very pronounced test of the Queen's constitutional statecraft. In his Irish Church policy she had no confidence whatever, and from those who were upon intimate terms with her this feeling of dislike was never concealed. Bishop Wilberforce tells us in his Diary that he dined with Her Majesty on March 20th (1869), and that she was very affable. "So sorry that Mr. Gladstone started this about the Irish Church—and he is a great friend of yours!" The Queen's part in what followed has been described elsewhere, and it serves to show how completely in touch she has always kept with these questions, with the leaders, and with that practical work of suggestion and compromise which finds no place in the *theory* of constitutional government, but which has had so large a place in its *practice* during her reign.

The whole Irish Church controversy, as described in Archbishop Tait's memoirs ; the Queen's correspondence with the Primate and the leaders of the two parties ; her prolonged efforts at warding off a collision between the two Houses ; her personal objection to disestablishment, and equally strong appreciation of the fact that her people had expressed a distinct desire to carry it out ; her arguments against any useless opposition to this admitted mandate, and her efforts to compromise between the extremists of both parties in the State ; illustrate the utterly erroneous view of the Queen's constitutional government which is held in so many quarters. When writers like Mr. Justin McCarthy and many of his American *confrères* endeavour to minimize the Queen into a mere automaton registering the will of the people, they make a mistake which can only be explained upon the ground of superficial Radicalism or prejudiced Republicanism. In the one case ignorance is implied, in the other partisan narrowness—and neither are serviceable guides to the reader. She bends, it is true, to the will of the people properly expressed, or, to use a better phraseology, she harmonizes this popular desire through and with the constitutional attributes of the Crown. To do this constantly and without public friction requires a degree of judgment, a process of discussion and consideration, a measure of compromise between herself and her advisers, a harmonizing of the two branches of the legislature, which can only be understood by those who read the constitution midway between high and dry theory and actual practice, and who comprehend the personal power and influence of a British Sovereign.

Moreover, the prerogatives of the Queen are so admittedly strong that they afford an immense reserve power which must be taken into account. Mr. Gladstone's description of those powers has been already quoted, and in the Session of 1871 he used one branch of Her Majesty's prerogative to the very fullest degree. His Government's Army Regulation Bill, abolishing purchase in the army, had made but slow progress through the Commons. The opposition to it was very keen, and, under Mr. Disraeli's clever management, very effective. It finally passed, though in such an attenuated form that the House of Lords felt justified in throwing it out. But the Premier believed that the sentiment of the country was with him ; that it was time to give the poor but able and promising officers in the army a chance for promotion ; and he seems also to have had the sympathy of the Queen in this particular enactment. Hence the unusual step of announcing that the standing royal warrant, under which the purchase of promotion was legal, had been cancelled by Her Majesty. It was, moreover, a curious step for a Liberal leader to advise and carry out. To strengthen by such a precedent the authority and prerogative of the Sovereign was a vivid illustration of the value of these reserved powers and an admission of their availability in time of need by the leader of a party generally opposed to their use. Mr. Disraeli, while criticizing the Premier's action from a political standpoint, did not attempt to deprecate the Queen's constitutional power in this connection. "I am not here," he declared, "to dispute the prerogative of the Crown, but that is a very delicate matter, and I very much doubt the wisdom of the Minister who attempts to cut the Gordian knots which every now and then have to be encountered in dealing with popular assemblies by an appeal to the prerogative of the Crown. I hope the prerogatives of the Crown may long exist, and be long exercised for the advantage of the country, for the maintenance of our liberties, and the general interest and welfare of the community at large."

That this criticism was, in the main, a party one is indicated not only by the concluding words, but by the use of the same prerogative powers by the Lord Beaconsfield of a half-dozen years later. During the diplomatic and warlike troubles of that period he more than once acted through the Queen's authority and consulted Parliament afterwards. It was in this way that the troops were brought from India to Malta, and the world shown an immense reserve force in the British Empire, which Europe, at least, had never before recognized. But Disraeli had always possessed strong monarchical principles—in this respect pre-senting one of a very few points of resemblance to his great rival. In one of his novels he declares that "the tendency of advanced civilization is, in truth, to pure monarchy," and this he describes as a system of government which "requires a high degree of civilization for its full development. It needs the support of free laws and manners, and of a widely diffused intelligence."

It was during this period that the publication of the Prince Consort's Memoirs, under the authority and responsibility of the Queen, revealed the real extent of Royal power and influence within constitutional limits, and led to several criticisms of intended severity from the school of thought which wants the Sovereign to be a mere nonentity, a figurehead, and ceremonial device, and yet pretends to believe that the people under such conditions can regard the Crown with reverence and their ruler with respect. At the time this bubble was pretty well pricked and exploded by the practical evidence afforded in the Memoirs of the Queen's ability and authority, as well as by the common sense of leaders in politics and the press who understood the advantages of the existing system, and of Disraeli's summary statement that "the House of Commons is the House of a few, the Sovereign is Sovereign of all." Amongst the replies which "Verax" —one of the critics referred to—drew upon himself was a stirring article in the *London Quarterly* of April, 1878. "The danger," said this writer, "to which we are exposed arises not from any unconstitutional encroachment on the part of the Crown, but from the ignorance and cowardice manifested in these 'common suppositions' of which 'Verax' makes himself the mouthpiece. For ignorance of the grossest kind it is to suppose that the occupant of the oldest throne in Europe, surrounded by a boundless prestige, possessed of a vast, if undefined, prerogative, and commanding countless sources of influence, could ever sink into the capacity of a mere mechanical register of the will of Parliament; or that, if she did, the people would be likely to pay the homage of an ungrudging, unstinted, and unwavering loyalty to what they would recognize to be nothing but a clockwork figure."

But though this is all true, what has been already stated must be borne in mind, that during the Queen's reign her *power* has, with one or two exceptions, always taken the form of *influence*. It has not been diminished on that account. The authority of George IV. or William IV. never equalled in any form the influence of Queen Victoria, and yet she has kept strictly within the limits of the constitution, and has enforced her will through her Ministers and not over them. Writing in 1857, Greville tells us that Lord Clarendon—then Foreign Secretary —talked one day about the Queen and explained how well and usefully she exercised her functions. "She held each Minister to the discharge of his duty and his responsibility to her, and constantly desired to be furnished with accurate and detailed information about all important matters, keeping a record of all the reports that were made to her, and constantly recurring to them, *e.g.*, she would desire to know what the state of the Navy was, and what ships were in readiness for active service, and generally the state of each, ordering returns to be submitted to her from all the arsenals and dockyards, and again, weeks or months afterwards, referring to these returns and desiring to have everything relating to them explained and accounted for; and so throughout every department."

This, of course, is simply one more indication of Her Majesty's influence within the constitution. That she thoroughly understood the apparent limitations of her power, while steadily increasing the practical area of her influence, is shown in one of her letters to Napoleon III., dated November 26th, 1855, and dealing with the difference between his position as an irresponsible potentate and her own as a constitutional ruler. "I am bound by certain rules and usages," wrote the Queen. "I have no uncontrolled power of decision; I must adopt the advice of a Council of responsible Ministers, and these Ministers have to meet and to agree on a course of action, after having arrived at a *joint conviction* of its justice and utility. They have at the same time to take care that the steps which they wish to take are not only in accordance with the best interests of the country, but also such as can be explained to and defended in Parliament, and that their fitness can be brought home to the conviction of the nation." This was an eminently fitting lesson in constitutionalism to the reigning monarch of France, but Her Majesty might also have pointed out, as she no doubt did in private conversation, that such a form of government lent stability and popularity to the Throne, while not diminishing the real influence of an able and intelligent Sovereign—

though it might prove a most desirable check upon one who was narrow-minded, unprincipled, or reckless. Certainly no one had felt the personal power of the Queen's displeasure, for a time, so severely as had Lord Palmerston, yet in a letter to Sir Charles Phipps on November 22nd, 1863, he eulogized her in most effective and accurate words.

" As to the Queen," he wrote, " her steady adherence and studious observance of the principles and practice of the constitution have, during the whole of her reign, been appreciated and admired by men of all political parties.

" One great security for the Throne in this country is the maxim that the Sovereign can do no wrong. This does not mean that no wrong can be done; but it means that as the Sovereign accepts and acts by the advice of those Ministers who, for the time being, enjoy the confidence of the Crown, it is those Ministers, and not the Sovereign personally, upon whom must fall the blame or the criticism which any acts of the royal prerogative may produce. There is scarcely any action of the power of the Crown to which some persons or some parties would not object ; and if the objectors could throw upon the person of the Sovereign the blame which they may be led by their view of the matter to attach to the action of the prerogative, the result would be very injurious to our monarchical institutions. A strict observance of these fundamental principles does not, however, preclude the Sovereign from seeking from all quarters from whence it can be obtained the fullest and most accurate information regarding matters upon which the responsible Ministers may from time to time tender advice, and upon which it is not only right but useful that the Sovereign should form an opinion, to be discussed with the Ministers, if it should differ from the tendered advice."

It will be observed that this experienced statesman does not for a moment dispute the right of the Sovereign to differ from her Cabinet, and to consequently cause its retirement, and this, as well as the general constitutional position of the Queen, has much bearing upon a recent political crisis in Canada. Another point which should be borne in mind is that the Queen has been, and must be, a politician in the noblest sense of the word. A partisan the Sovereign cannot be, without personal and national degradation, but an independent study, a close and continuous observance and knowledge of the politics and parties of the day, is a necessity, and part of the life-work of one whose interests are so intimately bound up with the welfare and honour of the country. To this political experience and information garnered by the Queen, from the days of Wellington's helping hand to this period of the supremacy of Lord Salisbury, is due the tactful guidance which has brought England through so many political crises, and has enabled the Crown to maintain itself in perfect harmony with the people—a condition curiously illustrated by recent cheers for the Prince of Wales from a mob which was calling for the destruction of the House of Lords. As far back as 1846 the same feeling was shown in the statement by a bigoted Radical organ—the *Examiner* —made during the Corn Law crisis, that "In the pages of history the directness, the sincerity, the scrupulous observance of constitutional rules which have marked Her Majesty's conduct in circumstances the most trying will have their place of honour.   Unused as we are to deal in homage to royalty, we must add that never, we believe, was the heart of a monarch so devoted to the interests of a people and with so enlightened a sense of their interests."   This is high praise, indeed, and it helps to indicate the basis for the present constitutional position in England and throughout the British Empire, so beautifully described by Lord Tennyson :

> " It is the land that freemen till,
>   That sober-suited Freedom chose,
>   The land where, girt with friends or foes,
> A man may speak the thing he will.
>
> A land of settled government,
>   A land of just and old renown,
>   Where freedom slowly broadens down
> From precedent to precedent.
>
> Where faction seldom gathers head,
>   But by degrees to fulness wrought
>   The strength of some diffusive thought
> Hath time and space to work and spread."

Three summarized conditions are essential to a clear comprehension of the Queen's constitutional work and place, and they should be kept clearly in mind.   The first is that she has vast dormant powers only occasionally exercised, but obviously available should they be required in the joint interest of the Crown and the people against hasty legislation, rash and dangerous diplomacy, or a too ambitious personality.   The second is the equally great influence of the Sovereign as distinct from her power, and its effect upon the history of the Victorian era.   The third is the immense fund of knowledge, experience, and political insight which has gradually accumulated in connection with the mental personality and character of Her Majesty.   Under the first head comes such incidents as the Bedchamber Question, the dismissal of Palmerston, and the abolition of Purchase.   Under the second is included an immense amount of foreign negotiation and correspondence hardly more than referred to as yet ; the personal choice of a Prime Minister in political crises such as those of 1852, 1859, and in 1880 when Lord Granville and Lord Hartington were both summoned as being the nominal leaders of their party before Mr. Gladstone was given his opportunity ; the exclusion of objectionable Ministers, as in the case of Mr. Labouchere in 1892, who was doubtless omitted from the Ministry by Mr. Gladstone, not because of any direct refusal to have him on the part of the Sovereign, but because of a general knowledge that he was objectionable to her ; the personal aid of the Queen in forming Cabinets, as during the organization of Lord Aberdeen's Ministry, the obtaining of Lord Palmerston's co-operation on another occasion, and the persuasion of Lord Rosebery, in 1892, to take office as Foreign Secretary; the general right to be consulted, to advise, to warn, and to encourage.

Under the third heading comes the willingness and pleasure with which a patriotic Minister is able to receive benefit by the cordial assistance of a permanent chief of the Government and nation who has no personal or political end to gain, and no ambition to attain except the welfare of the people as a whole. And in these later days of Queen Victoria's reign he has the privilege of dealing with a Sovereign who has been served for more than half a century by the great minds of the nation, and been in close intercourse with the great men of the world; who has possibly known his grandfather intimately, and been in personal touch with the politics of what now seem like other ages; who has an experience that he cannot pretend to, a knowledge more varied than he can hope to attain, a position where impartiality is a stereotyped quality, and patriotism an educated personal necessity. And certainly he will not, and no one in close contact with the State and the Sovereign has ever attempted, to minimize the beneficial influence and power thus wielded, within and through the Constitution, by Queen Victoria.

CHAPTER XVII.

THE PRINCE OF WALES.

THERE were popular rejoicings in England when the Prince of Wales was born. There was wide popular gratulation when the heir to the Throne married the charming daughter of the Danish King. There was universal rejoicing throughout the land, and a sympathetic thrill of pleasure through all the vast Empire of the Queen, when he recovered from his serious illness in 1872. There have been great popular receptions given the Prince in Canada, and in India, and in every important place within the bounds of the United Kingdom. For over half a century he has, in fact, been the centre of observation, the theme of constant discussion in public and private, in the press, on the platform, and even in the pulpit. The light which illumines a throne, and at the same time often shadows with silent and suppressed suffering those immediately surrounding it, has shone upon him during all these years with continuous intensity.

If, during this period, the nation has given much it has also exacted much. If the people have, as a whole, rejoiced with the Prince in his rejoicings, and sorrowed with him in his sorrows, they have also awarded him the sternest criticism—sometimes with an undue severity characteristic of British prejudice and British convictions, when once fairly aroused. But as a rule the people of the United Kingdom understand the responsibilities and limitations of the Prince's position. They know the burdens he has to bear in acting upon multitudinous occasions as the representative of his royal mother. They appreciate the importance of his duties as leader of society, and the nature of his success as a leader in British sports. They know his skill as a public and after-dinner speaker, and realize something of his wonderful tact and distinct diplomatic achievements at home and abroad.

Outside of the British Isles and the British Empire the Prince of Wales has hardly received the measure of consideration and respect to which he is entitled by virtue of personality as well as position. In the United States the wells of public opinion are poisoned by a cable system which magnifies every floating story; seizes upon every figment of imagination contained in a Reynolds' newspaper, or voiced in the columns of some low society sheet; serves up spicy paragraphs of lying gossip; distorts innocent and natural actions by ill-natured innuendoes and suppositions. And this condition is further intensified by an absolute ignorance of the functions and work of royalty, or of the character of

CARDINAL NEWMAN.

CARDINAL MANNING.

British institutions and British public life. The press of the Republic is, above all things, sensational, and nothing seems more pleasant to the people of a democracy which lives upon a belief that the United States is the only home of liberty in the world, and bases its Constitution upon the fiction that all men are born free and equal, than stories, and even slanderous statements, indicating the decadence of British royalty and the degradation of the British aristocracy.

To a certain extent this trouble has reached into Canada upon the wings of a cable news system controlled by Americans. Indirectly it has affected Australasia. But in British countries its nature is modified by a general knowledge of the difficult position and arduous labours of the heir to the Throne, and is not, therefore, seriously injurious to good feeling and loyalty. And, as time passes, the good work done by the Prince of Wales in wide and far-reaching concerns is permeating more and more the heart of all British peoples. His few mistakes are fully condoned, and the one time numerous and unpleasant hints regarding the follies of a distant youth are now almost obliterated from memory and public sentiment. They will inevitably be revived by the American press from time to time, and will probably always find a place in American national opinion, but there the evil ends.

No heir to royal power in Great Britain or elsewhere has ever had such beneficial and bright surroundings as those which blessed the early career of the Prince of Wales. Reared amid the domestic life of a home which has ever since been a pattern to the people of the realm ; trained by parents who were imbued with the loftiest ideals of Christian life and morality ; educated under the watchful supervision of a Princely father whose knowledge was as wide as his experience was varied and valuable ; surrounded by tutors such as Charles Kingsley, and by guardians such as General Bruce ; brought up amidst the advice of men like Bishop Wilberforce, and Baron Stockmar, and others of high attainment and character, who were frequently consulted by the Queen ; it is apparent that everything was done to make him a prince among men as well as a Prince in rank and position.

Every opportunity of travel was given him. As a child he accompanied the Queen and Prince Consort to Scotland and Ireland, to the Channel Isles, and to the English Lake country. In 1857, with the Hon. F. Stanley—now Earl of Derby—he travelled through Switzerland and Germany under the care of General Grey, Colonel Ponsonby, and his tutors. After his return he again visited Ireland, and especially the Lakes of Killarney. In 1858 he went to see his sister, the Crown Princess of Prussia, at Berlin. Early in the next year he visited Rome, and was received by the Pope with great courtesy. From thence he went to the south of Spain, saw the Alhambra, and was entertained by the King of Portugal at Lisbon. Then came education of another kind. A year at the University of Edinburgh ; a period at Christ Church and Pembroke College,

Oxford; and another at Trinity College, Cambridge, completed his academical course. In 1860 he made a tour of Canada and visited the United States under the care of the Duke of Newcastle.

Then came the great misfortune of his life. The death of the Prince Consort amid all its far-reaching consequences had no more important one than the leaving of the young Prince without a father's guiding hand. As Harriet Martineau well said three years afterwards: "It seemed as if he, on reaching manhood, was fated to lose his best and most needed personal friends. He has lost his father, and General Bruce, his governor, and now the guardian and companion of his early travels"—the Duke of Newcastle. Very wisely, however, and despite the distractions of a personal sorrow too intense for words, the Queen at once arranged a foreign tour for him, and the young Prince was sent to the East for five months, attended by his governor, Colonel Keppel, Major Teesdale, and Dr. Minter. The Nile was visited, together with Cairo and the Pyramids, Thebes and Karnac. Then came a month in the Holy Land accompanied by Mr.—afterwards Dean—Stanley, and this was succeeded by a visit to the Viceroy of Egypt, and the Sultan at Constantinople. It was about this time that Laurence Oliphant met the Prince at Vienna *en route*, and, after accompanying him as far as Corfu, made an interesting reference to his character and attainments.

"I was delighted with him," says the genial author, "and thought he was rarely done justice to in public estimation. He is not studious, nor highly intellectual, but he is up to the average in this respect, and beyond it in so far as quickness of observation and general intelligence goes. Travelling is, therefore, the best education he could have, and I think his development will be far higher than people anticipate. Then his temper and disposition are charming. His defects are rather the inevitable consequence of his position, which never allows him any responsibility or forces him into action."

Since that time the Prince of Wales has assumed an ever-increasing load of responsibility, and has never been accused, even by his sternest critics, of inaction or indifference to his endless routine of public duty and ceremonial. Meanwhile, also, the constitutional training of the heir apparent had not been neglected. To Prince Albert this was a naturally congenial part of his son's education, and one which he personally supervised. Men like Canon Kingsley were employed for instruction in purely historical matters, but the practical application of these teachings lay in the wise advice, and no doubt frequent conversations, of the Prince Consort. So far back, indeed, as 1849, when the boy was only five years old, his father asked Baron Stockmar to prepare a memorandum on the subject, and the views pronounced in the following paragraph may fairly be said to have constituted the basis of the Prince's training in this connection:

" The Prince should early be taught that thrones and social order have a stable foundation in the moral and intellectual faculties of man ; that by addressing his public exertions to the cultivation of these powers in his people, and by taking their dictates as the constant guides of his own conduct, he will promote the solidity of his empire and the prosperity of his subjects. In one word, he should be taught that God, in the constitution of the mind, and in the arrangement of creation, has already legislated for men, both as individuals and as nations ; that the laws of morality which He has written in their nature are the foundations on which, and on which alone, their prosperity can be reared ; and that the human legislator and sovereign have no higher duty than to discover and carry into execution these enactments of Divine legislation."

Such were undoubtedly the constitutional principles taught to the youthful Prince, and, though not perhaps immediately applied or practised by him, they have borne the most ample fruit during the last two decades of a public life which formally opened in February, 1863; when the heir to the throne took his seat in the House of Lords amidst every sort of pomp and ceremony. A month later his marriage with the Princess Alexandra was celebrated, and marks the introduction into his life of an influence which cannot be over-rated, and of a popularity for his beautiful bride which commenced in the words of the Poet Laureate's welcome :

" Clash, ye bells, in the merry March air ;
Flash, ye cities, in rivers of fire ;
Welcome her, welcome the land's desire ;
Alexandra ! "

and has since continued in the hearts of the British people and the homes of the British Empire. The first public speech of the Prince in England was given on May 2nd, following his marriage, at the Royal Academy banquet, and has been since succeeded by such multitudinous functions, speeches, and ceremonies that his personality is as familiar to the people of the United Kingdom as his name is in the literature and public prints of nearly half a century. In this sort of work, which included much of travel, and toil of a nature not always appreciated— because not understood—the years passed rapidly away. Prince Albert Victor was born in March, 1864 ; a visit in September was paid to Denmark and Sweden; a tour of Cornwall was made in the summer of 1865. In 1867 the Princess was laid up with a severe attack of rheumatic fever which left her lame and delicate for many months. During May of this year the young Prince visited Napoleon III. at Paris, and helped the Queen to lay the first stone of the Royal Albert Hall at Kensington. In 1868 a visit was paid to Ireland and Wales, and a prolonged tour of Europe commenced, which included France and Germany, Austria, Denmark, and Sweden, and was continued into Egypt, Syria, and Turkey. After more than six months' absence the Royal couple reached England in May, 1869, and were soon performing once more their many acts of ceremonial and kindly patronage. Another visit to Ireland was made in 1870, and various visits paid from time to time at the homes of nobility and gentry in different parts of the country.

During these years the Prince of Wales had done much and seen much, but it is a question whether he had really settled down to the serious business of royal life and the great responsibilities, but ill-defined duties, of an heir to the Throne. With his thirtieth year, however, came that crucial point which meets every man at some period of his life, whether he be prince or peasant, peer or pauper, and which in this case proved the metal to be genuine and the man worthy of his high post and calling. That prolonged and historic illness; the anxiety and loyalty of an entire nation; the devoted attendance of his Royal mother, and wife, and sister; the narrow escape from an early death and the closing of what could not yet be termed a great career; the wonderful enthusiasm which stirred the heart of England during the Thanksgiving services in London; had the effect which might have been expected in rousing all the best instincts of his nature and developing the teachings of his great and good father.

> " Bear witness that rememberable day,
>   When, pale as yet, and fever-worn, the Prince,
>   Who scarce had plucked his flickering life again
>   From half-way down the shadow of the grave,
>   Past thro' the people and their love,
>   And London roll'd one tide of joy thro' all
>   Her trebled millions and loud leagues of man."

Since that eventful period the ever closer attention of the Heir Apparent to his duties has been such as to win the admiration and popularity of the whole people; his devotion to wife and family and home—when it was possible to escape to Sandringham from his burdened life of ceremony and public work—has won him equal respect from all who understand the true circumstances of the case; whilst his leadership of society and sport has tended, upon the whole, to clarify the one and elevate the other. Not that the Prince of Wales has ever been one of those persons who believe they have a certain mission in life which it is their duty to force forward upon all occasions and in the teeth of all prejudices. His urbanity and tact, combined with his high position, have, however, given him the widest possible influence, and this has generally been used to frown down cant and hypocrisy, to promote generosity and cultivated tastes, to encourage a hearty and really English mode of living. He has always played cards, and admired beauty—whether in woman or in art, in literature or the drama. He has enjoyed the theatre as well as the opera, the Derby and the Doncaster as well as the debates of Parliament. He has appreciated the society and friendship of Mr. Reuben Sassoon as he has that of Lord Rosebery or Lord Carrington. But it has all been in an open, honest, hearty manner, and with a *bonhomie* characteristic of the Prince and impossible of repression even by his life of dignified ceremonial, and constant round of public work.

Criticism he has had, and will probably always receive. To please everyone he would have had to be at once the chief of saints and the prince of sinners. But a steadily growing volume of popularity has been his, and the keener the modern search-light upon his life the better the people seem to like him, and admire his thoroughly typical English tastes and habits. One of his great friends during an earlier period was the learned, eloquent, and popular Bishop Wilberforce, whose Diary contains many homelike sketches of the Prince at Sandringham, and the domestic, happy life of its inmates. Writing in 1864, he speaks of a visit there and of the Prince's dogs and horses and gardens; his simple country life, and rides and drives and walks; the various family excursions and picnics. In 1872, he says that "the Prince shines as a host in the midst of his family, and the Princess is charming." The Bishop's death in 1873 closed this long friendship, and evoked the following striking and sympathetic letter to the Rev. Basil Wilberforce:

"MARLBOROUGH HOUSE, July 23, 1873.

"MY DEAR WILBERFORCE,—Although I have only had the pleasure of meeting you but rarely since we were at Oxford together, I must intrude on your great grief in begging you and your family to accept from the Princess and myself our deepest sympathy and condolence at the irreparable loss you have sustained. I have had the advantage of knowing your lamented father from my earliest childhood, and during the last few years have seen a great deal of him, and I can never forget the many pleasant and instructive hours I have spent in his company when he was a guest in our house and elsewhere. His loss will be felt throughout the length and breadth of the land, as no one worked harder in his sacred calling than he did, and no one has left a higher name behind him than he has. I feel that I have lost a kind and valued friend, and can hardly realize the thought that we are to meet no more in this world.

"Hoping that you will forgive my trespassing upon you at such a time, believe me, my dear Wilberforce,

"Yours very sincerely,

"ALBERT EDWARD."

Such a friendship and such a letter indicate the cosmopolitan and broad nature of the Prince as truly as his Imperial sympathies in later years proved his clear and statesmanlike grasp of the national situation. During the next two years he worked hard in promoting the success of the Vienna International Exhibition as President of the English Commission; showed his love of art by helping the Landseer Exhibition of paintings; devoted much time to the study of manufactures and industries and paid a State visit to Birmingham, where Mr. Joseph Chamberlain was then Mayor; became President of the Royal Commission to inquire into the housing of the artisan classes, and spent much time in studying and promulgating schemes which, in some measure, he had already put into effect at Sandringham; was appointed Grand Master of the English Freemasons, and spent some time in Sheffield studying its famous steel industries.   In 1875 he made a prolonged tour through India, thus bringing England into touch with the swarming millions of her Eastern Empire, and helping to transmute ignorant fealty to an invisible power into personal loyalty to a beneficent sovereignty.

Upon his return the Prince settled down to a new course of public work. Under his auspices the Norwich Hospital was rebuilt, the foundation stone of a new Post-office at Glasgow laid, a Training Ship for boys established by the Marine Society, a statue to Prince Albert unveiled at Cambridge, the British Commission of the Paris Exhibition assiduously and successfully supervised, the Midland Counties Art Museum at Nottingham opened, together with the new docks at Great Grimsby, and a new harbour at Holyhead, the foundation stone laid of the Chelsea Hospital for Women, and that of the South Kensington Institute of Science and Art.   These functions are selected as being merely indicative of the nature and variety of his duties.   In such cases the co-operation or patronage of His Royal Highness meant thousands of pounds to each particular charity or interest, to say nothing of the inevitable donation from the Prince himself of anywhere between £50 and £200.   The aid of the Prince and Princess of Wales, in fact, almost ensures success to any enterprise which they may patronize, and consequently increases the responsibility of choice and the necessity of discrimination.

With the Fisheries Exhibition of 1883 began that series of efforts to embody in practical public form the resources and development of the British Empire, which owe so much to the work and direction of the Prince of Wales.   He was naturally inspired by the example of the Prince Consort in this connection, and was helped by his own preliminary experiences at Vienna and Paris.   Speaking of the latter, while laying the foundation stone of the Melbourne Exhibition in 1879, Sir George Bowen declared it to be well known that the success of the Parisian enterprise was due "in no slight degree to the personal tact and energy of the Prince of Wales."   After several years' work as President, His Royal Highness opened "the Fisheries," as it was popularly called, in the presence of a distinguished gathering, and with the support of most of the members of the Royal family.   An extract from his speech illustrates the nature of the occasion: "In view of the rapid increase of the population in these sea-girt kingdoms, a profound interest attaches to every industry which affects the supply of food; and in this respect the harvest of the sea is hardly less important than that of the land.   I share your hope that the Exhibition now about to open may afford the means of enabling practical fishermen to acquaint themselves with the latest improvements which have been made in their craft in all parts of the world; so that without needless destruction, or avoidable waste of any kind, mankind may derive the fullest possible advantage from the bounty of the waters.   I am glad that your attention has been directed to the condition of the fishing population."

By October following, the five months' run of the Exhibition had resulted in the presence of 2,703,000 visitors, a substantial financial success, and much valuable aid to the fishing interests of the country. The Health Exhibition of 1884 owed its general plan and inauguration to the Prince of Wales, though the death of the Duke of Albany prevented his active participation in its later development. He, however, formally inaugurated the work of the International juries on June 17th, and the result of the whole undertaking was an impetus to science and education, and a great aid to the public comprehension and use of health-saving appliances and methods. In the succeeding year came the Inventions Exhibition, the very name of which implies its scope and importance; and in 1886 the crowning achievement of all—the Colonial and Indian Exhibition. It was a great undertaking, and for two years was the subject of strenuous labour and thought on the part of the Prince. No new idea is easy of accomplishment, and to obtain the co-operation of all the various Governments of the British Empire in united and harmonious work and monetary subscription was in itself a great victory, to say nothing of the success which followed in a financial sense ; in the attendance and patronage by millions of visitors ; in the knowledge thus disseminated regarding the resources and products of the Empire; in the communications created and promoted between all its distant portions ; in the increase of loyalty and unity, and the furnishing of the first substantial basis for the succeeding movement towards a better and greater relationship. Speaking at Marlborough House to the Royal Commission, of which he was the head and the practical organizer, on March 30th, 1885, the Prince indicated thus his views and objects :

"In conclusion, let me express the hope that this great undertaking, and the many occasions for friendly intercourse with our fellow-subjects from India and the Colonies which it will afford, may convey to them the assurance that, while we are deeply moved by the spirit of patriotism they have lately shown in desiring to bear their share in the graver trials of the country, we on our part wish to participate in every effort to further and develop their material interests—interests which we feel to be inseparably bound up with the prosperity of the Empire. We must remember that, as regards the Colonies, they are the legitimate and natural homes, in future, of the more adventurous and energetic portion of the population of these Islands. Their progress, and their power of providing all that makes life comfortable and attractive, cannot, therefore, but be a matter of serious concern to us all."

These words show how fully the heir to the British Throne has grasped the Imperial nature of his position and duties, and they are only a few out of many similar expressions of his sympathy and interest. It must be remembered, too, that in 1885 the tide of Imperial knowledge and sentiment was only beginning to rise, and that it is due to this initiatory practical action and the hard personal work and great influence of the Prince that success eventually came to his enterprise. The Exhibition was attended by five and a half millions of people, and promoted a correspondingly wide interest in the Colonies, while it was succeeded by the Imperial Institute, the Colonial Conference, and various Trade Congresses of the Empire. Speaking at St. James' Palace on January 12th, 1887, after " the Colinderies " had come and gone, the Prince told his newly-organized committee for the creation of an Imperial Institute, or permanent exhibition of the arts and industries and interests of the Empire, that " no less than 16,000,000 persons from all parts of the kingdom have attended the four exhibitions over which I presided, representing fisheries, public health, inventions, and the Colonies and India, and I assure you I would not have undertaken the labour attending their administration had I not felt a deep conviction that such exhibitions added to the knowledge of the people, and stimulated the industries of the country. I have on more than one occasion expressed my own views, founded upon those so often enunciated by my lamented father, that it is of the greatest importance to do everything within our power to advance the knowledge as well as the practical skill of the productive classes of the Empire."

Six months later the foundation stone of the Imperial Institute was laid by the Queen amid most imposing ceremonies, accompanied by the presentation of an address from the Prince of Wales as President of the Committee, and the Institute, in which he stated that " it has been our desire, in pursuance of the ideas which gave birth to the Colonial and Indian Exhibition of 1886, to combine in some harmonious form a broader and more enduring representation of your Majesty's Colonies and India, as well as the United Kingdom ; and our confident hope is that this Institute may hereafter not only exhibit the material resources of the Empire, but may be an emblem of that Imperial union of purpose and action which we believe has gathered strength and reality with every year of your Majesty's reign." The opening of the magnificent building in 1893, which the Queen honoured by her presence, was the occasion for another striking demonstration and evidence of Imperial feeling, and of national regard for Colonial well-being, unity, and advancement. It proved the accuracy of the Prince of Wales' statement at another function, that " we are, in fact, a vast English nation, and we should take great care not to allow those who have gone forth from among us to imagine that they have in the slightest degree ceased to belong to the same community as ourselves." And, as evincing the sincerity of his feelings on this subject, the action of the Prince regarding a proposed testimonial to himself in connection with his work on behalf of the Colonial and Indian Exhibition should be recorded here. The Earl of Cadogan had assumed the chairmanship of a large and influential committee for this purpose, and money was freely coming in, when a letter was received from His Royal Highness declining with every possible appreciation to accept anything of the kind, but suggesting that what had already been contributed might go to the funds of the Imperial Institute. The following resolution was at once passed :

" Resolved, that this Committee, believing it to be the wish of the subscribers to mark their high sense of His Royal Highness's great services in the manner most acceptable to himself, acquiesce in the suggestions contained in his letter. They desire at the same time to record what they are assured will be the unanimous feeling of all the donors, that the step thus taken by His Royal Highness will, if possible, add to the appreciation entertained of his disinterested and public-spirited efforts, not only on behalf of an Exhibition by which many millions of Her Majesty's subjects have already derived so much advantage, but to further a project which will at once be a graceful memorial of Her Majesty's long and happy reign, and conduce to the permanent consolidation of the Empire."

Meanwhile other interests had not been neglected, and the Prince during these years found a constantly increasing burden of duties—a burden which he always accepted cheerfully, and carried off with a degree of tact, and apparent, if not real, pleasure, which brought him an increased popular regard as warm and sincere as the affection long since won by the charming courtesy and graceful, kindly deeds of the Princess. Every sort of charity and benevolent institution —asylums and homes and refuges for the blind or convalescent ; hospitals and deaf and dumb institutions ; educational and intellectual and literary under-takings ; arts and crafts and all manner of industrial interests ; orphanages, commemorations, and women's agencies or institutions ; religious, moral, and social organizations ; volunteer and rifle associations, or naval and military organizations ; all came under the influence of a judicious and careful patron-age and royal support. In a volume dealing with this subject, fifty closely printed pages record the known donations of the Prince and Princess of Wales to charitable or otherwise useful associations, and cover an expenditure of hundreds of thousands of dollars. The following random and very partial list of something over $100,000 in amount, gives some idea of the way in which these public demands upon his purse are met by the Prince :

Earlswood Asylum for Idiots	£ 472
Gordon Boys' Home	210
Cambridge Asylum for Soldiers' Widows	315
Bengal Famine Fund, 1874	500
Bishop of London's Fund, 1864	1,000
Cholera Relief Fund, 1866	275
Duchy of Cornwall Donations	500
Indian Famine Fund, 1877	525
Irish Relief Fund, 1879	200
Fund for the Unemployed, 1886	262
Sandringham Charities and Schools—Annually	600
Sheffield Inundation Fund, 1864	200
Sick and Wounded Fund, 1870	210
St. Patrick's Benevolent Fund	315
Royal Agricultural Society	367
Convalescent Homes	270
Deaf and Dumb Institutions	260
Duchy of Cornwall Donation	2,589

National Training School of Music	£ 300
Royal College of Music	1,300
School of Mines	600
St. Mary the Less School	295
Society to Aid Foreigners in Distress	315
London Fever Hospital	250
Norfolk and Norwich Hospital	240
Some other Hospitals	2,700
Whitechapel Hospital	210
Infant Orphan Asylum	210
Sundry Orphanages	1,000
Chester Cathedral	305
Cornish Bishopric Fund	500
South London Church Extension	500
St. Paul's Cathedral Completion Fund	552
St. Peter's Church Endowment Fund	200
Truro Cathedral	700
Copenhagen English Church	250
Hyde Park Corner Improvement Fund	500
Imperial Institute	2,000
Royal Albert Hall	1,000
Volunteer Associations	625

Amid all his innumerable engagements and interests the Heir Apparent has, however, always been the same in manner and style of bearing, combining with rare skill the dignity of a Prince, and the jovial manner of a popular English gentleman. A martinet in discipline and etiquette, and a master in ceremonial and heraldry and all the pageantry of a Court, he yet rules this realm of society and Royal functions with a strong but pleasant manner, which, while strengthening his personal popularity, fully maintains the dignity and high traditions of his environment. At Marlborough House he is the central figure in a great world of society, and art, and science, and literature, which, in all its variations, receives a share of support and attention—and of an inner circle of personal friends which includes Lord Carrington, the late Governor of Victoria, Sir Frederick Johnstone, the Marquess of Londonderry, late Viceroy of Ireland, Lord Rosebery, the Earl of Warwick, Mr. Christopher Sykes, the Duke of Devonshire—better known as Marquess of Hartington—Lord Cadogan, Viceroy of Ireland, and the Duke of Abercorn, who has twice held that position.

At Sandringham he is to be found during a part of the year surrounded by his model cottages and well-managed estate, his shorthorns and thoroughbreds —a type of those representative country gentlemen whom hard times and agricultural depression are now so greatly reducing in number. Between these two extremes of modern life he is constantly travelling in order to lay corner-stones, open public buildings, inaugurate public enterprises, or preside at some one of his innumerable committees—everywhere distributing his patronage with unfailing grace and good humour. One day it is a speech at the Royal Academy of Art, or perhaps of Music; another he is heading a movement to honour the memory of the noble-hearted priest who died among the lepers; again, he is presiding at a Colonial banquet or an International Medical Congress; addressing the Rifle volunteers, or opening a city of London church; inaugurating the Darwin memorial as a tribute to science, or attending the consecration of Truro Cathedral as a tribute to what should be its twin brother—religion; presenting new colours to an old regiment, or unveiling a statue to Sir Bartle Frere; attending the West Norfolk Hunt dinner, visiting the Derby, or opening the Great Northern Hospital in London.

To clearly understand the character of the Prince of Wales, Sandringham —his country seat in Norfolk—has, however, to be seen and inspected. The lot of the labourers on the estate is a happy one, and their welfare is so carefully looked after that the cottages they live in have been all rebuilt, and the neighbouring village is prevented from having a public house—though the Prince has established a workingman's club, where a glass of good beer can be obtained under certain restrictions, coupled with plenty of wholesome entertainment in the winter time. The kennels and aviary, the stud, the model farm, and the dairy —including a splendid herd of Jersey cattle—are all alike managed with recognized ability. But it is in the home life of the place that we find the real keynote. Kindness, hospitality, and thoughtfulness pervade the great establishment, and the first-named quality controls the entertainment of visitors as it does the treatment of domestics, and even the management of racehorses or thoroughbred cattle. All the churches on the estate have been restored at the Prince's expense, and that at Sandringham village contains many memorials to those who have gone, including the Princess Alice, the Duke of Albany, the greatly esteemed Emperor Frederick, and last, but not least, a simple marble cross to the memory of Blagg—the groom who was stricken down with typhoid fever at the same time as the Prince—and bearing the significant words, "One was taken and the other left."

In his family relationship the Prince has for many years been all that a man should be, and the education of his sons, while not perhaps of the same ideal character as his own at the hands of the Prince Consort, has been of that hearty, simple, English character which, as the British world likes to believe, assures the reasonable possession of good morals, good common sense, and a sound English education. The daughters came under the more direct control of the Princess, and received all the advantages of her own beneficent home life and experience in distant Denmark, and the training necessary to enable them to fill a similar place with grace and knowledge. Prince George early showed a resemblance to his father in character and hearty temperament, but Prince Eddie, as the late Duke of Clarence was called, became the pet of his mother and of the Queen, and was, during his short lifetime, the possessor of a tender and affectionate disposition, which all too surely accompanied a fatal delicacy of physique. A faithful son, a good father, and a staunch friend the Prince of Wales in truth has been, and the tribute of the *Times* in this connection—given on March 10th, 1888, during the celebration of the Silver Wedding of the heir to the Throne—was most thoroughly deserved :

" The care which has been taken in the education of the young Princes to fit them by study and varied experiences for the duties of their high position is significant of the strong sense which has ruled the Prince of Wales' family. And here it is impossible to omit a respectful reference to the Princess, who, if she has performed her public duties with a grace which has compelled even the sourest socialist to speak well of her, has played with no less perfection the part of wife and mother. What the country has gained by this example of a happy, strenuous family life in the highest place, it is difficult to state too strongly. At a time, so to speak, when all our institutions are being cast into the furnace, it is of enormous value to see, in the family next the Throne, a type of life which, aiming at no impossible or ascetic standard, is yet such as may be regarded without blame and imitated without harm. A Prince less genial, less capable, less hard-working ; a Princess less gracious, and less devoted to the duties of her home, might have done much injury, not only to the monarchy, but to what may be called the religion of the family throughout England."

The fact of the matter is that the life of the Prince of Wales has been a practical embodiment, in his own high sphere, of the jovial yet dignified and honourable life of the average English gentleman. It has had to be adjusted to innumerable demands upon his time and to the ceremonial etiquette of his position, but aside from that he has represented the English character and lived the English life. Hence his popularity with the English masses. Even the matters for which he has been condemned freely and criticized most harshly have not seriously detracted from this popular sentiment. Two of these occurrences are memorable—the baccarat case and the winning of the Derby. Of the former too much has been said and written, and it is certainly not necessary here to add to the controversial reams of rampant abuse or milk-and-water defence. Those who believe all card-playing to be vicious, and any game of chance in which money is involved to be gambling, will hardly be persuaded that the now historic game of baccarat was anything but wicked, under whatever conditions or circumstances.

Those who consider games, like wine, to be good or bad, according to their use or misuse ; who realize that a Prince must have some amusement as well as a peasant ; who are not prepared to condemn off-hand either the race-course, the theatre, the game of cards, or the ball-room ; who understand that a private game of baccarat in a private house, with a group of private friends, is not gambling after the Monte Carlo type, and cannot properly be termed setting a bad example to the nation; who appreciate the very English quality of standing by a friend, and like the Prince all the better for having tried to save Gordon-Cumming from the consequences of his weak folly and meanness—such persons will find plenty of room for defence of the Prince and even for considerable admiraation of his manly course throughout the entire affair. Between the religious press and the Nonconformist pulpit, which so greatly criticized the Prince in this connection, and the almost equally large sporting and society class—an honourable and representative one in its way—which defended him strongly, was a large and undecided portion of the people. Some played cards, but did not believe in dancing; others went to races, but would not have "gambled" under any consideration; others indulged in the theatre and cards and the ball-room, but drew a very sharp line at the race-course.

Amongst these people severe criticism of the Prince of Wales would be simply ignorant prejudice or hypocrisy, and probably they were very generally indifferent to the issue. However, the storm came and went, natural reaction followed the excitement, and the public came ultimately to comprehend that while the heir to the Throne did his public duties so admirably, ruled society so well, and upheld with dignity the functions of royalty amid myriad temptations to idleness or worse, he was entitled to have his private recreations, even though particular individuals did not quite approve their nature. So with his success in horse-racing. The winning of the Derby—the blue ribbon of the turf, as Lord Beaconsfield first called it—is the end and aim of all true British sportsmen, and a magnificent experience for any man to go through. When Lord Rosebery won it, there were many protests from those who could see no good in an event which unquestionably produces much yearly gambling and betting, but which, in itself, is the climax of the most manly and thoroughly English of all pleasures and sports. The hunting-field and the country races, developing by gradations into the great national fête at Epsom Downs, have done much to promote English physique and health and muscle, to say nothing of the characteristics of sporting honour which have made the English race-course so famous all over the world. It had long been the ambition of the Prince of Wales to win the Derby, and his victory in 1896 with Persimmon marked not only the greatest race in the history of the Downs, but one of the most popular events in the life of the Heir Apparent.* To quote the London *Mail* of June 4th—and it was typical of the average newspaper of the moment:

"There is no man in England better loved of the people than the kindly gentleman and thorough good fellow who is one day to rule over them. . . . It was a gallant race and a sportsmanlike victory; but the roar of delight that went up from two hundred thousand English throats when Persimmon passed the post meant a good deal more than that the Prince of Wales had won the Derby. It meant that the people of England, a sturdy

*The author saw the race, heard the storm of applause, witnessed the intense pleasure of the Prince, and will never forget the wonderfully spontaneous loyalty of that vast gathering, many of whom had lost money upon the result.

race that reck little of thrones and princes when royalty is not royal by desert as well as blood, have taken the Prince to their hearts as friend and comrade.   When they cheered his victory they were not applauding the accident of royalty, but voicing heartfelt regard for the man who has borne himself in his high estate as an Englishman, a gentleman, and a friend to every worthy cause and every honest sport.   He stood amongst them with no imposing array of armed guards and liveried courtiers, with none of the gaudy trappings of royalty, and standing thus was more secure in his future kingship than any autocrat that ever circled his throne with a million swords.   Even so stands the throne of England to-day, founded on the love and reverence of the people."

Meanwhile various important events had occurred.   Prince Albert Victor, Duke of Clarence and Avondale, the favourite and most delicate son of the Princess, had reached man's estate, had taken part in a number of functions, and become engaged to a charming second cousin—the Princess May of Teck.   All the world looked bright and the sky serene, when death suddenly stepped in, and removed him from the pleasures and the burdens of a great position, one which his health might perhaps have prevented him from adequately filling.   But it was none the less a great sorrow to the family, where, as in the case of the Duke of Albany with the Queen, he left a blank which it was hard to fill.   With it, however, came the mournful pleasure of a world-wide sympathy, and renewed evidences of the stability of the Throne and the popularity of the Royal family.   So pronounced indeed were these expressions that a formal letter of thanks was published, the Prince and Princess of Wales stating themselves as " anxious to express to Her Majesty's subjects, whether in the United Kingdom, in the Colonies, or in India, the sense of their deep gratitude for the universal feeling of sympathy manifested towards them at a time when they are overpowered by the terrible calamity which they have sustained in the loss of their beloved eldest son."   Following this came the active part taken in public affairs by Prince George, as the new heir presumptive to the Throne; his creation as Duke of York and eventual marriage to the Princess May.   Before this had happened, however, Princess Louise of Wales had been married to the Earl (afterwards Duke) of Fife, and, in 1896, the Princess Maud—gay, vivacious, and popular— was wedded to Prince Charles of Denmark.

During all these years of change and work and pleasure, of restricted responsibility and unlimited duties, the Prince of Wales has been steadily acquiring prestige and diplomatic influence abroad.   Like the Queen, he has come to be a recognized power in international politics, although, unlike her, he has no real place in such a field.   But his relationship with some sovereigns is so close, his friendship with others is so great, his tact is so admirable in matters of importance as well as in trifles, that he has been able to do much good.   He is known to be exceedingly popular with the excitable and sensitive French people; he is said to have reconciled the hot-headed German Emperor with his English mother, the Empress Frederick ; he is stated to have acquired considerable influence over the young Czar of Russia ; he is actually becoming, after long years of misrepresentation and abuse, somewhat popular in the United States.

At home the Prince has also made his mark as an effective, though not eloquent, public speaker. To be both an orator and a prince would be about the most dangerous combination which could beset a modern leader. It is probable that the conjunction would not last long. The heir to the throne should be cautious in his language and measured and dignified in style. This the Prince always is. He never uses a wrong word, or says too much or too little. He speaks to the point, with directness and precision, and has to deal in the course of a year with almost every conceivable variety of subject and occasion. He is a wide reader in a sort of general way, and there are few new books of importance which are not looked over or read, and possibly discussed, at Sandringham. Mr. Chauncey M. Depew, with characteristic American misapprehension, has stated his surprise at meeting " a thoughtful dignitary filling to the brim the requirements of his exalted position. In fact, a practical as well as a theoretical student of the mighty forces which control the government of all great countries, and their best history."

Politically, the Heir Apparent is an observant, impartial, and non-partisan leader of the nation. No one really knows his party views, though he undoubtedly has opinions of his own, and perhaps very strong ones. His chief known principle is Imperial unity ; his chief practical work has been the promotion of popular knowledge, and the alleviation of existing troubles amongst the working classes ; his chief social aim seems to have been the removal of class animosities, the diffusion of good manners, and the cultivation of more rational habits than those of the days when hard drinking, intoxication, and blasphemy constituted the correct social code. His friendships are of the most cosmopolitan order, so far as politics are concerned, and, if Lord Randolph Churchill was upon intimate terms with him in days gone by, so also was the Earl of Rosebery. He attends the House of Lords during all important debates, but never votes upon party questions. One of the rare matters of a parliamentary nature in which he has shared is the prolonged agitation for legalizing marriage with a deceased wife's sister, and upon this subject the Prince has taken strong ground, and has even used his personal influence.

The career of the Prince of Wales can be summarized as in many ways a great one ; while his character and life may be regarded as typical of a large English class, and as having made him a real leader of the people rather than of any parties, or classes, or divisions in their midst. He learned much from his father's teaching, much from his Royal mother's example, much from his wife's co-operation and noble character. He has done much for the unity of the Empire, much for charity and the poor, much for industry and the workingman, much for society and sport. He has shared in many great events, encountered wide and varied experiences of life, participated in a multitude of gorgeous functions and ceremonies, seen many foreign and interesting lands, met the greatest and best, as well as the most curious and striking, men of recent years. He has worked hard at many things, and has acquired an influence in many directions which is more absolute than that of the Czar, and certainly more beneficial. Speaking in April, 1894, Lord Herschell, then Lord Chancellor, referred to the Prince's willingness to assist every good and charitable cause. " He had peculiar reasons for knowing that His Royal Highness, when he thought a cause a good one, was not content with merely giving his occasional presence on State occasions, but found no details too irksome, no attention too great, if he could thereby promote the object in view."

But with all his laborious leadership in Royal work, he has never lost his pleasure in the lighter side of life. It is this many-sidedness to which, in fact, he owes his success, and for which he has earned the right to a place amongst men who are great by personal power as well as by inherited rank. The Prince of Wales would be the last to claim personal greatness, but history will compare him favourably with the heirs to the Throne in all past ages of English annals, and will point to his dignified, tactful, and useful tenure of an exceptionally difficult place during very many years of stirring and critical national life. In shaping the destiny of England and the British Empire he has thus had no small share—partly by what he has done and partly by what he has not done—and in its future, both as Heir Apparent and possible Sovereign, he can do still more to weld together its vast Imperial interests, to promote its social welfare, to elevate its masses and harmonize its classes, and to carry on the great work of his queenly mother by keeping the Throne and the people in happy unison and loyal co-operation.

HIS MAJESTY, EDWARD VII.,
KING OF GREAT BRITAIN AND IRELAND. EMPEROR OF INDIA.

HER MAJESTY ALEXANDRA QUEEN CONSORT.

CHAPTER XVIII.

The Court and the Sovereign.

UPON the immediate environment of the Sovereign depends, to an immense degree, the morals and manners of a nation. The men and women who constitute the Court make or mar much more than the mere passing fashions of the hour. For this reason—even had there been no other—the British people are under deep indebtedness to Queen Victoria. For the last half century things have gone so smoothly in Court circles that the public has become oblivious not only to the vast difference between the present and the past, but in some degree to the importance of the conditions which now prevail. They have forgotten the anxiety, and patience, and reflection which have gone into the creation of the existing system. They are apt to overlook the potent influence of the Royal example and opinion in bringing to the surface the best that exists in the nation, and in subduing those elements of evil which are always struggling to find a place, and a high place, in the upper social circles of such a great world-centre as London.

The Court of England has never before been of the kind which stands in the forefront of the nation during these closing years of the century. As with all society, in all degrees, the circle surrounding the Sovereign, or in attendance upon the Prince and Princess of Wales, may at times be flippant or foolish, and may even seem more intent upon display than upon serious service to the State. But compared with the surroundings of Elizabeth or Charles II., or of some of the Georges, it is as light to darkness, and in a positive sense it really represents the meeting together of those who hold high place in the government and literature and life of the country and the empire, instead of a gathering of pleasure-hunting sycophants, intent only upon providing amusement and getting some themselves. This result and the accompanying improvement in modes of life and social custom have been largely due to the Queen. To quote Mr. Walter Bagehot—writing in 1861 :

" The Crown is of singular importance in a divided and contentious free state, because it is the sole object of attachment which is elevated above every contention and division. But to maintain that importance it must create attachment.

" We know that the Crown now does so fully ; but we do not adequately bear in mind how much rectitude of intention, how much judgment in conduct, how much power of doing right, how much power of doing nothing, are requisite to unite the loyalty and to retain the confidence of a free people."

A Court must lead the people, in a moral sense. Even where it simply embodies a national reaction, and represents the prevailing mode of life, as during the reign of the second Charles, it none the less accentuates the surrounding good or evil, and furnishes a high example for its continuance and expansion. And in this way Her Majesty has led in the beneficial change which began in 1837 with her transfer from the simple life of Kensington to the intricate and stirring life of Windsor. She set the fashion for a better mode of living and a higher code of manners and morals. Partly because of her youth, partly because of her beauty and attractiveness, partly because of her loneliness in the lofty elevation of the Throne, men's minds were attuned in a readier and truer obedience to royal precept and example than might otherwise have been the case, and the consequent purification of the Court and improvement in social customs went on together and apace.

How much a sovereign can influence these matters is shown by the history of Elizabeth's reign. The social life of her time was one of light-hearted enjoyment. Responsibility was shunned and pleasure sought, even at the expense of principle and honour. In this seeking after enjoyment the Queen led with vigour, and her rapid-moving Court, in all parts of the country, set the pace for a life which suited the passing inclinations of the people, and was more or less oblivious to refinement and discriminating taste. She is said to have boxed the ears of an offending courtier, to have rapped out frequent oaths, and to have uttered every sharp, amusing word or phrase that occurred to her. Coarse manners in the Court and community—despite the polished graces of a Raleigh or an Essex—were naturally attended by more or less of coarse morals, and the condition of things at that period probably merited the vigorous onslaughts of Roger Ascham. But Queen Elizabeth was popular, partly because of her undoubted ability, partly because of her intensely English pride, partly because of the national achievements of her reign.

The Court of Queen Anne was, on the other hand, extremely moral and formal, so far as she could control its character. But her personality was not strong enough to make this influence spread very far, and Lord Chesterfield at the time ridiculed it in most unbridled language; although he proffered what was really a compliment in saying that " Her drawing-rooms were more respectable than agreeable, and had more the air of a solemn place of worship than the gaiety of a Court." Bishop Burnet furnishes another kind of criticism :

"Queen Anne is easy of access, and hears everything very gently ; but opens herself to so few, and is so cold and general in her answers, that people soon find that the chief application is to be made to her ministers and favourites, who in their turns have an entire credit and full power with her. She has laid down the splendour of a Court too much, and eats privately ; so that *except on Sundays,* and a few hours twice or thrice a week at night in the drawing-room, she appears so little that her Court is, as it were, abandoned."

That her efforts at making virtue fashionable and profligacy unpopular were not altogether successful was due partly to personal deficiencies and partly to the spirit of an age which boasted the political dominance of Bolingbroke and Oxford and Rochester, and the dramatic pre-eminence of a Congreve. The reign was glorious through external victories, and when the Court did meet at Kensington Palace, in occasional moments of festivity and frivolity, it was brilliant by virtue of wits, and writers, and poets who have marked the period by their achievements. But Queen Anne was not a leader of her people in any personal sense of the word. And it was much the same with the first three Georges, so far as the influence of their Courts was concerned.

During the reign of George I., Vauxhall and Ranelagh were types of fashionable life ; and the Mohocks and other bands of bullies, who scoured the streets of London at night, illustrated a degree of brutality, and ignorance, and indifference to morality such as is now hard to comprehend. Kensington Palace remained at this period, and during the reign of George II., the abode of the Court, with an occasional sojourn at St. James and Hampton Court. The society which gathered there was of a dull and uninteresting nature. It neither led the fashion, in any widely popular sense, nor did it voice the principles of a higher culture or a better social system. So with the circle surrounding George III. and his Consort at Buckingham Palace. It was distinctly, aggressively, moral in tone, and the domestic example afforded was excellent in a somewhat narrow and dreary way. But the influence which the Court wielded for good was more than counteracted by the example of the Prince of Wales and his friends at Carlton House.

Of the royal surroundings during the latter's Regency and reign the less said the better. It was simply endured by the people ; and from its influence the future Queen Victoria was mercifully shielded through the care of a wise mother. Manners, during this period, were almost as coarse as in the reign of Elizabeth ; and the Journals of Lord Auckland tell us a very characteristic anecdote of the Duke of Cumberland—the brother of King George III. At a reception given by the Duke, he was told that he ought to say something to Mr. Gibbon, the historian. " Well," said the Prince, with graceful familiarity, " I suppose you are at your old trade, scribble, scribble, scribble." Lord Selborne, in his recently published " Memoirs," says of the nephew and successor of the same royal personage, that at a dinner given the Duke of Wellington upon the occasion of his installation in 1833 as Chancellor of Oxford University, " the Duke of Cumberland distinguished himself by swearing all the evening."

Such were the precedents, and such the manners, very largely prevalent when the Queen came to the Throne, and introduced a new era in social morals and national tastes.

Her personality had much to do with the result. Youth and beauty were potent influences, no doubt, in making the Sovereign popular during the early years of her reign, but without tact and charming manners, mingled with determination, they would have been useless. Those were the days of hard drinking and hard swearing. Holland House was in the prime of the famous literary circle where Brougham and Sidney Smith, Macaulay and Monckton Milnes, held sway in the genial presence of their hostess. Lady Blessington guided a larger circle of men of fashion at Gore House, and while herself writing and speaking continually against the contemporary fashionable women permitted and encouraged the dandies and authors of the day in so-called smart jokes and sayings of a similar or worse character. Count D'Orsay and Benjamin Disraeli, Thomas Slingsby Duncombe and Lord Chesterfield, Lord Ranelagh and Lord Edward Thynne, were typical beaux of the day, and it was of the first-named that a then popular poem spoke :

> " Patting the crest of his well-manag'd steed,
> Proud of his action, D'Orsay vaunts the breed ;
> A coat of chocolate, a vest of snow,
> Well brushed his whiskers as his boots below ;
> A short-napp'd beaver, prodigal in brim,
> With trousers tighten'd to a well-turned limb."

Duels were the fashion, and Almacks the social resort and rage of the hour ; runaway matches and Gretna Green marriages were matters of frequent occurrence. Pugilism was very fashionable, as were " breakfasts " from 4 to 6.30 p.m., Sunday dinner parties, and coaching or hunting. Much of this, of course, could hardly be called objectionable, but the general *tone* of society could, on the other hand, hardly be called creditable. With the Accession an immediate change came about in the Court, and soon filtered down into all the highways and byways of what is termed society. Harriet Martineau declares that "one of the strongest and most genial influences of the period was the young Queen. At first she was in high spirits—liking to see and be seen ; driving in the parks when they were most thronged ; dining at the Guildhall, and saying as she went down to open Parliament, 'Let my people see me.'" Lady Granville, in writing to her brother the Duke of Devonshire, at different times in 1837, speaks of Her Majesty as "a little love of a Queen," and as being " perfect in manner, dignity, and grace, with great youthfulness and jovousness." In October, 1839, she declares that " the Queen looks lovely, much more delicate without looking ill. Lord Melbourne appears to be in as great favour as ever, and I think their relative manners in a difficult position perfect." Such characteristics naturally and quickly produced a gayer Court and a more refined society. Writing his daughter on August 4th, 1877, Chief Justice Lord Denman thus describes a Royal dinner party :

"Now for a description of the Queen's dinner. The Palace (Buckingham) has been much maligned, and is really much handsomer than I expected. The hall and staircase are magnificent. A splendid room hung with green silk first receives you, then a round room with a vaulted roof. . . . In about five minutes folding doors to the right were thrown open and the Queen came *tripping* in with the Duchess of Kent and all her ladies.

"She was led in (to dinner) by some foreign nobleman. The party was, I think, twenty-six in number. The conversation was confined to small knots, but was lively and incessant, though carried on in subdued tones. It was very different from the kingly table I remember, where the Royal host used to drink to the general health of the whole table, and singly with most of his company, and more than once.

"The Queen wore all black, with a train, her hair as usual, with thin rings of curls hardly larger than a shilling on the cheeks—that is, one just below each ear; a little flowing black gauze was fastened in the hair behind. No human countenance was ever more *expressive of happiness* and good nature; she had something to say to everybody; not the smallest constraint with anyone."

These dinners must have become more and more imposing as time went on. The Baroness Bunsen, writing in 1842, speaks of one at which the King of Prussia was present at Windsor as a scene like a fairy tale: "of indescribable magnificence, the proportions of the hall, the mass of lights in suspension, the gold plate on the table glittering with a thousand lights." Royal balls were also frequent in those days, and this mingling of the Queen with society had an effect which isolated example might not have had. Some were great functions and some comparatively small affairs, but at them all Her Majesty danced with more or less freedom. The Baroness quoted above—wife of the Prussian Minister of many years standing at St. James'—tells us, in 1847, of "a small dancing party, only Lady Rosebery and the Ladies Primrose (probably the late Premier's mother and sisters) coming in the evening in addition to those at dinner. The Queen danced with her usual spirit and activity and that obliged other people to do their best, and thus the ball was a pretty sight, inspirited by excellent music."

Meanwhile the whole condition of the Court, with its myriad officials and loose management—its lack of order, and method, and system—was being reformed and reorganized under the judicious oversight of the Queen and the Prince Consort. Departments were adjusted and given strictly specified functions; officials were gradually rearranged as regarded position, or dispensed with entirely; the great officers of State—appointed by incoming Ministries—such as the Lord Steward, the Lord Chamberlain, and the Master of the Horse, were given defined duties, and much friction thus prevented; rules of administration were introduced and uniformity of system gradually established. In the course of time order, comfort, and economy became the condition throughout all the Royal palaces and great functions of the Court, instead of a state of affairs described by Sir Theodore Martin as one which "daily experience proved to be incompatible with the comfort no less than with the dignity of the Court." The appointment of a chief part of the officials, despite the "Bedchamber question," has been, and is, in the hands of Her Majesty, though, no doubt, she is very glad to take advice in many cases. There are Lords and Ladies-in-Waiting, a Master of Ceremonies, a Marshal, many aides-de-camp, gentlemen ushers, grooms of the privy chamber—who on great occasions stand on the staircases or in corriders where the Queen passes—crowds of heralds, bodyguards, pages, inspectors, and minor servants, while the Ladies-in-Waiting and those of the Bedchamber are representative of the greatest families in England.

The chief State officer, in this latter connection, is the Mistress of the Robes, who must always be a Duchess, and who attends the Queen on all state occasions, enjoys precedence over all other ladies about the Court, and deals with Her Majesty's personal bills and accounts—dresses, bric-à-brac, etc. The Duchess of Roxburgh for many years held this and other posts in the Court, and has only very recently died. Lady Churchill, the Dowager-Marchioness of Ely, and the Dowager-Duchess of Athole have long been favourite attendants, while in earlier days Lady Canning and Lady Waterford held a high place in the Queen's estimation. Lady Lytton—widow of the late Ambassador at Paris—and Lady Ampthill, whose husband was for a long period Ambassador at Berlin, have been recent appointments. But the chief permanent official in connection with the Court and about the person of the Sovereign is her private secretary and keeper of the privy purse. The post has been filled for many years by the late General Sir Henry Ponsonby, a most careful, able, and faithful servant; a man of power in many different directions; an official of great industry, and who was implicitly trusted by the Queen in the myriad matters, important or of complicated unimportance, with which he had to deal. In the earlier years of the reign, General Grey and Sir Thomas Biddulph were in similar ways entrusted with wide and varied work.

Such is the Court in an official sense. It consists of a large body of public servants trained in the dignity and ceremony of Royal life, and fulfilling the functions which have enabled the Queen to represent the nation with appropriate symbols and surroundings of power, while promoting morality and a better social code through the high character of her attendants and officials. The social side of Court life has been referred to so far as concerns its dependence upon the character of the Sovereign. In that respect it has had every advantage. If it were really true that no man is a hero to his own valet, then the highest compliments which can be paid the Queen are those proffered in private letters by her attendants—some of which have only seen the light many years after the death of the writer. In one such letter, dated August 2nd, 1842, and written to Mrs. Jameson in connection with the latter's catalogue of London Art Treasures, the Hon. Amelia Murray says that:

" I was gratified to see that your catalogue elicited one of her beaming smiles, such as are rarely bestowed save upon her own husband. Few are yet sensible what a fascinating creature she is ! *The perfect truth* and simplicity which are united to such depth and strength of character give an interest to every look and a charm to every word she utters. But I must stop. If I once allow my feelings full vent in speaking of my dear young mistress, I know not how to stop.

"But I think, my dear Mrs. Jameson, you know me well enough to believe that it is, indeed, out of the fulness of the heart that the pen writeth, and that only a hearty appreciation of her character could make me admire my Queen as I do."

Combined with her pronounced charm of manner, the Queen has always had a strong desire for knowledge and an apparently keen pleasure in meeting able or distinguished men. Hence the intellectual as well as social tone of the Court—a feature which increased in after years, as the gay and bright side of life lost its attractions to the Royal widow. Sir Archibald Allison, the veteran Scotch historian, tells us in his Memoirs of staying at Balmoral in 1849, and of Her Majesty's conversation upon the early history of Scotland, her close questions about the battles of Selkirk, Falkirk, and Bannockburn, and her desire to know the exact localities in which they were fought; and he adds that "Such was the rapidity of her thoughts and the quickness of her apprehension that it was all I could do to keep pace with them, and I felt not less fatigued when the conversation closed by the mental effort required to carry it on than charmed by the grace and condescension of Her Majesty's manner." General Sir James Hope Grant, writing privately after his return from leading the Chinese campaign of 1861, gives an interesting sketch of Court life in its more general sphere. On reaching Buckingham Palace he was ushered into the long and beautiful gallery where guests were received, and where some had already gathered. After waiting twenty minutes or so, the Queen entered, accompanied by King Leopold of Belgium, Princess Alice, and the suite.

"Her Majesty, in passing, gave me a very graceful bow, and Prince Albert came up and shook hands with me. There was no particular constraint in the conversation. After dinner I was talking with Colonel Biddulph, when he suddenly warned me that Her Majesty was coming up to speak to me. I looked up and saw the Queen advancing towards me Nerves are very singular ! I must confess I felt very awkward. I did not know what to do with my hands. Her Majesty, however, was most graceful and affable in her manner, and after a few words of conversation with her I felt quite at my ease. Her figure was very pretty and graceful and young-looking for her age, and her voice was beautifully melodious. . .

" The Queen, after talking to me for a considerable time (upon various weighty matters), bowed and retired."

This nervous sentiment of the old soldier has been shared by many others before and since, and Laurence Oliphant, versatile, travelled, and *blasé* as he was, describes his presentation at Court (1851) in most amusing terms—indicative indeed, of peculiarly mixed feelings. " I found everybody in uniform ; the few who were in civil costume looked like servants of the Royal household. The

Queen looked me in the face much harder than I expected, and I repaid the gaze with such a will that I forgot to kneel, ultimately nearly going down on both knees, after which, finding the backing-out process rather irksome, I fairly turned tail and bolted." These functions, stereotyped and even wearisome as they may be in some respects, are more valuable than is, perhaps, generally supposed. Presentation to the Queen or the Prince of Wales is, of course, a compliment and an honour—but it is more than that. Properly controlled and guarded, as it is, the function promotes a certain sifting of society, and enables the Sovereign to stamp discredit upon practices and persons whom it may be in the interest of social and moral improvement to so mark. All names have to be submitted to the Lord Chamberlain for Her Majesty's consideration, and have to be presented by some recognized personage—official or social. Hence the value of this side of Court life, and the effect it has gradually had in purifying manners and customs through the various grades affected by Royal approval or the reverse.

It must be remembered that this influence has been a very wide one. The Queen only visited great country houses where the proprietors were distinguished by the higher graces of life as well as by worthy deeds or lofty position. She refused to receive formally or otherwise those who had any public stain upon their characters and life, or any scandal connected with their names. She has always discountenanced divorce and refused to allow persons in that condition— no matter how much distinguished otherwise—place or room at Court. In a society constituted as that of England is such a line of action constitutes a powerful lever for good, and as the salons of Holland House and Gore House gave way to those of Lady Palmerston, or Lady Derby, or Lady Waldegrave, and they in turn to the crushes and crowds which seem to be the "up-to-date" ideal of social life, the influence of the Royal stamping, and of the receptions and entertainments given by the Princess of Wales, has become more and more pronounced.

There is, of course, much to condemn in the social life of England to-day, and much that the Queen's influence can never reach or control, but so far as a high example, an absolute discretionary power in the head of the State—nobly exercised for the benefit of the nation in a moral and cultured sense—can reach, there the Court of Queen Victoria has been a power indeed, and one which few will dispute as weighty and ever-widening in its scope and action. When it is compared with the brilliant and beautiful, but corrupt and immoral, Court of France during the Second Empire; with the good but not very potent or popular example of that given in Louis Philippe's reign; with the minor Courts of Germany or that of Prussia during the first half of Her Majesty's era; with the absence of all rule or example—unless it be that of fashionable depravity—in the ranks of many another European Court; then we understand better the good that has been and the evil that has not.

The influence wielded has therefore not been restricted—certainly not to the narrow limits of the *levée* or drawing-room, which to many seem to compose the Court. It includes the personal example of the Sovereign; the work of a vast number of Royal officials; the effect of the Queen's known opinions and wishes upon society; the gathering together of leaders in every class of British life by means of Royal functions, State dinners, and receptions; the invitations constantly extended by the Queen to great men and eminent women, to meet her and discuss leading subjects of the present and the past; the entertainments given to foreign monarchs, statesmen, or generals; the encouragement and recognition accorded to merit in every kind of achievement and good work; the example given to all countries and peoples, and especially to the Colonies of the Crown, in Royal dignity and honour and purity; the splendour which should surround a throne and reflect the lustre of the nation and empire over which the sovereign reigns, and which in this case she so truly represents. Moreover, the Court of to-day, and of a good many years past, includes the hospitable receptions and parties at Sandringham, and the circle surrounding the Prince and Princess of Wales. Here are to be found remarkable men of every kind—in literature, art, music, inventions, learning, and politics. Clever women are always included, and the circle, without being too cosmopolitan and wide, is yet sufficiently so to be always interesting and instructive. It numbered in recent years such attractive or prominent personalities as the Duke and Duchess of Sutherland, Lord and Lady Dudley, Lord and Lady Spencer, Lord and Lady Charles Beresford, Lord and Lady Alington, the late Lord Dalhousie, Lord and Lady Carrington, Lady Mandeville, Lady Lonsdale, Lord and Lady Londonderry, Lord Randolph Churchill, and Lord Rosebery. These made up the social and more or less permanent element. The floating element of men and women of the passing day is interesting, but would be too numerous and many-sided to describe here.

An important power in connection with the Court and society, which is more often personally wielded by the Queen than is popularly supposed, arises out of her position as the fountain of honour. It is commonly thought that the Prime Minister suggests the honours to be bestowed upon leaders in all the various lines of British life and action, and that the Queen merely assents. This may in a sense be true. But the Prime Minister would not suggest a name which he knew to be unpleasant to the Sovereign, and if he accidentally did so would promptly withdraw it. From time to time he unquestionably receives suggestions from her, and in such cases they do not, of course, require his confirmation or approval, though no doubt it is always given. On the other hand, the Queen spontaneously, and of her own free will, confers many honours—as, for instance, the Order of the Garter given to her Premiers, and notably to Lord Palmerston, Lord Beaconsfield, and Lord Rosebery, and the peerages conferred upon Mr. Disraeli and offered to Mr. Gladstone. In very many other cases the initiative has been her own. But, taken in her Sovereign capacity or as the result of Ministerial recommendations, these honours have been a source of great good to the community and the nation under her wise dispensation.

To understand how clearly this statement has been demonstrated by history, it is only necessary to read a list of some of the titles conferred by preceding Sovereigns—and the reasons for such honours. With the Queen, however, they have proved another potent influence for good, and have given another incentive to right living and noble work by those who are very properly ambitious to be recognized by the State and by their Sovereign. When men like Lord Tennyson, and Lord Kelvin, and Lord Shaftesbury, and dozens of similarly noble-minded leaders in every branch of the national life, are proud to accept honours from Her Majesty, it is evident that the purity and beneficence of this Royal function and power is sincerely respected, and of great value and influence. So with appointments such as that of Poet Laureate. Wordsworth voiced with Royal approval and patronage the natural beauties of England and the charms of the English home; Tennyson sang the noblest attributes and aims in man and woman with a poetic imagery and power which have wielded wider influence for good than any other single force of the century—aside, perhaps, from that of the Queen herself; Austin has acclaimed the rural loveliness of his native land and the patriotism of his fellow-subjects. He has now been given a great opportunity for doing good through the production of poetry which shall sing the notes of a nobler life, and better aims, and greater principles than yet prevail. All these things have therefore worked together for the same end—the elevation of the people and the nation.

Intimately connected with the work and functions of the Court is the cost of its maintenance and that of the monarchy. The Sovereign must have a Court and regal surroundings suitable to the nation thus ruled and represented. To quote Mr. Gladstone in his famous speech on the Royal grants in 1889: "I am averse to all economy which would prevent not only the dignity, but which would impair the splendour of the Court. In a society constituted as this society is, the Court ought to be a splendid Court. And I will go further and say that a Court amply provided, but not extravagantly provided with means, worked in a genial spirit, and conforming to a high moral standard, is one of the most powerful, one of the most inestimable agencies which, in a country like this, you can bring to bear upon the tone of society, and by means of which you can raise the standard of conduct throughout the community." But there are always malcontents in every nation who are unable or unwilling to appreciate the excellences of any existing institution, and who much prefer to live in a discontented dreamland of their own imagination—generally a very distorted and diseased region. They would make reckless changes without caring or knowing what would follow, and where they do plan for the future it is generally done upon some utterly unstable and worthless basis.

For instance, many Radicals will say with an air of the most convincing force that the President of the great American Republic receives £10,000 per annum, while the Civil List of Queen Victoria amounts to the tremendous figure of £385,000! The fact is, of course, that to make any comparison of the cost of government in the two countries one has to add to the President's salary and allowances those of the vice-president, making a total of £16,000, together with the payments to State governors, senators, representatives in Congress, and State legislators—a sum total of £683,275 as the cost of *government* in the United States. If to this is added the enormous expense of electing a President every four years—estimated at £4,000,000—to say nothing of the loss occasioned by the disturbance in business, the comparison is still more to the point. Moreover, the Civil List of England is in a very peculiar state. It is in reality, though not in form, the income arising from the Queen's own inherited rights and property.

When Her Majesty came to the Throne an act was passed by Parliament, with her previous consent, taking over during her reign the hereditary estates of the Crown, and giving in place of their revenues a permanent yearly grant of £385,000. In after years this grant was added to by special sums, amounting, all told, to £188,000, which were given to various members of the Royal family. This, with an expenditure of some £100,000 upon the Royal Palaces and military escorts, etc., constitute the cost of the British Court and monarchy—a total of £673,000. Here, however, comes the fact so often forgotten or ignored, that the Crown lands already mentioned as held in trust by the nation, and subject to being handed over at the close of the present reign to Her Majesty's successor, now afford an annual income of some £490,000 to the country, and if deducted, as should be the case, from the total Royal expenditure, leave the cost of the monarchy to the tax-payers at the trivial sum of £183,000. Compare this with the great European Powers, where the personal Civil List in Germany amounts to £615,000, in Austria to £775,000, in little Italy to £650,000, and in poverty-stricken Spain to £400,000, while the Russian Czar has an income of at least £2,000,000!

Supposing, however, the amount is taken as it stands, and £673,000 estimated as the cost of monarchical institutions to the British people and Empire, few men of sense and knowledge can be found in Great Britain to seriously criticize or denounce the expenditure. The British nation, indeed, understands thoroughly the value of the monarchy as affording a dignified method of government; a stable and continuous and impartial head of the State; a representative of the nation of which it may be proud abroad, and which facilitates diplomacy and helps negotiation; a Court which surrounds the Crown with splendour, and contributes to the development of the higher social instincts of the people. Personally, the Queen has given the nation a noble example of Royal economy and business-like management, without undue parsimony or any inefficiency in Monarchical state and court ceremony. Harriet Martineau, writing in 1849, described Her Majesty's earlier characteristics in this respect :

"She had her allowance of money from an early age; her way of spending much of it was known at Tunbridge Wells and other places of summer sojourn ; but nobody ever heard of her being a sixpence in debt for an hour.

"The energy and conscientiousness brought out by such training are a blessing to a whole people.

"At first the Queen was very rich ; many persons thought much too rich for a maiden Queen whose calls could as yet be nothing. But in the first year she paid her father's heavy debts—debts contracted before she was born. Next she paid her mother's debts— debts which she knew to be incurred on her account. She did much for the family of William IV. Next she married, and nothing was said about any increase of income. Now she has a large family of children, and such claims and liabilities as grow up out of twelve years of sovereignty—and still we hear nothing of any Royal needs or debts."

In these and following years the entire Court was rearranged, Balmoral and Osborne bought and rebuilt out of the Queen's private means, while every call of State ceremony, and the expense of receptions to great visiting sovereigns were met without a word of debt or difficulty. We know also from Sir Robert Peel's statement in Parliament that the very large public expenditure upon the national receptions given for national reasons to King Louis Philippe of France and the Emperor Nicholas of Russia were paid by the Queen out of her own income, without calling upon Parliament for an additional penny. With, in fact, much greater responsibility, much more of pomp and ceremony, an infinitely more brilliant Court, an immense external empire and consequent important additional functions, much higher prices and more expensive surroundings, Queen Victoria has received and expended annually about one-half what her predecessors did from the accession of George I. to the death of Wiiliam IV. The story of immense savings in the possession of Her Majesty may consequently be considered as pure fiction, even without Mr. Gladstone's testimony to the contrary, or Mr. Labouchere's conclusive statement in the *Forum* of October, 1891—written by a confirmed Radical in policy, and a Republican in principle, upon the result of a Committee of Parliament appointed in 1889 to consider the provision required for the Prince of Wales' children. "The Committee was informed," he states, "under a pledge of secrecy, of the total value of Her Majesty's investments. As I was a member of the Committee, I cannot, of course, violate this pledge; but I do not think that I am breaking confidence in saying that the amount was surprisingly small."

There are many other considerations in connection with the Court which might be dwelt upon. The *risque* conversation so popular nowadays in certain circles is absolutely frowned down, just as the swearing and drinking of a past generation have been crushed out of sight. So with the position of women in society, in the world, and in politics. Her Majesty is distinctly and beneficially of the old school in this respect, and her feeling undoubtedly still predominates in the best homes and around the happiest hearths of her vast dominions. "Women are not made for governing," she wrote to King Leopold on February 3rd, 1852, "and if we are good women we must dislike these masculine occupations." That she herself has shown such signal and necessary skill in that connection is only one of the exceptions which may be said to prove the rule. Physical and family reasons; the loss of that chivalry and refinement in social intercourse which it has been one of the Queen's great aims to promote and increase; the bitterness inherent in public controversies which would, as a result of female suffrage, soon shadow and darken the home life of the nation; the strain upon family ties and domestic harmony which would inevitably follow; the probable introduction of all manner of religious and moral issues into politics and Parliament, which it is impossible for any influence to settle other than the steady and persistent voice of the pulpit, the power of the Church and schoolhouse, the purification of social ethics, and the gradual elevation of public sentiment through high example and individual exertion; all these things Her Majesty has felt and understood. She knows that ordinary legislation is only effective when it represents a majority in public opinion, and that moral legislation has to voice an overpowering moral sentiment before it can be successfully enforced. Hence the fact that woman's political influence lies not in forcing legislation through Parliament, but in moulding public opinion through its preliminary stages of the home, the family, the school, and the Church.

— In these latter directions women reign supreme. The ideal mother, the sweet old-fashioned woman above whose head hovers a halo of religion, and around whose life or memory clings the youthful recollection of everything that is good and beautiful, has more influence in moulding the destinies of the country than she would have if twenty votes were hers, or her presence a familiar one at all the polling booths and public meetings of a county. The gentle mother who thus instructs her children in the higher ideals of life, the beauty of poetry, the eloquence of nature, the charm of art, the spirit of music, the love of country and home and people, exercises a nobler power for good than is possible in any other direction. Such a woman is able to make men say as did the late Lord Langdale: "If the whole world were put into one scale and my mother in the other, the world would kick the beam." So in a different sphere with the noble-minded nurse who devotes herself, like Florence Nightingale, to the service of humanity upon the battlefield, or like many a more obscure heroine, cares for the sick at home or in the hospital. Her work does more to soothe and heal individual suffering, to remedy the horrors of war and disease and pestilence, to add to the strength and vitality of a nation, than could the devotion of many women to politics and so-called equal rights for the sexes.

And, in these days of bewildering restlessness, woman wields many a force in society and the world which might be all-powerful for good, if only guided in the right direction. The bright and spirited woman of society can do her share of public work, and wield an ever-widening influence, by the exercise of quiet tact, skilful conversation, and a dignified personal bearing. To smooth the rough edges of modern life and manners, to cultivate the virtues of courtesy and kindliness, to modify the harshly drawn lines between wealth and poverty, to soothe the rasping miseries of the working classes, and give an impetus to the sympathies of those who dwell in luxury, are surely objects sufficiently high and vital for any woman to be proud of helping forward. In such work lies the true mission of those who wish to influence their day and generation, and not in the promotion of new elements of discord and the stirring up of fresh discontents. The women of to-day should be a balm for the suffering of restless humanity, and the guardians of all that is peaceful and pure, rather than the participators in political struggle, and seekers after wild vagaries of ceaseless change and electoral reform. But above all these considerations is perhaps the fact that woman holds in her hand the powerful social and national lever which surrounds and controls the question of marriage. If the men of this and other generations once understood that looseness in life, the habit of drinking, the many instincts of vulgarity, or evidences of weakness, which are so apparent in the society of the time, were really bars against admission to the homes of their country, and the society and friendship and favour of its women, a change would come over the whole spirit of modern life beside which all the possible exertions of the voting and speaking representatives of the sex for a century would be of the most trivial and unimportant nature. The fact is that woman's power lies in her personal influence —the force of natural superiority inherent in her sympathy, and tact, and womanliness of character—not in fancied equality or similarity with man. As Lord Beaconsfield so well said in "Coningsby": "Man conceives fortune, but woman executes it. It is the spirit of man that says, 'I will be great'; but it is the sympathy of woman that usually makes him so."

No one in all history has so well illustrated these facts as Queen Victoria. Her beautiful home life as a child, a wife, a mother, and the regnant head of a great family circle ; her devotion to husband and children ; her love for domesticity amid all the distractions and attractions of what was for twenty years the most brilliant Court in the world ; her deep religious sympathies and intense earnestness in the education of the Royal family; her womanly sympathy with sickness and sorrow and suffering in all its myriad shapes ; her high example of what a womanly woman can be, and do, without infringing upon the duties and work of man, has done more to advance the good of her people and the welfare of women in their various spheres of national life than any other force in all the centuries. In the sympathetic influence which she had over Prince Albert, and the warm co-operation which she gave him in every high ideal and noble ambition which he strove to execute, there dwelt a power which moulded the character and life of the young Prince, and helped him to leave a name and fame as one of the purest, brightest, and noblest personalities in all the Royal annals of England—a character which Tennyson so truly designates in those well-known words :

> " And, indeed, he seems to me
> Scarce other than my ideal knight,
> Who reverenced his conscience as his king;
> Whose glory was redressing human wrong;
> Who spake no slander, no, nor listened to it;
> Who loved one only, and who clave to her."

And thus it happened that the Queen as a woman, and apart from her power as a Sovereign, has wielded such vast influence—first by the force of domestic example, then by the power of personal sympathy in the great and beneficial aims of the Prince Consort, and finally by the potency of a woman's work in the realms of philanthropy, charity, and personal kindliness. Hence it was that the British people of both sexes have been so greatly helped in upward development and progress by their Sovereign.

Those of the upper classes have benefited by a distinctly better social code and a more refined mode of life. Those of the lower classes have benefited through legislation modifying hours of labour in factory and shop and other branches of work; through laws affecting their treatment at home and their freedom abroad; through the better and brighter homes which have grown out of the Royal example, and been helped by the Royal sympathy with all proposals—public, individual, or Parliamentary—for the amelioration of grievances and the abolition of abuses; through the spread of knowledge amongst the masses, and the consequent improvement in the character of the workingman; through the progress of Church work and missions, and the personal part taken by the Queen and Royal family in encouraging every pursuit, and institution, and popular idea which has promised to elevate the life and improve the surroundings of the population as a whole.

Hand in hand, the Queen and her Court have, therefore, during sixty years cultivated beneficial reforms and opposed injurious fads. The dignity of the monarchy has been strengthened by the splendour of the court; its influence has been enhanced by the example set through the high places of the land and in the immediate environment of the Sovereign; its popularity has become deep-seated in the hearts of the people through the personality of the Queen; while its beneficence has been felt in all ranks and classes of the British Empire as a result of the moral code enforced by the Queen, and the domestic example set by her to the nation and the world.

CHAPTER XIX.

IRELAND AND THE MONARCHY.

THE Queen has visited Ireland three times during her reign. She has sent the Prince of Wales on several state visits to the Kingdom at periods when royal duty to a troubled country must have come in serious conflict with natural fears for the safety of a son and heir to the Throne. She has given at least one of her children an Irish name, and two of them Irish titles. More she would have done had the exigencies of political struggle allowed her Ministers to exercise a far-sighted policy of consistent conciliation instead of the see-saw practice of alternating suppression and surrender. The Irish people have always been naturall inclined to support monarchical institutions with enthusiasm. Their character-istic impulsiveness and imagination; their liking for pomp and splendour; their tendency to pursue the personal and sentimental in politics, rather than the materialistic and economic; their loyalty to leaders rather than to abstract principles; all tend to promote the popular idealization of a sovereign— and especially when that sovereign happens to be a woman.

These facts were fully indicated in 1837, when Her Majesty came to the Throne. She was young, she was charming; she was, above all, understood to sympathize with the Irish masses. The Roman Catholics had not many years before been admitted to general equality with Protestants in public life, and the Queen, shortly after her accession, addressed a letter to the Lord Lieutenant of Ireland—Lord Mulgrave, afterwards Marquess of Normanby— through the Home Secretary, and expressed an earnest desire "to see her Irish subjects in the full enjoyment of that civil and political equality to which, by a recent statute, they are entitled"; and added that "she is convinced that when invidious distinctions are altogether obliterated, her throne will be more secure and her people more truly united." The effect of this and many flying rumours was electrical. Daniel O'Connell, the uncrowned king of a fiery and impulsive populace, surrendered at once, and declared that the Irish people must hereafter be " friends of the Queen."

This unscrupulous orator, who had called Lord Anglesey a scoundrel, and described the undoubtedly able Marquess of Wellesley as "a mere driveller"; who had styled Wellington " a stunted corporal," and Copley, the future Lord Lyndhurst, " no great things"; who denounced Disraeli as descended from the

H R.H. PRINCE ARTHUR, DUKE OF CONNAUGHT.

H.R.H. PRINCE ALFRED.
DUKE OF EDINBURGH AND SAXE-COBOURG-GOTHA.

H.R.H. PRINCESS ALICE.

impenitent thief; who cared for nothing, and attacked every one, actually wrote to a friend on June 28th, 1837, in the following terms:

"It being now certain that the young Queen (whom may God bless!) places full confidence in that ministry which was the first during six centuries to desire honestly and faithfully to serve the people of Ireland, we must all with one accord rally round the throne of the Queen and support this government. The time is come . . . to aid in ameliorating and consolidating the institutions of the country, by selecting such representatives as will support and give full effect to the benevolent intentions of the Sovereign."

And a few months later he was presented at Court by Lord Morpeth, the Irish Secretary—writing shortly before the event to a friend: "I wish to tell you, in the strictest confidence, that the Queen has expressed a wish to see me. She is determined to conciliate Ireland." That this was no mere passing impression and illusion of sentimental loyalty is evident from other correspondence of a similar nature. What follows is important as illustrating the influence of royalty in those days upon the susceptible Irish people, and as indicating the still greater power which may be wielded by the Crown and the Royal Family in the future.

October 23rd, 1838. "It is quite true that our gracious and beloved Queen is actually and sincerely friendly to the rights and liberties of the Irish people. . . . We never had a sovereign before who was not an actual enemy to our people; the change is propitious, and should be cherished."

August 5th, 1839. "As to the Queen, I have it from a source of the best authority that she is perfectly *true*. But will she be able to resist both Houses of Parliament, should the Tories get a majority in the Commons?"

June 28th, 1841. "We have just been up with the address to the Queen. . . . . View of the dear little Lady. She is looking very well, and read the answer most sweetly."

That O'Connell misunderstood the attitude of the Queen is, of course, evidenced by his subsequent Repeal agitation and its memorable termination under the auspices of Smith O'Brien and Gavan Duffy. That Her Majesty, however, sympathized with the Irish people in many ways, and sought by every means in her power to ameliorate their sad condition during the years between 1841 and 1849, is equally certain. But little could be really done for some years after the outburst of personal loyalty above quoted. The Government of Lord Melbourne might have taken advantage of it had the Prime Minister been a man of energy and constructive statesmanship. An earlier visit of the Queen to Ireland might have done much to cement and strengthen the popular loyalty. Modified measures in the direction of local and county government might, perhaps, have been possible. Above all, O'Connell might have been definitely won over, and the Repeal movement checked or altogether prevented.

Little, however, was done excepting a reform of the tithe system and the granting of relief to paupers from the rates. Then came the famine of 1846; the flame of European revolution in 1848; the rumble of discontent and rebellion, which found vent in Ireland during the latter year. It was, indeed, a time of wretchedness. As Mr. (now Sir Charles) Gavan Duffy declared during a speech in Dublin early in May: " The graves of Skibbereen, the exiles in Canada, the Coercion Bill in the south, the fever in the west and in the north, and bankruptcy everywhere, are witnesses that Ireland needs new guidance." And then, with an Irish vehemence and thoughtless enthusiasm which afterwards brought himself, and D'Arcy McGee, and Smith O'Brien, and many a more humble and less responsible person, into trouble and transportation, or even death, he defied a recent proclamation of the Lord Lieutenant, tore it to pieces upon the platform, and declared that " we have vowed to resist and overthrow this system of foreign domination, or die." The storm gathered and burst, and its chief victims—as usual in such cases—were the unfortunate peasants who had been led away by the facile oratory of men who may have felt what they said, but had certainly not measured what it meant.

Meanwhile, England, and those in positions of authority and wealth, had been bending every energy to the relief of Ireland in its period of famine and disaster. During four months following September, 1846, 500,000 persons in that country were living upon English funds; Parliament had voted over £2,000,000 for purposes of relief; the Queen had issued a Letter of appeal, which brought in private subscriptions of £171,000; while from other collections came £263,000. To these funds Her Majesty contributed £2,000, Prince Albert £500, and the Queen Dowager £1,000. In response to the Queen's Letter, money or provisions also came in from all parts of the Empire and the United States. From British North America came £12,463; from the American Republic £5,852 and £100,000 worth of food; from India £5,674; from the Cape £2,900; and from Australia £2,282. Parliament also voted £620,000 to Irish railways in order to supply work to a part of the population, while other large sums were granted the poor-houses and various other public institutions.

But the suffering had been intense, the loss of life dreadful to contemplate, the emigration had run up into millions, while the rebellion of 1848 had indicated a natural, though regrettable, feeling of disaffection and still surviving misery amongst the masses. England's humanity and England's aid—proffered at a moment when her own people were enduring the hardest of hard times —were seemingly forgotten. It was at this period that the Queen proposed that she and the Prince Consort should carry out their long-contemplated visit to Ireland. Such a suggestion—the bringing of a ray of sunshine to the Irish people after their long struggle with starvation and sorrow—was not only a kindly but a courageous act. Only a short time before Her Majesty had been fired at upon Constitution Hill by an Irishman named Hamilton, and Ireland itself was known to be still seething with suppressed discontent, and the after effects of the famine.

The proposal was at once approved by the Prime Minister, but its details were found to be rather difficult of arrangement. As Prince Albert said in a letter to Lord John Russell: "Although a State visit has long been expected, I am sure that the present state of distress will be considered a sufficient reason for its not taking place." He points out that such a method of travelling through the country might be conducive of ill-timed prodigality, and that the Queen is so anxious to visit the people that she is "willing to sacrifice her personal convenience by taking a long sea-voyage for the purpose of visiting Cork, Waterford, Wexford, Dublin, and Belfast." The announcement of the proposed journey was received with many expressions of satisfaction in Ireland, and by anticipations in England which, in some cases at least, would have led a stranger to suppose that the Sovereign was about to go into a most wild, inhospitable, and distant—if not barbarous and dangerous—portion of her dominions. The four elder children accompanied the Royal party, and the younger ones were left at Osborne with Lady Lyttelton, who records in her diary on August 1st, 1849, in a somewhat tragic manner, that "It is done! England's fate is afloat."

Two days later the Royal squadron steamed into the Cove of Cork—now the harbour of Queenstown—amid showers of rockets and roaring bonfires all along the coast, which the enthusiastic peasantry piled higher and higher with turf, faggot, and tar-barrel, as the feeling that their Queen had put implicit confidence in their loyalty came more and more home to them. The morning of the landing at what is now Queenstown was dreary, and the air heavy with probable rain, but just as the Queen set foot on shore the sun broke out through the clouds with sudden and unusual splendour—typical indeed of the bright and sunny welcome accorded by the people wherever they had the opportunity given them of seeing their Sovereign. From Cove, which was so soon to change its name, the Queen and her party passed up the beautiful River Lee in the Royal yacht, amidst the cheering of great crowds along the banks, the firing of cannon, and the ringing of bells. At Cork—the supposed centre of disaffection, and still the home of great antagonism to British rule and British union—the streets, balconies, windows, and roofs were obscured with a delighted, cheering population.

To quote the Queen's Journal, she found herself surrounded by "a noisy, excitable, but very good-humoured crowd, running and pushing about, laughing and talking and shrieking." The beauty of the women she particularly noticed. It was "very remarkable, and struck us much; such beautiful dark eyes and hair, and such fine teeth; almost every third woman was pretty, and some remarkably so. They wear no bonnets, and generally long blue cloaks; the men are very poorly, often raggedly, dressed; and many wear blue coats and short breeches, with blue stockings." After addresses had been received from the Mayor and Corporation, the Protestant Bishop and clergy, the Roman Catholic Bishop and clergy, the county officials and others, the Queen drove for two hours through the principal streets, and found them densely crowded and decorated with flowers and triumphal arches. "Our reception," she says, "was most enthusiastic, and everything went off to perfection and was very well arranged." On the following morning the Royal squadron left the magnificent harbour and started for Waterford, which was duly reached in the afternoon.

Here, where the last of the Stuart kings had embarked as a trembling fugitive to France in 1690—after his defeat at the Boyne—Queen Victoria was received with the most loyal enthusiasm. In the great harbour of Kingstown—the seaport of Dublin—which was next reached, the sea was alive with boats, yachts, and steamers. "The wharves where the landing place was prepared," says Her Majesty's Journal, "were densely crowded; altogether it was a noble and stirring spectacle. The setting sun lit up the country, the fine buildings, and the whole scene with a glowing light which was truly beautiful." In the morning the landing was made under a salute from all the men-of-war in the harbour. The *Times* described it as "a sight never to be forgotten—a sound to be recollected forever. Ladies threw aside the old formula of waving a white pocket-handkerchief, and cheered for their lives; while the men waved whatever came first to hand—hat, stick, wand, or coat—and rent the air with shouts of joy, which never decreased in energy till their Sovereign was out of sight." From Kingstown to Dublin by rail was a matter of fifteen minutes, and from the station to the Viceregal Lodge in Phœnix Park—which was traversed in carriages—every window, roof, and platform was crowded with cheering people, while the hedges in the suburbs were festooned with flowers, and the very poorest cottages had their wreaths and decorations of flowers or evergreens.

In a centre of supposed disaffection, where revolt and martial law had actually existed a short time before, the sensitive populace was now thoroughly aroused, and all the kindly, genial, and natural loyalty of the race spontaneously poured out as an offering to their Queen. "It was," Her Majesty writes, "a wonderful and striking spectacle, such masses of human beings, so enthusiastic, so excited, yet such perfect order maintained." The four days which followed were one continued jubilation. The chief public institutions were visited, a great *levée* was held by Prince Albert at which 4,000 persons were present, a review of 6,000 troops was held in Phœnix Park, and the Royal Irish Academy, the Royal College of Surgeons, and the Royal Dublin Society were visited. At the latter, the Prince Consort declared in his speech that: "It is impossible not to feel deeply the marks of enthusiastic attachment which have been displayed to the Queen and myself by the warm-hearted inhabitants of this beautiful island; and I most sincerely hope that the promise of a bountiful harvest may be the harbinger of a termination to those sufferings under which the people have so lamentably, and yet with much exemplary patience, laboured."

A drawing-room was then held at the Castle by the Queen, and of this function the Marchioness of Waterford tells us in her Diary that it was immensely crowded, and that " the mob (outside), with their jokes, and speeches, and quizzes, and cheers, were much more alarming than a quiet set of *gobemouches* in London. The Court in the Throne-room looked much better than I ever saw it. .   . It must have been 2 a.m. before the Queen got home." This was followed by a visit to Carton, the seat of the Duke of Leinster—whom Her Majesty has described as "the kindest and best of men." In this connection Lady Waterford gives us a pretty picture. " To-day," she writes, " we went with the Primate to Carton. . . . After lunch we drove—the Queen in an open carriage, Lord Jocelyn, Prince George of Cambridge, Lord and Lady Clarendon, Sir George Grey and I, in a large jaunting-car. The Park was full of people, rushing in every direction after the Queen, and cheering tremendously. The Queen kept looking over the back of the carriage with a longing eye at the car, and when we got out at the cottage said she would return in it, which she did, to the great delight of the people." Then came the departure from Kingstown, amid scenes of exuberant loyalty very similar to those which marked the landing. Storms of cheers from dense crowds on shore were answered by the dipping of the Royal standard from the yacht in a sort of stately recognition, while the Queen waved her own handkerchief in a much more popular acknowledgment. Lady Caledon, in a letter written on the following day, described the scene and summarized the visit, in a rather interesting way :

" The Queen embarked at Kingstown about six o'clock. The sight was splendid She was very sorry to go, I am told, and her thanks and pretty speeches were quite overwhelming. As she stepped on board the band played the National Anthem, the artillery fired, the men-of-war manned their yards, and the people cheered as if they would break their hearts ! Altogether it was a sight such as I shall probably never see again—*most* magnificent !

" If the Queen had stayed longer it would really have been dangerous, for the loyalty of the people had got to a perfect frenzy, and they thought nothing of throwing themselves under the wheels of her carriage as she went along. She fully intends coming again, and is in a perfect state of enchantment ; her idea of Ireland now is so different from that she had formed before. She has left £1,000 to be given to the public charities."

On August 11th the Royal party arrived at Belfast, where an enthusiastic reception was a matter of course. Only a few hours were spent there, but it was long enough to receive many important deputations and addresses, to drive through the town in Lord Londonderry's carriage, to be met with abundant cheers, and crowds, and decorations, and triumphal arches, and to visit some of the local industries. " The reception of the Queen," wrote Sir James Clark, who had accompanied Her Majesty in his capacity of physician, and who was a close and impartial observer, " has been most enthusiastic from the moment of her first setting foot in Ireland to her quitting, and certainly by none more than by the industrious inhabitants of Belfast. The effect produced by the visit was most satisfactory." There was, indeed, no room for doubt as to its success. Dark fears had been entertained about the result, and Sir Archibald Allison says, in his Memoirs, that the Queen, " inspired by that courage which is inherent in her race, no sooner beheld the Irish rebellion extinguished than she resolved to visit Dublin, the headquarters of the disaffected, and Glasgow, the principal seat of revolutionary designs in Scotland. Both visits proved eminently successful. She experienced a cordial and magnificent reception in the Irish capital." Of the Queen's own feelings we can only surmise, but one of the many poetic broadsheets which were scattered throughout the streets and homes of Dublin at the time gives the popular idea of her impressions :

> " A thousand anxious cares I had,
>   A thousand doubts and fears ;
> Would Dublin meet me, wildly glad,
>   Or darkly drowned in tears ?
>
> I knew not which to dread the more—
>   An angry people's frown,
> Or adulations sickly roar
>   From helots grovelling down.
>
> Both fears alike I now reject—
>   One hour has testified
> Enough to Irish self-respect,
>   And Irish proper pride."

Of course, comments differed, though the great majority agreed upon the practical benefit of the visit. Lord Houghton—then Mr. Monckton Milnes—wrote a friend on August 17th, in pronounced contradiction of the poetic sentiments above quoted, that " the Queen's reception in Ireland has been idolatrous, utterly unworthy of a free, not to say ill-used, nation. She will go away with the impression that it is the happiest country in the world, and doubt in her own mind whether O'Connell or Smith O'Brien ever existed." This rather sarcastic commentary, however, is hardly borne out by the facts, at least in its latter statement. The Queen's judgment and experience were even then quite sufficiently apparent to prevent her from making any such optimistic mistake as that indicated. Of the general result Sir George Cornewall Lewis wrote on Sept. 4th that, " everything turned out better than the most sanguine expectation could have anticipated. The people were enthusiastic, there was no dissentient minority, and the Queen and Prince were most gracious in manner and expression, and were really pleased. . . . I am rather sanguine as to this visit giving an impulse to the Irish mind in the right direction." What the calm and philosophic mind of Lewis was able to see, the observation of Lord Clarendon—the Lord Lieutenant to whom the successful arrangements were so greatly due—amply verified.

" In short," he writes, " the people are not only enchanted with the Queen and her gracious kindness of manner, and the confidence she has shown in them, but they are pleased with themselves for their own good feelings and behaviour, which they consider have removed the barrier that existed between the Sovereign and themselves, and that they now occupy a higher position in the eyes of the world. . . . The presence of the Sovereign cannot, of course, produce social reformation, nor at once remove evils that are the growth of ages ; but it will produce more real good here than in any other part of Her Majesty's dominions. The Queen's visit, moreover, will be associated with a turn in the tide of their affairs, after four years' suffering, together with an unprecedented influx of strangers and expenditure of money ; and as they will contrast this year with the last their conclusions must be unfavourable to political agitation. So, even I, who am never very sanguine about things here, cannot help sharing in the feelings of hopefulness that pervade the whole country."

Following this visit the Prince of Wales was created Earl of Dublin as a compliment to Ireland, and at a later date the Royal infant who was afterwards made Duke of Connaught became possessed of the name of Patrick in addition to his other designations. For a time affairs really did go on in quieter and more peaceful paths than the Irish people had been accustomed to, and in 1853 another Royal visit was paid to Dublin. It had been intended by the Queen and Prince Albert to go in July so as to open the important Art and Industrial Exhibition in which they had both taken a warm interest, but a severe epidemic of measles had laid the Prince of Wales and other members of the family on sick-beds and delayed the visit a couple of months. On August 30th, however, they reached Kingstown, and in the journey through the now familiar streets of Dublin which followed, the Queen was greeted with an enthusiasm almost beyond that of the previous occasion. A State visit was paid next morning to the Exhibition, and each succeeding morning during their stay was spent in its inspection. The products of Irish industry were found to be very attractive and important, and the Queen expressed in her Journal great appreciation of the good results which should follow, and of the generosity of Mr. Dargan, who had put up the building at his own expense. " I would have made him a Baronet," she writes, " but he was anxious it should not be done."

Monckton Milnes, writing in his genial style from Dublin at this time, declares it to have been so damp and cold that for days he had to have a fire in his bedroom, when " there comes the magical little Queen with her luck, and to-day is a real warm autumn day." He adds that on her arrival " there could not have been less than a million souls out altogether ; there was no great shouting, but much eager satisfaction and earnest interest." He also expressed the belief that the effect of Her Majesty's visit to the Exhibition could hardly be exaggerated, and speaks of the brilliant smile which broke over her face when speaking to Mr. Dargan.

On September 3rd came the departure once more. " A beautiful morning," writes the Queen, " and this the very day we are going away, which we felt quite sorry to do, having spent such a pleasant, gay, and interesting time in Ireland. . . . At half-past five we started for Kingstown. We drove gently, though not at a foot's pace, through Dublin, which was unusually crowded (no soldiers lining the streets), to the station, where again there were great crowds. In eight minutes we were at Kingstown, where again the crowds were immense and most enthusiastic. The evening was beautiful and the sight a very fine one —all the ships and yards decked out and firing salutes, and thousands on the quay cheering." In this way ended the second Royal visit. The last one paid by Her Majesty in person will always bear for her a melancholy memory. It was not long after the death of the Duchess of Kent, and in little more than three months Prince Albert was to also pass away. Accompanied by the Prince, Lord Grenville and Lady Churchill, Dublin was reached on August 22nd, 1861, and the Queen, after being formally received by Lord Carlisle, as Lord Lieutenant of Ireland, was once more welcomed with enthusiastic cheers by the people.

Drives through the city and surrounding country, dinner parties, and a review of the troops at Curragh filled up some days. The Queen had also the pleasure of seeing the Prince of Wales in camp, going through the regulation duties of a young military officer, and learning by practical experience the details of military life and work. On the 26th the Royal party took the train for the Lakes of Killarney, accompanied now by Prince Alfred, Princess Alice, and two others of the family. Her Majesty's Journal contains many shrewd comments upon the places and people which were passed on the way. The first part of the journey was not attractive. " It is astonishing," writes the Queen, " how wanting in population this part of the country is—large plains, a good deal cultivated, here and there a small house, with a few cabins, but no villages, and hardly any towns, except the few close upon the railway. . . . We stopped at Thurles, close to the town. The crowd was tremendous, very noisy, the people very wild and dark-looking—all giving that peculiar shriek which is general here instead of cheers—the girls were handsome, with long dishevelled hair." At Killarney station they were received by Lord Castlerosse, Mr. Herbert of Muckross, and the various local dignitaries, and were then driven to the beautiful seat of Mr. Herbert, which commanded a capital view of one of the lakes— owned entirely by him—and from which the Royal party left, a little later, for their two days' tour of the lovely surrounding scenery. The Queen's own words in a letter to King Leopold of Belgium will best describe her impressions:

" We spent the 27th on the lakes, lunching at a cottage (Glena Cottage) belonging to Lady Castlerosse, and taking tea at another lovely spot—indeed, nothing could be lovelier Imagine three different lakes connected by channels or passages with each other—the mountains rising from the margins of the lakes to heights of from two to three thousand feet, covered with wood of all kinds : the lakes studded with islands and fringed with pro-

DANIEL O'CONNELL.

CHARLES STEWART PARNELL, M.P.

montories and rocks of the most picturesque shapes, covered with arbutus, yew, and holly trees, all growing wild to a great height, and down to the very water's edge. It is all really wonderfully beautiful, but the air has no lightness or freshness in it, and reminds one of the tepid waterfall of Devonshire. . . . The next morning we took a most beautiful drive all around this lake (Muckross) and in the afternoon went upon the water. There were at least a hundred and fifty boats out, which had a pretty effect. People live on the water there, and the boatmen row beautifully. I wish you could see these lakes; you would be delighted, and it is so quickly done."

The return journey was then made as rapidly as possible, and Dublin passed through without stopping. The importance of these visits can hardly be over-estimated so far as immediate results were concerned. And even the permanent effect was pronounced in many ways. By them the instinctive loyalty and naturally affectionate disposition of the Irish people were stimulated, and had other influences of a malignant nature not been developed in the unscrupulous hands of the wire-puller and politician Ireland might have been to-day united, peaceful, and contented. Unfortunately, the Queen's popularity was clouded, though it could never be totally obscured, by the wretched distortions of the agitator and the ignorance of the peasantry, while the historic bitterness and prejudices lying fallow in the hearts of the populace were constantly stirred up and revived with the object of maintaining the antagonism against England. What was possible to do in modifying these troubles Her Majesty had done, and when the sad time of bereavement and retirement came to her she was able to send the Prince of Wales upon many occasions to bear that wand of peace and amity which she was so anxious should produce some fruit. But more than occasional Royal visits—useful and beneficial as they were—was required to remove the hostility of centuries, the inherited and almost inherent prejudices of a people, and the mistakes of English and Irish leaders.

The Prince of Wales, however, has done much good service in the cause. On the 9th of May, 1865, he opened the International Exhibition at Dublin, after loyal and enthusiastic demonstrations in the streets, and in the presence of a dense and representative assemblage. The Lord Mayor and Corporation were present in their civic robes, together with the Lord Mayors of London and York, the Lord Provost of Edinburgh, and the Mayors of Cork and Waterford and Londonderry. The Duke of Leinster, the Earl of Rosse, and the chief of the Irish nobility were also there. When the Prince had taken his seat in the chair of State, an orchestra of 1,000 voices sang the National Anthem, and 10,000 voices in the audience responded with cheers. Various addresses were presented, and several short speeches made by the Prince before he finally declared the Exhibition open in the name, and under the patronage, of the Queen. During the evening a ball was given at the Mansion House, and the city brilliantly illuminated. On the succeeding day His Royal Highness reviewed a large body of troops, and was received with great enthusiasm by the immense throng of specta-tors present.

In 1868 the Prince of Wales—accompanied this time by the Princess—paid a much longer and more important visit to Ireland. It was in every way a not-able and interesting event. They landed at Kingstown on April 15th, and were enthusiastically welcomed in Dublin, where no troops lined the way and every confidence was placed in the loyalty of the populace. At night the city was brilliantly illuminated, and during the next two days the Royal party drove to the Punchestown races in open carriages, and attended a gorgeous function in St. Patrick's Cathedral, where the Prince was installed a Knight of St. Patrick and belted with the same sword which had been worn by George IV. At a banquet given by the Lord Lieutenant in the evening, His Excellency spoke of the shouts of acclamation which had been ringing for several days in their ears, and declared that they would fairly indicate to their Royal guest " the kindly nature of the Irish people, and the attachment that may be awakened in their generous and warm hearts." Following this came an incessant round of banquets, receptions, concerts, balls, and " entertainments," together with the inspection of museums, libraries, hospitals, colleges, and schools. Then there was the visit to a really exquisite flower show, to the Catholic University, to Trinity College, where the degree of LL.D. was conferred upon the Prince, the Duke of Cambridge, and Lord Abercorn. Visits were also paid to Lord Powerscourt's beautiful place in County Wicklow, to Maynooth College, to the Duke of Leinster's place at Car-ton, and to Christ Church Cathedral on Sunday. It must all have proved a tremendous pressure upon the young Prince. To quote the *Times :*

" There were presentations and receptions ; receiving and answering addresses ; pro-cessions, walking, riding, and driving, in morning, evening, military, academic, and medi-æval attire. The Prince was invested as a Knight, robed as an LL.D., and made a Lord of the Irish Privy Council ; he had to breakfast, lunch, dine, and sup with more or less publicity every twenty-four hours. He had to go twice to races with fifty or a hundred thousand people about him ; to review a small army and make a tour in the Wicklow Mountains, of course everywhere receiving addresses under canopies, and dining in state under galleries full of spectators. He visited and inspected institutions, colleges, universi-ties, academies, libraries, and cattle shows. He had to take a very active part in assemblies of from several hundred to several thousand dancers, and always to select for his partners the most important personages. He had to listen to many speeches sufficiently to know when and what to answer. He had to examine with respectful interest pictures, books, antiquities, relics, manuscripts, specimens, bones, fossils, prize beasts, and works of Irish art. He had never to be unequal to the occasion, however different from the last or how-ever like the last, whatever his disadvantage as to the novelty or the dulness of the matter or the scene."

It was, indeed, an ordeal, and a continuous one, during ten crowded days. Whether the Prince was with Cardinal or Chancellor, rector, mayor, or Commanding Officer, president, chairman, or local deputation, he had to hold his own without self-assertion or apparent effort. Men who have gone through two successive functions will know what they mean when spread over many days. But more important than even the personal responsibilities of the moment was the undoubtedly favourable impression which the youthful heir to the Throne everywhere made, and the good he undoubtedly did. Had the statesmen of that day been able to look forward and face some present difficulties in order to avert future dangers, much might have been achieved in the direction of permanent and attached relations between the two peoples by the establishment in Dublin of a Royal residence. But Lord Palmerston was busy stemming the tide of electoral reform, while Mr. Gladstone was industriously striving to push it to the front. Lord Derby and Mr. Disraeli were deep in the same difficulty, and within a few years all parties were fighting for or against the disestablishment of the Irish Church. So a great opportunity was lost, and much of the benefits of the happy and popular tour of the Prince and Princess of Wales were lost, through the inability of political leaders to embody in immediate practical form the sentimental feelings of a sensitive race.

Seventeen years later, when the prolonged labours of selfish and treasonable agitators seemed to have been successful, and to have finally wrecked the loyalty of the Irish people and destroyed the good done by the visits of the Queen and the Prince, it was announced that another Royal tour was to be made in Ireland. It was not a pleasant or apparently propitious time. Charles Stewart Parnell had in his own quiet and secretive but able way held the control of Irish action and policy in his hands for many years. The no-rent campaigns, the boycott battles, the shooting of landlords, the work of the Land League, the Fenian conspiracies, the murders of Lord F. Cavendish and Mr. Burke, had all occurred —whether with or without his knowledge or assent it is useless to discuss here. Home Rule was about to be taken up by Mr. Gladstone, though no announcement had yet been made, and Ireland was in a seething state of political and national uncertainty, if not distinct disaffection. In the midst of such conditions, on April 9th, 1885, the Prince and Princess of Wales and Prince Albert Victor landed at Kingstown, and, as might have been expected, and was probably hoped by themselves and the Queen, the feelings of disloyalty and discontent became merged in the spontaneous and hearty enthusiasm of the people as a whole.

Addresses were presented at Kingstown, and by the Citizens' Reception Committee of Dublin, in place of the recreant Mayor and Corporation. A more important one than either of these was an address of the Chamber of Commerce, in the course of which it was stated that " we earnestly desire that your present visit may be productive of so much pleasure to your Royal Highnesses that you may feel encouraged to honour Ireland hereafter by visits of more frequent occurrence and of longer duration. We venture to assure you that it would be a great gratification to Her Majesty's loyal subjects in Ireland if a permanent Royal residence should be established in our country, and if some members of the Royal family should see fit to make their home among us for some part of every year." This was, of course, too important a suggestion of national policy for the Prince to deal with in his reply, and he judiciously passed it over. None the less it represented a feeling, and voiced a practical proposal, which should have received a wider national consideration than was the case.

After a visit to the Agricultural Show, the Prince walked unannounced through the slums or poorer parts of the city, and everywhere charmed the people by his unaffected manner, his unguarded condition, and his evident interest in their welfare and knowledge of sanitation, and the construction of their humble dwellings. Cheers and the most cordial welcome greeted him all along his course. On the 10th of April as many as thirty addresses from public bodies were received, and answered by the Prince in words which won the warmest applause from the deputations. " In varied capacities," he observed, during his reply, " and by widely different paths, you pursue those great objects which, dear to you, are, believe me, dear also to me—the prosperity and progress of Ireland, the welfare and happiness of her people. . . . From my heart I wish you success, and I would that time and my own powers would permit me to explain fully and in detail the deep interest which I feel not only in the welfare of this great Empire at large, but in the true happiness of those several classes of the community on whose behalf you have come here to-day."

Then followed the laying of the foundation stone of the new Museum of Science and Art, for which function most elaborate preparations had been made. A visit was also paid the Royal University, where, with all possible ceremony, the degree of Doctor of Music was conferred upon the Prince and Princess. Dublin Castle had been their home while in Dublin, and here various State functions were now held, such as a *levée*, a drawing-room, and a State ball given by the Lord Lieutenant. Many other institutions were visited and ceremonies performed, before the Royal party left on the 13th for Cork—once more a centre and hotbed of discontent. Attempts were made at Mallow and Dundalk, as well as at Cork, to resent the visit of the Prince, but they were overpowered by the better sense and kindliness of the mass of the people. At Dundalk, indeed, Mr. Redmond, M.P., distinguished himself by a public speech, in which he hoped that " the Russian bear would soon stick his claw into the British lion," while at some other hotly Nationalist places in Kerry decidedly unpleasant indications of feeling were exhibited. In one village along the railway a Parnell banner was carried inscribed, " Charley our Prince"; at another black flags were hoisted, and in still another cheers were raised for the Mahdi and Parnell.

But these were isolated instances of folly, and at Tralee, Limerick, Killarney, and other places in the south the reception was respectful where not enthusiastic. The visit to Derry and Newtoun-Stewart and Belfast evoked, of course, both enthusiasm and loyalty. And, in his farewell speech at Carrickfergus, on April 27th, the Prince made some remarks which indicate the nature of the reception generally accorded, and illustrate the substantial loyalty of the great Irish majority, when properly elicited by kindliness and Royal appreciation of the people and country.

"My visit has been necessarily brief," he observed, "but in the time which has been at my disposal I have had an opportunity of seeing much of the occupations and of observing some of the habits of the people. We have everywhere been greeted with a kindness which has made a great impression upon us, and of which the remembrance will never pass away. From the addresses which I have received, from the decorations of the towns and country which have gratified my eye, and from the marked expressions of good will which I have heard from vast numbers of the people in all parts of Ireland, I rejoice to gather that in the heart of the country there is warm attachment to the Crown and Constitution of this realm; and I hope that every year may add to the knowledge of the advantages of that Constitution, and diminish the influence of those who seek to foment disloyalty among us."

Such has been the Royal record in Ireland. These visits of the Queen and Prince Albert and the Prince and Princess of Wales did much good at the time, and perhaps prevented much and incalculable harm which might have otherwise developed. They were successful in evoking loyalty and winning popularity. They were evidences of Royal courage and good will to the people which should have left a permanent impress upon even the mercurial Irish temperament. The visit of the Queen in 1849, after a rebellion and one of the most frightful famines in all history; her third visit in 1861, after the Clerkenwall outrages had alarmed England and stirred up the worst elements in Ireland; the tour of the Heir Apparent and his gentle wife in the teeth of a supposed universal discontent and savage hatred of England; indicate great personal bravery and the fullest recognition of the Royal responsibility towards Ireland.

But these royally made efforts had one vital defect. They were not continuous nor permanent. It was not the fault of the Sovereign. It was, however, the distinct fault of her advisers, and the result of those party politics which, in the case of Ireland, have proved such a bane and curse. The suggestion of a permanent Royal residence in Dublin was wise and salutary when it was made in 1885, and still more so in principle, when a meeting of Irish Peers and Unionist members passed a resolution in May, 1889, urging the abolition of the office of Lord Lieutenant, the performance of its duties by the Secretary of State, and the establishment of a Royal Irish residence. Supported by the Dukes of Leinster and Manchester, Lords Belm ore, Mayo, Pembroke, etc., together with members of Parliament such as Colonel Sanderson, T. W. Russell, and Lord

Dunsany, it is curious that no practical discussion of its terms should have ever taken place.

Whether the Royal Prince who might under such a proposal reside in Ireland should live there for a couple of months or a longer period; whether he should be Lord Lieutenant and Viceroy without political duties and without being subject to partisan change, or should merely have a local residence and social duties; whether such change would add a little to the cost of Irish government or not; there is no reason to doubt that it would have a pronounced effect upon the susceptible and impressible Irish people. Had the Queen been able to influence her Ministers in this direction before the political spectre of Home Rule grew great upon the horizon, she would have achieved a splendid success, and perhaps have saved Ireland from much of suffering and perplexing trouble. As it is, however, Her Majesty has done what she could, and if some of her statesmen had only achieved as much in practical work, or even a fraction of it, the situation in recent years would have been greatly different, and we might have seen an approximation to what may even yet be possible—the condition of Ireland as witnessed by a Saxon Prince many centuries ago:

> " I travelled its fruitful provinces round,
> And in every one of the five I found,
> Alike in church, in palace, and hall,
> Abundant apparel and food for all.
> Gold and silver, I found, and money,
> Plenty of wheat and plenty of honey;
> Found God's people rich in pity,
> Found many a feast and many a city."

Loyalty to the person of the Sovereign and to the principle of monarchy would have brought stability of national thought and confidence in national institutions. This in time would have promoted public confidence and credit; encouraged financial investment and commercial development; aided in producing contentment and individual prosperity; encouraged the maintenance of law and order, and by deprecating outrage and agitation would have gradually brought Erin into a condition of national equality with England and Scotland, and made the country what it should be—a garden of productiveness and pleasure, the home of genial liberty, and the lasting abode of light-hearted satisfaction and enjoyment.

THE RIGHT HON. SIR JOHN A. MACDONALD, G.C.B.

THE RIGHT HON. SIR WILFRID LAURIER, G.C.M.G.

CHAPTER XX.

CANADA UNDER THE QUEEN.

THE influence of the Queen's name and personality and position has been very great in the making of Canada and the moulding of its peculiar national sentiment. In earlier years, before Confederation gave the people of British North America an impetus towards united development, the feeling of loyalty to the Sovereign, and a desire to maintain British institutions—incomplete as they then were—constituted a chief bond of connection between the scattered provinces and afforded a powerful protection against the assimilating influences of the preponderating mass of population to the south.

It was fortunate that some such influence permeated Canadian thought in the stormy days when the Queen came to the throne, and during the period in 1849 when a genuine annexation cloud floated over the country. The French-Canadian is naturally monarchical in principle. He is the French peasant of days long prior to the Revolution, transported to Canadian soil and imbedded in the midst of a British community. So, also, in what was then called Upper Canada, the governing classes and a large part of the population were immediate descendants of United Empire Loyalists—men who had lost all for king and country during the revolt of the thirteen colonies. The rebellion of 1837 was consequently a fiasco, so far as it was directed against the Sovereign and in favour of a republic. The mass of the people would have nothing to do with it, even though there were admitted abuses to be rectified and admittedly justifiable demands for self-government still ungranted. And, both the omissions of Downing Street, and the somewhat high-handed conduct of local governments, were remedied or reformed within the following decade under the quiet action of constitutional authority and legal procedure.

That such a result was possible—that the discontent against local and galling restrictions did not swell the rebellion to formidable dimensions—was due in the main to that principle of loyalty to institutions described by Mr. D'Arcy McGee, in 1863, as a popular belief that "the equal union of authority and liberty is found possible only under the forms of constitutional monarchy," and to feelings such as were embodied in the speech of the Governor of Lower Canada addressed to both Houses of the Legislature on August 18th, 1837 :

"The mournful intelligence has reached us of the demise of our late deservedly beloved Monarch.

"Few kings have reigned more in the hearts of their subjects than William IV. The warm and lively interest he always took in every matter connected with the welfare of his Canadian subjects cannot fail to increase their feelings of regret for their loss. The succession of our present gracious Sovereign Queen Victoria to the Throne of the British Empire has not produced any alteration in the course that had been previously prescribed for my adoption."

This feeling of sympathetic allegiance does not seem to have been obliterated by the continued opposition of the Governors to popular reform and responsible government, although the general discontent had culminated in a restricted rebellion. Canadians, as a rule, laid the blame where it was due. Ignorance of local conditions amongst politicians at home, coupled with complications in Imperial politics and changing views upon questions of colonial policy, were the chief reasons. And since those days we are better able to appreciate the situation. England herself was not enjoying the full measure of popular rule which Canadians in some cases demanded. Ireland was a sore spot in the body politic, and all statesmen were afraid of giving too much freedom to people who might use it, as the Irish were doing and the Americans had done, against the unity of the Empire. The United States was a living lesson in the possibilities of separation. The French-Canadians were an unknown factor in such a connection, although they had loyally stood by England in defence of their religion and language against possible submersion by the American colonies. Opinions upon the value of colonies, and upon the proper relationship of the colony to the Crown, were in a state of ebb and flow—a condition of confusion which lasted off and on for over forty years. And, above all, British America was almost unknown, and its history, people, and resources were as little understood in England as they were in the Colonies themselves.

Plenty of reasons, therefore, existed for caution on the part of Downing Street, and for opposition to hasty change on the part of Her Majesty's earlier representatives. And, moreover, the latter, when they reached Canadian shores, became impressed with the reasonable fear that, as things then were, too great a lessening of their own prestige and authority, or too much approximation to what were called American ideas and American methods, might result in a serious movement for separation. Time has proved the mistake of this view, but it has also caused justice to be done to the motives of men like Sir Charles Metcalfe, who, in one of his last addresses in British America—spoken in 1843 to the Councillors of the Gore District—urged that every privilege had been granted to the people compatible with the maintenance of British connection ; claimed that the Imperial Government had no desire to interfere unnecessarily in local colonial affairs ; and added that "it can never consent to the prostration of the honour and dignity of the Crown, and I cannot be the traitor that would sign the death-warrant of British connection."

There is no doubt that this Governor-General studied the question of responsible government very closely, and that he acted honestly and patriotically in periods of intense pain and amid circumstances of heroic self-sacrifice—he was dying slowly from a cancer in the face. And it appears that his general course commended itself to the Queen. Her Majesty is known to have then and ever since looked earnestly and fully into all matters which came within the wide sphere of her duties, and when Sir Robert Peel wrote in 1844 to advise the conferment of a Peerage upon Sir Charles Metcalfe because of his great services, and as "aiding him in the discharge of a most important public trust," and in "giving confidence and animation to his Canadian friends and supporters," the Queen hastened to respond in a letter which declared that " he richly deserves this mark of the Queen's entire approbation and favour." Later on, in November, 1845, when Lord Metcalfe was forced by the progress of his disease to tender a resignation, which was to take effect whenever he found himself unable to further conduct the public administration, Lord Stanley—then Colonial Secretary, and afterwards Earl of Derby and Prime Minister—wrote that

" Her Majesty is aware that your devotion to her service has led you, amidst physical sufferings beneath which ordinary men would have given way, to remain at your post to the last possible moment. The Queen highly estimates this proof of your public spirit; and in accepting your proffered resignation, which in the present circumstances she feels it impossible to decline, has commanded me to express her entire approval of the ability and prudence with which you have conducted the affairs of a very difficult Government, her sense of the loss which the public service is about to sustain by your retirement, and her deep regret for the cause which renders it unavoidable."

Now that the partisan strife of those days is merged in the broader appreciation of historic retrospect, it is probable that the great majority of Canadians will endorse the Queen's view of Lord Metcalfe's sturdy British pluck and devotion to duty. In details he may have been, and was, mistaken, but in loyalty to the great principles of British union he stands as one of the heroes of Canadian history. Meanwhile party government in England had passed to the Liberals, and Earl Grey came into the Colonial Office with many new ideas and theories. Some were good and some the reverse, but the general principle was one of letting the colonies do pretty much as they liked. This was gradually developed by the teachings of the Manchester school into the cultivation of a popular belief that the colonies were not much good to England, and could leave the Empire at any time without causing it serious injury.

Lord Grey's first step, in the appointment of the Earl of Elgin to succeed Lord Metcalfe, was a good one. The policy of the new Governor-General also proved to be excellent. It enforced the British principles of his predecessor, conciliated the reforming elements in the country, and made commercial arrangements with the United States which were both beneficial and honourable. But Lord Elgin had much to contend with at home. The utterances of

English statesmen looking forward to the eventual independence of the colonies had helped the movement for annexation, which arose in Canada in 1849 as a result of the commercial and business troubles following the abrogation of the old-time British preferential arrangements. The Prime Minister—Lord John Russell—had actually himself referred in speeches to the probability of separation, and Lord Elgin's published correspondence with the Colonial Secretary abounds in vigorous protests against this and similar utterances. The narrowness of view which thus stamped the statesmen of the day is shown by a letter from Sir George Cornewall Lewis—September 28th, 1848—in which he speaks of the uselessness of settling, or even retaining, Vancouver's Island. "For practically," he observes, "it is in a different world from our provinces on the western coast of North America. If any people can colonize it with advantage it must be the Americans." Other politicians, such as Cobden and Bright, Lord Ashburton—the hero of the miserable treaty which goes by his name—Lord St. Vincent, Lord Ellenborough, Sir George Campbell, Mr. Lowe, and even Lord Monck himself, were tainted by this weak and wicked principle of disintegration.

They held, in part or in whole, the doctrines of the rising Manchester school, and thought that colonies were of little value to the motherland—more of a burden than a benefit. To them the United States was a great allied power, without aggressive ambitions and willing to work in harmony with a glowing future of Anglo-Saxon unity. True, it had purchased Louisiana from France, and obtained Florida from Spain; it had annexed, or was about to annex, Nevada and California, Utah and New Mexico, Arizona and Texas—to say nothing of the future purchase of Alaska, and the extension of the Maine boundary line at the expense of Canada. But it had not yet gone in for high protection, and was not therefore touching the pockets of English patriots who were not possessed of sufficient sentiment and national sense to appreciate the fact that trade and territory were, ere long, to be synonymous terms. This class, however, limited as it was in numbers, had great ability, and was aided by the circumstances of the time in cultivating a wide sweep of anti-colonial thought. What they knew, or cared, for the early history of Canada and its struggles for British connection, and battles for the British flag, amounted to less than nothing. Commerce and peace at any price was too often their motto, and the time has now come for men to measure the possible disasters around which the glamour of Bright's eloquence and Cobden's high character have thrown a web of sophistry and misplaced admiration. These men were narrow in view and local in their comprehension of England's destiny. What cared they for those earlier days?

> "When men bore deep the impress of the law
> Of duty, truth and loyalty unstained.

> Amid the quaking of a continent
> Torn by the passions of an evil time,
> They counted neither cost nor danger, spurned
> Defections, treasons, spoils; but feared God,
> Nor shamed of their allegiance to the King."

They argued that the American people were not aggressive and did not want Canada, and if they did want it, and took it, the loss would only involve a transfer of useless territory to a friendly and brotherly power. Such were the weak and wretched sentiments which Lord Elgin had to controvert, and which in modified and varied forms controlled English politics, and colonial policy, until the rise of Mr. Disraeli and the steady pressure of the Queen's Imperial sentiments had produced a final and crushing effect. Her Majesty showed an early, and indeed, continuous interest in Canada. The sending of the 100th Regiment to the Crimea had given her special pleasure, and in December, 1858, it was arranged that the Prince of Wales—then only seventeen years of age—should perform his first public military function by a review of the Canadian contingent at Shorncliffe. After the review was over, the Prince presented the troops with a new set of colours, and then addressed Colonel de Rottenburgh and his officers and men, in words illustrative of the Royal idea—antagonistic as it then was to the prevalent Manchester school principle.

" It is," said the youthful heir to the Throne, " most gratifying to me that, by the Queen's gracious permission, my first public act since I have had the honour of holding a commission in the British army should be the presentation of colours to a regiment which is the spontaneous offering of the loyal and spirited Canadian people, and with which at their desire my name has been specially associated. The ceremonial on which we are now engaged possesses a peculiar significance and solemnity, because, in confiding to you for the first time this emblem of military fidelity and valour, I not only recognize emphatically your enrollment into our national force, but celebrate an act which proclaims and strengthens the unity of the various parts of this vast Empire under the sway of one common Sovereign." Two years later arrangements were made by the Queen and Prince Consort for a tour through British America by the Prince of Wales, and a visit to Cape Colony by Prince Alfred. It was a far-sighted policy, and one full of Royal belief in the Colonial future as well as of self-sacrifice in sending their sons upon what seemed in those days journeys of grave import, if not serious danger.

The Prince of Wales' visit to Canada was not altogether without precedents, though rather distant ones. Prince William Henry had visited the Provinces in 1787, while Prince Edward, Duke of Kent, and father of Her Majesty, had spent some years in Nova Scotia as commander of the forces, and had been present at the inauguration of the Constitution of 1791—in which George III. took such an interest, and wherein he had so actively used his influence to promote the liberties and privileges of the French Canadians. Prince Edward, in particular, had done much to make the British Provinces better known to the authorities in England. His correspondence with De Salaberry during the war of 1812; his efforts to have justice done that distinguished officer after the victory at Chateauguay; his letter upon the proposed new constitution written to Chief Justice Sewell in 1814; all indicate the truth of Lord Durham's statement that " no one better understood the interests and character of the Colonies " than he. But neither of these princes had been heir to the Throne of the Empire, and they had not therefore, at the time, represented the highest elements of monarchy and royalty as did the Prince of Wales.

Nor did they embody the Imperial spirit in the manner which made Prince Albert exclaim in a letter written on April 27th, 1860: " What a charming picture is here of the progress and expansion of the British race, and of the useful co-operation of the Royal family in the civilization which England has developed and advanced! In both these young colonies our children are looked for with great affection and conscious national pride." The immediate occasion of the visit to Canada was an invitation and promise to open the great Victoria Bridge across the St. Lawrence at Montreal. But some kind of an intimation had been made during the Crimean war that as soon as the Prince was old enough a tour of British America might be arranged. The Queen was able to look ahead, if her Ministers were not, and she foresaw the desirability of cultivating and strengthening the inherent loyalty of what might some day be a great people. Taking advantage, therefore, of what seemed propitious circumstances, the Canadian Legislature, on May 4th, 1859, passed a unanimous Address, and sent it to London in the care of the Speaker of the Assembly, Mr. (afterwards Sir) Henry Smith. In it they invited the Queen herself, accompanied by the Prince Consort, and such members of the Royal family as it might please her to attend upon the occasion, and urged that an opportunity be thus given the inhabitants of Canada to testify their loyalty to the Throne and Empire. Though it was pretty well understood that Her Majesty could not come in person, this was, of course, the best way of presenting the request, and it elicited a most favourable response—received by the Governor-General from the Duke of Newcastle in time for the opening of Parliament in 1860. In the course of the reply it was stated that :

" Her Majesty values deeply the attachment to her person and the loyalty to the Crown which have induced this address, and I am commanded to assure the Legislature, through you, how lively an interest is felt by the Queen in the growing prosperity of Canada, in the welfare and contentment of her subjects in that important province of her Empire, and on the completion of the gigantic work which is a fitting type of the successful industry of the people. It is therefore with sincere regret that Her Majesty is compelled to decline compliance with this loyal invitation. Her Majesty feels that her duties at the seat of the

Empire prevent so long an absence, and at so great a distance, as a visit to Canada would necessarily require.

"Impressed, however, with an earnest desire to testify to the utmost of her power her warm appreciation of the affectionate loyalty of her Canadian subjects, the Queen commands me to express her hope that when the time for the opening of the bridge is fixed it may be possible for His Royal Highness the Prince of Wales to attend the ceremony in Her Majesty's name, and to witness those gratifying scenes in which the Queen is herself unable to participate. The Queen trusts that nothing may interfere with this arrangement; for it is Her Majesty's sincere desire that the young Prince, on whom the Crown of this Empire will devolve, may have the opportunity of visiting that portion of her dominions from which this address has proceeded, and may become acquainted with a people in whose rapid progress towards greatness Her Majesty, in common with her subjects in Great Britain, feels a lively and enduring sympathy."

Read between the lines, and in connection with the ignorance and lack of Imperial sentiment then so pronounced, this letter, as well as the policy involved, is seen to be the product of the Queen's own heart and mind. It was not the kind of an idea or document which the Duke of Newcastle would at that time have initiated, though he afterwards became a warm and sincere friend of Canada, and an active participator in the work of creating a new Dominion which the 1st of July, 1867, saw completed. Nor was it the sort of policy which Lord Palmerston or Mr. Gladstone, or even the Mr. Disraeli of those days, would have propounded. But it was unquestionably great in its inception, and more than successful in its application and results. By the 9th of July all arrangements had been made, including the acceptance of an invitation from President Buchanan to visit the United States, and on that day the Prince left for his ship, the *Hero*, after being accompanied to Plymouth by the Prince Consort, and to the Royal yacht which was to transfer him aboard by the Queen, Princess Alice, and Prince Arthur. In replying to a farewell address at Davenport he declared that he went to "the great possessions of the Queen in North America with a lively anticipation of the pleasure which the sight of a noble land, great works of nature and of human skill, and a generous and active people, must produce." The voyage to Newfoundland took two weeks, and in that loyal and ancient colony the reception was enthusiastic to the last degree.

Halifax was reached on July 30th, and here His Royal Highness was formally received by Lord Mulgrave, the Lieutenant-Governor—afterwards Marquess of Normanby—and by guards of honour and multitudes of people. His suite throughout the ensuing tour consisted of the Duke of Newcastle; the Earl of St. Germains, Lord Chamberlain to the Queen; General Bruce, the Governor of the youthful Prince; Dr. Auckland, his physician; together with Major Teesdale, V.C., and Captain Grey, two of his Equerries-in-Waiting. A loyal address was presented by the Mayor and City Council of Halifax, which included a reference to "the grandson of that illustrious Duke (of Kent) whose memory is gratefully cherished as the warm and constant friend of Nova Scotia." A triumphal procession to the Government House, an address from the two Houses of the Legislature, and a great State dinner in the evening; a review of the troops next day; an illumination of the city at night, together with a ball in the Provincial Buildings; a *levée* during the succeeding day, with an entertainment to the volunteer officers by the Prince; a grand display of fireworks and an illuminated fleet in the harbour; filled up and completed the three days' visit.

Of a similar nature was the reception given at St. John, New Brunswick. It was, however, specially marked by a most able sermon preached before the Prince in the Anglican Cathedral by Bishop Medley, and by words of warm appreciation spoken by the former in reply to an address from the Provincial Government, and in connection with the volunteers. "Every visitor to your shores," remarked the Prince, "but more especially the son of your Queen, must earnestly pray that your peaceful avocations may never be disturbed; but in case such a misfortune should await the Empire, I rejoice to observe the self-relying spirit of patriotism which prevails; and I see in the discipline of your volunteers the determination to protect the national honour which is manifested in every portion of the Queen's dominions." At Indiantown, and Truro, and Pictou, his welcome was equally warm, though naturally not as elaborate. In Charlottetown, the capital of Prince Edward Island, the decorations were really beautiful and the reception more than enthusiastic, while everywhere the speeches of the young Prince were characterized by taste, good feeling, and royal dignity. On August 13th he arrived at Quebec, and was welcomed in his ship by the Governor-General of the Canadas, Sir Edmund Head; by royal salutes from many cannon, the sight of gaily decorated houses and crowds of cheering people on the shores; and by a visit from the members of the Canadian Ministry, of whom George E. Cartier and John A. Macdonald, A. T. Galt and John Rose, were the chief. Before leaving the ship, however, a trip was taken up the beautiful Saguenay, and, at last, on the 18th of August, the heir to the Throne landed below the heights and ramparts of historic Quebec.

He was received by the Governor-General; Lord Lyons, the British Ambassador at Washington; General Sir W. Fenwick Williams, the Commander of the Forces; Sir E. P. Taché, and Sir A. N McNab; the military and civic officials of Quebec, and enthusiastic crowds of people. An address was presented by the Mayor, Mr. Hector L. Langevin, on behalf of the city, in the course of which he declared that in the Province of Lower Canada would be found "a free people, faithful and loyal, attached to the Sovereign and to their country." The Prince would find himself in this most ancient city of Canada amid a population "testifying by the heartiness of their acclamations and good wishes that, though they derive their origin from various races, and may differ in language and religious denominations, yet they have but one voice and one heart in expressing loyalty to their Sovereign, and in welcoming him who represents her on this occasion." Many other addresses were presented during the following days, including one from the Legislative Council and another from the Assembly—the united Parliament of Upper and Lower Canada having its meeting place in Quebec at this time. The first was presented by Mr. N. F. Belleau and the second by Mr. Henry Smith, both of whom were knighted by the Prince. In replying to the latter address, His Royal Highness declared that Canada might be "proud that within her limits two races of different language and habits are united in the same Legislature by a common loyalty, and are bound to the same Constitution by a common patriotism." A visit to the Falls of Montmorenci and a splendid ball at the Citadel followed, and then came more addresses and speeches and processions and all the routine of exuberant loyalty. The reply to one of these addresses was interesting :

"I accept with the greatest satisfaction," said the Prince, "the welcome which you offer me in your own name as the Catholic Bishops of the Province of Canada, and on behalf of your clergy, and I assure you that I feel deeply the expression of your loyalty and affection for the Queen. I rejoice to think that obedience to the laws and submission to authority, which form the bond of all society and the condition of all civilization, are supported and enforced by your teaching and examples.

"The assurance that you enjoy the free exercise of your religion, and that you partake in the benefits and protection of the British Constitution, is a pledge that your hearts, and those of your fellow-subjects, of whatever origin they may be, will ever be united in the feelings you now express, of attachment to the Crown of Great Britain."

Three Rivers was next visited, and then Montreal, where the reception was one long-continued ovation. Here the Crystal Palace was duly inaugurated and the great Bridge opened with all possible pomp and ceremony. Everything was done as royally as money and taste, though without much experience in such stately matters, could do—even the carriage conveying the Prince of Wales to the bridge being lined with crimson velvet and beautifully decorated. Many addresses were presented, and the Anglican Cathedral was attended on Sunday as it had also been in Quebec. Fireworks and illuminations in the evenings and the inevitable State ball ensued, and on August 30th the departure was taken for St. Hyacinthe, Sherbrooke, and other places. Ottawa was finally reached, and the usual loyal reception given. Here the Prince laid the corner-stone of the Parliament Buildings of a future united and continental Dominion of Canada. Then came the visit to Kingston and Toronto, and the regrettable incident connected with the Orange arches. The Duke of Newcastle had heard that some demonstration of this nature was possible, and at once wrote the Governor-General that it would be his duty to advise the Prince of Wales not to pass under arches of the nature proposed, or to visit the towns where such semi-religious demonstrations were decided upon.

Sir Edmund Head at once, and very properly, wrote to the mayors of Toronto and Kingston that : " You will bear in mind that His Royal Highness visits this colony on the special invitation of the whole people, as conveyed by both branches of the Legislature, without distinction of creed or party ; and it would be inconsistent with the spirit and object of such an invitation, and such a visit, to thrust on him the exhibition of banners and other badges of distinction which are known to be offensive to any portion of Her Majesty's subjects." But the religious and party feeling of the day ran high, and the Orangemen, getting the erroneous impression that it was Roman Catholic protests which had caused this communication instead of a settled and proper policy of impartial bearing, persisted in their attitude. A landing was consequently not made at Kingston, although many addresses were received on board ship. At Belleville, and Cobourg, and Port Hope an enthusiastic welcome was given the Prince, and Toronto fairly outdid anything yet attempted in Canada. There the Mayor, Mr. (afterwards Chief Justice, Sir) Adam Wilson, read an eloquent address, to which the Prince responded in rather striking and impressive terms :

" You will not doubt the readiness with which I undertook the duty entrusted to me by the Queen of visiting, for her, the British North American dominions; and now that I have arrived at this distant point of my journey, I can say with truth that the expectations which I had formed of the pleasure and instruction to be derived from it have been more than realized. My only regret is that the Queen has been unable, herself, to receive the manifestations of the generous loyalty with which you have met her representative—a loyalty tempered and yet strengthened by the intelligent independence of the Canadian character.

" You allude to the marvellous progress which a generation has witnessed upon this spot. I have already been struck throughout my rapid journey by the promise of greatness and the results of energy and industry which are everywhere perceptible, and I feel the pride of an Englishman in the masculine qualities of my countrymen ; in the sanguine and hardy enterprise ; in the fertility of conception and boldness of execution which have enabled a youthful country to outstrip many of the ancient nations of the world."

It is impossible here to refer at length to what followed—the addresses and entertainments, the State ball, and other events—or to more than mention the visits to London, Stratford, Woodstock, Sarnia, Paris, Niagara Falls, Queenston, St. Catharines, and Hamilton—which preceded the partial tour of the United States. Everywhere the reception to the Prince indicated deep popular loyalty and evidenced a continuous enthusiasm. It was a sincere and spontaneous expression of regard for the Sovereign, the Royal family, and British connection. Needless to say, the visit was keenly watched by the Queen and Prince Consort, and not the least of the Duke of Newcastle's responsibilities had been his honourable task of keeping Her Majesty fully informed of its progress and success. Writing from Halifax early in the tour, he spoke of the probability that newspaper reports and correspondence will have said more than he can possibly write, but expresses the strong belief that " good has already been sown broadcast by the Prince's visit, and he humbly prays that a rich harvest may arise from it to the honour and glory of your Majesty and your family, and the advantage of the mighty Empire committed to your rule." As the Duke passed on through the country he seems to have more and more understood what its possibilities were and what Imperial unity might really mean in the future. After the border had been crossed he wrote from Dwight, in the State of Illinois, on September 23rd, a brief summary of the tour, which must be given here :

" Now the Canadian visit is included, he may pronounce it eminently successful, and may venture to offer Her Majesty his humble but very hearty congratulations. He does not doubt that future years will clearly demonstrate the good that has been done. The attachment to the Crown of England has been greatly cemented, and other nations will have learned how useless it will be in case of war to tamper with the allegiance of the North American provinces or to invade their shores. There is much in the population of all classes to admire and for a good government to work upon, and the very knowledge that the acts of all will henceforth be more watched in England, because more attention has been drawn to the country, will do good. . . . It has done much good to the Prince of Wales himself, and the development of mind and habit of thought is very perceptible."

The Prince of Wales reached England again, after his United States tour, on November 15th—the voyage home taking twenty-seven days. As was to have been expected in this period, the comments of the English press dwelt more upon the result of the American than the Canadian visit—where, indeed, they were not confused altogether. But some good was done, and the very great advantage was gained of making the Queen more practically and personally interested in her Canadian provinces than was before possible. In the Colonies the visit was of great value, and increased the substantial basis of loyalty which alone enabled their people to resist the unfriendly abrogation of the Reciprocity Treaty by the United States in 1866, and the accompanying pressure for annexation. One indirect and partial result of the visit was the confederation of the Dominion, and the Canada of to-day. With this latter great event in the history of British America the Queen had also a direct, as well as an indirect, interest. There can be little doubt now that the Royal visits to Canada and South Africa were the first links in the chain of Imperial sentiment which was to eventually consign the disintegrationist school to a dishonoured grave. During the years in which Canadian federation was in a state of ebb and flow, Mr. Cardwell, Lord Carnarvon, and the Duke of Buckingham were successively Secretaries of State for the Colonies. To Lord Carnarvon belongs the most of the credit, so far as English co-operation and impetus went, for its eventual success. Speaking in the House of Commons on February 14th, 1867, he declared that " We are laying the foundation of a great state—perhaps one which at a future day may even overshadow this country. But come what may, we shall rejoice that we have shown neither indifference to their wishes nor jealousy of their aspirations, but that we honestly and sincerely, to the utmost of our power and knowledge, that we honestly and sincerely, to the utmost of our power and knowledge, fostered their growth, recognizing in it the conditions of our own greatness."

Lord Carnarvon, however, had not always been an Imperialist, and, as in the case of the Duke of Newcastle, it seems not improbable that the Queen had exercised an influence in the moulding of his views. It was far otherwise, indeed, with many of his colleagues and contemporaries. On the very day the extract just quoted was spoken, Earl Russell, with all the prestige of an ex-Prime Minister attached to him, declared that confederation " would place the colonies on such a footing that in the event of their ever being desirous of severing the connection, they would be able to choose their future position in the world regardless of any external disturbing influence, and to make their own arrangements in harmony with their own wishes and feelings." This open encouragement of independence was followed by similar speeches in the Commons from Mr. Bright, Mr. Fortescue (afterwards Lord Carlingford), and others. But, fortunately, Canadian loyalty was too well secured for this sort of thing to break or diminish it seriously, and in this condition the personality of the Queen was perhaps the greatest factor, helped as it had been by the visit of the Prince of Wales.

Meantime Confederation had, in the main, been adjusted, and the successful Canadian statesmen—Macdonald, Cartier, Galt, Tupper, and Tilley—who had been in London for some time arranging the details were received by the Queen, just before their departure, at a special Court. Sir John (then Mr.) Macdonald, in a letter to his sister, dated March 21st, 1867, describes the event. " I went in first, as head of the Conference. There were only in the room the Queen, Princess Louise, and Lord Carnarvon, the Colonial Secretary. On entering, the Queen put out her hand, on which I knelt and kissed it. On rising, she said, ' I am very glad to see you on this mission.' I bowed. ' I hope all things are going well with you.' I said I was happy to inform Her Majesty that all things had been prosperous with us, and by the aid of Lord Carnarvon our measure had made great progress and there had been no delays. Her Majesty said, ' It is a very important measure, and you have all exhibited so much loyalty.' I replied, ' We have desired in this measure to declare in the most solemn and emphatic manner our resolve to be under the sovereignty of your Majesty and your family forever.' And so ended the audience. She had kind words for all those who followed me, Cartier, Galt, Tupper, and Tilley." But it had not been all clear sailing, and in the arrangements as a whole Sir John was obviously hampered in his ambitious and Imperialistic designs by the prevalence of the opposite principle. In a letter to Lord Knutsford—published in Mr. Pope's work, and dated July 18th, 1889—he states that a great opportunity was lost in 1867, and proceeds to say that:

" The declaration of the B.N.A. Provinces that they desired as one Dominion to remain a portion of the Empire showed what wise government and generous treatment would do,

THE DUKE OF RUTLAND, K.G., G.C.B.

THE DUKE OF DEVONSHIRE, K.G.

and should have been marked as an epoch in the history of England. This would prob-ably have been the case had Lord Carnarvon, who as Colonial Minister had sat at the cradle of the new Dominion, remained in office. His ill-omened resignation was followed by the appointment of the Duke of Buckingham, who had as his adviser the then Gov-ernor-General, Lord Monck—both good men, certainly, but quite unable from the constitu-tion of their minds to rise to the occasion. The Union was treated by them much as if the B.N.A. Act were a private Bill uniting two or three English parishes. Had a different course been pursued—for instance, had united Canada been declared to be an auxiliary kingdom, as it was in the Canadian draft of the Bill—I feel sure (almost) that the Austra-lian colonies would ere this have been applying to be placed in the same rank as ' The Kingdom of Canada.' "

In a postscript, Sir John adds that it was not the Duke of Buckingham himself who caused the change from kingdom to Dominion. " It was made at the instance of Lord Derby, then Foreign Minister, who feared the first name would wound the sensibilities of the Yankees." To those who know the curious char-acter of the late Earl of Derby, this characteristically timid, if not cowardly, conduct will be easily understood. He was one of the Manchester school disciples, and there is little doubt, from a perusal of modern colonial history and a comprehen-sion of English foreign policy, that he did more harm to the loyalty of the external Empire—and to the Imperial principle at home through his desertion of Lord Beaconsfield in 1878—than all the others put together. His high position and peculiar qualities contributed to this unfortunate result. Hence the loss of this splendid opportunity for consolidating the Empire by gradually gathering a group of sister kingdoms around the Throne of the motherland. But Sir John Mac-donald, as the work of his life proceeded, had the consolation of knowing that public sentiment and the public men of England were forced to grow steadily and surely up to his broad view of the Imperial situation. By the Queen he was always highly appreciated, and her action in calling him to the British Privy Council and making him a G.C.B. indicated this feeling to what was, in those days, a remarkable extent. Her Ministers made the formal recommendation and received the popular credit, but it is not improbable that the real initiative came from the Crown.

It certainly did in the peerage conferred upon Lady Macdonald in 1891, and the accompanying letter, in which Her Majesty, without the usual Royal and formal style, declares that " though I have not the pleasure of knowing you personally, I am desirous of writing to express, what I have already done (by a cable to the Governor-General), my deep sympathy with you in your present deep affliction for the loss of your dear distinguished husband. I wish also to say how truly and sincerely grateful I am for his devoted and faithful services, which he rendered for so many years to his Sovereign and this Dominion. It gives me much pleasure to mark my high sense of Sir John Macdonald's distin-guished services by conferring on you a public mark of regard for yourself as well as for him."   A few years later Her Majesty was showering every possible token of sympathy upon the family and country of Sir John Thompson.   The kindly telegram and personal letter to his widow ; the almost Royal honours conferred upon the memory of the Canadian statesman who had thus died so near the Throne of his Empire ; the Queen's personal compliment to Canada in the sending of the stately "Blenheim" to bear his remains home to their last resting place ; the placing of a wreath by her own hands upon his coffin at Windsor ; the permission afterwards given to Mr. F. M. Bell-Smith—a Canadian artist worthy of the honour—to paint the scene and herself as the central figure ; illustrated Her Majesty's practical Imperial sympathies.

But this is anticipating a story which should include many more incidents of Royal interest in Canada than space can possibly permit.   Following the Prince of Wales' visit came a brief one from Prince Alfred in 1861, and again in 1878 ; a longer tour by Prince Arthur in 1869, and as Duke of Connaught in 1890 ; a hasty visit from Prince Leopold in 1880, and the residence of Princess Louise in the Dominion as the wife of the Governor-General, the Marquess of Lorne.   Prince Leopold's tour in 1880 was carried out in strict privacy, owing to the state of his health, and although he visited Montreal, Ottawa, Toronto, and other cities, he was unable to participate in public functions or do more than study the country for the noble purposes which he had mapped out for himself. With all possible care, however, he was laid up for a time while fishing on the lower St. Lawrence, and was tended with assiduity by Mrs. Stephen—wife of the future Lord Mount Stephen—at their summer residence.   For this personal kindness she afterwards received a charming letter of thanks and appreciation from the Queen.   The death of the Prince a few years after this visit adds a most mournful shade to the fact that he desired to be appointed Governor-General in succession to Lord Lorne, and to the knowledge that his lovable character and high gifts would have enabled him to do much good in that important position.   The addresses to Her Majesty passed in 1884 by both Houses of Parliament at Ottawa, and by the Legislature of Quebec, dwelt with deserved eulogy upon these recognized qualities of the young Prince, and illustrate the influence which he might have so increasingly wielded.

The reception given in Canada to the Marquess of Lorne and the Princess Louise, when, during 1878, they came to fill the vice-regal position, was warmly enthusiastic.   Abundant preparations had been made for the event in all the cities through which they were to pass, and at Halifax they had the Duke of Edinburgh with them during the local ceremonies of welcome.   But he could not leave his ship to go further into the country.   At various places along the route to Montreal loyal demonstrations were made and everywhere people showed their pleasure at having a daughter of the Queen in their midst.   At the commercial metropolis of the St. Lawrence, amongst many addresses and functions was one of the former presented by the Ladies' Educational Association to the Princess. To it Her Royal Highness read a reply in which occur some thoughts well worthy of remembrance and attention to-day. "The fruits of education," she observed, "are so attractive that we are often tempted to force them prematurely, without sufficient tillage, and thus lose sight of the true objects of education, which consist much more in the development of the intellect than in the mere putting in of superficial knowledge and of 'cramming.' Hence our necessity of grounding in the rudiments of knowledge, and thoroughness in all that is done. Knowledge thus got never dies. Knowledge got otherwise never lives."

At Ottawa a similar reception was given, and Royalty for the first time was duly installed in the local home of Her Majesty's Canadian representative. In reply to one of the addresses presented, Lord Lorne look occasion to pay a most eloquent tribute to the qualities and work of his predecessor. "A thousand memories," he very truly declared, "throughout the length and breadth of the land speak of Lord Dufferin. It needs with you no titular memorials, such as the names of streets and bridges, to commemorate the name of him who not only adorned all he touched, but by his eloquence and his wisdom proved of what incalculable advantage to the State it was to have in the representative of the Sovereign one in whose nature judiciousness and impartiality, kindness, grace, and excellence, were so blended that his advice was a boon equally desired by all, his approbation a prize to be coveted, and the words that came from his silvery tongue, which always charmed and never hurt, were treasures to be cherished." Naturally, the Princess Louise spent a part of her time in England, where she must have been greatly missed by the Queen—whose children had all one by one left their Royal home with the exception of Princess Beatrice. But with certain exceptions, chiefly in connection with an unfortunate accident in Ottawa which caused her some sickness and pain, the Princess seems to have liked Canada, and she certainly left behind her many pleasing memories amongst those who had the privilege of knowing her, to say nothing of the general and personal appreciation of the people at having the cultured and clever daughter of the Queen in their midst. And this feeling was thoroughly voiced in the Parliamentary address presented to Lord Lorne and the Princess on their departure from Ottawa in May, 1883. "The presence of your illustrious Consort in Canada," it was stated, "seems to have drawn us closer to our beloved Sovereign, and in saying farewell to your Excellency and Her Royal Highness, whose kindly and gracious sympathies, manifested upon so many occasions, have endeared her to all hearts, we humbly beg that you will personally convey to Her Majesty the declaration of our loyal attachment, and of our determination to maintain firm and abiding our connection with the great Empire over which she rules."

In 1890 the Duke and Duchess of Connaught returned home from India, where His Royal Highness had for some years commanded the forces in one of the presidencies, and received wherever they stopped a thoroughly Canadian welcome. In Toronto many addresses were presented at the Pavilion, which was beautifully decorated for the purpose, and much respectful enthusiasm was shown by the crowds everywhere. The Prince's reply to an address from the Imperial Federation League was specially noteworthy. "We can never forget," he said, " that at the time of the Egyptian war we had standing side by side with our troops representatives of the Canadian militia and Canadian boatmen. We had representatives of the Australian militia, and we had also representatives of our brave Indian troops. I, for one, hope some day that we may see some sort of federation similar to what you wish, but I believe it can only come at the desire, the expressly desired wish of the Colonies, of which there are many in Her Majesty's Empire, and I am certain that no one will more readily take them into their arms than the Queen and the people of Great Britain."

Coming to other details, it may be said that in 1880 Her Majesty commissioned Mr. L. R. O'Brien, President of the Royal Canadian Academy, to paint her a view of the historic citadel at Quebec, and four years later sent some copies of her work, " More Leaves from the Journal of a Life in the Highlands," to Mr. (now Sir) J. A. Chapleau, Secretary of State, for presentation to the principal Canadian libraries. Each book bore the Queen's autograph, and in an accompanying letter it was stated to be her desire to thus show her interest in the literary culture of the Dominion. In 1882 the attack upon the Queen by Roderick Maclean aroused the loyalty and sympathy of Canadians to an unusual degree, and loyal addresses were passed by the Dominion Parliament and the Legislatures of Quebec, Nova Scotia, New Brunswick, Manitoba, and British Columbia. From the women of Canada an address signed by 50,000 persons was sent, through the Governor-General, and obtained from Her Majesty, through Lord Lorne, a personal response. " I have received with feelings of the sincerest gratification," wrote the Queen, " the loyal and affectionate address presented to me by the women of Canada. I wish that you would convey to the signers of that address my heartfelt thanks for the cordial and friendly expression they have used toward me, and to assure the women of the Dominion of my earnest wish to promote their happiness and welfare."

In November, 1885, when the Canadian Pacific Railway was completed and opened to traffic, the most important and immediate congratulation was from the Queen. Lord Lansdowne wrote at once to his Premier, Sir John Macdonald, announced the receipt of the cabled message, and proceeded : " Her Majesty is pleased to add that she has watched its progress with much interest, and that she hopes for the future success of a work of such value and importance to the Empire." During 1886 the Queen was much pleased with the Canadian section of the Indian and Colonial Exhibition, and after the opening ceremonies cabled to Lord Lansdowne at Ottawa as follows :

" London, May 5th, 1886—Opening of the Exhibition went off splendidly; delighted to see so many of my Canadian subjects.

"VICTORIA R. and I."

During the Colonial Conference of 1887 Her Majesty followed its deliberations with interest, and received many Canadians of prominence at Windsor or Buckingham Palace. The people of Canada, on their part, have never been behindhand in their open, honest loyalty. The celebrations in the Dominion during the Jubilee were ample illustrations of this fact, and the addresses of congratulation from the two Houses of Parliament were representative of the sincere and strong public feeling. One paragraph must be quoted :

" From a few scattered provinces it has become a great federation, stretching from ocean to ocean, and linking by its iron path the European to the Asiatic portions of your Majesty's domain. It has been the good fortune of the people of Canada to enjoy from time to time the honour of the presence and countenance of several members of the Royal family, and this relationship not only deepened their loyal devotion to the head of the British Empire, but enhanced their regard for the wife and mother and their veneration for the memory of the husband and father. Our earnest prayer is that He who is the Ruler of all nations and the King of all kings may uphold, direct, and preserve your Majesty for many long years to reign over a prosperous and contented people."

The loyal resolution of 1890 was couched in still stronger terms, and was intended to indicate to the American people the absence of any important annexationist feeling in Canada. But it really required no resolution of stereotyped loyalty to embody the true sentiment of the Dominion. It might have been needed, and is needed, to convince that unreasonable and unreasoning sentiment in the minds of the American people which seems to exist wherever Canada is concerned. The hearts of Canadians, however, are so closely linked to their Sovereign by ties of sincere affection and profound respect that they themselves require no special assertion of the fact. They believe in the institution of a limited monarchy as the only means of preserving a really dignified democracy, and conserving a permanent British connection and an all-powerful British Empire. They have a land that is " rich in heart, in home, in hope, in liberty," and they have had all these elements of national greatness and individual benefit developed under the rule of their Queen and through the practical working of monarchical institutions—institutions which rest upon the free will of a free people, and interpret the best thoughts and aspirations of modern civilization, while combining the wealth of historic tradition with the impetus and freshness of vast new regions and rising nations all over the world.

CHAPTER XXI.

AUSTRALASIA UNDER THE QUEEN.

WHEN the Queen came to the Throne, Australia was an unexplored continent, with a few settlements scattered here and there along its shores ; New Zealand was practically unknown to civilization, and did not yet form a part of the British Empire ; Tasmania was a struggling penal colony under the designation of Van Diemen's Land. During the following fifteen years the people of Australia and Tasmania had to face many hardships and to endure the stigma which the transportation system threw upon all their struggles. That shadow remained long after the cessation of transportation ; but the discovery of gold, the granting of constitutional government, and the rush of population into the new El Dorado, did much during the early Fifties to modify a difficulty which time, and progress, and the character of the people has since obliterated.

For a considerable period, however, the colonies had much trouble to contend with. The convict element was always an unpleasant one, although many included under that designation had been sent abroad because of very minor offences, and for causes which sometimes did not reflect a criminal character, or even action, as now understood. Still there were many difficult and unruly subjects to deal with ; and, in 1840, when General Sir Charles Napier was requested to take the Governorship of South Australia, the condition of the colony was said to be so mutinous and insubordinate that he asked for troops to take with him. They were refused, and he naturally declined a position which Mr. (afterwards Sir) George Grey ultimately accepted. In New South Wales and other settlements the state of affairs was better, but not as well as it might have been. Meanwhile the dangers from extreme heat, unknown tropical insects and snakes, and little understood fevers, together with the heavy, unavoidable hardships of pioneer life, combined to merit the verses long afterwards dedicated to the people of Australia by the Countess of Jersey—one of which reads :

"They battled with ocean, tempest, and storm,
  With loneliness, hunger, and heat ;
With nature in many a perilous form,
  And never acknowledged defeat.
They won from the haunt of the savage and beast
  The pasture, the grain, and the gold,
And made a new home for the highest and least
  Of the country they loved of old."

THE HON. SIR HENRY PARKES, G.C.M.G.

THE RIGHT HON. CECIL J. RHODES, P.C., M.L.A.

The Queen's personal interest in these new countries was early aroused. When, in 1851, the Port Philip dependency of New South Wales was organized into a separate colony, it was by the express wish of Her Majesty named Victoria. So, in 1859, with the settlement of Moreton Bay, when its name was changed to Queensland. Speaking at Brisbane, upon appointment as Governor of the new Colony, Sir George Bowen declared, on 12th December of that year, that the name selected was "entirely the happy thought and inspiration of Her Majesty. Other designations had been suggested to her, but the Queen spontaneously determined to confer her own royal title upon the new province of her empire." A little later the Legislature passed addresses to the Queen which referred to "the loyalty which will bind us and our posterity in duty and allegiance to your Majesty and your Majesty's successors." The Duke of Newcastle, as Colonial Secretary, said in reply:

"I am commanded by the Queen to inform you, and through you the Parliament of Queensland, that she has received the addresses with great satisfaction. Her Majesty does not doubt that the feelings of the Parliament and people of the Colony towards herself and the Mother Country are fitly symbolized by its name; and she trusts that, under the Divine blessing, they may long continue to form a band of union between the two countries, and so contribute to the honour and welfare of both."

Meantime New Zealand had been partly settled by a well-educated and intelligent class of persons, and would have progressed in peace and prosperity had it not been for land troubles with the Maoris, and a constantly changing policy amongst the earlier Governors. Hobson, and Fitzroy, and Gore Browne, and Grey each had different ideas, and each mixed up the relationship of the colonists with either the Home Government or the natives. With the Maoris the result was war after war, and the almost complete disappearance of as fine a race of aborigines as ever graced a beautiful climate and country. Yet at first everything promised well, and in 1840, when the treaty was made with the natives which recognized British sovereignty, the original document in the Maori tongue declares that "Victoria, the Queen of England, in her kindly regard for the chiefs and tribes of New Zealand; in her desire also to guarantee to them their rank as chiefs and their land, that peace may be sure to them and quiet possession; has thought it desirable to send a chief to regulate affairs with the aborigines of New Zealand."

For years following the Maoris were taught to regard the Queen personally as their ruler and governor, who, though far away, was still ever mindful of their interests, and ever willing to listen to their appeals should wrong be done them. But they were a warlike race of men with many excellent qualities, in the wilder sense of the phrase, and with an irresistible tendency to fight amongst themselves, or with the settlers who might come into collision with their peculiar customs or claims to possession of the land. More use might have been made of the Queen's name and prestige during these troubles than was ever attempted, yet many chiefs remained loyal in the wars which broke out from time to time.   In 1861 an address was presented to Sir George Grey of such an eloquent nature that he at once sent it home for the Queen's perusal and received in reply a letter from the Duke of Newcastle, which stated that Her Majesty was "greatly gratified and touched by the feeling and poetic address of the New Zealand chiefs, and desired me to tell you so.   It was at Her Majesty's suggestion that I sent a copy of it to *The Times*, so that it might be read and admired by all her subjects."

The influence of a potent name and personality amongst such peoples as the Maoris was naturally remarkable, and history will record with sorrow the fact that in this connection the Sovereign's prestige was not always used as it might have been.   As with the Indians in Canada, the natives in Hindustan, and the countless races of Africa, so it was with the aborigines of New Zealand. It is, indeed, a question if the Queen's name is not better known and more important to large masses of the world's population than is the name of the country over which she primarily reigns.   The nature of this feeling was curiously shown in an address presented to Her Majesty in 1869 on behalf of certain loyal Maoris, and through the Governor of the day—Sir George Bowen:

"O, my guests," said Kawana Hunia of the Ngatiapis:
"She is our Queen as well as your Queen—Queen of Maoris and Queen of Pakeha.
Should wars arise we will take up our rifles and march whithersoever she shall direct.
My cousin Wiremu went to England and saw our Queen.   He returned.
When you landed in this island he was already dead.
He died fighting for our Queen.
As he died we will die, if need be—I and all my chiefs.   This do you tell our Queen.
I have said."

The orphan son of one of these chiefs—Albert Victor Pomare—was afterwards educated and supported by the Queen in Auckland.   These troubles, however, have long since passed away.   Those of the natives who remain live in peace and reasonable prosperity, while the people of New Zealand are to-day face to face with very different problems from any encountered by a previous generation.   As in Australia, so in these islands a thousand miles away, questions of socialism and the most advanced forms of experimental legislation have taken the place of pioneer struggles, and war, and discomforts.   They are being carried out under the British constitutional system and the special local influence of the Queen's representative.   And, upon the whole, they are not unduly straining the ties of union, while many and varied tendencies are making for closer and better connection with the Mother Country.

Of these influences the Queen in her home, and family, and royal position, and through the local power of the Governor, has been one of the strongest and

Her character has helped to mould the principles of the people; her constitutional rule has trained them in the work of government, and contributed the element of dignity to the otherwise preponderating ideas of extreme liberty and equality; her life has won their affection and her reign has proved their loyalty. Such an influence was needed in all these southern Colonies to an extent greater than can be understood at a glance. To the peculiar circumstances connected with early Australian organization was added the tremendous influx of a rough though hardy population during the days of the gold fever. Then came a time of bounding prosperity, and a development only possible in a country so naturally great and rich. Constitutional government was granted to the Colonies one after the other, and with it came a certain amount of reckless legislation and the growth of a somewhat wild democracy. But, thanks to the influence of the Governors, as representing the Queen, the substantial dignity of monarchical institutions and the inherent respect for Parliament felt by all British peoples, these early difficulties were kept under control, and the various settlements given an opportunity to grow into powerful, law-abiding, and loyal communities.

As time passed on, the discovery of gold was assisted by the raising of sheep and cattle, until the two and then three millions of Australian people upon the mainland came to boast with truth of having the greatest individual wealth of any country in the world, and a civilization of a new, buoyant, and aggressive type. Noble cities, such as Melbourne and Sydney, grew into proportions worthy of the natural beauties surrounding them, while the banking institutions and other concerns connected with the concentration and accumulation of wealth seemed to rest upon a basis as solid and substantial as those of the motherland itself. With all this material success came a personal confidence dashed with egotism, an individual education curiously mingled with ignorance through a too local limitation of studies, a political development which included much British loyalty with a strong strain of independence, and a somewhat narrow view of external issues. It was natural that such should be the case. The utterances of British statesmen preaching independence during twenty years had caused an ultimate reaction in the Colonies, and the formation of a noisy, though never very influential, body of men, who advocated the policy which by that time had lost all favour in England and been relegated to the dust-bin of forgotten fallacies. And the isolation of Australia was a natural encouragement to thoughts of independence.

But several influences were stronger than both these elements combined. The personality of the Queen had gradually grown into the hearts of the people, and her reign, as it progressed, transfused stereotyped loyalty of expression into the voicing of a sincere sentiment and warm allegiance. The steady development of Imperial feeling in England had some effect upon the colonists, despite the difficulty of immediately comprehending the change which it implied. The administration of Colonial affairs in the hands of men like Lord Derby and Lord Granville exercised a retrogressive and exasperating influence, but this in time was more than checkmated by the rise to power in England of leaders such as Lord Rosebery, and the sending out of more representative men as Governors. A more just appreciation of England's place in the world and a better knowledge of the history of the Empire began also to permeate the minds of the people, who in some of the Colonies had actually not been taught history in their schools; and, finally, the practical experience of their defenceless position against any great Power brought and sustained the conviction that union with Great Britain was really essential to their safety.

English statesmen had always appreciated the danger which the Colonies ran in the event of a war into which the Empire was plunged—to say nothing of the infinitely greater dangers from foreign ambition and aggression were they independent. But for a long time the Australians did not realize the situation. Mr. Spencer Walpole tells us, in his " Life of Lord John Russell," that " there is still amongst Lord John's papers a singular document which purports to be a translation of a series of confidential questions issued by Napoleon III. on the possibility of a French expedition, secretly collected in different ports, invading, conquering, and holding Australia." From the Emperor's general character this is not improbable, despite his admitted desire to maintain an English alliance. There were times of *pique* and anger at the prejudices of the English press which overpowered even his friendship for the Queen and his loyalty to their alliance. It may be, also, that this incident occurred after Sedan, when, according to the Emperor Frederick's diary, Napoleon had sought to stem the tide of German invasion by an alliance against England.

Speaking in December, 1889, Sir George F. Bowen, an experienced Australian administrator, stated that : " I was Governor of Victoria in 1878, when a war with Russia seemed imminent, and when it was also believed on good grounds that it was intended by that power to send a strong squadron and military force to attack and lay under contribution the chief cities of Australia. I can bear witness that the almost universal feeling of the colonists then was to throw in their lot with the mother country, and to make the most determined exertions for common defence." But it remained for the Soudan war to evoke the genuine British patriotism of the people, to drown the voice of ignorant independence, to diffuse a knowledge of their Imperial position amongst the masses, and prove to the world that Australia, as well as all the other colonies, intended to remain British despite distance in space and mistakes at home, or local prejudices amongst themselves. There was intense admiration felt in the southern continent for General Gordon, but this in itself was hardly sufficient to account for what occurred in 1885—although three years later a statue was unveiled in Melbourne which had been subscribed to by 100,000 people in the Colony of Victoria.

The inspiration first came to Mr. Walter Beade Dalley, acting Premier of New South Wales, and a most eloquent and loyal Irishman. He cabled the Colonial Office an offer of 500 infantry and 400 artillery, expenses paid, and after some brief delay the contingent was accepted for active service in the Soudan.

Had the delay been slightly longer the Home Government would have been in a quandary, for similar offers came pouring in from Canada, from Victoria— 700 men fully equipped—from Queensland, from South Australia, and elsewhere. They could not have been all accepted, because they were not really needed. The result, however, was marvellous in its evidence of wide and impetuous loyalty. People in Australia contributed everywhere to a " patriotic fund " for the maintenance of the troops, and many single offers of £1,000 a year while the contingent was engaged in the Imperial service were received. Within a few days £50,000 had been subscribed, and cablegrams of congratulation came from the Queen, Lord Wolseley, and Lord Rosebery. On March 3rd the detachment of 800 men, with ample stores and provisions, sailed from Sydney amid scenes such as the colony had never witnessed and may never see again. Thousands had volunteered to go, other thousands had subscribed money for expenses, and many more thousands assembled to see the contingent depart. The troops had been first reviewed in the presence of an immense multitude by Lord Augustus Loftus, the Governor of the colony, and on the succeeding day services had been held in all the churches for the volunteers, special sermons being preached by the Anglican and Roman Catholic Archbishops. Amid dense masses of cheering people the troops were finally escorted to the men-of-war, accompanied by the Governor, the Ministers, and all the Colonial leaders. When they reached the quay His Excellency the Governor addressed them in words significant of the concentrated enthusiasm of the occasion :

" Soldiers of New South Wales ! I have considered it my duty, as the representative of Her Majesty, to say a few words to you at this solemn moment before your embarkation. For the first time in the great history of the British Empire a distant colony is sending, at its own cost and completely equipped, a contingent of troops, who have volunteered with an enthusiasm, of which only we who witnessed it can judge, to assist the Imperial forces in a bitter struggle for the suppression of unspeakable cruelty and for the establishment of order and justice in a misgoverned country. . . . The eyes of your gracious Queen will be bent upon your exertions, and in every part of the world where our flag floats men, women, and children will eagerly read of your exploits, and pray for your success.

" Soldiers ! You carry in your keeping the honour of this great colony, which has made such great sacrifices in order to send you to the front with an equipment of which the nations most practised in war might well be proud. You will have the glorious privilege of helping to maintain the honour of the Empire. In your ranks are numbers who are voluntarily leaving the paths of fortune, worldly advantages, the comforts of home, and the sweetness of domestic life for heroic service in a bloody war in which already many brave men have been stricken down.

" You are doing this to show to the world the unity of the mighty and invincible Empire of which you are members. Your country charges itself with the care of the dear ones you leave behind, and all that generosity, tenderness, and gratitude can do to care for them and succour and console them will be looked upon as a labour of love by the nation."

It goes without saying that the Australians did their fullest duty in the Soudan, and shared in all the hardships and much of the scattered fighting of the ensuing campaign. That the result was not brilliant was the fault of the Home Government and its shilly-shally policy, and not of the brave troops under Lord Wolseley. But the action of the colony was none the less appreciated at home. As the Prince of Wales said during a speech in March, 1885 : " This in itself shows that they cling to the motherland. Long may that feeling exist ! Such spontaneous feeling on their part is most gratefully received through the length and breadth of our country." It also did great good in Australia. Mr. Dalley, who was afterwards created an Imperial Privy Councillor, and honoured by a memorial in St. Paul's Cathedral when he died a few years later, declared with truth that "we have awakened in the Australian Colonies an enthusiasm of sacrifice, of heroism—of all the nobler qualities which are to the loftier national life what the immortal soul is to the perishable body of humanity." And when the troops arrived again at Sydney they were welcomed by all that was notable and great in Australasia. The colonies, including New Zealand, joined their political, military, and naval forces in receiving the contingent, and it was clearly demonstrated that the latter had returned home not only crowned with England's gratitude and encompassed with the sympathies of an empire, but to give an impetus towards a national British feeling and the movement for a local Australian federation.

Meanwhile, Royal influence had not been idle in the promotion of that personal loyalty which only the presence of members of the Queen's family could create. It had always been the Prince of Wales' desire to visit Australia, but distance and the many demands upon him at home prevented it. Speaking at the laying of the foundation stone of the Melbourne Exhibition on February 19th, 1879, Sir George Bowen referred to the Prince's interest in the Colonies, and stated that he was well known to be animated by " a desire to visit in person, should high reasons of State permit it, our Australasian Colonies, as he has already visited India and Canada." Upon various occasions since then His Royal Highness has made statements to the same effect, and in speaking at a Colonial banquet in London on July 16th, 1881, he repeated his regret at not having been able to accept the pressing invitations of two years before to visit the exhibitions at Sydney and Melbourne, adding that " though I have not had the opportunity of seeing these great Australasian colonies, which every day and every year are making such immense development, still at the International Exhibitions of London, Paris, and Vienna I had not only an opportunity of seeing their various products there exhibited, but I had the pleasure of making the personal acquaintance of many colonists—a fact which has been of great importance and great benefit to myself." And in the Colonial Exhibition of 1886 the Prince was instrumental in rendering Australasia, as well as other parts of the Empire, a most substantial service.

If, however, the heir to the Throne had been unable to go, Prince Alfred was sent on a tour of the Australias in 1867-8, and the two sons of the Prince of Wales in 1881. The Duke of Edinburgh was only twenty-three when he started on his long cruise in H.M.S. "Galatea," but his succeeding experiences in varied countries and amongst all sorts and conditions of men must have been sufficiently interesting to hold a prominent place in his memories of the past. Arriving at Adelaide, the capital of South Australia, on Oct. 31st, the Sailor Prince was given a most hearty welcome, accompanied by the usual addresses, illuminations, ringing of bells, cheering crowds, decorated streets, the *levée* at Government House, the State Ball, and other functions and visits. Nearly three weeks were spent here or in the neighbourhood in a round of loyal festivities. On November 23rd Melbourne was reached, and an equally generous and enthusiastic reception given. The routine of welcome and ceremonial was, of course, much the same, but it included a visit to the gold mines in the vicinity of what one of the addresses described in words giving much Australian history in a nutshell: " The year prior to the birth of your Royal Highness, the site of this city was a trackless forest and the Colony an unexplored wilderness." Not the least interesting incident in Victoria was a loyal document prepared and presented by the Chinese residents of Castlemaine, and of which the following extract may be given :

" Your benign love is liberally diffused and extends to all things. The blessings and happiness you confer are as the ocean. They mollify and enrich us, who are of another country, although the subjects of this.

" Prolong your stay with us, until the customs of the people, in every nook of our shores, are inquired into and known by you ; then all will be exhilarated with delight. When you return to the Royal Court and take the corner place, we hope you will sit down in joy, with universal peace prevailing.

"Oh! how excellent and admirable! How worthy of praise is he to whom with veneration, awe, and humility we present our address."

All this and much more Oriental imagery was poured out upon the young Prince before he was finished with the peculiar people who embody in lofty language what they seem unable and unfit to have in their lowly lives. In Tasmania, which was visited during January, a most enthusiastic welcome was received—the Mayor of Hobart stating what was, and is, the sentiment of his colony when he spoke in the civic address of " the close identity which happily unites Her Majesty's dominions in all parts of the globe in sentiment, interests, and institutions." Sydney, the capital of New South Wales, was the next centre visited, and here the Prince was given a naval and city illumination, and a nightly display of fireworks.   He also held a *levée* on January 23rd, reviewed a body of troops, attended the horse races, paid a visit to the exquisite Botanical Gardens, and attended a great cricket match and a Citizens' Ball.   A very amusing trip was then taken to the up-country districts in Queensland, and before Brisbane, the capital, was reached, on February 23rd, the Prince had more than one rough-and-ready experience.   Loyal entertainments were given here and in some smaller places, until on March 10th a village near Sydney, named Clontarf, was visited for the purpose of attending some special local fête.   Accompanied by the Earl of Belmore, Governor of New South Wales, Sir Alfred Stephen, Sir William Manning, and other local dignitaries, the Duke had left the luncheon table and was watching a large party of the black natives, who were about to perform their " Corroboree," when a man walked out from the surrounding crowd till he came close up to the Prince, and then, drawing a pistol, shot him deliberately in the middle of the back.   He was, of course, seized, and proved to be a Fenian, who boasted his object to be assassination, " for the good of his country." The Duke of Edinburgh was at once carried to a house near by and carefully tended through the illness which followed.   His escape from death at such close quarters was really marvellous, but good does sometimes come out of evil, and the ensuing evidences of loyalty to the Royal House of England were very sincere and pronounced.

Addresses poured in from all quarters, and public meetings in every part of the country ratified the public feeling and testified sympathy with the Prince, and condemnation of his cowardly assailant.   The latter, a man named O'Farrell, was tried and executed, despite an appeal for mercy from the Duke, while the citizens of Sydney established a handsome hospital, to which £5,000 were subscribed before the subscription lists could be printed, as a memorial of the Royal visit.   By the 6th of April the Duke had recovered sufficiently to sail for home, but owing to his still weak condition it was thought better for him to avoid the excitement of his promised visit to New Zealand.   And, as the "Galatea" sailed away from the land where, despite one dark blot, so much of kindness and hospitality and loyalty had been shown the young Prince, the scene of the departure was well described in the poetic enthusiasm of Judge Francis:

> " Up with the flag ! the flag of old renown,
>   Tossed on all oceans, waved by every wind ;
>   Britannia's flag, signed with the triple cross—
>   Shake forth the Royal Standard on your towers
>   In all its wealth of blazonry, while far
>   And near, from battlement and pier and mast,
>   Ten thousand varied banners flaunt in air !
>   All pomp of gorgeous spectacle, all forms
>   Of duteous homage, crowd the closing scene.

We gave him of our best,
Heart welcome, and the unstudied courtesies
Of a free people not too proud to bend
In loyal homage to Victoria's son."

The visit of Prince Albert Victor—then only seventeen—and Prince George of Wales to Australia, in 1881, was part of a prolonged cruise around the world in H.M.S. "Bacchante." On board ship the two Princes were midshipmen and nothing more—subject to all the rules and work of a busy life, the performance of many duties, and the study of practical seamanship in all its details. On shore, in the various parts of the British Empire which they visited, the Royal position was reassumed, and its varied duties performed with more or less of boyish dignity and efficiency. The elaborate volumes which have since been published under the editorship of Canon Dalton—who was their chaplain during the tour—and which include the copious notes and journals of the two Princes, reveal them in a most favourable light, and indicate the wisdom of their father's care in giving them such a moral and mental training as this voyage involved. Some four months were spent cruising in Australian waters, and amongst the Australian people. Albany and Adelaide in the Western Colony were first visited, and various trips into the wild up-country taken. Then came the visit to Melbourne and Ballarat, a descent into one of the gold mines, and a reception at Sandhurst—of the enthusiasm of which the Royal Diary says: "We never saw anything to equal it." The hospitalities of Melbourne were simply innumerable, and are quite beyond the possibility of describing here.

As the Governor, Lord Normanby, said at a banquet given by the Corporation: "It is the innate loyalty and affection entertained by the inhabitants of these colonies towards the Throne and the institutions of the old country which causes them to give a warm reception to the Governor for the time being. . . . Loyalty is innate amongst us, but still is somewhat of a visionary character." Hence the welcome given the Princes, and the great value of such visits in transmuting a visionary sentiment into a personal affection. Sydney and other places in New South Wales, Moreton Bay and Brisbane, were next visited, and then the two Princes returned to their work-a-day life on board ship and sailed away to the Fiji Islands. Since that time various invitations have been sent to the Royal family to repeat these visits, but circumstances have prevented action as yet—the latest being a cabled intimation from Lord Hopetoun, then Governor of Victoria, to the Colonial Secretary in December, 1893, that: "The Colony of Victoria, in concert with the other colonies of Australasia, cordially invites their Royal Highnesses the Duke and Duchess of York to visit these parts of Her Majesty's dominions. Her Majesty's subjects in Australasia have a most gratifying recollection of the former tour made by their Royal Highnesses the Duke of Clarence and the Duke of York, and the colonies are deeply impressed with the advantage of such visits in knitting together more closely the distant parts of the Empire." The Duke of York was unable for domestic reasons to accept the invitation, but is understood to have promised a future visit.

Meanwhile many events had occurred which tended in different ways to train the public mind in what may be termed intellectual as well as sentimental loyalty. Knowledge of the true meaning of monarchical institutions and British power naturally helps in the first direction, and therefore the world-wide celebration of the Queen's Jubilee in 1887 had a practical result, as well as a most loyal echo in the land of the Southern Cross. Lord Brassey, who was in the country at the time, and who has since assumed the Governorship of Victoria, has described some of the demonstrations which took place. In Melbourne, he saw 5,000 colonial militia march past like a wall to the tune of " The Old Folks at Home." He saw the great Parliamentary buildings of that capital dedicated forever to the name of the Queen ; heard thousands of people at a Jubilee concert sing " God Save the Queen" four separate and distinct times ; besides listening a little later to the swelling words of the same National Anthem from 30,000 school children. He accompanied the Governor of South Australia through a remote district where the railway was being opened for the first time, and during the whole of one night and day, wherever a village or tiny community was passed—and whatever the hour—as the train drew into the station, he heard children's voices singing the soft and almost continuous strains of " God Save the Queen." And in the same colony the Government prize offered for the best Australian Jubilee Ode was received for one in which occur the following ringing lines :

> " Full grown and strong, yet still her mother's child,
> As loving now as when in childhood's days
> Her mother helped her with her judgment mild,
> With kindly words, encouragement, and praise.
> Stand out, fair land ! and let the nations hear
> Australia hail her Sovereign's jubilee—
> Australian men and women, far and near,
> Send your Godspeeds across the Southern sea."

Speaking at a great banquet during the opening of the Melbourne Exhibition in 1888, Lord Carrington, the new Governor of Victoria, spoke of the liberty inherent in British government, and of the feeling that " when we instinctively rise to our feet at the sound of the grand old anthem, and drink to the health of the Queen, we are recognizing our common unity of purpose." And then he pointed out the Imperial nature of that toast. "We are not only honouring the illustrious lady who so worthily wears the crown of King Alfred, but through her we drink to the common weal of all British people ; to law, to order, to freedom, and to justice, to Judges on the Bench and to Ministers and Parliaments elected by and answerable to the people; through her we drink to our sovereignty over, and our friendship with, the native Princes and the native races of India; we drink to Australasian unity, to the South African Confederation, to the Dominion o Canada, to our West Indian possessions, and to every law-abiding, self-govern. ing community of hardy pioneers who are to be found under the British flag doing their duty in the cause of liberty, in the furthest portions of the habitable globe." Typical this speech is of the process of Imperial education which went on all over the continent as a consequence of the Jubilee, and as a legitimate result of the personal loyalty which the Queen had herself won, and which mem· bers of her family had helped to increase. And no better proof of the strength of this feeling, and of the value to the British Empire of Her Majesty's life and work, could have been given than the following Address passed in July, 1887, by that most radical and democratic legislature—the Parliament at Sydney:

We, the members of the Legislative Council and of the Legislative Assembly of New South Wales, in Parliament assembled, desire to approach your Majesty and to offer our loyal and heartfelt congratulations on the completion of the fiftieth year of your Majesty's beneficent reign. We humbly trust that the Almighty may long preserve your life, that the weight of your great sorrow may be lightened by wise counsels giving happiness to your people; that you may at all times be sustained by the loyal attachment and affection of your subjects in all parts of your Empire; and we dutifully assure your Most Gracious Majesty that in no portion of your vast dominions are the sentiments of loyalty and love for your Throne and person more warmly cherished than by the inhabitants of New South Wales."

Not a tittle of the popular demonstrations and expressions of loyalty can, of course, be quoted or referred to, but it can easily be seen what a beneficial and permanent effect they must have had when considered in all their wide area and application. They undoubtedly influenced the tendency of the ensuing move- ment for Australasian federation, and prevented it from drifting into dangerous byways of separationist argument or policy. The formation of the Federal Council, in which sat representatives from Queensland, Victoria, Tasmania and Western Australia, paved the way for the Conferences of 1890 and 1891, although, its composition being only partial, it was unable to do very much seri- ous work or legislation. One feature of the session of 1888 was, however, the appointment of a committee to prepare an Address of congratulation to the Queen, which, as eventually presented, expressed unfailing loyalty to Her Majesty's Throne and person, and the hope that she would regard with satisfaction the efforts being made to promote a union of the Australasian Colonies. The work of the Melbourne Conference in 1890, at which were to be found representative politicians from each of the seven colonies—including New Zealand—was equally auspicious in its loyal expressions, and, as finally passed, the resolutions com- menced with an assurance of devoted attachment and loyalty. Sir Henry Parkes, in one of his speeches, spoke of prayer as " the soul's sincere desire, uttered or unexpressed," and declared that "My whole being trembles with an unuttered prayer that the whole of the British possessions may remain forever forming parts of one beneficent empire." And so with many of the other leaders present.

The Conference of the succeeding year at Sydney was a still greater and more representative event. The chief men of Australasia were present, and it is not too much to say that loyalty to the Queen controlled more than one narrow or local conception of what a federation should be, and guided the deliberations of the gathering in the direction of British unity rather than Australian independence—or the aspiration towards that end. Speaking at the magnificent banquet which preceded the meetings of the Conference, Sir Henry Parkes—who until his recent death, and despite the ups and downs of Colonial politics, was the grand old man of the Southern continent—observed, amid ringing cheers, that :

"Under the sway of Queen Victoria, they of Australia were as happy and as free a people as they could be; they desired no change. In the words of Burke, change is an ill sound to happy ears; they desired no alteration from the happy condition of Australian life. He, for one, believed that, instead of lessening the ties which held the nation together, the meeting of the Federation delegates in Sydney would be a cementing of the fabric which encompassed the Empire of the Queen. That young English maiden, who was in early morning awakened to be informed that she was Queen of the Empire, had passed through the trying stages of a maiden in a high station, of a wife, of a mother, and a sorrowing widow, and in all she had ever earned the deepest sympathy and the strongest admiration of those under her rule. He would not dwell on the womanly qualities of Queen Victoria, but he would request that great company to drink to the health of the Queen, one of the greatest constitutional sovereigns that ever lived."

Another striking incident of this period—the turning point of Australian national life—was the centennial celebration of the foundation of New South Wales as the first and parent colony. During the lengthened and varied proceedings, the Governors of all the colonies, the Admiral in command of the Fleet, the Duke of Manchester, and the Earl of Carnarvon, together with the Premiers and Ministers, and the majority of all the Australian legislators, took part in one way or another. An imposing statue of the Queen by Mr. J. E. Boehm, R.A., was first unveiled in Sydney by Lady Carrington, amid every formality of State and evidence of popular enthusiasm. It took the place of one which had been originally sculptured by Marshall Wood and afterwards destroyed in the fire of 1882. The ceremonies and events of the next few days were typical of Australian openhanded hospitality and generosity, and of the national ability to celebrate a great anniversary or occasion in a broad and comprehensive spirit. The culmination was a State banquet, at which nearly a thousand guests, representative of all the progress and opinions of Australasia, sat down under the chairmanship of Lord Carrington. The speeches were permeated with a desire to find some common ground for Imperial unity and action, and those of Sir Henry (now Lord) Loch, the Governor of Victoria; Sir William Jervois, Governor of New Zealand; Sir Anthony Musgrave, Governor of Queensland; Sir William Robinson, Governor of South Australia; Sir Henry Parkes, Lord Carnarvon, Sir William Fitzherbert, Sir Samuel Griffith, Mr. (now Sir) E. N. C. Braddon, Sir John Robertson, and other representatives of various colonies; urged Imperial Federation with strength and vigour.

Perhaps, however, the central incident of the occasion was a cablegram from Her Majesty, which Lord Carrington read in proposing her health: "The Queen warmly congratulates the Australian Colonies on the splendid material and social progress achieved during the past hundred years. She deeply appreciates their loyalty, and she has watched with sincere interest the excellent administration of their Governments, and she prays that their prosperity and close attachment to the mother country may continue to increase as hitherto." It is hardly necessary to say how this tactful and sympathetic message was received. A poetic speaker upon the succeeding day described it as coming suddenly and acceptably—like a streak of beauteous and brilliant light—upon the assembled multitude of distinguished people. As in so many other cases in Her Majesty's career, it was the right word in the right place, and higher praise it is difficult to give.

In these various continental meetings and discussions New Zealand had taken some part, as a rule, but it was not always the part of one really anxious for closer relations. The fact is that a thousand miles of stormy ocean rolling between, and the existence of many difficult and self-raised local problems and experiments, had made these beautiful islands—the Britain of the Southern seas—more inclined to stand alone within the Empire than to join in a confederation of the Australasian Colonies. Loyal New Zealanders believed in many cases that such a federation would result in ultimate separation from England; others feared the consequences of inter-colonial free trade; others, again, foresaw an overshadowing of local influence and prestige, and the submerging of New Zealand under the strong waves of an Australian nationality. But whatever the reasons, the people have certainly not taken kindly to the idea, and to-day are in the throes of more experimental and theoretical, democratic and socialistic, legislation than any other country or nation in the world. The leaders are perhaps of a somewhat demagogic character, but aside from the veteran politician, Sir George Grey (ex-Governor and ex-Premier), they remain apparently attached to British connection. Motives cannot, of course, be gone into or judged, but in this they no doubt represent the sentiment of the people as a whole. The Earl of Onslow, who was appointed Governor in 1889, and who some years later described his Government by saying that the Prime Minister had been an itinerant vendor of useful articles, his Minister for Defence a workingman, and his Minister for Lands a Scotch shepherd, put a finger on one of the causes for this quiet conquest of a crude democracy by the Crown, when he declared at the opening of the New Zealand and South Seas Exhibition that :

"It is difficult adequately to represent a Sovereign whose life, conduct, and accomplishments have been the admiration of all contemporary sovereigns and a subject of envy and reproach to all republics. It is now ten years since I first had the honour of serving Her Majesty, and since I first had the opportunity of studying her wonderful acquaintance with the politics of all Europe and the growth and constant change of her Colonial and Indian Empire. In her retirement she has probably more leisure to indulge in that careful study of all that is going on around us than would be the case were the splendour of her Court greater or the ceremonials more frequent."

In 1890, New Zealand celebrated its jubilee of fifty years of life under the British Crown, and received the hearty congratulations of the Queen on its "prosperity and good government," as well as her "warm wishes for continued welfare." And, as the years roll on in New Zealand and Australia, they continue to bring many changes, and the ever present ebb or flow of Conservative sentiment and Liberal action. But through it all the Queen's personality stamps a steadily increasing principle of loyalty in the hearts of the people, and is proving a powerful lever in the maintenance and strengthening of British connection. This influence has been aided by the steadying effect of the financial crisis and collapse which came to Australia, and which had struck New Zealand some years before as the result of too lavish a public expenditure. It has checked the buoyancy which sometimes degenerated into bombast, the confidence which bordered upon bravado, the patriotism which through self-satisfaction and ignorance became mere localism, the material prosperity which strangled the higher and nobler objects of a national life. With this negative force has come the positive one of appointing a superior type of men to the governorship of the colonies, and the useful vice-regal work of Lord Jersey, Lord Hopetoun, Lord Kintore, the Earl of Glasgow, Lord Gormanstown, and Lord Brassey.

In the far Southern seas able members of the Imperial Upper House have thus found room for statecraft and the exercise of qualities of tact, and heart, and hand, as representatives of a noble Sovereign and a great motherland. Through them the Queen is yearly exercising a wider influence and power upon Australasian life and character, and this deputed force, added to that of her own reputation and splendid reign, is proving a very powerful factor in the developments of the present and future, as it has been in the history of the past.

SIR CHARLES TUPPER, BART, G.C.M.G , C.B., M.P.

THE HON. GEORGE BROWN.

CHAPTER XXII.

South Africa under the Queen.

IN no country of the British Empire has the dismemberment craze of 1850 and 1870 wrought so much harm as in South Africa. Nowhere have racial troubles been so prominent, and a firm hand and firm policy so necessary to peace and the very preliminaries of prosperity. When, in 1806, the Cape finally became British territory, troubles had immediately arisen between the English settlers, the former Dutch or Boer owners, and the myriad tribes of surrounding natives. At the time of the Queen's accession, the whole region was in a state of turmoil. War with the natives seemed a normal condition of affairs; heavy expenditures had made the very name of the colony distasteful to ministers at home; while governors and generals had to leave the country one after the other, in a state of mingled disgust and disappointment with their work and its results.

The complications were still further increased, about 1837, by the abolition of slavery, the consequent discontent of the Boer settlers—who were determined to have slaves, and to treat the unfortunate natives as they liked—and the movement northward which was at once commenced by them. This "trekking" resulted in the foundation of the Transvaal and the independence of the Orange Free State, and marks one of the most disgraceful incidents in the whole history of the "Little England" school. It is hard to look back upon that period with equanimity. Earl Grey, as Colonial Secretary, threw a firebrand of folly into Australia and the Cape by his efforts, in 1849, to continue and increase the export of convicts to the Colonies. He was checked, and the transportation system finally stopped a few years later; but not before his policy had aroused much and keen ill-feeling. Meantime, in South Africa, fierce wars were being waged with the natives, mainly because of the absence of organized policy and the constant vacillation of the Colonial Office.

The natural difficulties of government were enhanced a thousand-fold by the anti-colonial feeling in England, which about this time commenced its sweep of supremacy. To this school of thought colonies were an unmitigated burden, and under no circumstances should British responsibilities be added to in the future. Hence the inevitable troubles along fluctuating frontiers in different parts of the world, and especially amidst the seething mass of African races. Finally it was decided in 1851 that, as the Boers in what was called the Orange River Sovereignty, and in the Transvaal districts, were making difficulties, it would be wise to give them their independence—without regard to the Englishmen settled amongst them. To this end Sir George Russell Clerk, a former Governor of Bombay, was sent out in 1853, and he very soon carried the policy into effect. A feeling of dismay was general at the Cape, and the indignation of the deserted British subjects extreme when, on March 11th, 1854, the flag of the new republic was hoisted in place of the Union Jack. The British element in the abandoned countries at once sent a deputation home to protest; and in the meantime a number of enthusiastic meetings were held, in the confident belief that England would never permanently consent to such an action. At one gathering, in the town of Smithfield, the following quaint resolution was carried:

"Resolved, that this meeting, before separating for the day, do with heart and lungs, nurtured and invigorated by the untainted air of freedom, and with right, true, loyal feelings, join devotedly, first in our most beautiful and sacred National Anthem, and then sincerely and vigorously in three hearty cheers for our beloved Sovereign Lady Queen Victoria; and may her reign and that of her children be long and permanent, happy and glorious, over the Orange River Sovereignty."

But it was not to be. The anti-colonial sentiment was in full swing under the effect of temporary free-trade prosperity, and the teachings of Mr. Bright, Mr. Cobden, and narrow-minded *doctrinaires* such as Mr. Goldwin Smith. The Duke of Newcastle, who at heart was an Imperialist, and in after years showed himself a true Briton, could only say that Cape Town and the harbour of Table Bay was really all that England required in South Africa. A languid debate in the Commons showed that the Government policy was almost unanimously approved, and Tories, like Sir John Pakington and Sir Frederick Thesiger, joined Liberal disintegrationists in denouncing Imperialism and sneering at colonization.

Not long afterwards representative institutions were given to Cape Colony, and Sir George Grey was despatched as Governor and High Commissioner to try to soothe the bitter racial prejudices and modify the general conditions of discontent. This great pro-consul was the type of man who makes or saves empires. During his long official career he was doomed to coldness and ingratitude from governments, but could always depend upon the approbation and sympathy of the Queen. To Her Majesty, in these years of "Little England" supremacy, there must have been much that was painful and opposed to her more far-sighted statecraft in the policy of the Home Government towards the Colonies. For instance, in 1857, an urgent despatch came to Sir George Grey from Lord Canning, telling him of serious troubles in India— the rising at Meerut, the fall of Delhi, and a possible rebellion of all the native forces in Central India. To the accompanying appeal for aid Sir George at once responded by ordering *on his own responsibility* the transports, which were in Simon's Bay *en route* to China, to proceed to Calcutta. The troops, thus diverted from their destination at a tremendous personal risk to the High Commissioner, were those which arrived in time to enable Sir Colin Campbell to relieve Lucknow; and, in the words of Lord Malmesbury—afterwards Foreign Secretary—they " probably saved India."

In addition to sending the China army, Sir George also despatched his own forces—the Royal Artillery, etc.—together with great quantities of military stores and £60,000 in specie from the Cape treasury. Little public attention was paid to these services. The Government said nothing publicly, though privately they were impelled to profess thanks. But the Queen and the Prince Consort were delighted with his conduct, and fully appreciated its value. On October 20th, 1857, Mr. Labouchere, Colonial Secretary, and afterwards Lord Taunton, despatched the following significant letter, in connection with his official acknowledgment of what Sir George had done:

" In writing to me on the subject of your last despatch, the Queen has commanded me to express to you in a private letter ' her high personal appreciation of your services, and her gratification at the loyalty of her subjects at the Cape.' You will at the same time receive Her Majesty's approbation of the measures you have adopted in an official form."

Meanwhile, Sir George Grey was getting into deeper and deeper water with the administrations at home. His action in connection with India was only one of several which, to the current conception of colonial government, seemed decidedly dangerous. The fact of the matter was that he possessed many of the qualities of an Imperial ruler, and few of those which enable a man to become the mere registering machine of distant and contradictory, and perhaps ignorant, orders. And he was tremendously popular in South Africa. So much was this the case that his scheme of local confederation, broached in 1859 to the infinite disgust of the Home Government, might really have been achieved had he received Imperial support. He was, however, too far in advance of his time; and even Lord Carnarvon, who, twenty years afterwards, tried to carry the scheme out on his own account, was, as Under-Colonial Secretary, mainly instrumental in recalling one whom he did not hesitate to designate as " a dangerous man."

The particulars of this recall, the protests by the population of South Africa, and its reversal at the direct instigation of the Queen, are very interesting. Through indirect communication from Mr. Greville, the well-known diarist and Clerk of the Privy Council, Sir George Grey heard afterwards that when the question of his recall had come up in the Cabinet, Lord Derby—the Prime Minister—accompanied by Mr. Greville, visited the Queen at Windsor, and informed Her Majesty of the decision arrived at. To this she was very unwilling to assent. " The great services which Sir George had rendered, especially in the late trying crisis in Imperial affairs, had disposed her strongly in his favour, and it was with feelings of repugnance that she contemplated his removal." Lord Derby, however, pressed his advice, and ultimately Her

Majesty yielded.   Shortly afterwards Lord Palmerston came into power, and
when Sir George Grey landed at Liverpool he received the news of his reappointment.   This had been the first act of the Duke of Newcastle as Colonial
Secretary, and upon the direct request of the Queen.   And before he went back
to his post Her Majesty received him with all honour and cordiality.   Mr. W.
L. Rees states in his elaborate biography of Sir George Grey, that the Prince
Consort on this occasion informed the Governor of the Queen's " approval of the
measures taken by him, and the policy of Confederation which he had pursued,
expressing without hesitation her opinion that the plans proposed were beneficent, worthy of a great ruler, honourable to herself, and advantageous to her
people."   His Royal Highness added that the Queen had read all Sir George
had written upon colonial subjects, that she regretted having been led to consent
to his recall, and that she had personally obtained the reversal of the decision.

Speaking at Sydney, New South Wales, in 1891, Sir George Grey referred
to this matter, and to what might have occurred had the views of Her Majesty
and the result of his own work been allowed free play :

" When I was a representative of the Queen in Africa I had arranged a federation of the
different States there, all having agreed to come into it except one; but the plan was regarded
with disfavour both by the Ministry and the Opposition of the day in England, and the
consequence was that I was summarily dismissed.   One person in the Empire held that I
was right in the action taken, and that person was the Queen.   Upon her representation I
was reinstated.   Her Majesty, together with the Prince Consort, held that it was necessary
to preserve to the Empire openings for the poor and the adventurous, and experience had
shown that the Queen better represented the feelings of the British people on that question
than did the Ministers of the day.   The Queen held, rightly, that the energies of the British
race should spread the Empire as instinct moved them, so long as no wrong was done to
other people."

As if to accentuate the expression of their Imperialistic sentiments, the
Queen and Prince Albert had also arranged at this interview to allow Prince
Alfred to visit South Africa, and thus in person testify their appreciation of
colonial loyalty and their practical disapprobation of the movement then going on
in the political circles of England.   While the Prince of Wales was voicing their
feelings in British America, another son was to represent them in the dominions
of the Crown in Africa.   The Governor at once returned to the Colony, and was
welcomed by every demonstration of popular pleasure—a feeling which was added
to, if possible, by the announcement that for the first time in its history a British
Prince was to visit South Africa, and in person receive the tributes of loyal respect
felt by the people for their Sovereign and her family.   On July 24th, 1860, the
Royal midshipman arrived at Table Bay in H.M.S. " Euryalus," and on the
succeeding day entered Cape Town amidst the wildest enthusiasm and a mingling of races, colours, creeds, languages, and dress, such as the Bridge of Galata
could only equal.   Boers, English, Germans, Zulus, Kafirs, and a hundred native

varieties joined in the welcome. At night the capital was brilliantly illuminated, and a local record declares that " never since the Cape became a British Colony were the streets so gaily decorated." Several days were spent at Government House in a round of balls, dinner-parties, receptions, drives, and excursions, and then the Royal visitor embarked for Port Elizabeth, from whence it was proposed that he should travel through the country parts of Cape Colony, and visit Kaffraira, the Orange Free State, and Natal.

Sir George Grey tells us that it was amusing and instructive to see the instant transition, when they stepped aboard the " Euryalus," from the Royal Prince to the simple midshipman. On land he was the Queen's son and representative, taking precedence of even the Governor; on the ship he was only a young and very minor officer. On August 6th the party arrived at Port Elizabeth, and were loyally welcomed. Between that place and Grahamstown the journey was one continued ovation to the Prince. Wherever they passed an isolated house, a small village, a rural inn, or even a native hut, the people endeavoured to show their pleasure by decorations and every means at their command. Grahamstown was entered under triumphal arches and amid waving flags, cheering crowds, and stirring strains of military music. King William's Town was reached six days later, and from here Sir George Grey wrote to a friend, in a letter preserved by the Prince Consort amongst his private papers, that "nothing can be more gratifying than everything connected with Prince Alfred's journeys here. He is a noble young fellow, full of life and fun. He is received everywhere with transports of delight. He rides as fast and far as I can myself, delights in every style of life, wins the hearts of all the native chiefs, gladdens the Europeans by the interest he takes in their prosperity and by the good influence he exercises over the natives, as also by turning out in dress, and even in minute articles of equipment, a thorough South African sportsman."

From William's Town the expedition was continued to Bloemfontein through ten days of constantly changing scenery, sometimes lovely and sometimes sombre, through grassy and woodless plateaux, over rapid mountain torrents and through deep wooded ravines. Much hunting was done by the young Prince, and the rough-and-ready life enjoyed with a zest which the luxuries of Buckingham Palace or Windsor had perhaps never afforded him. Through the Drakensberg Mountains, and many settlements, native villages, and mission stations, the journey proceeded, Prince Alfred being everywhere received with respectful curiosity, mingled with popular acclamations. At one place the natives danced with enthusiasm, and sang a chant of welcome, consisting chiefly of the words: "We have seen the child of heaven. We have seen the son of the Queen." On August 23rd Bloemfontein was reached, and the feeling of the people summed up in the motto of a triumphal arch, " Loyal though discarded." After traversing the Orange Free State, Natal was reached a week later, and at Pietermaritzburg a most loyal welcome received. From D'Urban, on the coast, the party re-embarked for Cape Town on September 5th, after an overland tour of 1,200 miles—summed up as follows by a local history of the trip:

"It was certainly a progress such as no Royal Prince had ever made before—among wild beasts and wild men, over mountain ranges and desert tracks and fertile pastures; from the homes of European civilization to the huts of barbarism, from the centre of the hostile hordes who for so many long years waged war upon our advancing colonization to the rapidly progressing prosperity of Natal, then (though not now) Britain's youngest colonial settlement in Africa. And wherever he appeared the welcome that greeted him was alike cordial and enthusiastic. The English settler and the Dutch boer were equally sincere in their fervent loyalty; and the natives, whether aboriginal, Hottentot, Fingo, Kafir, Basuto, or Zulu, were more loudly demonstrative still."

Amongst those who returned to Cape Town with the Royal party was Sandilli, a prominent native chieftain. His admiration of the way in which the Queen's son—the admired and fêted guest of Southern Africa—resumed his place on board ship and performed his routine duties found expression in an Address, the translation of which declares that when the son of a great Queen becomes the subject of a subject in order to learn wisdom it is easy to understand why the English are a great and mighty nation. "What we have now learned," he concludes, "shall be transmitted to our wondering countrymen and handed down to our children, who will be wiser than their fathers, and your mighty Queen shall be their Sovereign and ours in all time coming." The few days afterwards spent at the Colonial capital were filled with fêtes, and dinners, and balls, together with the more important laying, by Prince Alfred, of the first stone of the great new harbour works. Beneath the shadow of the curious flat-crested mountain, under the hot rays of a Southern sun, and in the presence of the largest gathering ever held in South African history, this important ceremony was performed. Following it came the laying of the foundation stone of the Alfred Sailor's Home and the inauguration of a new Library and Museum. To the latter the Prince presented Knight's Shakespeare and Pictorial History of England, and from the dais he gave to the people and Legislature of Cape Colony a splendid portrait of the Queen. In acknowledging the gift, Mr. Porter, Attorney-General of the Colony, spoke of the visit and its results in historic words:

"In welcoming Prince Alfred to the Cape, where we are still in many respects in the day of small things, we could not, of course, aspire to emulate the splendour of the reception which the Prince of Wales will have received in the great Colony of Canada. . . . But what the Cape people could do they have striven to do with heart and soul, and if they have in any degree succeeded in testifying their love and loyalty towards Her Majesty the Queen their sense of the honour that was done them by the visit of her son, and their respectful affection for His Royal Highness himself—a feeling which his simple dignity and constant courtesy has strongly and universally excited—if, I say, they have in any degree

THE RIGHT HON. W. E. FORSTER, M.P.

THE RIGHT HON. SIR GEORGE GREY, K.C.B.

LORD KELVIN, G.C.V.O., L.R.S.

LORD LISTER, F.R.S., D.C.L., LL.D.

succeeded in these things, then they have fulfilled their whole desire and have received their high reward. Let His Royal Highness be assured that he carries away with him the heartiest good wishes of all ranks, races, creeds, and colours in South Africa; that the people here, confident that, in after life, he will tread no path but that of honour, will watch with interest his future career, and that they will ever reckon it as one of the many services rendered to them by their Governor, Sir George Grey, that through his instrumentality the auspicious visit of Prince Alfred was arranged—a visit which has, as it were, annihilated ocean spaces and brought us in feeling so close to the old mother country that we seem to see her cliffs again."

In this otherwise accurate speech a very natural error is made in attributing the Royal visit to Sir George Grey's influence. The latter was merely the occasion—not the cause. His presence at Windsor had enabled the Queen to discuss with him a tour which was really a part of the Imperial policy mapped out by herself and the Prince Consort, and which, through this and coming years, resulted in Royal visits to Canada and South Africa, India and Australia. But Her Majesty none the less appreciated the services of the Governor, and after the Prince had returned home he received a letter saying that: "The Queen is anxious to express personally both the Prince Consort's and her own thanks for the very great kindness shown our child during his most interesting tour in that fine colony, and she trusts that the effect produced on the nation and people in general will be as lasting and beneficial as it must have been on Prince Alfred to have witnessed the manner in which Sir George Grey devotes his whole time and energy to promote the happiness and welfare of his fellow-creatures." To follow the further administration of this great but peculiar man, in either South Africa or New Zealand, is, of course, impossible. For many years after he left the Cape, in 1861, everything was in confusion, but Sir George Grey has lived —though in a somewhat disappointed and erratic seclusion—to see at a great age most of his earliest proposals adopted and his views of Colonial administration accepted. There are some important exceptions, but into them it is unnecessary to go.

During his long cruise in the "Galatea" as a captain of Her Majesty's Navy, Prince Alfred—then Duke of Edinburgh—once more visited the Cape. He landed at Cape Town on August 19th, 1867, and was received in State by Sir Philip Wodehouse, the Governor, by a motley but enthusiastic crowd of people, and with loyal decorations throughout the city. Memories of his former visit were many, and a warm personal affection and interest was shown. Addresses were, of course, very numerous, and the usual *levée* and State ball were held. But the public ball arranged by the citizens was perhaps the most splendid affair of the kind, and is described as one of the most successful and brilliant fêtes ever witnessed in Cape Town. A local Ingoldsby gave an amusing description of it at the time, in which the last verse declares that:

" There were gardens and bowers,

And fountains and flowers,
And mosses, and ferns, and glass prisms in showers,
And calico, too—
Glazed, pink, white, and blue—
And mirrors, and curtains, whose hanging so nice is,
And gas-lights in all sorts of shapes and devices;
Supper-rooms, whist-rooms, and rooms for potation,
And nice little corners for quiet flirtation."

Various other functions were participated in or performed, and on September 7th the Duke sailed for Simon's Bay, and from there took a prolonged hunting trip into the interior. Many elephants and much other game were bagged, and at the end of the month a farewell visit was paid the capital and a ball given by His Royal Highness to those who had proffered such loyal and kindly hospitality. A *levée* at Government House was also held, and then the departure amid long lines of Cape Mounted Rifles, volunteer cavalry, cheering people, singing school children, and bands of music, closed the second Royal visit to this land of mixed races and—of too frequently mixed government. During the ensuing ten years South Africa passed through alternate stages of neglect and interference. The Manchester school was still predominant in England, and all the waste of energy and money in forced or unorganized action, which resulted from its policy of vacillation and indifference, had a naturally disastrous influence at the Cape, though counteracted to some extent by the loyalty of the people and the personal qualities of some of the Governors. By 1874, however, the reaction at home against the anti-Colonial principles had taken firm root, and the policy of Mr. Disraeli as Premier soon began to prove the fact. Lord Carnarvon became Secretary for the Colonies, and with a broadened mind and the wider Imperial patriotism which time had commenced to develop amongst English leaders he saw that local confederation was the best policy for South Africa. But the scheme which the Queen had approved nearly a quarter of a century before, and which Sir George Grey might then have carried out, was now neither popular nor immediately practicable. For peculiar reasons of a local nature and temperament the people resented the Colonial Secretary's advice and would have none of his policy. Mr J. A. Froude, the historian, and a trusted friend of Lord Carnarvon's, was sent to the Cape, and Sir Garnet Wolseley to Natal, but they could do nothing to calm the curious excitement. A conference held in London in 1876, and presided over by General Wolseley, came to the same negative ending.

Meanwhile, Sir Bartle Frere had been filling the difficult post of Governor and High Commissioner. His policy of conciliation and union might ultimately have won the day had the Transvaal annexation been sustained at home. But Mr. Gladstone's bitter attacks upon that action, his subsequent success at the polls, and the natural encouragement thus given to the Boers, brought on the ensuing war and the disaster of Majuba Hill, accompanied by the unfortunate surrender of the British Government, the recall of Sir Bartle Frere, and the utter disorganization of existing relations throughout South Africa. Had the bold and determined policy commenced in 1878 been carried out, the countries up to the Zambesi would by now have been united in some form of federal or Imperial combination, and Cecil Rhodes, instead of fighting Matabeles in a miserable corner of the country, might have been using his superb abilities in manipulating the details of a great confederation.

While, however, these conditions were still in the latter stages of development, Prince Albert Victor and Prince George of Wales paid a visit to the Colony during their cruise around the world in the "Bacchante." They were received on February 21st, 1881, by Sir Hercules Robinson, who had not long before succeeded Sir Bartle Frere. Of the latter the Royal Diary says: "Ask any colonist haphazard—Afrikander or English—his opinion of Sir Bartle Frere, and in ninety-nine cases out of a hundred you will be told that he was conscientious, able, far-seeing, magnanimous, truthful, and loyal." During their stay the Princes made the occasion a private rather than a State visit, and for that reason saw much of the country and probably enjoyed it much more than would otherwise have been the case. They studied the natives and visited Cetewayo, who had not yet been reinstated in a pórtion of his territories. To the natives, says the Journal, "the Queen" represents an ideal English power, far off in the distance, but whose real behests, when once clearly understood and plainly given, "they would no more think of disobeying than civilized nations would disregard those of Heaven or of the Almighty." Unfortunately, both of these things are sometimes done. The significant statement is also made that "all natives, the Basutos, Zulus, Bechuanas, invariably profess their desire to come under ' the Queen' in preference to the Cape Colonial authority."

Ostrich-farming was studied, bok shooting and other kinds of hunting indulged in, Simon's Town visited, the hospitalities of several local gentlemen— Boer and English—accepted, and the shores of Africa left at the end of March with the general impression that it "is a quarter of the world where England has not been happy." Of course, their visit had occurred at a specially unfortunate period, and one which it is probable can never again be equalled in its tangle of conflicting policies, interests, and uncertainties. During the eight following years Sir Hercules Robinson—now Lord Rosmead—did much to pacify the antagonistic races and weld together diverse interests. Fortunately for all concerned, he was given a comparatively free hand in carrying out the policy which he has himself described in a sentence: "As Governor of a self-governing colony, I have endeavoured to walk within the lines of the Constitution; and as Her Majesty's High Commissioner for South Africa, I have, whilst striving to act with equal justice and consideration to the claims and susceptibilities of all classes and races, endeavoured at the same time to establish on a broad and secure basis British authority as the paramount power in South Africa."

He early set himself the difficult task of checking Portugal and Germany in acquisitions which might have forever stopped the northern expansion of British interests, and eventually succeeded, during the administration of Lord Salisbury, in taking possession of Bechuanaland and extending the British sphere of influence up to the Zambesi.   When he left the Cape, in 1889, to the administration of Sir Henry Loch, two notable developments of the time must be mentioned. One was the ever-increasing complexity of government as fresh annexations and new responsibilities were assumed.   At this period Cape Colony was under responsible government and Natal only partially so—the latter having a Governor of its own.   Basutoland, Pondoland, the British Protectorate and the " Sphere of British influence," were under the Governor of Cape Colony as High Commissioner, while the Crown colony of Bechuanaland was under him as Governor of the Cape.   Zululand and Amatongaland were under the joint control of the Governors of Cape Colony and Natal, while Swaziland was controlled by alternate British and Boer Committees.   The Transvaal and the New Republic (a part of Zululand) were under British suzerainty, so far as their foreign relations were concerned, while the Orange Free State was entirely independent.   Little wonder, therefore, that the Government of South Africa was complicated and difficult !

With the arrival of Sir Henry Loch came a fresh era and a more important one for both the Colony and the Empire.   It was auspiciously opened.   In reply to the addresses at Cape Town, His Excellency very truly said of the reception given him that " I feel it was an expression on the part of the people of this great country of loyalty to the Empire and devotion to the Queen, who is regarded not only by her own subjects, but by the whole civilized world, in the highest and truest sense, as the representative of social and material greatness."   During his succeeding administration the second development which has been referred to took place—the rise of Mr. Cecil Rhodes into political power and Imperial fame. This remarkable man had already organized personal wealth and become a millionaire.   He now proceeded to organize the Chartered Company and to acquire vast interests in Matabeleland and Mashonaland and in all the undefined interior right up to the Zambesi.   Not satisfied with this, he organized political victory, as he afterwards organized military success.   On July 17th, 1890, he became Prime Minister of the Cape, and for three years his Ministry was mainly as follows—with " a purely South African policy," and as an objective point in the distance " a red line from the Cape to Cairo ":—

Prime Minister	Hon. Cecil J. Rhodes
Treasurer	Hon. J. X. Merriman
Colonial Secretary	Hon. J. W. Sauer
Attorney-General	Hon. J. Rose-Innes
Commissioner of Crown Lands	Sir James Sivewright
Secretary for Native Affairs	Hon. P. H. Faure

Three years later this Cabinet was reorganized, and Mr. Merriman went into violent opposition, being succeeded by a former Premier, Sir J. Gordon Sprigg. Six months afterwards Natal received full constitutional government, and Sir John Robinson, who had represented that Colony at the London Imperial Conference of 1887, became Prime Minister. Mr. Rhodes' administration was wonderfully successful. With the help of Mr. J. H. Hofmeyr, the loyal leader of the Dutch elements at the Cape, he conciliated local interests, while winning, in his other capacity of President of the South African Company, the fullest confidence of the Imperial authorities. By these means, and the co-operation of Sir Henry Loch, he brought into the politics and business of these varied territories a degree of united labour and harmonious action which would have before seemed almost impossible. During March, 1890, the Governor unveiled a statue of the Queen, erected in the gardens of Parliament House, Cape Town, as a memorial of the Jubilee, and, in doing so, spoke of the heart of the country as pulsating with the awakened knowledge that she possessed a great future history and a power of pushing enterprises of civilization and wealth—with British help—into vast unknown regions. He concluded by declaring that:

"The statue which I have now the honour to unveil represents, in the person of the Queen, the emblem of the Empire's greatness—an Empire strong in the love and loyalty of her children.

"We speak of the unity of South Africa; in that unity I not only include this great country, and our sister Colony of Natal, but those important and friendly States which have a like interest with ourselves in its progressive prosperity, and who are alike secure from external danger through the power of that Empire which has done so much throughout the world for the advancement of civilization, and in the defence of freedom—a Power represented by one who unites all creeds and all parties in love and respect for the Queen, the Wife, the Mother, and the Woman. God save the Queen."

The Cape *Times*, in commenting upon the speech and the ceremony, declared that they came at a moment when there is "opened to us a future of prosperity which was never dreamed of before." Wool, diamonds, and gold had, in turn, succeeded each other in South African production, and of these gold was about to prove the greatest. In 1894, owing mainly to the discoveries in the Transvaal, South Africa produced over £7,000,000 worth of the precious metal, and eclipsed Australia, as well as all other countries, in its current annual production. While this material development was going on, Mr. Rhodes was pushing national affairs into a state of continuous progress and expansion. Unity of peoples, construction of railways and telegraphs, promotion of an internal customs arrangement, preferential trade within the Empire, and extension of communication through the continent to Egypt, was his policy. It was ambitious in design and great even in its partial execution. It is said to have had the hearty support of the Prince of Wales, who did, early in 1895, preside over a London meeting addressed by Rhodes and Jameson. It probably had the sympathy of the Queen, who about the same time made the great colonist a member of her Imperial Privy Council. In the person of the Duke of Fife, who acted as chairman of the Chartered Company, the policy, as a whole, was brought very near to the Royal family.

That it has not completely succeeded is only an accident of to-day, and the result of a delay to which it was naturally subject so long as the Boers and the Transvaal were allowed to exercise a sort of dominating weakness in the counsels and policy of Southern Africa. Much, however, was done despite pessimists and remnants of the Manchester school, such as Mr. Labouchere; and the subsequent Matabele war and Jameson raid. As Lord Knutsford pointed out in a speech in June, 1894, the Cape Customs Union Act had brought several of the countries into close commercial connection with each other, while the definite incorporation of Zululand in the Empire and the onward sweep of the Chartered Company promised to bring about his own dream of " one great federated South Africa from the Cape to the Zambesi." To so great an extent can the influence of one man extend that about this time, when Mr. Rhodes proposed that in future, throughout all territory held by the South African Company, British goods should have a preference by Act of Parliament, as well as by the policy of the Company, the *Times* declared him a man of genius and spoke of his powers as the founder of new States, but went on in sarcastic enquiry to doubt "whether the policy of the Empire should be controlled by the ideas of Mr. Rhodes." And in obedience to the still dominant free-trade views of England this splendid Imperial opportunity was allowed to slip by. The South African statesman, however, has never been afraid to speak his mind, and a few months before this he had handled the proprietor of *Truth*—January 6th, at Cape Town—in a way which is also applicable to the free-trade *doctrinaires* who refused to support his Imperialistic conceptions :

" It is an anomaly that a cynical sybarite in London, who devotes his time to the vilification of anyone who becomes above the average, and includes in that the family of our Sovereign—it is an anomaly that that man should appeal to a working community. The electors of Northampton require to be educated, they require to be told that the ' little England ' he advocates is destruction to their industry, and to have pointed out to them the necessity of the mother country, in its own future interests, keeping in with the colonies. If she does not, with foreign powers becoming more and more exclusive, England will be in a position similar to that of a ship out of which the provender has been taken, but in which the rats are left."

The Transvaal has proved a temporary check to this policy, and in 1896 Mr. Rhodes is no longer President of the Chartered Company nor Premier of Cape Colony. But he is none the less the greatest man in South Africa. Two incidents must be mentioned as illustrating his broad Imperial views. In 1893, during the crash of banks and general collapse of Australian finances, he cabled the Governments of those colonies an offer of financial aid from the then redundant revenues of South Africa should they find themselves really in need of assistance.   It was refused, but will live in history and in Australian hearts as an indication of kindly sentiment and a common nationality.   A year later he sent Mr. Hofmeyr and Sir Henry de Villiers to attend the Conference at Ottawa, in which Imperial interests and colonial trade, cable and steamship communications were to be discussed.   They came pledged to support and forward better trade relations, and in doing so indicated the nature of the South African leader, as they proved his far-sighted statesmanship.

Meantime, Royal influence in South · Africa had not been wanting. The Jubilee celebrations were as enthusiastic and harmonious as in any other part of the Empire.   The confidence of the natives in the great Queen, whom they could not perhaps understand, but for that very reason could respect in still greater measure, grew stronger as the memories of Majuba Hill and the defeat of the British became fainter.   The knowledge of Her Majesty's Imperial sympathies and her action regarding Sir George Grey no doubt impressed themselves upon the minds of succeeding Governors, and, once the burden and dead-weight of the anti-Colonial ascendency had been removed from British politics, were asserted, consciously or unconsciously, in the expansion of territory and development of unity.   Sir Bartle Frere picked up the threads of Imperial policy dropped by Grey, and he is known to have always been in pronounced favour with Her Majesty and the Royal family.   Speaking at the unveiling of his statue on the Thames Embankment in June, 1888, the Prince of Wales referred to him as "a great and valued public servant of the Crown, and at the same time a highly esteemed and dear friend of myself."

Sir Bartle Frere failed, it is true, to carry out his own policy, but, despite the Gladstone Government and the Transvaal surrender, Sir Hercules Robinson and Sir Henry Loch have in recent years carried it on to a great though not final conclusion.   They are now both Peers of the realm—an honour rarely conferred upon previous Colonial governors.   The statue of the Queen erected in Cape Town during 1890 was duplicated by a splendid memorial of the same nature in Pietermaritzberg, the capital of Natal.   The occasion of its unveiling by the Governor on July 8th of the same year brought together a great gathering of people, as well as of Ministers and members of the Legislature and public bodies.   And Her Majesty's personal interest in South Africa has been shown not only in her influence upon the policy of the Governors and the loyalty of the people, but in occasional bits of correspondence which have been allowed to creep into publicity through the memoirs of public men during the last half century. This interest has been also felt by the Royal family.   The visits of the Duke of Edinburgh speak for themselves, as did that of the Prince of Wales' sons. Speaking of the heir to the Throne in this connection, Sir Donald Currie, who has had so intimate and important a part in the development of South Africa, said in June, 1894, that:

" The Prince of Wales is always anxious to learn, from whoever may be Secretary of State for the time, what is going on in every part of our Colonial Empire, and it has been my duty on more than one occasion to communicate to His Royal Highness events of interest which have taken place in South Africa. I hold it to be a great advantage that we have in the Royal family of this country men—aye, and I may say ladies, too—who devote themselves zealously to the discharge of the great duties of their office in order that they may bear witness to the Colonies and foreign nations alike of the unity of the British Empire."

To this much troubled and harassed part of her realms the Queen has therefore given a stable centre of authority for the people of all races and creeds to look up to and respect ; has shown them sympathy in their sorrows, and tried to help them in their complex difficulties ; has rewarded and personally encouraged their public men and Governors ; has enabled them to be loyal to her personality and to their allegiance even when suffering from the effects of popular English neglect and ministerial indifference or incapacity. Hence the present power of the Crown in South Africa and its increasing prestige in the expanding future.

H.I.M. VICTORIA,
EMPRESS FREDERICK OF GERMANY AND PRINCESS ROYAL OF ENGLAND.

H.R.H. PRINCESS LOUISE, MARCHIONESS OF LORNE.

H.R.H. BEATRICE, PRINCESS HENRY OF BATTENBERG.

CHAPTER XXIII.

INDIA UNDER THE QUEEN.

THE direct share taken by the Queen in governing India has been keen in the interest displayed and great in the result achieved. Her Majesty's correspondence with British statesmen in India and with British leaders at home ; her advice during critical periods, such as the Indian Mutiny ; her wise selection of representative Indian leaders for Imperial honours—specially created by herself for the purpose of rewarding their services ; her acceptance of the title of Empress, and her despatch of the Prince of Wales and Prince Albert Victor at different periods to personally represent her before the people ; have combined to make the Queen a potent force in the control and maintenance of British power in the vast Eastern Empire.

During the first twenty years of her reign the Governors-General sent out to represent the Sovereign, and to carry on the policy of the East India Company, had duties of the greatest magnitude. It was an era of war and force and annexation, combined with vigorous efforts to create and maintain respect for law and order ; to repress individual caprice and religious license ; to extend commerce and improve finance and taxation. The legend of British rule was impressed deeply upon the minds of the masses, the names of great viceroys were slowly and surely enshrined in the history of the peninsula, while the British flag floated over constantly growing territories and expanding populations. Lord Auckland and Lord Ellenborough, Lord Hardinge and Lord Dalhousie, and Lord Canning succeeded one another amidst these conditions and marching events, and with each of them the Queen maintained a close relationship in both correspondence and advice. Between 1842 and 1844 Lord Ellenborough's letters to Her Majesty are of special interest. They deal with our relations with Russia, the Afghans and Herat, the campaign in China, the deplorable Afghan war, the annexation of Scinde, and various details of defence and military arrangement.

Writing on October 20th, 1843, the Governor-General very accurately pointed out to the Queen that "in Europe peace is maintained by the balance of power amongst the various States. In India all balance has been overthrown by our own preponderance, and to exist we must continue to be supreme. The necessity of our position may often render necessary here experiences wholly unsuited to the state of things which prevail in Europe." Some months before this—

January 18th—Lord Ellenborough hinted quite plainly at the assumption of a dignity which it took nearly a quarter of a century in time, the changes caused by a great rebellion, and the appearance of a really Imperial statesman at home, to bring about. "Lord Ellenborough," said the letter, "cannot but feel that the anomalous and unintelligible position of the local government of India excites great practical difficulties in our relations with native chiefs, who in an empire like ours have no natural place. All these difficulties would be removed were your Majesty to become the nominal head of the empire. The princes and chiefs of India would be proud of their position as feudatories of an Empress."

And then he goes on to make some suggestions as to legislation. But Lord Ellenborough had too much imagination and personal will to commend him to the Court of Directors of the East India Company. Like Lord Beaconsfield in his later Imperial aspirations, and Lord Durham, and Sir George Grey, and Lord Elgin, in their colonial ideas and principles of policy, he was ahead of his time, and although the Queen might sympathize with many of his suggestions the Company did not like all the details of his policy. In this they may have been quite right, but the situation presented by Lord Ellenborough's recall in 1844 illustrated the weakness of the dual control which the mutiny of 1857 finally put an end to. His last letter to the Queen as Governor-General is interesting :

"Amidst all the difficulties with which he has had to contend in India, aggravated as they have been by the constant hostility of the Court of Directors, Lord Ellenborough has ever been sustained by the knowledge that he was serving a most gracious mistress, who would place the most favourable construction upon his conduct ; and he now humbly tenders to your Majesty the expression of his gratitude, not only for those marks of royal favour which it has been intimated to him that it is your Majesty's intention to reward his services, but yet more for that constant support which has animated all his exertions, and has mainly enabled him to place India in the hands of his successor in a state of universal peace, the result of two years of victories, and in a condition of prosperity heretofore unknown."

During the Marquess of Dalhousie's great viceroyalty the letters which passed between the Sovereign and her representative were many. When, after eight years of arduous service in the annexation of vast territories, and the extension of beneficial laws and government, he returned, broken in health—and, as it turned out, on the verge of death—the Queen despatched a letter of welcome which must indeed have been pleasing to the worn and wearied statesman. In his reply he declared that "such gracious words from a Sovereign to a subject as those with which your Majesty has greeted his return to England create emotions of gratitude too strong and deep to find fitting expression in any other than the simplest words. Lord Dalhousie therefore respectfully asks permission to thank your Majesty from his inmost heart for the touching and cheering welcome home which he feels to be the crowning honour of his life."

But it was not in correspondence of this complimentary nature—valuable as such amenities were—that the great weight of the Queen's influence was chiefly felt.

As the terrible days of the mutiny came and went Her Majesty's letters to Lord Panmure, the Secretary for War, to Lord Palmerston, the Prime Minister, or to Lord Canning, the Governor-General of India, became stronger in their terms and more pronounced in advice and commands. When the troubles commenced Lord Panmure wrote announcing the Cabinet's decision as to the despatch of certain troops, and the next day, 29th June, 1857, received the following letter. It is too characteristic and valuable to give in any but a complete form :

"The Queen has to acknowledge the receipt of Lord Panmure's letter of yesterday. She had long been of opinion that reinforcements waiting to go to India should not be delayed. The moment is certainly a very critical one, and the additional reinforcements now proposed will be much wanted. The Queen entirely agrees with Lord Panmure that it will be good policy to advise the East India Company to keep permanently a larger portion of the royal army in India than heretofore. The Empire has nearly doubled itself within the last twenty years, and the Queen's troops have been kept at the old establishment. They are the body on whom the maintenance of that Empire mainly depends, and the Company ought not to sacrifice the highest interests to love of patronage.

"The Queen hopes that the new reinforcements will be sent out in their brigade organizations, and not as detached regiments. Good commanding officers, knowing their troops, will be of the highest importance next to the troops themselves.

"The Queen must ask that the troops by whom we shall be diminished at home, by transfer of so many regiments to the Company, should be forthwith replaced by an increase of the establishment up to the number voted by Parliament, and for which the estimates have been taken ; else we denude ourselves altogether to a degree dangerous to our own safety at home, and incapable of meeting a sudden emergency, which, as the present example shows, may come upon us at any moment. If we had not reduced in such a hurry this spring, we should now have all the men wanted !

" The Queen wishes Lord Panmure to communicate this letter to Lord Palmerston. The accounts in to-day's papers from India are most distressing."

What the Queen requested was partially done, but as the days passed into months and the ever-spreading horror in India became more and more visible at home, her dissatisfaction with the Government's mode of meeting the crisis increased. On July 11th Sir Colin Campbell started to assume command, and for some weeks afterwards Her Majesty was very anxious and greatly troubled over the increasingly bad news. On the 17th of the month she wrote Lord Palmerston a letter, which intimated—according to Sir Theodore Martin's " Life of the Prince Consort "—that he under-estimated the danger, and was not taking adequate military precautions. The Premier's reply was a characteristically light one, concluding with an expression of belief that the measures of the Government were sufficient and would "follow each other step by step."

But this was not satisfactory to the Queen, and on the succeeding day she sent an elaborate Memorandum upon the subject for communication to the Cabinet. It commenced with the plain and clear-cut statement that " the Queen is anxious to impress in the most earnest manner upon her Government the necessity of our taking a comprehensive view of our military position at the present momentous crisis, instead of going on without a plan, living from hand to mouth, and taking small isolated measures without reference to each other." This vigorous expression of a not very complimentary opinion was followed up by denunciation of the recent policy of reducing the army below the Peace establishment, and of now meeting the Indian crisis by sending out a few regiments at haphazard, instead of adequately reorganizing the entire service. " The present position of the army," continued Her Majesty, " is a pitiable one. The Queen has just seen, in the camp at Aldershot, regiments which after eighteen years' foreign service in most trying climates, had come back to England to be sent out, after seven months, to the Crimea. Having passed through this destructive campaign, they have not been home for a year before they are to go to India for perhaps twenty years. This is most cruel and unfair to the gallant men who devote their services to the country."

A few days afterwards the Cabinet decided to call out the militia, and, in replying to a communication from Lord Palmerston to this effect, the Queen, on August 2nd, declared it to be a most necessary measure, and expressed the hope that it would be carried out on " a proper and sufficient scale." But there was evidently much doubt in her mind. " She must say," the letter continues, "that the last accounts from India show so formidable a state of things that the military measures hitherto taken by the Home Government, on whom the salvation of India must mainly depend, appear to the Queen as by no means adequate to the emergency. . . . The Queen hopes that the Cabinet will look the question boldly in the face." And then, with a spirit worthy of the Stuarts in their best days, Her Majesty speaks approvingly of vigorous resolutions in the House of Commons, and concludes with the remarkable rebuke to a powerful Minister : " It is generally the Government, and not the House of Commons, who hang back." The importance of this firm counsel and criticism is shown in the military activity which followed, and in a letter from Lord Clarendon, the Foreign Secretary, in which he speaks of reading " with melancholy satisfaction your Majesty's warning to the Cabinet," and declares he will " use his utmost efforts " to bring about a better condition of affairs.

So bad did things look during the succeeding month, however, that an intimation came from the French Government that it would like to send out some extra troops for the protection of the Pondicherry settlements, and from King Leopold of Belgium, offering the assistance of two regiments completely equipped. The French Emperor also offered to use his influence—then very considerable—

with the Sultan and the Egyptian Pasha to allow British troops passage through Egypt, and declared that he was quite willing they should proceed through France, if that would facilitate matters.   But the tide soon turned, and within two months the Queen's correspondence is largely taken up with approval of Lord Canning's conciliatory policy, and condemnation of the wild though natural desire for vengeance which took possession for a time of the English mind—both in England and in India.   Writing to Her Majesty on September 25th, the Governor-General declares that " there is a rabid and indiscriminate vindictiveness abroad, even amongst many who ought to set a better example, which it is impossible to contemplate without a feeling of shame."   He points out the wickedness and unwisdom of hanging or shooting 50,000 mutineers, as many demanded, and adds, with absolute truth and far-sightedness, that " for the Sovereign of England to hold and govern India without employing, and to a great degree trusting, natives, both in civil and military service, is simply impossible.   The Queen's reply is interesting :

" Lord Canning will easily believe how entirely the Queen shares his feelings of sorrow and indignation at the unchristian spirit, shown, alas ! to a great extent here by the public towards Indians in general, and towards Sepoys *without discrimination !*   It is, however, not likely to last, and comes from the horror produced by the unspeakable atrocities perpetrated against the innocent women and children, which make one's blood run cold and one's heart bleed !   For the perpetrators of these awful horrors no punishment can be severe enough, and, sad as it is, *stern* justice must be dealt out to all the guilty.

" But to the nation at large ; to the peaceable inhabitants ; to the many kindly and friendly natives who have assisted us, sheltered the fugitives, and been faithful and true ; there should be shown the greatest kindness.   They should know that there is no hatred to a brown skin—none ; but the greatest wish on their Queen's part is to see them happy, contented, and flourishing."

In this letter breathes the sympathy of a woman united with the spirit of a statesman.   So in many others of that anxious period.   On January 19th, 1858, after the news of Lucknow, the Queen wrote in characteristic terms to Sir Colin Campbell, expressing her " feelings of pride and satisfaction " at the glorious victories of himself and his "heroic troops."   And then came a word of personal regard, which the stern and rugged soldier must have greatly valued : " But Sir Colin must bear one reproof from his Queen, and that is that he exposes himself too much.   His life is most precious, and she entreats that he will neither put himself where his noble spirit would urge him to be—foremost in danger—nor fatigue himself so as to injure his health."   After an expression of grief for the gallant men who had fallen—notably General Havelock—the letter concludes with the intimation of the Queen's " great admiration and gratitude to all the European as well as native troops who have fought so nobly and gallantly," and with the fervent wish that " the God of battles may ever attend and protect Sir Colin and his noble army."

During the year following the Mutiny occurred the prolonged **Parliamentary** debates and anxious Cabinet discussions upon the assumption of the Government of India by the Crown in place of, and from, the East India Company. In this, as in the previous period, Her Majesty took an influential and intelligent part. Sir Archibald Allison, in his Memoirs, tells us that a friend of his, on returning from active work in India during the rebellion, dined with the Queen at Buckingham Palace. After dinner " Her Majesty took him aside and conversed with him in the most animated way for nearly an hour on the Indian campaign—with the whole particulars of which she showed a thorough acquaintance." The same knowledge was very clearly exhibited during the India Bill debates. She protested to Lord Ellenborough against clauses in his bill which provided for the election of certain members of the proposed Indian Council by certain selected British cities. Eventually, of course, the absurd proposition had to be withdrawn. Meantime various political troubles and changes had occurred at home, but, strengthened by the Queen's confidence, and the knowledge that his pacific policy towards the natives must eventually be approved by the people, Lord Canning held to his post, and did not resign, as had been usual upon a change of government. Then occurred Lord Ellenborough's curious conduct as head of the Board of Control which still managed Indian affairs for the Home Government.

Details of the political storm which he raised need not be gone into, but in returning certain papers to Lord Derby—who was now Premier—after the trouble was all over, the Queen, on May 21st, condemned her late Minister frankly and fully. "Lord Ellenborough must be taken to have acted hastily," wrote Her Majesty, " in at once condemning Lord Canning, and unfairly to him in doing this on private information, without hearing the Governor-General on the other side. It is always dangerous to keep up a private correspondence with inferior officers, allowing them to criticize their superiors, but it is subversive of all good government to act at once on the opinion given by inferiors." About this time the Queen also wrote Sir Colin Campbell advising him of her intention to make him a Peer of the United Kingdom in consideration of his " eminent and brilliant services "; and on receipt of the draft of the new Bill dealing with the Government of India—which had replaced previous legislative attempts in the same direction—she advised Lord Stanley, who had meanwhile succeeded Lord Ellenborough at the Board of Control, that it was " a great improvement on the former ones," and that she was consequently " not sorry for the delay and discussion which have led to a more mature measure."

Eventually the Bill passed through Parliament, and then came the question of formally transferring the Government of India from the Company to the Crown, and terminating a long period of great but unequal administration of expanding territories by a brilliant though hydra-headed commercial corporation. Much depended on the form of the Proclamation and the prestige of the proceedings, though neither fact seems to have been appreciated by Her Majesty's Ministers. The sensitive feelings of the Mahomedans, the natural soreness of multitudes of Hindoos, the necessity of using comprehensive and careful language, and the assumption of a dignified position by the Crown, seem to have been far more apparent to the Queen than to her advisers. When the Proclamation was prepared Her Majesty was paying a brief visit in Germany, but the moment it was submitted to her by Lord Malmesbury, the Minister in attendance, she declared it to be conceived in a spirit, and clothed in language, utterly unworthy of the occasion. The following day it was returned to Lord Derby with the following letter:

"Bebelsberg, 15th August, 1858.

"The Queen has asked Lord Malmesbury to explain in detail to Lord Derby her objections to the draft of the Proclamation for India. The Queen would be glad if Lord Derby would write it himself in his excellent language, bearing in mind that it is a female Sovereign who speaks to more than a hundred millions of Eastern people on assuming the direct government over them, and after a bloody civil war giving them pledges which her future reign is to redeem, and explaining the principles of her government. Such a document should breathe feelings of generosity, benevolence, and religious toleration, and point out the privileges which the Indians will receive in being placed on an equality with the subjects of the British Crown, and the prosperity following in the train of civilization."

The Memorandum forwarded by Lord Malmesbury indicates the full scope of the Queen's objections. The draft Proclamation had spoken of the power which the British Government possessed for the "undermining of native religions and customs." This reference the Queen absolutely disapproved. "Her Majesty would prefer that the subject should be introduced by a declaration in the sense that the deep attachment which Her Majesty feels to her own religion, and the comfort and happiness which she derives from its consolations, will preclude her from any attempt to interfere with the native religions." So with a statement of the Government's policy being, in part, "to relieve poverty." "The Queen thinks," wrote Lord Malmesbury, "that this part of the paragraph should be extended, and that, in speaking of future prosperity in India, a direct mention of railways, canals, and telegraphs should be made, with an assurance to those prejudiced populations that these works are the basis and will be the causes of their general and individual welfare." Other suggestions were made, and the Proclamation, as eventually amended and issued, was worthy of the occasion and the Royal statesmanship. Lord Canning received it in October, together with the information that his rank had been raised to that of viceroy, and he at once made arrangements for its being read in English and in all the native languages —at the various seats of government and Provincial headquarters from the Indus to the Irrawaddy.

He was quick to see the effect of the religious clause, and wrote the Queen that " to the good effect of the words in which religion is spoken of in the Proclamation Lord Canning looks forward with very sanguine hope." At a mass meeting held in Calcutta shortly afterwards, a native merchant of high position declared that " a nobler production it has not been my lot ever to have met with." It must be added that the whole policy was a wise one, and that the natives could understand and obey and respect a Royal government, where the previous system had seemed utterly incomprehensible. As the *Times* correspondent said during this period, the masses " have a very decided notion that the Queen has hanged the Company for offences." The fact is that the natives did not comprehend " John Company," and do not now understand Parliamentary rule, but they did appreciate the Queen's Proclamation, as they now do her style and title of Empress. On December 2nd the Queen replied to Lord Canning, and her letter may be said to close the era of the Mutiny and its immediate consequences :

" It is," wrote Her Majesty, " a source of great satisfaction and pride to her to feel herself in direct communication with that enormous empire which is so bright a jewel of her crown, and which she would wish to see happy, contented, and peaceful. May the publication of her Proclamation be the beginning of a new era, and may it draw a veil over the sad and bloody past !

" The Queen rejoices to hear that the Viceroy approves the passage about religion. She strongly insisted on it. She trusts also that the certainty of the amnesty remaining open till the 1st of January may not be productive of serious evil. The telegram received to-day brings continued good news, and announces her Proclamation having been read and having produced a good effect.

" The Queen concludes with every wish for Lord Canning's success and prosperity, and with the assurance of her undiminished and entire confidence."

Following this came the establishment by Her Majesty of the Order of the Star of India for the purpose of rewarding services in the Eastern Empire. The idea seems to have been her own, and in its finally successful form has worked much good. Lord Canning highly approved of the proposal, and in 1861 the first investiture of distinguished Anglo-Indians and native princes took place. Since then this Order and that of the Indian Empire and the Imperial Order of the Crown of India have enabled Her Majesty to confer honours which the Oriental mind knows how to appreciate, and to give jewelled ribands and collars which have done more to crystallize the loyalty of native chiefs and princes into practical shape and action than all the talk of Parliamentary liberty and civilizing British influences could have achieved in centuries. So with the title of Empress which the Queen received and accepted in 1876. But prior to that event came the important visit of the Prince of Wales to India, preceded, in 1869, by the brief but beneficial tour of the Duke of Edinburgh. It had been a sort of preliminary step, and the welcome given during this very informal visit of young Prince Alfred was taken as an assurance for the future. There can be no

JOHN, LORD LAWRENCE.

THE RT. HON. SIR RICHARD TEMPLE, G.C.S.T., F.R.S.

MAJOR GENERAL CHARLES GEORGE GORDON, C.B.

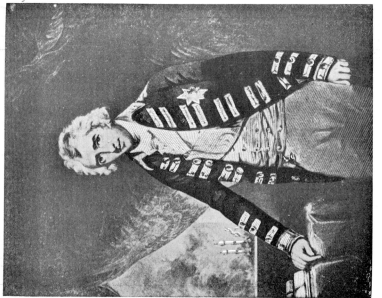

RICHARD, MARQUESS OF WELLESLEY.

reasonable doubt that these acts of Imperial policy had been in Her Majesty's mind, and probably in that of Mr. Disraeli, for years. As already mentioned, the change of title was proposed many years before by Lord Ellenborough, and the visit of the heir to the Throne was simply a part of the line of action which had included the Royal tours to Canada and South Africa during 1860, and the Duke of Edinburgh's various Colonial visits.

No doubt, also, the Queen's constant correspondence with her Indian viceroys had kept her well in advance of public opinion or knowledge at home, and had enabled her to see the importance of touching the Oriental imagination as well as the very changeable convictions of an ignorant population upon such subjects as national interests or sound administration. Writing from Osborne to the Viceroy of India on January 3rd, 1865, Her Majesty indicates the way in which she was, and is, kept informed of every passing event and tendency. "The Queen has to thank Sir John Lawrence for two interesting letters . . . as well as for enclosures and beautiful photographs which give a good idea of the splendid ceremony which took place at Lahore. The Queen highly approves Sir John Lawrence's addresses, and is truly rejoiced to see the good and friendly feeling which seems to pervade the chiefs, and cannot fail to lead to lasting good." Two years later another letter indicates how continuous the reports were, and how Her Majesty utilized every opportunity of obtaining information :

"Balmoral, Oct. 4th, 1867.

"The Queen is quite shocked to feel how long it is since she has received Sir John Lawrence's last satisfactory letter, and that she has not yet answered him. But she has very little time, and consequently misses the day for the mail. The Queen thanks Sir John much for his letter, and for the very interesting photographs of the tomb of her dear friend Lady Canning. She had the pleasure of seeing Lady Napier here the other day, and of hearing much that was most interesting about India from her.

"The Queen trusts that the misery caused by the terrible famine has passed away, and that her Indian subjects are in a state of prosperity. She rejoices to hear of the general state of tranquillity in the country. With every good wish for the happiness of her Indian Empire, and for the health of Sir J. and Lady Lawrence, the Queen concludes her letter."

The inference derivable from a study of this and much similar correspondence is almost a certainty. The policy of Mr. Disraeli, or Lord Beaconsfield, as he soon became, was, so far as India is concerned, as much that of the Queen as it was his own. It may be also said that the even wider question of whether that great Minister did not originally imbibe his Imperialism upon general issues from the Queen herself is one which can be very strongly supported in an affirmative sense. But, however that may have been, the policy was duly inaugurated in 1875 by elaborate preparations for the Prince of Wales' tour of the Indian Empire. The announcement was first made on March 20th, and caused much popular surprise, together with comments of a somewhat mixed nature.   The *Times* very accurately declared that the visit would enable the Prince to bring " the whole historic inheritance of England into contact with the most venerable heritage of Eastern antiquity and civilization."   But there was perhaps too much imagination in the policy for immediate English appreciation, and it remained for the future, and history, to do it full justice.   A mass meeting in Hyde Park even protested against this message of conciliation and friendship, and it was naturally difficult for people ignorant of Eastern etiquette and manners to understand the necessity of including £40,000 worth of presents in the Royal baggage.

Before the time of departure came, however, public opinion had adjusted itself to the new situation, and to the fact now brought into light by Royal intervention and influence, that India was a mixed multitude of varied and sensitive races, capable of being governed by courtesy, tact, and prestige, but incapable of imbibing loyalty unless the objects of that sentiment were presented in an Eastern fashion, and with a basis of Oriental pomp and reality.   By the 10th of October, when the Prince embarked at Brindisi, the feeling had risen into enthusiasm in many quarters—though there was still a substantial undercurrent of murmurs.   Dean Stanley spoke from the pulpit of this first visit made to India by the heir to the English Throne since the greatest of his ancestors (Alfred the Great) had a thousand years before so ardently longed to explore those fabulous territories.   An address was presented by the Corporation of London congratulating the Prince upon his desire to become " personally acquainted with the country, the customs, and the sympathies of the millions of Her Majesty's subjects in India."   The escort finally chosen to accompany His Royal Highness was composed of the Duke of Sutherland, a travelled and cultured nobleman, Lord Alfred Paget, the Earl of Aylesford, Lord Carrington, the future Governor of New South Wales, Sir Bartle Frere, the eminent Indian administrator, who had not yet tried his hand at the complex difficulties of South Africa, Lord Suffield, Major-General Sir Dighton Probyn, the gallant Lord Charles Beresford, Mr. (now Sir) Francis Knollys, Canon Duckworth, William Howard Russell, the famous war correspondent, and Sir Joseph Fayrer, M.D.

Details of the voyage, or of the journey through India, are as impossible to give here as it would be to describe the enthusiasm of the receptions, the value of the visit, and the pleasures and dangers of the sport enjoyed.   At Bombay, the Prince laid the foundation stone of the new docks, and was welcomed in opening the South Indian Railway by 6,000 natives singing loyal songs.   But the great event at this early rampart of British power was a reception given by the Royal visitor to the rulers and chiefs of Western India. Amidst the roar of guns, the flashing of countless gems, and all the dark oriental magnificence of an Indian Durbar, the Prince was welcomed to the soil of the Eastern Empire in a gathering that outrivalled even the historic splendours of the Court of Akbar or of

Aurungzebe. The viceroy, Lord Northbrook, was, of course, present, and to him much credit was due for the arrangements which were so often tested during the ensuing tour. At Lucknow, the Prince became acquainted with many more chiefs, and varied nationalities and industries; laid the foundation stone of a memorial to those who had fallen in its defence during the Mutiny; received an address from the municipality, and a crown set with jewels for presentation to the Queen. Here, also, it was announced that the Maharajah of Cashmere had given thousands of pounds in honour of the visit, besides recent gifts of £50,000 for promoting religion, and large sums for founding a Sanskrit scholarship. This same ruler was with difficulty persuaded to cut down his personal gifts to the Prince from £50,000 to £5,000. And at a later period he showed his broadness of mind, as well as generosity, in sending £200 to the Bishop of Calcutta with the request that it be used in erecting a tablet in the Cathedral of the capital as a memorial of the Prince's tour.

At Calcutta, His Royal Highness visited many charitable institutions, and presided at a great assembly or Chapter of the Order of the Star of India, when the dignity of knighthood was bestowed upon various Princes and Anglo-Indian statesmen. The new Zoological gardens were opened, the University of Calcutta inspected, and a statue to Lord Mayo unveiled. Madras, Agra, Lahore, Umritsur, Benares, Cawnpore, Delhi, and many other places were visited, and everywhere the dignity of the British Sovereign was brought home to the Eastern people by the bearing of her son and heir; the greatness of the Monarchy and the Empire was impressed upon them by the magnificence of his suite, and state, and ceremonial pomp—the only method they were capable of comprehending; while the Queen was transmuted from an intangible though powerful figure into a splendid reality, through the flesh and blood presentment of the Prince of Wales. The effect was greatly strengthened by the immediate co-operation of the native princes, and by the tact of the Royal visitor, who seemed to understand just how to preserve his own dignity while flattering their natural tendency to pride and pomp. On one occasion, for instance, the Maharajah of Puttiala wore £100,000 worth of jewels in his turban, supplemented by a scattering of pearls rubies and emeralds over his person to an almost fabulous amount. This same ruler presented the Prince with a sword studded with gems from hilt to point, and worth at least £10,000.

Everywhere the latter's tact and genial dignity had its effect, and an officer of great experience said afterwards that the single action of asking the haughty Maharajah of Scindia to ride down the lines with His Royal Highness at Delhi, was worth a million sterling in money—to say nothing of the prestige won through the following salute and obeisance from that hitherto intractable ruler. The words spoken by the Maharajah of Jeypore, at a local banquet, undoubtedly voiced a general sentiment in this connection: " Your Royal Highness's happy temperament and hearty sympathy for native chiefs and the people of India have made a deep impression on our minds, and it gives me unspeakable pleasure to be able to say that all my brother chiefs, and the native gentleman I have met recently, have one and all expressed similar feelings regarding your Royal Highness, and I would devoutly express a prayer that the presence on India's soil of the heir to England's throne may be productive of the richest blessings to princes and people, and may have issues promotive of the highest welfare of this great country." To bring out such utterances from national leaders, to unite the Imperial power and the vast dependent and complex nationalities of India, to bring home to the masses, as well as the Eastern classes, the personal reality of British sovereignty, was a great mission and a valuable work. And apart altogether from his personal tact in council and conversation, his dignity in durbar and ceremonial, his bravery and coolness upon the hunting field, there is no doubt that the mere presence of the Prince did much. With these other conditions also in action, a great and permanent service was done for England and the Empire, for peace and unity. To quote Sir Madhavo Rao, one of the really great statesmen of Hindostan:

"It was their privilege to see a Prince who was heir to a sceptre whose beneficent power and influence was felt in every quarter of the world, which dispelled darkness, diffused light, paralyzed the tyrant's hand, shivered the manacles of the slave, extended the bounds of freedom, increased the happiness and elevated the dignity of the human race. The visit to Baroda would never fade in their memory. The occasion would be commemorated by history, and would ever be associated with a renovated strength and a renewed stability of the State."

And so it was everywhere, whether in Baroda or Madras, Bombay or Bengal, Bareilly or Allahabad, Cashmere or Gwalior, Nepaul or Ceylon, Indore or Jeypore. Writing in a private letter, shortly after the Prince had returned home to receive a great ovation at Portsmouth, and to meet deserved congratulations from all who were able to appreciate the situation, Dr. Alexander Duff, the eminent Nonconformist divine, declared that, " taking it all in all, in its varied and multiplied bearings and aspects, it is to my own mind the most remarkable tour to be found in the annals of all time." History will, and does, indicate the substantial accuracy of this estimate, and will render full justice to the value of this portion of the current Imperial policy. So also with the creation and proclamation of the Queen as Empress of India. When Parliament met early in 1876 the Queen's speech referred to " the hearty affection " with which the Prince of Wales had been received in India, and after mentioning that no formal addition had been made to the style and title of the Sovereign at the time of the assumption of direct government by the Crown declared that the present was a fitting opportunity for supplying the omission. At first the idea was popular, and up to the time when Mr. Disraeli introduced his measure in the Commons there seemed no likelihood of opposition or serious criticism.

It was pretty well understood amongst the leaders that the Persian or Hindustani for Queen is a word signifying "inmate of a royal harem," and that for many years past it had naturally been very little used. In fact, the Duke of Argyll himself, when at the Indian Office in the previous Government, was known to have altered the wording of a telegram to " Empress of Hindostan," while the late Lord Mayo, as Viceroy of India, was understood to have strongly favoured a settled and comprehensive title. Mr. Disraeli, in his speech, was brief and to the point. The measure was intended to gratify the sensitive and imaginative minds of the people of India, to mark the recent Royal visit, and to indicate that the separatist school of politics in England was dead, and the British occupation and rule of the Eastern Empire supreme and final in its nature. He intimated that the policy had the Queen's approval, and earnestly asked for the unanimous support of Parliament. It would be an act which might " add splendour even to her Throne, security even to her Empire." But to the surprise of most people the proposal encountered a fractious opposition, unreasonable speeches, and a party division.

It eventually became law by a majority of seventy-five in the House of Commons, and has since shamed opponents and critics by its successful application and use. The Imperial diadem made Her Majesty an equal, in the important matter of titles, with the Emperor of Russia ; it raised her far above the haughty and more or less ignorant Princes of India ; it brought those great feudatories face to face with a situation of supremacy which it was necessary for the native mind to recognize ; and gave an environment of dignity and splendour to the Crown which the Eastern mind alone knows how to appreciate. To quote Sir Edwin Arnold, the Queen's name is now infinitely more potent in Hindostan than the Company's ever was, and " Maharani Kajai," or " Victory for the Empress," is a battle-cry which would be joyfully shouted by all the war-like races of Rajpootana, Kattiawar, the Punjaub, the Deccan, or the Mohamedan Northwest, should the occasion ever arise.

Closely linked with this development of Imperialism was the purchase of the Suez Canal shares, the subsequent practical acquisition of Egypt, and the securing of the trade route to India. Following the precedent already set, the Duke of Connaught was some years afterwards sent out to the East, and spent a period of useful military service in the north of India. Speaking in London, in March, 1886, His Royal Highness referred to the many native chiefs and gentlemen he had met, and described their good feeling and loyalty, generous kindness, and love of hospitality. He spoke also of the active work undertaken by the Duchess amongst the schools, the Zenanas, and the Indian ladies generally. During the succeeding year he was appointed Commander-in-Chief of the Forces in Bombay, and proved a most capable and popular officer. Shortly after his arrival he opened the Soldiers' Industrial Exhibition at Poona, and held an investiture of the Order of the Indian Empire on behalf of the Queen. Upon this latter occasion, and in response to a loyal address from the inhabitants of the same place, a letter was read from Her Majesty, expressing appreciation of their loyalty and affection, drawing attention to the fact that during her reign the Presidency of Bombay had been blessed with almost unbroken peace, and expressing pleasure at that part of the address which referred to the visit of the Prince of Wales and the appointment of the Duke of Connaught. Prince Arthur remained at his duties in Bombay for three years, returning home by way of Canada in 1890.

During 1889 Prince Albert Victor of Wales—who had recently been created Duke of Clarence and Avondale, and was taking up his all too brief round of duties as heir-presumptive to the Throne—visited Southern India, where he did a good deal of hunting and shooting, participated in many functions, and made friends of many princes and chiefs, to say nothing of masses of the people. Accompanied by Sir Edward Bradford, V.C., Captain Holford, and Captain Havey, the Prince reached Bombay on November 9th, and was welcomed by the Duke of Connaught, and Lord Reay, the Governor of the Presidency. All kinds of pomps and ceremonies and sights filled up the following days—ranging from a grand durbar to a ride upon an elephant. Then came a visit to Hyderabad and Madras, Mysore and Trichinopoly, Rangoon and Mandalay. At Calcutta, illuminations, and fêtes, and entertainments, of all kinds of vivid Asiatic splendour, were the order of the day, accompanied by such pleasures as juggling, music, Nautch-dancing, snipe-shooting, and polo. From the capital the Prince went to Benares, where tiger hunting was indulged in, and to Lucknow, which the memories of Havelock, and Outram, and the mutiny made so interesting. Thence to Cawnpore and Agra, Lahore and Peshawur, Rawul-Pindi and Delhi, Jeypore and Ajmere, Oodeypoore, Bareilly, and Baroda. At the latter place the Prince visited the Gaekwar's marvellous new palace, saw his famous jewels—one diamond was worth £80,000— and his carpets wrought in seed pearls. Bombay was reached again at the end of March, and a splendid farewell demonstration given the Royal visitor. Of his many hunting episodes and ceremonial functions a record is unnecessary, but the spirit and value of the young Prince's speeches may be gathered from that delivered in Madras :

" Ever since I landed in India I have been greeted by its people with an enthusiastic kindness and good will to which I know I have no personal claim ; but I can assure you that it is all the greater delight to me when I realize that in the reception given to myself your loyalty and devotion to Her Majesty the Queen-Empress are made so unmistakably clear. It has always been my greatest ambition to see this vast and interesting country, and I had long looked forward to the time when this wish might be gratified. Now that this opportunity has come I feel confident, from what I have already seen, that my expectations, though large, will be far more than realized, and that my tour will give me a life-long interest in the country, its people and its institutions, which could not have been acquired otherwise than by a personal visit."

Meanwhile the Queen's Jubilee had been celebrated throughout India with much loyalty and magnificence. The great princes held durbars, and gave entertainments, and much money to charitable, religious, or military objects. Royal salutes from myriad guns ; processions of school children singing the National Anthem in their varied native tongues; fireworks and illuminations in all the large cities ; festivities and State functions, presided over by the various Governors, from the Viceroy downwards ; speeches and thanksgiving services, and endless decorations and Eastern evidences of enthusiasm ; were everywhere the order of the day. The statement of the Maharajah at Bhownugger, that the Queen is " the best Sovereign who has ever wielded a sceptre in this world," was a fair indication of the trend of the loyal utterances expressed in a thousand quarters. Yet it is a question how far such manifestations may be taken or how deep they really go.*

No student of life and thought in India will depend too largely upon demonstrations of this kind—remarkable as they undoubtedly are from alien and

---

*Letter to the author from the Right Honourable Lord Harris, G.C.I.E., lately Governor of Bombay—February 2nd, 1896.

" India is so vast as to population, and so split up by differences of race, religion, and caste, that only the most audacious will venture to speak for India as a whole. The most experienced civil servants, with from thirty to forty years' service, would qualify this opinion by limiting it to that part of India which they knew best. And my five years of Bombay do not justify my giving an authoritative opinion.

" You must remember that to millions the Kaiser-i-Hind can be little more than a title deserving undoubtedly of the utmost respect, but not an idea that can be easily embodied. There are many millions who have but a smattering of education, and who can know nothing of the details of Her Majesty's career. To such the Queen would be no more than *The Authority* to whom appeal can be made in distress, and who has the power to overrule local decisions.

" But to the educated classes the Queen-Empress is much more than this. She is the Queen Mother. The family tie has still a most powerful influence amongst natives ; it is a part of their religion, and respect for the head of the family encourages respect for the head of the nation. At the time of the Duke of Clarence's death the Hon. Mr. Ranade made a most sympathetic and touching speech to the effect that the family tie influenced the natives of India, that they regarded the Queen in the light of a mother, and that her bereavement was a cause of distress to them—arising out of a feeling of respectful family affection.

" That, I think, describes more accurately than any words of mine how intense is the loyalty of the natives of India to their Queen-Empress ; and it goes without saying that that feeling has been immensely enhanced by the lively interest that Her Majesty has always taken in her Oriental subjects, and by the justice, impartiality, and purity of her rule over them. They would also appreciate at its full value the domestic purity of Her Majesty's life as a great and shining example."

mutually antagonistic races to the head of a conquering and paramount power.*
But the pivotal point in this connection is the fact that the princes, both Hindoo
and Mahometan, British and feudatory, are loyal to the Crown, and that this
loyalty has been deepened, and harmonized, and utilized, by the Imperial policy
indicated in these pages, and by the Queen's life and reign and personal influence. Her Majesty rules the minds and convinced loyalty of the chiefs, and they
rule the massed millions of people—outside of the three great Governments of
Bombay, Bengal, and Madras, and, in many cases, within them.

The Queen has been very fortunate in her direct representatives, as well as
in the subordinate officials who have wielded such vast powers in a manner so
generally beneficial. Lord Canning was succeeded in 1862 by the Earl of Elgin
and Kincardine, whose brilliant career in Canada and elsewhere gave promise of
a great vice-royalty. Death came, however, and made way for Sir John (Lord)
Lawrence, who distinguished himself by a policy of " masterly inactivity,"
so far as the complex web of Central Asian politics was concerned. To him
succeeded the Earl of Mayo, who won great popularity, and met a violent death
at the hand of some wretched fanatic ; the Earl of Northbrook, who abolished
the most unpopular of Indian taxes—that on incomes—and mitigated the horrors
of the Bengal famine ; Lord Lytton, who carried out the Imperial ideas and
policy of 1874 and 1880 up to the hilt, and made a specially pronounced impression upon the natives by his gorgeous proclamation and elaboration of the
Queen's new title ; the Marquess of Ripon, who excited so much attention and
raised such keen discussions by his policy of giving the natives greater control
over their Government ; the Earl of Dufferin, who followed Dalhousie and other
great pro-consuls in annexing new territories, made Burmah a British possession,
won increased fame and popularity by his eloquence, and received a marquessate
from his Sovereign ; the Marquess of Lansdowne, who proved a dignified and
capable administrator ; and another Earl of Elgin, who in 1896 still holds the
reins of power. To these men the Queen and the British nation owe much, as
they also do to administrators and governors such as Sir Richard Temple, Sir
Charles Aitchison, Sir David Barbour, Sir Stewart Bayley, Sir Auckland Colvin,

---

*Letter to the author from the Earl of Northbrook, G.C.S.I., formerly Viceroy of India—December 31st, 1895.

" India is so large a country, and the mass of the people are so ignorant of things remote
from their homes, that it must be very difficult to form a reliable opinion of the influence
exercised by the name of the Queen. The security of the British Empire in India mainly
depends, in my opinion, upon the general impression which prevails that our rule is a just
one, and that any disturbance of the peace will be promptly repressed. The contentment
of the mass of the people is principally secured by a moderate apportionment of the land
tax ; and the native Princes will be loyal to our rule so long as the promises made to them
in the Proclamation issued in the name of the Queen when the direct government of India
was transferred from the East India Company to the Crown are faithfully kept."

Sir W. W. Hunter, Sir Alfred Lyall, Sir Henry Durand, Sir Roper Lethbridge, and a host of others.

During the years which have followed the Mutiny and the inauguration of the Queen's direct rule there have been troubles, and discontents, and even plots amongst what Lord Dufferin calls these " tessellated nationalities." There have been famines, and silly agitations, and a sometimes disloyal press. But through it all has loomed the force and blessing of " an external, dispassionate, immutable authority." The reception given to members of the Royal family; the of the Queen's Jubilee; the offer of enormous sums of money and celebration bodies of troops by the native Princes during the Russian war-scare; the great service of native soldiers in Egypt and the Soudan; all indicate the substantial and practical loyalty of the people—so far as 250 mixed millions of the human race can be moved at all by considerations of common interest and feeling. And, though it may be impossible to fully estimate the value of the Queen's name and personality in this connection, it is not impossible to realize that certain causes have their natural effects, whether in England or India, Canada or Africa.

Her Majesty's quickly cabled sympathy in their sorrows, and pleasure in their successes or joys, coupled with the personal example of her own life, and the halo of respect surrounding her great name, have naturally pronounced effects upon the people as a whole. The influence of that distant throne, shadowed from their sight as it may be by stormy seas, has come home to them in the person of the Viceroy and different Princes, and with its mystical surroundings of splendour and power is perhaps more impressive than would be any local presentment of an Imperial Court. And, above all, the weight of the Royal policy which was inaugurated by the visit of the Duke of Edinburgh in 1869, continued in the historic tour of the Heir Apparent, and voiced in the assumption of the Imperial title, will roll on through all future years, gathering force through the passage of time and by the steady decadence of these local, narrow, and " little England " views which the Queen's whole career has done so much to check and nullify—if not destroy.

CHAPTER XXIV.

The Queen's Influence Upon Foreign Affairs.

IF it be true, as Carlyle says, that "the history of mankind is the history of its great men," the phrase indicates not only the high place which Queen Victoria must take in the annals of the century, but the wonderful experience which she must have obtained from her intercourse with the national leaders of her era. In the realm of foreign affairs alone she has had to encounter the keen intellect of a Napoleon III., the haughty mind of a Nicholas I., the shifty diplomacy of a Louis Philippe, the genius of Bismarck, the skill of Guizot, the experience of Metternich, and the ability of a whole host of passing Ministers and Chancellors and Ambassadors. Nor have these encounters been mere ornamental meetings, or discussions between a figurehead Sovereign and polite but smiling diplomatists or rulers. The Royal correspondence shows how real has been the Queen's influence, how strongly her voice has been raised from time to time, how close has been her touch with contemporary history, how real her intercourse with its makers and leaders.

At home she has been confidentially served by a series of able but diverse men. The Secretaries of State for Foreign Affairs during a sixty years' reign have included the brilliantly rash Palmerston, the courteous Granville, the cold and cautious Aberdeen, the dignified Clarendon, the philosophic Derby, and such variously qualified leaders as Malmesbury, Russell, Iddesleigh, Rosebery, and Salisbury. With them in the practical working of British policy, and in more or less intimate relations to the Queen, have been the ambassadors in foreign lands. These men, through the days when Lord Stratford de Redcliffe ruled Turkey, or Sir Hamilton Seymour held high place in Russia; when Lord Odo Russell conducted British affairs in Berlin, or Lord Cowley and Lord Lyons, Lord Lytton and Lord Dufferin, handled the difficult diplomacy of Paris; when Sir John Crampton, Sir Edward Thornton, or Lord Sackville acted in a similar capacity at Washington; when the ever-shifting scene of British policy was being guided and controlled from Downing street in all its varied embodiments at Pekin or St. Petersburg, Vienna or Washington, Paris or Constantinople; have been in direct or indirect, but always constant, communication with Her Majesty. And the Queen's interest in the vital issues presented by her servants at home or abroad has never been perfunctory or formal. It has been a close and anxious study of details, and participation in the settlement of many a pressing and serious question. To quote Mr. W. M. Torrens, in his able " Life of Lord Melbourne":

VISCOUNT PALMERSTON, K.G., G.C.B.

THE MARQUESS OF DUFFERIN AND AVA, K.P.

"Although entailing oftentimes a serious addition to the other cares and labours of State, the Queen has invariably desired to be made fully acquainted with the nature and character of diplomatic dealings of importance with foreign powers; and it is no more than a just acknowledgment of steadfastness of royal patriotism to say that no Minister who succeeded Melbourne ever failed to find the ready and cordial sympathy in the nation's wants and wishes which is the best guerdon of a nation's trust and loyalty."

During the first years of her reign the young Queen did not take a very active part in the conduct of Foreign Affairs. But as time went on, and she grew into her duties and recognized the important possibilities of her position, her interest naturally increased in all the varied forms of public work. At first, also, Prince Albert did not take strong ground in this direction, but satisfied himself with laying up a firm foundation of knowledge and judgment. In those days he learnt much from the Queen in connection with English ideas, and life, and constitutional government. "He takes the greatest possible interest in what goes on," she wrote to King Leopold in 1839, "feeling with me and for me, yet abstaining, as he ought, from biassing me either way." As time passed, however, and the Royal couple came into closer touch with the diplomacy and rulers of Europe, they took a continually deeper interest in its concerns, and the Prince developed unusual ability in dealing with problems of State. Writing on 14th September, 1844, Her Majesty refers to the dark cloud which had hung over the relations of France and England as a result of the Tahiti question, and declares that "the good ending of our difficulties with France is an immense blessing; but it is really and truly necessary that you and those in Paris should know that the danger was *imminent*. . . . We must try to prevent these difficulties for the future."

During these years, as well as at the present time, the burden of despatches and correspondence connected with Foreign Affairs was enormous, and all that was important had to go through the hands of the Queen. Lord John Russell informed Prince Albert in 1849 that during the previous year 28,000 despatches had been received or sent out of the Foreign Office, and in his reply the Prince spoke of these as having all come to the Queen as well as to the Minister. Taking into consideration the fact that these documents dealt with problems from Peru to Pekin, and of every conceivable character and condition, it is not difficult to comprehend the work which the Queen had to encounter before she thoroughly mastered the state of the world's diplomacy and international relationships. With the Prince's help it was made a little easier, but there is no really royal road to learning, and certainly none to experience. Writing of this period (1848-9), Sir Theodore Martin speaks of the great necessity which existed for tact and statesmanship, especially in connection with the revolutionary movements of the moment, and of "the enormous pressure of work and of anxiety" which it imposed upon the Head of the State:

"However we might as a nation desire to see other nations as free in their institutions and fortunate in their government as ourselves, it could only be from within that these blessings could be secured. . . . In the meantime sound policy demanded that nothing should be done by us to offend or alienate the existing governments, who, if they should succeed in subduing the revolutionary forces which were now arrayed against them, would not be likely to forget that we had borne hard upon them in their hour of trouble. The necessity for this line of policy—a deviation from which might have left us without allies among the Sovereigns of Europe—was constantly present to the minds of the Queen and Prince. Every communication on foreign affairs, every phase of the almost daily changes in the current of events, therefore engaged their most anxious attention."

At this time, also, commenced Her Majesty's difficulties with Lord Palmerston. Their personal aspect need not be considered here, nor is it necessary to trace their development through the various complications with Portugal, France, Italy, Hungary, and Greece. Upon the whole, Lord J. Russell, who was Prime Minister at the time, seems to have been in complete accord with the Queen's views, and to have recognized the frequently headstrong rashness of Palmerston's policy and mode of action. Writing to the latter on October 1st, 1848, Lord John observed: "That the Queen is constantly suffering under uneasiness is too true, but I own I cannot say it is always groundless. It is surely right that a person speaking in the name of Her Majesty's Government should, in important affairs, submit his despatches to the Queen, and obtain the opinion of the Prime Minister, before he commits the Queen and her Government. This necessary preliminary you too often forget; and the Queen, naturally, as I think, dreads that upon some occasion you may give her name to sanction proceedings which she may afterwards be compelled to disavow. I confess I feel the same uneasiness; but as I agree very constantly with you in opinion, my only wish is that in future you will save the Queen anxiety, and me some trouble, by giving your reasons before and not after an important despatch is sent."

About the same time that this letter was written the Queen objected to the sending of Lord Normanby as the English representative at a proposed conference on Italian affairs. She feared that he shared Lord Palmerston's views upon the situation, and sent for Lord John Russell, who stayed three days at Windsor, and thoroughly discussed with her the whole question of Austrian difficulties, Hungarian victories under Kossuth, and Italian opportunities and ambitions. The conference was not held, but Lord Normanby remained Ambassador at Paris, and three years later indirectly contributed to Palmerston's fall and the close of this period of difference between the Sovereign and her Foreign Minister. On December 4th, 1851, Her Majesty wrote the Premier from Osborne that she had learned with astonishment and concern the news of the *coup d'etat* in Paris, and that she considered it "absolutely necessary" that the British Government should remain passive and neutral. She also expressed the hope that the Ambassador would be very cautious and keep entirely aloof. Meanwhile, Lord Palmerston had personally expressed his sympathy with Louis

Napoleon to the French Ambassador in London, and followed it up, despite the Queen's letter, by an official despatch to Lord Normanby, which was not submitted to either Queen, Prime Minister, or Cabinet, and in which he repeated his approval of the Napoleonic policy.   Hence the immediate and necessary dismissal of the Foreign Minister, and the vindication of the Queen's opinion as to his rashness and the risk of compromising and dangerous policies.   Indeed, he had already been obliged to recall or cancel at least two important despatches, and if it had not been for Her Majesty's continued scrutiny and intervention many evils might have resulted.   Still, Lord Palmerston was a great Minister, and it only required this period of what may be termed discipline and control to bring him to a recognition of the real responsibilities of his position and the dignity of his Sovereign.

Prince Albert, in writing Lord John regarding the dismissal, declared that the Queen felt that " we were entering upon most dangerous times, in which military despotism and red republicanism " would be the chief powers on the continent, and to both of them the Constitutional monarchy of England would be equally hateful.   It was, therefore, necessary that the calm influence of our institutions, rather than the personal predilections and policy of a Minister who was intensely disliked in Europe, should prevail.   To this the Premier replied that he " perceived the Queen had become more and more uneasy, and, having given Lord Palmerston a special caution on the 29th of November, it appeared to me that I could not allow any further indiscretion on his part to commit the Queen and the Cabinet."   So far as can be now judged this incident closed the chief difficulties—though not all differences—between the Queen and Palmerston, and the latter eventually became one of her most trusted and valued Ministers. The famous document of Royal instructions issued in 1850 to the Foreign Office seems also to have been regarded in the spirit, if not the letter, and from that time on, for nearly half a century, Her Majesty has exercised an ever-increasing influence upon British foreign policy.   Writing on February 3rd, 1852, the Queen told King Leopold of her dislike to seeing women taking part in politics, but added, of her own exceptional position, that " there are times which force one to take an interest, and therefore I feel this interest now *intensely*."   This feeling is almost immediately indicated by the following extracts from the Diary of Lord Malmesbury, who was at the time Foreign Secretary, and therefore in a position to know what he was talking about :

" October 24th, 1852.—The Queen writes anxiously about the national defences. Universal apprehension of war, if the French Empire is proclaimed."

" November 3rd.—Called on Disraeli, just returning from Windsor. He had had a discussion of two and a half hours with the Prince upon the national defences. Disraeli, in very low spirits, said it would destroy his budget."

" November 9th.—The Queen sent for Lord Derby and me to Windsor, to talk over the Memorandum (*re* new titles of Louis Napoleon). Satisfied with it."

" December 18th.—The Queen had told him (Lord Derby) to send Lord Aberdeen as well as Lord Lansdowne, and they went down. The Queen asked who was likely to form a Government, and Lord Derby told her Lord Aberdeen had, he believed, coalesced with the Whigs, and was ready to be Prime Minister. The Queen *objected* to the idea of Lord Canning being Foreign Secretary, no doubt partly in consequence of his anti-Bonapartist speech when I announced the Empire."

The Crimean war period which followed thoroughly illustrated the wisdom of the Royal anxiety concerning the defences—as the succeeding Indian mutiny vindicated the Queen's suggestions as to the desirability of maintaining the military forces on a substantial and reorganized basis after the conclusion of the conflict with Russia. When the crisis came with the Czar in 1853, Her Majesty wrote Lord Aberdeen on September 25th, dealing with various despatches just received, discussing the uselessness of further correspondence with Russia, and putting plain questions in a very plain manner : " Ought not the points of difference to be now prominently laid before our allies, and, in conjunction with such as have either the honesty or the courage to avow the same opinion with ourselves, ought we not to point this out to Russia, with a declaration that such demands are unsupported by existing treaties, inadmissible by Turkey, if she has any regard for her independence, and inadmissible by the Powers, who have an interest and a duty to guard this independence, and that the continuance of the occupation of the principalities, in order to extort these demands, constitutes an unwarrantable aggression upon Turkey, and infraction of the public law of Europe."

Action was taken, but the little hope that existed of maintaining peace was soon dissipated, and a war entered upon with light hearts and pleasure amongst the masses of England, which they came out of with glory to the national arms, but disgrace to the national defensive organization, as well as to the statecraft which had paid due attention to neither the advice and protests of the Queen nor to the ordinary dictates of governing common sense. During this struggle, as in the negotiations which preceded and followed it, the personal relations of the Royal family of England and the Emperor and Empress of the French had been a recognized European factor. The old-time influence which the Queen had possessed over King Louis Philippe, and which had done so much to preserve the peace and promote friendly relations between France and England, was even greater in the case of Louis Napoleon, and seems to have been based upon his absolute confidence in her goodness, and admiration for her personal qualities. One of the ways in which this intercourse was utilized to keep the machinery of diplomacy working smoothly and without friction is seen in the following private letter, written just after a visit of Prince Frederick of Prussia to Paris, and the announcement of his engagement to the Princess Royal :

" Windsor Castle, December 31st, 1856.

" SIRE AND DEAR BROTHER,—I am glad to seize the opportunity of the new year to thank your Majesty for your kind letter, while begging you to accept all our good wishes as well for your own happiness as for that of the Empress and your son. The new year again begins amid the din of warlike preparations; but I hope that with these preparations matters will stop, and after the friendly communication which has taken place between yourself and Prussia I have every confidence that it will be possible for you to arrange a pacific solution of this Swiss affair, unfortunately envenomed, though it be, by wounded *amour propre* on every side.

"I am very happy that the difficulties which arose about the execution of the Treaty of Paris are now entirely at an end, and that what is expressed in your Majesty's letter as a hope is now a reality. Nothing, I trust, will hereafter take place to trouble that good understanding between us which furnishes so important a guarantee for the welfare of Europe.

"We were gratified to learn that you liked our future son-in-law so much. He has written to us full of gratitude for the kindness of the reception you gave him, and full of admiration for all he has seen in Paris. . . . I embrace the Empress, and subscribe myself, sire and dear brother, ever your Imperial Majesty's very affectionate sister and faithful friend.

" VICTORIA R."

Many, indeed, were the times during these years when the relations of the two countries were endangered by either the prejudiced attacks of English papers and politicians upon the Emperor, or the bitter enmity of French officers and leaders against England. When these somewhat frequent incidents occurred Napoleon sought relief and pacific explanations by either visiting or writing the Queen, and the result was invariably a renewal of the *entente cordial*. The Swiss episode referred to above is a forgotten and now unimportant one, but the Treaty of Paris, which the Queen speaks of, and which terminated the Crimean war, owed its final acceptance, in the form which the British Government wished, very largely to Her Majesty's influence upon Napoleon and her judicious manipulation of his admitted desire to preserve an English alliance. Coupled with this was the recognized ability of Prince Albert and the Emperor's respect for his views and frequently asked advice. Speaking of Napoleon's visit to Osborne, in 1857, Lord Malmesbury says in his Diary that "the object of the visit is kept very secret, but I have no doubt it is to discuss the subject of the Principalities." The French Government at this time wanted Moldavia and Wallachia to be united under one Hospodar, or Prince, while the British Government thought separate rulers would be safer, and perhaps less accessible to external Russian influences. Lord Malmesbury adds that "the Emperor has long been very much dissatisfied with Lord Palmerston, and I suppose he has come to try to settle matters with the Queen." In this case he succeeded, and the Principalities were united for a brief period in their stormy career. To-day, after coming through all the storm-swept waters of the Eastern Question, they are known as the peaceful and prosperous Kingdom of Roumania.

A curious international incident occurred in 1859, which illustrates both the

Queen's attitude toward Napoleon III. and her active participation in foreign affairs. It must, of course, be borne in mind that while she personally liked the Emperor, and earnestly strove to keep the two countries upon good terms through him, she was not at all desirous, after the Crimean period, of any allied relationship which might involve England in French complications. Hence it was that in the war between France and Austria, when Italy was made a sort of pawn to the players in that peculiar struggle, Her Majesty deprecated strongly Lord Palmerston's desire to aid Napoleon by various indirect ways and means. Hence it was that she did not share the surprise and disappointment of her Ministers at the Peace of Villafranca—a feeling which Lord John Russell expressed in a letter to the Queen on July 7th, 1859, by the remark that "the Emperor must either give independence to Italy, or be stigmatized as the betrayer of the Italian people." It was this distrust of Napoleon's policy—arising more from a knowledge of the national conditions by which he was constantly forced forward than from any personal prejudice or disbelief in his frequently good intentions—which enabled Her Majesty to write such an authoritative letter to Lord Palmerston, on July 18th, as that from which the following is an extract:

"We did not protest against the war, and Lord Palmerston personally wished France success in it. We can hardly now protest against the peace, and Lord Palmerston will, the Queen is sure, see the disadvantage which would accrue to this country should he make it appear as if to persecute Austria were a personal object with the first Minister of the Crown. The Queen is less disappointed with the peace than Lord Palmerston appears to be, as she never could share his sanguine hopes that the '*Coup d'Etat*' and the Empire could be made subservient to the establishment of independent nationalities, and the diffusion of liberty and constitutional government on the Continent. The Emperor follows the dictates of his personal interests, and is ready to play the highest stakes for them, being himself entirely uncontrolled in his actions. We are cautious, bound by considerations of constitutional responsibility, morality, legality, etc. Our attempts, therefore, to use him for our views must prove a failure."

But Lord John Russell, who was now Foreign Secretary under Palmerston, was bent upon finding some means of reversing or rearranging the terms of peace. To this end he proposed a scheme for the settlement of Italian affairs, and submitted drafts of the despatches to the Queen before sending them to the French Government. In returning them, on August 24th, Her Majesty refused her sanction on the following expressive grounds: "Either it is expected that our advice will not be listened to, in which case it would not be useful, and hardly dignified, to give it, or it is expected that France will follow it. If, on finding herself cheated, Austria were to feel herself bound to take up arms again, we should be directly responsible for this fresh war. What would then be our alternative? Either to leave France in the lurch to refight her own battles, which would entail lasting danger and disgrace on this country, or to join her in the fresh war against Austria—a misfortune from which the Queen feels herself equally

bound to protect her country." Lord John referred the matter to the Cabinet as a whole, and its decision was in favour of the Queen's position. So it was with the Emperor's effort to have an European Congress deal with the Italian question, and thus save him from the difficulties of his position.

The British Cabinet at first favoured the idea, but wiser counsels from higher quarters finally prevailed, and the scheme fell through. Her Majesty's letter to the Foreign Secretary on November 18th shows the basis for her wise interference upon this occasion, in a single paragraph : " The whole scheme," she wrote Lord John, " is the often attempted one, that England should take the chestnuts out of the fire, and assume the responsibility of drawing the Emperor Napoleon from his engagements to Austria and the Pope, whatever they may be, and of making proposals which, if they led to war, we should be in honour bound to support by arms." Then followed the long negotiations relating to Italy, the French occupation of Rome, the rivalries of France and Austria and Prussia, and the private declaration of the Queen, on February 5th, 1860, that, despite her warnings to the Government, "we have been made regular dupes of." Fortunately, however, Her Majesty had prevented any serious British entanglement, and the only unpleasant result was Napoleon's effort to annex Savoy and Nice—to which the above remark referred—as a reward for his services to Sardinian independence and expansion. Yet all this time there is little doubt of the Emperor's real desire to act with England. Upon occasion, as the Queen had said, it was in order to have his chestnuts pulled out of the fire by someone else, but underlying it all was " the profound conviction " that the harmonious action of the two countries was indispensable and their antagonism a calamity—as he told Lord Cowley after the passage of the Cobden trade Treaty of 1860. The policy of the Queen was to conserve this feeling of friendship, while refusing to be an instrument of French aggression or ambition. That she succeeded against the French-Italian sympathies of Palmerston, who was Prime Minister during the period, is a strong proof of her power in foreign affairs and knowledge of foreign conditions.

The details of diplomacy in these years indicate therefore that more than once the Queen prevented her Ministers from drifting into war with Austria. So it was with Prussia in the succeeding period, and during the prolonged and complex Schleswig-Holstein embroglio. Her Majesty seems, however, to have always stood upon the sound basis of argument and discussion with her Cabinet and not upon the platform of prerogative—strong as her power in that connection might really be. Hence it was that no further personal trouble occurred with Lord Palmerston, however much the Premier and his Sovereign might differ. He undoubtedly now recognized both her ability and right to intervene, but there seems to have developed a tacit understanding on both sides—either in the case of a difference with Lord John Russell or with the Prime Minister—

that the Cabinet should decide the issue as a whole so long as it possessed
the unmistakable support of Parliament and the people.   In no other way could
the Government have been carried on, and it is the highest tribute which could
possibly be paid the Quean's statecraft that she was usually sustained in her
conclusions by the Ministry—even against the two chief men in its ranks.

The Schleswig-Holstein question is too large a one to deal with in detail,
but it may be said roughly and briefly that Denmark possessed the best right to
the two Duchies, and Prussia the power which enabled her to ultimately take
them.   By the protocol of 1850, partly negotiated, and signed by Lord Palmerston as British Foreign Secretary, the union of Denmark and the Duchies had
been practically admitted by the great Powers and confirmed by the Treaty of
1852, which was signed by Lord Malmesbury.   Thus, both parties in England
were pledged to a recognition of the Duchies' incorporation with Denmark.
But there was the inevitable loophole, or opening for the diplomatic wedge, in
both these arrangements.   They were accepted subject to a reservation of the
rights of the Germanic Confederation—of which Holstein had once been a member.   And, as the years passed on, the question became complicated by Danish
efforts to make the Duchies a closely incorporated part of the monarchy, and
the opportunity which this gave the two great rivals, Austria and Prussia, to
gain a point with the various German States through intervention on behalf
of the German inhabitants of Schleswig and Holstein.   Ultimately the Duchies
were occupied by the allied troops of the German powers, and Denmark appealed
in vain to the signatories of the treaty of 1852.   During the whole of this period
English sympathies were with Denmark, and the British Government openly
showed its feelings in the same direction.   Could they have obtained French
assistance, war would have probably resulted.   More than once this seemed
probable.   Lord Malmesbury's Diary contains some interesting references to the
Queen in this connection :

" December 5th, 1863.—I returned from Windsor.   The Queen sent for me before dinner
and spoke of the Danish question ; though she is annoyed about it, she told me that it
was not my fault, that I could not do otherwise than sign the treaty of 1852, which had
been drawn up by Palmerston."

" January 29th, 1864.—The Prussians and Austrians are advancing towards the Eider
with the intention of entering Schleswig ; the Danes are preparing to resist, but can have
little chance unless England or France come to their assistance, which the latter, it is said,
is ready to do, but the Queen *will not hear* of going to war with Germany.   No doubt this
country would like to fight for the Danes, and from what is said I infer that the Government is inclined to support them also, but finds great difficulties in the opposition of the
Queen."

Very many signs go to prove this statement of Lord Malmesbury's.   The
private correspondence—since published—of both Lord Russell and Lord Palmerston indicate their very strong predilections in the direction of war.   Writing

on April 18th, 1864, the latter declared that "public opinion in this country would be much shocked if we were to stand by and see the Danish army taken prisoners, and Denmark thus laid prostrate at the feet of Germany." The Queen, however, watched matters very closely, and on May 5th Lord Granville writes to Lord Russell that: " Last night the Queen sent me your two draft despatches to Vienna with a message. Her Majesty does not like Lord Palmerston's conver. sation with Apponyi (the Austrian Ambassador), nor the embodiment of it in a despatch with the Cabinet's adoption and approval." Eventually the conver- sation was disregarded, and the despatch, which had threatened, under certain contingencies, the sending of a British fleet to the Baltic to prevent the entrance of the Austrians, was modified to an extent which saved England from isolated action and probable war.

But in addition to the Queen's influence upon her own Government in favour of peace was the fact that she did not exert her personal influence with Napoleon against it. He was left, so far as she was concerned, to the clever manipulation of Count Bismarck, who now first came to the surface of affairs in Prussia, and by keeping the French Emperor from an intervention which would have forced England into the struggle got the united German troops into the Duchies, while by his brilliant diplomacy he kept the Prussian troops in permanent occupation, and manoeuvred the Austrian forces out of the territory—thus giving his country an im- portant advantage over its great rival, a pronounced increase of prestige amongst the German states, and its first impetus towards the headship of the Confederation and the Imperial supremacy of to-day. The Queen's intervention with her Government, therefore, prevented war with the united forces of Austria, Prussia, and the German States, while her non-interference with Napoleon possibly allowed him to make the great tactical mistake of his life, in letting Prussia obtain the supremacy in Germany and enabling Bismarck to create his conquering edifice of a few years later.

As things now stand, this was a great service to England. Any policy which might have hopelessly antagonized the united Germany of to-day would have been dangerous, if not disastrous. Count Vtzthum von Eckstaedt, who, during these years was Minister for Saxony at the Court of St. James, blames the British Ministry in his memoirs for holding out delusive hopes to Denmark, declares that for a time war seemed iminent, and attributes the ultimately peace- ful result to the steadfast support and intervention of the Queen. As a German he felt proportionately grateful, and adds : " Maligned, insulted, and reproached for German sympathies, Her Majesty has checkmated the dictatorship of her Prime Minister and beaten him three times in his own Cabinet on the question of war or peace. The Queen has recognized the true interests, the true wishes, of her people." Count Beust, the eminent Austrian statesman who was ambas- sador in London at the time, also tells us in his Memoirs that :

"The Queen was thoroughly versed in the Schleswig-Holstein question. . . . Consequently my task was not difficult, but I can say that I performed it skilfully. I maintained, with all the eloquence of conviction, that all Germany would rise as one man if an armed intervention of France or England (which at that time seemed imminent) were to take place; and I have been assured on very trustworthy authority that in this case the Queen followed the example of her grandfather, George II., who in the early part of his reign refused to be fettered by constitutional trammels, and frequently carried his point by a personal decision."

During the years which follow we have only been allowed occasional glimpses of the Queen's part in foreign affairs. Her influence unquestionably grew with every passing year; increased with her own Ministers and foreign rulers by the force of garnered experience; and was enhanced by the marriages of her family into the Royal houses of Europe. From the letter published recently by Prince Bismarck, without Her Majesty's permission and in defiance of all diplomatic etiquette, we know that she used her personal influence with the Emperor William against renewed war with France in 1875. Dr. Busch tells us, in his Life of "the man of blood and iron," that the Queen wrote twice to Prince Bismarck in 1877 asking him to intervene on behalf of peace between Turkey and Russia. He does not, however, publish the letters, and adds that she finally wrote the Emperor, holding him and Germany responsible for the coming conflict. There is inherent probability in the latter statement, but not much in the former. Correspondence of such a nature between the British Sovereign and any foreign Minister—no matter how great a personality he possessed—would hardly be the correct thing. And Her Majesty has always been punctilious to an extreme degree in matters of the kind. We know, however, that she sympathized strongly with Lord Beaconsfield's policy in Turkey and at the Congress of Berlin, while her letter to General Gordon's sister declares that she not only took a keen interest in the lamentable Soudan war, but strove to obtain more prompt and active steps for his rescue at the hands of Gladstone's Ministry.

Of this latter situation Lord Randolph Churchill spoke on May 20th, 1885, when he declared that "I cannot help thinking that, if under Providence, we are extricated from the great difficulties which surround the nation, it will be peculiarly owing to the wise and sagacious counsels which Her Majesty, from her long experience of public affairs, and from the great influence which she is enabled to command by reason of the unparalleled manner in which she has filled the position of a constitutional sovereign, is able to give." Of course, it is not possible for Ministers or ex-Ministers of the Crown to publicly state that they receive and desire the advice of their Sovereign, but from this and many similar utterances, or letters which might be quoted, it is clear that they come as near to making the assertion as is advisable. The monarchs of Europe, as well as the political leaders of to-day, are indeed the veriest tyros in experience, knowledge, or statecraft, when compared with the Sovereign of Great Britain.* She has seen Nicholas I., Alexander II., Alexander III., and now the youthful Nicholas II. upon the Imperial throne of Russia. She has followed the politics and participated in the international policy of that Empire for a quarter of a century before the present Czar was born. She has seen the Papal throne occupied by Gregory XVI., by the veteran Pius IX., and by Leo. XIII. She has been in close touch with all the foreign relations of France during two Republics and the reigns of Louis Philippe and Napoleon III. She has had frequent communication with the Emperor Francis Joseph of Austria, and probably understands the complex mechanism of that empire better than any living personage outside of its own veteran sovereign. She has known Frederick-William III. of Prussia; has lectured Frederick-William IV.; has been upon most intimate terms of friendship and correspondence with William I. of Germany; and has combined the family and State relationship with the Emperor Frederick, and the present youthful ruler.

Wars have been prevented upon more than one occasion in Europe by her advice and influence over her own Ministers; diplomatic troubles and friction which might have led to war have been soothed by her personal and foreign influence upon far more frequent occasions than history will yet reveal to us; a conflict over the Trent affair with the United States was unquestionably averted by the intervention of Her Majesty and Prince Albert; while many now incomprehensible pages of British history in its connection with foreign countries are unquestionably due to the Queen's influence or intervention, and to the heavy veil of secrecy which necessarily hangs over such incidents—a veil which the Prince Consort's Memoirs were allowed to partially lift, and which diaries like those of Lord Malmesbury, or incidents such as that recently connected with Prince Bismarck, have slightly raised again. To an extent far greater indeed than is generally known or even fancied, the Queen has been her own Foreign Minister. Lord Palmerston was the strongest and most popular political personality in England during the years preceding and following the Crimean war, yet he had to bend under her displeasure in 1851, and in the time of his dominant Premiership had to more than once submit his views and those of his Foreign Secretary to the wiser and more logical opinions of the Queen. Lord Beaconsfield was the other great Minister of the reign who pre-eminently prided himself upon a knowledge and love of foreign affairs, and the whole world knows how sincerely he and his Sovereign worked together in the direction of Imperial expansion and prestige. Speaking on September 26th, 1871, at Hughenden, and before assuming his second and great Premiership, Mr. Disraeli—as he then was—referred in weighty words to the position and duties of the Queen:

---

*Hence the utter folly and ignorance of a typical despatch to Canadian and American newspapers—preceding the Czar's English visit of 1896—to the effect that a visit of Lord Salisbury to Balmoral was in order to "post the Queen" so that she would not "make any mistake in the event of the Czar's conversation trenching upon high politics."

" Those duties are multifarious ; they are weighty ; they are incessant. I will venture to say that no head of any department of the State performs more laborious duties than those which fall to the Sovereign of this country. There is no despatch received from abroad, nor any sent from the country, which is not submitted to the Queen ; the whole of the national administration of this country greatly depends upon the sign-manual ; and of our present Sovereign it may be said that her signature has never been placed to any public document of which she did not approve. Cabinet councils . . . are reported and communicated on their termination by the Minister to the Sovereign, and they often call from her remarks that are critical and necessarily require considerable attention."

And then the speaker declared that " such complete mastery of what has occurred in this country, and of the great important subjects of State policy, foreign and domestic, for the last thirty years," is possessed by the Queen that " he must be a wise man who could not profit by her judgment and experience." Since this speech another quarter of a century has passed away, and the great statesman who expressed the opinion has long ago become but a sacred memory to his followers and friends, and his career a brilliant page in history. His interest in foreign policy has passed to Lord Salisbury and Lord Rosebery, and they in time have come under the influence of Her Majesty and the control of her still more ripe experience and rich stores of knowledge. It is in this connection impossible to overestimate the value to the nation of the Sovereign's position abroad. To quote an American paper which cannot be accused of friendliness to England or the British Monarchy—the New York *Sun* of January 12th, 1896 :

" She does not fear to remind her grandson, the German warrior, of his duties ; she looks upon her relative by marriage, the Russian Czar, as a youngster in need of guidance ; she is on the best of terms with the Emperor of Austria, and with the King of Italy, and the King of the Belgians, and the Kings of Portugal, Denmark, and Sweden. No British states-man could speak to these monarchs as the Queen can speak to them, in a motherly, or sisterly, or a cousinly, or a collateral way. They would not take from any man, not even from a king, such words as Her Majesty can pen to them, or utter in their presence. Thus Her Majesty possesses a power unlike that of any other sovereign in Europe. She is a veteran diplomatist. When negotiations are afoot, when there is a time of danger, she can make her influence felt from the Thames to the Oxus."

In these, and in many other ways, Her Majesty has added to the dignity of the Crown and the nation a personal prestige which immensely increases the power of the Empire for good, and the effect of its decisive action during any critical period. Her life-long impartiality as between rival and European nations has also enhanced the weight of her opinion, and the close relations with France which were cultivated from time to time during the reigns of Louis Philippe and Louis Napoleon are quite sufficient answer to hints of undue German tendencies during the reigns of the recent Emperors. And, as time passes on, and the veil is lifted upon the diplomacy of the last thirty years, it will be seen how great and beneficial has been this continually growing influence of the Queen upon the more important international complications and events of the period.

H.I.M. WILLIAM II.,
GERMAN EMPEROR AND KING OF PRUSSIA

PRINCESS ALIX OF HESSE, EMPRESS OF RUSSIA.

CLAREMONT, AN EARLY ABODE OF QUEEN VICTORIA.

CHAPTER XXV.

The Queen and the United States.

THE impression made by the Queen's life and reign upon the people of the United States has been of an extraordinary nature. There is only one other name within the realm of England and the sweep of British power which commands anything like a similar measure of respect. But Mr. Gladstone, with the exception of his attitude during the Civil War, has usually supported measures of change, and democracy, and so-called reform; has gone out of his way to praise American institutions, and flatter American prejudices; has appealed to a side of political opinion in England which all Americans consider it a duty to support—without always knowing the reason why. The Queen, however, has voiced for sixty years that monarchical principle which the citizens of the United States are taught to look upon as either tyranny or impotence. She is surrounded by an aristocracy which the American press would lead its people to regard as permeated with corruption and immorality. She is, above all, the head of a nation which embodies in its modern history all the heaped up prejudices—national, educative, journalistic, and political—of the American people.

Yet the Queen is very popular in the United States. It is not popularity in the sense of that word as used in England. It is rather a feeling that Her Majesty in some way represents the best home life of her people, and is in person an embodiment of virtue, a living example to her subjects. Mixed up with this, in an unacknowledged and perhaps hardly realized degree, is respect for her great position and her lofty state surroundings of dignity and ceremonial. To quote Mr. G. W. Smalley—usually a very able critic—"there seems to be in America an odd mixture of personal respect and even admiration for the Queen, with an impatience that her subjects should translate respect and affection into loyalty." The fact is, that through the antagonism felt for England there has struggled a ray of peace and friendliness in this liking for England's Queen. Through ignorance of British institutions, and the profound belief that a monarchy is opposed to democracy, has grown a gradual perception of the truth that the Queen, in her position, adds to democracy the two qualities of dignity in administration and stability in foreign policy, which the United States so greatly lacks.

These things are hardly confessed in the press, nor do they appear very much in public addresses, but the ideas have entered the homes of the country, and find occasional expression in the pulpit—coupled, of course, with that curious deification of democracy for which, in speech, the Americans are so well known, and to which, in practice, they are so often indifferent. But this feeling for the Queen is not extended to her ancestors, or to her family. American literature teems with unpleasant statements about the monarchs of England and the general institution of monarchy. American newspapers are filled with scandalous stories about the Royal family, or insinuations which are worse and more silly than the stories. The editorial statement of such a high-class paper as *The New York Tribune*, that the English juror who, during the trial of Gordon-Cumming, examined the baccarat chips used by the Prince of Wales was, "in reality, fingering the fragments of the crown of England," illustrates one phase of the situation. The abuse once lavished upon Prince Albert, the miserable fictions told about the Prince of Wales, the brutal remarks in papers like *The Minneapolis Tribune* about the life and character of the Duke of Clarence, the eagerly seized upon and utterly false stories of little Prince Edward's deafness and dumbness, indicate other points of view.

That the Queen has remained high above this stream of misrepresentation and cabled calumny is a tribute to her life and work of the loftiest import. And aside from the national American prejudice against monarchy, her sphere of labour has been a very difficult one. She has always endeavoured to keep the Empire and the Republic upon good terms, and perhaps to this recognized fact, coupled with a knowledge of her impartial position between the Liberal party, which the American generally likes, and the Tories, whom he usually detests, is due a large share of her popularity. Certainly the relations between the two countries have been sufficiently complicated and difficult to manage. The War of the Revolution and the War of 1812 left rankling memories of bitterness on the American side, reciprocated in England more by a sort of good-natured indifference than by genuine hostility. When Sir Stratford Canning (Lord Stratford de Redcliffe) was appointed minister to Washington in 1819, his friend Henry Addington, wrote him that the American mission was "the most important, difficult, and dangerous of all on the list," and added, "if you can succeed in keeping those schoolboy Yankees quiet and saving us another hundred millions you will be England's *Magnus Apollo*."

This rather offensive phraseology was not used in a letter from Sir Robert Adair, who, about the same time and with prolonged diplomatic experience, voiced, however, the same idea: "Most difficult will be your task, difficult beyond that of any European mission." Two years later Sir Stratford himself declared that "the feelings of this nation are as pacific as they are ever capable of being—but so is gunpowder till the spark touches it." When the Queen ascended the throne matters were not very much improved. The miserable little rebellion which was taking place in Canada received the almost universal sympathy of

Americans, and the more practical aid of arms, and money, and men. The schooner "Caroline" was openly used for the conveyance of munitions of war to the rebels from American sympathizers and the New York State arsenals, while its ultimate seizure by Canadian forces was denounced throughout the Republic as unlawful and piratical. To quote Sir Francis Bond Head, in a dispatch to the Colonial Secretary dated 9th February, 1838: "The capture of the 'Caroline' has been productive of the most beneficial consequences. Before it took place American sympathy for our absconded traitors was unbridled and unchecked. The state arsenals were openly plundered, subscriptions were openly collected, provisions as well as munitions of war were openly supplied."

This difficulty passed away only to be succeeded in 1842 by the boundary question, which Lord Ashburton was deceived into settling with the surrender of undoubted Canadian territory; and by the Oregon dispute, over matters which the American press summed up in the belligerent motto, "Fifty-four forty or fight." Fortunately for British interests forty-nine degrees was ultimately agreed upon as the boundary. Then came the Central American and Monroe doctrine troubles of 1856, the San Juan dispute of 1859, and the refusal of the United States to permit any vessel which chose to fly the American flag—no matter how suspicious its character, or how close it might be to points of slave-trading importance—to be stopped by the British cruisers engaged in suppressing the iniquitous traffic in slaves. Curiously enough the Queen and the nation had to also face during the Crimean War an undoubted American sympathy with Russia.

Why it was so no one seemed to understand, though history will describe it as a survival of national hostility to England herself. It is interesting to note, in view of the occasional claim—the sincerity of which is so much to be desired —that the United States would help Great Britain in any serious European conflict, that at this time Sir John Crampton, the British minister, paid the passage money of some volunteers who wished to go and join our forces in the Crimea. Though the minister was fortified by an American judicial declaration that such an act was not illegal; though the British Government stopped further enlistment when it heard of the matter, and, without waiting for any communication from the United States Government, apologized for the unintentional offence; though any other nation in the world would have been amply satisfied, Sir John Crampton was promptly ordered out of the country, and the feeling of the people temporarily soothed by a gratuitous insult to Great Britain. Not only had Americans no idea of aiding England in that war, but their government and press went out of the way to show friendship and sympathy for Russia.

Then came the disastrous Civil War, and its effect in enhancing American prejudices against England. Meanwhile, however, the Queen had shown her friendliness toward the United States in many ways. Her natural antagonism to slavery revealed itself in undoubted sympathy for the North—so far as the war was fought for the suppression of that great crime against humanity. An extract from Mary Howitt's Diary throws a curious side-light upon this fact:

"December 3rd, 1852. The Queen has read 'Uncle Tom's Cabin,' as well as all her subjects. She and the Duchess of Sutherland, and others of the good and great about the Palace, have determined to make a demonstration in favour of the slave. Her Majesty in her own person can do nothing ; therefore, the movement comes from the Duchess of Sutherland. From her I received an invitation to meet a number of distinguished women at Stafford House, to take into consideration an address from the women of England to the women of America on the subject of slavery."

Eventually, the Committee then appointed obtained over 576,000 signatures to this address, and paved the way for the wonderful reception given Mrs. Harriet Beecher Stowe in 1856. Amongst the myriad social invitations which the famous authoress then received was one to visit Inverurie Castle, the seat of the Duke of Argyll, and it was while on their way to this destination that Professor Stowe records a meeting with the Queen. " None of the informal drawing-room, breathless receptions," says he, " but just an accidental done-on-purpose meeting at a railway station. . . . The Queen seemed really delighted to see my wife and remarkably glad to see me for her sake . . . the Royal children stared their big blue eyes almost out looking at the little authoress of 'Uncle Tom's Cabin.'" But pleasant as these personal courtesies were, Her Majesty had still more practical methods of creating good-feeling. Of these the visit of the Prince of Wales to the United States in 1860 was the most important. When the news reached Washington that a Royal tour of British America was possible, the President at once addressed the following letter to the Queen:

"To Her Majesty Queen Victoria :

" I have learned from the public journals that the Prince of Wales is about to visit your Majesty's North American dominions. Should it be the intention of His Royal Highness to extend his visit to the United States, I need not say how happy I should be to give him a cordial welcome to Washington. You may be well assured that everywhere in this country he will be greeted by the American people in such a manner as cannot fail to prove gratifying to your Majesty. In this they will manifest their deep sense of your domestic virtues, as well as their convictions of your merits as a wise, patriotic, and constitutional sovereign.

" Your Majesty's most obedient servant,

" JAMES BUCHANAN.

" Washington, June 4th, 1860."

The Queen, in her reply, expressed appreciation of the invitation, and intimated that the Prince would return from Canada through the Republic, though on leaving British territory he would drop all royal state and travel under the title of Lord Renfrew. A letter from Lord John Russell to the American Minister, in response to an invitation from the New York City Council, went more into particulars, and added that his Royal Highness " trusts to be enabled as a private gentleman to employ the small amount of time at his disposal in the study of the interesting features in the United States, and of the ordinary life of the American people." Needless to say, the two national characteristics of curiosity and hospitality prevented any such hope being realized. From September 20th, when he arrived at Detroit, after a prolonged series of Canadian ovations, until he sailed from Portland on October 20th, the Prince was given very little time for rest and hardly any for retirement. An immense crowd welcomed him at the border city, where, of course, the people were more or less familiar with what had been going on in the Canadas. Chicago, which was reached after a long and somewhat dreary railway journey, was less enthusiastic, but, no doubt, presented a more interesting subject for inspection and study to the visitor. At every station and cross-road on the way crowds of people had gathered to see him, but were very seldom gratified, and the published expression of a desire that the trip should be as private as possible prevented any public demonstrations in the great western city. But it could not control popular curiosity or hinder people from trying to see the Prince.

At Cincinnati the Duke of Newcastle, who acted as the Prince's guardian in the States, as well as in British America, wrote to the Queen that enormous crowds had turned out to welcome the party, while at St. Louis some 80,000 people were visible in the streets. According to the Duke, there was no enthusiasm, but great curiosity combined with courtesy and order. It is notable, as illustrating a curious public hostility to the British flag, that during the visit to this representative town not a single Union Jack was hoisted in honour of the heir to the British Throne. Somewhat similar conditions had prevailed in Chicago, and were repeated in many other places. Pittsburg, Harrisburg, Baltimore, and Washington were subsequently visited, and everywhere the reception was kindly and courteous, and marked by a steadily growing popular interest. The most important event at the American capital was a visit to the home and tomb of Washington at Mount Vernon. It was an interesting occurrence, but the difficulty of avoiding " gush " under such circumstances is illustrated by the terms of the *Times* correspondence : " Before this humble tomb the Prince, the President, and all the party stood uncovered. . . . There is something grandly suggestive of historical retribution in the reverential awe of the Prince of Wales, the great-grandson of George III., standing bare-headed at the foot of the coffin of Washington. For a few moments the party stood mute and motionless, and the Prince then proceeded to plant a chestnut by the side of the tomb. It seemed, when the Royal youth closed in the earth around the little germ, that he was burying the last faint trace of discord between us and our great brethren in the West."

In New York the reception was beyond all doubt enthusiastic, and the people appear to have at last awakened to what such a visit should mean, and would result in, if the spirit of its inception and intention was really carried out.   An American writer named Davis declared Lord Renfrew to be "an up and down and out and out Prince," and asserted that there was " not a living being more beloved by our people than his Royal mother, who, they think, cannot do wrong, even if she tried to."   Processions, dinners, and balls signalized the visit, and also marked the brief stay in Albany and Boston.   At the latter place occurred the most interesting event of the whole American tour—the singing by a thousand school children of an ode written by Oliver Wendell Holmes.   The following verses are very striking :

> " God bless our Father's land ;
> Keep her in heart and hand,
>   One with our own.
> From all her foes defend,
> Be her brave people's friend,
> On all her realms descend,
>   Protect her throne.

> " Father, in loving care
> Guard Thou her kingdom's heir,
>   Guide all his ways.
> Thine arm his shelter be
> From harm by land and sea ;
> Bid storm and dangers flee,
>   Prolong his days ! "

Harvard University, in the town of Cambridge, was seen, and then the Prince left for Portland, Maine, whence he sailed with the Royal Squadron, amidst farewells from roaring cannon, ringing bells, and cheering people.   To say that this American visit did good is, of course, the absolute truth.   But it was an evanescent benefit at best.   The Prince of Wales no doubt obtained a wide experience of new people and strange places; found himself dancing in ballrooms where everyone stopped to look at him, and visiting theatres where the whole house turned from the stage to the Royal box; passed unnoticed for a time amid the crowds of Philadelphia during an especially exciting election ; and probably learnt much in many directions of the working of Republican institutions.   Upon the relations of the two countries, however, despite the hopes of the Queen, and the belief of the Duke of Newcastle, that "the most important results will ensue from this happy event," there was no real impression made. The good that was done seems to have been largely counteracted by the hostility of a part of the press, and the untruthful stories circulated about the young Prince in a country which had not a basis of personal loyalty, or popular knowledge concerning England and its Royal family to go upon.   There was nothing in the nation as a whole, sentimentally or otherwise, to minimize the force of this ensuing newspaper campaign,* and the result was that a visit which should have conduced to the unity and friendship of two great nations only caused a fleeting exhibition of mingled curiosity and temporary personal enthusiasm.

Quickly following this event came the lamentable Civil War, and a record of international complications which show much injustice done to England's action and policy as distinct from England's sentiment. There is no doubt that a considerable body of British sentiment was with the South. There is even yet a feeling that both Washington and Lee fought for independence, but one succeeded and the other failed. Sir Henry Parkes, of New South Wales, in his autobiography says with truth that while he was in London " the recognition of the Confederates was loudly talked of, and in the great drawing-rooms few words of sympathy with the Federal cause were heard." Lord Palmerston, under certain contingencies, was in favour of interference; Mr. Gladstone at one stage of the rebellion spoke of Jefferson Davis as having made a nation ; and Lord John Russell, on September 17th, 1862, wrote Palmerston that " whether the Federal army is destroyed or not it is clear that it is driven back to Washington and has made no progress in subduing the important States. Such being the case I agree with you that the time is come for offering mediation to the United States Government with a view to the recognition of the independence of the Confederates." Seventeen thousand pounds were subscribed in England for the relief of the Confederate soldiers in Northern gaols, while the bulk of the great Reviews and many of the newspapers prophesied the destruction of the Union. And, finally, the " Alabama " escaped from Liverpool the day before the law officers of the Crown had concluded that it could be legally seized, and had issued orders accordingly.

Such is the case against England. Superficially, and seen after years of misrepresentation, it seems strong. Upon the other side is the fact that *action* was never taken by the British Government against the North, despite the strong current of popular feeling ; that leaders such as Bright, Disraeli, Forster, and Cobden worked strenuously against intervention or any recognition of the South ; that the middle classes as well as many of the aristocracy sympathized with the North, and were assisted by the heroic self-sacrifice of the Lancashire operatives, who would not raise a finger, although starving in thousands, for want of Southern cotton ; that the Queen undoubtedly favoured the Northern cause, and with her Government resisted all the pressure of Napoleon III. to join with him in recognizing the South ; that thousands of Canadians volunteered and fought in the Northern armies, and few, if any, in those of the Confederacy. In

---

*The author has an editorial yarn of this nature before him now in a largely circulated Western paper—the Minneapolis *Tribune*. It is too silly to quote, but accuses the young Prince of snobbishness, drunkenness, swearing at a man in the streets, and all manner of ignorant, clod-hopping actions.

a letter written on May 10th, 1861, Mr. W. E. Forster spoke of the attempted resolutions in Parliament—none of which ever passed—and declared of one which was then being proposed that "most men of influence wish him not to persist in bringing it forward." And then he continued almost in the spirit of a Northern abolitionist: "I cannot be longer without saying how intensely interested I am in this crisis of your country, and how much I, I may say we, sympathized with you in what must be your feeling. Terrible, however, as is civil war, I cannot say but I greatly rejoice in the outburst of patriotism throughout the North. I am doing what in me lies to help it."

The position of the Queen is indicated by three facts—her known antipathy to slavery, her influence in holding back the Ministry from action, and her refusal to join Napoleon III. in the proposed intervention. The first is proven by the incident already narrated, where the Duchess of Sutherland—a close friend to Her Majesty, and holding a Court post which absolutely prevented public action without the Queen's permission and favour—headed a national woman's petition against the continuance of slavery. The second is indicated by the little known fact that in September, 1862, when British intervention was almost decided upon by the Government, Lord Granville came to Gotha, where the Queen was then staying, as Minister in attendance. Immediately on his arrival a message arrived from Lord Russell, the Foreign Secretary, stating that the Cabinet was about to discuss the question of Southern recognition. In the state of political feeling then existing, and amid daily news of Southern victories, the result could hardly have been doubtful. Needless to say that the matter was at once discussed with the Queen, and equally needless to add that the following extract from a very long letter in reply to Lord Russell was dictated by Her Majesty's view of the situation. Lord Granville's position in the Cabinet would certainly not have warranted him in using such language upon his own responsibility: "It is premature to depart from the policy which has hitherto been adopted by you and Lord Palmerston; and which, notwithstanding the strong antipathy to the North, the strong sympathy with the South, and the passionate wish to have cotton, has met with such general approval from Parliament, the press and the public." Lord Palmerston, in his answer, said that the letter required serious consideration; and as we now know, the ultimate decision was against taking action.

The third point is of even greater importance. The relations of England and France were at this time very close, and the feelings of the Queen for Napoleon III. were personally very cordial, although always tinged with suspicion of his public motives and policy, as apart from his private and personal qualities. The Emperor was intensely anxious to intervene in favour of the South, and probably cherished those incipient ambitions for American territory which afterwards found vent in the unfortunate episode of Maximilian in Mexico. It might also have been a diplomatic advantage for England to have supported him in return for his assistance in the Schleswig-Holstein question. But, just as the Queen deprecated and averted hostile action against the Germans in the latter case, she seems to have also used her influence with her own Government in opposition to Napoleon's persistent efforts. Mr. Spencer Walpole, in his Life of Lord John Russell, says that in November—following the situation already indicated—the British Cabinet "refused to join France in the offer to mediate, which the Emperor of the French made alone." Had the Queen supported his suggestions with her own Cabinet they would probably have carried, and had England joined with France in an intervention favourable to the South, as desired by Palmerston and Russell two months before this date, it would have probably resulted in a general war and the eventual disruption of the American Union.

Thus, in face of much popular and class sentiment, and in the teeth of urgent French wishes and possible diplomatic benefits—to say nothing of intense suffering in the cotton districts—the British Government did not intervene, and by this negative policy probably saved the Republic. A prompt joint intervention in September, 1862, accompanied by the refusal to recognize an illegal blockade, would have given the Southern States money and supplies, and even without the aid of British or French troops would have afforded them an opportunity of using their victories and indefinitely prolonging the struggle, if not in the end winning their independence. What was the result of this refusal to carry out individual opinions and the sacrifice of many English material interests? The Trent affair, soon after, dragged the two nations to the point of war, and public opinion became so embittered in the Northern States that perhaps all time will not wipe out the feeling. The South was disgusted at the policy of inaction, the North angry at the supposed sentiment of sympathy with the Confederates. The Alabama claims were pushed to the front, and more than once threatened war. The treaty negotiated in 1865, by Reverdy Johnson and Lord Clarendon, was thrown out of the United States Senate with contempt, and Charles Sumner's speech upon the question set the whole Republic on fire with anger—even James Russell Lowell sharing in the national sentiment. A special correspondent of the London *Times*, writing after General Grant's death in 1885, declares from personal knowledge that all the members of Grant's Cabinet were then in favour of war, and that the President himself was the only cool and calm person amongst them. Yet so little did he know of England or English life that he believed the country of Victoria to be much the same as the country of George III., and actually said to the correspondent in question, that "I did not know you had to reckon with the people in your country"!

Between this period and the settlement of the points at issue by the Geneva arbitration, hostility was the order of the day in the United States, and it naturally aroused some feeling in England—but absolutely nothing in comparison.

Canada suffered severely in the abrogation of its Reciprocity treaty with the Republic, and the encouragement given to Fenian raids on the border. Misunderstanding was indeed rife in the United States, and it is to be feared always will be, concerning England's policy during the war. But, as the Queen had done her best to conciliate sentiment before the conflict by permitting the visit of the Prince of Wales; as she did her utmost to avert hostilities or dangerous British action during the struggle; so after it was all over she used every possible means to soothe the feelings of a hasty and misinformed nation, and make the relations of the two countries friendly and sympathetic. Her expression of womanly sorrow to Mrs. Lincoln, "the heartfelt sympathy of a widow to a widow," was a gracious way of indicating genuine British feeling regarding the deplorable death of the great President. Her treatment of George Peabody—the eminent American philanthropist—in 1866, was another instance of international regard, or disregard, of national divisions. Mr. Peabody had done much for the poor in London, and his gifts at this time were so generous and wisely distributed that the Queen decided to offer him some high British honour as an evidence of public appreciation. It was declined, but he received instead a letter which might well be prized, and considered as he described it in his reply, "an evidence of the kindly feeling of the Queen of the United Kingdom toward a citizen of the United States":

"Windsor Castle, March 28th, 1866.

"The Queen hears that Mr. Peabody intends shortly to return to America; and she would be sorry that he should leave England without being assured by herself how deeply she appreciates the noble act, of more than princely munificence, by which he has sought to relieve the wants of her poorer subjects residing in London. It is an act, as the Queen believes, wholly without parallel; and which will carry its best reward in the consciousness of having contributed so largely to the assistance of those who can little help themselves.

"The Queen would not, however, have been satisfied without giving Mr. Peabody some public mark of her sense of his munificence; and she would gladly have conferred upon him either a baronetcy or the Grand Cross of the Order of the Bath, but that she understands Mr. Peabody to feel himself debarred from accepting such distinctions.

"It only remains, therefore, for the Queen to give Mr. Peabody this assurance of her personal feelings; which she would further wish to mark by asking him to accept a miniature portrait of herself, which she will desire to have painted for him, and which, when finished, can either be sent to him in America, or given to him on the return which she rejoices to hear he meditates to the country that owes him so much."

The tact and timeliness of such a letter, and such expressions, are beyond all praise. With many similar instances, they explained the sentiment which began to prevail in the United States concerning the Queen, and about which General Meredith Read wrote Sir Theodore Martin on June 22nd, 1878, that "a feeling of affectionate respect has always been entertained towards the Queen in America.

This found expression when the President visited New-England last year on the anniversary of one of our Revolutionary battles, and Mr. Evarts, our Secretary of State for Foreign Affairs, proposed the toast of the Queen ; immediately, 40,000 people sprang to their feet and cheered enthusiastically." Similar manifestations took place at Norfolk, Virginia, about this time, and at the opening of the Philadelphia Centennial Exhibition. But all this was merely the beginning of a friendly, kindly sentiment, and it is still very far from having reached the desired end—a national friendship for Great Britain. A personal liking for England's Queen is, however, a long step in the right direction, and to its steadily growing strength may be due more of peace and diplomatic compromise than is generally understood, although a recent indication is afforded by the popular influence of the Prince of Wales' message during the Venezuelan controversy.

Meanwhile General Grant had been making his tour of the world. He was received in Great Britain with a warmth and kindly interest which seems to have astonished him greatly. Fed upon a mental and literary diet which for years had represented England as the bitter enemy of the Republic, and as lying in wait to do it an injury at every turn, he was naturally surprised to find himself received with almost Royal honours and fêted in every direction. Cheers came from the people, addresses from corporate bodies, receptions, banquets, and every form of entertainment from the leaders of the country—and especially from the aristocracy, whom he had been taught to think of as greatly disliking the American Republic. The Prince of Wales dined him and the Emperor of Brazil at the Mansion House, and it may be said here that upon his death in 1885 a telegram was sent to Mrs. Grant from the Prince and Princess, asking her to "accept our deepest sympathy on the loss of your distinguished husband. We shall always look back with gratification at our having had the advantage of knowing him personally." A further illustration of this Royal and national sentiment was produced by the assassination and death of President Garfield in 1881.

During the long illness and brave struggle which followed Guiteau's crime the feeling shown in England was really wonderful in its brotherly strength and sympathy. Mr. G. W. Smalley, the American correspondent, described it at the time as "a memorable demonstration." Of the Queen he declared that : " Her messages, and most of all that last outburst of womanly and wifely sympathy with the President's wife, are, and will remain, household words in America. I can only repeat what I told you some weeks ago, that those about the Queen describe her as passing agitated days, often talking of the President and Mrs. Garfield, impatient for the bulletins, and anxious for better news when a bad despatch arrived. Again and again she has broken through the etiquette that hedges a Queen to send her own messages, in her own name and in her own handwriting, to Mr. Lowell and to Mrs. Garfield." So, in a hundred other directions have England and the British Sovereign testified cordial feelings towards the United

States.   Actions and incidents which from any other nation would inevitably have caused war are passed over with good-natured indifference, or received with sincere sorrow and willing compromise.   The Canadian fisheries disputes and the rejection of the Chamberlain treaty by the Senate, the Behring Sea arbitration, the dismissal of Lord Sackville, and a dozen minor instances, illustrate a regrettable American hostility, while proving the British desire for friendly relations.

Yet while these things are occurring there has been no relaxation of British efforts to appease the unfortunate ill-feeling based upon the wars of long ago and cultivated by the mistakes of the time of civil strife.   American Ministers in London, such as Everett, Buchanan, Adams, and Motley, could never complain of their reception, but later ones, like Lowell, Phelps, and Bayard, have been fêted and treated more as great English leaders than as foreign ambassadors.   At the very time of the Sackville incident Mr. Phelps was being entertained in every direction, and before his departure he was invited to Osborne by the Queen, while his wife was visited by Lady Salisbury, Lady Rosebery, and the wives of other recent Foreign Secretaries for the purpose of presenting a gift of diamonds as a farewell compliment.   In the same spirit Mr. Bright had written not long before to the American Centennial Committee—Sept. 9th, 1887:

" As you advance in the second century of your national life, may we not ask that your country and mine may march in line in the direction of freedom and that policy which the moral law will sustain ?   May we not comfort ourselves with the belief that your country, under a succession of noble Presidents, with their Ministers and your Congress, and my country under a succession of patriotic Sovereigns with their Ministers and Parliaments, may assist and guide the growing millions for whom they act to nobler ends than have hitherto been reached ? "

Upon every side these personal tokens of regard have grown in England, from the memorials of Longfellow and Lowell in Westminster Abbey to the honorary degrees constantly conferred by the great universities on eminent Americans ; the banquet and receptions given to Captain A. T. Mahan of the " Chicago " ; the election of American Ambassadors to high honorary posts in England; and the sending by the Queen of a private exhibit of tapestries worth hundreds of thousands of dollars to the World's Fair.   There have been some pleasant reciprocal courtesies and much of the reverse.   To take the unpleasant topic first, it must be said that the American press does not try to educate the public into a friendly sentiment towards England, and that much of the friendly language used by American Ministers in London is either entirely changed when they return to the States, as in the case of Mr. Phelps before the Behring Sea arbitration, or else militates absolutely against future position or political popularity, as in the case of Mr. Lowell.   As President Grant thought so the American masses are taught to believe—that England is more or less of an aristocratic despotism tempered occasionally by public suffering and discontent.   To them the poet's wail is entirely true :

" Landless, joyless, restless, hopeless,
    Gasping still for bread and breath,
To their graves by trouble hunted,
    Albion's helots toil till death."

They do not comprehend the power of England, they utterly disbelieve in the loyalty of the Empire, they misunderstand the position and functions of the aristocracy, they read daily chapters of multitudinous misrepresentation concerning English leaders, politics, and history. The most extraordinary language is in constant use by public men and newspapers. The *Illustrated American* gravely tells its readers that the destiny of Great Britain is annexation to the Republic. " In the end, England must be American or perish." Congressman Wilson, in 1888, declared that should the Queen of England aim one unfriendly shot at the United States from one of her warships: " I predict that the echo which it would awaken would not cease to reverberate before Grover Cleveland, President of the greatest Republic on earth, would salute Charles Stewart Parnell as President of the youngest Republic on earth." Such bombast is more frequent than is generally supposed, and is embodied in legislation such as the Alien Labour Law, by which respectable Canadians are debarred from crossing the border for purposes of livelihood. And it produces such episodes as the speech of Mr. Andrew Carnegie at Dundee, denouncing the Queen and the " funny little monarchy," or that of Colonel Ingersoll in his insult to Canada and England by the declaration that " there isn't air enough upon the American continent to float two flags."

But this is the worst of it, and we must hope that better feelings will continue to grow and increase despite ebullitions of a dangerous spirit, and the still more harmful outflow of hostile literature and invective such as were aroused by the Venezuelan trouble. Ralph Waldo Emerson was able to appreciate the motherland, and no writer in the world has more truly portrayed its greatness and its great men than he. To him " England is the best of actual nations," and London " the epitome of our times." Nathaniel Hawthorne was able to live there several years, and to then write a charming book with a significant title—" Our Old Home." In erecting an American memorial to Shakespeare on the banks of the classic Avon, Mr. George W. Childs, of Philadelphia, received no more interesting tribute than a letter from John G. Whittier, the veteran Quaker poet: " I have just read of thy noble and appropriate gift to the birthplace of Shakespeare. It was a happy thought to connect it with the Queen's Jubilee. It will make for peace between the two great kindred nations, and will go far to atone for the foolish abuse of England by too many of our party orators and papers. As an American, and proud of the name, I thank thee for expressing in this munificent way the true feeling of all our people."

Such should be the spirit of United States citizens, and such it should in time become under the influence of moderation, education, and reciprocal courtesies. Speaking at one of these latter evidences, or efforts at international comity, Mr. Bayard told the distinguished gathering which had met in London to dine the officers of the "Chicago," that "the banquet is being given—it is a happy omen —on the birthday of that benign and gracious lady whose devotion to public duty, and whose pure and beautiful private life have endeared her not merely to those who have the good fortune to live under her benignant sway, but to all right-minded and right-thinking men and women in America as well as in England." This was indicated to a limited extent in the Jubilee celebrations of June 21st, 1887. On the preceding Sunday many services were held and special sermons preached in the Republic, though they were not as numerous as might have been desired. The Rev. Morgan Parker, of Philadelphia, told his congregation of the Queen's sympathy with the widows of Lincoln, Garfield, and Grant, and declared that during the dark days of the Civil War her sympathies were with the cause of union and liberty. In New York a great mass meeting was held, at which Mr. Seth Low, Mayor of Brooklyn, described Her Majesty as "a perfect type of Queen, ruler, and woman," and declared that the American people were "grateful for her friendship when America needed it, and grateful for her ready sympathy in our joys and sorrows." Still more important was the speech of Hon. A. S. Hewitt, one of the higher class of American politicians :

" I am introduced as Mayor of New York, but I am not here as Mayor of New York, but as an American citizen in whose veins blood is thicker than water. In the hour of our trial, when the flag under whose broad folds I was born was trailing in the dust, as a humble citizen it was my fortune to resort to another land on matters of great moment. There I learnt—and I know whereof I speak—that we owe to the Queen of England the non-intervention policy which characterized the great Powers of the world during our great struggle for life and death."

.It was a manly speech, and did good, though it proved a factor in Mr. Hewitt's defeat when afterwards standing for re-election—mainly because of being delivered under the auspices of St. George's Society, and to a gathering composed chiefly of Englishmen. Chicago, Boston, Pittsburg, and other places also celebrated the event. Of the Queen's share in moulding American sentiment and controlling international relations between the Republic and the Empire much more might be said. But the main facts are that she has always desired friendship betwixt the two countries, and has always striven to maintain it. The past therefore speaks for itself, and it would also speak for the future, were it not for that divided note which commenced at Bunker's Hill and continued in varied and discordant strains through the succeeding century. Her Majesty has done her best to pipe the tunes of peace and harmony—the song which should be sung :

"Two empires by the sea,
Two nations great and free,

> One anthem raise.
> One race of ancient fame,
> One tongue, one faith, we claim,
> One God whose glorious name
> We love and praise."

But the end is not yet certain. Despite the fact that American ideas of liberty were learnt from England, American law modelled after the British system, American literature in its higher sense derived from English models or inspiration, American learning and enterprising spirit inherited from the British race, the United States, as a whole, is not friendly to the idea of a British alliance or to the power and expansion of the British Empire. Despite the fact that, as Mr. Lowell says, Wolfe's victory above Quebec " made the United States possible," and that Americans admire Shakespeare—though they do not greatly cultivate his plays—and like Burns, or Tennyson, or Walter Scott, in differing degrees of fancy, they do not appreciate a sight of the British flag or comprehend the benefits of united thought and action between the two great English-speaking races. It may all come in time, and, if it does, Queen Victoria will hold the highest place in the international pantheon of the future. If the two peoples, however, do not grow into closer relations they must grow further apart, and the latter process indicates possibilities of hostile action and policy which all true subjects of the Republic or the Empire should try to avert. Let us hope that the better principle will prevail, and the national emblem of England become to the United States as sacred, if not as loved, as its own great flag:

> " With its red for love, and its white for law,
> And its blue for the hope that their fathers saw
> Of a larger liberty."

CHAPTER XXVI.

The Queen at Home.

THE home environment of British Monarchy is perhaps the most solidly magnificent in history or the world. In certain elements of histrionic splendour it may be inferior to the oriental surroundings of the Mogul Emperors of Hindustan, the early and greater Sultans of Turkey, or some of the present Princes of India. But in the massive proportions of royal Windsor, the lofty beauty and artistic grace of the interior of Buckingham Palace, the luxurious comfort of Osborne or Balmoral, it has a setting of combined historic and modern grandeur beside which all other royal environments pale into significance. Around this setting are grouped the great houses of British nobles, such as Wilton and Longleat, Haddon Hall and Hatfield House, Belvoir and Trentham, Lowther Castle and Welbeck Abbey, Arundel and Raby Castle, and a host of other structures which in beauty, or military strength, or historic memories, constitute worthy and solid surroundings to the royal abode at Windsor—in the same way that the aristocracy of Great Britain forms a suitable and splendid basis for the maintenance of the Court and the dignity of the Crown.

The first of these many houses of the Queen in personal interest is Kensington Palace. Plain, old, and unpretentious to a degree, it now stands amid beautiful grounds of a public character, and in the heart of a crowded residential suburb of London. Here, in the days when it formed the comfortable country home of the Duke and Duchess of Kent, Her Majesty was born in 1819. Here, after her father's death, she played and studied and lived the simple life of a child —and nothing more. Here, amid the sylvan glades of what were then private and retired grounds, the Duchess and her little girl roamed at will, breathing the fresh air and healthy instincts of the rural scenes, and, so far as the child was concerned, growing in strength and health and mental vigour. Though not now a royal abode except in the sense of being occupied by Princess Louise and the Marquess of Lorne, it is therefore important as having been for eighteen years the home of the future Sovereign. In an architectural sense it is a large quadrangular brick building of the most simple and homely character.

Historically, it was a private residence and the seat of the Earl of Nottingham, until the first years of the reign of William and Mary, when it was purchased by the Crown for £20,000. King William added the wings and made various alterations, and the house of to-day is pretty much as he left it. It was indeed

OSBORNE HOUSE, ISLE OF WIGHT.

BALMORAL CASTLE, SCOTLAND.

Windsor Castle

KENSINGTON PALACE

THE BIRTHPLACE OF QUEEN VICTORIA.

he principal home of Queen Mary and her strong-minded, able, and patriotic husband—royal consort in name, but Sovereign in reality—and the abode of Anne, of George I. and George II. Here their Courts were held in

"The tea-cup days of hoop and hood,
And when the patch was worn."

And within its walls were held many an important Council of State in the days of William, many an unimportant and more or less dull assemblage in the days of Anne and the first Georges. Here gathered the wit and wisdom of the Court of Anne, only to be dulled by formalism and by a moral strictness excellent in itself, but not properly applied, and not sufficiently forcible to be widely beneficial. Here met the still more stupid and narrow and gossipping Court of George I. and his immediate successor, and through its wide sweep of wooded land and artificial waters wandered the belles and beaux of a now forgotten period. Of the Palace itself, Leigh Hunt says that "it possesses a Dutch solidity; it can be imagined full of English comfort; it is quiet, in a good air, and, though it is a palace, no tragical history is connected with it; all which considerations give it a sort of homely fireside character, which seems to represent the domestic side of royalty itself, and thus renders an interesting service to what is not always so well recommended by cost and splendour. Windsor Castle is a place to receive monarchs in, Buckingham Palace to see fashion in, Kensington Palace seems a place to drink tea in."

From Kensington, on the day of her accession, Queen Victoria passed to the stately splendours of Buckingham Palace and thence to Windsor. Since then she has never resided within the familiar walls, though paying a brief and very occasional visit to the place. The London residence of the Queen is plain and solid-looking without, as are so many of the greater mansions of England, and brilliant within. The earlier building upon the site was known as Arlington House, and is famed in history as having seen the first cup of English tea made —from leaves brought home by the Earl of Arlington in the year of the great plague and at a cost of sixty guineas a pound. In 1703, the Duke of Buckingham rebuilt it under its present name. Long afterwards it was purchased by George III., who for some time used it as a royal residence. In 1775 Queen Charlotte occupied it and held her drawing-rooms there, while in the early years of Queen Victoria's reign it was repaired and improved at a cost of £150,000, and has since been the abode of Her Majesty during her visits to London—the scene of the gaieties and balls and functions of her earlier Court, and the occasional State events of later years.

It is difficult to describe such a building as this—not so much because of the mere grandeur of furniture, and colouring, and gilding, and surrounding brilliance, but because of the general idea of beauty conveyed, and the priceless nature of pictures and other items of luxury, or elegance, or taste, contained within its walls. The entrance through the central arch, for instance, has gates supposed to be the most beautiful in Europe; the great marble hall is surrounded with double columns of pure Carrara marble of a Corinthian character, while this particular roof is painted with armorial devices in royal blue and crimson, and green and gold. Opening from the hall is a splendid suite of rooms —the first being hung and carpeted in blue and drab, with pilasters of gold, and mahogany furniture. Then comes the room occupied by Nicholas I. of Russia in 1844, with its painted ceiling of white ground, with gold and royal blue decorations, its marble Corinthian columns and curtains of crimson silk, its carpet of crimson velvet and furniture of the same upholstery, with frames of burnished gold.

The centre room is sometimes used for banquets, is lighted by massive ormolu chandeliers, and supported by columns of Ionic granite. Here are seen collections of priceless and matchless china—Sèvres, Dresden, and Chelsea; a Roman mosaic table of great beauty, presented to the Queen by Pope Pius IX. in 1859, "in commemoration of the visit of the Prince of Wales"; an Oriental vase presented by Napoleon III.; a unique model of a mortar beautifully carved and worked, and given to the Prince Regent in 1812 by the Spanish nation as a memento of the raising of the siege of Cadiz; Genoa vases, life-sized paintings, and many other valuable and artistic things. In the succeeding room the ceiling is exquisitely painted, the curtains are of crimson silk, with borders of rose, shamrock, and thistle worked in gold, while the furniture is of rosewood gilt and crimson silk. Splendid paintings upon military subjects crowd the walls. In another and smaller room is a collection of rare old paintings, many of them fourteen hundred years old. It includes a large one placed here temporarily of the famous Soudan contingent from New South Wales, and illustrates not only the event, but the Queen's interest in the patriotic spirit which inspired it.

Leaving this suite of rooms the visitor, after retracing his steps, may perhaps, if he has been so specially and unusually favoured, ascend the grand staircase of white marble—richly carpeted in crimson upon State occasions—with its hand-rails of mosaic gold, and a roof painted in gold and cream, and supported by great marble columns. The East or promenade gallery is finally reached, and is found to be carpeted in crimson, with luxurious settees, and costly marble chimney pieces, and mantels crowded with Sèvres; cabinets of tortoise shell, buhl and inlaid ivory; pedestals and busts, together with Frith's famous picture of the marriage of the Prince of Wales. Then comes the State ball-room finished in 1856 at a cost of £300,000, hung with crimson velvet and floored with inlaid satinwood. The beautiful drawing-room follows with its superb decorations, ormolu chandeliers, curtains of gold silk, walls panelled in gold, furniture upholstered in gold, the floor carpeted in gold and white Brussels, marble chimneys with rarely beautiful sculptured figures, costly cabinets, Sèvres china, gold screens, vases presented to the Queen on her marriage by Prince William of Prussia (afterwards German Emperor), and paintings by Kneller, Lely, and others.

The Picture Gallery is filled with priceless and beautiful paintings—Titian, Teniers, Rubens, Rembrandt, Reynolds, Vandyck, and others, being prominent, and leads into the magnificent Throne room, with its ceiling emblazoned with shields and armorial bearings, a frieze illustrative of the Wars of the Roses, curtains of crimson silk edged with gold lace, and furniture to match, chandeliers and candelabra which at night throw a richly soft brilliance over occasional scenes of more than splendid appearance and reality. The Throne stands on a dais of carved and burnished gold, and is covered with crimson velvet and canopied with the same material. The Green drawing-room, which comes next, takes its name from the walls being panelled in striped green silk and gold, and its furniture being made to match. There are many more rooms of importance and interest, but a brief reference only can be made to one seldom seen,* and reserved for the exclusive use of Her Majesty and the royal family. It opens into the white drawing-room by touching a spring which moves a large cabinet and mirror as though it were a door, and closing behind the royal party as they pass through hides all trace of the entrance. This Closet, as it is called, contains a beautiful collection of enamels, many choice art treasures, inlaid cabinets, ormolu stands, carved or inlaid tables, and is hung with crimson silk and gold.

Such is a brief sketch of the interior of Buckingham Palace, which in magnificence is perhaps fully equal to that of Windsor, though it has, of course, no external or architectural pretensions to even compare with that colossal castle. The grounds, however, are very beautiful and extensive, and well fitted for the occasional garden-parties or Royal fêtes given by the Queen. One of these rare events—for Her Majesty has never cared very much for her London Palace since the gay days of her youthful reign and the happy years of her married life—occurred in June, 1889, and has been described at length by Mr. G. W. Smalley. The 5,000 guests, after their arrival and passage through seemingly endless lofty corridors, and lines of gorgeous guards or grave officials, found themselves suddenly on the broad gravelled terrace at the back of the buildings, and surrounded by all the loveliness of an English park in the leafy month of June—and in the heart of London's swarming population. Tents and many-coloured marquees, boats floating on the little lake with rowers in royal scarlet, gentle slopes of ground, broad stretches of exquisite turf, trees which seem like memorials of a primeval past, women without number arrayed in all the loveliest and most lustrous hues of soft and silken fabrics—everything most distinguished in English society and the British Court were there.

*The author cannot sufficiently appreciate the privilege of having been allowed so see this exquisite little room. It is a gem of artistic beauty and richness.

Presently the Majesty of England entered, proceeded by equerries and other gentlemen in attendance, and accompanied on this occasion by the King of Denmark, the King and Queen of the Belgians, the King of Saxony, the King of the Hellenes, the Prince and Princess of Wales, and a host of beautiful women or famous men.   Through the gaily-dressed multitude, where, as the Queen passes, every man bows his head and every woman courtesies, she proceeded with slow and graceful dignity, bowing now and then, and occasionally pausing to recognize some distinguished personage, or summon him, through the Prince of Wales, to a moment's audience and speech.   Of her appearance at the time Mr. Smalley says: "I do not think any enthusiasm of loyalty would lead the most devoted of her subjects to say that the impressiveness of the Queen's presence is due in any considerable degree to dress.   It does not matter what she wears.   I have said it so often that it is mere repetition to remark on the singular, the absolutely unique, distinction of her bearing and manner."   After a circuit of the grounds in this way Her Majesty retired to the royal pavilion, guarded and surrounded by a picked company of swarthy and splendidly uniformed Indian troops, and there received the many persons who were one by one summoned to her presence. Two hours later she left the grounds, returning through the same circuit, and amid quiet but none the less expressive evidences of loyalty.   Such is a summary of the function in these beautiful grounds which it took Mr. Smalley many interesting pages to describe.

From the grounds of Buckingham Palace to the lofty towers of Windsor is a rapid transition.   But once the latter is seen it is not difficult to understand the royal preference.   The Castle is indeed a noble pile of buildings, and in solidity of strength and external splendour well deserves the declaration of more than one visiting sovereign, that it is the greatest regal residence in the world. Its history is almost as old as the Monarchy, and fits in with many of the events which have made or moulded the national life.   Here rested King John during those vital days of conference at Runnymede.   Here lived William of Wykeham, the architect, and Geoffrey Chaucer, the poet. in times when it was not used by the Sovereign.   Here dwelt Henry I., and Edward I., and Edward III. Founded originally by William the Conqueror, it was added to and enlarged by succeeding rulers, until the enormous castellated and feudal-looking structure of to-day towers above wind and storm, or seems to loom out from amongst exquisite rural scenery, the peaceful work and quiet homes of Windsor town, and the games of Eton boys upon the green sward of their cricket grounds, like some gigantic personality amid a gathering of dwarfs.   Parts of the Castle owe their construction to Edward IV., Henry VII., and Henry VIII., and to Queen Elizabeth and her successors up to the time of George IV.   The latter sovereign employed as his architect Sir Jeffrey Wyatville, and his final improvements are estimated to have cost £900,000.   Queen Victoria restored Albert Chapel in honour of the Prince Consort, and in it is seen a marble cenotaph erected to his memory, and an altar tomb to that of the Duke of Albany.

The historic walls of Windsor, it is needless to say, enclose many grim memories of the stormy past; many pleasant reminiscences of royal pageants, and marriages, and festivities; many recollections of statecraft and kingcraft, plot and counterplot, Court life and domestic incident. It is in many ways representative of Great Britain and the nation. Here during portions of the year live the Sovereign and the Court, and at least one member of the Cabinet in constant attendance. Here is a garrison of troops, a guard of volunteers, a home for the old veterans who are styled Military Knights of Windsor—one of whom for many years was Colonel Fitzgibbon, of Canadian fame and achievement in 1812. Here are the Naval Knights for the sister service, while the ancient Beefeater elbows the modern policeman, and the Royal Buckhounds typify the national sport, as Eton near by represents the best bone and sinew of British youth, and Windsor town constitutes in itself a type of the commonalty of England resting under the staid shadow of constitutional sovereignty. All around the mighty towers are to be seen the beauties of rural England, the natural graces of rolling ground, and cultivated greensward, and winding river.

> " Earth has not anything to show more fair;
> Dull would he be of soul who could pass by
> A sight so touching in its majesty."

The Castle is famed for many things. In its stately chambers are gathered most exquisite oil paintings, miniatures, drawings by old masters, rare books, and priceless manuscripts, old china of untold value and beauty, bronzes, and ancient armour, old French and English furniture and tapestries of every description, gold plate, and carvings of the richest kind. Three of the ceilings now existing were painted by Antonio Verrio, while much of the carving was done by Grinling Gibbons. In the great corridor large pictures by eminent artists, from Sir David Wilkie to Sir J. Linton, illustrate the principal personal or family events in Her Majesty's reign—from her first Privy Council to the Jubilee service in Westminster Abbey. Here also are pictures by Hogarth, Reynolds, Gainsborough, and Lawrence; a casket of crystal carved two hundred years ago, and now containing General Gordon's Bible; numerous beautiful cabinets and quantities of costly Sèvres, Crown Derby, and other kinds of china or porcelain.

From the corridor and through the spacious castle branch off an almost illimitable series of lofty rooms, with carved woodwork, ancient tapestries, bronze, ormolu, or golden candelabra and chandeliers, emblazoned ceilings, walls lined with many-coloured silks or satins, and a general combination of richness and luxury, exquisite carving, gold and crimson and blue hangings, velvet and silk and satin furniture, decorations of every shade and colour, pictures, and statuary, and ornaments of almost indescribable beauty. In the Queen's private audience room are cases let into the carved satin-wood framework, and containing two hundred enamels from Henry VII. and Elizabeth of York to Queen Victoria and her descendants. Here, also, are cases of gems and the jewels of various Orders, which have been given to the deceased sovereigns of other lands. In the Throne-room is a chair of carved ivory and precious stones, presented to the Queen by the Maharajah of Travancore. The Rubens and Vandyck rooms contain magnificent collections of the respective Masters, while the King's Closet, or private reception room, contains furniture of solid silver, presented to Charles II. and to William III. by the Corporation of London. Throughout the crimson and green and white drawing-rooms are countless treasures of art, and china, and beauty, with furniture and walls and ceiling and floors made to harmonize with the colours after which they are called.

In another part of Windsor, and seldom seen by visitors, is the Trophy Gallery, containing innumerable articles of historic interest and importance, from the sword of Napoleon and the bullet by which Nelson was killed, to the golden and jewelled casket presented to the Queen in 1895 by the Ameer of Afghanis tan through his peculiar son, the Shahzada. Here are memories of a myriad battles, trophies of every land and clime, mementoes of England's leaders on sea and land, and proofs of the conquering prowess of her sons in all parts of the globe. To describe the Castle in further detail is impossible here, but it is of more than passing interest to note the difference in royal life during the earlier and happier days of the reign and in the latter portion of its more sombre greatness. In 1840, M. Guizot, then Prime Minister of France, sent home a letter from which the following is an extract:

"I write to you from Windsor. It is certainly one of the most delightful and picturesque castles in the world; its exterior is a Gothic fortress of the middle ages, the interior is a very elegant and comfortable modern Palace. . . . On my left (at dinner) sat the young Queen, whom they tried to assassinate the other day, in gay spirits, talking a great deal! *laughing very often, and longing to laugh still more;* and filling with her gaiety, which contrasted with the already tragical elements in her history, this ancient castle, which has witnessed the career of all her predecessors. It was all very grand, very beautiful, very striking."

A quarter of a century afterwards the great Castle had passed through a tragedy indeed, and the Queen had recovered slowly and partially from the loss of the husband whose life had been so precious to her. From Court gaieties and regal functions she had turned again to the relief of work and the quiet pleasures of intercourse with cultured and eminent men. Dean Alford's Journal of July 4th, 1865, gives us a quiet picture of this change, and describes the message calling him to Windsor, the reception in the Prince Consort's private sitting-room, "with many little comforts about," the Queen's entrance, and her "very kind and gentle manner, quite such as to lead one on and make one at home." Archbishop Tait, in his Diary, says:

" July 10th, 1871.—Last week telegraphed for to dine and sleep at Windsor on Wednesday. Her Majesty received me most kindly. After dinner she spoke very freely about the mistakes made in Convocation last spring, and in the Ritual Commission."

" May 22nd, 1881.—All day in Convocation on Tuesday till evening, when Lucy and I had to rush down to Windsor to dine with the Queen. . . . The Queen told me she was reading my Charges, which rather astounded me. I told her I thought she would find them rather heavy, but she denied the imputation."

But the favourite residence of the Queen for many years, and the one to which she goes for rest and the genuine pleasures of a temporarily retired life, is Balmoral. The healthful, beauty and invigorating air of this part of the Highlands induced Sir James Clark, the Royal physician at the time, to recommend the situation to Prince Albert as suitable for a summer residence, and after a brief lease of the place it was finally purchased in 1852 from the late Earl of Fife. There had been a small castle on the estate, originally built by Sir Robert Gordon, but it was soon replaced by a granite building in two great divisions, surmounted by a massive tower and turrets, and presenting a most stately and solid appearance. The view from the castle is magnificent, and those who know something of the beauties of Braeside and Deeside can appreciate the Queen's admiration for Balmoral and its surrounding scenery—apart altogether from many reasons connected with the memory of the Prince Consort which have made this country home of a decade so sacred to Her Majesty. Her first impressions indeed were quite enthusiastic, and are recorded in the Royal Journal of Sept. 8th, 1852: " Looking down from the hill which overhangs the house, the view is charming. To the left you look to the beautiful hills surrounding Loch-na-Gar, and to the right towards Ballater, to the glen along which the Dee winds, with beautiful wooded hills, which reminded us very much of the Thuringian Forest. It was so calm and so solitary, it did one good as one gazed around. All seemed to breathe freedom and peace, and to make one forget the world and its sad turmoils."

In the building and improvements which went on for some time after the first visit in 1849, the Queen took an active interest, although Prince Albert necessarily directed the operations, and in doing so, utilized to the full his naturally artistic tastes and clear ideas of beauty. Thus the castle grew as the result of their joint labours, and became to both a favourite and most home-like residence. Here, after the death of the Prince, Her Majesty came to bury for a while her sorrow and loneliness; here, during all the years that succeeded, she goes every summer or autumn for fresh air and rest:

" Away to the bonnie green hills,
        Where the sunshine sleeps on the brae,

> And the heart of the greenwood thrills
> To the hymn of the bird on the spray.
>
> Away where the clear brook purls,
> And the hyacinth droops in the shade,
> And the plume of the fern uncurls
> Its grace in the depths of the glade."

The main entrance to the castle opens into a great flagged hall containing innumerable stags' head trophies of Prince Albert's hunting, a statue of the great Argyll, and tattered battle flags from Waterloo and Sebastopol. In front of the grand staircase is a marble statue of the Prince in Highland costume, and an inscription stating that " his life sprang from a deep inner sympathy with God's will, and, therefore, with all that is true, beautiful, and good." Elsewhere is a bust of the late Emperor Frederick of Germany, whose betrothal with the Princess Royal took place here. Almost everything is Scotch, from the Royal Stuart tartan of the carpets, the frequent sound of the bagpipes, the Royal thistle upon the Queen's armchair, the Presbyterian service in the little church of Craithie, the cairns or commemorative piles of stones erected in various places around the castle, the reels danced in the ball-room, to the kilts worn by the male members of the Royal family, the Court, and the servants. Writing to his wife on October 19th, 1870, Mr. W. E. Forster, who was for the time Minister in attendance, describes the ordinary routine of life at Balmoral :

" After dinner the Queen favoured me with a long talk ; and somehow, I do not know how, I told her about the children, which interested her. I told her, too, about my father and mother, and altogether she was most pleasant and kind. The normal life here is breakfast at 9.30—all the household meals are very punctual—letters and work till 2. The Queen drives out about 11.30, and again about 3.30. She does not return till past dark, nor do we. Then the second post comes in . . . and there is the possibility of the Queen wanting me before dinner. Everything is so quiet and silent. . . . But telegrams and despatch boxes all through the day are fired at our fortress from the rushing crowd without."

If, however, Balmoral is a Scotch castle of the rural and sometimes rugged style, Osborne House, on the Isle of Wight, embodies all the home surroundings and domestic comforts of English life. It is now more than half a century since the Queen and Prince Albert went to see the mansion which then stood on the estate of Osborne, with a view to obtaining a private residence not too far from London, and yet within sight and sound of the sea. Sir Robert Peel had strongly recommended the location, and after some inspection and negotiation it was purchased, in 1845, from Lady Isabella Blatchford, the old house was pulled down, and the present handsome structure of white stone, with its two lofty towers, was erected. Soon after she had taken possession, the Queen wrote that: " It is impossible to see a prettier place, with woods and valleys and points of view which would be beautiful anywhere, but when these are combined with the sea (to which the woods grow down), and a beach which is quite private, it is really everything one could wish." Here the Prince Consort enjoyed himself to the full, not only in the artistic work of landscape gardening, and laying out grounds of beauty and taste, but in the more practical ways of model farming on a scientific basis, which he actually made to pay for the improvements and produce a profit on the expenditure. Writing in 1848, when obliged to leave Osborne for London, Her Majesty told King Leopold that "we are going to town to-day with great regret, as the occupation of farming, gardening, planting, improving, etc., is so very soothing, and does one's wearied, worried mind so much good."

In all this home work the Queen seems to have shared, and the result of their combined and sympathetic improvements was a place which constantly grew in charm of scene and in the pleasantness of its home-like surroundings. The Queen tells us in her Journals how greatly they learned to love Osborne, of their long walks in its grounds and woods, and of the special pleasure the Prince had in listening to the songs of the nightingales and in whistling to them, an encouraging note which was invariably answered. There are about 5,000 acres upon the estate, and the Queen could therefore take quite a long drive without leaving her own property. The house itself is imposing and substantial but not palatial, and the object of the Royal couple originally was to make and keep it a home rather than a palace. Comfort was considered more important than grandeur although there is necessarily a vast number of rare, or beautiful, or interesting things in the house, and a degree of luxury which is in keeping with Royal ideas of comfort. The frescoes of Britannia ruling the waves which may be seen on the grand staircase are particularly worthy of attention, as are Theed's "Psyche," and Delaroche's picture of Napoleon at Fontainebleau. It was at Osborne that the Royal children best liked to be, and where they all most thoroughly enjoyed their Christmas or other festivities. Here the Prince and Princess of Wales spent their honeymoon, and from Osborne Princess Beatrice was quietly married, at quaint and pretty little Whippingham Church, to Prince Henry of Batten. berg.

But the Queen is at home elsewhere than in Windsor, or Balmoral, or Osborne. For a decade past she has usually spent a month or two upon the continent during the inclemency of the early spring, and the place chosen has naturally been an object of interest. The south of France has been most favoured because of the absence of obtrusive curiosity or unnecessary hospitality, combined with the beauties of nature and health-giving characteristics of the places visited. Aix-les-Bains was chosen in 1885, 1887, and 1890. Grasse, the cradle of so much that is interesting in French civilization, and lying within a three hours' drive of Nice, was the next selection, while Hyères was chosen in 1892, Florence in 1894

—where Her Majesty was visited by the King and Queen of Italy—and Cimiez in 1895 and 1896.   The latter suburb of Nice is, of course, beautiful and picturesque to a degree.   The ranges of hills in the distance, their olive-clad sides and mazes of milk-white roads, the winding mule-paths, the valleys of flowers, the grottos, and sparkling springs, the slopes crowned and covered with orange and lemon groves, the tropical plants and spreading palms, the pretty villas and quaint cottages, all combine to make a scene of rare charm.   Here, as elsewhere in her visits abroad, the Queen has her own specially selected house, in some location where privacy is possible, her own attendants, and every device for the creation of home-like surroundings—even though they be only temporary.

It is impossible to leave this general subject without making a brief reference to Hampton Court.   Though no longer a royal residence it is still the property of the Sovereign, and around it clings such memories and illustrations of the past as make it exceedingly interesting.   Founded by Cardinal Wolsey in 1515, it soon became the scene of a boundless and splendid hospitality, and of festivities frequently attended by Henry VIII.— to whom he finally presented it as a gift.   This king passed much of his time here with his six successive wives, as did Edward VI.   Here Queen Mary spent her gloomy honeymoon with King Philip of Spain, and here Queen Elizabeth held many gay hunting parties, balls, and banquets, masques, and plays.   Here, also, lived at intervals James I., Charles I., Oliver Cromwell, Charles II., Queen Anne, and the first two Georges.   But George III. would have nothing to do with it, and the historic palace gradually became what it is to-day, a royal gallery of art, and the home of various aristocratic personages, who by virtue of service to the Crown or the State are considered deserving of some such reward at the hands of the Sovereign.

The State apartments are famous for their tapestries, for Verrio's painted walls and ceilings—once thought so artistically great—and for the magnificent collection of paintings by Sir Godfrey Kneller, Sir A. Vandyck, Sir Peter Lely, Tintoretto, Velasquez, Veronese, Salvator Rosa, Sir Joshua Reynolds, Gainsborough, Lawrence, Hoppner, Grenze, Holbein, and many others.   Here are the languishing beauties of the court of Charles II.—pictures by Lely which convey whole histories upon their canvas, and indicate the significance of their removal at the beginning of this reign from the walls of the private apartments at Windsor.   Here, also, is to be seen the curious astronomical clock made for the king in 1540, and which, after two centuries, was allowed for a time to fall into desuetude —meriting the poet's reproach:

> " Memento of the gone-by hours,
>   Dost thou recall alone the past ?
> Why stand'st thou silent midst these towers,
>   When time flies still so fast ? "

The palace itself is a handsome structure with a splendid Gothic roof to its great hall, which is considered pre-eminent for richness of decoration and elaborate workmanship. The grounds amidst which it is placed are very beautiful, and from here to Kew Gardens and Richmond are some of the loveliest spots upon the banks of the historic Thames. A word must also be said here about St. James' Palace. Originally built by order of Henry VIII., it was at times a Royal residence during nearly three centuries, and in the earlier part of her reign the Queen occasionally stayed within its walls, where drawing-rooms as well as *levées* were held. In the Chapel Royal she was married to Prince Albert, and here also several members of their family were wedded. But since the Prince's death, in 1861, the spacious rooms, with their splendid pictures of historic royalty, have been mainly used by the Prince of Wales for his *levées*—although the Court of St. James still remains the diplomatic designation of the Monarchy and Government.

With all these residences, it must be admitted that the environment of the British sovereign is sufficiently stately and dignified. And from unpretentious Kensington to glorious Windsor; from gorgeous Buckingham Palace to the lofty towers of Balmoral, or the cultured beauty of Osborne House; they all breathe the spirit and history of the Monarchy and of England—past and present. They give the surroundings which a great nation and the greatest empire in the world requires for its Royal representative and ruler. They contain the priceless memorials of past centuries, and the evidences of an advancing civilization and progressive history. They embody the growing culture of the country, and have for sixty years at least held within their walls the example, and life, and work which in a great Sovereign helps forward all that is good in the nation and elevating in the individual. They are, in a word, the golden setting to a ring of union between the Crown and the people, between monarchical institutions and the masses, between the Sovereign and the vast realms throughout the world. Their magnificence is to foreign rulers and States an indication of the place and dignity of Great Britain, and an evidence of the fact that a Sovereign ruling in the hearts of her people can live amid far greater surroundings of splendour and state than he who rules over their fears or governs by force of arms.

CHAPTER XXVII.

THE ROYAL FAMILY.

ENGLAND is the country of homes. From the stately abodes of its nobles and men of wealth to the ivy-covered walls of its workingmen's cottages the spirit of domesticity everywhere pervades the life of the people. In more senses than one an Englishman's home is his castle, and in no sphere of the modern national embodiment has this been more clearly shown and felt than in the palaces of the Sovereign. During her sixty years of royal power the Queen has won the deepest sympathies and regard of the nation by her love of home and its influences of purity, refinement, and culture. Her example has stamped upon the pages of British history, and the comprehension and conviction of British peoples, the fact that domestic institutions based upon lofty ideals and a worthy practice are the best and truest basis for national achievement and power.

Down through the great houses of the nobility this sentiment has spread into the villas of the middle classes, and the cottages of the artisan or labourer, until the British people have no better or more forcible element in their civilization than this belief in the sacredness of home and the pleasures of domestic life. There are, of course, shadows of sombre magnitude upon the scene. But any comparison of the small minority of dissipated peers and reckless commoners, of the debased poor in the slums of London, or the brutal workmen in other parts of the country, with what existed at the time of Her Majesty's accession, will indicate the marvellous change which has taken place in the manners, morals, and domestic life of both classes and masses. There have been several reasons for his change. The pulpit and the revived influence and work of the Church of England has done something. The spread of education has done much, though it must be remembered that culture and knowledge are by no means synonymous with good living and right dying, and that the Elizabethan period and Augustan age of Anne were distinguished by as much coarseness in manners and morals as they were by literary achievement and brilliant wit. The press has done something, though in these latter days its manifestations of sensationalism and pen pictures of evil in every form are in many cases more productive of harm than good.

But above these varying influences, though in touch with their better action and in harmony with the good they have done, was the example and life of the Queen, the ever-spreading influence of her family, the force of gentle precepts

H.R.H. PRINCE LEOPOLD, THE LATE DUKE OF ALBANY.

RIGHT HON. ARTHUR JAMES BALFOUR, M.P.

put into effective practice. Whether she was living at Windsor in royal state, at Osborne and Balmoral in domestic seclusion, or at Buckingham Palace on occasions of passing social splendour, the people have felt and seen the value of a noble home life, a truly Christian example, a model family environment. The Queen's happy marriage greatly aided in the process of popularity by which the first home in the land became the most respected, and the first family in the land the best trained and taught. Prince Albert was very fortunate in possessing her absolute trust and affection, the Queen was happy in his entire devotion, while the family was doubly blessed with the surroundings of such domestic harmony. The Prince Consort, indeed, during their twenty years of united life, had full experience of what Lord Beaconsfield so well describes in " Coningsby " as:

" The lot the most precious to man, and which a beneficent Providence has made not the least common ; to find in another heart a perfect and profound sympathy ; to unite his existence with one who could share all his joys, soften all his sorrows, aid him in all his projects, respond to all his fancies, counsel him in his cares, and support him in his perils ; make life charming by her charms, interesting by her intelligence, and sweet by the vigilant variety of her tenderness ; to find your life blessed by such an influence, and to feel that your influence can bless such a life ; this lot, the most divine of divine gifts, that power and even fame can never rival in all its delights."

This fact was one which the people could understand and appreciate, and it made other love matches in the Royal family of after years as popular and as potent for good as was the domestic happiness of the Queen and her husband. Much has been said elsewhere of the marriage and home life of the Prince and Princess of Wales, and much more might still be said. Sandringham is in many respects an ideal home, and the Princess has made its domestic surroundings as beneficial to her children and the nation as the Queen had done before her in other places and a higher sphere. Marlborough House is, of course, a great social centre and the scene of royal ceremonial and gorgeous fêtes, but it is in their Norfolk residence that the heir to the Throne and his wife and family are found at their best. Here, the second generation of the Queen's descendants through her eldest son have been born and nursed and educated. Here, the Princess has revelled in the pleasures of motherhood from the days when she would leave her guests for a few minutes to see that little Prince Eddie was properly bathed, until one by one her sons and daughters have left her—the firstborn to another world, and nearly all the others to homes of their own.

It was at Sandringham that Bishop Wilberforce, writing in his Diary on April 15th, 1871, said: " I saw the Princes again. Both interesting children. The eldest, Edward, has that inward look of melancholy which the Prince (Consort) had. George, full of fun, spirit, and life." It was here that Prince Eddie, or, as he afterwards became, the Duke of Clarence and Avondale, struggled with a life-long tendency to delicate health, and was watched over by his mother with such tender care, and an affection which is said to have been greater —and naturally so—than she felt for any of her other children. From here he went to the University, possessed of a genial and gentle manner, a modest amiability, and a sincerely Christian character, which had developed amid surroundings described by a writer in the *New Review*, who evidently speaks with authority. "There has probably never been a home in England," he declares, "where the parental and filial relationship was more unrestrained, or where the enjoyment of mutual affection between parent and child was so absolutely without a flaw. The mother was ever with them, playing or reading to them, encouraging their studies, taking a wise personal superintendence over everything that could in any way whatever affect the healthful development of her sons and daughters; and the fearless, open-hearted converse that grew up between the mother and her eldest son from childhood nothing afterwards ever came to spoil."

But the University training had to be gone through, and Prince Albert Victor—as he was known to the public—together with his brother, took a succeeding tour round the world, and later on went alone to India. Then the celebration of his coming of age occurred in 1885, and was marked by the receipt of a significant letter of congratulation from the veteran Premier, Mr. Gladstone. "There lies before your Royal Highness," said the writer, "the occupation, I trust at a distant date, of a throne which to me, at least, appears the most illustrious in the world, from its history and associations, from its legal basis, from the weight of the cares it brings, from the loyal love of the people, and from the unparalleled opportunities it gives, in so many ways and in so many regions, of doing good to the almost countless numbers whom the Almighty has placed beneath the sceptre of England." And then he wished the young Prince all possible influence and characteristics for good in the work he would have before him. The reply is interesting and modest in its terms, and is dated from Sandringham on the 9th of January:

"DEAR MR. GLADSTONE:

"I wish I were better able to answer your very kind letter, conveying, as it does, not only the best of good wishes, but carrying with them reflections on the past and advice for the future for which I wish to thank you. I assure you the letter shall have that attention which words from yourself must deserve. It admirably describes much which demands my most earnest thought on this perhaps the most important birthday of my life. Believe me, I am very grateful for your remembrance of me this day, and that among the many offerings which have reached me I prize nothing more than the letter you have so kindly written, for which pray accept my most sincere thanks. I am glad to believe that your health is restored, and I trust your many friends will have no cause for renewed anxiety on your behalf. With my most kind remembrances to Mrs. Gladstone, believe me, yours very sincerely,

"ALBERT VICTOR."

But the young Prince's life was destined to be very brief, and as melancholy in its sudden termination as Bishop Wilberforce thought the face of the little boy appeared to be in years long past. The engagement of the newly-created Duke of Clarence to the Princess May of Teck, the popularity of the proposed marriage, and the Prince's death amidst the preparations for a new and fuller life, form one of the saddest pages in England's royal history, and must have been the keenest of all griefs to the Princess of Wales. Meanwhile Prince George had been proving himself the exact reverse of his brother. He did not go to the University, he loved the sea, he was physically strong, he was fond of jokes and boyish tricks from his earliest years at home. Entering the navy in 1877, he went around the world in the " Bacchante " as a midshipman, and served through all the grades and work of a man-of-war. He has visited the West Indies, the Cape, Australia, Fiji, Japan, China, Singapore, Ceylon, and Canada, and during the many years in which he has been almost continually at sea has seen nearly every important country, or place facing the waterways of the world. From his early home training he has become a great reader, and is, of course, active in mind and body. Warm and constant in his friendships, endowed with much practical common sense and simplicity of tastes, he is the natural product of a beautiful home life and that manliest of all callings—the Royal Navy.

As Duke of York and heir presumptive to the Throne, he has had to retire from the sea, but his new career has developed in him distinctly popular qualities and a power of speech said to be superior to that of any member of the House of Hanover. His marriage with the Princess May a year after his brother's sad death has given him a beautiful home at York House—almost beside Marlborough House, and in front of St. James' Palace. There little Prince Edward has been born, and as the great-grandson of the Queen perpetuates in his own small person the direct succession to the Throne. In connection with this marriage a very passing reference must be made to the miserable slanders which alleged some previous union with a subject—who, as in all such cases, was unnamed and unknown, even to those who delighted in spreading the story. Perhaps all that is necessary is to quote the letter written by Sir Francis Knollys, Secretary to the Prince of Wales, in answer to an evidently sincere enquiry: "I am desired by the Prince of Wales to state that the report to which you allude is so obviously invented for the mere purpose of causing pain and annoyance to an innocent young couple that His Royal Highness has always declined to allow the story to obtain further currency by any contradiction from him. There is, of course, not the shadow of foundation for it ; but it is none the less cruel and malignant."

The Prince and Princess of Wales have much the same reasons for being proud of their family as the Queen and Prince Albert had. The three daughters —Princesses Louise, Victoria, and Maud—grew up to be most accomplished, cultured, and practical girls. Trained by a most kind but particular mother, they knew all about cookery and needlework, and much about fine arts and music, while their reading has been wide in one sense, though limited in another. It is said that all new novels were first read by a former governess before being placed in their hands—Mr. Stanley Weyman's "Gentlemen of France" being one of the books thus passed. The Princess Louise has now for some years been Duchess of Fife, Princess Maud has just left home to become the wife of Prince Charles of Denmark, and only one daughter remains to her who was eloquently and truthfully described by the late Sir Richard Burton during a public speech in 1887:

"That lady," he said, "has been the pivot of greatness and attraction for over twenty-four years with every eye fixed upon her; yet none have ever heard her say one word, none have ever seen her do aught but what befitted a Queen! And what perhaps all do not know is that although she may have been in public all day, perhaps tired, perhaps suffering, perhaps obliged to be in Society a greater part of the night, she never once omitted (so long as her children were little) to go into her nursery at a certain hour every evening, to hear them *say their prayers at her knee*, lest those little prayers should ever become a mockery."

Of the Queen's eldest daughter, the Princess Victoria, England had seen comparatively little between the days of childhood and those following upon the death of her husband—the Emperor Frederick of Germany. Her visits were frequent, but brief, and during the stormy years which came to the countries of the Germanic Confederation after her marriage to the Prince of Prussia, it was necessary that all her energies and devotion should be given to the people of her adopted land. But if she was not seen in person her influence was felt, and it was fully understood that the Court of Prussia and the social life of Germany soon became better and purer for the presence of the daughter of Queen Victoria. That she was greatly missed in the Royal circle at home indicates in some measure the place which she filled abroad. Writing to her from Buckingham Palace the day after the wedding—February 3rd, 1858—Prince Albert says: "My heart was very full when yesterday you leaned your forehead on my breast to give free vent to your tears. I am not of a demonstrative nature, and therefore you can hardly know how dear you have always been to me, and what a void you have left behind in my heart; yet not in my heart, for there assuredly you will abide henceforth, as till now you have done, but in my daily life, which is evermore reminding my heart of your absence."

The prolonged and valuable correspondence between father and daughter of which this letter was the commencement proves not only the ability of the Princess Royal—as she was called in England—but the respect in which her views were held by a Prince who was himself one of the most instructed statesmen of Europe. In December, 1860, for instance, the Princess prepared and submitted to her father an elaborate Memorandum upon the advantages of a law and system of Ministerial responsibility which it was proposed to tender the authorities at Berlin as a means of removing the fears then generally entertained in the Prussian Court respecting possible liberal or popular developments. Sir Theodore Martin declares that this document "would have been remarkable as the work of an experienced statesman ; and as the fruit of the liberal political views in which the Prince had been at pains to train its author, it must have filled his mind with the happiest auguries for the great career which lay before her." And, as her life opened out, it seems to have kept pace with her husband's growth in position as heir to the Throne of Prussia, as a distinguished commander in the war with France, as heir to the Imperial Throne, and finally, though briefly, as German Emperor. That her influence was considerable is shown not only in this important correspondence, but by Prince Bismarck's dislike and suspicion, and by the actions of her own son when that headstrong though able ruler ascended the Throne in 1888. Since that time the Empress Frederick has once more become a familiar figure in England and a frequent companion of the Queen's.

The career of the Duke of Edinburgh has not brought him into really close touch with the British people, although his abode at Clarence House—close to York House and St. James' Palace—has been a familiar centre of social influence, and his long experience in the Royal Navy has made him in many ways popular. Rising through all the various grades, His Royal Highness is now an Admiral of the Fleet. Beginning with his visit to the Cape in 1860, he has seen all parts of the world and roughed it in many a stormy sea and unpleasant port. Refusing the Throne of Greece in 1862, he is now Duke of Saxe-Coburg-Gotha, in succession to his uncle, the able brother of the Prince Consort. Receiving £15,000 a year from Parliament for his maintenance, he voluntarily surrendered this upon accepting his German sovereignty, and only retained £10,000, which had been afterwards granted upon his marriage with the Grand Duchess Marie Alexandrovna of Russia, daughter of the late Emperor Alexander II. It was a comparatively small amount with which to match the £20,000 paid for years by Russia as the allowance of his wife—chiefly spent in England, and still continued when they went to Coburg.

Their wedding in 1874 had been a gorgeous and popular event—the bride's trousseau costing £40,000, and her dowry, as distinct from her allowance, amounting to £200,000. Accustomed, therefore, to the wealth and luxury of the Imperial Court of Russia, the Duchess soon transformed Clarence House from its somewhat gloomy and old-fashioned condition into a tasteful, though not extravagant, home. During the prolonged absences of her husband she devoted herself to her children, and showed the possession of simple and domestic tastes. The children of the royal couple were brought up in the plainest possible way, their rooms being simply furnished, their lessons careful and continuous, their instruction in sewing and knitting and similar pursuits—so far as the girls were concerned—very complete. The Duchess herself is passionately fond of music, and one of her favourite accompanists upon the piano for a long time was Lady Randolph Churchill.   At Eastwell Park, in Kent, where they made their country home, the Duchess was extremely popular with the poor, and exceedingly charitable in a quiet, unobtrusive way.   She is also a great favourite with the royal family of Germany, and Prince Albert, the eldest son of the Duke and Duchess, has been largely educated there, and is now an officer in the army—no doubt with a view to his future rank as a German Prince.   Of their other children, Princess Marie is married to the Crown Prince of Roumania, and will bring English ideas of Court life and social development into action in that far-away and progressive kingdom; Princess Victoria Melita is married to the Grand Duke of Hesse, and thus succeeds the Princess Alice upon the throne of that small but historic principality; while the Princesses Alexandra and Beatrice are still little more than children.

In her day, the Princess Alice was perhaps the most loved and most popular of the Queen's daughters.   Her unhesitating self-sacrifice upon a myriad occasions—her devotion to her father in his days of sickness, to her mother in her days of sorrow, to the Prince of Wales in his period of fever and pain, to her husband and his people during times of war and poverty and humiliation, to her own children in that dreadful time of smallpox and death—have won for her a crown of public respect and admiration which history will preserve and increase. And this feeling her pathetic death in 1878 has made still more pronounced.   Let the Earl of Beaconsfield summarize her character and describe her death in words taken from an eloquent speech which he addressed to the House of Lords, and in which he voiced the current national sentiment:

"A Princess, who loved us though she left us, and who always revisited her Fatherland with delight—one of those women the brightness of whose being adorns society and inspires the circle in which she lives—has been removed from this world, to the anguish of her family, her friends, and her subjects.   The Princess Alice—for I will venture to call her by that name, though she wore a crown—afforded one of the most striking instances that I can remember of richness of culture and rare intelligence, combined with the most pure and refined domestic sentiment.   .   .   .   My lords, there is something wonderfully piteous in the immediate cause of her death.   The physicians who permitted her to watch over the suffering family enjoined her under no circumstances whatever to be tempted into an embrace.   Her admirable self-constraint guarded her through the crisis of this terrible complaint with safety.   But it became her lot to break to her son—quite a youth—the death of his youngest sister, to whom he was devotedly attached.   The boy was so overcome with misery that the agitated mother, to console him, clasped him in her arms, and thus received the kiss of death.   My lords, I hardly know an incident more pathetic."

The children of the Princess who has left such a noble name,

"A light, a landmark on the cliffs of fame,"

have all assumed high positions.   Her eldest son is, of course, the reigning Grand

Duke of Hesse; the Princess Victoria is married to Prince Louis of Battenberg—a brother of the Princes Alexander of Bulgaria and Henry of Battenberg; Princess Elizabeth has married the Grand Duke Sergius of Russia; the Princess Irene is wedded to Prince Albert of Prussia (brother of the German Emperor William); and Princess Alix is the wife of the Emperor of Russia. Hence an ever-widening influence, through her life and example, from the happy home teachings of the Queen and Prince Albert in days long gone by. Of a still briefer nature than hers was the career and work of Prince Leopold, Duke of Albany. But it was none the less a power for good. Married, in 1882, to the Princess Helen of Waldeck, he died in 1884, leaving two children, a widow who has since made herself widely popular, and a memory around which, as the *Times* put it, "there will long linger a serene and sunny radiance." Of his life and character something has been said elsewhere, and the universal sympathy with the Queen and appreciation of his brief life-work was so pronounced when the end came, that Her Majesty addressed to the nation one of those occasional letters in which she expresses such sincere gratitude for popular regard, and by which she wins in ever-increasing measure the affections of her people. It is interesting and pathetic in its terms, and indicates, what can readily be understood, how close to her heart was this delicate youngest son:

"Windsor Castle, April 14th, 1884.

" I have on several previous occasions given personal expression to my deep sense of the loving sympathy and loyalty of my subjects in all parts of my Empire. I wish, therefore, in my present grievous bereavement, to thank them most warmly for the very gratifying manner in which they have shown, not only their sympathy with me, and my dear, so deeply afflicted daughter-in-law, and my other children, but also their high appreciation of my beloved son's great qualities of head and heart and of the loss he is to the country and to me.

" The affectionate sympathy of my loyal people which has never failed me in weal or woe s very soothing to my heart. Though much shaken and sorely afflicted by the many sorrows and trials which have fallen upon me during these past years, I will not lose courage, and with the help of Him who has never forsaken me will strive to labour on for the sake of my children and for the good of the country I love so well, as long as I can.

" My dear daughter-in-law, the Duchess of Albany, who bears her terrible misfortune with the most touching, admirable, and unmurmuring resignation to the will of God, is also deeply gratified by the universal sympathy and kind feeling evinced toward her. I would wish, in conclusion, to express my gratitude to all other countries for their sympathy; above all, to the neighbouring one, where my beloved son breathed his last, and for the great respect and kindness shown on that mournful occasion.

" Victoria R. and I."

The character of Prince Arthur, Duke of Connaught and Strathearn, is known throughout the Empire, and has brought him a very large measure of popular affection and respect. Educated for the army at the Royal Military Academy, Woolwich, he served through the various grades until during the campaign in Egypt, in 1882, he commanded the 1st Brigade of Guards, and received the thanks of Parliament for his services. From 1883 to 1885 he commanded a division in the Bengal Presidency, and from 1886 to 1890 was Commander-in-Chief at Bombay. Since then the Duke has served at home in command of the South Military District and at Aldershot. Prince Arthur has a most popular personality, though on account of his serious military duties he has not come into as close contact with the people as some of his brothers. At Bagshot Park, their beautiful country home, the Duke and Duchess—during the brief intervals when duty permits the former to rest—have surroundings of mingled historic grace and modern comfort. The house itself is very old, and was a favourite residence of both James I. and the " Blessed Martyr."

Here the Duchess, who is a daughter of the late Prince Frederick Charles of Prussia, is greatly liked by the people. The Duke himself is affable in the extreme, and his house-steward once told a visitor that in his long period of service he had never heard or known His Royal Highness to say an unkind word or exhibit traces of ill-humour. As a soldier the Duke holds high rank in the consideration of those best able to judge. In 1893 a cruel and cowardly report was spread, and promptly cabled to the United States, that by orders from a " high personage " his troops had been so arranged at the battle of Tel-el-Kebir as to prevent him from incurring danger. Apart from the utter improbability of a British officer, royal or otherwise, being disgraced by such instructions, we know from the Queen's Journal—from which quotations have been given elsewhere—how intense was her anxiety during the progress of the battle and how great her rejoicing when the news came of his safety. The statement was emphatically denied by Mr. Childers, who had been Secretary of State for War in 1882 ; while Lord Wolseley declared it to be " absolutely untrue," and added that " no one ever even suggested that I should in any way deal with His Royal Highness differently from the other general officers in command of brigades ; nor did I do so. He took his chance like every one else ; and as I reported to you (Mr. Childers) at the time, I had no better brigadier in the force under my command."

If any further proof of the falseness of the insinuation were required it would be found in the statement of Major-General Herbert, who had fought at Tel-el-Kebir, and who told a Montreal interviewer that the " only fault of the Duke of Connaught while an action is in progress, as far as I could see, was his disposition to expose himself unnecessarily. He was away ahead of his brigade the whole time, and it is significant that his bugler was shot by his side. The Duke himself was in the hottest of the fire the whole time." Of a similar nature to this *canard* was the nonsense talked in certain circles about his appointment over Lord Roberts to the command at Aldershot. The fact is that the latter came home from India to rest, by order of his medical advisers, and could not have accepted the post under any circumstances. Next to him there could have been no better appointment than that of one who was both a keen and experienced soldier and a popular Prince. Of the Duke's interest in charitable matters one little incident will suffice. On March 21st, 1881, his cousin, the Duchess of Teck, wrote Prince Arthur asking him to try to obtain the support of the Lord Mayor in connection with certain village homes in which they were both interested. The next day a letter was despatched which had the desired effect, and in which the Duke said: "I know how fully your time is taken up, and yet I venture to think I shall not plead the cause of so excellent a charity in vain. We have, alas! daily only too many instances of how numerous is our criminal class, and it is in order to rescue children from swelling the ranks of this unfortunate class of the community that the Princess Mary Village Homes have been started."

When the Prince Consort died in 1861 the Princess Louise was only thirteen years old, though quite able to appreciate the loss in other than a purely family and personal sense. Her artistic tastes, and love of painting and drawing and sculpture, were of a nature which must have specially bound together the father and child, and which, as time passed on, continued to be carefully cultivated. Of the ability displayed by her in painting there are many evidences in various royal homes, and of her skill as a sculptor the statue of the Queen in Kensington Gardens will be a lasting memorial. But for many years, and up to her marriage with Lord Lorne in 1871, the Princess did much more than devote herself to artistic enjoyment and work. She went everywhere with the Queen, and practically succeeded to the place of companion and comforter which Princess Alice had for a time filled in the life of her bereaved mother. This devotion, and the ready sympathy and help which was always at the service of public interests and objects, soon made her one of the most popular and best liked of Her Majesty's children. From 1878 to 1883 the Marquess of Lorne acted as Governor-General of Canada, and much time was therefore spent by the Princess in the new Dominion.

She was everywhere loyally received, and did much travelling through the length and breadth of the country—making at the same time many charming sketches of its mighty mountains, its plains and forests and lakes. Speaking in 1879, Lord Lorne declared that the Princess Louise " would always associate herself gladly in anything tending to the welfare of the people of the Dominion. In so doing she will fulfil the wish of her father, the Prince Consort, whose desire it was that his children should identify themselves with the interests of our colonial Empire." Since leaving Canada both the Princess and her husband have done much to show their sympathy with its progress, and their appreciation of its people. There are many incidents and anecdotes which might be quoted in this connection as illustrative of personal kindnesses accorded to Canadians, but it is perhaps hardly necessary. The innumerable magazine articles, letters, and speeches of Lord Lorne upon Canadian topics sufficiently attest his interest, and, it may safely be said, his Royal wife's sympathy. Living quietly at Kensington Palace, the Princess has of late years taken a more or less active part in public functions and royal work, while her husband has recently obtained a seat in Parliament and is taking part in the politics which he undoubtedly likes to cultivate. In the course of time he will become Duke of Argyll and reign in the heart of those faithful clans who have been known to question whether the House of Hanover was as great as that of " the Maccallum More."

Less known personally than the Princess Louise to the masses of the public, but none the less regarded with deep respect, is the Princess Helena, who for many years has lived at Cumberland Lodge, near Windsor, with her husband, Prince Christian of Schleswig-Holstein, and their family. Devoted to the welfare of the working classes, and with untiring zeal in every philanthropic direction—especially in connection with nursing associations and needlework guilds—the Princess has done a good work in England. Visiting the poor, not only around Windsor, but even in the slums and alleys of the great capital ; helping little children in all kinds of organized and unorganized ways—by means of food, and entertainments, and country holidays ; arranging nurseries for the infants of unfortunate women who have had to work for a bare living ; and in a hundred other directions caring for the poor and the suffering; the Princess Christian finds a truly royal place in life and a home in very many hearts. To her own children she has been a model mother, and has brought them up in the best and most domestic English fashion. The two sons are soldiers, and one has seen much service in India, while the youngest of the daughters is wedded to Prince Aribert of Anhalt. Cumberland Lodge itself is a comfortable, unpretentious, but altogether charming English house, inhabited by a family which is equally English in its tastes and pursuits. Apart from her charitable work the Princess is passionately fond of music, and is skilled in playing various instruments, while Prince Christian—who is a warm favourite with the other members of the Royal family—is a great lover of such athletic and manly sports as hunting, shooting, and cricket, and is also very fond of his horses and dogs.

Of the Princess Beatrice the world has heard much—and it has never been of an unfavourable nature. Devoted to her mother, she seems to have fallen naturally into the place once taken beside the Queen by Princesses Alice and Louise. Unlike them, however, her union with the handsome Prince Henry of Battenberg, in 1885, was not allowed to affect this close companionship, and arrangements were made by which the newly married couple were to continue their residence with Her Majesty. The marriage was a quiet one, but it would indeed have seemed a scene of sorrow if the Queen had been obliged to lose her only remaining daughter and companion. To quote Lord Tennyson's Ode upon the occasion :

" The Mother weeps
At that white funeral of the single life,
Her maiden daughter's marriage; and her tears
Are half of pleasure, half of pain—the child
Is happy—ev'n in leaving *her!* but Thou,
True daughter, whose all-faithful, filial eyes
Have seen the loneliness of earthly thrones,
Wilt neither quit the widow'd crown, nor let
This later light of love have risen in vain,
But moving thro' the Mother's home, between
The two that love thee, lead a summer life."

An honest, straightforward, and genial man, Prince Henry appears to have won and retained the affection of the Queen, and to this fact was due the general happiness of the arrangement. The character of Princess Beatrice appears also to have been of a nature calculated to produce peace and comfort and surrounding harmony. Apart from her domestic tastes, she is perhaps the most accomplished musician in a most musical family; is a graceful composer, and has set to music many of Lord Tennyson's pieces; and is exceedingly fond of amateur theatricals, which in later years she has persuaded the Queen to once more tolerate, if not enjoy. Her Majesty has seen many painful incidents in connection with the national life, and has suffered much and frequently in her own family circle, but it is a question if she has seen any sadder and more painful occurrence than that of the death of Prince Henry of Battenberg. Spurred by the honest desire to achieve something for himself; goaded, no doubt, by the miserable insinuations of a discreditable section of the press; he volunteered to accompany Sir Francis Scott's expedition to Coomassie in 1895. Despite all the opposition of the Queen and his wife, he won his way, and died of fever in the jungles of Africa, before even reaching the destination of the troops. It was the sad waste of a life which was precious to his friends, and might have been made valuable to the nation. The public sympathy was, however, roused at once, though a little late, and people began to understand something of the self-sacrifice which Prince Henry's life had involved and really exhibited. From the Queen came an immediate response to the sentiment of the nation—dated Osborne, February 14th, 1896 :

" I have, alas! once more to thank my loyal subjects for their warm sympathy in a fresh grievous affliction which has befallen me and my beloved daughter, Princess Beatrice, Princess Henry of Battenberg.

" This new sorrow is overwhelming, and to me is a double one, for I lose a dearly-beloved and helpful son, whose presence was like a bright sunbeam in my home, and my dear daughter loses a noble, devoted husband, to whom she was united by the closest affection.

" To witness the blighted happiness of the daughter who has never left me, and has comforted and helped me, is hard to bear. But the feeling of universal sympathy so touchingly shown by all classes of my subjects has deeply moved my child and myself, and has helped and soothed us greatly. I wish from my heart to thank my people for this, as well as for the appreciation manifested of the dear and gallant Prince, who laid down his life in the service of his adopted country.

"My beloved child is an example to all in her courage, resignation, and submission to the will of God.   VICTORIA R.I."

Such, in great brevity, is the Royal family of England. Each of these domestic circles, whether it be the Prince and Princess of Wales at Sandringham or Marlborough House; the Duke and Duchess of Edinburgh at Clarence House, or in Coburg; the Duke and Duchess of Connaught at Bagshot House, or Aldershot, or in India; the Empress Frederick at Berlin, or in London; the Princess Christian at Cumberland Lodge; or the Princess Louise at Kensington Palace, and in far-away Ottawa; have their Courts, whether small or large, and their accompanying spheres of influence, whether great or little. So with the Duke and Duchess of York in the bewildering mazes of their public functions, and the blaze of light which illumines even their domestic retirement. So also with the more distant descendants of the Queen, whether seated near the throne of Roumania, wearing the Imperial crowns of Russia or Germany, married to the heir of the throne of Greece, or governing various German principalities. Everywhere they have borne the impress of the home surroundings which the Queen and Prince Albert first instituted amid the grandeur of Windsor, and carried into perfection amid the shades of Osborne, and upon the slopes of Balmoral. And, with hardly any exceptions, the example of the children, and the children's children, have been of the best, while their homes have spread further that environment of domesticity which has done so much to make and keep England great.

But the Royal family has not in any of its branches been content to live as merely passive examples of a happy home life. They have been everywhere amongst the people, strengthening their institutions, helping their charities, advancing their interests, and moulding their sentiments of loyalty and patriotism. The busy life of the Prince of Wales for a quarter of a century is a matter of history, and this career of royal work the Duke of York is now closely following. During two months of 1894, for instance, he performed many public duties. On April 3rd he laid the foundation stone of an institute to commemorate the Queen's Jubilee, Two days later he opened the Rutherford College at Newcastle, and on the 13th accompanied the Prince and Princess of Wales to inaugurate the new building of the Royal College of Music in London. On May 5th he presided at the annual dinner in aid of the Hospital for Sick Children—the contributions for the evening amounting to £10,000. On the 19th he opened the new lock and bridge at Richmond, and on June 11th attended the opening of the new home of the Missions to Seamen at Poplar. These, of course, only illustrate the many-sided Royal life, which also includes innumerable social functions, and private duties such as correspondence.

There are other, and more distant, members of the Royal family who have not been mentioned, but whose lives have done much more than merely mark time. Of these the genial, brave, whole-souled Duke of Cambridge is the chief. A cousin of the Queen, he has known and served her almost from infancy, and while there is nothing of the courtier about him there is a steadfastness of friendship, a depth of affection for the woman, and of almost chivalrous devotion to the Sovereign, which in these days is as rare as it is attractive. His services in the Crimea and as Commander-in-Chief of the army from 1856 to 1895 are matters of history, and there is little doubt that although a newer type of leader and one with more modern experience may have lately become desirable, the nation and the Empire owe an equal debt of gratitude to the veteran Duke in very many directions for his prolonged rule at the Horse Guards. Speaking of the popularity of the Royal family in a general sense, the *Times* of May 11th, 1893, declared in words which might well close this particular consideration of the subject, that " the feeling of loyal devotion to the Sovereign is curiously blended with a homelier interest in the persons, the characters, the fortunes of all the members of the Royal House. The domestic instincts of the masses of our people have led them, so to speak, to adopt the Royal family as their own, to share its hopes and fears, to rejoice in its prosperity, and to mourn in its adversity." This is really one of the secrets of the power of British royalty, and so long as it lasts national stability and popular loyalty will both alike be conserved.

CHAPTER XXVIII.

HER MAJESTY'S FRIENDS AND CONTEMPORARIES.

DURING her long reign Queen Victoria has seen more of the personal greatness and individual achievement of a remarkable age than has any other sovereign or personage in the history of the world. Not only has her position brought the leaders of the nation into contact and communication with her, but the increasing facilities for travel and intercourse have made her familiar with the men of the past and present generations in other countries, as well as with the interests and pursuits which they might represent. She has seen four sovereigns upon the throne of Russia, two upon that of Austro-Hungary, five upon the throne of Prussia, and three wearers of the Imperial Crown of Germany. Two sovereigns and six presidents have ruled in France; the United States has had seventeen rulers in quick and changing succession; while countries like Canada and Australia have risen from straggling and struggling settlements into great British states. She herself has had twenty Ministries at home and an almost countless number of governments in the Colonies, and has seen a constant succession of statesmen win their way upward upon the stage of affairs and pass away.

To-day very few of the leaders in the British Empire or the world were born when she came to the Throne. And it seems hard to realize that the men who have been making and moulding the destinies of nations for half a century have lived, and fought, and died within the period of her reign, while numbers who were unknown in 1837 have made history and passed away many years before 1896. Most of Her Majesty's British contemporaries in literature, and art, and science, and music, and history, and politics, have been personally known to her. Campbell, Southey, Wordsworth, Moore, and Tennyson; Hallam, Macaulay, Leigh Hunt, and Napier; Arnold, Grote, Milner, Alison, and Burton; Carlyle, Froude, Stanhope, and Strickland; Hood, Rogers, Landor, Montgomery, and Browning; Freeman, Green, Kinglake, and Matthew Arnold are a few of those who have written in living letters during the period now gone by. Novelists have been almost innumerable, but the names of Dickens, Thackeray, George Elliot, the Brontes, Lytton, Disraeli, Kingsley, Wilkie Collins, and Marryat will occur to every one. In science she has known or rewarded such men as Faraday, Brewster, Lyell, Kelvin, Tyndall, Spencer, Huxley, and Dawson. Wars and rumours of wars have brought upon the stage of affairs and into her presence a long succession of brilliant generals and able officers—men like Sir William

THE RIGHT HON. GEO. J. GOSCHEN, M.P.

ALFRED, LORD TENNYSON.

Gomm, Sir Daniel Lysons, Lord Strathnairn, Lord Clyde, Lord Napier of Magdala, Sir Richard England, Sir William Rowan, Lord Gough, Sir W. Fenwick Williams, the Earl of Lucan, Lord Cardigan, Sir Patrick Grant, Sir Richard Airey, Lord Sandhurst, Sir John Low, Lord Raglan, Sir Hope Grant, Sir W. J. Codrington, Sir Lintorn Simmons, Sir Paul Haines, Lord Roberts, Lord Wolseley, the Dukes of Cambridge and Connaught, and a myriad others who bring to memory all the conflicts of the period—east and west and north and south.

So with the Navy, and such names as Sir Provo Wallis, Sir Alexander Milne, Sir Sydney Dacres, Sir Edmund Lyons, Sir Charles Napier, Sir Astley Cooper Key, Sir Geoffrey Hornby, Sir Leopold M'Clintock, Sir John Commerell, Sir Michael Culme-Seymour, Sir Anthony Hoskins, the Earl of Clanwilliam, Lord Charles Beresford, and Lord Alcester. And, in every other walk of life, or place where genius finds an opportunity to expand into action and achievement, the Queen has met or known the leaders. The great bishops and divines of the Established Church, from the days of the Oxford movement and the secession of Newman and Manning; through those of Philpotts, and Wilberforce, and Temple, and Archbishop Tait, down to the present time; have been upon terms of more or less intimacy with the Sovereign. So with the other religious divisions, from the ministrations of Dr. Norman Macleod and the fiery personality of Dr. Chalmers, to the modern development of the Salvation Army and the work of a General Booth. Upon the stage she has known a myriad actors, and actresses, and singers, from Macready and Phelps and Mrs. Keeley to Sir Henry Irving, and from Neilson to Patti or Albani. Engineers such as Stephenson and Brunlees, painters like Landseer and Leighton, journalists such as Buckle, and Russell, and Forbes, caricaturists like Doyle, Leech, Furniss, Tenniel, and Du Maurier, have come and gone. So with the innumerable public men, and politicians, and leaders of this changing era.

It must, however, be remembered that while the Queen has known in some form or other most of the men and women of note who have distinguished her reign, only a limited number have been upon what may be called terms of friendship. From the great mass of them she has obtained amusement, or instruction, or experience; has listened to what they said, or watched what they did, or read what they had written; and perhaps granted them reward and recognition on behalf of the nation, or through her private allowances from the Civil List. Prince Albert used long ago to say that Her Majesty ought to be the best informed person in the realm, because everything comes under her observation, and because "Ministers go out, but the Queen remains." So, men of all classes have come and gone for generations, but the Queen still remains in the centre of intelligence and knowledge. During the first part of her reign statecraft necessarily required the closest attention from a youthful monarch, and the advisers who came into most direct and personal relationship with her were Wellington, Melbourne, and Peel.   They, in turn, were succeeded by Aberdeen and Palmerston.   It is needless to say much of Lord Melbourne here.   His life and the early history of the reign speak for themselves, and indicate the closeness of the friendship which existed for years between the sovereign and the statesman.   The Duke of Wellington was, up to the time of his death, almost a member of the royal circle.   No family ceremony or function was complete without him, no political crisis passed without his advice being obtained either directly or indirectly, no man in all England was so devoted to the Queen and the Prince Consort as was this great, loyal, and modest soldier.   Sir Robert Peel did not at first obtain either the sympathy or friendship of the Queen, but was accorded a simple constitutional toleration.   The peculiar circumstances which caused this feeling, combined with the natural difference between Melbourne's urbanity and his own brusqueness, were, however, soon forgotten, and became merged in a steadfast appreciation of the greater qualities which Peel afterwards showed and the personal patriotism which the Queen found to exist in his character and work. Writing to the Prince Consort after his defeat in 1846, the ex-Premier said:

" It was only yesterday that I was separating from the rest of my correspondence all the letters which I have received from the Queen and your Royal Highness during the long period of five years, in order that I might ensure their exemption from the fate to which in these days all letters (however confidential) seemed to be destined, and I could not review them without a mixed feeling of gratitude for the considerate indulgence and kindness of which they contained such decisive proofs, and of regret that such a source of constantly recurring interest and pleasure was dried up.   I can act in conformity with your Royal Highness' gracious wishes, and occasionally write to you without saying a word of which the most jealous or sensitive successor in the confidence of the Queen could complain."

But the personal relationship which was thus continued in kindly correspondence and intercourse came to an end with Peel's premature death in 1850. Unlike the great free trade leader, Lord Aberdeen seems to have won the trust and regard of the Queen from the very first, although, like Sir Robert, he retained it until his death in 1860.   It was, however, as the progress of this narrative will have intimated, a discriminating confidence.   Her Majesty knew the faults of the statesman, while she respected and esteemed the qualities of the man.   He had been her Foreign Secretary between 1841 and 1846, and history has so far recorded no serious differences of opinion.   During his Premiership and the Crimean war, Lord Aberdeen seems to have often received advice from the Sovereign, and to have been her personal friend as well as First Minister.   In 1844 he was offered by the Queen the home at Bagshot, now occupied by the Duke of Connaught, and on declining it was afterwards given the Ranger's House at Blackheath, which he used from time to time.   In December, 1854, upon the verge of retiring from office, he was made a Knight of the Garter, and about the same time the Queen wrote from Balmoral a personal letter urging him to take care of his health, in view of his past devotion to work and the impending events of the future. "The Queen must therefore," she said, "almost insist on his coming speedily north, where he will in a short time take in a stock of health, which will carry him well through the next winter and season." During succeeding years and at each visit of the Royal family to Balmoral, Lord Aberdeen found his relations with the Queen pleasantly renewed. In the autumn of 1857 she and the Prince Consort paid him the compliment of a private visit to Haddo House. But perhaps the best and most unusual evidence of her regard is the following letter written by Her Majesty upon his resignation, February 7th, 1855 :

"Though the Queen hopes to see Lord Aberdeen in a short while . . . she wishes to say what a pang it is for her to separate from so kind, and dear, and valued a friend as Lord Aberdeen has ever been to her since she has known him. The day he became her Prime Minister was a *very happy* one for her ; and throughout his ministry he has ever been the kindest and wisest adviser, one to whom she could apply for advice on all and trifling occasions even. This she is sure he will still ever be, but the losing him as her first adviser in her Government is *very painful*. The pain has been to a certain extent lessened by the knowledge of all he has done to further the formation of this Government in so loyal, noble, and disinterested a manner, and by his friends retaining their posts, which is a great security against any possible dangers."

With Lord Palmerston the Queen's relations were very varied. At first she entirely distrusted, and finally dismissed him ; then he became more careful, and she tolerated him ; finally, he emerged as a great statesman from out the shell of rashness and carelessness with which he had covered, or partially concealed, his really splendid abilities as a Foreign Minister. From that time, with isolated exceptions, Her Majesty trusted him sincerely, and regarded him with the warmest feelings of friendship. On April 2nd, 1850, Prince Albert wrote Lord John Russell, at the Queen's request, that to Lord Palmerston's management of foreign affairs since 1847 was due the fact that England, at the moment, was "generally detested, mistrusted, and treated with indignity by even the smaller powers." At this time there can be no doubt that he was bitterly disliked by the Queen and the Prince Consort. Greville goes into many details, and quotes conversations with Lord Clarendon and others in his Journal, which indicate the tenseness of the situation, even though we may not believe everything he penned, or like the spirit which dictates his writings. Then came the inevitable end, and Palmerston was forced to resign. Of the Queen's action in this matter Mr. Gladstone long afterwards wrote Mr. Holyoke, the well-known Radical, a strong expression of approval. "With a brevity beyond my power," says the latter, "Mr. Gladstone explained to me that the Crown did, in the case of Lord Palmerston's conduct, what the people would have done. The Queen deserves very high credit for her action in dismissing him ; reassuring the French people that England was neutral, intended no interference in their affairs, and lent no encouragement or sanction to the usurpation (Napoleon's *coup d'etat*) imposed upon them."

In the Aberdeen Administration Lord Palmerston was Home Secretary, and from 1855 until his death, in 1865, he was Prime Minister—with one year's interval—and away from the Foreign Office, though of course interested more or less in the management of Foreign Affairs. During this prolonged period he gained steadily in the good opinion of the Queen, as she did in his respect and appreciation. The close intercourse of Sovereign and Premier removed the past misunderstandings, so far as they may have been personal, while a better and fuller knowledge of the Queen's ability and experience unquestionably modified many of Lord Palmerston's more impetuous views. And then the latter's sincere patriotism and fervent Imperialism were brought into contact with much the same qualities in the Queen, and with the natural result of harmonized friendship. When the great Minister passed away, in 1865, Her Majesty could therefore join with deep sorrow in the national tributes to the genial, popular, and gifted statesman, and say with *Punch*:

> " He is down, and forever the good fight is ended,
>   In deep-dented harness our champion has died ;
> But tears should be few in a sunset so splendid.
>   And grief holds her wail at the bidding of pride."

Sir Archibald Allison tells us many stories of the Queen and the exercise of her personal influence. One of them concerns a bluff soldier whom she afterwards delighted to honour—and with good reason. It was at the close of the Crimean war, and Sir Colin Campbell was so jealous and angry at the appointment of a junior to the chief command there, after General Simpson's retirement, that he refused at first to go out again when it was thought that the war would be continued. " But," declares Sir Archibald, " he yielded his own inclination eventually to that of the Queen, who at Windsor, it is said, asked him to sit beside her on the sofa and burst into tears at his continued refusal. He respectfully kissed Her Majesty's hand, and said he could hold out no longer." It is not indeed difficult to understand a chivalrous soldier giving way at the sight of any woman's tears, though this statement is no doubt an exaggeration of what did actually occur. The Queen herself tells the story a little differently in a letter to Lord Hardinge, and states that after expressing the earnest hope that his valued services would not be lost to the country in the Crimea he replied that he would return immediately, " for that, if the Queen wished it, he was ready to serve under a corporal."

The feeling of personal loyalty, whether in this or other instances, is indeed fully exhibited throughout contemporary history. Writing to Lord Clarendon on August 30th, 1855, the Duke of Newcastle—who naturally felt somewhat bitter and pessimistic under the burden of unpopularity brought him by the Crimean war—referred to his travels in the East, and then added : " If I had not children at home, and a name to support in my own country, I should linger long in Circassia, or anywhere else, for I see no chance of public usefulness in such a state of things as we are now reduced to. I often think of our dear Queen, and feel how completely she is not only our main, but our only stay. There is still some chivalry and much loyalty in England ; and the throne, occupied as it now is, may keep us above the waters." The Queen's own letters have had a good deal to do with this sentiment of affection amongst her more prominent contemporaries. Nor did the sympathy thus shown and felt by her wait for expression until her own widowhood had come with all its burden of sorrow and loneliness.

To Thomas Carlyle the Queen has given one of the very few bright and pleasant notes in a discordant life. At her accession he had expressed a feeling of unusual sympathy for "the poor little Queen," and subsequent incidents increased what one must consider as almost a kindly idiosyncrasy. The bitterness of the Chelsea sage was indeed phenomenal. He once criticized Sir A. Panizzi, who had refused him some privilege at the British Museum, by declaring that " Intrinsically the blame is not in him, but in the prurient darkness, and confused pedantry, and ostentatious inanity of the world which put him there, and which I must own he very fairly represents and symbolizes." His vanity seems to have been equally pronounced, and while he considered Mr. Gladstone —according to Froude—" the representative of the multitudinous cants of the age: religious, moral, political, and literary," and Mr. Disraeli as "equally incapable of high or sincere purpose," he was yet able to say of an offer made to him by the latter in the Queen's name of a pension and a G.C.B. that "the accurate perception of merit in others is one of the highest characteristics of a fine intellect. I should not have given Disraeli credit for possessing it, had it not been brought home so directly to me." Sir William Fraser, who tells the story, states that, though refusing the honours, Carlyle was much impressed, and repeated several times the words " generous " and " magnanimous."

There is, of course, something not altogether ignoble in this full appreciation of the incident, but it remained for the Queen to draw him out to a further and really astonishing degree. Upon the death of his wife in April, 1866, Lady Augusta Stanley was instructed to write Dr. Carlyle (a brother) an expression of the Queen's sympathy and sorrow. " Her Majesty expressed a wish that as soon as I could do so I should convey to Mr. Carlyle the assurance of her sorrowful understanding of a grief which she herself, alas ! knows too well. It was with heartfelt interest that the Queen heard yesterday that Mr. Carlyle had been able to make the effort to return to his desolate home, and that you are with him." The rugged genius of a man who was, after all, great in many senses of the word was stirred by this action into real gratitude, and found voice in an immediate reply to Lady Augusta : " The gracious mark of Her Majesty's sympathy touches me with many feelings, sad, and yet beautiful and high. Will you in the proper manner, with my humblest respects, express to Her Majesty my profound sense of her great goodness to me in this the day of my calamity? I can write to nobody. It is best for me at present, when I do not even speak to anybody." A few years later he was honoured with a special invitation to meet the Queen at the Westminster Deanery. The message was personally conveyed by the Dean and Lady Augusta, and was received in a half-respectful, half-quizzical way, characteristic of the man.

Of this occurrence Mr. Froude says that it was through a genuine desire felt by the Queen to become personally acquainted with a man of whom she had heard so much, and that while no one could ever accuse Carlyle of being a courtier— certainly no one has ever done so—yet " for the Queen, throughout his life, he had entertained always a loyal respect and pity, wishing only that she could be less enslaved by the ' talking apparatus ' at Westminster." Lord Houghton, in writing to his wife about this time, says that " the talk of the town is Dean Stanley's five o'clock tea on Thursday to the Queen, Princess Louise, Mr. and Mrs. Grote, Sir Charles and Lady Lyell, Carlyle and Browning. Carlyle sat opposite Her Majesty, and prophesied to her for quarter of an hour, telling her, among other truths, that there were no poor in Scotland, which she contradicted. She pleased Browning by telling him she had much enjoyed some of his wife's poems." These incidents indicate the closeness of the friendship which existed for very many years between the Stanleys and the Queen.

The Dean was indeed a man eminently fitted for his position, and while a courtier in manner was none the less a strong and sincere Christian. His piety and learning were as great as the confidence felt in him by those in authority, and just as no better companion and chaplain could have been found for the young Prince of Wales when travelling in Palestine and the East, so the Queen herself could have had no wiser religious friend and adviser than he. Lady Augusta Bruce had been for some years a member of the Court circle, and a more or less confidential servant of the Queen, before she married the Dean, and this relationship was maintained until husband and wife had both passed away. Another loyal servant and friend was Archbishop Tait. From 1869, when he became Primate of all England, until his death in 1882, he was consulted either by the Queen or her Ministers in all the chief problems of the time. The part which he took in the settlement of the Irish Church question and his extraordinary position of mediator between the Queen and the Government, and the Queen and the House of Lords, shows the confidence which was placed in his ability and discretion. His Diary contains many affectionate or eulogistic references to Her Majesty, and his death-bed scene, as described by Dean (now Bishop) Davidson, is loyally significant.

During the weary weeks of half unconsciousness which preceded his death, many enquiries came from the Queen, until one afternoon the Marchioness of

SIR HUMPHREY DAVY.

ROBERT STEPHENSON, M.P.

SIR HENRY M. STANLEY, G.C.B., M.P.

THE MOST REV. EDWARD WHITE BENSON, D.D., LL.D.

Ely arrived from Windsor with a special message of regard and sympathy. When told of it, he roused himself and said he would like to see Lady Ely. To her he spoke of his love and gratitude to the Queen, and then tried to write a message.   Raising himself up he took the pen in hand, and, though unable to guide it alone, repeated the words aloud, and they were thus inscribed as a halting yet strong evidence of his feelings : " A last memorial of twenty-six years of devoted service ; with earnest love and affectionate blessing on the Queen and her family. —A. C. Cantaur."   The Archbishop was buried at his own wish, in Addington churchyard, although Her Majesty would have liked to have had his remains interred in Westminster Abbey.   She, however, sent two of her sons to represent her at the funeral, and England sent many of its foremost men ; while the Prince of Wales became chairman of the Committee which eventually established several memorials of his great life and work.

But although the Queen has known more or less intimately five Archbishops of Canterbury—Dr. Howley, Dr. Sumner, Dr. Longley, Dr. Tait, and Dr. Benson—four Bishops of London, six Archbishops of York, and a similar variety and number of Church and religious leaders in other directions, her acquaintance has not been limited to ecclesiastical dignitaries any more than it has to political leaders.   One of her warmest and most respectful admirers was Charles Dickens. In the earlier years of the reign his romantic nature seems to have been stirred to an unusual degree by the sight of the frail young Sovereign, and, like Carlyle, with the idea of her vast responsibilities.   Later on, when he had become a great writer and novelist, more than one opportunity of meeting as well as seeing her occurred.   During the month of March, 1870, the Queen sent for him in order to personally express her thanks for some photographs of American scenes which he had collected and presented to her.   He was received quietly and privately, and amongst other matters referred to was an alleged discourtesy shown Prince Arthur during a recent visit in New York.   Dickens begged Her Majesty not to confound the true Americans of that city with the Fenian portion of its Irish population.   She replied by simply expressing her belief that the people about the Prince had made too much of the affair.   Then, says Dickens' biographer, "She asked him to give her his writings, and could she have them that afternoon ? But he begged to be allowed to send a specially bound copy.   Her Majesty then took from a table a copy of her own book upon the Highlands with an autograph inscription ' To Charles Dickens '; and saying that ' the humblest ' of writers would be ashamed to offer it to ' one of the greatest,' but that Mr. Helps had remarked that it would be valued most from herself, closed the interview by placing it in his hand."

Another of the Queen's great contemporaries, and one whom she could indeed call a friend, was Lord Tennyson.   His personal loyalty was so sincere and spontaneous, his belief in monarchical institutions so strong and confirmed by experience, his admiration of Her Majesty's character and ability so marked and vigorous, that no crown of Laureateship or royal recognition was needed to inspire his muse, or to evoke those beautiful poems and references to his Sovereign which have become so historic and powerful in their influence upon public opinion. Two currents of thought seem to have bound them together in a common sympathy. One was his intense Imperialism, the other his conception of woman and her sphere. Like the Queen, he was a fervent lover of the Empire, and believer in its expansion. They both looked to the Colonies, in days when shallow littleness of view prevailed all around them, as the chief elements in England's future greatness. They both endeavoured to stem the tide of separationist opinion, and Tennyson's Ode to " that true North " and stern rebuke to the Manchester school theorists was one of the first strong impulses towards a change of sentiment.

The Imperial feeling now dominates British public life, and that it does so is due in the first instance to the Queen, Lord Tennyson, and Lord Beaconsfield. The great poet unquestionably thought much of the exceptional ability of Her Majesty,* but this did not prevent him believing in the home as the best and highest sphere of woman's work and influence, any more than it prevented the Queen from sharing the same general sentiment while performing to the full the necessary and exceptional duties of her lofty position. Upon this subject he always wrote strongly, and his winsome maidens are modest and trustful, just as his more matronly women are loyal and devoted wives, with all gentle, loving, and self-sacrificing qualities. He was a pronounced antagonist of the " new woman," as he was an earnest upholder of all that is truly womanly and therefore noble. To him the fostering of youthful goodness and manly greatness, ministering to the wants of the humble and poor, scattering the shadows of sorrow and softening the sting of suffering, constituted the highest possible ideal of woman's work. And in this view the Queen undoubtedly agreed, as did the bright and sympathetic spirit with whom he was blessed as a wife. The late Lady Tennyson's view upon another important subject is indicated by her request, in connection with the poet's state funeral in 1892, that a flag should be placed around the coffin, as representing " the feeling of the beloved Queen and the nation, and the Empire he loved so dearly." Her Majesty showed every possible sympathy and respect to his memory upon this occasion, as she had given him all possible honour during his lifetime. The Court Circular of October 7th declares that she received " with much concern the news of the death of Lord Tennyson, the Poet Laureate, for whom she had a sincere regard and great

---

*The present Lord Tennyson told the author, while in England lately, something of his father's admiration for the Queen's political ability, and permits the following quotation as being one of the Poet Laureate's last utterances : " The Queen has a wonderful knowledge of politics—quite wonderful ! and her sagacity seems unerring—what we call an instinct."

admiration." Upon his coffin were placed three wreaths from the Queen—one of laurel, one of flowers, and one of metal. The inscriptions were in her own handwriting, and read, in part, "a mark of sincere regard and admiration from Victoria R.I.," and "a tribute of affectionate regard from his Sovereign." To his son and successor came also a personal telegram of sympathy :

"Most truly grieved that the great poet and kind friend has left this world. He was ever so kind to me and full of sympathy. Feel so deeply for your dear mother, and yourself, his devoted son.

"V.R.I."

A very different type of man was Sir Bartle Frere. A great administrator of distant and Imperial possessions, he voiced and felt that sense of world-wide British power which no one appreciated more than did the Queen. In Africa and India he had distinguished himself, and, like Sir George Grey, more than once experienced the benefit of Royal sympathy and help. An undoubtedly good and conscientious man, he had also been selected as one of the Prince of Wales' companions during his State visit to the East in 1876. His biographer tells us that he had scarcely arrived from South Africa on October 5th, 1880— recalled by Mr. Gladstone's Government—when "an invitation came to visit the Prince of Wales at Abergeldie. Thither he went, and met with a cordial and gracious reception from the Prince, and also from the Queen, who twice sent for him to Balmoral, and showed him the greatest personal kindness. During his stay in South Africa he had, at the Queen's desire, *written regularly to her*, and she had evinced the greatest interest in, and clearest understanding of, what had passed there." It may be said here that Frere's policy of extension up to the Zambesi which Mr. Gladstone then disapproved of, but with which there is little doubt the Queen sympathized, was accepted by the same statesman in 1893 from the hands of Mr. Rhodes and Sir Hercules Robinson. Writing on October 16th, Sir Bartle declared that "nothing could be more kind or more constitutional than the kindness of the Queen to her recalled Governor, and I felt as I travelled home that there were other things besides Katie's dog who would gladly ' die for the Queen.' "

In the month of October, 1870, the Minister in attendance upon Her Majesty at Balmoral was Mr. W. E. Forster. He had just reached Cabinet rank for the first time in a career which had been strenuous, and which was yet to be stormy, and this was his first introduction to Her Majesty in his new capacity. His biographer, Sir T. Wemyss Reid, says that this first visit and the succeeding personal intercourse with his sovereign was to Forster a source of unalloyed personal pleasure. Strong as he seemed to be, rugged and stern as his nature appeared, it was really more or less of a mask for the warm and sympathetic feelings which his correspondence with Mr. Gladstone during the Irish coercion days now clearly demonstrates. The unique position of the Queen as a woman, and the ruler of the greatest Empire in the world moved him with a sense of pathos, and inspired him with a feeling of chivalrous devotion to the Throne. "From the time when he first came into contact with her, as his knowledge of Her Majesty increased, and as his opportunities of seeing her multiplied, his desire to do everything that lay within his power to lighten for her, by even the smallest degree, the burden of the Empire, became constantly more ardent." That his services were personally appreciated is evident from the following characteristic letter—written at the time of his death :

"Windsor Castle, April 7th, 1886.

"DEAR MRS. FORSTER:

"I purposly delayed writing at once to you, not wishing to intrude on your overwhelming grief for the loss of such a husband, so good and so devoted, fearing to add to the weight of your affliction ; but to-day I trust I may venture to express not only the deep sympathy I feel for you, but also the true and sincere concern I feel at the loss of one for whom I had the greatest regard and respect, and who served his Queen and country, bravely, truly, and loyally. We can ill afford to lose so honest, so unselfish, and courageous a statesman as he was, in these days, and his public loss is very great.

"But I ought not to speak of such feelings when I think of you, from whom the light and joy of your life has been taken. Still, I think that the appreciation of those we have lost by others, and by the Sovereign he served so well, is soothing to the bleeding heart.

"My daughter Beatrice feels deeply for you, and shares my sorrow at dear Mr. Forster's loss. Pray express my sympathy to your children ; and praying that God may give you peace and strength to bear up, believe me always,

"Yours very sincerely,

"VICTORIA R. and I."

Of a similar nature was Her Majesty's tribute to Mr. W. H. Smith, the greatly respected Conservative leader—as Mr. Forster was for many years one of the Liberal chiefs. "Courteous, yet strong, transparently sincere," Mr. Smith lived a life of earnest labour, and died on July 7th, 1891. To his funeral was sent a wreath from the Queen, inscribed as "a mark of sincere regard, and gratitude for devoted services to his Sovereign and country. From Victoria R. and I." To his widow came a Peerage, as Viscountess Hambledon, and a letter of sympathy, just as similar honours, about the same time, were conferred upon the widow of Sir John A. Macdonald in far-away Canada. In her letter to Lady Macdonald the Queen said: "I feel most deeply for you, and fear that his unceasing devotion to his country and Sovereign has shortened his most valuable life. I cannot sufficiently express my sense of gratitude to him for his invaluable services, or how deeply I mourn his loss, which is so great to the country." It must be remembered, in connection with these very real evidences of Royal feeling and sympathy, that for sixty years the Queen's Ministers have taken turns in personal attendance upon Her Majesty, whether she was staying at Osborne, or Windsor, or Balmoral, or upon the Continent, and that she has thus come to intimately know all the political leaders of all parties during the prolonged period of her reign. Some, of course, she liked more than others, and some impressed themselves more by their ability, or manners, or character, than did the others.

It was probably this intercourse of Sovereign and Minister, coupled with the latter's brilliant and sparkling daily letters, or reports from the House of Commons, which first brought Disraeli into favour, and changed an alleged— though not proven—dislike into undoubted appreciation. His motto of "a smile for a friend and a sneer for the world" was one which others besides Vivian Grey acted upon, and it certainly had the desired effect in many a high quarter. But more was required than mere address and ambition to gain the genuine and personal confidence of Queen Victoria. And as time passed, Disraeli showed himself to possess that divine quality of sincere patriotism which enables a man to make ambition serve great ends and wit to work wonders of personal influence. The combination is not often seen, but he had it. His appeal to young men in a speech on October 3rd, 1844, indicates this as well as did his policy of thirty years later: "I give to them the counsel which I have ever given to youth, and which I believe to be the wisest and the best—*I tell them to aspire*. I believe that the man who does not look up will look down, and that the spirit which does not dare to soar is destined perhaps to grovel. . . . When they have wealth, when they have authority, when they have power, let it not be said that they were deficient in public virtue and public spirit. When the torch of knowledge is delivered to them, let them also light the path of human progress to educated man."

This real feeling of the statesman as against superabundant brilliancy and apparent lack of principle in younger days ultimately made way amongst the people, and in the teeth of hostile and bitter prejudice—such as that of the Duke of Bedford, who once openly expressed his dislike at Disraeli's companionship with his son. So with the Duke of Argyll, who had been almost a life-long critic of the statesman, but who, on May 2nd, 1892, declared he had "no doubt whatever of the earnest patriotism of Mr. Disraeli. He was a great patriot." So, also, with the Queen in her later and frequent association with Lord Beaconsfield, the honours she heaped upon him, the favours and confidence she exhibited towards him, and the deep personal sorrow she felt and showed at the time of his death. Of his great rival, Mr. Gladstone, little need be said here. He was never to the same extent a personal friend of the Queen's, but he was to fully an equal degree a devoted believer in Monarchy, an admirer of Her Majesty's constitutional services to the nation, and a loyal, courteous servant of the Sovereign and the country, as his conscience appeared to guide him. One thing must be said, however, regarding a current popular impression that Mr. Gladstone was disliked by the Queen because he was at times uncivil to her. Such a thing as rudeness from any politician would be almost impossible to one so hedged in with personal and

Royal dignity as she is, and in any repeated form it would be absolutely impossible. But from a man like Mr. Gladstone, who is almost ideally chivalrous in his treatment of the humblest woman, to a Sovereign whom he not only admires as a ruler, but reveres as a woman, the very supposition is preposterous.

To the Queen's relations with her living Ministers, and ex-Ministers, it is impossible to refer at length. Her favourite statesmen have unquestionably always been those who showed a broad and Imperial spirit, and hence her sympathy with the Palmerston of later years, the Lord Lytton who proclaimed her Empress of India with such gorgeous and wise ceremonial, the Prime Minister of the same period, and Lord Salisbury, Lord Rosebery, and Mr. Chamberlain in the present time. To Lord Rosebery she has shown much favour, and he has received not only the unusual compliment of being given both the Order of the Garter, and the Thistle, but, if apparently reliable authority is to be accepted, has once, and perhaps oftener, been personally asked by Her Majesty to assume the portfolio of Foreign Affairs.

But amidst all this panorama of passing greatness, which any glance at the Queen's contemporaries and friends must reveal, the names of those faithful personal servants who are not statesmen or public leaders, but who yet have a real and great place in the government of the realm, must not be forgotten. General, the Hon. Charles Grey, Sir Thomas Biddulph, Colonel Sir Charles Phipps, Sir Arthur Helps, General Sir John Cowell, and the late General Sir Henry Ponsonby were men whose close secretarial relations with the Queen brought them onerous and important duties, and a life of ceaseless work and much anxiety. The last named Private Secretary possessed great ability and tremendous industry, and yet his double duties—he was also Keeper of the Privy Purse, or Treasurer to the Queen—were almost more than he could perform. They are now being carried on by Sir Fleetwood Edwards and Sir Arthur Bigge. To the Queen the loss of these successive personal servants and devoted friends must have been a more important and trying evidence of the passage of time than even the death of her Ministers and other leaders.

It is, however, only one more indication of the solitary splendour which surrounds the closing years of a long reign to an extent far beyond even that which greeted its opening in the May-day of youth and the first flush of pleasure and power. To the Queen all those who have been mentioned in this brief review have brought in some measure of their wealth of learning, or experience, or genius, and laid it at her feet, as have very many others who are known to history and fame both within the Empire and without. They have combined to surround her personality with a degree of knowledge and experience which makes even the briefest consideration of her relations with the contemporaries of her reign, a revelation of personal tact, and kindliness, and patriotic statecraft.

CHAPTER XXIX.

MODERN DEMOCRACY AND THE QUEEN.

DEMOCRACY may, or may not, be the dispensation of this age. But there can be no doubt of its potency in controlling legislation and in affecting public opinion. Of course it assumes different forms in different countries, and likes to rule in England through an aristocratic environment and under the ægis of a constitutional sovereign, as in the United States it prefers to reign through the picturesque fuss and fury of great national electoral conflicts, and under the brief rule of partisan leaders. In both countries, however, the press is the vital factor in controlling and representing the popular will and the democratic spirit. Parliaments or Congresses may come and go, but the newspapers continue to voice in differing degrees the feelings of the people, and to practically rule their convictions upon many important subjects.

Oratory has not, of course, lost all power, as the career of Mr. Gladstone and the rising of Mr. Bryan indicate, but it is checked in manifestation by the ever-present reporter, and weakened in its influence by the cold criticisms of the morning paper. In the United States, however, democracy has a fuller fling and wider freedom than in Great Britain. Whether for good or ill "the voice of the people is the voice of God," and this uncontrolled popular power has placed the American democracy more or less at the mercy of the demagogue. In Great Britain the people rule, but it is in a more guarded and modified manner. Hedged in by monarchical forms and constitutional precedents ; influenced largely by historic associations and sentiments of inherited loyalty ; bound by strict codes of political honour and etiquette ; controlled by parties which are led by men of culture and wide experience ; the democracy of the British people finds expression in a dignified system of government where the masses rule by, and through, the classes, under the stability of monarchical institutions, and over vast dependencies and interests which naturally tend to sober the judgment of the people as a whole, and control any hasty manifestation of temper or popular passion. It is indeed

> "That sober freedom out of which there springs
> Our loyal passion for our temperate kings."

British democracy is therefore, in its modern development, a combination of restricted privilege and dignified liberty ; of monarchical influence and popular control ; of mingled Conservatism and Reform—two principles which Emerson has somewhere described as making each a good half, but an impossible whole. It is not without its abuses and grave defects, but, as under many previous conditions in England, the constitution is able to adjust itself to the permanent necessities of the time—as opposed to those passing fancies of the hour which a democracy under republican forms is so apt to make paramount. Edmund Burke once declared that " the distempers of Monarchy were the great subjects of apprehension and redress, in the last century (seventeenth), in this the distempers of Parliament." In the early years of George III., when this was written, 160,000 voters in England represented 8,000,000 of people ; the great landowners held the counties, and many seats in Parliament were looked upon as hereditary possessions ; the cost of one contested election in the County of York had amounted to £300,000 ; and town corporations were in the habit of letting their representation to the highest bidder for the benefit of the town funds.

It is very different now. Then the aristocracy ruled, and very often wisely and well. They governed at times in spite of both King and people, and it was not an unusual thing in the reign of George III. to find him with the people and against the peers. Now the latter have lost much of their old-time power, while, however, obtaining a very distinct personal ascendency. So with the Sovereign, whose rights have been restricted in practice though not in principle, but whose influence has expanded out of all proportion to the apparent loss. Meanwhile Parliament steadily gained in power, and during the present century has distinctly advanced the force of the popular will—with the exceptions which must always attach to the complexities of a party system and the influence of the modern caucus. But while this process was going on, the Queen, by her wise rule and work, and the inherent force of her character and conduct, had fused into the rising tide of democracy a belief in the principle of constitutional monarchy and a living element of personal loyalty. The representative position of the Crown was perhaps the first consideration which thus sank into the minds of a thoughtful people. As some writer well puts it :

" On our Queen's head our laws have placed the crown,
By honouring her we to our laws bow down."

The sovereign, indeed, represents much to British citizens. The continuity of their institutions through a thousand years of steadily developing national life is one consideration which the patriotic spirit can hardly overlook. To quote Dr. Creighton, the eloquent Bishop of Peterborough, in a recent speech—June 18th, 1896—" National character is the abiding product of a nation's past ; and that conception of the past is most valuable which accounts not so much for the present environment of a people, as for the animating spirit which produced it, and which must still exist if it is to be maintained." The Sovereign represents, therefore, a most glorious history, and in her present position voices the struggles of the past for liberty as distinct from license, for evolution as opposed to revolution. She represents stability, and to the genuine conservatism of the English mind, and the ever-widening business interests of the English people, nothing is more important than a stable system of government. She represents impartiality and dignity, and to a country which is divided between two great political camps, and agitated by various partisan issues, the presence in the constitution of an absolutely impartial monarch is, indeed, vital. To a people who possess a great and extended Empire and potent interests in every capital and country of the world, dignity in government is also essential, and this the sovereign has given to them in the fullest degree.

In a democratic age personal popularity is a most important factor in government, and this element the Queen has all her life possessed—and has continuously increased by her own individual character and achievements, and by the merits and work of the members of her family. In a country where the aristocracy has been so powerful and is still so strong ; where the national Church has had so much to do with national administration, and is still so influential ; where the people are yet so divided in opinion and sentiment ; it rests very largely and very often with the Crown to turn the scale in favour of political sobriety and national dignity. By the exercise of tact and conciliation, by persuading and guiding, instead of dictating, the Queen has thus frequently attained important and beneficial ends for the whole community, as distinct from sections and divisions. She has, in short, incorporated the monarchical sentiment with English character and life, and in doing so has combined the two separate, but not necessarily hostile, elements of democracy and monarchy in a common national repudiation of Republicanism.

It is a curious situation, and one which Americans, for instance, have never understood, and perhaps never will. In Canada and Australia also, it would be well if the principle underlying this condition were more clearly comprehended. There is, in fact, no more danger of Great Britain becoming a republic than there is of the United States accepting a British monarch—though a dictator is not an impossibility in the latter case. It was tried once in England, and not even the memories of Hampden, or the genius of Milton, have made the experiment popular. And, it may be frankly stated, the example of the United States, with all its past record of boundless development, and many evidences of national patriotism and greatness, has not been such as to evoke any wide desire for imitation. As Mr. Augustine Birrell recently, and very neatly, put it, the English republicans fleeing to America in the days of Penn are now replaced by American republicans fleeing from the *ennui* of Washington to the aristocratic halls of the Old Land—and all agog for presentation at Court.

Of course these people do not represent the Americans as a whole, any more than the dissipated and more or less worthless younger sons who try to make a precarious livelihood upon the prairies of Canada or the States represent the sturdy and really typical Englishman. But it must still be confessed that American democracy is disappointing. It has shown great qualities in the struggle against secession, in more than one memorable political battle, and in the generous and hospitable character of its people. These qualities, however, are inherent in the race—not in democracy as such. So with the national ingenuity and cleverness, the individual inventive skill, the wonderful flow of popular oratory, and the keen business instincts of the nation. To quote a writer whom all Americans respect and admire—Ralph Waldo Emerson :

" The spirit of our American radicalism is destructive and aimless ; it is not loving ; it has no ulterior and divine ends ; but is destructive only out of hatred and selfishness. On the other side the conservative party, composed of the most moderate, able, and cultivated part of the population, is timid and merely defensive of property. It vindicates no right, aspires to no real good, it brands no crime, it aspires to no generous policy, it does not build, nor write, nor cherish the arts. From neither party when in power has the world any benefit to expect in science, art, or humanity, at all commensurate with the resources of the nation."

This keenly bitter and incisive criticism boldly reaches into the heart of existing conditions, though it does not touch the causes. Why should not a great people, with all that makes for wealth, and luxury, and personal development, possess a wide culture as distinct from mere book education ; and a constructive national policy as distinct from tariff tinkering and the struggles of demagogues ? The Republic has produced great men, and the production has not ceased, although it may be somewhat obscured by party narrowness and a localism which shuts the leaders within State limits of representation. The real difficulty is the fiction that a democracy must recognize no class—with its inevitable corollary that when the classes develop, as they must do, no responsibility accompanies their establishment. Hence the creation in the United States of a powerful moneyed class utterly irresponsible and indifferent. Hence the almost absolute exclusion of the cultured and wealthy part of the population from politics. Hence the power of the demagogue and the rise of free silver and similar agitations.

In England it is very different. The Throne is there a secure and stable symbol of national power. The aristocracy forms a natural, harmonious, and dignified environment for the Sovereign, and is composed of a recognized class with some privileges and rights, which do not injure anyone else ; and many responsibilities which unquestionably benefit the whole nation when properly sustained. The people find their place and power in the House of Commons, yet, strange as it may seem, they choose very many of their representatives from the class which is peculiarly fitted by tradition, and surroundings, and education, for the work of statecraft as distinct from the sphere of the demagogue. In January, 1866, the London *Review* drew attention to the fact that, " the

Duke of Devonshire has in the House of Commons a brother and three sons; the Marquess of Abercorn, a brother and two sons; the Duke of Buccleuch, two sons; the Marquess of Salisbury and the Earl of Derby, each two sons; the Marquess of Westminster, two sons and a nephew; the Marquess of Ailesbury, the Duke of Richmond, the Duke of Rutland, and the Duke of Newcastle each two brothers; the Earl of Enniskillen, an uncle and a brother; Earl Cowper, the same; Lord Feversham, a brother and a son; and Earl Fitzwilliam, an uncle and a son." In the Parliament of 1891 Lord Henry Brudenell-Bruce, Lord Weymouth, Lord Brooke, the Hon. Bernard Coleridge, the Hon. W. H. Cross, Lord Lewisham, Lord Hartington, Lord Arthur Hill, Lord Burghley, Lord Ebrington, Mr. W. Beckett, Lord Bective, Lord Curzon, Lord Newark, the Hon. W. St. J. Brodrick, the Earl of Compton, Viscount Baring, the Hon. W. H. James, the Hon. S. Herbert, Lord Lymington, the Marquess of Granby, the Hon. R. Wynn, Lord Wolmer, the Hon. C. R. Spencer, the Hon. F. C. Morgan, Lord Grimston, and Lord Elcho, were a few of the Peer's eldest sons, or heirs, who held seats in the House of Commons.

With them were seated a very large number of members of the aristocracy who were not heirs to a place in the peerage, but were either closely connected with it by birth or through the associations of a country life which includes most of the influential families of England—titled or untitled—in one general aristocratic class. The point to be borne in mind is, therefore, the undoubted fact that, whether in the Cabinet or in Parliament, the people rule in Great Britain, and are content to rule, through a class which is in the main a trained, cultured, and patriotic body of men, having recognized duties and responsibilities in social life, in political possibilities, and in their position as landowners or possessors of accumulated wealth. And, so long as this class is more or less instinct with a patriotism inspired by hereditary recollections and surroundings; so long as it rises to the level of its opportunities and does not shirk the duties which fall upon its members; so long will the aristocracy help to maintain the Monarchy in close touch with the popular interests. To quote the well-known Radical, Mr. Joseph Cowen: "Ancient order and modern progress are not incompatible. Our workmen are neither barbarians nor incendiaries. They are Englishmen first and operators afterwards." They are, therefore, willing that the democracy should be organized, and tempered, and trained by the classes, in the interest of stability and educated government, and under the sceptre of a sovereign whose qualities made the erratic George Augustus Sala once declare that: "When I had any politics at all I was one of the people called Radicals, and a very bitter and perhaps blatant Radical to boot; but I have never swerved in my loyal love and reverence for the gracious lady who rules this vast Empire so mildly and so wisely."

Of course these views are not characteristic of all the Radicals of England

—to say nothing of the people as a whole. There is at times much froth and foam upon the surface of politics, and the English democracy shows occasional signs of the condition so largely prevalent in the United States. One of the Socialist speakers during the Trafalgar Square demonstrations of November, 1886, for instance, advised workingmen to unite and " tell the aristocrats that they would no longer submit to the gross injustice, the pauperism, and the robbery of the upper classes. They would tell Lord Salisbury and Lord Randolph Churchill that they were upstarts and robbers, interlopers and hypocrites." And he concluded with these interesting lines:

> " Raise up the banner of freedom,
> March onward and never fear,
> Show tyrants you no longer fear them,
> And the wealth of the robbers we'll share."

But this sort of thing only creates amusement or contempt amongst the great mass of the people, and ten years after the above little diatribe Lord Salisbury himself was in office with one of the largest majorities in English history. The idea that freedom cannot exist without being unrestrained, or that liberty is a farce unless it becomes license, is therefore fully controverted by the record of British democracy and the position of the British sovereign. Of a similar nature and destiny is the favourite cant of demagoguery, that only those who rise from " the people " are able and willing to legislate for the people. If, as Lord Beaconsfield once said, social legislation is the most beneficial form of national activity, then no greater name than that of the Earl of Shaftesbury can be seen upon the roll of those who have worked for the people and with them. The fact is that true democracy is not to be found in mere destruction, or in Hartley Coleridge's dictum, "I hate property; I haven't any," but rather in that admirable analysis by the great Italian agitator, Mazzini :

" Liberty is not the negation of all authority ; it is the negation of every authority that fails to represent the collective aim of the nation. . . . I am a democrat, wishing to advance and make others do the same, in the name of those three sacred words, Tradition, Progress, Association. I believe in the great voice of God which the ages bring to me through the universal tradition of the human race. It tells me that the family, the nation, and humanity are three spheres through which human individuality must labour to the common end—the moral perfecting of itself and of others, or rather of itself by others and for others ; that the institution of property is destined to be the sign of the material activity of the individual ; of his share in the improvement of the physical world, as the right of suffrage must indicate his share in the administration of the political world ; and that it is precisely from the use, better or worse, made of such rights in those spheres of activity that the merit or demerit of the individual before God and man depends. . . . Dreams of communism, or absolute fusion of individuality in the whole, are only transitory incidents in the march of the human race."

This is a very fair, though unintended, representation of the conditions of

British national life. Tradition is a strong auxiliary force behind the Throne and the aristocracy; progress is the watchword of the people, and is only controlled and directed, not really checked, by the other elements in the constitution; while the power of association mellows the relationship of these differing elements, and in some measure fuses them into one harmonious whole. Before dealing with the present place of the Sovereign in this connection, a word must be said about the way in which the aristocracy of to-day lives up to its duties and responsibilities. Earl Grey referred to what has since become in great degree a fact, in a private note which he wrote to Princess Lieven during the crisis of the Reform Bill in 1831. He declared that the great measure in question "takes from the Peers a power which makes them odious, and substitutes for it an influence which connects them with the people, at the same time preserving their relationship with the Crown, and thus making them, as they ought to be, a connective link between the Crown and the people."

It is very easy in these days to accept reports of the evil conduct or dissipated lives of certain Peers, or scions of the aristocracy, as being typical of the whole class. In countries where no ancient, time-honoured, and traditional element has ever existed, or been possible under new and varied conditions, it is hard to understand the gradual development through many centuries of these class divisions of England. And it is not always remembered that such classes are inevitable and unavoidable—the only difference being that in the British Isles they are hereditary, while in the United States or British Colonies they are the more or less passing product of quickly won wealth. Speaking of one of the great English families—the Russells—a few lines from the *Times* of January 15th, 1891, indicates a strong and permanent source of aristocratic strength: "The calm judgment of history will declare that whatever the source of the influence of the family, it was exercised, on the whole, in a spirit of enlightened patriotism, and regulated by an honest love of the constitutional liberties of Englishmen. The burial place of the Russells at Chenies, where lie the remains of a long line of nobles who, as statesmen, churchmen, soldiers, sailors, diplomatists, have served their country in various capacities from generation to generation, is *characteristic* of this country."

So it has been with countless individual members of the class during this century as well as in past ages. The great majority of the Cabinet Ministers and political leaders have belonged to the aristocracy; the hard work and thankless task of political life has seldom been shirked by its sons—of whom each passing Parliament has been full; the field of diplomacy, from the days of Canning to those of Dufferin, is stamped with the evidences of aristocratic work and skill; the Colonial and Imperial field from Calcutta to Capetown, and from Ottawa to Melbourne, has felt its influence. Everywhere throughout England the wealthier Peers have devoted themselves to the welfare of the people around them, and of this fact some illustrations will readily occur.   The Earl of Derby in 1863, during the terrible cotton famine in Lancashire, devoted much time and large sums of money to the aid of the distressed.   So with the Duke of Westminster during many past years, and not only upon his own model estates, but amongst the charities of London, and in sympathetic causes such as that of the Armenians.

The third Duke of Sutherland, who died in 1891, and who in his time had entertained the Prince and Princess of Wales, the Shah of Persia, the Khedive of Egypt, and Giuseppe Garibaldi at his princely houses of Dunrobin or Trentham, spent many years of labour and much money in the reclamation of waste lands, and the extension of railways in the northern part of Scotland, as well as in promoting the comfort and well-being of the people.   In these ways he is stated to have expended over a million pounds sterling upon works not personally profitable, though productive of great good to the country, and of an immense amount of employment to the poor.   In a similar connection the Duke of Bedford, another large landowner, stated during a recent speech that his family had spent upwards of £1,600,000 since 1816 upon estate improvements in Bedfordshire and adjoining counties, with the net result that there was a deficit of £7,000 between the revenue and expenditure of those particular properties.   How different this is from the conduct of wealthy Americans such as the Astors and the Vanderbilts, Carnegie, or Ross Winans !

And, as an illustration of the way in which aristocratic families may become a part and parcel of the people while remaining aloof from the peerage itself, the by no means isolated case of Sir Watkin Williams Wynn may be mentioned.   He was very popular in Wales, and on his seventh election to Parliament, in 1868, told his constituents that : "It is a position which for more than a century and a half has been the most prized distinction of my family ; it was preferred by my great-grandfather to an earldom, by my father to an earldom, and by myself to a peerage."   Yet he was essentially an aristocrat, and as much liked by the Royal family—the Princess of Wales was godmother to his daughter—as he was influential amongst the people.   Nothing can, indeed, better indicate the active personal work of the aristocracy than such incidents as these, especially when in 1895 we find eleven peers acting as mayors of as many important towns—from the Duke of Norfolk in manufacturing Sheffield, to the Earl of Derby in populous Liverpool.

With them, in this union of work and influence all through rural England, is the Established Church and its clergy.   Playing a great part in the making and moulding of English institutions, the Church of England is now taking a perhaps greater part in revived religious administration amongst the people, and in keeping the popular feelings in harmony with the Crown and Constitution. The noble cathedrals, the beautiful parish churches, the sweet music, the sympathetic co-operation in so many districts of the clergy and landlords, all have

their natural effect upon the minds of the masses, and while attuning their sentiments in a religious direction have the further influence of promoting loyalty and
good feeling between the classes. Indirectly, the Church acts somewhat as the
Primrose League does, with its pronounced admixture of aristocracy and democracy, and as the Woman's Liberal Federation has tried to do. Needless to
say, the Queen has always sympathized much with the Church of which she is
the national head, and has done what she could during the struggles of the last
half century to encourage movements intended to enhance its usefulness or to
strengthen the hands of its clergy. In replying to an address presented by the
Canterbury Houses of Convocation on March 2nd, 1893, Her Majesty said:

"I receive with much gratification your loyal and dutiful address, and thank you sincerely for your renewed assurances of devotion to my Throne and person. The continued
progress made by the Church of England in the work of the moral and social improvement
of my people affords me great satisfaction. It is with regret I hear that many of the clergy
are suffering from the effects of the agricultural depression at present prevalent in my kingdom, and on all matters that concern the welfare of the Church of England you may rest
assured of my continued sympathy and interest. I thank you for your prayers on behalf of
myself and my beloved family, and trust that, by the blessing of God, prosperity may be richly
granted to the Church of Christ in my dominions."

Supported, therefore, by sentiment and traditional loyalty; by the aristocracy
—a phrase which covers the county families as well as the peerage; and by the
Established Church; the Crown would hold a strong position in England, even if
the sovereign were not personally popular. The position might not be impreg-
nable, as the fate of Charles I. has shown, but in these days of settled government, innumerable and vital precedents, and Parliamentary supremacy, much,
indeed, would be required to make the people move as a whole against their
monarch. Popular unanimity could, of course, overthrow the constitution, but
such a condition is practically impossible, and anything short of it would involve
civil war. Strife of that nature would break the thread of England's Imperial
power, would shatter her vast fabric of financial credit, would place her immense
commerce at the mercy of her rivals—and nothing less than a national earth-
quake would make the Englishman of to-day risk such possibilities. The only
way in which monarchical institutions can be injured in Great Britain is, therefore, by a gradual process of undermining, and this the Queen has not only prevented during her reign, but has altogether averted, so far as can now be seen, by
making this part of the constitution not only a basis for loyalty, but a symbol
of popular power, a principle of recognized public liberty, a source of national
self-respect and dignity, a subject of almost personal love and of undoubted
regard.

Against this wall with which the Queen has surrounded the monarchy
such puny waves of anger or agitation as Sir Charles Dilke once tried to arouse,

or which Mr. Labouchere feebly stirs up to-day in his little kettle called *Truth*, have about as much influence as King Canute had in his traditional dealings with the Atlantic Ocean. The fact of the matter is that while Tadpole may worship registration, and Taper adore a cry, and Labouchere think himself a Radical king, all parties and sections in Great Britain are monarchist in principle. And this despite occasional attacks upon the Civil List, now as in the past six hundred years, or characteristic English grumblings about the expense of the monarchy. Servility is not loyalty, and no true Englishman or Briton is ever servile. Love of freedom is not republicanism, and Britons now have that well-ordered and stable freedom which is suited to themselves, their Empire, and their vast financial interests. From the first Her Majesty has governed from a standpoint which assumes the interest of the Crown and the people to be identical, and in doing so she has favourably developed the modern conception of constitutional sovereignty during a period in which different ideals of royal work and duty might have created an eventually fatal antagonism between the two.

Acting, therefore, upon this general principle, that change in itself is not necessarily an evil and is very often a great benefit, the Queen has not only ruled constitutionally, but has used the vast power with which she is endowed within the constitution to further the good of the people; to prove that the Sovereign is a central object of rational loyalty, raised far above the party principles around which factions rally; to make the Crown an embodiment of the national sentiment and life; to unite all the people in support of its honour and prestige, as involving the reputation and good name of the nation; to link the people with the monarch, and, through her or him, to the other masses of British subjects all over the globe. In his Manifesto to the French nation on September 14th, 1887, the Comte de Paris showed how this interpretation of monarchical institutions had done more than influence the British people. He threw to the winds the old French idea of a sovereign who was above the people, but not of them; who represented nothing but his own selfish interests and personal will, and was surrounded mainly by sycophants and favourites; who might do great deeds if he possessed a phenomenally great mind, but who was just as likely to drag his country in the mire as he was to lift it to the clouds. "France must be shown," declared the Orleanist claimant, "that the principle of historic tradition, with its marvellous suppleness, can adapt itself to modern institutions; that it will bring to the government of our democratic society the steadying element which is lacking under the Republican system and that it will play in that society a rôle not less efficacious than in the old European monarchies which have peaceably transformed themselves."

Had France adopted the system which Queen Victoria has developed with the help of her statesmen and people, the country might have been saved an immensity of trouble and turmoil. But, as Lord Beaconsfield has somewhere

said, such a plan of government needs the support of a widely diffused intelli
gence, and this the French peasant can hardly boast of as yet.   To Great Britain
the essential value of the Queen's services during these sixty years is, therefore,
the consolidation of sentiment around a stable throne and centre.   And this has
not been achieved by any mere negative existence or policy.   The sovereign has
had her own personal opinions and political preferences; she has intervened in the
formation of governments, and the dismissal of individual ministers; she has
taken a pronounced place and share in the control of foreign politics; she has
held an independent but powerful position between the leaders of parties, and
amidst the quarrels of the two houses of Parliament; she has demonstrated to the
full the value of Prince Albert's statement, that through all changes the Queen
remains at the seat of information, the constitutional arbiter between warring
factions, and the permanent representative of the national honour.   As the *Times*
put it on December 5th, 1868: "To discern the real meaning of popular or parliamentary contests, to act as the interpreter of the national mind, to select its truest
representatives, and to give effect to its will, are offices involving grave responsibilities, and calling for more than ordinary intelligence and judgment.   To do
these things is part of the business of an English monarch."   And in performing
them the Queen has added dignity to democracy, stability to monarchy, and
personal popularity to the national instinct of loyalty.

In England, therefore, the student of democracy will find a general and
passionate fondness for freedom, but, in the words of Emerson, a nation wherein
"the frame of society is aristocratic and the taste of the people is loyal."   He
will find that every commoner, when he becomes rich, tries to strengthen the
aristocracy by purchasing land and winning a title.   He will find the historic literature, the greater romances, the cathedrals and churches, the universities and
great public schools, the national music and drama, all building into the perpetuation of monarchical institutions and an aristocratic framework in a country
where there is no doubt that the labourer dearly loves a lord, and where, as Mr.
Gladstone once put it, the majority of the people will usually select an aristocra
if other things are at all equal.   He will find a condition of politics where politicians
are not placemen, and where leaders like Peel, and Bright, and Chamberlain, and
Hartington, will sacrifice party or position for the sake of what they believe to b
the national welfare.   He will find a class of public men who combine culture
with statecraft, and will see in Mr. Gladstone a leader as devoted to Dante or
Horace as he was to politics; in Mr. Morley, a better writer perhaps than he is a
statesman; in Lord Rosebery, a man who is able to write a brilliant book
upon Pitt or make a great oration upon Burns; in Mr. Balfour, a profound delver in the realm of metaphysics and the author of the "Foundations of Belief"; in the Duke of Argyll, a peer who has been as distinguished in the literature of science and philosophy as he is in statesman-

ship; in Mr. Bryce, Lord Playfair, and Sir John Lubbock, men who are as well known in literature as they are in politics. He will remember Lord Beaconsfield and the great Earl of Derby, and many others, and will naturally feel that this is indeed a different democracy from that existing anywhere else.

He will see a country where the Sovereign and the governing classes have more than once kept the peace when the first hot wish of the people was for war. He will remember the national desire to help Italy and Hungary in 1848, and Poland and Schleswig-Holstein in the "sixties," even at the expense of wars with Austria, or Russia, or Prussia. He will, perhaps, remember that statement of Mr. Gladstone to Lord Houghton, in which he said that " I have been in a hurry for forty years," and will probably reflect that constitutional checks may, after all, be very valuable in these rapidly moving times. He will still find traces of Robert Lowe's bitter and famous detestation of unbridled democracy, and may be told that after a tour of the United States in 1856 the latter returned home with almost a horror of universal suffrage—although a life-long Liberal in politics. He will find, in short, a reasoning democracy which somehow feels with Tennyson, though in a vague and undefined way, that:

> " Not he who breaks the dams, but he
>   That thro' the channels of the state
> Convoys the people's wish is great,
>   His name is pure, his fame is free."

And above all, and through all the interests of the nation will be seen the influence of the Queen, the work of the Royal family, the stamp of monarchical institutions. To the labours of Royalty in England the life of an American President is simply a holiday and sinecure. Always before the people, always participating in public ceremonial, always sharing in the national interests and concerns, a position has been won for the monarchy which made Mr. G. W. Smalley tell the readers of *The New York Tribune*, during the mourning for the Duke of Clarence, that " the anti-monarchical sentiment seems to have not much more hold on life than the Prince who is dead. . . . It is not heard of, at any rate, amongst the articulate classes. It is not visible amongst the poorer classes." And then he continues, in words which, coming from an American republican, and a close observer, may well close any consideration of the relations held by the people toward Queen Victoria's interpretation of monarchy : " The flood-tide of English democracy pours steadily along, rises higher and ever higher, but so far from submerging the Throne or sapping its foundations seems to bear it on its surface, as if it were indeed, and as in this nation of seamen it should be, the Ship of State."

H.R.H. PRINCE GEORGE OF WALES,
DUKE OF CORNWALL AND YORK.

H.R.H. PRINCESS MAY OF TECK,
DUCHESS OF CORNWALL AND YORK.

CHAPTER XXX.

The Queen and the Empire.

THE relationship of the Monarchy to the Empire is a subject intimately connected with Queen Victoria's interpretation of monarchical institutions. If the Queen has been instrumental in weaving the Monarchy into the hearts of the British people at home, she has been not less influential in creating throughout the expanding Colonial empire a feeling in which personal affection has done more to keep those rising democracies in harmony with the British ideal of constitutional monarchy than any other single factor. The net result is an empire of great states and scattered communities, separated by the oceans of the world, and composed of varied races and nationalities, but all united in peaceful allegiance and sympathetic loyalty to the Crown of England.

There is no possible comparison in this connection with any other past or present empire. Rome was a vast military camp, the product of conquest, and maintained by the force of a militant race. Greece was not in the main an empire at all. Spain had vast imperial possessions, but they were held for the purpose of wringing wealth from inferior peoples who naturally broke away at the first opportunity from an allegiance which was hateful and oppressive. France, towards the end of the eighteenth century, had a colonial empire as large as that of England, but she was unable to hold it against the power which swept the seas. Great Britain, it is true, lost the United States, but apart from that deplorable event she has built up and maintained a vast and complicated system of Imperial supremacy. Its creation was due, in the first place, to British sailors and soldiers, and to the pioneers of the forest and prairie. Its maintenance has been due to the power of trade, and money, and sentiment—but more to the latter than the former. Commerce and finance, for instance, may bind the interests of the American republic with those of England, but events have shown that antagonistic feelings and national prejudices are more powerful than even individual interests. And so it would have been with the Colonies had not the force of a common allegiance, and increasing regard for British institutions, kept their growing populations under the folds of that flag which Rudyard Kipling has so beautifully apostrophized:

"Winds of the world, give answer! They are whimpering to and fro—
And what should they know of England, who only England know?

Never was isle so little, never was sea so lone,

But over the scud and the palm trees an English flag has flown.

The dead dumb fog hath wrapped it—the frozen dews have kissed—
The naked stars have seen it, a fellow-star in the mist.

What is the flag of England? Ye have but my breath to dare,
Ye have but my waves to conquer. Go forth, for it is there! "

To-day the echoes of a world-wide sentiment tell us that the principle of a limited monarchy is well suited to British peoples everywhere, and that personal loyalty to the present Sovereign is one of the strongest links in a silken chain of Imperial unity. Canadians, as a rule, feel with Principal Grant, of Kingston, that "we have a fixed centre of authority and government; a fountain of honour above us that all reverence, from which a thousand gracious influences come down to every rank; and along with that immovable centre representative institutions so elastic that they respond within their own sphere to every breath of popular sentiment." So with the Queen, whose "virtues transmute the principle of loyalty into a personal affection." From Australia comes the resolutions of countless public bodies and the more significant utterances of public men such as the late Sir Henry Parkes—when speaking at the Federation Conference of 1891: " We seek no separation. We only seek to draw closer the bonds of Empire. We seek to draw closer the bonds of true loyalty and to continue to share in the rights and privileges that belong to every British subject. . . . We claim to take our place side by side with England; to share all her difficulties, and honours, and glories; and to be equal in everything beneath the sway of the British Crown and under the beneficent rule of our sovereign lady the Queen."

From South Africa comes the loyal Imperialism of Cecil Rhodes and Sir Gordon Sprigg, while the speeches of Indian chiefs and Princes teem with the evidence of such feelings as those expressed by the Maharajah of Cashmere, when he said in open Durbar on October 4th, 1885, that: " Foremost in all circumstances will be the duty of giving substantial proofs of unswerving and devoted loyalty to her Imperial Majesty's Government, and, when necessity shal arise, in placing all the resources of the country at the disposal of His Excellency the Viceroy, and personally joining the British army with my whole military force. . . . I know that the paramount Power and the public will watch with interest the progress of measures of reform, and I am fully alive that they will estimate me, not by the splendour of my retinue, but by the amount of happiness which I secure to my subjects." And, despite the restlessness recently referred to by Lord Lansdowne, and engendered by the diffusion of superficial and imperfect western knowledge amongst peoples who are essentially Eastern in life, and thought, and character, there is no real reason to apprehend trouble or serious disaffection amongst the myriad millions of India.

But neither the Imperial greatness of to-day nor the Imperial sentiment of the present period have been developed without difficulties and dangers, which at one time seemed to involve the absolute disruption of the British Empire. Of the forces working for union during the past sixty years the most potent has been the personality and position of the Sovereign. Of those working for disintegration the chief has been the Manchester school of economists and theorists. The Queen has been a rallying point for loyalty throughout all the dark days of early struggle and political dissaffection in Canada, and through the later events of American commercial coercion, or efforts at annexationist conciliation; throughout all the gloomy days of South African wars, and maladministration, and Imperial indifference; throughout the times of Australian conflict with the transportation system and struggles with a stormy and rough mining democracy; throughout the days of West Indian decadence, or New Zealand's contests with powerful Maories, and its more recent struggles with the crude vagaries of socialism run mad.

Everywhere, the name, and qualities, and constitutional action of the Queen have permeated Colonial politics, preserved Colonial loyalty, helped the British sentiment of the people, and developed their constitutions along British lines. The Edinburgh *Review* declared recently, and with accuracy, that "the true symbol of the union of the Empire is the Crown. The Crown is the keystone of the arch. The loyal attachment of the Colonies to the person of their Sovereign is more than a mere sentiment, for it springs from the confidence of the people in the justice and liberality of the British monarchy, which unites them all to a common centre without impairing their local freedom." So with Lord Salisbury's description of the monarchy on June 28th, 1894, as "that form of government which was in his view the only centre around which they could rally the vast multitudes of different creeds and races which acknowledged the beneficial sway of Queen Victoria." Undoubted fact, however, as this may now appear, it has not always seemed such, and its present recognition is largely due to the Queen's own convictions upon the general questions of Imperial unity and supremacy. How far the personal influence may have been felt by leading statesmen during the anti-colonial period can, of course, only be estimated from what may be called collateral evidence.

Her Imperial views we know from various letters and references in contemporary and private correspondence. Her new policy in sending the different members of the Royal family to visit the Colonies from time to time we can now thoroughly appreciate. The weight of her views upon foreign affairs and her influence in home politics has been indicated in various historic events. It is, therefore, not unreasonable to suppose that opinions voiced lately by the Prince of Wales' remark, that he "regards Canada and Australia as being as much part and parcel of England as Surrey or Yorkshire," should have had a more potent force in guiding Imperial policy than is seen in any known incidents, such as the appointment of Lord Lorne to Canada, the reappointment of Sir George Grey at the Cape, or the expressed approval of Sir Bartle Frere's schemes of expansion. The views of English statesmen in this connection indicate a steady change, which must bear some relation to their close and constant intercourse with Her Majesty, because it must be remembered that upon this general question of Imperial supremacy and expansion there was for twenty years an utter deadness of public opinion, and the most entire political indifference. Hence there was no popular force to help the process by which a leader like Disraeli changed from writing of "those wretched Colonies which hang like a millstone round our necks," to the statesman who, as Lord Beaconsfield, regarded them as the keynote of his policy and later life work.

During all these years the Queen was in keen and clear-cut antagonism to the Manchester school, which found its time of triumph between 1850 and 1870. Isolation was the watchword of this party or school of thought; trade, the central idea and principle; manufactures the Mammon which was worshipped with a devotion unsurpassed in narrowness and bigotry by even the sentiment actuating the Hindoo who throws himself under the wheels of the car of Juggernaut. Their policy in a nutshell was the gradual abandonment of all external possessions which did not bring in direct pecuniary returns to England; the isolation of the British Isles from European complications and interests; the establishment of a powerful naval force in the narrow seas surrounding the shores of the United Kingdom; the turning of the whole country into one vast workshop, which was to labour in an industrial sense for all the rest of the world and supply its wants for considerations of cash. Rising in some measure out of the free trade idea, it was based upon ignorance of the Colonies, misapprehension of their great destiny and resources, belief in the ultimate victory of free-trade, and joy over the apparently easy conquests of foreign markets and the undoubted expansion of commerce. From Australia there had come suddenly an almost unlimited supply of gold; from within the Kingdom came the triumphs of steam in the railways, and its external manifestation in great steamers; from out of the American Civil War came the transfer of an immense transporting interest to British ships. Intoxicated by these and other events many British leaders and a portion of the public were inclined to ask why they should look into an unknown future, or trouble themselves with vast Colonial responsibilities? The present was prosperous, and sufficient unto the day was the good thereof. To men like Bright and Cobden, and, upon a lower level, Mr. Goldwin Smith, the traditions of the past were nothing; the fruits of a hundred national victories upon land and sea were small in comparison with a present expenditure of a few million pounds; the prestige of great possessions and an historic empire, or a sentiment of common allegiance, were merely the foolish expressions of a jingoism which did not pay any cash dividend; the possibility of foreign nations adopting protection and manufacturing for themselves, or competing even within the limits of England itself, was never dreamt of by these and other theorists.

It is wonderful now to see how far this dismemberment craze spread. It affected many besides the special free trade leaders. Lord Ellenborough, in 1845, told the House of Lords that "he hoped the Government would communicate with the North American colonies with a view to separation." Lord Brougham at the same time declared that " he was one of those who desired a separation of Canada from the mother country. Lord Ashburton and Lord St. Vincent shared the same opinion. Lord Derby, the eminent Conservative leader, went so far, in 1864, as to say of the North American colonies, that "we know these countries must before long be independent states." Mr. Lowe said at a later date that " it is perfectly open to Canada to establish herself as an independent republic." Lord Monck, after his return from the new Dominion, of which he had been Governor-General, told the House of Lords that its people " should be taught to look forward to independence." Sir George Campbell said in the Commons that Canada was " a burden and a risk," and that he would let it go free without more delay." The *Times*, the *Examiner*, the Westminster *Review*, and the Edinburgh *Review*, all held similar opinions, the last named, in January, 1865, declaring that the proclamation of a Canadian federation "falls welcome on our ears as the harbinger of the future and complete independence of British North America." Sir William Molesworth drew attention in 1851 to the increasing expenditure upon the military defence of the colonies from £1,800,-000, in 1832, to £3,000,000 in 1846. He urged a policy which was carried out twenty years later—the relief of the mother country from all such expenses, and the removal of the Imperial troops from the colonies. In this he was supported by Lord Stanley—the Lord Derby of an after time ; by Lord John Russell, who expressed views favourable to independence ; by Mr. Cobden and others. Mr. Edward Baines, M.P., according to his biographer, always believed the Canadian provinces to be of " no real value to the Empire," while Earl Grey, in January, 1885, told an interviewer that " from 1850 downwards the tendency of English administration of both parties has been to throw away with both hands all that remained of Imperial unity." This tendency was further helped, and the work of the cotton manufacturers (amongst whom the Manchester school first developed its theories) was advanced by the ignorance of colonial conditions everywhere prevalent. Robert Lowe's lines upon a famous Secretary for Foreign Affairs are far more appreciable to the Colonial Secretaries of that period, and to such narrow-minded *doctrinaires* and permanent Colonial Office officials as Sir Frederic Rogers and Sir Henry Taylor :

> " Of foreign affairs our new Minister, Canning,
> Is said by his friends at all times to be planning,
> But his ignorance of them too plainly declares
> That to him they must always remain ' *foreign affairs*.' "

Both parties in the State share the blame, and both share, though in hardly equal proportions, the recovery from a condition of surprising blindness. In 1868 Sir George Grey returned home from the Colonies and travelled through England, pointing out the alarming eventualities which the continuance of such ideas would make certain, and obtaining the signatures, as one result, of 100,000 persons to a protest against Colonial abandonment. It was about this time, also, that Mr. Froude wrote the following important letter to Sir George :

"My Dear Sir,—Lord Salisbury tells me that Lord Carnarvon means to take up the subject in the approaching session. Lord Salisbury himself, however, is desponding, and confirms the impression which I have received from other quarters, that the Conservative party in the House of Commons is not to be relied on. The hope is that on both sides of the House there is still a patriotic section. Enough may be done now to keep the economists in check. Hereafter we may see a fresh organization and the old Imperial temper revive.

"If mischief can be prevented meanwhile, this will be the happiest result. The Tories, if they moved now, would do it only as a party dodge, and rather discredit than further a nobler line of policy.

"Lord R. has remonstrated earnestly with the Government *in private*. You will have seen Mr. Foster's speech at Bradford.

"Faithfully yours,

"J. A. Froude."

From this time onwards, however, the tide began to turn. The troops were removed, it is true, from the Colonies, but the development of Australia, the loyalty shown by Canada, the efforts of a few staunch English leaders, the increase of foreign industrial competition, the growth of trade within the Empire, the expansion of telegraph and postal services, all began to slowly have a centripetal influence. But above all these minor forces was the influence of the Queen's Imperial spirit. There is no other way of accounting for the change in the convictions, and utterances, and policy of the statesmen of the period. It seems probable that constant advice from the Queen to her Ministers, and the consistent pressure of her views upon each successive statesman in attendance upon her—even apart from the natural potency of a knowledge of her strong feelings—have been largely responsible for the result. Men are easily moved from such a quarter, and especially if their opinions are negative rather than positive. If this impression is a correct one, and innumerable side-lights of historical reference bear it out, Her Majesty has been mainly instrumental in preserving the unity of the Empire and in creating that Imperial spirit which has led in recent years to the utter repudiation of the Manchester school, and to the acquisition of 2,000,000 square miles of territory with a hundred millions of new subjects.

Hence the pleasure of the Queen in Lord Salisbury's foreign policy of expansion, in the opening of the Indian and Colonial Exhibition, the holding

THE MARQUESS OF LORNE, 9th DUKE OF ARGYLL, K.T., G.C.M.G.

THE MARQUESS OF LANSDOWNE, G.C.M.G., G.C.S.I.

of the Colonial Conference of 1887, and the inauguration of the Imperial Institute. Hence her appreciation of the Ottawa Conference of 1894, which Lord Rosebery declared to have "permanently stereotyped the defeat of those who would limit the British Empire to two small islands," and of the sympathetic loyalty of the Colonies as testified during the Jubilee and shown upon a myriad other occasions. Hence the change of tone in English society which Mr. Goldwin Smith has found so singularly distasteful, and which probably causes much of his misrepresentation of the English aristocracy. Hence, in all likelihood, the Queen's dislike of Mr. Labouchere and his exclusion from the last Liberal Cabinet. A Radicalism which in 1885 did not prevent Dilke and Chamberlain from being admitted to the Government would hardly, in 1895, keep Labouchere out, unless it were the reiteration in *Truth* of such statements as the remark that " Colonial loyalty is a spurious article," or his declaration that " we are always being compelled to put our hands in our pockets on account of these British bantlings, who will never be anything but bantlings and ne'er-do-wells." These opinions had probably more to do with the result than has been suspected. Hence the Queen's warm sympathy with Lord Beaconsfield and her affection for Lord Tennyson.

Hence, also, one of the most important of modern developments—the change in the character, position, and duties of the Colonial representatives of the Queen. To say that a sovereign who objected to Lord Normanby as Ambassador at Paris, and to Lord Canning as Foreign Secretary; who dismissed Palmerston from office in his day of greatest popular influence, and sent Sir George Grey back to the Cape after his recall by a previous Ministry; has often given more than a passive acquiescence in the appointment of Colonial Governors, is to make a very reasonable statement indeed. With the warm interest which the Queen has always felt in Colonial matters—a sympathy well expressed by Prince Albert in April, 1860, during a public speech in which he said: "How important and beneficent is the part given to the Royal family of England to act in the development of those distant and rising countries which recognize in the British Crown, and their allegiance to it, their supreme bond of union with the Mother Country and with each other"—it is only natural to suppose that she should be concerned in the personality of those who represent her, and the name of England, in different parts of the world. Especially would this be the case as regards great territories such as Canada and Australia.

Both the position and character of the Governors have greatly altered during the past half century. Sir George Gipps, Sir Charles Fitzroy, and Sir William Denison, in New South Wales; Sir Charles Hotham, Sir Henry Barkly—who went out at the height of the anti-Colonial feeling, and was termed in official circles "the last Governor of Victoria"—Sir Charles Darling, and Sir George Bowen, as well as Lord Lisgar in Canada, were types of the old school of trained

Governors. They were men who spent their lives in the Colonial service, and went with impartiality from a self-governing people to a Crown colony. They were excellent public servants, but they hardly represented the Crown with that dignity of environment and social splendour which are required in a new and democratic community. With the rise of Mr. Disraeli in 1867, however, came a change, and the Queen began to appoint noblemen to the positions which fell vacant. Lord Belmore went to New South Wales, Lord Canterbury to Victoria, and the Marquess of Normanby to Queensland. As time passed on and the experiment was found to succeed, rank, wealth, and social qualifications became more important considerations than Colonial experience—except in a storm-centre such as South Africa. Lord Dufferin, Lord Lorne, and Lord Lansdowne were sent to Canada, and the Earls of Hopetoun, Onslow, Kintore, Glasgow, and Jersey to Australia or New Zealand. So with Lord Carrington, Lord Brassey, Lord Hampden, Lord Gormanston, and Lord Lamington.

It was a most important departure, and must beyond doubt have been warmly approved, if not originally suggested, by the Queen. It brought the aristocracy into touch with the democracy of the Colonies, and showed the latter the type of men who really constitute the House of Lords. It gave the members of that body a wider scope of knowledge, and experience, and work, and sent them back to their legislative functions with a clear insight into the Imperial position and responsibilities of England. It gave the Colonies an opportunity of utilizing the social culture and ethics of an old country in the development of the necessarily crude society of new and struggling communities. It brought them into touch with a Court which on a small scale was similar to that of the Queen at home, and which might be made both useful and beneficial to the people. It enhanced the dignity of a great office, and lent prestige to the communities over which men of high rank and prospects were proud to preside. By this process of mutual elevation it did good to the governors and governed, and emphasized Lord Elgin's statement in a letter written during September, 1852, that : " I believe there is more room for the exercise of influence on the part of the Governor under my system than under any that was ever before devised ; an influence wholly moral—an influence of suasion, and sympathy, and moderation, which softens the temper, while it elevates the aims of local politics." It naturally flattered the sentiment of the people in the Colonies, and showed a growing appreciation at home of their position and prospects. It evoked from Sir Henry Parkes, who in New South Wales had seen many Governors, the following interesting reference :

" One of the uppermost thoughts of the Colonist, whatever his rank in society, is of the importance of everything belonging to his Colony, including his own position in life and his relations to the head of the government, whom he prefers to regard as the representative of his sovereign rather than as governor. He is sensitive to a fault of any manifestation of English feeling which may seem to belittle the conditions of his existence as a subject of the Queen in a remote part of the empire. In numberless cases this deep-rooted sentiment exists in rough, practical minds which are quite unconscious of it, though it manifests itself to all around them on the faintest provocation. With regard to the governor, as a rule he receives an amount of dutiful attention which the same man would not have received in any other capacity. For the time being he is felt to be the essential and the highest part of the fabric of law and order. No name is above his—and his name is a symbol of respect for authority, and of loyalty to the throne and the empire. The people of one Colony cherish this sentiment towards the governor of every other colony. The people of New South Wales would feel acutely any slight or supposed slight offered to their governor in Victoria, and in like manner the people in Victoria would feel any supposed indignity of a like nature in New South Wales."

The influence attached to the position of Governor in a great Colony is indeed very important, though regulated in some measure by the personality of the individual. Lord Loch, and Lord Rosmead (Sir Hercules Robinson), in South Africa illustrate this fact, as did the popularity of Lord Carrington in New South Wales. When he and Lady Carrington left for England on November 1st, 1890, the streets of Sydney were lined with troops, the carriage while it stood waiting was piled high with bouquets of the choicest Australian flowers, and as it passed through the streets to the station was literally bombarded with floral tributes. Lord Dufferin's name to this day is one to conjure with in Canada, and he did more to promote a British sentiment and increased loyalty in the Dominion than can be easily described. Lord Aberdeen has recently shown that the Governor-General can exercise the right to practically dismiss his ministry under certain circumstances, and to influence the decision of its successors in more than one important direction. This authority in any Colony is enhanced by personal distinction—whether the distinction be one of high social rank or of individual achievement—and has therefore been usefully assisted by the system of appointing ambitious and youthful peers to the position. It has given an opportunity for men who have ability to obtain experience, and for men who will eventually rise to high political place in England to commence their career in the Colonies. Of this ability Lord Onslow, Lord Jersey, Lord Hopetoun, and Lord Carrington, are distinct examples.

And the opportunity is appreciated and understood. Lord Lytton, when Secretary of State for the Colonies, nearly forty years ago, told Sir George Bowen that it was "a grand thing to have been the founder of the social state of so mighty a segment of the globe as Queensland; and it is perhaps, more sure of fame a thousand years hence than anything we can do in the old world." To represent the Majesty of England and the Empire is great in itself; to represent the personality of the Queen is a still more difficult responsibility; to carve a name and fame upon the trunk of a vast Colonial tree of continuous growth and expansion is of more than ordinary personal importance. There are difficulties of course. The welding together of the interests of monarchy and democracy has

never been an easy task, even in England, with all the skill and individual influence of the Queen, and it is still less so in the Colonies. But the general position and work, the representative capacity and present importance of a Colonial
governor, is eloquently voiced in the following words of Lord Kintore, November
9th, 1890 :

"Unsubstantial, phantasmal and impersonal as we may be individually, we nevertheless symbolize and represent in our uninterrupted succession, some of the most solid
realities of which the modern world can boast—for are we not the living proofs and exponents of the love of a mighty nation for the children she has sent forth to enlarge her dominion and enhance her renown ; the affection of great colonies for a mother country that
has endowed them with freedom and legislative independence ; the reverence of a free
people for constitutional liberty as secured by monarchical government ; the recognition
by the owners of a continent of their right to share a still mightier *imperium* ; the love and
loyalty towards the purest woman and most duty-bound sovereign that ever wore a crown
or wielded a sceptre ; the unswerving confidence of the community in their ability to
vindicate their independence, to elaborate their own destiny, and to guard and embellish
to the uttermost the glorious inheritance with which providence has endowed them."

Another element in the Queen's Imperial influence which must be remembered, is the conferring and distribution of honours. Whether given by the
advice of a Colonial ministry, the Governor, or Governor-General, the Imperial
cabinet, or through the personal action of Her Majesty, they have all the force
of a high recognition of local services, the stamp of Imperial approval for Colonial
labours, the effect of coming through a Sovereign whom all her subjects regard
with affection and respect. Whether these titles be conferred upon eminent
politicians or scientists, physicians or jurists, educationists or literary men, they
prove the advantage of having in the State a fountain of honour which at the
source is absolutely free from suspicion, and is thus enabled to give a natural
and Imperial, and world-wide recognition to services rendered the country or
the Empire, or to unselfish labours for the good of humanity at large. Writing
to the Duke of Newcastle—then Colonial Secretary—the Earl of Elgin, on
February 18th, 1853, gave a characteristically wise estimate of the Canadian
situation in this respect :

"Now that the bonds formed by commercial protection and the disposal of local
offices are severed, it is very desirable that the prerogative of the Crown, as the fountain of
honour, should be employed, in so far as this can properly be done, as a means of attaching
the outlying parts of the empire to the throne. Of the soundness of this proposition as a
general principle, no doubt can, I presume, be entertained. It is not, indeed, always easy
to apply it in these communities, where fortunes are precarious, the social system so much
based on equality, and public services so generally mixed up with party conflicts. But it
should never, in my opinion, be lost sight of, and advantage should be taken of all favor-
able opportunities to act upon it."

Since that somewhat distant day unavoidable mistakes have been made,
but upon the whole, the distribution of these tokens of distinction has been care-

ful, wise, and useful. No one can deny that the G.C.B. conferred upon Sir John Macdonald at the advice of Mr. Gladstone, or the peerage given Lady Macdonald by the Queen in person, were not deserved and valuable compliments to Canada, as well as to its Prime Minister. Most people will regret that sturdy and loyal servants of the Crown like Alexander Mackenzie and George Brown did not see their way to accept the distinction of knighthood which Lord Lorne so gracefully pointed out to the former in 1882, was a personal and not hereditary dignity—the recognition by the sovereign of the position occupied by a man amongst his fellow-countrymen, and consequently, "a recognition by the first and abiding representative of the people of that people's election." The peerage conferred upon Sir George Stephen was a royal and fitting reward to a man who had risen from the most humble position into a place where he could wield the power of capital and credit, and help to create the greatest of Canadian practical undertakings—the Canadian Pacific Railway. Honours given to men like Sir William Dawson, Sir Daniel Wilson, Sir Henry Joly de Lotbiniere, Sir George Cartier, Sir Antoine Dorion, Sir Leonard Tilley, Sir John Thompson, Sir Charles Tupper, Sir William Van-Horne, Sir Casimir Gzowski, or Sir Oliver Mowat, are compliments to the country as well as to the men who have won them, and as the last named has well said, " the Queen is not the Queen of England, Scotland, and Ireland only, but the Queen of Canada as well, and by our common constitution the Queen of the realm is deemed the fountain of honour."

Many other Canadians have more imperial honours, from the Victoria Cross worn by Surgeon-General Reade and the late Colonel Dunn, to the lofty position of Admiral of the Fleet attained by Sir Provo Wallis. They show the practical unity of British peoples and indicate how much closer the tie of mutual work and achievement might yet be drawn. So it has been in South Africa where knighthoods conferred upon men like Sir Gordon Sprigg or Sir John Robinson and admission to the Imperial Privy Council granted to Cecil Rhodes or Sir J. H. de Villiers have been fully appreciated. And in Australasia the same fact is evident, although a few recipients of the dignity have not always lived up to it. Sir Henry Parkes, Sir John Robertson, Sir James McCulloch, Sir Graham Berry, Sir Henry Wrixon, Sir William Windeyer, Sir James Patterson, Sir George Dibbs, Sir John Hall, Sir Frederick Whittaker, Sir Julius Vogel, Sir Arthur Blyth, and Sir Dillon Bell, practically represent the history of the Australasian colonies. Writing to Sir Alfred Stephen, perhaps the most eminent of Australian jurists and one of the only two local recipients—Mr. W. Bede Dalley, was the other—of a place in the Imperial Privy Council, the Hon. G. H. Reid, now Premier of New South Wales, who has not been supposed to be very much in sympathy with Imperial ideas, some years ago penned a letter of remarkable congratulation :

"In the very striking honour which has been conferred upon you, Sir, the splendour of the compliment is free from the alloy of an expectation of services to be rendered in return. Policy the most sordid may affix a decoration to the breast of a powerful and ambitious subject; but only a generous and high-minded impulse can have moved the Queen's Government to disturb your modest and well-earned retirement with an especial mark of Imperial favour. Even the most ardent Republican or socialist can reverence the title of 'Right Honourable' when it is conferred upon a right honourable colonist at the close of a right honourable career. . . ."

Not less important than these means of keeping the Monarchy and the Colonial Empire in touch is the fact that the foreign policy of England to-day is essentially guided and controlled by Colonial contingencies and requirements. "Which is the Empire, Britain or Canada?" asked Mr. Phelps, the American representative at the Behring Sea Arbitration. "The key of India is in London," said Lord Beaconsfield in 1878; and "the Eastern question is India," echoed Lord Rosebery in 1891. "A consideration of which in office I am especially sensible," said Lord Salisbury in 1892, "is the large portion of our foreign negotiations which arises entirely out of our Colonial connections." Throughout this external policy the hand of the Queen and the influence of her experience is felt to-day as it was in the time of Palmerston—but more silently and perhaps even more strongly. Necessarily, therefore, Her Majesty's share in the Imperial interests of Great Britain is not restricted to the appointment of Governors, the distribution of honours, or the reception of distinguished people from the colonies. It is and has been, one of advice and practical sympathy from before the time, nearly forty years ago, when she astounded a newly-returned Governor with her knowledge of complicated South African affairs, to the day when she showered every possible compliment and honour upon the memory and remains of the Canadian Premier who had died at Windsor Castle.

The new evolution of British foreign policy also helped in the development of the equally new school of Imperial statesmen. Lord Salisbury, Lord Rosebery, and Mr. Chamberlain are indeed types of men whom the Queen delights in, and who resemble, in their wide sympathies, the genius and loyalty of Lord Beaconsfield. She has seen thirty colonial secretaries come and go, and a countless number of colonial governors, yet, during all that time, has never, so far as we can tell through many passing glimpses of Royal statecraft, failed in wise counsel and Imperial ideas. To the influence of her example as a woman, the general prestige of her personality, the weight of her experienced advice, the power of her position as a central embodiment of the Empire, must, therefore, be added the continuous pressure of her views upon British leaders during a period of disintegration, and the force of that loyalty which her career and character have created in the most distant dependencies of the Crown. These considerations all combined illustrate the position of the Queen and the Monarchy in the new Empire which has developed out of the chaotic conditions of sixty years ago.

H.R.H. PRINCE EDWARD OF YORK.

H. R. H. PRINCE ALBERT VICTOR,
THE LATE DUKE OF CLARENCE AND AVONDALE.

CHAPTER XXXI.

A Glorious Sunset.

THE celebration of the fiftieth anniversary of her accession, when, to quote Dean Alford, "she who was the darling of our hopes became the Queen of our realms," marked a great epoch in the Queen's life as it did in the history of modern England. The occasion served to intensify public loyalty, whilst proving to the world outside the British empire the real strength and importance of that sentiment. As Lord Salisbury said at the Guild-hall banquet in August, 1887, it was really "a festal year of English loyalty, the loyalty of the most loyal and most powerful people on the earth. The sight we have seen, the unbidden enthusiasm we have witnessed, will remain engraven on the memory of all who have passed through this year." But while an important period was closed by these celebrations, a not less important decade in the Queen's long reign was commenced. In Her Majesty's speech to Parliament at this time she had expressed her hope that "I may be spared to reign over a loving, faithful, and united people."

For ten years more of crowded work and development this wish has been granted, and the longest reign in British history reached by the Sovereign who has done so much good, and won a regard so far-reaching and remarkable. Only the barest outline of the events of this last decade can be given, but they were of a nature to touch the most vital points in the structure of the empire, as well as in the home life of the Queen. Lord Salisbury's brilliant administration of six years came to an end in 1892, and Mr. Gladstone once more assumed office, and undertook his pathetically futile and final struggle for the achievement of Irish autonomy. With him in the Government were Sir William Harcourt, the Earl of Rosebery, Mr. Asquith, Lord Ripon, Mr. Campbell-Bannerman, Lord Herschell, Sir George Trevelyan, Mr. Fowler, Earl Spencer, and Mr. John Morley. His majority, however, was small; his wonderful efforts to carry Home Rule through the Lords unsuccessful; his backing from England weak, though it was strong from Scotland, Wales, and Ireland; and his eyesight a constant source of trouble. In March, 1894, the veteran statesman resigned, and Lord Rosebery took the helm of state for a brief and unsatisfactory period of political weakness—relieved by the cheerful brilliance of his personal leadership and the continuity in his foreign policy.

With the elections of the succeeding year came the overwhelming defeat of the Liberals, the practical burial of Home Rule, and the accession to power of

Lord Salisbury, with a Cabinet which the Liberal-Unionists joined in force, and in which the Premier, the Duke of Devonshire, Mr. Chamberlain, and Mr. Balfour constituted a sort of internal governing committee. This event stamped the rise of Mr. Chamberlain as a Conservative leader, while his tenure of the Colonial Office has so far marked him out as a far-seeing Imperial statesman. Lord Halsbury, Lord Cross, Sir M. White Ridley, Lord Lansdowne, Lord G. Hamilton, Sir M. E. Hicks-Beach, Lord Balfour of Burleigh, Lord James of Hereford, Mr. Goschen, Lord Cadogan, and Lord Ashbourne were others who made up a most exceedingly able administration—in its individual capacity. In his general policy Lord Salisbury has absolutely proved the statement of his predecessor on March 23rd, 1891, that " our Foreign policy has become a Colonial policy, and is in reality much more dictated from the extremities of the empire than from London itself." South Africa was one element in this problem, while India entered largely into the Turkish situation, as Canada and British Giuana did into the Venzuelan trouble.

Meanwhile much had happened in the Royal family and to the Queen— apart from the latter's steady devotion to duty and consistent sympathy with all good work and imperial achievement. In 1888, Cambridge bestowed its LL.D degree upon Prince Albert Victor and Lord Salisbury, amid much ceremony, as it had upon the Prince Consort and Lord Palmerston nearly quarter of a century before. The Queen visited Glasgow, opened its international Exhibition, and paid a brief visit to Paisley, In the succeeding year she journeyed to Spain, and met Queen Christina; received the Shah of Persia; and shortly afterwards welcomed the Emperor William II. of Germany upon his first state visit to England—an occasion of much pomp and great naval and military reviews; attended the wedding of Princess Louise of Wales to the Earl of Fife; paid a first personal and state visit to the Welsh principality, and was most loyally received; allowed Prince Albert Victor to make his tour of India; and was presented with loyal addresses from the colony of Victoria. In 1890 Her Majesty unveiled the Jubilee statue to the Prince Consort, visited Southampton, and once more received the German Emperor. Writing at this time to a friend, Lady Waterford states that:

" I have been on a visit to Osborne to dine and sleep. I specially enjoyed it, indeed I did *much* want to see the Queen again. I was agreeably surprised to see her looking so well, such a smooth face, and if wider in figure not strikingly so; her expression is really charming, with the old attraction."

During 1891 a summer visit was paid to southern France; the German Emperor entertained in the most regal manner at Windsor, in London, and at Lord Salisbury's place; Derby visited, the French fleet inspected, and the Duke of Clarence betrothed to the Princess May of Teck. The succeeding year opened with the merry marriage preparations, but soon merged into the period of pain and sorrow, which followed the sad death of the young prince on January 14th. The sickness was very sudden, and while thinking and talking of the coming wedding the country was shocked by the posted telegram from the Prince of Wales to the Lord Mayor of London: "Our beloved son passed away at 9 o'clock." The demonstrations of sorrow were unusually keen. It seemed to be generally felt that the loss of this favourite grandson would be especially trying to the Queen; and to the people in all parts of the Empire there was also something peculiarly pathetic in this young life cut off upon the very verge of a new period of happiness, and of constantly increasing responsibilities as heir presumptive to the throne. So strong and sincere was this sympathy that the Queen issued from Osborne on January 26th, a letter of appreciation and thanks to the nation:

"I must once again give expression to my deep sense of the loyalty and affectionate sympathy evinced by my subjects in every part of the Empire on an occasion more sad and tragical than any but one which has befallen me and mine, as well as the nation. The overwhelming misfortune of my dearly-loved grandson being cut off in the flower of his age, full of promise for the future, amiable and gentle, and endearing himself to all, renders it hard for his sorely stricken parents, his dear young bride, and his fond grandmother to bow in submission to the inscrutable decrees of Providence.

"The sympathy of millions which has been so touchingly and visibly expressed, is deeply gratifying at such a time, and I wish both in my own name and that of my children, to express from my heart my warm gratitude to *all*."

"These testimonies of sympathy with us, and appreciation of my dear grandson, whom I loved as a son, and whose devotion to me was as great as that of a son, will be a help and consolation to me and mine in our affliction. My bereavements during the last thirty years of my reign have indeed been heavy. Though the labours, anxieties, and responsibilities inseparable from my position have been great, yet it is my earnest prayer that God may continue to give me health and strength to work for the good and happiness of my dear country and empire while life lasts.

"VICTORIA, R.I."

Following this sad event, Prince George was created Duke of York, and took up the active duties of his new position. A year later he was married to the Princess May. Meantime the Queen had opened the Imperial Institute on May 10th, 1893—after a prolonged period of retirement. It was one of the most brilliant functions in which even Her Majesty has ever participated. The state procession, the beautiful decorations, the splendid throng of guests, the Imperial importance of the occasion—all lent brilliance to the ceremonies and pleasure to the Prince who thus witnessed the achievement of his great aim, and the successful end of much thought and toil. The enthusiasm of the reception given to the Queen and the Prince of Wales was, as usual, very great.

On July 6th, the sailor son of the Prince of Wales was married to his second cousin Princess Victoria May of Teck—already so well known to the nation as Princess May. Not since the marriage of the heir-apparent or the

Queen's Jubilee had London been so crowded.   Between eleven and twelve the Royal party proceeded from Buckingham Palace to St. James' Chapel amid dense crowds of cheerful and cheering people, and the fluttering of endless flags and decorations.   The old, old, ceremony was performed by the Archbishop of Canterbury, in the presence of the Queen and a great throng of her greatest subjects, and concluded with the booming of cannon, the strains of sweeter music, the sound of wave upon wave of applause from without the chapel, and the echoes of the Primate's voice as he delivered his brief homily.   "High is your estate," said he, "high are your claims, and therefore high should be your duty.   The light that beats upon you must teach discretion, but let it kindle earnestness, yea, and enthusiasm, that it should illuminate only what is good and fair to see.   To you are looking a glorious Empire, and a strenuous and laborious people, and they look that you should carry forward that high tradition which makes a people proud.   Marriage is the foundation of the family, and upon the ties, and loves, and strength of the family is built a nation's greatness." After the event, and the ensuing popular rejoicings, and congratulations from all parts of the Empire, came another letter to her people from the Queen, in which she spoke of the universal loyalty shown, and declared that : " It is indeed nothing new to the Queen ; for in weal and woe she has ever met with the warmest, kindest sympathy, which she feels very deeply.   She knows that the people of her vast Empire are aware how truly her heart beats for them in all their joys and sorrows, and that in the existence of this tie between them and herself lies the real strength of the Empire."

The following year was marked by the unveiling of a statue of the Queen at Aberdeen : by Royal telegrams of sympathy upon such diverse events as the death of some blue-jackets on the Gambia, and the assasination of President Carnot of France ; by Her Majesty's presence at the marriage of Princess Victoria Melita of Edinburgh to the Grand Duke of Hesse ; by her opening of the great ship canal at Manchester ; by the brilliant wedding of Lady Margaret Grosvenor, the daughter of the Duke of Westminster, to Prince Adolphus of Teck ; by the memorable death of Sir John Thompson at Windsor ; and by the birth of a son and heir to the Duke and Duchess of York.   This latter event deserves more than a passing notice.   Not only was the birth of a great-grand-son in direct succession to the throne an unique national occurrence, but it served to illustrate and complete the domestic interests of the Royal family.   In moving an address to the Queen in the House of Lords on June 28th, Lord Rosebery declared that "no more gratifying guarantee could be given of the permanence of the form of government under which the people of these islands live and which seems best suited to them."

He added that the sympathy of the Queen and her family with the objects and pursuits of the nation had sweetened the air of the three kingdoms.   Lord

Salisbury stated that the event would give the people "great confidence that they would in the far future enjoy the form of government which had conferred so much greatness on this little island." Mr. Balfour, in the House of Commons, declared that "the succession of our sovereigns is the thread on which the history of this country hangs, and they might express their hope that the infant just born would some day, as the sovereign of these realms, continue the great traditions of his ancestors." Sir William Harcourt spoke words of similar import, and observed that "it must bring joy to Her Majesty's heart to feel that the succession to the throne of this great Empire is secured in her descendants to the third generation." And the interest of the whole occasion was well summed up by the *Times*:

"Never before in the history of these islands has the reigning sovereign seen three male descendants in the direct line of succession. The fact is without precedent and scarcely less unprecedented is the close family affection which binds together every branch which issues from the parent stock. "Never in any former reign have sovereign and subject been more closely bound together by ties of mutual regard, never has the example of the throne been more looked up to by the nation as in every way worthy to be imitated."

Events now hurried on to the Inter-Colonial Conference, when, as the *Times* put it, "For the moment Ottawa has, so far as Colonial interests are concerned, taken the place of London as the centre of the Empire," and where strong resolutions of Imperial loyalty were passed; to the sad death of Prince Henry of Battenburg, and the marriage in July, 1896, of Princess Maud of Wales to Prince Charles of Denmark. This royal wedding was celebrated somewhat unusually, in the private chapel of Buckingham Palace, and in the presence of the Queen. The state procession, the popular enthusiasm, and the loyal decorations were, however, much the same as upon other similar occasions, while the Archbishop's address was a model of brevity in language and beauty of thought. With this occurrence, and the approach of a new and more splendid anniversary in a great reign, this study of the Queen's character and career must draw to its close.

No brief summary can do justice to the life of such a sovereign. Her name is known in the farthest confines of the earth, and a visitor amongst the Khirgese of Central Asia has stated that "they had not the remotest idea of where or what England was, but they had heard of Queen Victoria." Her fame is secured in the designation of an era and in the pages of an almost universal literature. Her work has included the most complex details of diplomatic negotiation and personal influence, the threads of legislative action in many parliaments, the monotonous but important study of dispatches, as well as in the more interesting discussions with countless Ministers upon an infinite variety of subjects. Her influence has increased with each passing year and in ever widening centres of British dominion, until the citizen of an empire which now embraces 400,000,000 of people, and one-fourth of the earth's surface, can look up with affectionate loyalty to his sovereign, whether he be living in the valleys of the Indus or upon the plains of the Saskatchewan, at the diamond fields of the Cape of Good Hope, or upon the sheep ranches of Australia.

But if the name, and fame, and influence of the Queen constitute so potent a factor in the British life and policy of the Nineteenth Century, they also represent much in the present and the future. She voices to us now in this sixtieth anniversary of her accession, a glorious history, a most ancient dynasty, a stable system of government, a trained and cultured freedom, the home happiness upon which all society must ultimately rest, the progress and unity of a vast and increasing Empire, and what Lord Rosebery has termed " the most consistently great, and most consistently good reign," in all our annals. She gives to us the future legacy of a great example ; the influence of wise teachings in a widely scattered and powerful Royal family ; the strength of constitutional precept, and the potent evidences of a prolonged and wise administration to her suceessor ; the blessings of a royal system of precedent and practice which can hardly be broken even in the most distant time ; the great heritage of sympathy between the Crown and the people, and of loyalty to a common centre of allegiance and respect from one end of the British realms to the other. She leaves us a successor—in the day when change must come and ring down the curtain upon her beneficent life and reign—who has been not only trained in the arts of government and the love of peace, but who has become habituated to the wise exercise of much Royal power, and has obtained an assured place in the hearts of the people.

The Queen has, in a word, given free government to a free people, a noble example of purity and domestic goodness to the nation in days of much moral stir and stress, a legacy of love and loyalty to the whole vast empire, a memory of work done and righteous influence used, which will affect and control all future development amidst the countless masses owing allegiance to the British Crown, and will stimulate their children, and their children's children to revere the memory and study the reign of Queen Victoria.

THE MARQUESS OF SALISBURY, K.G.

THOMAS CARLYLE.

CHAPTER XXXII.

The Diamond Jubilee.

THE 22nd of June, 1897, will live in British history as the greatest day in a thousand years of development. It marked the highest point yet reached by British power, and liberty, and expansion, while it embodied a new departure along lines of Imperial growth which indicate still more potent possibilities of future unity and greatness. It stamped with unique and marvellous loyalty, affection, and veneration, the career, personality, and prolonged reign of the Queen-Empress. It brought together from the ends of the earth and the uttermost isles of the seas such profound proofs of popular homage, such evidences of Imperial strength, such tokens of loyalty to the Sovereign, to monarchical principles, and to British world-wide unity as would have been deemed the veriest vision of a disordered fancy a decade since, and may now be recognized as firmly establishing the British Empire in its position as the greatest national power of to-day and in the history of the world. To quote the inimitable words of Rudyard Kipling :

> " Take hold of the wings of the morning,
> And flop round the earth till you're dead,
> And you won't get away from the tune that they play
> To the bloomin' old rag overhead."

For many months before the opening of a day which must stand through all the centuries to come for the accumulated power, and dignity, and expansion of the nation during a strenuous period—with the help of a woman's lofty influence and regal example—the British world was ringing with notes of preparation. The machinery of popular government in different continents and distant countries was brought to bear in the production of countless addresses from parliamentary, provincial, municipal, and religious bodies, and from public meetings of every kind and description. The loyal addresses passed during this Jubilee year would alone provide a printed pathway around the waters of the world. The Parliament of Canada, the Legislatures of Australia, New Zealand, Tasmania, Cape Colony and Natal, the Councils of India, the Provincial Legislatures of Canada, the great cities of the Empire at home and throughout the world, vied with each other in these preliminary evidences of public admiration and loyalty.

Some of the popular addresses were perhaps more significant than even those passed by legislative bodies. When the Africander Bund, led by Mr. Jan Hendrick Hofmeyer, presented to the new Governor at the Cape an address of loyalty and congratulation it meant much. It represented a feeling of allegiance which was superior even to the racial feud which has, during the past year, been so rampant between the Dutch and the English in South Africa. It embodied a sentiment of Imperial unity which must have been very strong to enable a purely Dutch organization to join its English fellow-subjects in such an expression of loyal sympathy, and to a little later help in passing through the Cape Parliament an unanimous resolution in favour of contributing to the support of the Imperial navy.

Equally striking was the loyal address from the Roman Catholic hierarchy of the Province of Quebec. In this document the ecclesiastical representatives of another conquered, but now friendly and loyal people, declared that in 1775, in 1812, and in 1837, the Church and the great mass of French-Canadians had proved their allegiance to the Throne, as they now desired to indicate their affection for their Sovereign. " From the distant country watered by the Ganges, from the great rivers and plains of America to the British Isles, your first and most brilliant Crown, comes to-day the unanimous and spontaneous cry from a hundred million breasts. Your faithful subjects spread over five continents and the isles of the ocean, chant with filial and patriotic pride, like a prayer addressed to Heaven and a homage to the Throne, this solemn acclaim, which sums up the dearest sentiment of their hearts: ' God Save the Queen.' "

Signed by Cardinal Taschereau, Archbishops Duhamel and Bégin, Bishops Lafleche, Moreau, Lorrain, Gravel, Blair, Labrecque, Emard, Larocque and Decelles, this address was in many ways noteworthy. So also with a meeting held at Haidarabad, in far-away India, where all classes and races were represented, and resolutions were passed amid great enthusiasm that on Accession Day prayers should be offered in all places of worship, that all the poor should be fed, and that a girls' school should be established and called the Victoria Diamond Jubilee School. From the one-time rebellious Maoris of New Zealand came a loyal address. The spontaneous way in which the Canadian Parliament and Provincial Legislatures sang the National Anthem, and in which public meetings, and every occasion upon which a few people were gathered together throughout the Empire, joined in similar and repeated strains, was another indication of the vast undercurrent of loyalty which rolled in ever-increasing volume from shore to shore, until it broke in a crested wave of enthusiasm on Jubilee Day.

Even more practical proofs soon began to pour in. Lord Hampden, Governor of New South Wales, was able to announce to Mr. Chamberlain a gift from the pastoralists of that colony, and Victoria, and Queensland, of many thousand sheep and cattle, in response to the Princess of Wales' appeal for a Jubilee dinner to the poor of London. Her Royal Highness's letter in this connection constitutes in itself one of the most sympathetic and pleasant features of the spontaneous outburst of charity and brotherly love which marked the whole course of events at this time;

> "Marlborough House, Pall-Mall, S.W.
> April 29th, 1897.

"My Lord Mayor,—In the midst of all the many schemes and preparations for the commemoration of the Queen's Diamond Jubilee, when everybody comes forward on behalf of some good cause; when schools, hospitals, and other charitable institutions have been so wisely and liberally provided for; there seems to me to be one class that has been overlooked, viz.: the Poorest of the Poor in the slums of London. Might I plead for these, that they also should have some share in the festivities of that blessed day, and so remember to the end of their lives that great and good Queen whose glorious reign has, by the blessing of God, been prolonged for sixty years?

Let us, therefore, provide these poor beggars and outcasts with a dinner or substantial meal during the week of the 22nd of June. I leave it to your kind and able organization to arrange that the very poor in all parts of London should be equally cared for. I, myself, will, with pleasure, head the subscription list with £100. You are at liberty to make any use you think best of this letter, and

> Believe me, yours truly
> "Alexandra, Princess of Wales."

The contributions to this Fund, to the Prince of Wales' Hospital Fund, and to the Queen's Jubilee Nursing Institute Fund, were more than generous. They marked an enthusiasm in Great Britain which must have been intense and personal in its nature, as well as charitable in result. No other event could have produced it. To the first named Fund came not only the bountiful Australian gift, but countless contributions from many people—enough finally to feed 300,000 persons, as perhaps they had never been fed before. From one firm, for instance, came ten tons of golden syrup, and from another enough cocoa for 5,000 cups. To the Hospital Fund, so enthusiastically launched and aided by the Prince of Wales, the London Council voted £5,000, the Peabody Trustees gave £10,000, Baroness de Hirsch contributed £4,000, the Grand Lodge of Freemasons £2,000, and through a Masonic gathering, presided over by His Royal Highness, came another £3,500. And so, with many minor and personal subscriptions the amount rose until a short time before the Jubilee Day it amounted to a total of £19,800 in annual sums promised, donations of £117,000, and commuted subscriptions for investment of £20,000—a total of £157,000 or $785,000. To the Queen's Nursing Fund the gifts totalled over £50,000, or $250,000—Irish subscriptions alone amounting to £18,000.

The same practical spirit of loyal philanthropy showed itself everywhere.

Lord Wimborne, Mayor of Poole, offered that town Poole Mansion for use as a hospital, and £1,000 as a cash subscription. At Grimsby, stones were laid in an extensive almshouse scheme. Lord Carrington gave the town of High Wycombe the site for a new town hall. Lord de la Warr contributed £500 cash and an acre of land worth £1,000 to the Bexhill Cottage Hospital scheme. Mr. E. D. Stern, of Chertsey, offered five and a-half acres of land to that town for public use. The famous brewers of Dublin, the Guinness family, gave £2,000 to charitable purposes. Mr. H. O. Mills, of Bristol, contributed £10,000 towards the proposed local Convalescent Home. The Jewish community of London prepared to raise £20,000 for a Jewish Hospital. Glasgow citizens raised £14,700 at a public meeting to rebuild the Royal Infirmary. Provost Mackenzie of Paisley endowed an Eye Infirmary with £4,000. At St. Helens, in Lancashire, £7,000 was contributed towards a local recreation ground; to Dorking Lord Ashcombe gave a similar ground, nine acres in extent; to Northampton Lord Spencer gave eight and a-half acres of land.

These few instances of generosity, however, afford but the barest hint of the national overflow which took place from heart and purse. Outside the United Kingdom the feeling was not evidenced by such large local expenditures, owing to the absence of that enormous accumulated wealth which gives England so conspicuously the control of the financial world. But something was done. Whether intended as a Jubilee offering to the Mother-Country or coming merely as part of a settled Canadian policy, the Government of the Dominion fairly electrified the statesmen of the Empire by offering, and putting into practice, a tariff preference of one-eighth per cent. upon British goods imported into Canada. The Parliament also voted $5,000 for a statue to the Queen in Ottawa, and $26,000 for the military contingent at the Jubilee, while the Postmaster-General arranged for the special issue of a series of Jubilee stamps.

The New Zealand Legislature voted the necessary expenses for its Premier, military contingent and a team of marksmen. The Melbourne City Council granted £1,000 to the Queen's Fever Hospital Fund. The Cape Parliament voted £25,000 as a Jubilee Memorial to be expended on hospitals and similar institutions. Preparations were made to erect a magnificent statue of Her Majesty in the Punjaub, and meetings were held all over India for purposes of more or less permanent and charitable celebration. The general feeling was well expressed by the *Melbourne Age* on February 29th:

"Such functions as those which will celebrate Queen Victoria's sixty years' reign are not merely empty glitter and no more. They are the external symbols of the feelings that lie at the core of millions of hearts; and it is just as important to the unity, and even to the growth of empire that those feelings should find expression in form and colour as that the chosen orators of the nation on great occasions should speak 'the thoughts that breathe and words that burn,' their indelible marks on popular apprehension. In other words, great pageants do not merely celebrate history, they make it; or, at least, they assist in its making. Every part of the Empire will have its own method of expressing its joy, its own illuminations, its own literary and oratorical glorifyings. The shouts that will arise on the banks of the Thames, must find their echo on the banks of the Yarra, and the united burst of patriotism will meet, and fill the world with a new sense of British ubiquity and sovereignty."

But after all this was merely preliminary to the tremendous manifestation of power and patriotism which was slowly gathering its world-wide momentum and force. London became a scene of bare scaffolding and ugly structures which were to eventually develop into many miles of coloured drapery and buildings almost concealed by masses of people and waving flags and banners. Through all the complex arrangements for an event which was to bring many millions more of people into a centre where the population already numbered six million souls, the government and city officials acted in a way which in its result must form one of the marvels of the century. Just as no other country could have such a demonstration or gather together such a multitude, so no other city on earth could have handled the throng as was done throughout the week of jubilee in London. The Prince of Wales, by his executive skill, and influence, and experience, did much to help and direct the authorities, and to him was partly due the Queen's popular and wise decision to have the procession pass through some of the poorer parts of the city.

As the eventful day approached the excitement and interest was universal and sympathetic throughout all the vast bounds of the Empire. London was radiant with streamers and transparencies, mottoes and bunting, spangled cloth and rich tapestries; the gorgeous decorations and electric illuminations of the rich, the little oil-lamps and coloured lights and fluttering flags of the poor or humble. Miles and miles of brilliancy, sparkle, brightness and colour met the bewildered eye; while the greater illuminations on public buildings or important private houses were beautiful and costly beyond compare. Such was the eve of the great day in the Empire's capital. In countless other cities similar preparations were in progress, and from Melbourne to Ottawa, from Dunedin to Cape Town, from Calcutta to Halifax, the pulse of loyalty and unity was beating high. To quote the words of Sir Lewis Morris:

> "Time's finger writes it on the storied page.
> This is the golden link which binds in one
> All British hearts beneath the circling sun."

Sunday, the 20th of June, was Accession Day and the Queen, with several members of the Royal Family, attended a solemn thanksgiving service at Frogmore. An official service for the Lords and Commons was held at St. Margaret's, Westminster, while Her Majesty's Judges, the Lord Mayor and Corporation of

London attended at St. Paul's Cathedral. A special service was also held in every Church of England edifice throughout the world, and in accordance with an idea suggested by Mr. Barlow Cumberland, of Toronto, President of the Sons of England Benefit Society, members of that organization throughout the Empire, together with masses of citizens outside their ranks, attended church in a body and at four o'clock, by the sun, circled the world with a simultaneous girdle of the strains of " God Save the Queen." During the Royal service in the morning a most impressive scene followed the Queen's period of silent prayer. With tears in her eyes and all the solemn appreciation which a Sovereign who is also a true woman might be expected to feel on the eve of such a tremendous event, she kissed the Duke of Connaught and other relatives who were present, and then slowly and almost sorrowfully withdrew from the sacred edifice.

At noon on the succeeding day, Her Majesty left Windsor Castle and travelled to London in a special carriage, beautifully arranged and exquisitely furnished —itself one of the myriad sights of the time to those who might get a glimpse at either exterior or interior. The station at Paddington was transformed into a crimson reception-hall resplendent with gold and fragrant with flowers. From there the Queen drove to Buckingham Palace through the long lanes of a cheering multitude, triumphal arches, and many profuse decorations—though the latter were not yet as they would be on the morrow. At four o'clock Her Majesty received the representatives of the Empire and the Royal or special envoys of foreign States in the Throne Room of the Palace. The British Premiers present were as follows :

United Kingdom	Marquess of Salisbury.
Canada	Hon. Wilfrid Laurier.
Newfoundland	Sir William Whiteway.
New South Wales	Hon. G. H. Reid.
Victoria	Sir George Turner.
Queensland	Sir Hugh Nelson.
Tasmania	Sir E. N. C. Braddon.
South Australia	Hon. C. C. Kingston.
Western Australia	Sir John Forrest.
New Zealand	Hon. R. J. Seddon.
Cape Colony	Sir Gordon Sprigg.
Natal	Hon. Harry Escombe.

Within a few hours of this event the whole external Empire was made aware of the signal honour conferred upon its chosen chiefs by the Queen, in calling them to her Imperial Privy Council—an honour only given in the Colonies before this Jubilee year to Sir John A. Macdonald and Sir John Thompson of Canada, W. Bede Dalley and Sir Alfred Stephen of Australia, and Cecil Rhodes of South Africa. Lately, however, three distinguished colonial jurists—Sir Henry Strong, of Canada, Chief Justice Way, of South Australia, and Sir H. de Villiers of the Cape—had been appointed to the Judicial Committee of the Privy Council. Mr. Laurier also received the insignia of a G.C.M.G. In the evening a Royal banquet was held and a State reception given to the Diplomatic Corps.

With the dawn of light on the 22nd of June everything was in readiness for the greatest celebration and function the world has seen. The decorations were completed, and the Jubilee colours of red, white, and blue were to be seen in every direction, and in every form of varied beauty or ugliness. Costly flowers and tinsel imitations, fir and evergreen and laurel, pennons shields and standards, Venetian masts and wreaths and festoons, coloured globes and balloons, garlands and myriad flags, everywhere presented a brilliant wall of colour, behind, and above, and around a vast sea of faces along the six miles which the procession was to take. Without any serious accident, without disorder or apparent difficulty, the millions of spectators were placed in line, or seat, to await the commencement of the day's proceedings. At St. Paul's Cathedral the stands and seats prepared for them soon held the great and representative personages of British life and modern achievement. The brilliant robes of the Peers, the beautiful dresses of the Peeresses and a myriad other ladies, the lawn sleeves and sombre gowns of the Bishops of the Church, the diplomatic uniforms of varied colour and degrees of brilliance, the splendid robes of the Catholic clergy, the quieter dresses of the Commoners and Dissenting ministers, the scarlet uniforms of the officers, the jewelled and superb costumes of Indian princes, and the stately gold-laced garb of the Privy Councillors, mixed and merged into one blaze of gorgeous colour.

Above this display of individual splendour towered the Corinthian columns and turrets of the great Cathedral. In front, and down through Ludgate Hill, winding along Fleet Street and the ever-crowded Strand stretched a long and longer avenue lined with column after column of the best troops of England—a thin red line now prepared to meet and honour its Sovereign, as it ever is to defend the interests and integrity of the Empire. Through this line of scarlet from Victoria Embankment and Pall Mall came the first part of the procession—the Colonial Contingents and the Colonial Premiers—in the following order :

Detachment of Royal Horse Guards.

Canadian Mounted Troops.　　Premier of Canada.

New South Wales Mounted Troops.

Premier of New South Wales.

Victoria Mounted Troops.　　Premier of Victoria.

New Zealand Mounted Troops.

Premier of New Zealand.

Queensland Mounted Troops.　　Premier of Queensland.

Cape of Good Hope Mounted Troops.

Premier of Cape Colony.
South Australian Mounted Troops.
Premier of South Australia.   Premier of Newfoundland.
Premier of Tasmania.
Natal Mounted Troops.   Premier of Natal.
Premier of Western Australia.
Mounted Troops of Crown Colonies.
Rhodesian Horse.   Colonial Infantry.

It was a striking part of a wonderful scene. The picturesque Mounted Police of Canada, and the Dominion cavalry looking so like the best types of the home soldier; the Australian troops with their different coloured uniforms and feathered and slouched hats; the Zaptiehs from Cyprus with their dark blue uniforms, red fezzes and sashes; the wiry little Dyaks of Borneo in their vivid uniforms; the West Indian troops in their scarlet and white; the coal-black troopers from the distant Niger or the African Gold Coast; the strange-looking Chinese Police from Hong-Kong and the Malay contingent from the Straits Settlements; the Malta Artillery, the Canadian Highlanders, the Ceylon Light Infantry, the Natal cavalry and the Cape Colony troopers; marched by in precise order, but in a most bewildering succession of surprises to the eager, cheering multitude.

The Premiers, each in his new Privy Council uniform with its profusion of blue and gold braid, were received with immense enthusiasm. But all agree in awarding the honours of popular acclaim to the Canadian Prime Minister. With Lady Laurier he was given one continuous ovation from the Embankment to the Cathedral. He was first in the procession, with a handsome presence and a genial smile, while the news of Canada's preference to British goods had by now filtered slowly down into the minds and hearts of the masses. It was, therefore, not surprising if a cordial reception had been given him as well as to the other Colonial leaders. But there was more than cordiality, both in the special welcome to him, and in the more general greeting to the others. It was a feeling of almost personal affection for these British representatives and soldiers from all parts of the world—a feeling which embraced the humblest private in the ranks as it did the Prime Minister in his royal carriage. In the welcome to Sir Wilfrid Laurier it culminated—so far as that word can be used of anything in the day's proceedings apart from the Queen herself.

The press upon this point was unanimous. To Lord Roberts and the Canadian Premier came the secondary receptions and greetings of the Jubilee—to one as representing all that was gallant and proud in the life of a British soldier, to the other as representing, for the moment, all that was Imperial and world-wide in the mind of the British citizen. Mr. Henry Norman in *The News*, declared of this part of the Procession that "here was in truth a reminder that the British Empire keeps and is kept by not only the 'pink-faced Englishman,' but the black man, and the brown man, and the yellow man, in their millions. * * * We give them liberty, they give us loyalty. In their strange faces and hard, discoloured palms the strength of empire goes around the world." *The Chronicle* described the Colonial Contingents as being greeted with "a continuous roar of cheering, better maintained and far more hearty than that which greeted the familiar faces of their own soldiery. Mr. Laurier was one of the stateliest figures in the Procession, and he was received with an unmistakable enthusiasm." *The Standard* stated that they were received "with something like passionate emotion. The bronzed sons of England and the Colonial Premiers went by amidst a roar of cheering." This popular acclaim meant much in an Imperial sense, but in still another sense was the military part of the great procession important. There were home soldiers as well as colonial, and the splendid sight of nearly 50,000 of the best troops of Great Britain gathered upon this occasion to swell the glory of the Jubilee, justifies, in some measure, the description of this preliminary portion of the scene by Mr. Julian Ralph, correspondent of the New York *Journal*:

"For seventy-five minutes these brilliant, gorgeous, gold and silver-plated be-feathered or fur-topped men swung by, all flashing back 'the arrows of the sun' and setting old London agog by the unexpected size, grandeur, colour, and splendour of the show. London had expected a show in which there would be only one great figure, the Queen, but the scheme grew, and swelled, and altered, until the Queen, at last, became merely the proud captain of a multitude of shining, gilded, steel-toothed war-dogs, gathered from every corner of the globe."

But after all is said and written of the Imperial enthusiasm displayed, the military power indicated, and—at a later period—the marvellous evidences of naval strength exhibited; the central figure of the day, and personal embodiment of every loyal and proud feeling in the minds of her myriad subjects, had yet to come upon the scene. Following the Colonial procession, after a few minutes interval, came a contingent of the brilliant Life Guards, headed by Captain Ames—the tallest man in the service—and succeeded in steady progress by regiment after regiment of cavalry and artillery—the ever popular Dragoons, and Hussars, and Lancers receiving many and constant cheers.

The Duke of Westminster, as Lord-Lieutenant of London, the Aides-de-Camp to the Queen—including Lord Charles Beresford—Field Marshals Sir Lintorn Simmons and Sir Donald Stewart, the Sheriffs of London in all their gorgeous array, hundreds of Royal Equerries and military Attachés, and a brilliant contingent of officers from the Imperial Service Troops of India, followed in rapid succession. The latter, splendidly mounted and clad in gorgeous and beautiful native uniforms, were alone enough to glorify any pageant. Then came the carriages with certain foreign Envoys, followed by those containing various members of the Royal family, each drawn by four magnificent horses, with postilions clad in scarlet liveries. Forty British and foreign Princes came next, and preceded the special Royal escort from the regular Indian Army. The gorgeous cavalcade of Princes fairly gleamed and sparkled with jewelled Orders, and presented a sight far too brilliant to take in during what might be termed the flash past. But now, for a minute along the whole route, the people became intensely, solemnly quiet, and no amount of splendour would avert or distract the concentrated attention of all hearts and minds from the central figure of a great world-wide concourse of humanity. The Queen left Buckingham Palace at eleven o'clock amid the roar of guns, the pealing of countless bells, the thunderous music of massed bands, and the strained expectancy of probably five million people in London alone. Just at the moment of starting Her Majesty touched an electric bell, and instantly, to forty British governments and peoples in every part of the world there flashed the simultaneous message:

"From my heart I thank my beloved people. May God bless them.

VICTORIA, R. I."

Immediately preceding the Royal carriage rode Lord Wolseley as Commander-in-Chief of the Army. Upon its right hand rode the Prince of Wales and the Duke of Connaught, and on the left, the veteran Duke of Cambridge. Behind it waved the Royal Standard, followed by various stately officials, and a Royal escort of the Irish Constabulary and Horse Guards. Her Majesty was dressed in black with a black hat trimmed in white, and carried a white sun-shade. The weather had up to now been doubtful, and the sky cloudy, but curiously enough, as the Queen entered her carriage the sun broke through the clouds, and from that time onward the great demonstration proceeded amid a brightness of sunshine only equalled by the light of loyalty which illuminated the six miles of serried masses. With the Queen, in her carriage were the Princess of Wales and Princess Christian (Helena) of Schleswig-Holstein.

It is impossible to describe here in detail what followed. That steady, stately drive through millions of cheering people has never been equalled or approached in the history of the world. The Jubilee of 1887 came the nearest perhaps to doing so, and the Czar's recent coronation next so far as mere grandeur was concerned. But this combination of almost barbaric military pomp and splendour, with absolutely unique popular love and veneration, and the consciousness that the same pulsing sentiment of loyalty was echoing in numberless British throngs around the world, could not occur in any other age or empire.

To quote an intelligent and certainly not over-friendly critic, Mr. Chauncey M. Depew:

"I can conjecture no tribute like the popular ovation to the Queen ever being given to any human being. Respect, reverence, love, or gratitude are words too tame, and there is no intermediate expression between them and adoration. This practical age does not worship. But, leaving out the idea of divinity, yesterday's greeting to the Queen and Empress is its equivalent. That she was deeply moved was evident, but she seemed more absorbed by the significance of the event than conscious of her past."

The personal pleasure, Imperial pride, and dominating national passion of loyalty which were concentrated in the reception thus given made it beyond doubt the most marvellous popular manifestation in the world's annals. It was a tidal wave of enthusiasm surrounding and enclosing the great little woman in black, who embodied to her people everything that was noble and historic in all this sweeping panorama of power. From Buckingham Palace Her Majesty drove by way of Constitution Hill, Piccadilly, St. James's Street, Pall-Mall, Trafalgar Square, and the Strand to the ancient city boundary at Temple Bar—where the Lord Mayor went through the famous formula of handing his sword to the Sovereign and receiving it back again—thence by Fleet Street and Ludgate Hill to St. Paul's Cathedral, where a brief open-air service was performed by the Archbishop of Canterbury, assisted by various other ecclesiastical dignitaries. Reference has already been made to the splendour of this particular scene, but two events may be mentioned here. One was the unique picture presented by the dignified Primate of all England calling for three cheers for the Queen, from this special gathering of all that was great in modern British life. The other was the fact that here, as elsewhere along the route, the Canadian Premier had been received with a great outburst of cheering. As the *Times* said: "Sir Wilfrid Laurier was one of the few notabilities of the day who were instantaneously recognized—a surprising fact considering how little he has come into contact with the London public."

From the Cathedral, the Queen and her escort of a mile long passed amid renewed salvos of artillery and a constantly growing volume of cheers, down King William Street to London Bridge and thence through South London and a part of the poorer population of the city to Westminster Bridge, Whitehall, the Mall, and Buckingham Palace—which was reached at a quarter to Two. The central event of the Jubilee was thus finished, but the glory of the event will long remain in men's minds. One more description may be given here. Mr. G. W. Stevens in the *Daily Mail* said:

"Riding three and three came a kaleidoscope of dazzling horsemen, equerries, aides-de-camp, attachés, ambassadors and princes, all the pomp of all the nations of the earth—scarlet and gold, purple and gold, azure and gold, emerald and gold, white and gold—always a changing tumult of colours that seemed to live and gleam with a light of their own. It was enough. No eye could bear more gorgeousness. * * * The roar surged up the street, keeping pace with the Queen's carriage. We all stood up. The enthusiasm swelled to delirium. * * * You could not look at anybody but the Queen, so very quiet, so very grave, so very punctual, and so unmistakably every inch a lady and a Queen. It was almost pathetic, if you will, that small black figure in the middle of those shining cavaliers, this great army, this roaring multitude; but it was also very glorious."

Following the great pivotal event of an Empire's celebration came a series of Royal functions and popular ceremonies. The evening of the 22nd was devoted by Her Majesty in person to rest, but throughout the British world the celebration continued in the shape of countless illuminations and other forms of popular demonstration. At Buckingham Palace the Prince of Wales presided over a second Royal banquet and participated in a State concert, while London was ablaze with light and the streets thronged with moving masses of people. On Wednesday morning Her Majesty received separately at the Palace the two Houses of Parliament, and in response to their addresses of congratulation declared that "I have been deeply touched by the numerous manifestations of loyalty and affection to my Throne." A State reception followed to the Chairmen and Conveners of the County Councils of Great Britain, and the Mayors and Provosts of the United Kingdom. In the afternoon a great garden party to 6,000 guests was given at Buckingham Palace and the Queen received the personal homage of a multitude of representative men and women. Another Royal banquet was given in the evening, whilst Lady Salisbury held a Ball at the Foreign Office, attended by the chief visitors and Royal guests of the occasion.

The Queen travelled to Windsor in semi-state on Thursday morning and visited Eton, where she was enthusiastically received by the college boys. In the evening a banquet was given at the castle and Her Majesty reviewed a torchlight procession of Eton boys. On Friday, June 25th, the Queen, with the Prince of Wales as inspecting officer, reviewed the fire brigades of England, and in the evening gave a State banquet in St. George's Hall to which all the Imperial and Royal guests were invited. Then came the wonderful naval review off Spithead on June 26th. Here the Prince of Wales took the place of his Royal mother and inspected a vast fleet of 166 warships manned by 45,000 sailors and with a British tonnage of 600,000 tons. If the Jubilee Procession in London had been an outpouring of popular affection for the Queen and a splendid display of Imperial power and military strength, this function was an equally important evidence of absolute British supremacy upon the seas of the world. The fleet marked the great naval triumph of England and yet was only composed of the first line of maritime defence—an unique aggregation of sea-power without the weakening of a naval station or defence in any part of the globe. The Colonial Premiers, with Mr. Chamberlain, in the yacht *Wildfire* followed the vessels bearing certain Royal guests, and preceded those with the

Houses of Lords and Commons and the Foreign Ambassadors. Steaming through the five miles of warships, the waving flags, the serried masses of sailors, and roaring guns gave sights and sounds to the visitors which could hardly fail to leave a life-long impression.

Meanwhile a myriad minor events had transpired. Those connected with the entertainment of the Colonial leaders were second only in picturesque interest to the events of the Jubilee proper, and in real importance might perhaps be placed with the greater of the Royal functions. On June 12th the Liverpool Chamber of Commerce banquetted the Premiers, and listened to a great speech from the Duke of Devonshire (the Lord Hartington of earlier British politics) in which he expressed himself in sympathy with the idea of a commercial union within the Empire. On the following day (Sunday) the Earl of Crewe—formerly Lord Houghton, and Viceroy of Ireland—entertained the visitors at Crewe Hall. On Monday, they were welcomed by the Lord Provost of Edinburgh; on Tuesday by the Lord Provost of Glasgow; on Wednesday by the Lord Mayor of Manchester; on Saturday by Prince and Princess Christian at Egham, Surrey; on Monday by the Lord Mayor of Birmingham; on Tuesday by the British Empire League—which had arranged these functions—to a water party on the Upper Thames; on Saturday, July 3rd, by the Earl of Jersey, at Osterley Park, to a Garden Party. On July 4th the Duke of Devonshire gave a magnificent fancy dress ball at Devonshire House. On the 2nd of the month the Canadian troops were specially reviewed by the Queen at Windsor Castle, and on the following day the Prince of Wales inspected all the Colonial troops at Buckingham Palace and presented a Jubilee medal to each man present. Other functions too numerous to even give a list of took place, including a splendid reception at the Imperial Institute by Sir Donald Smith, the Canadian High Commissioner, in honour of Sir Wilfrid and Lady Laurier. One very important Banquet given by the Royal Colonial Institute on June 18th, presided over by Prince of Wales, and attended by Lord Salisbury, Lord Rosebery and many other public leaders must be mentioned, as well as an equally splendid dinner given by Mr. Chamberlain, and a luncheon by Lord Rosebery in honour of the same distinguished and much fêted guests.

Meantime the progress of loyal rejoicing fairly girdled the world, while the strains of the national anthem echoed wherever the flag of England flaunts in the wind until one could almost fancy the waves of sound beating down the walls of Windsor. The procession in London on Jubilee Day was duplicated in equally enthusiastic fashion from the Himalayas to the Rockies. The celebrations in Canada were worthy of its place in the Empire; and the message of Lord Aberdeen in response to the Queen's greeting well voiced the feeling of its whole people: " The Queen's most gracious and touching message shall immediately be made known to Her Majesty's people throughout the Dominion. It will stir afresh hearts already full. We offer our glad tribute of loyal devotion and affectionate homage. God save and bless the Queen." Halifax and Victoria, Montreal and Toronto, Winnipeg and Hamilton, Ottawa and St. John echoed the cheers of the Empire's Capital. Canada spoke, indeed, with one clear, unbroken voice, and in the beautiful words of Mrs. Jean Blewett:

> " The shadows all have swiftly fled,
>   Our song goes ringing, clear and sweet,
>   From the Atlantic at our feet,
>   To the Pacific at our head :
>   It is the year
>   Of jubilee,
>   Ring out glad song o'er land and sea :
>   God save our good Victoria !
>   God save the Queen ! "

But so it was everywhere. In Cape Town, as the leading city of South Africa, the festivities were upon an unprecedented scale in the annals of the Colony, and included a united thanksgiving service of Dutch and English, succeeded by a long procession. At Durban in Natal ; from the Mauritius, with its mixed religious population ; in Mombassa and Zanzibar on the East Coast ; to Freetown and Lagos on the West Coast, the occasion was kept with unbounded loyal rejoicings. From Aden, from Ceylon, from Singapore, from the Malay States came the same story. Throughout India most elaborate and gorgeous eastern demonstrations were held. Churches, mosques, and temples were filled with vast multitudes praying for the great Empress whom they had never seen, and splendid shows, loyal speeches, and munificent charities—even after the terrible strain of the late famine—attested the universal desire to mark the great event. In Australian capitals such as Melbourne and Sydney similar demonstrations occurred, and in many parts of the Island-Continent and New Zealand the celebrations continued for a week.

If, therefore, wealthy Britain laid at Her Majesty's feet the greatest and costliest demonstration in all history, and a subscription to charities aggregating over a million pounds sterling, the external empire, with its more limited capital but tremendous potentialities, was able to contribute proofs of an affectionate loyalty which presaged a measure of unity and strength sufficient to enable the noble woman, who presides over the vast destinies of four hundred millions of the human race, to hold during her lifetime and hand to her successor an Empire solid in the sentiment of kinship or allegiance, and permeated with sympathetic loyalty and fellowship.

PRINCE CONSORT'S SARCOPHAGUS IN THE ROYAL MAUSOLEUM, FROGMORE,

Photo by J. Russell and Sons, Windsor.

THE FUNERAL OF QUEEN VICTORIA AT COWES.

The Royal Coffin Descending the Hill From Osborne into Cowes, on Friday Afternoon, Feb. 1st, with **Her** late Majesty's Equerries and Aides-de-Camp, walking by the side of the Gun Carriage.

CHAPTER XXXIII.

The Close of a Noble Life.

When the Queen drove through the cheering and cheerful millions of her subjects during the Diamond Jubilee everything seemed to promise a peaceful end to her eventful life and reign. The whisperings of war were hushed, no signs of rebellion or disaffection were visible within the far-flung bounds of her Empire, the influence of the Royal personality was as powerful in Europe as the prestige of her great fleets, or the loyalty of her myriad subjects, was marked. And, for a year or two this state of affairs continued. An aftermath of the Jubilee was a characteristic letter from the Queen to her people issued on the 16th of July, 1897. It referred in tactful language to the wonderful demonstrations of loyalty which had then taken place in British countries around the world, and continued in part as follows:

"It is, indeed, deeply gratifying after so many years of labour and anxiety for the good of my beloved country to find that my exertions have been appreciated throughout my vast Empire.

"In weal or woe, I have ever had the true sympathy of all my people, which has been warmly reciprocated by myself. . . . I shall ever pray God to bless them and to enable me still to discharge my duties for their welfare as long as life lasts."

With the passing of this great event, when "The tumult and the shouting dies—the captains and the kings depart," there came a time in which the central figure of it all retired to Balmoral and Osborne for a brief period of rest and recuperation. But the cares of statecraft and government could not be entirely disposed of. Apart from the study of despatches, the signature of documents and the ever-present mass of correspondence, out of which some considerable proportion always received personal attention, there was the consideration of those new matters of public importance which so constantly arise. There seems little doubt that the Queen hoped in the last years of her reign to do something effectual towards conciliating Ireland and Irish opinion. She had determined that no citizen of her Empire could say that everything within her power had not been done in that direction. The Prince and Princess of Wales had already paid a most successful visit to Erin and now it was decided to send the Duke and Duchess of York upon a similar tour. The visit lasted through August and September of this year, and included Dublin and Killarney, Londonderry and Belfast—the south, centre and north of the country and every class and creed of its peculiar population. To the Queen the time must have been one of anxiety, as it has always been impossible to say just what the excitable and irresponsible element amongst the Irish people might do at such junctures. But everything went off with success, and the personal loyalty of the crowds seemed as marked as their political disloyalty is sometimes loud.

On October 27th, following the return of the Royal tourists, came one of those sad events which the Queen in recent years has had so frequently to face. The death of the Princess Mary, Duchess of Teck, her "beloved cousin, to whom the Queen was warmly attached," as the *Court Circular* very correctly puts it, was one more loss from the ever-narrowing circle of friends or relations whom she could meet upon anything like an equal or confidential footing. The Duke of Cambridge still lived, but the Empress Frederick was far away in her German home, and public duties kept the Prince of Wales and the Duke of Connaught from having any continuous intercourse with their Royal mother. To the Princess Henry of Battenberg (or Princess Beatrice as she is still popularly known), and, in lesser measure, to the Princess Louise, remained the privilege and duty of being constantly with the Queen. But the death of the Duchess of Teck, with all her lovable qualities and goodness of hand and heart, was none the less a distinct loss to the much-diminished Royal circle.

Like so many other similar griefs, however, it had no effect upon the Queen's continuous participation in public affairs, and, a few weeks later, she marked her interest in the patriotic ambitions of Mr. Cecil Rhodes by sending a cable message to the Chairman of a banquet at Buluwayo, in far-off Rhodesia, which is significant as shewing her appreciation of the Imperial policy involved in his great Cape to Cairo project : " The Queen desires to convey to her people at Buluwayo her hearty congratulations on the completion of the Railway." During the succeeding year events involving personal sorrow came quickly upon top of one another. In July, 1898, the Prince of Wales suffered the accident to his knee which caused so much alarm at the time, and seemed capable of serious consequences which were, fortunately, not realized. On September 10th occurred the sad and cruel assassination of the Empress of Austria.

It was the cause of much natural grief to the Queen, not only from personal sentiment, but because of her long and intimate relations with the now widowed Emperor, Francis Joseph. The published official announcement was sufficiently explicit regarding the shock which the event must have been to her : " The Queen yesterday evening received with feelings of the utmost consternation and sorrow the startling news of the terrible crime which has caused the death of the Empress of Austria. The Queen mourns profoundly the loss of Her Imperial Majesty, with whom she has been on terms of friendship for many years." About the same time there passed away the Queen of Denmark, who, as a Royal personage born within a couple of years of the time when England's

Queen saw the light of day; as a life-long friend and near relation; as mother of the Princess of Wales and grandmother of the Duke of York; held a place very near to the heart of the aged Sovereign. And, as if to accentuate the fact that death has the same power over persons of all grades, the veteran Sir George Grey died during the same month. Though far away in New Zealand, and not in any personal sense now associated with the Queen, he had yet been for many years a living link with earlier days of rule when he was one of her favourite statesmen and a much-regarded friend of the Prince Consort—a period which was the birth-time of great problems and issues in the far East and in distant South Africa.

At the opening of the year 1898 the Queen paid one of her periodical visits to Netley Hospital, and brought pleasure to many a poor and maimed soldier of the realm. A Drawing-Room at Buckingham Palace followed, and on March 11th Her Majesty left London for Nice, receiving on the way the homage of the authorities at Cherbourg. There she remained until April 30th, having the Princess Beatrice with her, the Marquess and Marchioness of Salisbury in a Villa in the immediate neighbourhood, and visits from the King of the Belgians, the Queen of Holland, and President Faure, of France. Meanwhile the expedition of General Kitchener to Khartoum had commenced, and was followed by his triumph at Omdurman, the evolution of the Fashoda affair, with its anxious moments of possible war with France, the gradual passing of the storm-cloud, and the arrival of Lord Kitchener in England to receive his well-won honours, and to visit the Queen at Balmoral on October 31st. During April the illness of Mr. Gladstone had brought many inquiries from Her Majesty at Nice, and his death on May 19th, following, caused her genuine personal sorrow for a statesman whose old-fashioned and deferential manners toward women, and undoubted loyalty to the Queen herself, could not fail to charm even a Sovereign who had never concealed her dislike for some of his political policies. A telegram was instantly despatched to Miss Gladstone: "I am deeply grieved at sad news. Beatrice and I wish to express our deepest sympathy to your dear mother and all of you." A little later, on May 28th, the Queen wrote to Mrs. Gladstone in words which were significant of her personal feelings, and were penned in a guarded language which omitted any reference to great or patriotic services rendered the country and the Empire—words such as she had used at the time of Lord Beaconsfield's death:

"My thoughts are much with you to-day when your dear husband is laid to rest. To-day's ceremony will be most trying and painful for you, but it will be at the same time gratifying to you to see the respect and regret evinced by the nation for the memory of one whose character and intellectual abilities marked him as one of the most distinguished statesmen of my reign. I shall ever gratefully remember his devotion and zeal in all that concerned my personal welfare and that of my family."

During the year which followed the Queen was much in retirement. The Prince of Wales had taken upon his shoulders all the ordinary functions of Royalty, and was now being greatly assisted by the Duke of York, who had steadily grown in general popularity. On January 9th, 1899, however, Her Majesty presented a medal at Osborne for distinguished service to some soldiers from the Soudan, and on March 10th left for the Riviera with the Duchess of York and other members of the Royal family. At Cimiez she remained until May 2nd. On May 15th the Queen paid a semi-state visit to the metropolis in order to lay the corner stone of a splendid building which was intended to house a fine art collection at South Kensington, and to perpetuate popular study along artistic lines. Vast crowds were massed along the route from Buckingham Palace, and much enthusiasm greeted the aged Sovereign. In the Pavilion, erected where the future Victoria and Albert Museum was to be built, the gathering was a most brilliant one, and included the Prince of Wales, the Duke and Duchess of York, Lord Salisbury, Lord Rosebery, Mr. Chamberlain, the Duke of Devonshire, the Duke of Cambridge, and many others. The Queen's speech in concluding the ceremony was characteristically appropriate, and declared of the proposed structure that: "I trust it will remain for ages a monument of discerning liberality and a source of refinement and progress."

On May 24th the Queen's 80th birthday was celebrated throughout the Empire with most unusual fervour and enthusiasm. From Bombay to Montreal, from Sydney to Cape Town, from London to Land's End, came the evidences of strong and sincere loyalty. There was more than that, however. There was a feeling of deep affection, the principal cause for which is well explained by the *Times* in a tribute of remarkable and accurate judgment: "With a consummate tact, of which she alone among Sovereigns seems to possess the secret, never abating one jot of the dignity of the Crown nor one tittle of her own self-respect, she has taken the people into her confidence, making them partakers, as no monarch ever did before, of her own joys and sorrows, and giving them, in return, a sympathy as timely, as gracious and as genuine as ever flowed from a true woman's heart." One of the most valued tributes of the time was a message from President McKinley speaking of " the regard and affection " cherished by the American people towards Her Majesty.

As the year waxed and waned the South African crisis grew into acute being, and finally developed into war. To the Queen such a situation involved much mental tension and serious additional work. Deeply and specially interested in all matters affecting the Colonies, her already published opinions regarding South African policy had shown a true grasp of the situation half a century before, and there can be no doubt that she followed closely and clearly the intricate phases of the Chamberlain-Kruger negotiations. Much nonsense

THE NAVY'S TRIBUTE TO THE GREAT QUEEN. THE TORPEDO BOATS LEADING THE WAY IN FRONT OF THE "ALBERTA."

From a Sketch by S. M. Lawrence, our Special Artist.

PLACING THE COFFIN ON THE GUN-CARRIAGE AT VICTORIA STATION, PREVIOUS TO THE PROCESSION THROUGH LONDON.

Drawn by Frank Dadd, R. J.

has been written in this connection about her opposition to the war. Like every good woman or humane man, the Queen abhorred war in principle and practice. But her first interest throughout her reign was always the interest of her own people. She was never cosmopolitan, she was always Imperialistic and patriotic. An insult or injury to her nation and Empire was as quickly resented by her as it would be by the humblest of her subjects, while her sense of responsibility could not but be infinitely greater. Issues involving war and peace were therefore simply matters of duty and national honour, not of private dislike to war or womanly aversion to its inevitable sufferings. Had Mr. Chamberlain carried out a policy to which she was opposed, he would probably have suffered the fate of Lord Palmerston half a century before; but such an alternative was rendered most unlikely by the fact that the patriotic, Imperialistic, British view of any great question was almost certain to be the Queen's own opinion.

From the first Her Majesty took a marked public, as well as personal, interest in the development of this crisis. On September 30th she presented new colours at Balmoral to the Seaforth Highlanders, and on November 20th and 21st received the German Emperor and Empress at Windsor. The functions were splendid and the greetings cordial. But there was much more than mere ceremony in this visit. The South African war had not only commenced; it was in one of its dark and disastrous phases. Europe was in a state of restless readiness to take advantage of any weakness shown by Great Britain and of any possible alliance of hostile nations. France was eager for intervention and Russia not apparently averse—and intervention of any kind would have meant intense humiliation to England or the beginning of a great European conflict. At this crisis the Emperor William came to Windsor, and, after prolonged private conferences with the Queen and the Prince of Wales, left the country a friend and practical ally. The inference is natural, and it is that one more exercise of the Queen's tact, personal influence and *prestige* had averted once again a great danger from the peoples of her Empire.

Meanwhile, everything that could be done to show the Queen's appreciation of her troops was done. In June she had reviewed a division under Sir Redvers Buller, and on July 1st, the Honourable Artillery Company of London. A couple of weeks later she presented new colours to the Scots Guards, and on November 11th reviewed the Household Cavalry before its departure for the seat of war. During the next few months Her Majesty remained at Windsor so as to be near her advisers, and on the day after Christmas entertained a large gathering of soldiers' wives and children at the Castle. The first important action of the year 1900 was the despatch of congratulations to Sir George White upon his repulse of a severe attack on Ladysmith. A little later she sent a characteristic message to Mrs. Vernon, whose gallant son, Captain Ronald

Vernon, had lost his life in one of the most heroic of the Mafeking sorties : "Her Majesty knows that in such moments words can do little to bring real comfort. But Her Majesty feels that in your sadness there will be the lasting bright thought that your son gave his life in devoted and self-sacrificing service to Queen and country." On January 30th she wired General Buller an expression of deep admiration for the conduct of the troops at Spion Kop ; on February 2nd she thanked the defenders of Mafeking for a message of loyalty ; on February 6th she expressed British gratitude to the Greek nation for its evidences of unbounded sympathy in the sorrows of the moment ; and a little later was able to congratulate Lord Roberts on the relief of Kimberley, and the Canadian people on the gallantry of their sons at Paardeberg. The little bugler, Dunn, who had so distinguished himself at Colenso was received at Windsor on February 19th, and two days earlier the Queen made a personal appeal to her old soldiers to re-enlist for home defence. It was done in the form of a letter to Lord Wolseley, the Commander-in-Chief, and contained the following strong sentence : "Confident in their devotion to country and loyalty to her Throne, the Queen appeals to them to serve once more in place of those who, for a time are absent from these Islands, and who, side by side with the people of her Colonies, are nobly resisting the invasion of her South African possessions."

Meanwhile, the battle had occurred in which the Irish Regiments had so specially distinguished themselves, and the Queen, ever quick in her tactful sympathy, telegraphed Sir Redvers Buller : "I have heard with the deepest concern of the heavy losses sustained by my brave Irish soldiers. I desire to express my sympathy and my admiration of the splendid fighting qualities which they have exhibited throughout these trying operations." A few days later she inspected at Windsor a company of the Berkshire Volunteers, who were about to proceed to the front, and early in March, one of the most wise and gracious acts of her reign was announced as impending. Since the visit of the Duke and Duchess of York to Ireland, it seems obvious that the situation there had specially pressed itself upon the Queen's attention. The necessity for a hurried and continuous despatch of troops to South Africa also brought home to the mind of the Sovereign, as it did to the people generally, the fact that tens of thousands of British soldiers had to be retained in Ireland at a moment when the splendid gallantry of Irish troops at the seat of war revealed the dormant military possibilities of the "distressful isle."

On the fifth of the month it was announced that Her Majesty had decided to abandon her usual health visit to the Italian Riviera, or Southern France, and proposed instead to pay a state visit to Ireland. The statement was received with unusual and sustained enthusiasm. She had just returned to Windsor from Netley Hospital where a personal interest had been shown in every one of the 500 patients in that great military institution. Almost immediately afterwards she entered London in state, and was welcomed by dense crowds of people delighted at not only seeing their Sovereign again, but in seeing her look so well. She spent three days in the metropolis, and on March 10th inspected the 2nd Battalions of the Grenadier and Scots Guards before their departure for the seat of war.

Simultaneously with the announcement of the proposed visit to Dublin came an Army Order, specially issued by Royal instruction, that the Queen "is pleased to order that in future, upon St. Patrick's Day, all ranks in Her Majesty's Irish regiments shall wear, as a distinction, a sprig of shamrock in their head-dress to commemorate the gallantry of the Irish soldiers during the recent battles in South Africa." The effect of this rare act of Queenly kindness and tact was instantaneous, and a sort of electric thrill of sympathy seemed to run around the globe. On the ensuing 17th of March, and during the celebrations following the relief of Ladysmith, every part of the Empire showed a "wearing of the green," and a flying of the flag by myriads of friendly hearts who had hitherto regarded or worn the emblem as a hostile and anti-British one. This little action of thoughtful kindness had, in fact, changed the character of a national celebration and affected all, except the most extreme of American or home Irishmen.

On the news of Ladysmith's relief arriving the Queen instantly cabled Sir Redvers Buller and Sir George White. To the latter she expressed a few simple and heart-felt words : " Thank God that you and all those with you are safe after your long and trying siege, borne with such heroism. I congratulate you and all under you from the bottom of my heart. Trust that you are all not very much exhausted." Shortly afterwards Her Majesty visited the 400 soldiers laid up in Woolwich Hospital and, in passing through the arsenal works, was enthusiastically welcomed by 20,000 workmen, as well as by the great crowds of people along the entire route to the Hospital. A reception of the Australian Delegates visiting England in connection with the details of their Commonwealth measure followed, and on April 2nd, the Queen left Windsor for Ireland. She arrived at Kingstown on the succeeding day, and made her state entry into Dublin on April 4th. Accompanied by Princess Beatrice and Princess Christian, preceded and surrounded by much of pomp and ceremony, but by little of military show or strength, she drove slowly through the streets of Dublin amid a cheering, seething mass of humanity, which appeared utterly oblivious of politics, or Home Rule, or the hated Saxon, and sang with vim and enthusiasm the National Anthem and " Soldiers of the Queen." To the formal welcome and address of the Lord Mayor, Her Majesty's reply was as follows :

" I thank you heartily for the loyal welcome and good wishes which you have tend-ered to me on behalf of yourselves and your fellow-citizens on my arrival in the ancient capital of my Irish dominions. I come to this country to seek change and rest, and to revisit scenes which recall to my mind, among thoughts of the losses which years must bring, the happiest recollections of the warm-hearted welcome given to me and my beloved hus band and children. I am deeply gratified that I have been able at this time to see again the mother-land of those brave sons who have recently borne themselves in defence of my Crown and Empire with a cheerful valour, as conspicuous now as ever in their glorious past. I pray that the Almighty may ever bless and direct you in the high functions which you exercise in the benefit of your fellow-citizens."

One of the features of the welcome so spontaneously offered by the warm hearts of her Irish people was the gathering of 8,000 school children in Phœnix Park, who had come from every part of Ireland, and whose enthusiasm was intense. Another was the brilliance of the continuous stream of illuminations in the evening, and the good nature of the great masses of people trying to crush their way through the streets of the city, and happy, indeed, if they had obtained a fleeting glance at the Sovereign. During the next few days the Queen took long drives through the city and surrounding country, received deputations, and constant cheers from crowding people at every point of depart-ure, visit and return. On the 7th she accepted a beautiful bouquet presented by the Lord Mayor and Lady Mayoress on behalf of the children of Ireland, and drove slowly through an assembly of 52,000 children gathered from all parts of the country. A passing cloud came in the midst of these splendid exhibitions of loyalty through the distressful news of the attempt on the Prince of Wales' life at Brussels. But, though enough to unnerve most rulers in the position of Her Majesty, it had absolutely no effect upon her public programme, or the entire freedom and unguarded character of her movements abroad.

Many drives and a few private visits followed during the weeks which passed until April 27th, when the Queen departed for England. Formal invi-tations to Belfast and other places were reluctantly declined ; forty-two addresses were received on April 18th from all kinds of public bodies in Ire-land ; a bouquet was accepted from the wives and widows of non-commissioned officers and men in South Africa ; Lord and Lady Cadogan were ceremoniously visited at Dublin Castle ; it was announced that an Irish Regiment of Foot-Guards would be formed with the designation of the Queen's Guards ; a review of 6,000 troops was held in the presence of 200,000 spectators by Her Majesty, and with the Duke of Connaught—who had been appointed in January to the command of the Forces in Ireland—at their head. The visit of three weeks' duration had been an unqualified success, and, coupled with preceding acts of courtesy and kindliness, won the Queen a place in Irish hearts throughout the world which can hardly now be undermined by the influence of politicians or politics or the changes of death and time.

Immediately upon her return she again visited the sick and wounded at Netley, and early in May came to London, where an enthusiastic welcome awaited her every appearance. A Drawing Room was held at Buckingham Palace; Sir George White was invested with the Star of the Royal Victorian Order —specially created in 1896 as a personal method of awarding services; on May 17th the Queen attended the christening of the Duke and Duchess of York's youngest child; and late in the month visited the Victorian Barracks at Windsor to inspect a draft of the Grenadier Guards who were about to leave for South Africa. The fall of Pretoria was celebrated quietly by Her Majesty at Balmoral on June 7th, but with loud rejoicings and bonfires by her tenantry and with a roar of congratulatory voices which echoed around the British world.

Expressions of renewed loyalty and of unique rejoicing came to the Queen from British countries and islands everywhere. On June 7th the Canadian Parliament passed a resolution congratulating her "on the approaching termination of the war in South Africa as foreshadowed by the recent successes culminating in the fall of Pretoria," and this was duly replied to. Her Majesty had already shown marked interest in the wonderful sympathy shown by the Colonies in the struggle, and the evidence thus afforded of genuine and growing Empire unity must have proved balm to a heart otherwise so sorely wounded by the sad losses in the campaign. When the first Contingent had been contributed by Canada a despatch was received by the Governor-General on Oct. 24th, 1899, declaring that: "Her Majesty the Queen desires to thank the people of her Dominion of Canada for their striking manifestations of loyalty and patriotism in voluntarily offering to send troops to co-operate with Her Majesty's Imperial forces in maintaining her position and the rights of British subjects in South Africa." When the Canadian troops distinguished themselves at Paardeberg another message came declaring the desire of the Queen "to express to the people of Canada her admiration of the gallant conduct of the Canadian troops in the late engagement, and her sorrow at the loss of so many brave men." Similar messages were sent to the Australian Colonies at opportune moments duriug a war in which their troopers proved themselves second to none in the Imperial service.

Late in June, 1900, the Khedive of Egypt visited London, and was received in state by the Queen at Windsor and by the City at the Guildhall. On July 9th Her Majesty gave a formal assent to the Imperial enactment creating the Commonwealth of Australia, and adding one more link of accomplishment to the chain of Imperial ideas which had so early permeated the mind of the Queen. The influence of her life and character and reign had indeed been no inconsiderable factors in producing the sentiment of loyalty amongst the Colonies of that Southern Continent which had enabled them finally to harmonize divergent interests and petty localisms in one general union of states around the Throne of Victoria. The signing of the Commonwealth Bill was a memorable and historic event, and the Queen showed her usual tact in presenting the table upon which the document was signed, and the pen which was used in the operation, to the new Commonwealth. They were given the Earl of Hopetoun, as the first Governor-General of Australia, to take with him to the seat of his Government.

His appointment was in itself an exceedingly wise one, and, as a well-known *persona grata* to the Queen, it is most probable that the choice was hers. It was an exceedingly popular one in the Colonies concerned, and the announcement made at a later date that British troops to the number of a thousand, and representing every branch of the service at home, would accompany him to take part in the initiatory celebrations of the union, which was to be proclaimed on the first day of the new century, made it still more acceptable. The sending of the soldiers at such a juncture, when Australian breasts were throbbing with military ardour and patriotism, looks very much like one of those touches of imagination which are so essential to great statesmanship and so characteristic of the life and administration of the Queen.

The second son of the Queen, Prince Alfred, Duke of Saxe-Cobourg and Gotha, and better known as Duke of Edinburgh, passed away on July 31st. He had for several years dropped out of the public life of England, and come to be regarded as in some sense a German ruler and Prince; but to the Queen he could never be anything but the son of whom we catch such frequent glimpses in Her Majesty's published journals and in Sir Theodore Martin's book—the sailor son who saw much service in many parts of the world, and had rightly risen to a high place in the Royal Navy. He had been ill for some years, and though ignorant himself of the real nature of the trouble, his family, and, no doubt, his mother, knew of it. Thoughtful of others, as she always was, the Queen caused the announcement in the *Court Circular* that her health had not suffered, and that she was bearing up well "under this fresh grievous loss." She was, however, "full of solicitude for her dear daughter-in-law and grand-daughters, who have but a year and a half ago had to mourn the loss of an only son and brother." Her Majesty was "much soothed and touched by the universal expressions of sympathy with her in her affliction."

During August the Chinese crisis reached its acute stage, and it can be readily believed that the dreadful fear which over-shadowed the civilized world regarding the fate of the Europeans in Pekin must have found more than a mere echo in the Queen's heart. To her some at least of the Ambassadors and their

FROM OSBORNE TO WINDSOR. THE COFFIN, DRAWN BY BLUEJACKETS, APPROACHING ST. GEORGE'S CHAPEL.

Drawn by our Special Artists, Mr. Maynard Brown and H. C. Seppings Wright.

THE CORTÉGE PASSING THROUGH HYDE PARK.

Drawn by our Special Artist, Mr. Robert Lillie.

wives were known personally, and certainly Sir Claude and Lady MacDonald. The awful fate which threatened, and seemed to have overtaken them, could not but cause painful moments in the Palace as it did in so many cottages. Immediately on receipt of the news of rescue Her Majesty sent the following despatch: "I thank God that you and those under your command are rescued from your perilous situation. With my people I have waited with the deepest anxiety for the good news of your safety, and a happy termination to your prolonged and heroic defence. I grieve for the losses and sufferings experienced by the besieged." On September 18th it was announced that the Queen had consented to a visit of the Duke and Duchess of York to Australia for the purpose of opening the first Parliament of the new Commonwealth in the spring of 1901. It was stated that:

"Although the Queen naturally shrinks from parting with her grandson for so long a period, Her Majesty fully recognizes the greatness of the occasion which will bring her Colonies of Australia into federal union, and desires to give this special proof of her interest in all that concerns the welfare of her Australian subjects. Her Majesty at the same time wishes to signify her sense of the loyalty and devotion which have prompted the spontaneous aid so liberally offered by all the Colonies in the South African war, and of the splendid gallantry of her Colonial troops."

Few really thought of such a possibility at the time, but it afterwards seemed almost prophetic that the announcement should also include the condition that at the time fixed for the departure of the Duke of York, " the circumstances are as generally favourable as at present, and that no national interests call for His Royal Highness' presence in this country." The intelligence was received with immense enthusiasm in Australia, where preparations were already being made for the celebration of the inauguration of the Commonwealth on January 1st. The opening of Parliament was arranged for the April following, and during the next three months the Colonies under the Southern Cross were in a perfect turmoil of discussion and preparation. In Canada the natural wish was widely expressed that the Royal visitors should be invited to return home by way of the Dominion, and receive the welcome which its people would desire to accord them. It came to be generally understood that some such arrangement would be made, and that an official invitation had been given by the Canadian Government.

On October 29th death again visited the Royal circle, and this time took away an active and gallant young Prince who had made his mark in the military service, and had now been on duty in South Africa for quite a long period. He had shared with his comrades, as a member of Lord Roberts' staff, the dangers and privations of the war, and now he had to share in the sufferings of enteric fever, and meet the fate of so many others who had in this way laid down their lives for the country. Prince Christian Victor was the eldest son of Prince and Princess Christian (Helena) and grandson of the Queen. He had served in three Indian border expeditions, and in the Ashanti and Soudan wars and was, personally, a general favourite. The *Court Circular* declared regarding the event in words of personal force and meaning that: " The Queen deeply mourns the loss of so dear a grandson, and brilliant officer of great promise. She suffers doubly in the grief of his afflicted parents and family, who were so devoted to him. The Prince, who was born in Windsor Castle, was in his 34th year, and was universally loved and respected. He had taken part in the whole campaign, and had gone through the greatest hardships and dangers. The Queen and all her family were looking forward to his happy return, when suddenly his life is thus cut short." By special orders from Her Majesty he was buried in a soldier's grave at Pretoria, and in a manner befitting the quiet, kindly and modest char-acter of a young Prince who was intensely anxious to do his full duty as a soldier, and to rank as one rather than as a scion of royalty.

In November the troops began to return home, and this evidence of the practical end of a painful war was, no doubt warmly welcomed by the sorrowing Sovereign. She had shared to the full in the anxieties of the period when for weary weeks soldiers were being slaughtered in thousands, and the garrisons of Ladysmith and Kimberley and Mafeking were guarding the honour of their Queen and Empire in the midst of shot and shell and continuous privation. She had suffered with her people, but had also shared in their grim determina-tion to meet and overcome any new developments of military science, or any possible combination of hostile forces and nations which might be brought to bear against their country. She had taken a personal interest in, and had a personal knowledge of, many of the gallant officers who fell in fights from Magersfontein to Pretoria, from Elandslaaghte to the final relief of Ladysmith.

Now the war seemed nearly over, and it was fitting that the first formal Royal welcome to returning troops should be given to a mixed body of invalided Colonial soldiers gathered together at Windsor to parade before their Queen. There were to be seen members of Lord Roberts' picked Body-Guard of Col-onial fighters, men who combined polish with persistent pluck; dashing Aus-tralian troopers who neither asked nor gave quarter; farmers of the Natal Mounted Rifles, who had guarded advanced posts in their beautiful Colony in days when the enemy seemed to be sweeping everything before them; sporting planters from Nepaul in distant India, who appeared in the quilted head-dress of Lumsden's Horse; men of the Imperial or South African Light Horse, and of Roberts', Kitchener's, and Strathcona's Horse. The Queen was accompan-ied by Princess Beatrice and others of her Household, and, after asking several men personally about their wounds, and making various inquiries about the

Colonies represented, Her Majesty addressed the parade with a few brief fare-well words: "It is with the greatest pleasure I welcome you here to-day, and I thank you all for your loyal service, and I wish you God-speed and a safe return home."

The 1st Life Guards returned on November 29th after a year's arduous service in South Africa, and were accorded a fitting popular welcome. They were received at Windsor with great simplicity and in the most private manner. In their travel-stained and war-worn uniforms they paraded before the Queen, who was accompanied by Princess Beatrice and Princess Alice of Albany. From her carriage, and in the most simple and sincere language, Her Majesty said to them: "It is with feelings of great pleasure and deep thankfulness that I welcome you home after your gallant and arduous services in the war in South Africa, just a year after I bid you farewell. Alas! the joy at your safe return is clouded over by the memory of sad losses of many a valuable life which I, in common with you all, have to deplore." On the day following the Queen received a detachment of the Royal Canadian Regiment, which was returning home by way of London. The Contingent was commanded by Colonel W. D. Otter, who was accompanied to Windsor by Colonel W. H. MacKinnon, lately in command of the City Imperial Volunteers. They were received by Her Majesty in the quadrangle of the Castle at 12 a.m., and presented, according to the London *Times*, an eminently soldierly appearance—wiry, robust, and smart. The Queen was accompanied by Princess Beatrice and Princess Alice of Albany, and attended by Colonel Lord Edward Pelham-Clinton, Lieut.-Col. Sir Arthur Bigge, K.C.B.; Lieut.-Col. Arthur Davidson, M.V.O., and Colonel the Hon. H. C. Legge, M.V.O. As the Contingent was marching past the Royal carriage, the Queen saw that a man in khaki, with the maple-leaf badge on his hat and supported by crutches, was struggling to keep in line. It was Trooper Armstrong, of the Mounted Rifles, from New Brunswick, who had lost a leg at Heidelberg. With her usual quick graciousness she at once sent an Equerry to bring up the maimed soldier, and then expressed to him a few words of kindly sympathy. To Colonel Otter and the Royal Canadians she said: "I am glad to see you here to-day, and to express my warm thanks for the admirable services rendered in the war by the Canadian troops. I wish you all a safe and happy return to your homes." Colonel Otter declared in reply that "we have been proud to fight for the flag under which we hope that we may live all our lives," and, after the officers had been presented to Her Majesty, the ceremonies terminated.

But the end of all the Queen's gracious actions and kindly thought for others was now coming. A final function of importance was the reception to Lord Roberts on January 2nd at Osborne House, his cordial welcome home by the Sovereign to whom he had rendered such loyal and self-sacrificing service, the conferment upon him of an Earldom and the ribbon of the Garter. Thence he went to London to be acclaimed by the people and to be entertained by the Prince of Wales at Buckingham Palace by request of the Queen. Minor matters occupied the next two weeks, and many will be the cherished memories of last kindly letters, little gifts of a few pounds each, a portrait here, a message there, sent out by Her Majesty during this period to mark her appreciation of incidents in connection with the South African war. On January 1st she had raised the Duke of York to the rank of Rear-Admiral, and on the same day despatched a telegram to the Governor-General of Australia in words of appropriate meaning and force: "Accept my heartfelt congratulations for the New Year, and for the welfare of my new Australian Commonwealth." Lord Hopetoun's reply to this last personal communication from the Queen to her subjects has since become of mournful interest :

"On behalf of self and Ministers for the Commonwealth I express the deep gratitude of her subjects throughout Australia for the Queen's gracious message read by me at the inauguration of the Commonwealth to-day. They humbly join Her Majesty the Queen in the hope that Divine Providence may grant increase in prosperity and well-being to her devoted subjects of this new nation within the Empire; and it is the earnest and unanimous hope of these subjects that their noble and gracious Sovereign may be long spared to watch over and encourage the development of her Empire in peace and mutual trust and love."

Meanwhile, the Queen's strength had been very slowly fading. The anxieties of the war, the death of so many relations, the dangerous illness of her much-loved daughter and eldest child, the Empress Frederick, the death of the Dowager Lady Churchill, long a devoted friend and personal attendant—holding to Her Majesty, in fact, much the relation of the Marchioness of Ely, who had passed away a dozen years before—all these things were, almost imperceptibly, having their effect upon the wonderful physique of the aged Sovereign. Early in January rumours began to develop as to the state of her health, and they flew on wings of lightning speed to the four corners of the world. But similar reports had risen before and been disproved by time, and continued personal activities. Besides this, her people had come to believe that the Queen bore a charmed life, and as year after year, decade after decade, generation after generation, came and went, the death of the great little woman at Windsor was put out of men's minds and thoughts. Had she been really considered immortal in the life of this world, as she must be in its history, the shock could hardly have been greater than that felt on January 18th, when the official announcement was made that Her Majesty's condition of health was not satisfactory.

Throughout the British Empire, and in a lesser degree throughout the civilized world, almost the sole topic of thought and speech during the next few days was the news from the bedside at Windsor Castle. Even yet British peoples did not quite grasp the situation, and it was not until the Prince of Wales, at 4 p.m. on January 22nd, telegraphed the sad warning to the Lord Mayor of London that the life of his beloved mother was in the greatest danger, that a distinct realization of the issue came to many minds, and hope was really abandoned.

Two hours later came the final telegram from the Prince announcing the Queen's death, and stating that she was surrounded by her children and grand-children. Everything had been done that medical skill and science could do, and Sir James Reid, Sir R. Douglas Powell and Sir Thomas Barlow had been most devoted in their attendance and labours. Around the bedside, when the greatest of England's rulers passed away, were gathered the Prince and Princess of Wales, the Princess Louise, the Princess Beatrice, the Duke of Connaught, the Duke and Duchess of York, the German Emperor, the white-haired Bishop of Winchester, the Royal Physicians, and other faithful attendants. The end was peaceful and a suitable setting for the sun of such a life. Pathetic, it could not help but be, as the head of a mighty Empire lay amid surroundings telling in every detail—even to the portrait hanging opposite her dying eyes—of the hus-band whose love and memory she had so deeply cherished, and beside whom she was to soon rest in the stately mausoleum at Frogmore. Not the least import-ant of the events connected with that historic scene was the presence of William II. of Germany. He had hurried to England immediately upon learning that the sickness was serious, and acted through all that trying time, as well as in the succeeding period of funeral preparation and mourning, like an affectionate son, rather than as the powerful Sovereign of a rival nation.

As Sir James Reid held up his hand to inform the sorrowing family at the bedside that all was over, and the broken prayers of the aged Bishop of Win-chester ceased, the news travelled quickly through the Palace, and fifteen min-utes later was made officially known by a medical bulletin, and the already-mentioned despatch to London of the Heir Apparent. Bells immediately began tolling throughout all the vast confines of the Empire, and their echoes found a place in many millions of hearts, as well as in every form of external and pub-licly expressed sorrow. From Australia and Canada, India and the Cape, New Zealand and all the Isles of the British seas, came pouring in messages of sor-row and sympathy. The electric wires of the world bore such a burden as they had never known, and the bonds of a common sympathy knit anew the affec-tionate allegiance of distant peoples to the Throne of the Empire. Symbols of mourning and all the draperies of public grief gave quick vent to the feelings of the masses. In Sydney and Melbourne, Toronto and Montreal, Cape Town and Calcutta, as in London and Edinburgh, the streets assumed the appear-

ance of a sorrow which was as sincere as its expression was wide and spontaneous.   The new King, whose familiar and famous title of Prince of Wales was
now to be merged in that of Edward VII., King of Great Britain and Ireland,
Emperor of India, left Windsor early the next morning and, accompanied by
the Duke of Connaught, the Duke of York, the Duke of Argyll and Mr. Balfour,
proceeded to attend the first Privy Council of a new reign.   Amidst a scene of
brilliant impressiveness, His Majesty took the oaths, and then delivered a brief
speech, which can be truly described as at once wise, resolute, touching and sincere.   His reference to the event which was in every man's mind, and to the
conditions of the immediate present, may properly be given here :

" My first melancholy duty is to announce to you the death of my beloved mother, the
Queen, and I know how deeply you and the whole nation, and I think I may say the whole
world, sympathize with me in the irreparable loss we have all sustained.   I need hardly
say that my constant endeavour will be always to walk in her footsteps.   In undertaking
the heavy load which now devolves upon me, I am fully determined to be a constitutional
Sovereign in the strictest sense of the word, and so long as there is breath in my body to
work for the good and amelioration of my people."

To the House of Commons, as well as to the Upper House, a Royal message was sent on January 25th, which stated that the King was fully assured
that each of these bodies would "share the deep sorrow which has befallen His
Majesty and the nation by the lamentable death of his mother, the late Queen.   Her
devotion to the welfare of her country and her people, and her wise and beneficent rule during the sixty-four years of her glorious reign, will ever be held in
affectionate memory by her loyal devoted subjects throughout the dominions of
the British Empire."   In the Houses of Parliament, called together to receive
the formal announcement of death and accession, and to make the formal reply
of sorrow and congratulation, there was a scene of sombre splendour as the
nation's representatives gathered in silent black-garbed crowds to listen to their
leaders express an Empire's grief.   Lord Salisbury and Mr. Balfour were equal
to the emergency, and their speeches were really adequate appreciations of the
dead Sovereign's life and influence.   Lord Salisbury's tribute was peculiarly
striking and obviously sincere.   After speaking of her glorious reign and splendid character, he proceeded to say :

" Being a constitutional monarch, with restricted powers, she had reigned by sheer
force of character, by the lovableness of her disposition, and by her hold upon the hearts
of her subjects.   The example which she set of governing by esteem and love would never
be forgotten, nor how much she assisted in the elevation of her people by their simple contemplation of her brilliant qualities as wife, mother and woman.   Her wonderful powers
of observing with absolute strictness the limits of her power as a constitutional Sovereign,
and at the same time maintaining steady and persistent influence over the actions of her
Ministers, inspired the greatest admirations.   She always maintained a vigorous supervision

FUNERAL PROCESSION OF HER LATE MAJESTY THE QUEEN.

COFFIN GOING UP THE STEPS, ST. GEORGE'S CHAPEL, WINDSOR.

Photo by J. Russell & Son, Windsor.

GENERAL VIEW FROM THE WEST END.

THE FUNERAL SERVICE AT ST. GEORGE'S CHAPEL, WINDSOR.

Drawn by F. C. Dickinson.

over public affairs, giving her Ministers the benefit of her advice and warning them of dangers. No Minister could disregard her views or press her to disregard them, without feeling that he had incurred a great danger. He had always said that when he knew what the Queen thought he knew for a certainty what her subjects would think, especially those of the middle classes."

The papers of the Empire teemed with tributes, personal and general, and with many significant references to the now recognized stability and permanence of monarchical institutions amongst its peoples as a result of the Queen's life and reign. The *Spectator* spoke of the "perfect simplicity and sincerity" of her character; the *Saturday Review* referred to what was in her case the insufficiently noticed "subtle, strong influence of sex" in raising and protecting the dignity of British womanhood; the *Speaker* dealt with her even-balanced patriotism, which kept the nation's unity absolute in every great crisis. Foreign respect was shown in a very generally appreciative press; in the official expressions of sorrow; in the announcement of attendance by Sovereigns or their heirs at the funeral from half the capitals of Europe: in the special interest and continued presence and sympathy of the German Emperor, and his orders that all flags should be half-masted throughout his dominions in remembrance of "my beloved, highly-honoured and never-to-be-forgotten grandmother, Victoria." The Parliament of France immediately adjourned on receipt of the news, and all public functions were cancelled. The veteran Emperor of Austria telegraphed his heartfelt condolences to King Edward, and declared that "the deceased Sovereign was for many years a loyal and gracious friend to me, and those mutual feelings of friendly sympathy have ever formed the basis also of our political relations." From all Europe came expressions of sympathy or sorrow. President McKinley offered the King his "sincere sympathy and that of the American people in your personal bereavement and in the loss Great Britain has suffered in the death of its venerable and illustrious Sovereign, whose noble life and beneficent influences have promoted the peace and won the affection of the world." The United States Senate and House of Representatives passed resolutions of regret, and the flag flew at half-mast over the White House at Washington for the first time in connection with the death of a foreign ruler.

In Canada, every Province and Government, every city and large municipality, every important Church, society or institution, passed resolutions of sorrow and sympathy. Especially significant and eloquent in its terms was a *mandement* from Archbishop Bruchési, of Montreal, read in all the churches of his ecclesiastical jurisdiction on January 26th, and in which occur the following words: "No message, amongst all those we have read in the despatches, appears to us more touching than that of Leo XIII., giving echo to the profound sorrow of the British nation, and recalling with gratitude all that a Queen, of a creed other than his, had done to secure full liberty to the Catholic Church throughout her vast Empire." The Hon. G. W. Ross, Premier of Ontario, expressed himself with still more effect when he declared that : "An evangel of peace in the councils of the world, she was equally an evangel of tenderness and womanly sympathy in the homes of her own people. In no other person, certainly in no other ruler during the Christian era, were found combined so much greatness and sagacity in matters of State, and so much goodness and virtue in daily life and action."

The funeral commenced on February 1st, and was the most splendid, and at the same time sombre spectacle witnessed in the world's history. In the stately, and yet simple pageant from Osborne House to the Royal yacht at Cowes, the dead Sovereign was borne upon a simple gun carriage, preceded by officers, soldiers, and massed bands, followed by King Edward, Emperor William, the Duke of Connaught, the Crown Prince of Germany, Prince Henry of Prussia, and a number of Royal ladies in deep black, and with heavy veils, many dignitaries and more officials. All were walking, while reverent crowds stood along the line of route, seeing the sorrowful procession as through a mist of tears, and feeling a personal, as well as a national loss. At Cowes the coffin and the gun carriage were placed on board the *Alberta* in a magnificent catafalque, and then, on the route so often passed before by the Royal lady, when she had reviewed so many mighty fleets, and had witnessed the splendours of the Jubilee demonstration of a nation's greatness, there now passed the little yacht which bore her remains to their last resting place. Between ten miles of black-hulled battle-ships and cruisers, with sailors in solemn silence manning the yards, with the drooping flags and emblems of mourning, with minute guns booming from ship to ship and shore to shore, with requiems wafted through the air like one continued wail of sorrow, the procession of mourners passed in their tiny vessels, and the Queen of the Seas received the last tribute of respect from her powerful Navy.

On the succeeding morning the coffin was removed from the *Alberta* and, in draped trains, mid mourning villages and silent masses of people, the Royal party with its sorrowful burden passed slowly to Victoria Station, and thence to Windsor through three miles of a sad-coloured city, through millions of black-garbed mourners, ranging from the wealthy man or women in the castle windows to the poorest person and the wildest *gamin* standing silent in the crowded streets. Everywhere was silence, sombreness, sorrow. Apart from this pathetic evidence of a nation's feelings the procession in dignity, in splendour, and in embodied force and power, was worthy of the occasion. More could hardly be said. Yesterday, the sailors had paid their last tribute. Now, 30,000 soldiers of the Queen added their homage along the line of route to that of the motion-less and serried masses behind them. In the *cortège* were volunteers, militia, members of almost every regiment in the army, soldiers from India and the Colonies. The King rode with the German Emperor and the Duke of Con-naught, while following him was such a gathering of Princes and foreign rulers, or future rulers, as even London had never seen—the Kings of Belguim, Portugal and Greece, the Grand Duke Michael of Russia, the Crown Princes of Prussia, Roumania, Greece, Denmark, Norway, Sweden, Siam and the Archduke Franz Ferdinand of Austria, being the chief. Queen Alexandra and her daughters, with the other female members of the Royal family followed in closed carriages, while elsewhere in the procession were Field Marshal Earl Roberts, the Duke of Cambridge and Lord Wolseley. It was a military funeral, as became the daugh-ter of a soldier and the Sovereign of a great people who had just passed through stormy scenes of war and suffering.

In the superb St. George's Chapel at Windsor, surrounded by the pomp and splendour of mediæval times, and with the living greatness of England around her, the burial service of the Established Church was read by the Bishop of Winchester over the remains of the Queen. From here to the last resting place at Frogmore the body was carried on February 4th, and there, mid simple and private ceremonies, deposited where the heart of the woman and Queen had so long rested, and where already the epitaph was engraved over the tomb of the husband which was now to be her own : " Here at last I shall rest with thee ; with thee in Christ I shall rise again." Meanwhile over the length and breadth of the Empire, the 2nd of February had been observed as a day of universal mourning, and the million-tongued voice of pulpit and forum had acclaimed the merits of the woman and the greatness of the Sovereign. She still lives, how-ever, in the hearts of her subjects, in the best and noblest memories of a mighty epoch ; and in this fact realizes in some measure her own heart-felt wish as well as the sentiment of her favourite poet ;

> " Twilight and evening bell,
> And after that the dark,
> And may there be no sadness of farewell
> When I embark."

DESCENT OF QUEEN VICTORIA FROM EGBERT (A.D. 827).

1. EGBERT. 2. ETHELWOLF. 3. ALFRED THE GREAT. 4. EDWARD THE ELDER. 5. EDMUND 6. EDGAR. 7. ETHELRED. 8. EDMUND IRONSIDE. 9. Edward (not a king). 10. Margaret, wife of Malcolm, King of Scotland. 11. Matilda, wife of HENRY I. 12. Matilda or Maud, Empress of Germany and wife of Geoffrey of Anjou. 13. HENRY II. 14. JOHN. 15. HENRY III. 16. EDWARD I. 17. EDWARD II. 18. EDWARD III.

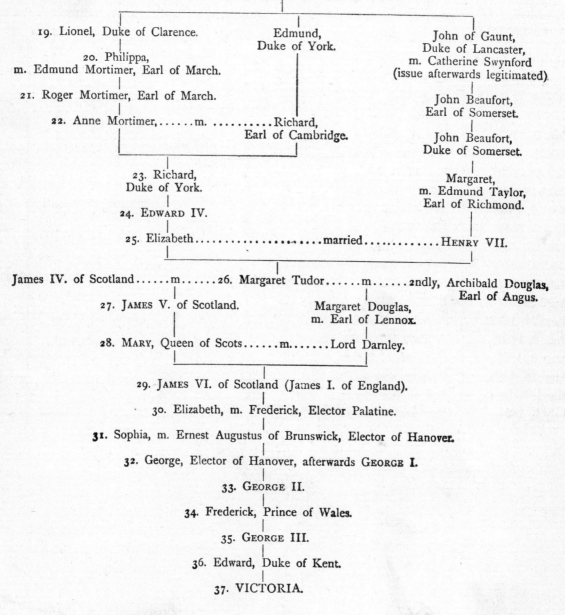

19. Lionel, Duke of Clarence.

20. Philippa, m. Edmund Mortimer, Earl of March.

21. Roger Mortimer, Earl of March.

22. Anne Mortimer,......m. ....Richard, Earl of Cambridge.

Edmund, Duke of York.

John of Gaunt, Duke of Lancaster, m. Catherine Swynford (issue afterwards legitimated).

John Beaufort, Earl of Somerset.

John Beaufort, Duke of Somerset.

23. Richard, Duke of York.

24. EDWARD IV.

Margaret, m. Edmund Taylor, Earl of Richmond.

25. Elizabeth....................married............HENRY VII.

James IV. of Scotland......m......26. Margaret Tudor......m......2ndly, Archibald Douglas, Earl of Angus.

27. JAMES V. of Scotland.

Margaret Douglas, m. Earl of Lennox.

28. MARY, Queen of Scots......m.......Lord Darnley.

29. JAMES VI. of Scotland (James I. of England).

30. Elizabeth, m. Frederick, Elector Palatine.

31. Sophia, m. Ernest Augustus of Brunswick, Elector of Hanover.

32. George, Elector of Hanover, afterwards GEORGE I.

33. GEORGE II.

34. Frederick, Prince of Wales.

35. GEORGE III.

36. Edward, Duke of Kent.

37. VICTORIA.

THE QUEEN'S PRIME MINISTERS.

DATE OF APPOINTMENT.	PRIME MINISTER.	DURATION.	
		Years.	Days.
April 18, 1835.	Viscount Melbourne	6	141
Sept. 6, 1841.	Sir Robert Peel	4	303
July 6, 1846.	Lord John Russell	5	236
Feb. 27, 1852.	Earl of Derby	0	305
Dec. 28, 1852.	Earl of Aberdeen	2	44
Feb. 10, 1855.	Lord Palmerston	3	15
Feb. 25, 1858.	Earl of Derby	1	113
June 18, 1859.	Lord Palmerston	6	141
Nov. 6, 1865.	Earl Russell	0	242
July 6, 1866.	Earl of Derby	1	236
Feb. 27, 1868.	Benjamin Disraeli	0	286
Dec. 9, 1868.	William Ewart Gladstone	5	274
Feb. 21, 1874.	Benjamin Disraeli, Earl of Beaconsfield	6	67
April 28, 1880.	William Ewart Gladstone	5	57
June 24, 1885.	Marquess of Salisbury	0	227
Feb. 6, 1886.	William Ewart Gladstone	0	178
Aug. 3, 1886.	Marquess of Salisbury	6	15
Aug. 18, 1892.	William Ewart Gladstone	1	193
March 3, 1894.	Earl of Rosebery	1	121
July 2, 1894.	Marquess of Salisbury	———	———